English
COMPOSITION

Executive Editor: Katherine Cleveland

Editors: Laura Brown, Caitlin Clark, Caitlin Edahl

Designers: Bryan Mitchell, James Smalls, Patrick Thompson, Tee Jay Zajac

Cover Design: James Smalls

VP Research & Development: Marcel Prevuznak

VP Sales & Marketing: Emily Cook

A division of Quant Systems, Inc.

546 Long Point Road

Mount Pleasant, SC 29464

Printed in the United States of America 🇺🇸

ISBN: 978-1-946158-02-4

Table of Contents

Table of Contents

Chapter 1
Why We Write

Lesson 1.1
Writing Situations and Purposes

"Writing, the art of communicating thoughts to the mind through the eye, is the great invention of the world . . . enabling us to converse with the dead, the absent, and the unborn, at all distances of time and space." Abraham Lincoln, 1832

Composing a strong piece of writing is often viewed as an art, which can be intimidating if you don't consider yourself a writer. However, we are all writers in ways that we may not immediately recognize. Think about the last time you sent a text message, left a voicemail, wrote a note, or mailed a card. In each of those instances, you made decisions as a writer.

All texts—from tweets to emails to complex scholarly articles—can be traced to a basic starting point: an author wants to communicate something to an audience. From there, different situations and purposes shape the writing.

It's important to understand this commonality among texts so that you can recognize the different elements that shape them. These are key considerations for both critical reading and effective writing.

In this lesson, you will think about writing situations and purposes as you explore the following questions:

When and Where Do We Write?
What Purposes Drive Our Writing?
What Considerations Affect How We Write?

When and Where Do We Write?

Remember that writing is all around us. Consider how many times you read each day without thinking about it: when you read the cereal box in the morning, when you check your email, when you drive on the highway and look at the signs for different exits, when you are shopping and look at a sale sign, and all the times you read at work.

Similarly, you likely encounter writing situations more often than you think. Whether it involves posting pictures or submitting job applications, our writing is affected by our environment.

Throughout this course, you will consider when, where, and how different types of writing are used. You will also explore new concepts as they are applied to three writing environments: academic, professional, and everyday.

- **Academic Writing**: includes texts intended for instructors or students
- **Professional Writing**: includes texts intended for managers, coworkers, or customers
- **Everyday Writing**: includes texts intended for anyone

Learning about how writing functions in these environments will help you understand and improve your skills in both writing and critical thinking.

> Reflection Questions
>
> What have you written recently? Emails? Blog posts? Image captions? Make a list of these items, and think about the choices you made as you wrote. What messages were you trying to convey? In what writing environment would you classify the writing: academic, professional, or everyday?

On Your Own

Complete the table below by first reading the definition and example of each writing style. Then, fill in your own example of a text that corresponds to each writing environment. For inspiration, think about your own writing.

Environment	Definition	Example	Your Example
Professional	A text intended for managers, coworkers, or customers	A proposal for a plan to market a new product	
Academic	A text intended for instructors or students and often directed by specific prompts and requirements	An analytical essay discussing perspectives on climate change	
Everyday	A personal and/or informal text intended for anyone	A text message to a friend you have not seen in a while	

What Purposes Drive Our Writing?

The **purpose**, or goal, of a piece of writing plays a critical role. The most common and broadly-defined goals of writing include expressing, communicating, informing, and entertaining. In this chapter, we will take a closer look at specific purposes that fall under these broad categories. For example, if your big-picture goal is to express your opinion on a movie, your more specific purposes will include *summarizing* what you know about that movie and *responding* with your feelings and conclusions.

Most writing is driven by a combination of several purposes. Here are some common purposes that can work together to achieve a bigger writing goal:

- **Writing to Discuss**: presents issues or interprets something you have read or studied
- **Writing to Respond**: expresses your thoughts and opinions about something you have read or studied
- **Writing to Summarize**: presents a small, generalized overview of a larger amount of information
- **Writing to Describe**: explains the appearance of someone or something using words that appeal to the senses

- **Writing to Argue**: convinces the audience to adopt a belief or take an action
- **Writing to Propose**: gives suggestions and solutions to an issue or problem
- **Writing to Analyze**: examines something you have read or studied
- **Writing to Evaluate**: creates criteria for judging something you have read or studied

Do not view these purposes as a defined list of standalone writing strategies. Instead, consider this list as a toolbox that you can consult both before and during writing.

Writing Environment: Academic

Be on the lookout for purpose indicators in essay prompts and assignment details. **Look for key words in the examples below.**

> Write a five-paragraph response to the novel *White Oleander*. Summarize the major themes and discuss how they affect your perspective.

> As you explore Chapter 7 of your textbook, evaluate the approaches to sustainable oil drilling. Expand your knowledge with further research, and choose one approach that you think is best. Write a proposal to decision-makers in your state for implementing that approach. Use your research as evidence to support your argument.

Writing as Powerful and Influential

Think about the different types of writing you have encountered over the years. Some texts are extremely powerful and meaningful to their readers. Here are some examples:

The Declaration of Independence: The founding fathers of the United States wrote this declaration of America's freedom from the king of England.

Bible, Torah, and Quran: These texts have shaped entire cultures and been a place for Christian, Jewish, and Muslim people to find faith and inspiration.

Treaties: Various treaties throughout history have outlined the terms by which peace is declared after war.

Banned Books: Many books have been banned, whether from school reading lists or from even being printed. Sometimes, this is because they are considered too vulgar or morally inappropriate. Other times, they go against the predominant religious or political values of a country. Whatever the case, these books possess such power that people feel threatened by them.

Reflection Questions

Think about the situations in which these influential texts were created. Where and when were they written? Who wrote them, and who was the audience? In what writing environments would you classify them?

Group Activity

Divide into small groups of 3-4 people. On separate sheets of paper, write down 1-2 compliments about each person in your group. When everyone is finished, hand each classmate the paper with the compliments you wrote about him or her. After reading what your classmates wrote about you, answer the following questions together as a group:

- How did these compliments make you feel? Did they change your mood?
- Was is easy or difficult for you to read the compliments? Why or why not?
- How does this exercise represent the power of words?
- How would you feel if someone had written negative words instead?

The following is an excerpt from Martin Luther King, Jr.'s famous speech, "I Have a Dream." Consider why these words were important when they were spoken and why they are still important today.

> And that is something that I must say to my people who stand on the worn threshold which leads into the palace of justice. In the process of gaining our rightful place we must not be guilty of wrongful deeds. Let us not seek to satisfy our thirst for freedom by drinking from the cup of bitterness and hatred.
>
> We must forever conduct our struggle on the high plane of dignity and discipline. We must not allow our creative protests to degenerate into physical violence. Again and again we must rise to the majestic heights of meeting physical force with soul force. The marvelous new militancy which has engulfed the Negro community must not lead us to distrust all white people, for many of our white brothers, as evidenced by their presence here today, have come to realize that their destiny is tied up with our destiny.
>
> They have come to realize that their freedom is inextricably bound to our freedom. We cannot walk alone. And as we walk we must make the pledge that we shall always march ahead. We cannot turn back.

Reflection Questions

After reading the excerpt from Martin Luther King Jr.'s speech, consider the following questions:

- Have you ever read something that made you cry? Why did it cause an emotional response?
- Have you ever read something that made you feel happy? What was it about that piece of writing that made you respond that way?
- Have you ever written something that made someone else emotional? What techniques did you use while writing it?

What Considerations Affect How We Write?

Your purpose and environment should influence and be influenced by genre, audience, and tone, so consider them as you think about your own writing.

Genre

The **genre** is the type of text you're writing. Examples of genres include emails, letters, poems, songs, stories, novels, papers, and more.

On Your Own

Read each purpose and identify its genre.

1. Thanking someone for a gift

    ☐ Business proposal
    ☐ Letter
    ☐ Novel

2. Presenting an idea to your boss

    ☐ Business proposal
    ☐ Letter
    ☐ Novel

3. Sharing a story you've imagined

    ☐ Business proposal
    ☐ Letter
    ☐ Novel

Audience

Your **audience** is made up of the people who will read your writing. For example, an assignment that you submit to a teacher will require more time and effort than a casual email to a friend. Friends, colleagues, teachers, managers, and members of your community are all examples of different audiences you might address while writing.

Think about this writing situation: Heidi has had a bad day, so she summarizes and describes her day in her journal.

> Today was a horrible day. I was late to work because my car broke down. I tried to call my boss, but my phone was dead. Because I couldn't start my car, I also couldn't charge my phone. I had to walk over a mile to the nearest gas station to use their phone. By the time I got ahold of my manager, he said that he had already written me down as a no-show! I can't believe it! Even though I've never missed one day of work, he still told me I was fired! I also had to have my car towed, which cost a ton of money. As if that weren't enough, when I finally got home and walked in the front door, I stepped right into a puddle my dog left because I couldn't get home in time to take him outside.

Now, imagine a new writing situation: Heidi has had some time to calm down. She wants to email her manager to ask him to reconsider his decision. How might Heidi's writing change for her new audience?

> **Group Activity**
> On a separate piece of paper, write the email to Heidi's manager from her perspective. As a group, compare the differences between the journal entry and the email. What specific details of the writing have changed?

Writing Environment: Academic

In school, you might think that your audience only includes your teacher. However, you should consider others who would also be interested in reading the different texts you create. An academic paper might be of interest to the following audiences:

- Your family
- People who will take the same class as you in the future
- Students who are studying the same subject as you
- Scholars or professionals in your field of study
- Publishers of journals in your field of study

Tone

Tone is the positive, negative, or neutral attitude that an author expresses about a topic. The tone of a research paper should be more serious than the tone you would use for a funny tweet or text. Within the general categories of *positive*, *negative*, and *neutral* are more specific tones, like *persuasive*, *informative*, *menacing*, *inspiring*, and more.

Writing Environment: Professional

Consider the following examples of emails to the CEO of a company. In the first example, the writer has not considered the audience, purpose, or tone of the piece. Reflect on specific ways the first example differs from the second.

Example 1:

> Dear boss,
> Do we still have that one meeting tomorrow morning? I don't know if I will be able to make it because I have to go to the dentist to get a new filling, and afterwards I'll be out of it from the laughing gas. Lol. I'll be in ASAP. I'll call you on your cell when I'm on the way. Thomas

Example 2:

> Dear Ms. Green,
> I wanted to let you know that I may not be able to make it to the meeting tomorrow at 9 a.m. because of a dentist appointment. I'm not sure how long it will last, but I will call the office as soon as I know. I will also bring documentation.
> Thank you,
> Thomas Martin

Lesson Wrap-up

Key Terms

Academic Writing: a text intended for instructors or students and often directed by specific prompts and requirements

Audience: the person or people who read or interpret a text

Everyday Writing: personal and/or informal texts intended for anyone

Genre: a type of writing

Professional Writing: a text intended for managers, coworkers, or customers

Purpose: the goal of a text

Tone: the positive, negative, or neutral attitude that an author expresses about a topic

Writing to Analyze: a writing purpose achieved by examining something you have read or studied

Writing to Argue: a writing purpose that convinces the audience to adopt a belief or take an action

Writing to Describe: a writing purpose that explains the appearance of someone or something using words that appeal to the senses

Writing to Discuss: a writing purpose that presents issues or interprets something you have read or studied

Writing to Evaluate: a writing purpose achieved by creating criteria for judging something you have read or studied

Writing to Propose: a writing purpose achieved by giving suggestions and solutions to an issue or problem

Writing to Respond: a writing purpose that expresses personal thoughts and opinions about a text

Writing to Summarize: a writing purpose that presents a small, generalized overview of a larger amount of information

Writing Application: Writing Situations and Purposes

Read the following letter and determine its purpose. The annotations will point out important clues in the writing.

Dear Mr. Turner,

My current position as a Marketing Associate for Berkeley Innovations has taught me so much about converting and growing new leads for various products. I have learned how to create email and web content that will attract new customers. I am also learning how to analyze the traffic on the company's website and social media sites. I now understand the role that social media plays in retaining customers.

> The audience is the author's manager (Mr. Turner).

Since starting at Berkeley Innovations a little over a year ago, I have secured accounts with Farmfield Co., Mandarin House, and Blue Technical Affiliates. All these businesses are leaders in their respective industries and have more than 200 employees. I have also updated our email subscription list and Twitter account every day for 10 months. According to the analytics, the Twitter account has attracted roughly 1,000 unique visitors to Berkeley Innovations' website per month.

> The tone of this piece is both informative and professional. It does not use slang or conversational language.

During my time with the company, I have done my best to educate current and potential customers about our company. I have met with customers in person, through video conferencing, on the phone, and via emails and text messages. I always try to turn a simple question about our company into a lead. In the past week alone, I have successfully upsold three customers on our products.

It is for these reasons that I am hoping you will consider me for a promotion. I am excited to move to the position of Marketing Manager with Berkeley Innovations, and I believe that I am now ready to take on the responsibilities associated with this position. I also anticipate the educational opportunities that this promotion would provide. I will be happy to discuss my request with you and answer any questions that you may have.

The purpose is to persuade Mr. Turner to promote the author.

Thank you for your consideration.

Sincerely,

The genre of this sample is a business letter, which is revealed in part by the format.

Mae Pierce

Learning Style Tip

If you have trouble writing for a specific purpose, try one of these strategies for getting started:
- Draw pictures to represent your ideas, and then use words to describe what you've drawn.
- Use your computer or phone to record yourself explaining your thoughts, and then transcribe them into words on paper.
- Write separate ideas on sticky notes. Then, arrange them on the wall, taking out the ideas that are not as strong and re-ordering the others in a logical way.

Further Resources

Check out these resources for more information on writing purposes, writing in the workplace, and the power of writing:
- Online Writing Lab at Purdue (https://owl.english.purdue.edu/owl/resource/625/06/)
- Writing in the Workplace (https://www.youtube.com/watch?v=JvAiE7owmeI)
- TED Talk: Lakshmi Pratury (https://www.ted.com/talks/lakshmi_pratury_on_letter_writing)

Lesson 1.2
Writing to Respond

We are constantly reacting to the world around us: what we see, hear, smell, taste, and touch. In other words, reactions are innate and unavoidable. Sometimes, we let our natural reactions show; other times, we change or hide them. However, sometimes our reactions are so strong that we have trouble controlling them.

Just as we naturally react to the world around us, we also have natural reactions to the written word. Good writing uses language and content that make you think and feel. Capturing these thoughts and feelings in words can be difficult, but it's always rewarding.

In this lesson, you will learn strategies for writing to respond in two phases:

Getting Started
Developing the Response

> Group Activity
> Work with several classmates to brainstorm the ways you see personal reactions made public. After you generate a large list, categorize the items into professional, academic, and everyday situations. Are different reactions appropriate for different environments? How so?

Getting Started

Before you can choose an approach for writing your response paper, it's important to understand the topic of your response. To understand what you're responding to, follow these three steps:

1. Closely read the text.
2. Write a summary of the text.
3. Review your summary and explore reactions, connections, and implications.

Closely Read the Text

Highlight, underline, and/or mark up important components of the text. Record notes, questions, insights, and other important thoughts you have while reading. Once you've finished reading, look back at your notes.

> To learn more about annotating a text, see Lesson 5.1.

Write a Summary of the Text

Use your notes as a helpful tool for summarizing the text. If you get stuck, go back to the text and re-read as often as needed. Writing a summary will help you stay focused on the **main ideas** of the text so that you can adequately respond to them.

Your summary should answer the following questions:

- What is the **thesis** and main topic of the text? (This might be an idea, person, group of people, movement, or historical event.)
- What is being explained or argued about this topic?
- What details are being used to support this explanation or **argument**?

> To learn more about writing to summarize, see Lesson 1.3.

Review Your Summary

Think about how the text makes you feel, but also consider how the author intended for his or her audience to react. Additionally, consider what questions the text raises. Last, consider the implications of the **purpose** and main ideas as well as possible connections to similar issues.

Think about your reactions as you read the following paragraph:

> Author Ray Bradbury once said, "Video games are a waste of time for men with nothing else to do." While video game sales remain on the rise in many countries, it is important to consider the very real danger that they pose to our citizens and our future. Children and teenagers are being irreparably harmed by overexposure to violence and mind-numbing activity brought on by excessive gaming. This damaging hobby can desensitize individuals to violence, making them less likely to find fault in vicious behavior. It can also lead to apathetic tendencies, lack of physical activity, and isolation.

Now, explore possible approaches to your response by thinking through the following questions:

> How does this text make me feel?
>
> What is the author's purpose for writing? How do I know?
>
> Do I agree or disagree with the main idea(s) in this text? Why?
>
> What **evidence** does the author use to back up his or her claims?
>
> Why does the author choose to organize his or her ideas in this way?
>
> How does the word choice affect my opinion?
>
> Who is the author? Why should I believe what he or she says?

On Your Own

Use the previous questions to brainstorm your response to an article, conversation, or social media post that you've recently encountered. Respond to each question with a brief sentence in the right column.

Question	Answer
How does this text make me feel?	
What is the author's purpose for writing?	
Do I agree or disagree with the main idea(s) in this text?	
What evidence does the author use to back up his or her claims?	
Why does the author choose to organize his or her ideas in this way?	
How does the word choice affect my opinion?	
Who is the author? Why should I believe what he or she says?	

Helpful Hint

Remember, you may be asked to respond to a text in a specific way. Other times, you will be able to choose the way you format your response. Some reactions will be personal while others may be analytical or academic.

Developing the Response

Now that you understand how to start this type of assignment, let's consider different approaches to the response.

Respond by Reflecting

One response method is to capture your natural reaction to what you've read and reflect on it. To do this, consider two things: how the text makes you feel, and (if the author is making an argument) whether you agree or disagree with that argument.

To capture your thoughts, try free-writing your response. **Free-writing** is a **brainstorming** strategy for getting your ideas down on paper. Sometimes, using **sentence stems** like the ones listed below can help get you started.

This makes me think . . .	This is interesting because . . .
I believe that . . .	I agree with the argument that . . . because . . .
This angers me because . . .	It sounds like the time has come to . . .
This frustrates me because . . .	This gives me hope that one day . . .

On Your Own

Using a sentence stem, free-write for ten or fifteen minutes in response to the paragraph below:

In a 2014 article published in *U.S. News and World Report*, Mark Edelman explains, "The college sports industry generates $11 billion in annual revenues. Fifty colleges report annual revenues that exceed $50 million." College athletes should get paid for the talent that they bring to a university. The athletes increase school spirit by encouraging unity and excitement. As Edelman indicates, some teams also generate revenue and increase publicity for their institutions. Additionally, college athletes work extremely hard to keep up with academic demands while facing pressure to provide skill and talent to their teams. Many college students choose not to take on this demanding work, so those who do should be rewarded.

The ideas you jot down while free-writing can be useful for shaping a more formal response. Consider the following reflection. In what ways is it responsive to the previous paragraph?

<u>The time has come to stop glorifying athletes more than other college students.</u> Yes, student athletes work hard, and they have a lot of responsibilities, but so do many other college students. Some students balance academics with heavy work schedules while others volunteer a great deal or have many personal obligations. No matter what other responsibilities students have outside of the classroom, they can result in a time-consuming and demanding schedule. If student athletes start getting paid to balance their heavy and demanding time restraints, so should other students who have challenging obstacles to navigate.

The first sentence indicates the writer's attitude.

The writer disagrees with the argument and counters it with his or her feelings.

Writing Environment: Everyday

The internet has become a popular outlet for response writing. Perhaps you are writing or responding to a tweet. Maybe you feel the need to write a formal complaint to an airline after they lost your luggage. Possibly, you loved your meal so much at the new restaurant in your neighborhood that you had to write a review online. No matter what prompts it, you will be taken more seriously if your response is well-written.

Respond by Comparing

If you feel that a reflective response won't do, a comparative response might be more effective. Writing always touches on topics and themes that exist both in other works and in the real world, and your response can bring attention to those topics and themes.

Here are some topics you could use for comparison:

Personal experiences	Plays	Song lyrics
Movies	Films	Current events
Short stories	Documentaries	Historical events
Novels	Television shows	

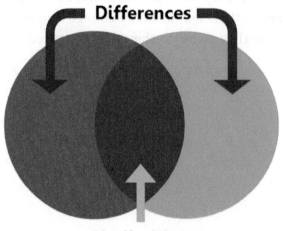

> **Group Activity**
>
> With a partner, complete a **Venn diagram** comparing the last thing you read in class to any piece of writing, film, or music that you're both familiar with. Consider comparing the characters, plots, themes, conflicts, settings, and/or languages.

The following passage compares two works.

> Khaled Hosseini's rich novel *The Kite Runner* has strong thematic connections to Francis Ford Coppola's blockbuster movie trilogy *The Godfather*. At the heart of both stories lie the intricate and heart-breaking complexities of a father-son relationship. Each story exposes the pressure and consequences that stem from navigating this difficult relationship as blind loyalty and fear encompass the central characters. Additionally, both stories are set to a backdrop of violence and chaos. Whether it is the partial history of Afghanistan's war-torn past in *The Kite Runner* or the harsh realities of mafia life in *The Godfather*, both works use external disarray to parallel the internal struggles faced by the main characters.

Respond by Critiquing

While some response writing requires reflection or comparison, other assignments may ask you to think differently. Just because a text is published, that doesn't mean you have to like it or agree with it. In fact, some instructors may deliberately assign a reading that they know will cause controversy or opposition.

To critique an argument, you should expand on your original summary with a thorough analysis of the author's main idea and his or her use of support.

To **analyze** is to examine and interpret something. In an analysis, you want to go beyond basic summary. **Summary** focuses on the *who, what, when,* and *where* while analysis focuses on the *why* and *how*.

> **Learning Style Tip**
>
> If you're a sensing learner, summary may be easier for you than analysis. If you're an intuitive learner, analysis may feel more natural than summary. However, both are important parts of writing. As you practice both summarizing and analyzing by asking yourself questions, you will feel more comfortable with using them in your writing.

Brainstorm your analysis by answering these questions:

- What is the goal or purpose of this writing? How do I know?
- How does the author defend his or her thesis? Is it effective? Why or why not?
- What are the different ways to interpret this text?
- What components of this text are unexplored or unanswered? Why might this be?
- Why does the author seem to be writing this piece? Can I detect any **biases**?
- What does this text imply? How and where do I see this?
- How does the author use language to achieve his or her goal? (Consider word choice and sentence structure.)
- How can I defend my analysis with evidence from the text?

> **Helpful Hint**
>
> Once you've thoroughly answered these questions, you may want to read the text one more time to be sure you haven't missed anything. Once you're content with your summary, move on to the analysis.

Writing Environment: Professional

Nearly every job requires you to ask *why* and *how* whether you're analyzing a text, a data set, or a situation. For example, research scientists might conduct experiments and then interpret the results. A sales assistant might find out the goals of customers in order to direct them to the right product. Both of these situations require analysis.

Lesson Wrap-up

Key Terms

Analyze: to examine and interpret something

Argument: a reason why you should think or act a certain way

Bias: a person's opinions and preferences

Brainstorming: exploring and developing ideas

Evidence: a piece of information, also called a supporting detail, that is used to support a main idea

Free-writing: a brainstorming strategy for getting your ideas down on paper

Main Idea: the statement or argument that an author tries to communicate

Purpose: the goal of a text

Sentence Stem: a word group that introduces or frames a statement

Summary: a small, generalized overview of a larger amount of information

Thesis Statement: a concise sentence or set of sentences that expresses the main idea of a longer work

Venn Diagram: a chart that uses overlapping circles to illustrate similarities and differences between two or more things

Writing to Respond: a writing purpose that expresses personal thoughts and opinions about a text

Writing Application: Writing to Respond

Read the following response essay. Which response method does the author use, and is it effective?

Poetry Night

Poetry Night with Anis Mojgani was a night full of imagery, metaphor, and rhyme. For the first hour of the program, students shared their poetry with the audience. During the second hour of the event, award-winning poet Anis Mojgani recited his poetry. I enjoyed Poetry Night much more than I thought I would.

As I listened to the student poets, I noticed that the meter of many of their poems used rhythms similar to rap and hip-hop. Love was definitely one of the most prevalent topics. Many of the poems dealt with issues like beauty, secret crushes, or longing for a soul mate. Other poems discussed ambition, peer pressure, societal issues, and forgiveness. I was impressed by how well people presented their work. Instead of standing still in front of the microphone and reading from a piece of paper, the speakers moved around the stage, motioned with

The author summarizes the event for the audience.

This sentence indicates that this student is using the "respond by reflecting" response method.

This student includes examples from the event to support his or her reflections.

their arms, and instilled feeling into their poetry. I could tell that they had worked to make their presentation pleasing and interesting. Seeing a passionate and thoughtful recitation of poetry was a new experience for me. <u>It showed me that speaking a poem is an art form, not just the poem itself.</u>

> The author goes one step further than simply reflecting on his or her feelings and analyzes the event.

The second half of the event belonged to Anis Mojgani. Taking his time, the slightly-built man with glasses and wild hair stepped onstage and took a long sip of water while the audience waited expectantly. Finally, he plunged into his first poem. His poetry overflowed with imagery that created clear pictures in my mind. Between poems, he made the audience laugh with humorous and whimsical observations. He finished with one of his most well-known poems, "Shake the Dust," an inspiring piece urging the audience to <u>"grab this world by its clothespins and shake it out again and again and jump on top and take it for a spin and when you hop off shake it again for this is yours."</u>

> Using a quote adds interest, demonstrates what the author is responding to, and includes the audience in the event.

Poetry Night with Anis Mojgani was overall an intriguing and thought-provoking event. I was not expecting much, but I received much. I had not heard, read, or written poetry in a long time, but this event inspired me to seek it out. I also realized that the music I listen to is just poetry set to music. As Gwendolyn Brooks said, "Poetry is life distilled."

> You can write in response to almost anything, not just a piece of writing. In this case, the author has responded to an event.

Lesson 1.3
Writing to Summarize

By the time someone says, "to make a long story short," it's probably too late because they have been talking for quite a while already. What they probably meant to do was give you a summary.

A **summary** is a small, generalized overview of a larger amount of information. Instead of recreating something in its entirety, summary captures the point (the "gist") with only the most relevant and important details.

In this lesson, you will learn two important aspects of writing to summarize:

When to Summarize
How to Summarize

When to Summarize

Although most writing has multiple **purposes**, some amount of summary is usually necessary no matter what. For example, in an email to your classmates, you might summarize what happened in class. In a job interview, you might summarize the education and experience that make you qualified. In both situations, you're creating brief versions of larger amounts of details.

Using summary makes the most sense when your readers need a broad overview of a **topic** but not every detail. Because summaries are general, they should be used when you need to **inform** your audience about important background information.

Sometimes, you know when to summarize because it's in the details of an assignment. In elementary or middle school, you were probably asked to write book reports. Similarly, college instructors may ask you to summarize an article for homework or a pop quiz. In cases like these, you're expected to write a detailed summary that could be one or more paragraphs.

For example, consider this prompt:

> Write a one-page summary of your favorite American novel. On a second page, write a reflection that explains why you chose it.
>
> For an assignment like this, you'll want to provide important details related to the **main idea(s)**, event(s), and/or character(s) from the text. The first two paragraphs of an assignment based on the prompt might look like this:
>
> In *The Great Gatsby*, author F. Scott Fitzgerald gives readers a glimpse into the American Jazz Age through the voice of the narrator and main character, Nick Carraway. Nick recounts the summer of 1922—a time of optimism, romance, recklessness, desire, and greed—in Long Island, New York. The story starts after Nick rents a house in the fictional West Egg district, where his wealthy neighbor, Jay Gatsby, often throws large, extravagant parties.
>
> Although Nick is from Minnesota, he does have a cousin, Daisy Buchanan, who lives in the upper-class East Egg district with her husband, Tom. Early in the novel, while visiting Daisy and Tom, Nick meets Jordan Baker, with whom he begins a summer romance. When the four attend one of Gatsby's parties, it doesn't take long for Nick to discover that Daisy and Gatsby have a romantic history.

In other cases, an especially brief summary may be necessary for providing background information about the main idea of a text. Rather than summarizing an entire book or article, you may need to summarize a particular idea or **fact** within that book or article.

For example, consider this prompt:

> Write a two-page analysis of the character development in one of the novels we read this semester. Support your claims with specific examples from the novel.
>
> For an assignment like this, your main goal is to **analyze.** However, you'll want to provide the reader with context (through summary) so that your main idea is clear. The introduction of the assignment might look like this:
>
> Like other protagonists in L.M. Montgomery's novels, Emily Starr is an idealist and optimist. Throughout the novel, Emily reaches for her dream of becoming a famous poet. In climbing the "alpine path," however, Emily is unknowingly limited by her belief that fame is synonymous with happiness. The idealism that first drove Emily to seek notoriety nearly extinguishes her artistic spirit, but ultimately, it rescues her from despondency.
>
> This paragraph includes a combination of summary and analysis. It references only the events that are relevant to the author's main idea: Emily Starr's development as a character.

Writing Environment: Academic

When instructors ask you to summarize and critique a text, they usually want to see how you apply course content to an outside reading, such as a scholarly article. For example, a sociology professor may ask you to summarize a news story and then analyze what sociological theory it demonstrates. A biology professor may ask you to summarize an article in a scientific journal and use the information in an experiment. In each case, the summary merely shows that you understood the article. The analysis (or critique) matters more and should make up the bulk of your writing.

How to Summarize

The key to summarizing is shortening. The length of a summary should be significantly more concise than the original text.

Use these strategies to create a concise summary:

- Use general words and phrases that encompass specific details from the original text.
- Only include information that is relevant to your purpose.
- Include the most important ideas and details from the original text.

Use General Words and Phrases

Consider the following excerpt from Franklin D. Roosevelt's 1941 "Four Freedoms" speech to Congress:

> In the future days, which we seek to make secure, we look forward to a world founded upon four essential human freedoms.
>
> The first is freedom of speech and expression—everywhere in the world.
>
> The second is freedom of every person to worship God in his own way—everywhere in the world.
>
> The third is freedom from want—which, translated into world terms, means economic understandings which will secure to every nation a healthy peacetime life for its inhabitants—everywhere in the world.
>
> The fourth is freedom from fear—which, translated into world terms, means a world-wide reduction of armaments to such a point and in such a thorough fashion that no nation will be in a position to commit an act of physical aggression against any neighbor—anywhere in the world.

Here's a summary:

> In his "Four Freedoms" speech, Franklin Delano Roosevelt explained that freedom of speech and worship and freedom from want and fear are the four freedoms essential for democracy.

> The excerpt from FDR's nine-page speech is fairly brief itself, so the summary above is even shorter while still comprehensive.

Only Include Relevant Information

Considering only relevant information is particularly important when you're using summary as a supporting detail. A **supporting detail** is a piece of information, also called evidence, that is used to support a main idea.

Take another look at this introductory paragraph:

> Like other protagonists in L.M. Montgomery's novels, Emily Starr is an idealist and optimist. Throughout the novel, Emily reaches for her dream of becoming a famous poet. In climbing the "alpine path," however, Emily is unknowingly limited by her belief that fame is synonymous with happiness. The idealism that first drove Emily to seek notoriety nearly extinguishes her artistic spirit, but ultimately, it rescues her from despondency.

> This writer summarizes only the events that are relevant to character development of Emily Starr. For the same assignment, another student might use summary that focuses only on events that support a claim about Perry Miller, another main character in the novel.

On Your Own

Chelsie is writing a persuasive email motivating her club lacrosse teammates to fire their current coach, who hasn't shown up to any of their games so far. She wants to include a reference to the Declaration of Independence, and she finds the excerpt below. What makes this excerpt relevant to Chelsie's cause?

> "We hold these truths to be self-evident, that all men are created equal, that they are endowed by their Creator with certain unalienable Rights, that among these are Life, Liberty and the pursuit of Happiness.—That to secure these rights, Governments are instituted among Men, deriving their just powers from the consent of the governed,—That whenever any Form of Government becomes destructive of these ends, it is the Right of the People to alter or to abolish it, and to institute new Government."

How can you summarize the main idea of this passage? Read the attempts below and circle the summary you think is best.

Summary 1

> Of course, people are made equal and have some God-given rights, like staying alive, being free, and trying to be happy. People make governments to protect these rights and agree to be governed, giving their okay to powerful people. If some government goes against these purposes, it is the duty of the people to replace that government.

Summary 2

> Obviously, everybody is equal and has certain rights from God, including living, freedom, and a chance to thrive. People make governments to protect these rights, pooling their power until their government works against it; then they have to change or overturn it.

Summary 3

> Clearly, people are equal and have rights, so they agree to make a government to protect those rights and should overthrow any government that doesn't.

Writing Environment: Everyday

If you have ever filled out an accident report, you know that it requires focusing only on the relevant details. This way of selecting details is a type of summary. The version you tell friends and family will include details about how you were thinking and feeling and what happened before and after the accident. However, the report will be shorter and only include a precise and objective account of the facts.

Include the Most Important Ideas and Details

In a longer, detailed summary of a text, focus on the main idea(s) and the most important details. To find these components, **annotate** each paragraph or section of the reading. In your **annotations**, identify the main idea and supporting details in each paragraph. Then, review all the main ideas and ask yourself these questions:

- What is the author's **thesis**? What main ideas are stated or implied in the thesis?
- What details does the author use to support the thesis?
- What is the purpose of the story? What main events illustrate that purpose?

Take a look at this example of an annotated paragraph.

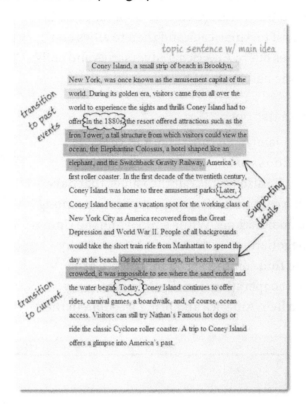

Lesson Wrap-up

Key Terms

Analyze: the process of thinking critically about a text and drawing inferences about its ideas

Annotating: a strategy for taking notes while reading

Annotation: an informal note or comment entered in the margin of a text

Fact: a piece of information that most people generally agree to be true

Informative Writing: a text that gives the audience information about a topic

Main Idea: the statement or argument that an author tries to communicate

Purpose: the goal of a text

Summary: a small, generalized overview of a larger amount of information

Supporting Detail: a piece of information, also called evidence, that is used to support a main idea

Thesis Statement: the major claim or idea supported by evidence in a piece of writing

Topic: the general subject of a text

Writing to Summarize: a writing purpose that presents a small, generalized overview of a larger amount of information

Writing Application: Writing to Summarize

First, consider the following preview of John F. Kennedy's Inaugural Address. The preview will show you the structure of the speech and anticipate major topics. Then, write your own summary of it.

> In his first speech as President of the United States, Kennedy knows that various factions around the world are curious about him, so he offers a series of pledges, first to Americans and then to allies and other groups. He also reaches out to America's adversaries and ends with two mottos that became hallmarks of his administration.

Compare your summary with this one:

> In his Inaugural Address on January 20, 1961, John F. Kennedy contrasts the military conditions of his day with those of the Revolutionary War era, but he also points out the values that have been preserved through the centuries. He urges cooperation among allies and promises aid to poor nations. While supporting the United Nations, he urges peace negotiations with America's enemies by encouraging each nation to find common ground, enforce arms control, and have scientific cooperation. Finally, he urges every citizen to ask how they can help America and bring freedom in the world.

This information about the speech provides context.

Summaries should be written from a third-person perspective.

The author uses original wording.

Lesson 1.4
Writing to Propose

After six weeks of cold water and broken tiles, Nick is beyond irritated with the showers in Thompson Hall. He rallies his fellow students, and they petition the campus housing director to update the facilities. Nick proposes the following changes:

- Showers should be completely refurbished within one academic year.
- Funds should be diverted from the planned updates to the auditorium and campus movie theater.
- In the meantime, Thompson residents should have access to hall bathrooms in a more updated dorm.
- If no immediate action is taken, Thompson Hall residents are prepared to go on a "bathing strike."

A **proposal** is a plan or suggestion submitted for consideration or discussion by others. Proposals usually include a request or recommendation intended to solve a problem or address a need. As a result, writing a proposal requires carefully studying a situation or problem and using persuasive tactics to convince your audience that your request or solution is worthwhile.

Formal written proposals are required for business and academic research, but you also make proposals in everyday situations. Recommending weekend plans with friends or simply suggesting a restaurant for lunch are examples of informal proposals. They attempt to solve a problem and demonstrate how your recommendation benefits others.

In this lesson, you will learn about the following aspects of writing to propose:

When We Write to Propose
Building a Written Proposal
Considering the Audience

When We Write to Propose

Formal proposals may be written to secure permission, assistance, money, or materials. In academics, proposals are often gateways for research or change. They present new ideas, theories, and breakthroughs while persuading the audience to take action. Here are some examples of academic situations that might require a proposal:

> A medical student proposes new methods for increasing the efficiency of emergency medical care in article for the *Harvard Medical Student Review.* She recommends that hospitals with specialized capabilities should accept transfer patients and not discharge them until their condition is resolved.

> Two professors present a paper at a conference for the National Association for Music Education, explaining the need to expand musical studies across all levels of education. Their research suggests a direct correlation between music education and the development of language skills. They propose using music to teach subjects like English, history, and social studies.

> The College of Agriculture proposes a community outreach program to the state government for educating urban neighborhoods about how to grow food. The proposal recommends an inner-city vegetable garden, growing classes, food preparation instructions, and free vegetables for members of the community.

In business, proposals often include requesting financial backing from investors or asking another department for support and cooperation to implement a new program.

Business proposals present plans and needs persuasively in order to capture attention and win approval. This requires a combination of clear, persuasive writing and concise presentation of **facts**. Here are some common types of business proposals:

Corporate research

> An aerospace engineer proposes a new research study on how to reduce the risks of taking electronic devices on commercial aircraft. Her proposal is addressed to airplane manufacturers and asks for both testing facilities and funding.

Project approval within a corporation

> After several employees are hurt in accidents at an auto-parts machining company, corporate headquarters asks the regional manager to investigate the causes of the accidents and submit a formal proposal for new safety procedures.

Client proposals to win bids and new business

> A national department store sends a Request for Proposal (RFP) to several health insurance companies. The insurance companies are expected to create "rate and benefit proposals." Each insurance company attempts to have the most cost-effective plans with the greatest number of benefits to win the store's business for the new enrollment year.

Small business loans/grants

> A young chef dreams of opening his own bistro and puts together a proposal asking for start-up funds from his local Small Business Bureau. His proposal lists his qualifications and experience. It also explains that he already has raised three-fourths of the money, proving he is committed to his project and is a good investment risk.

Nonprofit funding/grants

> A small not-for-profit farm that grows fresh produce for local food banks needs a new tractor. They apply for a State Agriculture Grant of $7,000, competing with other small farms that also need money for operating expenses.

> Helpful Hint
>
> When selecting a topic for a proposal, choose something interesting and meaningful to you. Your proposal will be more convincing if it's about something you really care about, and your enthusiasm will convince your readers to put your plan into action.

Building a Written Proposal

To write a proposal, follow these steps:

1. Get the audience's attention with a hook
2. Define/describe the problem/need
3. Propose your recommendation/plan for action
4. Provide supporting evidence
5. Anticipate objections to your proposal
6. Ask for support, assistance, and/or action

Get Your Audience's Attention

A **hook** grabs the audience's attention, often by making an initial appeal to their emotions. A shared personal experience or a brief story, or **anecdote**, may also be effective hooks.

> Helpful Hint
>
> When developing a hook for your proposal, consider your subject matter. Your hook should reflect the **tone** of your proposal. For example, if your tone is serious, don't start with a joke.

Define the Problem/Need

Following the hook, clearly define the issue and/or provide an overview of the problem. Include background information about the issue and its relevance.

Propose Your Recommendation

After presenting the background information, suggest a plan of action or your intended goal. Give a preview of the **supporting details** you plan on using to support your proposal.

On Your Own

Read the following descriptions of proposals. Identify the statement that does *not* propose a solution, plan, or goal.

> Healthy, fast-casual restaurants are becoming the most popular food franchises in America.

> Cyber-bullying ends when students, parents, and teachers recognize the symptoms and start working together to help both the bullied and the bullies.

> Life Source Opportunity Center hopes to convert their holiday food drive into a year-round food pantry through both charitable donations and state grants.

Provide Evidence

Provide **evidence**, or supporting details, for your ideas by discussing them in detail. Supporting evidence creates the bulk of your proposal. It should be fact-based, and it may include specific instances where the proposed action has proven effective.

Here's an example that uses evidence to support three ideas for protecting pets:

> Action 1: Microchip your pets. If they get lost, animal control or a veterinarian can scan the chip and contact you.
> Action 2: Use social networking to get the word out about missing pets. Pictures and descriptions can be sent to thousands of people instantly. Some social networking sites are even dedicated to finding lost pets.
> Action 3: Take advantage of free neuter and spay clinics. Many shelters offer these services for feral animals as well.

Anticipate Objections

Use a **counterargument** to effectively respond to weaknesses in the proposal. When you anticipate **objections** to your proposal, you are letting your audience know that you are aware of any part of your plan that might be perceived as weak or problematic.

Troubleshooting problems also shows that you've considered the issue from every angle. This improves your **credibility**: what makes you believable.

Ask for Support

In your **conclusion**, after recapping the main points of your proposal, make a last appeal to your audience's reason and emotions. Leave them confident they are making the right choice in reading and approving your proposal, and ask them directly to join you in your effort to make change.

Considering Audience

When you write, it is important to be aware of your **audience**: the people who will read your writing. If you know for whom you're writing, you can make the best decisions about what information to include. You can also adjust your tone and language.

Specifically for a proposal, your audience is a person or group of people with the power to support or implement your solution or recommendation. Addressing the wrong people costs time and money, and it can even defeat your purpose.

Before you start writing, consider who your audience is, what you want them to do, and what they need from you to be convinced. Use the following questions to clearly identify your audience and address their needs:

Who is Your Audience?

After you have chosen the subject of your proposal but before you begin drafting, make sure you know exactly who you are addressing. What does this group of people know about the subject, what do they know about you, and what will make your recommendation valuable to them?

Do You Have Multiple Audiences?

If your audience is made up of multiple groups of people, make sure your proposal addresses all of them. For instance, if you are recommending improvements in a local school district, you must consider students, teachers, parents, homeowners, and any others who might be impacted by the changes. Will traffic patterns be interrupted? Will local businesses be inconvenienced? Who will be paying for the improvements?

What Does Your Audience Need/Want?

Just as you hope to "get something" from your audience, your audience also wants something in return. What's in it for them? They want to invest their support, time, money, and materials wisely. Your audience is cultivating its own reputation by assisting and helping you.

On Your Own

An English professor regularly volunteers for literacy initiatives in a low-income, rural community. A local school asks him to research companies that might be willing to donate money to fund an after-school study program. He has several companies in mind.

After reading the descriptions of potential business donors, decide which company represents an audience whose needs would be met by assisting the local after-school study program.

- A dry-cleaning chain already donating to several school programs

- An international airplane manufacturer that has recently moved into the area and wants to be "accepted as part of the community"

- A car dealership known for its work with autism charities

What is Most Important to Your Audience?

What do members of your audience have in common? Why are these people all reading your proposal?

If your proposal is for school improvement, you're addressing any and all people who will be impacted by those improvements. Regardless of how they are otherwise different, what one feature do they share? This might be best illustrated by a **Venn diagram**. High school students who can drive, teachers, parents, administrators, local business owners, and homeowners are a diverse group, but they would all be affected by a new traffic light at the corner near the school. How will this change their route and driving patterns?

What is Least Important to Your Audience?

It is important to be concise when writing a proposal. Your audience does not want to feel that their time has been wasted. Define your need, propose your plan of action, and ask for your audience's consideration and/or help. Get to the point and make your case. Avoid technical explanations and long-winded arguments.

Also avoid **bias**; be honest, transparent, and clear. There is no need to criticize, assign fault to, or attack your opposition. Stay on track, focus your argument, and emphasize the benefits of your solution.

Lesson Wrap-up

Key Terms

Anecdote: a long example told as a story

Audience: the person or group of people for whom your writing is intended

Bias: a person's opinions and preferences

Conclusion: a paragraph that ties together the ideas in a paper and summarizes the main points, also called a concluding paragraph

Counterargument: when an author anticipates objections from the audience and refutes the objections with logic

Credibility: what makes someone or something believable

Evidence: the available body of facts or information indicating whether a belief or proposition is true or valid

Fact: a piece of information that most people generally agree to be true

Hook: the first sentence or two in a piece of writing that aims to immediately engage the reader

Objection: an expression or feeling of disapproval or opposition; a reason for disagreeing, or the action of challenging or disagreeing with something

Proposal: a plan or suggestion, especially a formal or written one, put forward for consideration or discussion by others

Supporting Detail: a piece of information, also called evidence, that is used to support a main idea

Tone: the positive, negative, or neutral attitude that an author expresses about a topic

Venn Diagram: a chart that uses overlapping circles to illustrate similarities and differences between two or more things

Writing to Propose: a writing goal that offers suggestions and solutions to an issue or problem

Writing Application: Writing to Propose

Read the following proposal. What is the problem, and what solution and/or plan does the author suggest for fixing it? Is it a persuasive argument?

Creating an Oasis in the Desert

Connie Wright is a single mom who lives in West Middleton with her two children. She usually grocery shops at the local Big Lots, which offers the barest of necessities. To reach the closest full-service supermarket, she must take a long bus ride

The proposal begins with an anecdote used as a hook to grab the reader's attention.

to get there and a taxi to get back home. In addition to the ten-dollar cab fare, the taxi also charges her an extra twenty-five cents for each bag of groceries. Connie's problem is that she lives in a desert, but not the kind with sand and cacti. She lives in a food desert, and she is not the only one.

A food desert is defined as an urban area or rural neighborhood without ready access to fresh, healthy, and affordable food. Food deserts are a major problem in the West Middleton area, where approximately 15,000 people live in a food desert or low-access community. Low-access communities are generally defined as those more than a mile from a full-service grocery store. Many of the residents do not own a car.

The second paragraph clearly defines the problem.

With the lack of affordable and fresh grocery options, coupled with an absence of reliable and affordable transportation, the citizens of West Middleton are desperate to find an oasis in this overwhelming food desert. A solution to this problem is the implementation of mobile farmers' markets or community-operated and -maintained produce gardens. These options could provide healthy food options to low-income families while simultaneously helping local farmers promote and sustain their businesses.

This paragraph provides a clear solution to the problem.

Mobile markets have already proven to be successful in neighboring cities such as Winnsboro and Easton. These mobile farmers' markets honor all government food assistance programs as payment. The "Mobile Veggies" program in Easton not only honors government assistance, they also have a "Free-to-Seniors" program supplemented by donations from the local farmers' market. "Farmers for Families," in Winnsboro, is a non-profit organization that has also incorporated a mobile farmers' market into existing free-standing farmers' market and community-supported agriculture programs to bring healthy, local food to those less fortunate.

This paragraph supports the solution with evidence of its success in other towns.

While there is yet to be a fully functioning program like these operating in the West Middleton area, residents can rest assured knowing that help is on the way. Erin Coffey and Tori Linn, recent graduates of the state university, are working towards starting a mobile farmers' market that will operate in the West Middleton area. Their intention is to provide locally sourced fruits, vegetables, dairy products, and meats by means of a retrofitted school bus. They will accept cash, credit and debit cards, or government assistance programs. They will also offer free cooking demonstrations and recipe cards.

This supporting paragraph shows that there is already local interest in creating mobile farmers' markets, making it an easy solution to implement.

Even with a mobile farmers' market, some families might still be unable to afford or find healthy nutritional options. Rosa Villacruz, the founder of Middleton Community Farm, may be able to fill the gap. She is opening her farm to the public in the summer of 2016. She will offer tours to the public and provide them with gardening and cooking instructions. Not only will gardens provide the community with fresher produce options, they will also provide members of the community with the necessary skills to begin their own urban farms.

This paragraph discusses a second solution: creating community gardens.

While mobile farmers' markets and urban farms can provide a community with healthier food options, they only solve one side of the equation. The people of the community must be willing to improve their dietary habits and be informed on how to fully utilize this new food source. If a rewards program is implemented (like Free-to-Seniors in Winnsboro), and Coffey and Linn's mobile market work together with Villacruz's community farm project, this unified network could bring the community together and entice people to maintain their new lifestyle changes.

This paragraph uses a counterargument to anticipate and address possible objections.

Food deserts are not a problem indicative of lack of food but of lacking proper access to the right food. Mobile farmers' markets and urban farms are feasible solutions. Mobile markets can cater to a larger radius, and the use of locally sourced goods will assist farmers in the promotion and sustenance of their businesses. Urban farms can ensure that the people who are unable to match the schedule or route of the mobile markets will still have fresh foods and learn the skills necessary to grow their own produce. Implementing mobile markets and urban farms can make an oasis in West Middleton's food desert.

This paragraph concludes the proposal by restating what the problem is and how it can be solved.

Lesson 1.5
Writing to Discuss

Let's talk. What have you recently discussed with your friends? Spouse? Boss? Although the word *discuss* sometimes has negative connotations, it simply involves exchanging ideas and information.

Discussion takes place in both formal and informal settings: watching a television show with your friends, meeting with colleagues to plan a project, or talking at the dinner table with your family. Although you engage in verbal discussion all the time, you may not often think about discussion as an approach to writing.

In this lesson, you will learn the following strategies for discussion writing:

Recognize Discussion in Writing
Generate Questions for Discussion
Respond to Your Questions for Discussion

Writing to discuss is often a goal of **expository writing.** You might be less familiar with expository writing than you are with other modes of writing. However, expository writing is just as prevalent in everyday life; it just tends to go by a few different names, like "example writing," or "illustration."

To learn more about expository writing, see Lesson 2.3.

Recognize Discussion in Writing

Discussion is an exchange of ideas or information surrounding a particular topic. It may be used to explain a situation or compare one theory to another.

Discussion is often used in texts that also include purposes like **writing to argue**, **writing to analyze**, and **writing to evaluate**. However, the discussion portion of these texts does not take a side. Instead, it explores all the points of view and information about the topic. A discussion may identify and consider subjective ideas, but it does so in an exploratory manner; it does not seek to drive home an **argument**.

Think about discussions you have in class or at work. Usually, discussions are not short, and they are not truly discussions if they are one-sided. Instead, the discussion leader seeks to keep the conversation going by encouraging everyone to contribute their ideas.

Discussion provides a platform for your ideas to flow.

Similarly, if you intend to discuss your subject in a piece of writing, include multiple details, explanations, and interpretations.

Consider the following passage written by a student who is thinking through two different perspectives on zoos.

> Those in favor of zoos say they educate people about animals. They also allow people to better enjoy the beauty of wildlife. Zoos can also protect endangered species by keeping them safe from hunters and poachers. Additionally, zoos make it easier for scientists to study animals and help certain species survive. Zoo animals also get proper nutrition and medical care for injuries.

> On the other hand, some say that zoos are unfair to animals and create major problems for them. Wild animals run in large spaces, but a zoo is a small, restricted area. When animals are held in captivity, they also lose important survival skills and can never be released back into the wild. In

zoos, animals are often not in their natural habitat and climate and cannot be outdoors year-round. Also, some animals, like orcas, often become depressed and die quickly in captivity.

This is not a polished discussion essay, but it's a good start. The writer is considering the issue from both sides and exploring multiple ideas.

Reflection Questions

How would you lead a class discussion about gender roles in the workplace? How would you engage your peers in the conversation? How would you keep the discussion moving while still allowing everyone to voice their opinions?

Generate Questions for Discussion

Just as a discussion leader poses questions for the class to consider, you can develop questions to direct your own discussion of a topic.

To get your ideas flowing for discussion, consider question like these:

In what ways . . . ?

If you could. . . ?

How do these. . . ?

Describe a time when this happened. . .

What connects to. . . ?

Imagine that you are leading a discussion about realism in American literature. You ask the class to read an essay that **analyzes** Edith Wharton's *The House of Mirth*. Here's an excerpt from the essay:

> Hardship. Unhappiness. Confinement. Rebellion. These are just a few of the words that describe a woman subject to the demands of the New York social elite in the early 1900s. These struggles are realities that Wharton, as a realist, aims to expose through dramatized accounts of her own experiences. In her novel, *The House of Mirth,* Wharton illustrates the conflict between woman and society through her depiction of the complex character Lily Bart.

To prepare for your discussion, you come up with this set of questions about the passage:

> What can be gleaned about Wharton's feelings toward "the demands of the New York social elite?"
>
> Where does the author get the idea of "confinement"?
>
> How do these ideas connect to your understanding of realism?

On Your Own

Read the passage below. Then, think of at least four questions that will generate discussion about the passage and write them in the space below.

> We should be doing everything in our power to spur on technological advances in energy instead of drilling for more oil. Some lawmakers believe that the solution is to ban automobiles with poor gas mileage. However, this is unnecessary. Car manufacturers are always improving their designs, and automobiles with bad gas mileage will naturally become impractical or obsolete. In the meantime, countries

with scientific resources should explore more seriously solar power, hydropower, and other alternative sources of energy. The massive amounts of crude oil needed to keep just one country like the U.S. functioning would not be remedied by continued drilling. Even disregarding the environmental damage it causes, continuing to depend so heavily on oil and neglecting alternative energy is like putting a band-aid on a broken leg.

Group Activity

Split up into groups of three or four and use your questions to discuss the previous passage. Which questions seemed to prompt the most responses? Which questions encouraged people to share different perspectives?

Developing your Questions

Use your questions from the previous activity to develop your ideas even further for in-depth discussion.

Question Development Checklist

- ☐ Your questions offer more than a "yes" or "no" answer.
- ☐ Your questions use description or analysis.
- ☐ Your questions include **examples** from the passage and/or direct quotes.
- ☐ Your questions link ideas together.
- ☐ Your questions attempt to define an idea or concept.
- ☐ Your questions demonstrate an understanding of an idea or concept.

Respond to Your Questions for Discussion

By skillfully answering questions you've generated, you are actively contributing to academic discourse. Follow these steps as you build your answers and discussion:

1. Divide the question up into separate pieces for dissecting and answering.

2. When answering, make sure you address the subject or theme as well as point of view.

3. Include **evidence** that illustrates your assertions in discussion.

4. Expand your answers to make sure they fully encompass well-developed ideas.

Lesson Wrap-up

Key Terms

Analyze: to understand something by looking at its parts

Argument: a reason why you should think or act a certain way

Discussion: an exchange of ideas or information surrounding a particular topic

Evidence: a piece of information, also called a supporting detail, that is used to support a main idea

Example: a specific instance or illustration that demonstrates a point

Expository Writing: writing that uses evidence to support a main idea

Writing to Analyze: a writing purpose achieved by examining something you have read or studied

Writing to Argue: a writing purpose that convinces the audience to adopt a belief or take an action

Writing to Discuss: a writing purpose that presents issues or interprets something you have read or studied

Writing to Evaluate: a writing purpose achieved by creating criteria for judging something you have read or studied

Writing Application: Writing to Discuss

Remember, nearly all writing has an argument, but in writing to discuss, persuasion is not the primary goal. Read the following essay and pay attention to how it discusses a medieval book of courtly etiquette.

Courting Princes

In the 16th century, Baldesar Castiglione wrote a book comprised of a series of discussions about the proper behavior of a courtier. It became one of the most influential and widely-known etiquette manuals in Europe. Centuries before, Ovid wrote *Ars Amatoria*, a collection of poems that describes how to win a female's attentions. Despite the significant time gap (1,526 years), Castiglione's *The Book of the Courtier* is very similar to Ovid's instructions on the art of love. However, in Castiglione's book, a prince is being courted instead of a woman. To be a successful courtier and win the approval of the prince, one must express nonchalance in intelligence, physical prowess, and appearance.

With the dawn of the Renaissance came a new ideal of courtly behavior and genteel manners. Intelligence was key for soliciting a prince because it was useful for battle tactics, diplomacy, and everyday affairs. However, Castiglione stressed how important it was to "practice in all things a certain nonchalance which conceals all artistry and makes whatever one says or does seem uncontrived and effortless" (67). Through the dialogue of the characters, he builds on the old values of being courtly by adding the quality of *sprezzatura*: doing something without seeming to put forth effort. Ovid also emphasizes this quality in *Ars Amatoria*. He urges his audience to "dissemble / Your powers, avoid long words / Don't look too highbrow" in order to win over women (lines 463-465 Ovid).

This essay identifies a similarity between two works, but arguing this idea is not its primary purpose.

Even in writing to discuss, a strong thesis like this one is best because it gives the essay structure.

This statement answers the discussion question, "What connects to The Book of the Courtier?*"*

Courtiers were also expected to be fit and skilled at various physical exercises, not only for a practical reason, like war, but also for entertainment, like hunting. However, according to *The Book of the Courtier*, even nonchalance during these highly physical activities is admirable for several reasons. First, sweating and brute strength are associated with peasants and considered crass and "too anxious" (Castiglione 62). Second, if a courtier is casual about his physical strength and abilities, it creates the illusion that he is even more formidable than he actually is. "How much more agreeable and admired is a warrior when he is modest, saying little and boasting hardly ever" (69). Similarly, Ovid encourages men to be fit and athletic so that they appear pleasing to women.

This essay both informs the audience about *The Book of the Courtier* and analyzes it.

Finally, to court a prince successfully and become politically and socially influential, a courtier must be clean and attractive. Castiglione writes that nobles should ideally be born with a good countenance, but if not they should do their best to be presentable and agreeably hygienic. However, they must still maintain masculinity. "I don't want him to appear soft and feminine as so many try to do, when they ... curl their hair and pluck their eyebrows" (61). This echoes Ovid's words in *Ars Amatoria*: "Don't torture your hair, though, with curling-irons: don't / pumice / Your legs into smoothness" (504-506).

Discussion questions attempt to define a concept or idea. What concept does this essay try to define?

Including examples and quotes from each source makes the discussion stronger and more balanced.

In Baldesar Castiglione's *The Book of the Courtier*, the most important quality of a courtier is nonchalance that implies natural ability. His statements promoting balance in all things closely mirror Ovid's advice in *Ars Amatoria*. This confirms the impression that "courting" a prince in 16th century Italy may have borne a resemblance to courting a woman in ancient Rome.

Lesson 1.6

Writing to Describe

Every writer is an artist. We start with an idea that only we can see and show it to others. Some artists use paint, but writers use words.

A **descriptive text** uses vivid details to illustrate an idea or experience. The key to using description is showing, not telling.

This lesson will cover the following topics:

Why We Write to Describe

How We Write to Describe

On Your Own

Examine the following photo. How would you describe what's going on?

Reflection Questions

Think of a person, place, or thing that you imagined as a child. Maybe it was an imaginary friend, a magical universe, or the Tooth Fairy. How would you describe it so that someone else could visualize it?

Why We Write to Describe

Descriptive writing provides readers with perspective by helping them develop a thorough understanding of the author's intended message. You could use description in a story to show your readers an important character, in a restaurant review to recount a meal, or in a presentation to express your vision for a project.

In any description, you'll need to use words and ideas that help readers understand your perspective. For example, it's not enough to simply "tell" your audience that you had an unpleasant experience at a concert. Instead, you should help them "see" what you saw, "hear" what you heard, and "feel" what you felt when you got lost in the crowd.

Effective descriptions can leave a lasting impact on an audience, which is often why description is an effective approach to **persuasive writing**.

Describing to Persuade

We all know that "a picture is worth a thousand words." That's why **visual arguments**—messages within photographs and illustrations—are often used for posters, magazines, and billboards. What makes them so effective?

Consider these images:

What messages do these images communicate? What do they mean to you? How would your perception change if details of the images changed?

Advertisers know that visuals are a powerful persuasive tool. For example, if someone tells you that the donuts at Sweet Mary's are delicious, you *might* go to Sweet Mary's one day if you feel like making the trek. However, if someone shows you a mouth-watering image of the famous Berry Berry Sweet Special, you might walk right out the door and head to Sweet Mary's without hesitation.

What makes a visual argument effective is the dominant impression it leaves on an audience. You are not going to stop visualizing that Berry Berry Sweet Special until it is in front of you. Good descriptive writing will impact its audience the same way a visual message would: with a dominant impression. In persuasive writing, use description as a lens for the perspective you want your audience to adopt.

Writing Environment: Professional

Most employers ask applicants to submit a résumé. More often than not, they also ask applicants to *describe* their strengths and weaknesses along with information that makes them stand out. Employers do this so they can compare one job candidate to the next.

How We Write to Describe

The goal of descriptive writing is to create an experience. If you've had a great dinner at a new restaurant, you might tell your friends about everything, from how the restaurant looked to how each bite tasted. When you get your hair cut, you might describe the style you want. In these situations, you're trying to use the right words to paint a specific picture for your audience.

> Group Activity
>
> Break up into groups of three. One of you will act as the storyteller, and the other two will act as illustrators. The storyteller will describe a person, place, or thing using only words. Without looking at the image, each illustrator will draw a picture of the person, place, or thing being described. When everyone is finished, compare the drawings. How were your interpretations different or similar? How could the description have been more effective?

The **dominant impression** of a text is the overall feeling it communicates. Take a look at the following sentences. What feelings do they convey?

> Beep beep. Someone had received a notification. The unexpected noise lasted what seemed like a lifetime as we sat frozen in our seats. When he pushed his gun-metal gray frames down the thick slope of his nose, glaring at the teenage girl behind the front desk, we knew we were about to hear him angrily mumble something under his bearded breath. I stealthily checked my phone to make sure that it was set on silent.

> After she finished spinning on her short legs, her pink tutu bouncing, she stared at her daddy with dark brown eyes, melting his heart. He thought to himself just how much she looked like her mother. It had been three years since he watched his wife's last breath flow out of her tired mouth. Now, his delicate ballerina danced her mother's memory back into existence.

On Your Own

Read the following passage. How would you describe the style of the writing? To what extent does it help you visualize the scenario?

> Not too long ago, we went to the park. While we were walking around, we saw a woman jogging. We looked at the ice skating rink. As we sat on a bench and enjoyed our lunch, the park animals tried to steal our food. It was a fun time.

Rewrite this passage using descriptive words to create a clearer experience and dominant impression for the reader.

Use Specific Details

In descriptive writing, you should include specific details. Carefully choose words and phrases that will accurately set the scene for your audience. Consider this sentence:

> The man was wearing a blue shirt.
>
> A statement like this only allows your reader to see a vague image. Include more details to provide a more specific image. Here's a better example:
>
> The somber gentleman wore a faded, baggy shirt issued by the county jail.

Writing Environment: Professional

Description is often used in medical professions. The following example is from a nursing student who assessed a patient and described his or her condition.

Skin, Hair, & Nails	Assessment
Skin color	Skin was flesh tone
Rashes or lesions	Rash was found on the upper arms
Skin temperature & texture	Skin temp was warm to touch and rough
Turgor	Turgor reflected that patient was slightly dehydrated AEN late return of skin to original state after being pulled for a few seconds.
Capillary refill (hands and feet)	Capillary refill was <4 seconds in hands but slightly longer in the feet.
Hair (note pattern, texture, color, infestations)	Consistent, black with gray, no infestations
Palpate scalp (note lesions and tenderness)	No tenderness noted upon palpitation

Figurative Language

Sometimes, we lack just the right words to describe how we feel about a topic. In these situations, we can use figurative language. **Figurative language** is a non-literal word or word group that writers use to emphasize an idea or detail.

Here are some elements of figurative language that you might use in descriptive writing:

Simile	I am hungry as a horse.
Metaphor	To me, the stationary store was better than Christmas morning.
Personification	The strong, healthy wave pushed the sailboat forward with all of her might.
Onomatopoeia	Thwack! The arrow flew from Robin's bow and buried itself deep in the wooden target.

The Five Senses

Although all five of our senses are actively working throughout the day, we don't always notice them because we are so used to using them. Good writers take advantage of this familiarity in descriptive writing.

When you appeal to the senses to describe an event or meaningful moment, you provide the audience with a way to relate to an experience that is otherwise unfamiliar.

Consider the five senses and what they often describe:

- **Sight:** color, pattern, size, shape, reminds me of.....
- **Sound:** pitch, sound, length, distance, reminds me of.....
- **Smell:** disagreeable/agreeable, reminds me of....
- **Taste:** bitter, sour, sweet, tangy, salty, reminds me of....
- **Touch:** hard, soft, smooth, bumpy, reminds me of....

On Your Own

Think about what your senses are telling you right now. Where are you? Are you sitting? Are you holding anything with your hands? What do you smell? What do you taste, hear, and/or see?

Write a paragraph detailing everything you're feeling with every sense at this moment.

Sight

What would your readers see if they were present in the moment you're describing? Who would they meet? How could you give them the same first impression that you had?

> His yellow, calloused fingertips wormed around the package for the last cigarette. Almost in slow motion, he tilted it up to his cracked lips surrounded by thin wrinkles. As he held up a glowing match, his eyes admired the moment like a child mesmerized by a fire place. He lowered the smoking cigarette to his side, carefully avoiding the oxygen tank that wrapped its tubing along his neck.

Sound

Sometimes, sound can be overpowered by other senses. Try closing your eyes and listening to your surroundings. Are you in a busy office or a quiet room? Is the noise harsh or soft? Piercing or muffled? Are there people talking or cars speeding by?

One method to describe sound is **onomatopoeia**: using a word that imitates a sound. Some examples are *buzz*, *sizzle*, and *pop*. Some sounds are familiar to readers, while others might be new.

Read the following passage, paying close attention to the sounds:

> As the hum of the motor stopped, Chris' key chain swung and clanked against his steering wheel. We hopped out of his truck, slamming the doors shut and hurrying into the hall. Inside, we could hear nervous chatter from fans impatiently waiting in line. The opening band started playing, but we could only hear muffled bass booming out of speakers behind closed doors. Chris was saying something to me, but I couldn't make out his words.

Further Resources

Check out this video (https://www.youtube.com/watch?v=_JznyeOiqYE) about using sound effects in film. Sometimes, we are so busy watching a movie, we forget about the influence of background noises, sounds, and music.

Smell

When describing scent, most people just say *good* or *bad*. However, this isn't description; it's opinion. One person might think the smell of cooking liver and onions is delicious, but someone else might find it disgusting.

Instead of basing description on opinion, think about specific details. Is it a strong odor or a subtle fragrance? Is it sweet, sour, or something else?

Further Resources

Ironically, as much as we might struggle to describe smell, it's the sense most strongly connected to memory. Read this article (http://www.bbc.com/future/story/20120312-why-can-smells-unlock-memories) about how our sense of smell can remind us of past experiences.

Taste

Similar to smell, it can be tempting to simply say something tastes *good* or *bad*. However, taste buds can detect a wide range of flavors, including bitter, sour, sugary, spicy, and salty.

Read the following description from Zitkala Ša's "Impressions of an Indian Childhood" and look for description that appeals to the reader's sense of taste.

> In the early morning our simple breakfast was spread upon the grass west of our tepee. At the farthest point of the shade my mother sat beside her fire, toasting a savory piece of dried meat. Near her, I sat upon my feet, eating my dried meat with unleavened bread, and drinking strong black coffee.

Further Resources

Think about foods that you don't like. Have you ever thought about why you don't like these foods? Read or listen to this story (http://www.npr.org/blogs/thesalt/2014/10/01/352771618/from-kale-to-pale-ale-a-love-of-bitter-may-be-in-your-genes) from NPR about how biology can impact taste preferences.

Touch

Think about the sensations that your fingertips feel when you touch something. These sensations usually involve the texture, temperature, weight, and size.

While touch is one of the more difficult senses to describe, we experience life through what we feel. Read the following passage, paying close attention to how it appeals to the sense of touch:

> My shoes dig into the freshly cut grass of the outfield. I can feel the metal cleats twist into the grass, breaking the fragile blades. I bend my knees, my left hand sweating inside my new leather glove. I drag the back of my right hand across my slick forehead and wipe it on my stark white pants, my stomach tight from nerves. I watch the bat make contact with the ball, and it bolts in my direction. I run toward it, right hand grabbing the smooth, hard sphere, and throw it to first base, feeling as if it is cutting through the thick, summer heat.

On Your Own

Imagine you are in the scene pictured below and describe what you're experiencing with thorough details.

Lesson Wrap-up

Key Terms

Dominant Impression: the overall feeling communicated by a text

Figurative Language: a non-literal word or word group, also known as a literary device, that writers use to emphasize an idea or detail

Metaphor: a type of figurative language that connects two dissimilar things

Onomatopoeia: a type of figurative language that uses a word to imitate a sound

Personification: a type of figurative language that gives human traits to something non-human

Persuasive Writing: writing that uses argument to influence someone's beliefs and/or actions

Sensory Detail: a description that appeals to the senses: sight, sound, touch, taste, or smell

Simile: a type of figurative language that indicates similarities between two things

Visual Argument: messages within photographs and illustrations

Writing to Describe: a writing purpose that explains the appearance of someone or something using words that appeal to the senses

Writing Application: Writing to Describe

Read the following narrative that uses description. Which senses does it appeal to? Does it successfully communicate a clear image to you, the reader?

Alaska

My contempt begins underneath a Christmas tree while I'm lying on my dad's pea green shag carpet. I'm the girl with braids holding a brunette Barbie that I'm making climb up the branches of the shedding tree. The irritable, well-dressed girl to my right is making her Barbie a bed out of discarded gift bows; she is my new step-sister.

The key word contempt *indicates an unpleasant dominant impression right away.*

After a few minutes of silent play, she looks directly at me and instructs me to take my Barbie to Alaska. I have to go there where nobody would ever want to move, where it's cold, and I have to put layers of coats on my Barbie so nobody sees her legs, she explains. Alaska isn't located under the tree. I have to get up and move into the hallway. But her Barbie gets to go live in Hawaii. Her Barbie is beautiful, she tells me. Mine isn't. She tells me her Barbie wins. After she says all this, I pick up my Barbie and move. I don't care at the time. Alaska seems like a place I'd rather be, anyway. I'm stuck there in the living room visiting my dad. Her dad isn't here, so I let her have Hawaii.

The introduction and first body paragraph use descriptive writing to set up a comparison that exists throughout the entire essay.

We leave our childhoods and become women. It's Christmas time once again, twenty-five years later, and we find ourselves back in that living room. It takes two trips to the minivan before all of my family is in the house. I grab the diaper bag, a sippy cup, and my son before yelling at his sisters to put on their coats. As we all pile into the house, the faintly burned scent of the apple cake baking in the oven tells me someone needs to get it out.

I collect myself in the bathroom, pulling back my dark hair sprigged with grey and wiping the eyeliner that's already coming off. The green carpet has been replaced with cherry hardwood, but the tree is stationed in the same exact place it was when we were little. Suddenly, I wish I could go home.

Moments later, as my children are running through the hall and my step-mom is nervously telling me it's okay, that they can't break anything, my step-sister walks in. She looks exquisite. Her sleek, designer handbag is all she carries. Her wine-colored blouse and form-fitting pants make her look ageless. She glides through the living room and sits down on the burnt orange couch, not saying a word to her husband. They have no children.

At one point in the night, as I chase my girls around and make sure they don't spill, break, or disrupt anything, I finally speak to her. She's staring at me as my four-year-old slathers my lips with her new chocolate-flavored lip gloss. I politely ask her how she has been, aware that we don't keep up enough with each other to know or care. She looks judgmental as I speak, as usual. She replies with, "Fine."

I make my way into the kitchen to help clean up our Christmas dinner, and my step-mother begins. "They're getting divorced."

"Oh," I say, "I'm sorry. I didn't know."

"This will be her third divorce, you know," her mom says to me.

"Yeah, that's sad," is all I can think to say to her.

"She can't have kids."

"Oh, no. Do they know for sure?"

"Yes. That's why he's leaving her."

For the first time that night, I feel guilty. And like a total hypocrite. My four children feel more present than ever. My worries about losing baby weight feel trivial.

As we continue talking, the baby falls asleep on my shoulder. Tonight, he seems lighter. My dad starts a conversation about summer.

"What are you guys going to do?" he asks me.

"I doubt much. The baby will only be about nine months old, so we won't be able to go too far this year."

"What about you?" he asks my step-sister as she reapplies her expensive lipstick.

"I'm flying to Hawaii," she says.

We pack up the minivan with my children and some leftover chicken, making sure two of the four are secured in their car seats while the other two bicker in the back seat. I grab my husband's hand and close my eyes to get a little rest on the drive before we get home, realizing that I'd take Alaska over Hawaii any day.

> The conclusion ties together the theme of location that began in the first paragraph. Is the dominant impression still "contempt," or would you use another word?

Lesson 1.7
Writing to Argue

Arguments often have a negative connotation in everyday life. However, a written argument reasonably, logically, and politely presents the reasons for and against a position, sometimes offering a solution. The main goal of an **argument** is to convince others to adopt our way of thinking or at least be willing to compromise on the subject.

This lesson will discuss the following topics:

When to Make an Argument
How to Approach an Argument
Strategies for Delivering an Argument

When to Make an Argument

You should use argumentative writing when you need to justify your opinion or understanding of something.

A basic rule of argument is that it involves at least two opposing sides, or viewpoints. Make an argument only when you are prepared to defend your opinion with reasonable claims. **Reasonable claims** use common sense to draw logical conclusions based on evidence.

For example, imagine your dog disappears one night. You and your roommate hear a strange whirring noise above the house and see a bright flash of light in the backyard. The dog yelps, so you run out back, but he's nowhere to be found. Your roommate concludes that your dog was kidnapped by aliens, but you think this is an unreasonable argument for several reasons:

- Your roommate doesn't know what noise an alien spaceship makes.
- Your roommate has no reason to assume that aliens would want your dog.
- The probability of a visit from aliens seems low since you have never seen one before.

You argue that a helicopter flying low to the ground scared the dog into hiding, and this is a more likely conclusion for several reasons:

- You know that your dog is scared of the sounds that helicopters and cars make.
- Your dog frequently hides when he is scared.
- Helicopters frequent your neighborhood more often than aliens do.

In the passage below, the writer argues against a deer-hunting ban to support this claim: "I love hunting, and it isn't right for anyone to deny me that privilege."

> In the past, whenever hunting has not been permitted, overpopulation of deer has become a problem. There's only so much food to go around, so when too many deer occupy an area, some of them will starve, which is a cruel way for an animal to die. Furthermore, when deer are starving, they will strip all low-lying vegetation and foliage, including bark from trees as high as they can reach. This leads to the loss of smaller wildlife that also depends on the vegetation for survival.

Writing Environment: Professional

Consider the following scenario; given the situation, what are possible arguments?

> Jana works nights at a gas station/convenience store in a neighborhood known for its high crime rate. She feels more secure when her coworker Danny has the night shift too. However, Jana's manager, wants to cut costs, so she decides to let Danny go. What should Jana do? She needs this job, but she's afraid to mind the store alone at night. How should she approach her manager? Consider possible arguments Jana could make to change her manager's mind.

Group Activity

Have you ever faced a difficult problem at work? How did you handle it? Knowing how to argue reasonably and respectfully is a wonderful tool. Discuss similar situations you've been in and how you approached them. Did you argue?

We Argue Opinions, Not Facts

Not all topics are appropriate for argument. Facts, for instance, are never up for debate. A **fact** is anything that can be proven. An **opinion** is anything that cannot be proven, and it is always around opinions that arguments revolve. Remember that you will *argue* over *opinions*, but you will *support* your opinion with *facts*. The more proven information you have behind your position, the stronger it will be.

For example, to say that animal testing is used to develop many products is a fact, so this is not debatable. If, however, we want to contend that animal testing should not be used to develop cosmetics, we could argue about that because that's an opinion. Again, we argue about opinions, but we back up our opinions with facts.

Helpful Hint

When trying to determine if a statement is fact or opinion, watch for words and phrases such as *should, ought to, better, worse, prettier, uglier,* or any other word that indicates a judgment.

On Your Own

Read the following statements and identify the one that states a fact.

☐ Dogs, cats, apes, and mice are all used for research.
☐ Testing on animals should be outlawed.
☐ Animals always suffer in research labs.

Read the following statements and identify the one that is an opinion.

☐ Animals sometimes suffer in research labs.
☐ Research methods have changed over time.
☐ Only mice should be used for animal testing.

If we build the argument around an opinion, how might that look? Let's say that we're going to write an argument against animal testing; the **thesis** might look like this:

> Testing on animals should be banned because it's inhumane, inaccurate, and unnecessary.

The opinion (the part we're arguing about) is that animal testing should be banned. Now, we need to support our opinion with facts. Remember, we want to be logical and reasonable. Here's how the first body paragraph of that argument might look:

> First, animal testing should no longer be allowed because it is often cruel. When drugs are being tested on animals, pain medications usually can't be used because they could interfere with the results of the test. According to *Pro and Con*, "The US Department of Agriculture (USDA) reported in 2010 that 97,123 animals suffered pain during experiments while being given no anesthesia for relief." These animals included primates, rabbits, guinea pigs, and hamsters ("Testing"). This should not continue; it's wrong to make animals suffer this way.

> The paragraph started with an opinion; then, it backed up that opinion with proven facts, including **statistics** from a reputable source.

We Argue Values, not Preferences

Once you've chosen an opinion to argue, make sure it's a value, not a preference.

If we wanted to argue that rock 'n roll has changed the face of American culture, we could find plenty of evidence to back that up. In other words, we could find information supporting the *value* of rock. However, we could never find enough evidence to prove that rock music is *better* than country music because that's a matter of preference. If you're a country fan, I'll never convince you that rock is better, nor will you convince me that country is better.

Always be careful when you find yourself saying that one thing is better than another because these types of comparisons often fall into the realm of personal preference, which isn't appropriate for argument.

On Your Own

Which of the following would make a strong argument? Identify the correct sentence.

☐ Modern art is ugly.
☐ Picasso is a much better painter than Goya.
☐ The study of great art should continue to be offered in high schools.

Now let's look at a weak argument:

> Mexican food is the best because it's colorful, fun, and tasty.
>
> Why is this a weak argument? This is a personal preference. You could never find facts to support the argument that Mexican food is the "best." Here's how the first paragraph of this argument might begin:
>
> First, Mexican food is great because it's colorful. With the colorful corn, black beans, red tomatoes, and bright yellow cheese, it's just fun to look at.
>
> Where is the author going from here? Do you see the problem? The author could talk about colorful, fun food of all kinds—Mexican, Chinese, Italian—but it proves nothing beyond his or her own culinary preferences.

How to Approach Argument

Analyze Opposing Views

Rationally and fairly weighing all sides of an issue is integral to argument. This means recognizing various perspectives and circumstances that could make one viewpoint more sensible than another.

Before you begin any argument, you should familiarize yourself with all sides of the debate. To convince an audience, you must make your case based on the strengths of *your* position, but you must also deal with the strengths of the *opposing* position. This can be accomplished with a **counterargument**, which is when an author anticipates objections and refutes them with logic.

How do you decide what the opposing views are? **Brainstorming** is a good place to start. For argument, you should have two columns: one *pro* and one *con*. Complete the following activity to practice brainstorming.

On Your Own

The table below includes the two sides of several possible debates about capital punishment. Can you think of any others? Fill in your answers.

Yes to the Death Penalty	No to the Death Penalty
Closure for the victim's family	It won't bring back the victim
An eye for an eye	Thou shalt not kill
It deters crime	An innocent person might be executed

Now, you can create a thesis using one side of the list and prepare counterarguments using the other side of the list. Brainstorming, of course, can be a much longer process, but this should give you an idea of the basics.

Offer a Solution

After you have examined all the viewpoints on an issue, you're prepared to offer a solution. Argument is an excellent way to offer a solution to a problem, which is why it's often combined with **writing to propose**.

To learn more about writing to propose, see Lesson 1.4.

To offer a solution, find **common ground**, which is a place where both sides agree.

Let's consider illegal immigration. There are many perspectives on this issue, but for the sake of this example, let's imagine there are two clear sides. One side wants to keep all non-Americans out; the other side wants to let everyone in. These two positions are plainly at odds, so for compromise to occur, we first have to find the areas in which both sides can agree.

On Your Own

Of the following possibilities, which is the best example of common ground for these two viewpoints? Identify the correct sentence.

☐ All people deserve the right to work and feed their families.

☐ Everyone has the right to enter and work in any country.

☐ Illegal residents should have as many rights as American citizens.

Once we've established something everyone can agree on, we can move forward toward finding a solution. Here's an example:

> A good first step toward solving the immigration issue might be to start with young adults who have lived in the United States for most of their lives. If a child moved here from Mexico when he was a baby and is now seventeen years old, should he be sent back to Mexico? In every way except the paperwork, this young man is already American. He has grown up in American schools, speaks English as well as anyone else, and thinks of the small town in which he grew up as his hometown. He's a good student and a hard worker and is proud of living in the United States. Shouldn't young people like him be allowed to stay? Despite where he may have been born, this is his home.
>
> Do you see how the writer is reaching out to the other side, appealing to their feelings of home and fairness? This could be common ground from which to start on the path to finding a solution.

Strategies for Delivering an Argument

Three important aspects of arguing appropriately include the following:

- Tone
- Evidence
- Credibility

Tone

In written arguments, the importance of tone cannot be overemphasized. In verbal argument, we can use gestures, body language, inflection, and facial expressions. In a written argument, we have none of these tools. As writers, we have only our words, and our words contribute to our **tone**, which is the positive, negative, or neutral attitude that we communicate to the reader.

Writing Environment: Everyday

Imagine you get into a disagreement with a friend. You can yell and get angry and still hug at the end and be friends. It's not so easy when writing. Think of how often emails and texts are misinterpreted. It's the same when writing an argument. You must be very careful not to offend or upset your reader. If you lose your audience before making your point, your argument has failed.

Consider the following two examples. Which has the more appropriate tone?

> We should do away with welfare. If people were allowed to starve for a while, they'd get off their behinds and get to work. Those of us who work and pay taxes shouldn't have to pay for all of these deadbeats who just want to manipulate the system and get by without ever having to do anything. It's just not fair! If I have to work, so should they!

Now, let's try that again with a more reasonable tone:

> Welfare should be restructured. It was never intended to be generational, yet those raised to see welfare as a way of life don't know any other way. Perhaps a first good step would be to change the way the program is administered. Instead of giving people money, the program should give out food.

▷ Do you see the difference between the two passages? Don't use your words to provoke someone's anger like in the first example. Keep it fair and reasonable.

> To learn more about tone and word choice, see Lessons 5.4 and 5.6.

Evidence

When you're trying to convince others to agree with your position, facts are necessary. Those facts fall under the broader category of evidence. Sometimes, it helps to imagine evidence in a courtroom setting. Think of yourself as a lawyer trying to convince a jury to agree with you. Now think of **evidence** as your expert witness, someone brought in to support and prove what you say.

Here's an example that uses evidence:

> School uniforms have proven beneficial in redirecting student energies in positive ways. According to Susan MacNeil, a school principal in Abbotsford, B.C., "Negative behaviour was what the norm was and it would be supported, whereas now? Not at all — polite and courteous behaviour is what's expected." She went on to answer those who consider uniforms an infringement on students' rights to express themselves: "I know for many [parents and students] they think it's just going to create an atmosphere for anonymity — it doesn't. What it does do is it takes away the draw of the eye to the garment and brings you to the face and to the personality of the child" (Cahute).
>
> Source: Cahute, Larissa. "Uniforms on Rise in B.C. Schools: Two Abbotsford public schools join the list in a move that parents hope will cut down on bullying." *The Province*, 5 July 2012, A3. *PressReader*, http://www.pressreader.com/canada/the-province/20120705/281526518155567.

A school principal is an expert source on this topic, so her views make the author's argument more convincing.

The types of information used for evidence include facts, statistics, **expert analysis,** and more. The sources of this information must be documented appropriately. You want proof that is academically acceptable, so be especially careful with websites. Stick with academic databases, school and government websites, and websites written by experts. Be very careful about blogs and websites that are pushing any kind of agenda.

To learn more about properly documenting sources, see Lesson 7.5.

Credibility

We have discussed the importance of acknowledging the opposing side in order to maintain honesty with the audience. In a broader sense, this honesty is part of **credibility**, which is your believability. Another way to think of credibility is trustworthiness; if it's ever lost, the argument is over.

A major part of maintaining credibility is avoiding **logical fallacies**. Let's say an article argues that legalizing casinos in your state is a good idea. It discusses how casinos will positively affect the economy, but it doesn't mention what can accompany casinos, such as crime, prostitution, and bankruptcy. The article is not being honest because it is arranging the facts to look better than they are. Not only is this dishonest, it's also unfair to the audience because they can't make an informed decision without knowing all the facts.

To learn more about logical fallacies, see Lesson 5.8.

Group Activity

Can you think of any industries that habitually use logical fallacies? Think of commercials you've seen that may misrepresent the whole truth. Discuss how likely you are to trust the people making these types of skewed arguments.

In order to honestly present the facts to your audience, you must also know them yourself and get them from a credible source. First, if you use information to support your argument, make sure that information is correct. Second, remember that using facts from a disreputable source can affect your own credibility as a writer.

Sometimes, using information from a disreputable source can actually support your argument. For example, if you want to argue that certain American news outlets are untrustworthy, to demonstrate your point you could include quotes from news stories that are clearly **biased**. However, to protect your own credibility, always explain why you're using biased information and how it supports your argument.

On Your Own

You must be wary of sources that are trying to sell you something, whether it's a product, an idea, or a philosophy. Which of the following sources might have agendas? Look up the organizations listed below; then, categorize them in the table below under "Credible" or "Questionable."

The American Heart Association

Democratic National Committee

Republican National Committee

WebMD

Nutrisystem

American Society for the Prevention of Cruelty to Animals

The American Professional Rodeo Association

Credible	Questionable

Lesson Wrap-up

Key Terms

Argument: a reason why you should think or act a certain way

Bias: a person's opinions and preferences

Brainstorming: exploring and developing ideas

Common Ground: areas of agreement in a controversy

Counterargument: when an author anticipates objections from the audience and refutes the objections with logic

Credibility: one's believability or trustworthiness

Evidence: the available body of facts or information indicating whether a belief or proposition is true or valid

Expert Analysis: an opinion or statement shared by someone who is knowledgeable about a topic

Fact: anything that can be proven

Logical Fallacy: a faulty or incorrect argument

Opinion: a personal belief or viewpoint that cannot be proven

Reasonable Claim: a statement that uses common sense to draw logical, evidence-based conclusions

Statistic: a number or percentage that represents research data

Thesis Statement: a major claim or idea supported by evidence in a piece of writing

Tone: the positive, negative, or neutral attitude that an author expresses about a topic

Writing to Argue: a writing purpose that convinces the audience to adopt a belief or take an action

Writing to Propose: a writing purpose achieved by giving suggestions and solutions to an issue or problem

Writing Application: Writing to Argue

Read the following essay and identify the author's argument. Is it persuasive, and do you agree with it? Why or why not?

Facebook: A Bane on Real Relationships

How many friends do you have on Facebook? Some have thousands, but are they really friends? Facebook hit the web in 2004 and was initially created by Mark Zuckerberg to help his college friends at Harvard stay connected. What started out as a

Beginning with a question gets the audience's attention.

small community is now a worldwide phenomenon with 1.59 billion active users ("Facebook"). That's an enormous number of people connecting, liking, and friending, but that's not all that people do. Facebook is also a place for drama, catfishing, bullying, and wasted time. Whether it's something as innocent as Candy Crush or as terrible as cyber stalking, Facebook creates an arena for disaster. Facebook has destroyed real relationships by encouraging narcissism, creating a false sense of friendship, and eliminating genuine communication.

First, Facebook has damaged genuine relationships by creating a culture of narcissism. According to the *American Heritage Dictionary*, narcissism means "excessive love or admiration of oneself." How many selfies are posted to Facebook every day? How healthy is it for someone to believe that he or she is the center of the universe? Yes, it's flattering and fun, but it isn't realistic. These people are in for a rude awakening when they interact with others in the real world. An unhealthy sense of entitlement often accompanies the narcissism that Facebook fosters.

Second, Facebook teaches users a false form of friendship. Leaving messages on people's walls and liking pictures and videos is not friendship. True friendship takes time to develop; it requires trust between two people who know each other. On Facebook, people can pretend to be whomever they wish. How many have loved and been hurt by people who don't really exist? Genuine friendship involves responsibility. Facebook is often all about the drama. People friend and unfriend all the time; this isn't friendship.

Last, Facebook destroys real communication between people. In the past, people would pick up a phone and call a loved one or get in the car and drive over to someone's house. Now, they post a picture or leave a message on Facebook. People engage less and less in person, losing the ability to communicate with others. At sleepovers, instead of talking with each other, children are texting each other and posting on Facebook while sitting in the same room! Our children are being trained to be more comfortable with virtual communication than social interaction, and Facebook is one of the primary culprits.

Many would argue that Facebook is a great way to catch up with old friends and to track down people with whom we've lost contact, and this is undeniably true. However, aren't we already friends with most of these people? They are friends IRL (in real life). Let's focus a moment on those words: "in real life." Herein lies the biggest problem with Facebook. It was created for college classmates and friends to keep up with one another. Its intention was to keep people in communication who already knew each other. So, in this sense, the site is doing exactly what it's supposed to do. But this is no longer the

---

The thesis states the author's argument: Facebook has destroyed real relationships.

Define any terms with which the audience might be unfamiliar.

This sentence indicates that the author has analyzed opposing viewpoints.

This argument would benefit from more evidence to support its claims. What kinds of evidence would you recommend?

How does the author's word choice contribute to the overall tone of the argument? Does the tone make the argument more or less convincing?

Here, the author uses a counterargument to acknowledge opposing viewpoints and then refute them.

main focus of Facebook, not even close. It's when we add so many online "friends" that Facebook begins whittling away at genuine relationships.

Facebook has entirely changed the landscape of friendship in a negative way. Genuine relationships are being ruined by self-centeredness; hollow, fake friendships; and the loss of honest communication. How much better would friendships be if the next time we wanted to say "hi" to friends, we closed all the apps and drove to their houses? What if, instead of hitting the "like" button, we ring the doorbell? What if, when our friends answer, we greet them not with an emoji but with a smile?

Works Cited

"Facebook." *Wikipedia*. Wikimedia, 24 Mar. 2016,
      https://en.wikipedia.org/wiki/Facebook.

"Narcissism." *American Heritage Dictionary*, 4th ed., American
      Heritage Publishing Company, 2001.

> Many do not regard *Wikipedia* as a credible source, which could hurt the author's argument.

Lesson 1.8
Writing to Analyze

Have you ever watched a police procedural TV show like *NCIS*? If you have, you know that investigators are called upon to analyze crime scenes all the time.

Analysis requires that we focus keenly on some part of the world around us and translate that intense examination into words. Think of analysis as the process of understanding something by looking at its parts; **writing to analyze**, then, means writing about those parts in order to deepen that understanding.

Crime scene investigations require very thorough analysis.

This lesson will discuss the following topics:

When to Analyze
Choosing an Approach to Analysis
Developing the Analysis

Group Activity

Using popular culture as a guide, list the things a crime scene investigator would need to notice at a crime scene. Can you think of any other jobs that require a similar degree of attention to detail?

When to Analyze

If you haven't already, at some point in the future you may decide to make a major lifestyle change, like losing weight or eating healthier. If so, you'll have to perform two acts of analysis. First, you'll need to look at your current lifestyle to figure out what factors have contributed to your present physical state. After this initial analysis, you'd need to establish a new, healthier way of life.

On Your Own

Practice analysis performing these two steps. List two general areas of your life that you need to evaluate. Underneath those areas, list facts about your lifestyle that relate to the category.

Lifestyle Area 1	Lifestyle Area 2

Now, using the same areas as before, list three things you are going to do differently for each one.

Lifestyle Area 1	Lifestyle Area 2

By both looking back at your old lifestyle and looking forward to your new one, you have analyzed your existence. In other words, you have broken your life (or potential life) up into parts in order to better understand your current and potential state.

In academic and professional life, we are often asked to react to the world around us. For example, in an art history class you might explain why a work of art inspired outrage when it was produced. In a business administration course, you might explain why a particular business plan is likely to be successful. These types of assignments can be difficult because they must be reinforced with logic and **evidence**, which conflicts with our natural desire to act intuitively rather than rationally.

Writing Environment: Everyday

Analysis is an integral part of human experience because it involves our capacity to think deeply about the world. However, when we interact with others, we often depend only on our emotional reactions. Think about some of the "discussions" you may have had with others online. Whether reacting to the latest Hollywood blockbuster or responding to a recent presidential debate, people often resort to name-calling and empty expressions of praise or blame.

Go to a website that features movies or video games. Then, look at the comments. Take note of the language that they use. Are they polite or rude? Are the commenters being logical and fair? Do they explain their points in detail?

When you try to understand how something works (or perhaps why it is not working), you are probably analyzing it, or breaking it down into parts. Although these sorts of tasks may seem tricky, you can build an analysis following these two main steps:

1. Choose an approach.

2. Develop your analysis with details appropriate for your approach.

Helpful Hint
Remember, most texts have multiple **purposes**. When you write to analyze, you will almost inevitably be **writing to describe** and **writing to summarize** throughout the text as well.

Choosing an Approach to Analysis

The first step in developing an analysis is deciding on an approach. In an analysis, the approach and tone of your writing will be either be informative or critical.

Informative

An **informative analysis** seeks to use **facts** to explain what something is or how it works while avoiding value judgments. If your approach is informational, your primary concern will be to provide **supporting details** that help the reader understand a **topic** or process.

One specific type of informative analysis is a **process analysis**, which requires breaking a procedure into steps and explaining each step in order. In a business class, you might be asked to write a process analysis for setting up a payroll system. You'll use specific, objective details to present and describe all the necessary steps.

Critical

A critical analysis, on the other hand, seeks to evaluate the topic in a way that could be argued. Writing that takes this approach to analysis is called a **critique**, which is a critical review of a subject's components.

The following examples prompt students to write critically.

> Explain what a recent climate change study means for coastal cities over the next decade.

> Discuss the most emotionally affecting moment in Toni Morrison's *Beloved*.

> Review the latest episode of AMC's *The Walking Dead*.

> Evaluate the career of a potential member of the NFL Hall of Fame.

Helpful Hint

Note that a critique will almost always seek to both analyze and evaluate.

To learn more about **writing to evaluate**, see Lesson 1.9.

Causal analyses explain how events lead to outcomes, such as a history paper that connects American foreign policy in the '80s to the rise of Al Qaeda. Causal analyses can be considered critiques because they are always arguable. In other words, even though a good causal analysis will be grounded in factual evidence, there are always other possible causes for complex phenomena like historical events.

Although critiques can include formal, objective analyses of data, like box office statistics, they're most often focused on subjective, opinionated reviews of topics, like book or movie reviews. For this reason, critiques often involve drawing inferences.

An **inference** is a logical conclusion based on both information from the text and your prior knowledge about a topic. When you make an inference, you make an assumption about what the author is saying or how the author wants you to respond.

Whenever you watch a movie, you make inferences about the characters: their backgrounds, emotions, relationships, and futures. Even though the story doesn't have time to include all of this information, you can usually fill in the gaps with your imagination and instinct.

Through making inferences, you can understand things that aren't stated outright.

For example, think about the last action movie you watched. You could probably identify the "hero" and the "villain" almost right away. Obviously, the movie didn't directly tell the audience, "This is the hero of the story." You had to make inferences about the characters based on their actions, words, and even their appearance.

Here are some examples of questions you can answer by making inferences:

> What is the author's purpose?
> What is the **main idea** of the text?
> How does the author feel about the topic?
> How does the author want me to respond?
> What will be the future or outcome of the topic?

For example, if you are tasked with analyzing the **tone**—the attitude that an author expresses about a topic—in a text, you'll want to pay close attention to the words and details that the author chooses to include. Here's an example:

> This charming cottage features all the little details that make a house a home.

> In this sentence, the author uses the words *charming* and *home* to describe the house and express a warm and inviting tone.

Developing the Analysis

To develop your analysis, use supporting details appropriate for your approach and combined purposes. It's important to choose and organize these details in a way that is most effective for your goal.

Organizing an Informative Analysis

One way to organize an informative analysis is according to category. In this case, you would likely be writing an expository essay, providing examples of each category to explain your points.

To learn more about **expository writing**, see Lesson 2.3.

For example, imagine you're writing about the history of punk rock. You would first break up the topic into a few categories:

- Visual art
- Music
- Politics

Then, you would discuss each category with specific details.

To learn more about **writing to discuss**, see Lesson 1.5.

Here's an example outline for a categorical analysis of the history of punk rock.

1. Introduction: Explain development of rock music in '50s and '60s

    a. Thesis: Punk rock is an important popular movement that found expression in visual art, music, and politics

2. Body Paragraph 1

    a. Punk rock and visual art: discuss do-it-yourself fashion, fetish wear, homemade zines (magazines made by fans), underground comic art

3. Body Paragraph 2

    a. Punk rock music: discuss various punk music styles, from three-chord rock to ska to hardcore to pop punk

4. Body Paragraph 3

   a. Punk rock politics: discuss anarchy as a movement and punk resistance to political regimes and capitalism in England and the United States

5. Conclusion: Explain that punk rock was more than just a musical style, and discuss artists and musicians still considered "punk" today

You might also organize an informative analysis sequentially. Think about how you would teach someone to bake a cake. You wouldn't start with icing it. Instead, you would organize the details in **sequential order**, presenting a sequence of steps or events in the order they should occur.

You could discuss the punk rock movement sequentially by covering its formation to its demise as in the following outline.

1. Introduction: Explain development of rock music in '50s and '60s.

   a. Thesis: Punk rock is an important branch of popular music that began in the late '60s and continued to flourish through the mid-2000s.

2. Body Paragraph 1

   a. Early precursors of punk (1967-1974): discuss The Velvet Underground and The Stooges as early American punk pioneers

3. Body Paragraph 2

   a. Punk in its prime (1974-1977): discuss The New York Dolls and the Ramones in New York, The Sex Pistols and The Clash in England

4. Body Paragraph 3

   a. American Hardcore (1977-1984): discuss Black Flag, Bad Brains, Fear, and The Dead Kennedys

5. Body Paragraph 4

   a. Pop Punk (1984-now): discuss NOFX, Offspring, Green Day, Blink 182

6. Conclusion: Explain that punk rock has a thirty-year history. Point at some of the ways today's bands continue to celebrate that history.

Organizing a Critical Analysis

On the other hand, if you are writing a critique, use a set of standards as the basis of your organization. These **standards** determine the categories of value and specific areas in which you will judge the topic.

If you are reviewing a horror movie, you would judge it differently than you would a romantic comedy. In general, horror audiences want to watch films that build suspense and feature relatable characters. Many horror fans also enjoy and expect high-quality special effects and makeup. This being the case, a horror reviewer could break up his or her review by the following standards:

- Suspense
- Characters
- Special effects

Let's reconsider the punk rock topic we talked about before, but this time imagine that we are writing a critique arguing that the Sex Pistols are the most important punk rock band of all time. We can see that this is obviously a critical assessment; the writer is making a claim about the Sex Pistols, not just writing about the band's history.

To make this critique work, the writer will need to establish his or her standards: the points of evaluation. These could include the same three categories of information as before:

- Visual art
- Music
- Politics

These categories were the basis of the informative analysis earlier in the lesson. However, a critique would use these categories to argue that the importance of a punk band depends upon its influence in these three areas.

Here's an example of how this might be broken down in an outline:

I. Introduction: Explain development of rock music in '50s and '60s. Explain that important punk bands made a mark on visual art and the music industry as well as in politics.

    a. Thesis: The Sex Pistols are the most important punk rock band of their era because of their impact on visual art, music, and politics.

2. Body Paragraph 1

    a. Sex Pistols and visual art: discuss the band members' styles, manager Malcolm McLaren's impact on fashion, their bizarre movie *The Great Rock n' Roll Swindle*

3. Body Paragraph 2

    a. Sex Pistols and music: discuss the greatness of the Sex Pistols' album *Never Mind the Bollocks, Here's the Sex Pistols* and its important three-chord anthems: "God Save the Queen," "Anarchy in the UK," and "Pretty Vacant"

4. Body Paragraph 3

    a. Sex Pistols and politics: discuss the Sex Pistols' struggle against Margaret Thatcher's conservative government, their chaotic protest concert played on the River Thames, their lasting impact on anti-corporate music movements

5. Conclusion: Explain why recognizing the multi-faceted impact of the Sex Pistols on punk rock is so important and why their legacy must not be forgotten.

Group Activity

As a group, pick a movie that everyone has seen and remembers. First, have everyone give it either a "thumbs up" or a "thumbs down," and record each response. Then, ask each person to discuss why his or her reaction is justified and record the reasons. Then, look at your list and try to group these reasons into categories, like "story," "acting," "special effects," and so on. This will help you start to visualize the way an experience can be "broken up" into parts.

Writing Environments: Academic

Sometimes, a project requires you to conduct both informative and critical analyses.

Imagine that you are asked to write a paper for a science class about an experiment you conducted during a lab. You are told that this paper is meant for a general audience, not just scientists, and your purpose is to explain the experiment's procedure and consider the results.

If you look at the purpose again, you'll notice that you are being asked to analyze in two ways, and this can make it easier to understand what to do.

First, you are being asked to break down the experiment you conducted into steps to explain how you did your experiment. This is a kind of process analysis that describes the methods used to achieve something. It is important to provide this kind of information in science classes because for experiments to be valid, they have to be repeatable.

Second, you are being asked to analyze the data you obtained to explain what it means. For a simple science paper, you might just break this up into two parts: discussing the results of the experiment and comparing those results to the hypothesis, or prediction, you made at the beginning.

Lesson Wrap-up

Key Terms

Analyze: the process of understanding something by looking at its parts

Causal Analysis: an analysis that explains how events lead to outcomes

Critique: a critical analysis of a subject's components

Evidence: the available body of facts or information indicating whether a belief or proposition is true or valid

Expository Writing: writing that uses evidence to support a main idea

Fact: a piece of information that most people generally agree to be true

Inference: a logical conclusion based on your prior knowledge and the information in a text

Informative Analysis: an analysis that uses facts to explain what something is or how it works

Main Idea: the statement or argument that an author tries to communicate

Process Analysis: an analysis that breaks up a set of events into steps and explains each in detail

Purpose: the goal of a text

Sequential Order: an organizational pattern that arranges ideas or events in the order that they occur (also known as chronological order)

Standard: a category of value used to judge a topic

Supporting Detail: a piece of information, also called evidence, that is used to support a main idea

Tone: the positive, negative, or neutral attitude that an author expresses about a topic

Topic: the general subject of a text

Writing to Analyze: a writing purpose achieved by examining something you have read or studied

Writing to Describe: a writing purpose that explains the appearance of someone or something using words that appeal to the senses

Writing to Discuss: a writing purpose that presents issues or interprets something you have read or studied

Writing to Evaluate: a writing purpose achieved by creating criteria for judging something you have read or studied

Writing to Summarize: a writing purpose that presents a small, generalized overview of a larger amount of information

Writing Application: Writing to Analyze

The following essay is a short, analytic critique that discusses the famous shower scene in Alfred Hitchcock's acclaimed 1960 movie *Psycho*. This essay is a critical analysis because it expresses the opinions of the author. It also establishes a set of standards for great horror movies and then explains how the shower scene meets those standards of excellence.

Cuts, Cues, and Narrative Crisis: *Psycho*'s Innovative Cinematography

In many of today's horror films, directors use expensive CGI shots of violence and mayhem and elaborately choreographed action scenes to show the audience the literal truth of a story. Unfortunately, this strategy can sometimes backfire. Terror is often established more effectively through less overt tactics, such as innovative editing techniques, insinuated violence, and unexpected plot twists. In the infamous shower scene of his 1960 masterpiece *Psycho*, Alfred Hitchcock masterfully utilizes each of these tactics to unnerve his audience.

This sentence establishes the standards by which the author will judge the movie scene.

When the shower scene starts, the film is about halfway over. The heroine, Marion Crane, has stolen $40,000 from her employer and fled to the Bates Motel. She has just met its very strange caretaker, Norman Bates. After an unnerving conversation with Norman over dinner, Marion decides to take a shower before heading to bed. Soon after entering the shower, she is mercilessly attacked by a shadowy figure.

This brief paragraph summarizes the scene.

One reason this scene is so unnerving is because of Hitchcock's masterful use of editing to convey Marion's horror. Having filmed over seventy takes of the stabbing, Hitchcock cuts rapidly between snippets of these sequences, all in time to the staccato violin of the soundtrack. The film is thus literally cut as the character is being stabbed, kinetically capturing the violence of the moment using the formal techniques of the medium itself. Viewers are overwhelmed by the immediacy of the event and feel like they are occupying the shower along with the victim.

Here is the first reason that the writer values Hitchcock's scene.

Another reason this scene works so well is that Hitchcock leaves much to the imagination. Though the audience sees Marion's body doubling over and hear her screams, they are never shown the actual stabbing or her wounds. At the end of the attack, the camera captures her dead gaze and the blood trickling down the drain. This might sound like a letdown, but because the actual attack was so shocking (given the editing discussed above), the viewers are so caught up in the moment that they think they see more than they do. This is effective because every person's mental vision of such a crime is different, so Hitchcock's suggestions allow every person's mind to visualize what is just off screen in a way that is uniquely disturbing to his or her own psyche.

Here is the second reason the writer values the shower scene.

The essay analyzes the movie scene by breaking it into three parts. Then, it breaks down each of those parts even more.

Finally, Marion's stabbing violates viewer expectations. Most American film narratives focus on a central character from beginning to end. Even if that person perishes, his or her fate is usually decided during the film's final moments. By killing off the "main" character so early in the movie, Hitchcock blindsides the audience. Viewers are left

The writer puts this point last because the final example is the one that is likely to stay with the reader after the essay is over.

wondering what can possibly happen next. After all, they thought Marion's narrative was the one that counted; no one seems safe.

In just one scene that suggests its content instead of showing everything, Hitchcock manages to terrify and confound his viewers. For a horror film to truly work, it must involve the audience and leave viewers feeling unmoored. This scene does both and is a testament to Hitchcock's greatness.

Here is the paper's conclusion, which ties everything up and explains why the essay's point is important.

Lesson 1.9
Writing to Evaluate

Before leaving for school or work, do you check yourself in the mirror? If so, you are in the process of evaluating whether you look good enough to leave the house. Questions that may or may not enter your mind are, "Am I dressed appropriately?" or "Do I look attractive?" You may even make specific judgments about your hair, face, or body.

Evaluation occurs naturally in our everyday lives. In more formal settings, **writing to evaluate** is used for interpretation and measuring value.

Writing Environment: Everyday

Before buying a car, people research its strengths and weaknesses and look at the price to decide whether or not it is a good value. In any situation where you are attempting to determine whether you will be receiving the best value for your money, you are in the process of evaluating the product or service.

Writing Environment: Professional

In the workplace, your supervisor may give you a performance review to determine how well you do your job. This review usually asks for recommendations for improvement and an overall evaluation of your performance.

Here is an example of an evaluation of an instructor by her supervisor. It includes areas of improvement and a summary or overall evaluation of the teacher's performance:

Instructor Annual Evaluation

NAME OF INSTRUCTOR: Ellen Smith

CLASS TAUGHT: ENG 121

DATE OF EVALUATION: 5/10/2017

Ellen provides detailed instruction and guidance for students. She also provides positive support and encouragement in her open discussions, emails, and assignment feedback. She passes quality assurance standards for our courses.

Areas of Improvement:

Ellen needs to be more aware of her students' motivations. She sometimes blames the students for not understanding assignments. She could benefit from more professional development. By taking more responsibility on herself as an instructor, her students may benefit more from her assignments.

Summary:

Please assign one of the levels below to this employee's overall performance:

- ● Needs improvement
- ○ Commendable
- ○ Exemplary

In this lesson, you will learn about the following aspects of writing to evaluate:

Forms of Evaluation

Building an Evaluation

Forms of Evaluation

Depending on the writing situation, evaluation is accomplished in a few different ways.

Analyze

When you **analyze**, you break down different parts to see how they interact with each other. This process is usually used in academia and laboratories.

For example, in an English class, you may be asked to critique a piece of literature. A **critique** is a critical analysis of a subject's components. Therefore, a literary critique or analysis will examine how parts of the text work together. On the other hand, scientists could analyze different properties of a chemical to discern how it affects the body.

Assess

When you **assess** something, you are making a judgment to determine its value. This process can be used at work or in school.

In the workplace, employees often undergo an annual assessment or review to determine whether or not their performances are an asset to the employer. Writers have to assess their **audience** in order to write a strong text. Your instructor must assess your performance in class in order to give you a grade that accurately reflects your performance.

Appraise

When you **appraise** something, you are determining its monetary value or worth. This process is used by many businesses like real estate companies, jewelers, car dealerships, and pawn shops.

For example, if you want to trade in your old car, the dealer will appraise it to see how much money it's worth. When people sell their houses, real estate agents help them determine how much the house is worth so that the owners can set an appropriate price.

Building an Evaluation

To write an evaluation, follow these two steps:

1.   Determine the standards for your evaluation.

2.   Analyze the subject of your evaluation with the standards in mind.

Determine the Standards

No matter the context, the goal of evaluation is to judge something. To do this, you first need to establish the standards by which that thing should be judged. **Standards** are the categories of value that you can use to judge a particular **topic**.

On Your Own

Think about your ideal manager. What standards would this person have to meet? Include at least three.

In your academic career, you have probably come across a rubric. Instructors often use **rubrics** to outline their expectations for student behavior, attendance, and/or performance. These expectations are the standards upon which your final grade will be measured.

When you are tasked with evaluating something, start by creating your own rubric. Make a list of standards that you'll use to judge the subject's strengths and weaknesses.

Here are some examples:

For a creative writing workshop, Ciara is analyzing a poet's literary techniques. She evaluates the work based on the following standards:
  o   Use of appropriate word choice
  o   Use of figurative language

While judging the effectiveness of a visual argument, Chris measures its effectiveness in the following areas:
  o   Reaching the target audience
  o   Appealing to *ethos*
  o   Appealing to *logos*
  o   Appealing to *pathos*

While reviewing a restaurant, a food blogger makes judgments based on the following observations:

- o   Atmosphere
- o   Customer service
- o   Menu

Reed and Caleb are interviewing applicants for an internship in their customer service department. At the end of the day, they evaluate each candidate based on these desired qualifications:

- o   Professionalism
- o   Verbal and written communication skills
- o   Organization and time management skills
- o   Relevant experience

Gather Relevant Details

Once you've listed your standards, you need to analyze the subject's components as they measure up to each one. Your list of standards should direct this process so that you can avoid placing too much focus on irrelevant items.

For example, if your instructor isn't going to add or deduct points for spelling, then he or she isn't going to spend much time reviewing your paper for typos. Likewise, you should focus specifically on only those components that are relevant to your standards. Later, these components will serve as **supporting details**, or evidence, for each of your claims. Without relevant evidence, your judgments aren't reliable.

If an employer is evaluating a candidate, she might look for indicators of professionalism in the following areas:

- Promptness of arrival for the interview
- Attire and professional demeanor during the interview
- Professional experience highlighted in the résumé

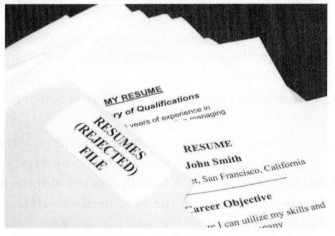

A résumé is one example of a text that undergoes strict evaluation.

Once you've listed each relevant detail, review it and rate it. How prompt was the candidate's arrival? What behavior indicated professionalism? What responses indicated a lack thereof? Consider as much as possible to ensure that your judgment is reliable.

Develop Your Claims

Finally, establish your claim(s) based on the evidence.

Remember that an effective paragraph includes a **main idea** and supporting details that support and/or prove that main idea. In your evaluation, each main idea should be a claim about how the subject measures up (or fails to measure up) to a standard. The rest of the evaluation should include supporting details that illustrate or support your claims.

If you are trying to make an objective evaluation based on **facts** and logic, it's especially critical to maintain a neutral tone and avoid bias as you present your evidence. **Tone** is the attitude expressed about the topic of a text. You should use words and details carefully to ensure that your tone is as neutral as possible. Here are some descriptions that could indicate a positive, negative, or neutral tone.

Positive	Negative	Neutral
excited	angry	objective
encouraging	disapproving	straightforward
confident	critical	direct

A **biased argument** is unreliable because it relies too heavily on a person's opinions and preferences.

Look at these examples:

Unbiased   The investigation revealed that the café manager had caused the fire by leaving a pot of boiling water unattended.

Biased   The investigation revealed that the negligent café manager must have thought talking on the phone was more important than monitoring the safety of his kitchen.

Do you notice the difference? The first sentence focuses on giving the reader information while the second sentence uses negative words to make the manager seem like a criminal. Unless a judge has convicted the manager of negligence or arson, the author should make his or her point using evidence, not emotional language.

Maintaining a neutral tone and an unbiased argument can be especially difficult when you're evaluating an experience. For example, food bloggers have a responsibility to their readers to distinguish between their personal preferences and objective facts.

Take a look at the following evaluation of a restaurant. How does this author balance her opinions with facts?

My husband and I visited Marion Diner on the recommendation of a friend who is also a local food blogger. As we were walking into the restaurant, we were greeted with the delicious scent of sautéed garlic and rosemary. The waiter was friendly and knowledgeable about the menu. She even recommended her personal favorites. The menu itself was not lengthy at all. Clearly, this restaurant focuses on a few key specialties and customer favorites. I was surprised to see the blend of fresh, healthy ingredients incorporated into traditional "diner food."

I ordered the Bleu Ribbon Burger with baked onion straws, and my husband had the Grandstand Salad. My burger was cooked perfectly although the onion straws were more seasoned than I would have preferred. I'm not a salad fan, but even I had to admit that my husband's meal looked great.

Overall, I would definitely recommend Marion Diner to anyone who's looking for a fresh twist on diner favorites.

Writing Environment: Academic

There are two different types of evaluations that are common within the academic system:

- Grade sheets
- Student evaluations of instructors

Here's an example of a grade sheet:

Discussions	20/20
Critical Analysis Essay	125/150
Literary Analysis Essay	150/150
Final Grade	A

Here's an example of a student's evaluation:

Please fill in the box that closely matches your opinion.

1. My instructor was readily available to me.

Strongly Agree ■ 5   Agree ☐ 4   Disagree ☐ 3   Strongly Disagree ☐ 2

2. My instructor provided feedback as to my improvement.

Strongly Agree ☐ 5   Agree ■ 4   Disagree ☐ 3   Strongly Disagree ☐ 2

3. My instructor helped me to understand the material.

Strongly Agree ☐ 5   Agree ☐ 4   Disagree ■ 3   Strongly Disagree ☐ 2

Other comments and feedback about this course:

I really enjoyed this class. My communications with my instructor were always professional yet personable. She made sure that I understood all of our assignments and when I did not, she provided one on one guidance. I wish I could take her for the second semester of this course.

As you can see in this evaluation, there is a point score and a place for additional comments. The points and comments all may be taken into consideration at the end of the year when the teacher receives his or her annual review.

Lesson Wrap-up

Key Terms

Analyze: to understand something by looking at its parts

Appraise: to determine the monetary value or worth of something

Argument: a reason why you should think or act a certain way

Assess: to determine the value of something by making a judgment

Audience: the person or people that your writing is intended for

Bias: a person's opinions and preferences

Critique: a critical analysis of a subject's components

Fact: a piece of information that most people generally agree to be true

Main Idea: the statement or argument that an author tries to communicate

Rubric: a list of standards used for evaluation

Standard: a category of value used to judge a topic

Supporting Detail: a piece of information, also called evidence, that is used to support a main idea

Tone: the positive, negative, or neutral attitude that an author expresses about a topic

Topic: the general subject of a text

Writing to Evaluate: a writing purpose achieved by creating criteria for judging something you have read or studied

Writing Application: Writing to Evaluate

Read the following annotated bibliography; what is it evaluating, and what techniques does it use to do this?

Jones, A. D. (1999). The types of motivation found in the classroom. *Educational Psychology,* 8(3), 120-125. Retrieved from http://www.articlehomepage.com/full/url/

According to Jones (1999), motivation is necessary for facilitating effective learning. Each individual has different personal motivations. Additionally, due to increasing globalization, a single classroom could contain many people from other countries who have different cultural values and ethics. Because of students' varied backgrounds, motivating them can be a difficult process. However, it is up to the instructor to create lesson plans that motivate and stimulate his or her students.

This text is evaluating the article cited above.

This text would be clearer if the author had provided a list of standards that he or she is using to judge the article.

Jones claims that everyone has his or her own individual motivations, such as fear, ambition, and acceptance. When students feel motivated, they will make an effort to learn new material. However, if they are unmotivated, they will not try to learn no matter how skilled their instructors are. This lack of motivation also extends to foreign students.

Some students who come to America for an education were raised in cultures that traditionally value male leadership. When they have a female instructor for the first time, these students might lose motivation and even rebel against the course requirements. Other students may come from educational backgrounds that discourage questioning the instructor. As a result, these students could appear to lack motivation since they don't participate in the same way as native students. Even though students come to school for the purpose of learning, it is up to the instructor to create a classroom environment that motivates them in the learning process. Jones claims that it is the instructor's responsibility to be aware of his or her students' motivations and to design and develop flexible lesson plans. Educators

The author analyzes Jones' article by breaking it into parts. This paragraph addresses one part of the article: the examples.

Here, the author begins assessing the article, using judgment to determine its value.

cannot assume that just because a student is in the classroom that he or she will learn the material.

Jones makes good points about motivation. He discusses types of motivations, cultural hindrances, and the responsibility of the instructor in this area. Even though the article is only a paragraph, it provides the audience with an overview of the importance of motivation. I will use this paragraph while developing my compare and contrast essay because of its simplicity and strong overview of the importance of motivation. In addition, it lists the different types of motivation, which I can use in my research.

Although the author did not provide a rubric at the beginning of this text, these final sentences provide clues about the standards he or she used to evaluate the article.

Chapter 2
Modes of Writing

Lesson 2.1
Descriptive Writing

Descriptive writing communicates the characteristics or qualities of a thing or event. The more you focus on effective description, the more your reader will understand and feel what you're trying to communicate. You don't have to be a natural storyteller, poet, or creative writer to use descriptive writing well.

Reflection Questions

Do you use description often? Why or why not? How would you describe the picture above to a friend?

In this lesson, you will learn about the following aspects of descriptive writing:

Key Elements of Descriptive Writing
Organizing Words, Sentences, and Paragraphs
Different Types of Description
Enhancing Description with Sensory Details

Key Elements of Descriptive Writing

When writing descriptively, keep in mind the following elements:

> Purpose
>
> Show, don't tell
>
> Pacing and emphasis
>
> Mood

Purpose

The choices you make regarding description will depend on your **purpose:** the goal of a text. For example, if you want a reader to feel sorrow over an individual's tragic illness, you could describe that person and his or her difficult experiences.

In contrast, if your purpose is to discuss scientific research about the illness, your description will likely sound and feel quite different.

Consider the differences between the following descriptions.

> The woman, who had recently become a grandmother, received the news of her cancer diagnosis. She eased into a chair, frowned, and said nothing.

> When informing a patient of the diagnosis of a malignant tumor, oncologists should provide thorough information while also maintaining a sympathetic demeanor.

Writing descriptively requires deliberate thought and effort. You can begin the writing process by observing and noting your own reactions to your subject, but don't forget to explore other perspectives as well.

Writing Environment: Academic

A composition or creative writing class might ask you to use creative description, such as describing a robin's feathers or how it looks when it flies. However, a biology class would require factual description, such as a robin's classification as a vertebrate, its eating habits, or its habitat. Again, what is most important is the purpose of the description.

Show, Don't Tell

When you're watching a movie or reading a book, you probably don't like to be told exactly what is going on. Instead, you want to draw your own conclusions based on the details of the story. Writing works the same way; it's more interesting to *show* your readers a topic rather than just *tell* them about it.

> **Telling:** John Nelson was afraid to go into battle.

> **Showing:** John Nelson balled his sweaty fingers into fists and dug his nails into his palms as the sound of gunfire approached.

On Your Own

Read the following descriptions and decide whether they show or tell. Check the box next to your answer.

The fabric felt like horsehair.

☐ Shows
☐ Tells

The fabric was rough.

☐ Shows
☐ Tells

He was not very eager to speak in class.

☐ Shows
☐ Tells

He kept his eyes trained on his pencil.

☐ Shows
☐ Tells

Group Activity

After examining the following photograph for several minutes, write three to four lines of description that *tell* readers about this scene and what the mother is doing, thinking, and feeling. Then, write three to four lines of description that *show* readers this scene and what the mother is doing, thinking, and feeling. Discuss the differences between each set of lines.

Pacing and Emphasis

At times, you may want to emphasize a certain point because it's important. You can do this by describing it thoroughly. A few words might be enough to describe less important points.

Spending a lot of time describing something could be a good idea if it's central to your writing topic, or you may want move quickly from one point to the next. By slowing down or speeding up your language and description, you are controlling the pace of your writing. **Pace** is the movement or speed of language as a description or argument advances.

> Helpful Hint
>
> It's easy to overdo description and assume that providing more information or details is always best. However, too much description can cause readers to become confused. Be purposeful with your description. Developing a particular point more than others can create a sense of emphasis and, therefore, indicate for readers that it is important.

Mood

Mood is the overall feeling or emotion of a text. Take a look at these examples that both describe a classroom:

> The room was empty, with pale walls lit by harsh fluorescent bulbs.

> The room, with golden walls and bright lights, was ready to be filled with students.

> ▷ In the second example, the author has used specific words to create a lighter, more welcoming mood.

Here are two more examples that have similar facts but evoke very different moods:

> While watching the election results, Lawrence slumped in his faded armchair, yawned, and waited.

> Lawrence sat on the edge of the chair and tightly crossed his fingers, his eyes fixed on the television screen.

Writing Environment: Everyday

Whether you're talking with a friend or explaining directions to a passerby, details can be the difference between clarity and confusion. However, if you're not used to observing and remembering details, using them in your writing can be difficult. Here are some tips:

- **Slow down.** Hurried activities don't allow you to observe what's going on around you. It requires time to see details and let them inform your thinking.
- **Empathize.** By empathizing—or imagining what others might think or feel—you can see the world from another point of view. Learn to see situations from others' perspectives, and you might pick up on new details you'd have missed otherwise.

Organizing Words, Sentences, and Paragraphs

Parts of Speech

Strong words are the building blocks of good description. Parts of speech work together within sentences to create effective description.

Four important parts of speech in descriptive writing are nouns, verbs, adjectives, and adverbs.

- **Noun:** A word that represents a person, place, thing, event, or idea.
- **Verb:** A word that represents an action, relationship, or state of being.
- **Adjective:** A word that describes a noun or pronoun.
- **Adverb:** A word that describes a verb, adjective, or another adverb.

Sometimes, one well-chosen noun or verb is more effective than two or three adjectives or adverbs. Using fewer words will also make your writing more direct and concise.

Consider these descriptions:

> The slippery mutant pursued the children through the cavern.

> The slippery mutant speedily ran after the frightened kids as they tensely ran along the damp, dank, and dark corridor.

> The first example is concise; it communicates its idea with just a few words. For example, the action verb *pursued* is just as descriptive as the longer phrase *speedily ran after*. When writing descriptively, try to avoid weak verbs like *run*, *is*, or *walk*.

Weak Verbs	Strong Verbs
ran	sprinted
went	explored
said	argued
walked	shuffled

Helpful Hint

Verb tense can make a difference in description. Present verb tense, for example, makes descriptions feel more immediate.

> The ship is traveling at full speed.

> Crows are gathering in the yard; their rustling feathers are the only sound.

Depending on the requirements of your assignment, try using past, present, and future tense to see what effect each has on descriptive writing.

Sentence and Paragraph Structure

Sentence and paragraph organization also contribute to the mood of a text. Sentence length and placement of information in a paragraph can put emphasis on certain ideas or words.

On Your Own

Read the two paragraphs below and identify the one that most effectively emphasizes the important ideas.

> After steadying the clanging symbols, the drummer banged out a series of resounding rhythms, causing audience members to rise to their feet, clap, and even shout at the top of their lungs. Louder and louder they cheered, until the arena was filled with the sound and the band knew they had given the best concert of the tour.

> The arena was filled with the sound of cheering. The band knew they had given the best concert of the tour. The drummer steadied the clanging symbols. Then he banged out a series of very loud rhythms. These rhythms caused audience members to rise to their feet, clap, and even shout at the top of their lungs. They yelled louder and louder.

Different Types of Description

There are two general approaches to description. The first type is called concrete. **Concrete descriptions** are descriptions that use physical and specific terms. The second type, called abstract, is the opposite of concrete description. **Abstract descriptions** are descriptions that use theoretical and nonspecific terms.

Think of abstract description as broad and concrete description as specific. Specific words can help readers *see* and *feel* while abstract language is more appropriate for conveying meaning.

Our brains naturally choose broad or specific language based on a situation. For example, we identify a group of trees as *woods* or *forest* in part because our brains would be overwhelmed by specifically naming every tree.

However, concrete description works well for *show, don't tell*. Readers can more easily understand and imagine a topic that is described with specific words.

Think of concrete and abstract as two ends of a spectrum.

Nature — Mysterious, wild woods — Dark forest — Stand of big trees — Those locust trees in my backyard on Robinson Street

Abstract → Concrete

> **Group Activity**
>
> As a group, find an image online and write two descriptions of it. In your first description, rely upon broad and abstract language. In the second description, utilize specific and concrete language.

Watch out for **clichés**, popular words or phrases that have been overused until they have lost their original impact. Clichés do little work for your description. Because they're so familiar, readers might skim right over what you've written.

Here are some examples of clichés:

> All's fair in love and war.

> He was faster than the speed of light.

> Live life to the fullest.

> **Helpful Hint**
>
> In order to avoid clichés, consider the significant aspects of what you're trying to describe. Clichés are vague; they say little about a specific person, place, or thing. Replace clichés with words or phrases that are unique to the situation you're describing.

Enhancing Description with Sensory Details

> *"The way to a reader's emotions is, oddly enough, through the senses."* Annie Dillard

Sensory details include descriptions that appeal to our senses: sight, sound, touch, taste, and smell. Sensory details work well in concrete description. They also help readers relate to a text because people relate to the world through their senses.

Figurative language—non-literal words or word groups—can also help you create interesting description. Metaphors and similes are two types of figurative language.

Metaphor: a direct comparison between two unlike things

> The car's engine is a purring cat.

Simile: a comparison between two unlike things using the words *like* or *as*

> Walking through that mall was like running a marathon.

Imagery can be used in both abstract and concrete description.

On Your Own

Read the paragraph below and identify the sentences containing sensory details.

> Samson decided to dress as a lumberjack for Halloween. He fashioned an ax out of smooth cardboard. Then he put on a scratchy, wool toboggan and rubbed a charcoal beard onto his cheeks. He also wore soft cotton flannel, which he stuffed with balled-up newspapers that crinkled and crunched as he moved. He was ready to go.

Writing Environment: Professional

You've probably heard the phrase "attention to detail." In the workplace, your ability to pay attention to details will enable you to be an informed and well-organized planner or manager. In fact, some jobs will require this skill as a necessary component. Consider the importance of detail for surgeons, lawyers, engineers, or graphic designers.

Further Resources

Learning to observe and communicate details not only makes you a better writer, but also it helps you establish your credibility in the workplace. Check out this story about former Apple CEO Steve Jobs and his attention to detail: (http://www.npr.org/sections/thetwo-way/2011/08/25/139947282/a-shade-of-yellow-steve-jobs-and-attention-to-detail).

Lesson Wrap-Up

Key Terms

Abstract Description: a description that uses theoretical and nonspecific terms

Adjective: a word that describes a noun or pronoun

Adverb: a word that describes a verb, adjective, or another adverb

Cliché: a popular phrase that has lost its original impact due to overuse

Concrete Description: a description that uses physical and specific terms

Descriptive Writing: writing that communicates the characteristics or qualities of a thing or event

Figurative Language: a non-literal word or word group, also known as a literary device, that writers use to emphasize an idea or detail

Metaphor: a direct comparison between two unlike things

Mood: the overall feeling or emotion of a text

Noun: a word that represents a person, place, thing, event, or idea

Pace: the movement or speed of language

Purpose: the goal of a text

Sensory Detail: a detail that includes descriptions that appeal to our senses: sight, sound, touch, taste, and smell

Simile: a comparison between two unlike things using *like* or *as*

Verb: a word that represents an action, relationship, or state of being

Writing Application: Descriptive Writing

Read the following essay that describes an experience in the author's life. What types of description does the writing use, and how does this variety contribute to the story's impact?

Saying Goodbye

I watch the scenery pass. What else is there to do?

There's the old diner where John and I always went after soccer practice to gobble down way too many greasy French fries. There's the library where I stayed up way too late working on class projects in high school. On this mid-winter morning, the sun shines warmly through the car window, yet I know that on the other side of the glass is a bitter cold that will make my bones ache.

The first paragraph sets a slow pace and establishes a melancholy mood.

As my mother drives us to the vet, I try to focus on those places and memories and not what is ahead of us. Next to me sits Brady, making almost no noise the entire ride, his ears bent forward, and his head resting between his brown front paws. He barely fits between my brother and me, and since his breathing is even heavier than usual, I can feel his ribs against my leg. On the other side of him Jake whistles, though I've asked him a million times to just stop it already. This is hardly a happy occasion.

This story uses present tense verbs to make the action feel immediate.

In reality, the car ride is pretty short. Usually we talk a lot, especially since my trips home from college are rare. But this time, we're quiet.

I catch my mom's hazel eyes in the rearview mirror in spite of her sunglasses. She had told me that Brady's pain needed to end and that it needed to happen today. But now she doesn't say anything. I kind of wish she would. I also wish there is a way for my own pain to end. I slide further down into my seat and look away from my mom's eyes. I think back to the research paper I've been writing.

Though this paragraph describes the author's feelings, which are unseen, it also describes actions that reveal his emotions: breaking eye contact and slouching in his seat.

It's about Chronic Obstructive Pulmonary Disease, or COPD. Brady is "Patient Y" in my paper. He's been having a harder and harder time breathing, and the doctor said his heart is really strained after all those years. You can see it in the way Brady walks, only to finally sit and rest or whimper and roll over whenever I crouch to pet him.

His COPD, my research tells me, is a growing problem in pets. In my paper, I am arguing that the issue really doesn't get the attention it deserves. It's a progressive disease, so people need to be aware of it; it gets worse over time. It doesn't help that Brady isn't moving around as much anymore: his bulging sides have become even pudgier. You can almost hear his legs creaking under his own weight.

Next to me, Brady starts coughing again. Each hack sounds like paper ripping or the crackling of little fireworks. I pat the top of his head. His hair always feels so soft; Mom and Jake have done a good job brushing his fur on a regular basis.

This simile helps the readers "hear" the moment.

Of any of us, I think I love Brady the most. He could be a real pain sometimes, always chewing on the painted baseboard in the dining room, eating chicken bones out of the garbage can, busting out of the house on his more mischievous days and taking himself for a walk. (One time we had to spend two days looking for the old mutt.) But even through all that, we loved him. I loved him. He was always there for me when I needed him.

Brady—a glorious mix between a Collie and a German Shepherd—would wait, panting and whimpering, at the door for me each afternoon when I still lived at home. And each day when I got off that chugging school bus, I darted into the house because I knew he was there for me, loyal as always.

A year or two after I started college, we knew it was time. His coughing increased and some afternoons he hardly moved at all. So, we sit in silence during this car ride and wait for the inevitable.

Finally, my mom turns our green sedan into the parking lot of a squat, red-brick building that looks like it could be a house. We get out of the car, still quiet. And Brady is quiet too. He knows.

After I get out of the car, he steps down from the side door, too. Then he whimpers and just stands there. He coughs again, this time like firecrackers. I bend down, wrap my arms around him, and lift him up. He shows no resistance.

We walk to the front door of the building and memories flood my brain. All I can think about are those days coming home from school. Then my mind quickly flashes to all those articles I had read recently on COPD. "This condition is non-reversible," they all seemed to say.

My mom lightly touches my forearm. I can feel her fingertips through my winter coat. "Sam," she says, "I'm so very proud of you. I know this is probably hardest for you."

I feel hot tears at the edges of my eyes. I find myself now gasping for breath a bit as well.

Inside the vet's office, in its small waiting room, we all sit on the floor with Brady. Mom pulls a cheeseburger wrapped in paper out of her purse. She places it on the laminated floor in front of Brady's muzzle, and he sniffs at it. Personally, I had not been able to eat that morning;

as I smell the cooked meat and the grease, I still do not want to eat. Brady moves his head to the side and just looks up at Mom.

I pet Brady for several minutes without saying anything. Then the vet enters the room and all of us turn our eyes to him.

Of course, losing a pet is hard. But what about when you grew up with that pet and he really does feel like your best friend? After today, he won't be greeting me whenever I come back home.

The vet just nods his head slowly and frowns. Wisps of hair fall over his eyes, and he doesn't bother to brush them aside. He just holds the door with one hand and waves us over with the other. I pick up Brady and follow the vet.

Afterward, my mom offers to take us out to lunch, but still I have no appetite.

I enter the silent house, sit down on the couch with my laptop, and begin working on my COPD paper. I find myself typing faster than ever before.

A week later, my instructor returns the assignment to me. Across the top in red marker is written a large *A*.

Here again the author "shows" Brady's lack of appetite in concrete terms rather than "telling" about it.

Lesson 2.2
Narrative Writing

Storytelling is a way to preserve history and tradition, impart wisdom, teach children, or simply entertain. We tell stories all the time.

Storytelling is part of daily life.

In writing, storytelling is used to transport readers into detailed moments that are relatable, personal, humorous, teachable, and more. **Narrative writing** is a form of storytelling because it conveys events that happen during a defined period of time. Frequently, narratives are descriptive and seek to communicate a message, lesson, or personal account.

In this lesson, you will learn about the following aspects of narrative writing:

Key Elements of a Narrative
Strategies for Getting Started
Organizing a Narrative

Key Elements of a Narrative

Narratives tend to focus on conveying a single experience, event, or idea. While there is rarely a set standard for all texts, most narratives contain the following parts:

An experience or significant event

A setting and timeline

Characters

Sensory details

Experience or Event of Significance

Most good narratives focus on a single story or moment. This moment does not need to contain a ton of action or plot twists to keep readers engaged. In fact, an overload of events can make it difficult to effectively deliver the story.

When you choose your story, focus instead on the message that you want to send. Consider a story that evokes a strong response or has a lasting impact. Sure, your story *could* be about a life-changing conversation on an airplane that prompted you to quit your job and go skydiving. However, a simpler event, like the two minutes you spent holding your newborn nephew, could be just as meaningful. Just be sure the story leads to a significant outcome.

Here are some more examples:

- The moment you first saw your parents as imperfect and how that changed your outlook
- An experience meeting your idol, which led you to realize that people aren't always what they seem
- The day you reluctantly agreed to try something new and ended up loving it, creating a thirst for adventure

On Your Own

Use the following table to think about significant experiences in your own life. In the *Moment* column, write short descriptions of personal experiences or moments. In the *Outcome* column, write about how your life, or someone else's, was changed by that experience.

Moment	Outcome

Setting and Timeline

All stories have a **setting,** or a time and place, in which the story exists. Some stories contain a setting of little importance, while other settings carry heavy significance. Consider how the setting of your narrative impacts, reflects, or symbolizes important components of your story. If your setting *does* reflect important story components, play around with the details of that setting and how they can add to your storytelling.

Here are some examples:

- The setting of a circus highlights your point in an argument with your mother about handling your dysfunctional siblings
- Your small, rural hometown is contrasted with your need to break free and travel
- The hustle and bustle of New York City symbolizes the chaos you felt when you moved away from home for the first time

Reflection Questions

Examine the details of the picture below. Think about how these details reflect the feelings that may come with moving to a new city.

Characters

A narrative usually includes **characters**. In a **non-fiction** narrative, your real-life friends or relatives may be characters. In a **fictional** narrative, you might build a world of talking animals or **personified** objects.

Characters come to life in well-written narratives. For effective **characterization,** consider incorporating these sorts of details about the star of your story:

Actions	Hopes, fears, dreams
Reactions	Motivations, beliefs, viewpoints
Dialogue	Strengths and flaws
Physical descriptions	Everyday situations (family, job, location)

Group Activity

On your own, find an image of a person, animal, or object. Then, as a team, choose a "character" from one of the photos and build his, her, or its story. What are the character's hopes and fears? Where does the character live? What does the character believe in? How is the character feeling right now? Why?

Sensory Details

Get your reader's attention by employing sensory details in your writing. **Sensory details** include descriptions that appeal to our senses: sight, sound, touch, taste, and smell. Don't simply tell the audience that you and your brother got into a fight. Illustrate the moment so that readers can see your red-faced brother and hear the door slam as he stomped out of the room.

Using sensory details adds life, sincerity, and relatability to your writing, allowing your readers to experience the story along with the characters.

Writing Environment: Everyday

As a way to explain yourself, you may need to recount a story verbally in an everyday conversation. Observe the narrative writing in the following response to this question: "Jerusha, can you please explain to me how my car got a dent in it?"

> "Dad, you know how I'm always allowed to borrow the car, right? Well, I tried calling you three times to see about taking it for a quick trip to Jasmine's. I wanted to go over there because she had just gotten into a huge argument with Ron, and she needed someone to talk to. I know I usually need your permission, Dad, but after I tried to reach you, Jasmine called again in a hysterical fit. I had no choice. I made a decision, grabbed the keys, and ran out the door.
>
> So, I'm driving toward Jasmine's, with my phone away and my seatbelt on, and I'm being careful not to speed. Then, the next thing you know, a basketball comes flying toward me from the right side of the street. I slammed on the brakes just as the ball made direct contact with the passenger door. Two kids came running toward me and began apologizing, quickly followed by their mother.
>
> The mom's name is Janice Mulroney, and here's her address and phone number. If you want to call her, she said she'll take full responsibility for the damage."

Strategies for Getting Started

Now that you understand a narrative's key components, consider ways to bring this strategy to life. First, narrow your **topic** and focus by considering the context of your writing. If you're using a narrative to explain a problematic situation to your manager, you don't have much to narrow down; your topic is the specific situation, and you'll probably want to focus on the most important details and possible solutions.

If you're writing a narrative essay for a school assignment or a job application, your may have more options. Carefully review the assignment details and decide how much flexibility you have in choosing your topic and focus.

Writing Environment: Academic

As you read the following essay prompts, think about how they should affect your approach to narrowing a topic and focus.

> Create a personal narrative that explores a time when you faced a major challenge. Explore how this hurdle changed you for better or for worse.

> Think of a change you want to see on campus. Illustrate why this change is necessary by providing a detailed account of a relevant personal experience.

> Write a two-page narrative about your first day in college. Include who you met, what thoughts were running through your mind, and how you felt at the end of the day.

Once you have a strong handle on your assignment guidelines, follow these steps:

1. First, brainstorm a list of meaningful moments, special places, personal values, and influential people in your life.

2. Next, for each item in your list, create a **mind map** like the one below. Write the topic in the center of the map. Fill in the surrounding shapes with memories and details that you associate with the topic.

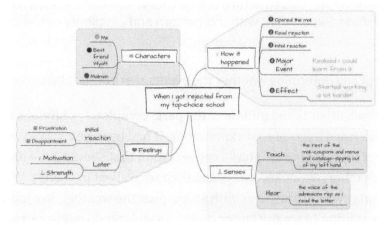

3. Finally, begin writing descriptive sentences for the topic. Use the ideas in your mind map as building blocks for these sentences. For each memory, add details about what you saw, heard, touched, tasted, or felt.

Weak Examples	Strong Examples
I was angry.	I slammed the car door with all of my strength.
The sun was hot.	The sunlight scorched everything it touched.
I heard the ocean from my bedroom.	The peaceful static of the ocean filled the room.
The rainbow had seven different colors.	The rainbow was bursting with colors I have only ever seen in my dreams.

Once you complete these steps, you will have a large bank of ideas and details to include in your writing.

Organizing a Narrative

You have a bank of ideas. Now what? There are numerous ways to organize your narrative. Consider the following components when piecing your story together.

Order of Events

Effectively organizing the events you describe can help your audience understand and stay interested in your narrative. Think about how much time passes between the first and last event in your narrative. How are you going to account for this passage of time? Is it important that your readers observe the events in the order that they occurred? Based on your responses to these questions, choose one of these two options for organizing your narrative:

- **Chronological Order**: This pattern simply tells the story in the order the events occurred. Often, this pattern makes sense when the story is leading up to a pivotal moment or when clarity is a major focus for your writing.
- **Non-linear Order**: This pattern is the opposite of a chronological pattern. Non-linear stories jump around to different times and places. They often include flashbacks and flash-forwards as part of their structure.
    - **Flashback**: A scene that takes your narrative backwards in time.
    - **Flash-forward**: A scene that takes your narrative forward in time.

> **Helpful Hint**
>
> A non-linear pattern is often used either to symbolize a component of your story or to better engage your reader. However, this structure can be tricky. You don't want a narrative that's impossible to understand. Experiment with this pattern and get plenty of feedback from others on its effectiveness.

Read the following excerpt and determine whether the events are ordered chronologically or non-linearly.

> We stood facing each other in the middle of the park, completely oblivious to the passers-by who must have been alarmed by our facial expressions. It had been years. What we needed to do was talk, but neither of us knew how to start a conversation that should have happened a decade ago. We looked at each other, we looked away, and then we walked in silence. We spent our remaining time that day filling awkward silences with safe topics: the weather, my job, and my children. Now, as I sit here waiting to see my father again, it's all I can do not to re-route my plans and run out of this restaurant, never dealing with the truth. Unfortunately, "never dealing with the truth" has become my life's motto, and being here is an attempt to change that. I occupy myself with the contents of the menu, I scan the bar in a minimal effort to people-watch, and I think about my upcoming presentation at work. But nothing can completely shield me from my looming fate. As I look up to ask a server about the specials, I am met with that familiar face. I desperately try to push back my feelings, but they betray me by leaking from my eyes. I grab the closest waiter and hear myself say, "Excuse me, ma'am, where's the bathroom?"

The Introduction

The first line in your story can be powerful. As you write the **introduction**, consider using one of the following strategies as a **hook** to immediately get your readers' attention:

Compelling quote or strong piece of dialogue

> "You must challenge yourself to do what you think you cannot," my history teacher reminded our class. Well, I certainly took that to heart.

In medias res

Latin for "in the midst of," this lets you begin your story right in the middle of the action.

> The doctor walked toward me with an expression of excitement. As he looked me in the eyes, I panicked. What? What piece of information was coming toward me? How was my life about to change?

"Triplets." He smirked as I dropped into the nearest chair.

Intriguing description

I whipped around the curves of the mountain road in the pouring rain, peering out of the fog-smothered windshield.

Thoughtful question

I was told that moving across the country would be "an exciting thrill," so why am I sitting here, still friendless and alone, on Week #5 in my new school?

Brief anecdote

I was five years old when I first spoke. The experts told my mom it might never happen, but as I watched my two-year-old brother toddle towards the uncovered pool, I looked at my mother and managed to eke out my first word: "Help!"

Writing Environment: Professional

There may be times at work when your colleague or supervisor asks you to write a narrative of something that you heard or witnessed. In cases like this, it is probably best to avoid a fancy introductory hook and get right to the heart of the story.

> **Helpful Hint**
>
> If you are stuck on how to start your narrative, skip the **introduction** and come back to it later. Use whatever idea you have in mind and start there. Sometimes, a good idea for your introduction stems from something that happens later in your writing.

The Climax

A major component of the narrative is the **climax**, the highest point of action or awareness. You may choose to follow the traditional narrative arc below as a guide for when to include this moment:

Your climactic point does not need to be directly in the middle of the narrative. Some narratives include the climax early and backtrack to how it happened, or they spend more time on the moments after the climactic point. Others work up to the climax for the majority of the narrative, only revealing it in the final paragraphs or words.

Consider what works best for your story, and think about how much time you want to dedicate toward other elements of the narrative arc.

On Your Own

Read the paragraphs below and identify the sentence that contains the climactic point.

> I walked through the cold, crowded streets, hands shoved in my pockets, hoping to make it home before dark. Strangers passed by, shoving, shoving, but never looking me in the eye. I turned right on Helm Street and was greeted with an angry specimen of a man. His frustration over our near-collision seemed unjustified. I bumbled a pathetic apology and picked up the pace to my apartment. Almost there, almost there. Almost avoiding . . .
>
> And then, with one quick turn, I'm hit with the image crowding my nightmares: my grim, fading face staring back at me in the reflection of the store windows, mercilessly exposing my sickness and decay. It's unavoidable, I realize, as I throw myself down on the couch and prepare for the evening's practiced routine of medication and loneliness.

The Conclusion

Sometimes, wrapping up a piece of writing can be the hardest part. Below are some do's and don'ts to follow when writing the **narrative conclusion**:

DO:

- ✓ Consider reflecting on the impact of your story.
- ✓ Consider reflecting on how your story may affect others.
- ✓ Consider a creative ending strategy such as leaving your reader with a final thought or question.
- ✓ Consider referencing the introduction of your story.

DON'T:

- ✗ Overwrite because you don't know how to stop.
- ✗ Stop abruptly because you don't know how to stop.
- ✗ Explicitly state the point of your narrative.
- ✗ Summarize the entire story you've just told.

Lesson Wrap-up

Key Terms

Character: a person or thing imagined or invented by an author for a story

Characterization: describing a character in a convincing way

Chronological Order: an organizational pattern that arranges ideas or events in the order that they occur (also known as sequential order)

Climax: the highest point of action or awareness in a text

Fiction: a text that deals with content imagined or invented by the author

Flashback: a scene that takes a text back in time

Flash-forward: a scene that takes a text forward in time

Hook: the first sentence or two in a piece of writing that aims to immediately engage the reader

In Medias Res: Latin for "in the midst of," this narrative technique starts a story in the middle of the action

Mind Map: a graphic organizer that uses shapes to illustrate connections between ideas

Narrative Conclusion: the end of a narrative, usually used to tie together themes, resolve issues, and/or leave the audience with a thought or question

Narrative Introduction: the beginning of a narrative, usually used to grab the audience's attention, introduce characters, and/or provide general information

Narrative Writing: writing that conveys events that happen during a defined period of time

Non-fiction: a text that deals with reality and facts

Non-linear Order: an organizational pattern that arranges ideas or events out of order

Personification: a type of figurative language that gives an animal or thing the attributes of a person

Sensory Detail: a description that appeal to the senses: sight, sound, touch, taste, or smell

Setting: the time and place in which a story exists

Topic: the general subject of a text

Writing Application: Narrative Writing

Read the following narrative and consider how the setting, characters, order of events, and other components work together to create a unified message.

"A Much Worse Crime"

It wasn't until I finally got up the courage to raise my hand that I learned of the high-pitched squeak that my voice makes when I'm terribly nervous. Dead giveaway. Just what I need.

"Yes, Audrey, so glad to hear from you. What are your thoughts on last night's reading?" asked Mrs. Richards.

"Umm, well," I yelped, cherry-faced and squirming in my seat, "I think the red hunting hat is a symbol of Holden's conflicting desires toward being a part of society."

This off-beat introductory description draws the reader in.

I'd done it. I'd challenged myself. I'd spoken in front of my classmates and shared an *actual, original* thought. I scanned the room to find twenty-four faces staring at me, and the only reason it wasn't twenty-five was because Hyde Gleason was too busy sleeping on his desk to be bothered with my awkward proclamation of self-assurance. Was it *that* shocking that Audrey actually had a voice, squeaky and painful, but in existence?

"Did she just talk?" Dane Palmer boomed, loud enough for the neighboring class to hear. "It's a miracle! I'm totally going to tweet this."

This dialogue characterizes Dane as a negative character.

"Enough, Mr. Palmer!" Mrs. Richards said crisply. "Unless you'd like to share your thoughts on the reading, too."

"Let's see," said Dane, proudly enjoying yet another glorious moment in the spotlight, "I think Holden just needs to chill out and make some friends." He looked my way, adding salt to my open wound.

As the class giggled, I sank lower and lower in my chair. Twenty-four minutes. That's how long I had to sit and agonize over my backfired attempt at dignity. After what felt like days, the bell rang, and I ran out of that classroom, head down and books in hand.

"Hey, Audrey," I heard Dane say, "I hear the choir is looking for sopranos! Why don't you go try out?" As his half-witted buddies laughed, I turned the corner just in time not to let them see my tears.

After being summoned to the dinner table that evening, I sat down, trying my best to hide my latest Dane encounter from my intuitive parents.

"How was school today, honey?" my mom asked me as she swatted my father's hand away from adding a third heaping spoonful of mashed potatoes to his plate.

Realistic descriptions bring the characters to life.

As she passed me the string beans, I said, "Fine. Good. Great, actually. Got an *A* on my biology exam."

Once again, my voice gave me away. It must have had that hint of sadness that only my mother can hear. I swear, sometimes she's just like our dog Sadie, acutely hearing what I do my best to keep quiet.

"Dane again?" she asked, frowning and looking me in the eyes.

I burst into tears for the second time that day. "I just don't get it. I mean, no one is perfect, and there are plenty of other people he could focus his attention on. Why me? What did I ever do to him?" As I tried to calm my erratic breathing, my father got up and gave me a hug. My mother looked at me with the face of unconditional love, and we all stayed like that for a few minutes.

After dinner, my dad offered to take a walk with me, telling me the fresh air would do me good. I agreed but decided to go alone. I wasn't exactly up for a father-daughter pep talk, but I thought wallowing in my self-pity for an hour or two might do the trick.

This phrase indicates that the story uses chronological order.

As I turned the corner a few blocks from my house, I walked past a shiny "Sold" sign on an otherwise brown and deserted front lawn. I heard yelling coming from inside the house but couldn't make out the words, only the jarring sound of two men screaming. I decided to respect their privacy and sped by without looking back.

After an hour of fresh air, I was starting to feel a bit better. However, my thoughts had been so consuming that I forgot to pay attention to where I was. When I looked up, I was twenty or thirty feet away from the house I had passed earlier. This time, two figures stormed out of the front door, so I quickly hid behind a shrub. My heart was racing and my palms were sweaty as I cursed Dane for putting me in this situation. Then, as I took a peek at the unfolding scene, there he was: Dane, tears streaming from his eyes, fear on his face.

The sensory details in these paragraphs help the reader visualize the setting.

I had heard him bragging at school about moving into a big house but hadn't cared to learn where. "Just my luck," I thought, "he's managed to seep even deeper into my life."

As I turned my ear to the yard, I heard, "I don't care that you're my son! I don't care that you're a football star! You're not good for anything!"

I stood there, frozen. Why wasn't I happy? Dane, the boy who had tormented me for *years*, was getting what he deserved. Wasn't he?

I listened as a barrage of nasty, abusive insults and threats were thrown Dane's way. I heard in shock as Dane's father berated his son, apparently for forgetting to unplug the toaster. However, Dane did not react with the shock I was experiencing; this was routine, practiced, *normal*. I had never heard such blind hate spewing out of someone's mouth. I had never witnessed someone so intentionally try to hurt someone else. It almost reminded me of . . .

In those moments, hearing Dane apologize, hearing him plead his innocence, hearing him sound defeated and broken, something happened that I never thought would: I began to empathize with my tormentor. I began to realize he was the casualty of a much worse crime.

This is the turning point in the narrative that conveys Audrey's significant experience.

I thought of eating dinner with my parents just an hour before. Then I thought of Dane's father. And I understood. I went home that night, hugged my parents a little tighter, and told them that I would be okay. And I actually meant it. My mother must have known, for she simply smiled and nodded.

The next day in school, there was Dane. Laughing, boisterous, and obnoxious as ever. He stuck out his foot to trip an underclassman, his buddies laughing as usual. But for the first time, I noticed the absence of joy in his smile. I hadn't noticed before, but something told me the emptiness had always been there.

When I got to English class, again I looked at Dane, but like last night I didn't see a tormentor; I saw a victim. That day, Dane ignored me. I wasn't part of his agenda, but he was part of mine.

After class, I approached him in the hallway when he was alone. He looked shocked to see me, but before he could get anything out, I simply said, "I saw you and your father outside last night. And I want you to know that I understand, and I forgive you."

And at that, I walked away. My voice didn't squeak, my hands didn't sweat, and, as it turned out, my tormentor didn't pick on me again. In fact, after several weeks of complete avoidance, Dane actually looked at me, and I think I even saw an apologetic smile creep over his lips.

> This phrase references the introduction, framing the narrative stylistically.

Lesson 2.3
Expository Writing

You might be less familiar with expository writing than you are with other modes of writing. However, expository writing is just as prevalent in everyday life; it just tends to go by a few different names, like *example writing*, *informative writing*, or *illustration*.

The word *expository* relates directly to the concept of exposure, or bringing something to light, as well as to the notion of an explanation, or conveying information to an **audience**. When you write an expository essay, you are *exposing* an idea to your audience by using evidence (also called supporting details).

Much like a photograph, an effective expository essay creates a clear picture of a central idea that the audience sees. It does this by presenting information in a tightly organized pattern. When you learn to organize your evidence for an expository essay, you can master writing assignments for all different purposes. You will also be able to express yourself more clearly in academic, professional, and everyday settings.

A photographer captures an image much like a writer captures an idea.

Reflection Questions

Have you ever been faced with a situation that required some quick thinking? Did you have a convincing set of evidence to get you out of trouble? If not, think about a scenario when evidence could have helped your cause.

In this lesson, you will learn about the following aspects of expository writing:

Components of Expository Writing
Structuring Expository Writing
Using Informative Details
Relating Exposition to Other Modes

Components of Expository Writing

Expository writing refers to any writing that uses evidence to support a main purpose. Whether you're instructing your audience on how to make or do something, informing your audience about a topic, or arguing a core belief, as long as you are providing evidence that relates back to your purpose, you are producing an expository piece of writing.

Group Activity

As a group, come up with a topic that you all know something about. Write down a short description of this topic. Then, gather details and **examples** of how this topic can be explained. When you're done, discuss why each one of these potential examples might be helpful in achieving your purpose.

The information you collect about a topic can serve as evidence that supports your main idea and strengthens its credibility. **Credibility** is what makes something or someone believable.

Primary Parts of an Expository Essay

Expository writing has two primary parts:

- A **main idea** expressed as a **thesis statement**. In expository writing, this is the essay's most general idea, and it requires support to be convincing.
- A series of **evidence**, accompanied by compelling details, that supports the thesis statement and informs, persuades, or instructs. This collection of evidence is typically referred to as the body of an expository essay.

> To learn more about thesis statements, see Lesson 4.3.

Writing Environment: Everyday

We use exposition all the time to explain something to those around us. If you have ever provided instructions for cooking a meal or justified a decision you've made by referring to the circumstances that inspired your choice, you've used this type of communication.

Organizational Strategies

Besides establishing a thesis and developing evidence, you need to decide how to organize your evidence so that it is coherent and convincing. This decision will depend on the writing task itself, but most expository writing follows one of the following **organizational patterns**:

Spatial Order: This organizational pattern is used to describe a subject's physical characteristics, usually from top to bottom, left to right, or front to back. Think about the way you scan a person, place, or thing with your eyes; that action is what spatial order tries to imitate.

Chronological Order: This pattern tells a story in the order the events occurred. For expository writing, this pattern is used when you are instructing the audience on how to do something. Imagine explaining how to bake a cake; you would need to tell your reader the steps and their order.

Order of Importance: This pattern organizes evidence from most important to least important or from least important to most important. In expository writing, it's usually best to order your points from least to most important. Putting your strongest pieces of evidence last makes it stand out to the audience. Assume you need to persuade the audience to use a new product. This structure lets you work up to your main point.

On Your Own

For each of the following topics, decide which organizational pattern would be most effective. After choosing one, make sure you consider why it would work best. There may be more than one way to approach each one!

Topic	Order	Rationale
Describing an experience that taught you the importance of cooperation.		
Explaining why an athlete or entertainer deserves more recognition.		

Presenting the traits that contemporary Western society considers physically attractive.		
Explaining the perfect vacation.		
Arguing that a local intersection needs a stop sign.		

Helpful Hint

When you think about order of importance, imagine a lawyer arguing his or her case to a jury. The lawyer will save the best piece of evidence for last so that when the jury leaves to deliberate, that final example will still be resonating in the jury members' minds.

Remember, organizational patterns refer to the overall strategy for a whole assignment. However, you could use other organizational patterns to connect ideas within the **body paragraphs** of an essay, where most of the evidence appears.

Sometimes, to persuade someone or explain something, you might use series of stories that illustrate each of your main points. These narratives are your evidence, and you would organize them chronologically in your body paragraphs each time you bring them up. We'll come back to this point later when we discuss how modes of writing relate to each other.

To learn more about the modes of writing, see Lessons 2.1, 2.2, and 2.4.

Group Activity

Discuss a time in your life when a major misunderstanding led to personal or professional problems. What kind of examples could you have presented to clarify your position or explain your situation? Come up with 3-4 examples and list them by order of importance. Why did you organize them this way?

Writing Environment: Academic

In school, if you are asked to explain a concept or discuss how one thing causes another, you will use expository writing to make your case. Take a look at these examples:

In a philosophy class, you might be asked to explain existentialism. To do so, you could break this philosophy into different features and explain each one in a separate body paragraph.

In a history class, you might be asked to explain how American foreign policy in the 1980s affected the current political situation in the Middle East. Each of your body paragraphs might discuss one policy decision and its results.

Structuring Expository Writing

Like many writing tasks, the way you frame your essay will have a strong influence on the impact of your work. Let's consider some ideas for opening and closing an expository essay.

The Introduction

An expository introduction needs to be more than just a thesis statement. In fact, your thesis statement should appear towards the end of your introduction. That way, it serves as a natural transition to the body paragraphs, where the evidence is located. What, then, should the rest of the introduction do?

An **expository introduction** serves two purposes:

- To get the reader's attention
- To provide important background information

There are several strategies for getting your audience's attention, including using a **hook**: a strong **quote**, an interesting question, a brief **anecdote**, or a **proclamation**. Just remember that most of your paper should be focused on presenting your evidence in the body paragraphs.

> To learn more about using introductory hooks, see Lessons 2.2 and 4.2.

Group Activity

Imagine your supervisor at work has asked you to create a presentation for the board of directors that explains why it's a good idea to move the office across town. As a group, brainstorm what kind of story you could tell that would hook them and get them interested in the new location even before you present the reasons.

When you write an expository introduction, also consider what kind of information your reader needs in order to feel comfortable with the evidence you provide later. Is your audience a specific group that is knowledgeable about the topic? Are you writing to a general audience that isn't familiar with the focus of your work? Considering the needs of your audience in advance and addressing them in your introduction is an essential part of effective communication.

Writing Environment: Professional

Sometimes, when you are tasked with constructing a business plan or writing other types of expository reports for work, lengthy introductions can be perceived as unprofessional. Always keep the context of your assignment in mind when you are planning your work!

Consider the following example of an introduction for a finance report. Note how brief it is and how it gets right down to business without any sort of hook:

> The following report offers data concerning the profitability of Bamco, Inc.'s line of dinner-themed ice cream products for the fiscal year 2015. It will focus on those figures related to the Midwest over the period January 3rd to March 31 in order to determine the effect that consumer complaints had on the products in question. The report will make recommendations that would improve the products' performance in the opening quarter of 2016.

> Helpful Hint
>
> Think of an expository essay like a conversation. Most of the time, you don't suddenly run up to someone, begin talking, and then run away again. Conversations, like essays, have introductions and conclusions. Use this idea to help you write the introductory and concluding paragraphs of your expository essay.

The Conclusion

Wrapping up an expository essay can be difficult. Many writers feel compelled to repeat themselves in their conclusions, restating all the evidence they presented in the body and reiterating their thesis statement. This kind of strategy is appropriate sometimes, but it can also bore readers if it is too repetitive. Instead, try asking yourself the following questions before writing your **conclusion**:

> Why is my main idea important?
>
> What do I want my readers to learn?
>
> What do I want my readers to take away?
>
> What do I want my readers to *do*?

Depending on the purpose of your essay, you might not have answers to all of these questions, but chances are you have answers to at least two of them. These answers can form the basis for your conclusion.

Additionally, your conclusion doesn't have to be overly long. Usually, several sentences that emphasize the importance and relevance of your main idea will work just fine.

> Helpful Hint
>
> Most expository essays need a title. Often, the best way to come up with a title is to write it after you've written the essay. Try to sum up your main purpose in a few words, perhaps putting a clever or poetic spin on it. Unless your instructor has requested a certain title, avoid calling your essay something like "Assignment #1" or "Expository Essay."

Using Informative Details

The most important skill to master when writing an expository essay is arranging your ideas in a logical way. If you dread writing, it's probably not because you don't have anything to say but because you have a lot to say and don't know how to put it all together.

Expository essays depend on making connections between main ideas and supporting details. A main idea, presented in a thesis statement, is broad and establishes a purpose or makes a claim. The more general an idea, the more **supporting details** it needs to back it up. **Major details** are anything that help explain or prove a main idea, while **minor details** support major details.

Consider this example of a thesis statement for an expository essay arguing that college students should avoid generating credit card debt:

> College students should avoid accruing credit card debt because their lifestyles encourage frequent spending, and the resulting interest can negatively impact their finances.

This statement is general enough that it naturally leads to more specific points about spending and interest rates. A statement like *credit cards have high interest rates* on the other hand, is too specific. It is a factual detail that can't produce a whole paper. After all, it's just *true*; it doesn't make a general claim that could be argued.

Basic Expository Outline

Here is what a simple outline of what an expository essay might look like. Depending on your topic and assignment, you might have more or fewer than three body paragraphs. Consider the placement of the details here as a way to support your main idea.

I. Introduction
      A. Thesis statement (main idea)
II. Body Paragraph 1
      A. Topic sentence (explains your first piece of evidence)
          1. Major details
             i.   Minor details
III. Body Paragraph 2
      A. Topic sentence (explains your next piece of evidence)
          1. Major details
             i.   Minor details
IV. Body Paragraph 3
      A. Topic sentence (explains your final piece of evidence)
          1. Major details
             i.   Minor details
V. Conclusion
      A. What should my audience learn, take away, and/or do?

One way to understand expository essays is to imagine them like our solar system.

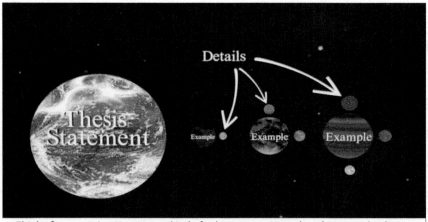

Think of an expository essay as a kind of solar system. Note that the example planets would make up the body of the essay.

Think back to the astronomy you learned in grade school. At the center of our solar system is the sun, the largest object in the system around which all the planets revolve. Your thesis statement is the sun because it is the most general, and hence the "largest" idea in your essay. Your evidence should orbit, or focus on, your thesis.

> **Helpful Hint**
>
> When you present evidence in your body paragraphs, you can use transitions like *first of all*, *second*, *also*, *next*, *in addition*, *furthermore*, *most importantly*, *last*, and *finally* to emphasize how your details connect. Think of these words as the gravitational forces that hold the whole system together!

In our solar system, the planets closest to the sun, like Mercury and Venus, are the smallest, while those further away, like Jupiter and Saturn, are much larger. This is similar to an expository essay organized by order of importance. The most important, or "biggest" pieces of evidence, come last and are "farthest away" from the thesis in the introduction.

Finally, every planet in the solar system has one or more small moons; they orbit the planets just as the planets orbit the sun. You can think of minor details as moons; they revolve around and explain the evidence in your major details.

> **Group Activity**
>
> Imagine you're a screenwriter working on a new TV show. You want to convince the show's producers to include a major event in the season finale. After deciding what this event should be and the reasons it should happen, use the previous outline to logically organize your points using order of importance.

Relating Exposition to Other Modes

As we discuss expository writing, it's important to understand that modes of writing don't stand alone.

For example, **descriptive writing** uses words that appeal to the senses to describe something. **Narrative writing** conveys events over a defined period of time. Both of these modes use evidence; descriptive writing uses sensory details, and narrative writing uses the events that make up a story. Understood in this way, both description and narration are types of expository writing.

However, unlike descriptive and narrative writing, expository writing always requires a thesis statement. The main points of descriptive and narrative writing are often implied rather than explicitly stated.

Lesson Wrap-up

Key Terms

Anecdote: a long example told as a story

Audience: the person or people meant to read and interpret a text

Body Paragraphs: the paragraphs between the introduction and conclusion of an essay that use supporting details to explore, explain, and/or prove the main idea(s)

Chronological Order: an organizational pattern that arranges ideas or events in the order that they occur (also known as sequential order)

Credibility: what makes something or someone believable

Descriptive Writing: writing that communicates the characteristics or qualities of a thing or event

Evidence: a piece of information, also called a supporting detail, that is used to support a main idea

Example: a specific instance or illustration that demonstrates a point

Expository Conclusion: the end of an expository essay, used to communicate the importance of the main idea and what readers should learn, take away, and/or do

Expository Introduction: the beginning of an expository essay, used to get the reader's attention and provide important background information

Expository Writing: writing that uses evidence to support a main idea

Hook: the first sentence or two in a piece of writing that aims to immediately engage the reader

Main Idea: the statement or argument that an author tries to communicate

Major Detail: a type of evidence that supports and proves a main idea

Minor Detail: a type of evidence that uses specific information to clarify a major detail

Narrative Writing: writing that conveys events that happen during a defined period of time

Order of Importance: an organizational pattern that arranges ideas from least to most significant, or vice versa

Organizational Pattern: the structure of a written text, used to arrange the main points of a work

Proclamation: a strong declaration of an opinion or fact

Quote: someone's exact words

Spatial Order: an organizational pattern used to describe a subject's physical characteristics, usually from top to bottom, left to right, or front to back

Supporting Detail: a piece of information, also called evidence, that is used to support a main idea

Thesis Statement: the concise sentence or group of sentences that expresses the main idea of a longer work

Writing Application: Expository Writing

Read the following expository essay and consider the techniques it uses to clearly communicate and support its main idea.

Billy's Bistro: A Bad Place to Work

A lot of my friends have been teasing me about quitting my job at Billy's Bistro. They have a point; I don't have much money since leaving, and just yesterday I had to borrow some cash for gas to get to class. That was pretty embarrassing, and for a minute I almost regretted my decision. However, people who know me best will realize just how bad the situation must have become for me to walk out.

For those who don't know, Billy's is in the center of town, so it gets a lot of business. I pulled in a bunch of tips every night, sometimes as much as $100, and I worked five nights a week. I'm sure management had no problem hiring someone else after I left, and some of my friends are even considering applying. Before anybody makes that mistake, though, I hope he or she will hear me out. Working at Billy's Bistro is not a good career choice.

> The writer uses two paragraphs to provide both a personal anecdote and background information to hook the audience. Finally, the author ends with her thesis, which indicates a persuasive purpose.

For one thing, many of the current employees at Billy's are unfriendly and will throw other people under the bus to save their own jobs. For example, two weeks ago a server totally forgot about one of her tables. I guess she was out back taking a break, but the customers she had abandoned were getting visibly frustrated about not getting refills, and one of them needed a new fork. I tried to help out by getting what they needed. I even made an excuse for my coworker by saying that she had a personal emergency. Later on, this same girl told my manager that I had taken her table and had told lies about her. I was threatened with being written up when what she should have done was share her tips. This kind of thing is always happening there; nobody on the staff wants to work as a team.

Even worse are the safety conditions at Billy's. The kitchen almost always has water on the floor because the dishwashers are overfilled, and the tile is extremely slippery back there. I slipped and sprained my elbow once, and on the day I quit, one of the busboys fell and hit his head. Luckily, he wasn't hurt badly, but he barely missed the sharp edge of a counter top. In addition, the cooks never use splash guards on the fryers, and that same busboy was burned by hot oil that splashed onto his arms. One of the cooks is also notorious for leaving knives right on the edge of on the main counter in the back.

By far the worst part of working at Billy's, though, is the management. Billy only hires female servers, and he makes us wear tight shirts and short skirts because he says it's good for business. I knew about this policy going in, but I didn't expect to be harassed by customers. Billy gets mad if we complain, though, and he tells us, "That's the price for big tips." He also refuses to work around any of our school schedules and gets mad if we can't work because we have class. He refuses to listen to any suggestions for improving the dining room or the way we do things. Once, he told me, "I'm the boss, and you're the help. Now go out there and look pretty." I'm not the type to go around demanding my way, but I refuse to have someone speak to me that way.

I know the money is good at Billy's Bistro, but no one should have to put up with those kinds of working conditions. If you are reading this, I hope you will avoid applying there. Getting a few extra dollars isn't worth the trouble!

The first body paragraph starts with a transition and establishes that the evidence in this paragraph will be the writer's negative experiences with other employees.

The essay uses order of importance, so the evidence about lack of safety at Big Billy's is more important than the unfriendly coworkers.

The transition here clearly announces that this is the author's most important point.

The author uses minor details about Billy's uncooperative attitude to clarify the major detail: the worst part is the bad management.

Lesson 2.4
Persuasive Writing

Do you ever think about the number of persuasive messages you are exposed to everyday? Persuasive messages make up the advertisements and campaigns we encounter while watching TV, listening to the radio, reading magazines, and browsing the internet. We are exposed to these messages everywhere: in school, on public transportation, and on our cell phones.

Persuasion is a powerful tool. If we know how to harness it in our writing and speaking, we're more likely to convince others to agree with us. This, ultimately, is the purpose of persuasion.

In this lesson, you will learn about the following aspects of persuasive writing:

Key Elements of a Persuasive Argument
Supporting a Persuasive Argument
Organizing Your Argument

Key Elements of a Persuasive Argument

Persuasive writing uses an **argument** to influence someone's beliefs and/or actions. Because they're so crucial to persuasion, arguments can't just *sound* convincing; they must also be strong and well-supported.

To write an effective persuasive argument, you'll need to understand three basic elements:

- The claim
- The support
- The counterargument

The Claim

Every piece of persuasive writing should include a claim. The **claim** is the writer's opinion or position on an issue, so it's directly related to what the writer is convincing the audience to believe or do.

Let's look at some examples of claims.

The extra food that the United States produces and ends up wasting should instead be distributed to poverty-stricken areas.

This is a direct claim that extra food should be redistributed, not wasted.

Illegal immigrants are helping the American economy by working for lower wages and taking jobs that most Americans refuse to do.

The claim in this sentence is implied. It is indirectly saying that America needs to let illegal immigrants keep working.

Read through the following claims and their goals for persuasion:

Claim	Goal
The right to vote in America is one of our many freedoms; in support of our nation, we all must vote.	This claim is trying to convince the reader to vote.
To halt climate change, all nations must act cooperatively to enact policies that protect the earth.	This claim is trying to convince the reader to spur support for climate change with political representatives.
Because marijuana continues to be a major source of revenue for dangerous drug cartels, the U.S. must treat it as an illegal substance.	This claim is trying to convince the reader to support the criminalization of marijuana in the U.S.
In today's evolving world, it is necessary for everyone to have some form of post-secondary education.	This claim is trying to convince the reader that higher education after high school is necessary.

Now, it's time to turn your claim into a polished thesis statement. In persuasive writing, the **thesis statement** is the clear, logical viewpoint or opinion on an issue. This thesis statement will direct your persuasive writing just as a GPS directs a traveler.

Here are examples of thesis statements for different topics.

Topic	Thesis Statement
Climate change	As the world's climate continues to undergo startling changes, people who are concerned by this issue must communicate with their local and state representatives.
Football and concussions	Because there is not enough conclusive evidence that contact sports cause brain trauma, football should not be banned in the U.S.
Standardized testing	Testing is not an accurate measure of every student's ability; therefore, American schools must cease excessive standardized testing.

To learn more about thesis statements, see Lesson 4.3.

Group Activity

Practice writing a claim by choosing a controversial issue and expressing your opinion. Think about what you want your reader to believe or do. Then, write these things in direct, simple language.

When you're done, share your claims with your group, and offer one another feedback. Can any of the claims be made stronger? If so, how?

The Support

Once you have developed your claim, you need to support it. The support is your evidence or reasoning to justify what your claim is asking of the reader. Your evidence should be substantial and needs to include information from trustworthy sources. Later, this lesson will cover supporting persuasive arguments in more detail.

Just as these columns support the roof, your evidence will support your claim.

The Counterargument

A **counterargument** is an argument given to negate the opposition's opinions.

Every complex issue has at least two sides, if not more. Sometimes, there are valid arguments for both sides of an issue. Look at these opposing viewpoints concerning illegal immigration:

Side A	Side B
There is an economic burden on U.S. citizens because many illegal immigrants send their income back to their home countries.	There is no economic burden on U.S. citizens because illegal immigrants often spend money in U.S. businesses.
It is an economic burden on the U.S. because there are not enough jobs for illegal immigrants; they are taking jobs away from American citizens.	There is no economic burden on the U.S. because illegal immigrants work for lower wages than most Americans, and these immigrants take jobs that many Americans will not take.

Often, our opposition has valid arguments, so how do we handle these arguments? If the opposition's argument is valid, we need to step in with our own counterargument that says, "I understand your point; however . . ."

Here is an example that uses counterarguments based on the previous table:

> Illegal immigration has placed some economic burden on the U.S., but illegal immigrants spend money in American businesses daily while working for lower wages than most Americans will accept. Additionally, many illegal immigrants take jobs that most Americans have refused. Overall, illegal immigrants are helping the U.S. economy.
>
> These persuasive statements partially concede to the opposition's argument by saying, "Illegal immigration has placed *some* economic burden on the U.S." However, these statements also use counterarguments:
>
> "illegal immigrants spend money in American businesses daily"
>
> "illegal immigrants work at jobs that many Americans have refused"

Think about your own experiences with persuasion on a regular basis. You are probably more likely to listen to an argument when your point of view isn't ignored. The counterargument does just that: it acknowledges the opponent's views and then disputes those views.

Writing Environment: Everyday

We frequently try to persuade others to accept our opinions, even in simple situations like the one below:

> Person A: "I don't understand why you're not coming with all of us on the trip to Washington, D.C. It's going to be great!"
>
> Person B: "That trip's going to be so boring! I have no interest in government and politics."
>
> Person A: "Oh, it won't be that bad! We'll ride up together in Janet's car. There's a ton of stuff to do in D.C. We can plan it all on the ride up."
>
> Person B: "Still sounds boring to me."
>
> Person A: "Adam went last month and had an awesome time exploring Georgetown! We'll do more than just see the White House. Come on, everybody else is going. Please?"
>
> Person B: "Okay, okay, I'll go. But I'm picking the restaurants."
>
> Person A: "Okay, deal!"

Supporting a Persuasive Argument

Support is used to convince the reader that a claim is valid. In order to support your argument, you must have evidence. **Evidence** is a piece of information, also called a supporting detail, that is used to support a main idea. Evidence for your argument often comes in the form of facts, opinions, statistics, expert analysis, and examples.

First, let's look at facts vs. opinions.

Facts: a piece of information that can be proven true or false

> Nine people were killed at a church in Charleston, SC, on June 17, 2015.

Opinions: a statement, usually a personal belief or perspective, that cannot be proven true or false

> Americans need to take action to stop mass shootings.

Both facts and opinions should be considered in effective persuasion. We all agree that shootings are tragic, but to persuade someone that we need stronger gun control laws will take effectively worded opinions supported with sound, factual evidence.

Helpful Hint

Opinions help us form ideas for persuasive writing. It's stimulating to discuss opinions with friends, but in formal writing our opinions are more effective when they're supported by factual evidence.

On Your Own

Read the following statements and decide whether they are facts or opinions. Check the box next to your answer.

> Frogs are classified as amphibians.
> ☐ Fact
> ☐ Opinion

> Fridays are the best day of the week because we can wear jeans at work.
> ☐ Fact
> ☐ Opinion

> Women make better soldiers than men because women have more patience.
> ☐ Fact
> ☐ Opinion

Helpful Hint

Consider your audience; will they be more effectively persuaded by logical, researched facts; strong, emotional opinions; or both?

Now, let's examine the use of statistics and expert analysis as evidence. Statistics and expert analysis are difficult to refute, but finding them usually requires careful research.

Statistics: pieces of information based on a collection of data. The numbers used in statistics are powerful, so make sure they come from reliable sources.

> In 2013, 41.3 million immigrants lived in the United States.

Expert Analysis: pieces of information from someone knowledgeable about a topic. It wouldn't be wise to ask a car mechanic to design and build a space station; the same logic applies to using expert analysis. Do not use an expert on gun control to support your claim about illegal immigration.

> "The evidence that we have is that illegal immigration across the southwest border is at its lowest level since the early 1970s," states Doris Meissner, director of the Migration Policy Institute.

Your persuasive writing will be much stronger if you cite a reliable source. Compare the reliability of the following citations.

Strong Source	Weak Source
"According to *Time* magazine"	"I think"
" weapons expert Joe Lasky says"	"My friend Dean says"
"The U.S. Census Bureau reports"	"I believe . . . because I say so"

Last, let's consider how to use examples as evidence. **Examples** are specific instances or illustrations that demonstrate a point. Providing an example helps the reader understand a topic more thoroughly.

Think about the math courses you've taken in the past. Hopefully, with each example the instructor shared, your understanding of the topic increased. It's the same in persuasive writing; examples help your reader understand your claim as well as other pieces of evidence.

Consider these strong and weak examples for an essay that supports gun control:

Strong	The weapons of the 21st century are far more sophisticated than when the Second Amendment was ratified in 1791. Then, the weapons of choice were the Kentucky rifle (firing two to three shots per minute) and the six-pound field gun (firing one shot every two minutes).
Weak	The Second Amendment was ratified in 1791. George Washington was the president. John Fitch was granted a patent for the steamboat. Some Americans were involved in another battle as the Northwest Indian War began in Ohio country. Weapons were needed.

The strong example illustrates the factual difference in weapons and sets up the argument for a revision of the Second Amendment. The weak example uses factual evidence, but these facts are irrelevant to a claim about restricting gun use.

The strongest way to support your beliefs or opinions in persuasive writing is to use multiple types of evidence. Find valid statistics and quotes from experts, use your opinions effectively by supporting them with facts, and provide examples that clearly illustrate your point of view. Using evidence will make you more persuasive.

Organizing Your Argument

At this point, you've completed the following steps:

- Chosen an issue
- Determined the claim you want to make about that issue
- Written a thesis statement

Now, it's time to organize your argument within a logical structure.

The Introductory Paragraph

The **introduction** in persuasive writing should describe the issue in a way that is memorable and thought-provoking. Think of the introduction as an upside-down triangle. Using broad, general statements, describe your issue and gradually narrow to your specific thesis statement (the claim).

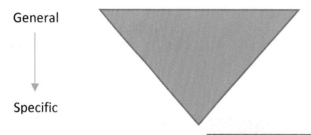

General

Specific

To learn more about introductions, see Lesson 4.2.

Compare the two introductory examples below and consider why one is weak and one is strong:

Weak	I think the death penalty should be banned. If a bad guy harms people, he should be placed in prison with no chance of parole. Who are we to kill a person? I think that would make us just as bad as the bad person.
Strong	A young girl is out shopping with her mother. Suddenly, a masked man with a gun enters the store with the intent of committing armed robbery. The robbery goes awry, and he fires his weapon several times. One of the bullets strikes the young girl, killing her. With heinous crimes like this one occurring daily, all states must enforce the death penalty to deter criminal acts.

Writing Environment: Everyday

In an editorial, the author shares an opinion on a current event or a controversial topic and calls his or her audience to action. If there is an issue that you feel strongly about, you can write an editorial for your local newspaper.

Support in your Body Paragraphs

The body of your persuasive writing is where you will present your arguments and counterarguments. This is also where you will use the facts, statistics, quotes, and examples you compiled during your research.

There are two common methods for organizing these **body paragraphs**:

- Acknowledge your opposition in the initial body paragraph, and then use the remaining body paragraphs for your counterarguments.
- Concede to your opposition at the beginning of the first body paragraph and immediately present your counterarguments. Then, continue your argument in the remaining body paragraphs.

Following are some techniques writers use to communicate their arguments effectively within these paragraphs. Using these strategies can lead to more compelling writing.

- **Tone**: the positive, negative, or neutral attitude that an author expresses about a topic. Use a tone that will appeal to your audience and support your purpose. Some examples of tone are formal, serious, sarcastic, or neutral.

  > With heinous crimes occurring daily, all states must enforce the death penalty to deter criminal acts.

- **Similes**: comparisons between two unlike things using *like* or *as*

  > The thesis statement will direct your persuasive writing just as a GPS directs a traveler.

- **Repetition**: occurs when a sound, word, phrase, or line is repeated to stress meaning or to create an engaging rhythm.

  > Martin Luther King, Jr. proclaimed, "Now is the time to make real the promises of democracy. Now is the time to rise from the dark and desolate valley of segregation to the sunlit path of racial justice. Now is the time to lift our nation from the quicksands of racial injustice to the solid rock of brotherhood."

- **Parallelism**: uses similar grammatical patterns to emphasize related ideas. Often, parallelism and repetition work together.

  > "We choose to go to the moon . . . because that challenge is one that we are willing to accept, one we are unwilling to postpone, and one which we intend to win," said President Kennedy about the space race during a speech at Rice University in 1962.

Let's take a look at an example of a body paragraph that combines many of these strategies:

> The Second Amendment of the U.S. Constitution states, "A well-regulated militia, being necessary to the security of a free state, the right of the people to keep and bears Arms, shall not be infringed." This Amendment was ratified on December 15, 1791. Has America changed since 1791? When America's forefathers wrote these words, they were still reeling from the Revolutionary War. Militias had been formed to fight for America's independence and protect citizens against invasion. The world of the 21st century is completely different from the world of 1791. The weapons of the 21st century, handguns and assault rifles, are completely different from the weapons of 1791: the Kentucky rifle and the six-pound field gun. The Kentucky rifle fired two to three shots per minute; Media Matters for America states that assault weapons fire thirty-round magazines in five seconds. Has America changed since 1791? ABC News states, "Access to weapons with high capacity magazines played a major role at Sandy Hook and in other mass shootings." Responsible citizens and lawmakers must put a stop to high-powered weaponry use on American soil by revising the Second Amendment to manage the sophisticated weapons of the 21st century.

This paragraph uses facts, quotes, examples, parallelism, and repetition to support its argument.

Group Activity

Partner with a classmate or friend. Ask your partner to take the opposition's viewpoint on your issue. Have this friend play "devil's advocate" and challenge your evidence. As you discuss, take note of any areas where you can strengthen your argument. If necessary, revise it to be clearer, more relevant, and easier to understand.

The Concluding Paragraph

A **persuasive conclusion** often leaves the audience with a compelling thought, question, or call to action. Before you write the conclusion, look back at your introduction. Sometimes, a good persuasive conclusion is written in the opposite order of your introduction. Start with a strongly reworded version of your thesis statement. Compare the introductory thesis to the concluding thesis.

Introduction Thesis	Football is a risky sport, but because there is not enough evidence that it causes serious brain injuries, it should not be banned.
Conclusion Thesis	Because there is not enough conclusive evidence that contact sports cause brain trauma, football should not be banned in the U.S.

Use the rest of your conclusion to summarize your main points and express your call to action. Here's an example:

> Because the death penalty is a cruel and unusual punishment that ends human lives, it should be banned. Who truly has the right to decide another person's time to live or die? We need to focus on rehabilitating criminals, not eliminating them. In order for America to eventually ban the death penalty, our society needs to dedicate time, funding, and educational resources to crime prevention.
>
> This concluding paragraph begins with a restated thesis statement. Then, it summarizes the main points: human rights and rehabilitation. Last, it ends with a call to action: dedicate time, funding, and education to help prevent crimes and eventually ban the death penalty.

Writing Environment: Professional

There may be times at work when you need to compose persuasive writing. For example, asking for a raise requires sound persuasive techniques, like facts, not overly emotional statements. A polished and professional request is more likely to succeed.

> Mr. Smith:
>
> I take pride in my professionalism. I am consistently on time to work, and I am never absent without prior notice. My tasks are completed thoroughly and before the deadline. For example, I researched and presented the Meyer project a week before the initial deadline. For these reasons, I believe I deserve a raise.

Lesson Wrap-up

Key Terms

Argument: a reason why you should think or act a certain way

Body Paragraphs: the paragraphs between the introduction and conclusion of an essay that use supporting details to explore, explain, and/or prove the main idea(s)

Claim: a writer's opinion or position on an issue

Counterargument: anticipating objections and refuting them with logic supported by evidence

Evidence: a piece of information, also called a supporting detail, that is used to support a main idea

Example: a specific instance or illustration that demonstrates a point

Expert Analysis: an opinion or statement shared by someone who is knowledgeable about a topic

Fact: a piece of information that can be proven true or false

Opinion: a statement, usually a personal belief or perspective, that cannot be proven true or false

Parallelism: a method for showing a relationship between ideas by using similarly structured words, phrases, or clauses

Persuasive Conclusion: the end of an essay, which leaves the audience with a thought, question or call to action

Persuasive Introduction: the beginning of an essay, which describes an issue and states the author's claim

Persuasive Writing: writing that uses argument to influence someone's beliefs and/or actions

Repetition: when a word, phrase, or sentence is repeated to stress meaning or create an engaging rhythm

Simile: a comparison between two unlike things using *like* or *as*

Statistic: a number or percentage based on a collection of data

Thesis Statement: the concise sentence or group of sentences that expresses the main idea of a longer work

Tone: the positive, negative, or neutral attitude that an author expresses about a topic

Writing Application: Persuasive Writing

Read the following persuasive essay about gun control, paying close attention to how it's structured and the supporting details it uses.

Keep the Safety On

Your friends have decided to go see the latest Oscar-winning movie. Just as the previews end, shots ring out through the movie theater. Scenarios like this are becoming all too familiar in America. After each shooting, there are cries for better mental health care and stiffer gun control regulations. However, after a few weeks, things seem to stall, and the shootings continue. Due to the increased number of mass shootings and gun-related fatalities in America, U.S. lawmakers need to create stricter background checks and increase the requirements for owning a firearm.

The introduction begins by describing the issue in a memorable, thought-provoking way.

This sentence is the persuasive thesis and includes the author's claim.

Feeling safe and protected is crucial to humans. Many Americans own guns for just this reason: to protect their homes and loved ones. Ironically, many of the guns purchased for protection end up harming someone. "One in three homes have guns," which results in an "average of 55 people committing suicide and 46 people being shot or killed accidentally with a gun" every day, reports the Bureau of Alcohol, Tobacco, Firearms and Explosives (BATF). It's too easy for untrained citizens to accidentally harm themselves or others with their guns. The FBI "counted 172 cases of mass killings from 2006-2011," reports USA Today. Public massacres like Sandy Hook Elementary only "account for one in six mass killings." The other mass killings are a result of "family breakups, estrangements, and family arguments." The very guns that are purchased for protection are responsible for the majority of mass killings and suicides in America. Don't we want our homes and loved ones to be safer?

These first few sentences acknowledge the opposition's argument and then refute it with facts and statistics.

Gun advocates frequently argue that it's not the gun that kills, it's the person using it. This statement is true; however, recent history proves that American laws are not doing a thorough job of regulating who owns and uses a gun. Two of America's largest mass shootings, both on school campuses—Virginia Tech in 2007 and Sandy Hook Elementary in 2012—involved shooters with serious mental health issues. The Virginia Tech shooter had been suffering from severe depression and anxiety. He was ordered to seek outpatient treatment. Because he was not technically institutionalized, he was still permitted to purchase handguns: a Glock 19 and a Walther P22. Both weapons are ideal for conceal-to-carry purposes and both use a minimum of fifteen-round magazines. The Virginia Tech shooter killed thirty-three people, including himself. The Sandy Hook Elementary shooter killed twenty-seven people, including his mother and himself. Six adults and twenty-two defenseless students between the ages of six and seven lost their lives. It took a twenty-year old just five minutes to fire one hundred and fifty-six shots: one hundred and fifty-four from an AR-15 assault rifle and two from a Glock.

The author begins this paragraph with another counterargument.

The final sentences in this paragraph use parallelism as a persuasive technique.

According to law enforcement reports, the Sandy Hook shooter suffered "significant mental health issues that affected his ability to live a normal life." He'd been diagnosed with sensory-integration disorder, Asperger's Syndrome, and OCD. Under Connecticut law, he was old enough to carry a rifle or shotgun but not to own or carry a handgun. His mother legally owned the weapons. He shot her four times in the head.

This paragraph begins with expert analysis from law enforcement.

Ninety percent of Americans support background checks for weapons' purchases, but it is clear that background checks alone are not preventing people from obtaining and using guns to commit crimes.

According to the Council on Foreign Relations, "the U.S. has the highest homicide-by-firearm rate among the world's most developed nations." The U.S. should follow Japan's lead: Japanese laws require gun owners to have formal instruction in gun safety and to pass a battery of tests. Additionally, firearms must be inspected annually. The Council on Foreign Relations reports, "Japan's gun-homicide rate is the lowest in the world at 1 in 10 million." Obviously, these horrific mass shootings and homicide rates can be reduced in America, as well.

Because of the escalating incidents of mass shootings and gun-related fatalities in America, U.S. citizens and leaders need to come together to create stricter background checks and require more training for gun owners. Citizens and lawmakers continue to cry out for something to be done to halt these deaths, with little happening due to political division. However, for the sake of safety, we need to overcome our differences. People should not have to hear the pop of gunfire and fear for their lives.

The author begins the conclusion by restating the thesis.

Chapter 3

The Writing Process

Lesson 3.1
Pre-Writing

You're sitting at your computer, ready to write the first essay of the semester, but the cursor blinks at you, and you don't know where to begin.

You're ready to take a final exam; you've studied hard, but you're worried you'll forget everything you know before you get to the end of the test.

You're planning a birthday party; you're excited, but you're worried you'll forget to send invitations or order the cake.

If you've ever found yourself in a similar situation, you're not alone. Taking on a big project or assignment requires learning and keeping track of a lot of information, organizing that information, and turning it into a final product.

To do lists help you stay organized and on task.

Fortunately, you don't have to accomplish all of these tasks at one time; you can break them down into a process. In any of the previous examples, you could begin your process with the same first step: pre-writing.

Pre-writing is the first stage of the **academic writing process.** Pre-writing involves making decisions and planning ideas that will allow you to meet the expectations of an assignment or project.

This lesson will discuss the following concepts:

Why We Pre-Write

How We Pre-Write

How to Transition from Pre-Writing to Drafting

Why We Pre-Write

While it might be tempting to dismiss pre-writing as "extra work," effective pre-writing often doesn't take very long, and it can make the rest of the writing process go faster and smoother.

Pre-writing is used for three main reasons:

- To generate ideas for writing
- To determine what you know and what you need to learn
- To identify connections between ideas

Let's practice so you can see how pre-writing helps you in academic, professional, and everyday life.

On Your Own

Read the following scenarios and identify which method you think would be an effective pre-writing step.

Mary has studied hard for a history exam that she knows will have two essays. She doesn't want to write the essays until she has finished the multiple-choice section of the test, but she's worried she will forget some key facts. What should Mary do?

- ☐ Write a quick list of key facts and information she can refer to later.
- ☐ Focus on the essays since they're probably worth more points than the multiple-choice questions.
- ☐ Ask her teacher for more time.

Andrea feels overwhelmed because she has to give a speech at her sister's wedding. She's already decided to put together a video, along with the speech, that includes interviews with family and friends. However, before she can even get started on that, she needs to write her speech, find someone to revise it, figure out who should be in the video, and write down a list of questions she wants to ask them. She doesn't know how she will keep track of all these tasks! What is the first thing Andrea should do?

- ☐ Start working and hope she doesn't forget anything.
- ☐ Make a to-do list.
- ☐ Re-think her decision to include a video.

Xavier has been invited to a job interview at a tech company. He's spent some time on the company's website in order to learn more about what they do and what they are looking for, but he can't seem to find the details he needs. What should Xavier do?

☐ Call the company and ask them to update their website.
☐ Decide not to go to the interview because he feels unprepared.
☐ Create a list of questions to ask during the interview.

As you can see, pre-writing strategies are helpful in all kinds of situations.

Writing Environment: Professional

Pre-writing techniques are often helpful in the workplace. On a busy day, you can brainstorm a list of the tasks you need to accomplish. If you're preparing for a meeting or sending an email to colleagues, creating a list or outline of the topics you plan to discuss can help you cover a lot of information in an organized manner. Your notes can also be easily turned into a PowerPoint presentation or meeting minutes.

Now, let's look at a few different approaches to pre-writing.

How We Pre-Write

There are several different styles of pre-writing. You can use them individually or in combination as you generate and develop your ideas for your writing.

Brainstorming is a general term to describe pre-writing that explores or develops ideas. As a technique, brainstorming involves writing down words, phrases, or ideas that come to mind as you think about a particular **topic**. Brainstorming helps you assess what you already know about a situation.

Imagine that you've been asked to write an essay about your favorite television show. You might start by brainstorming a list of shows you could potentially write about:

The Walking Dead
Friends
M*A*S*H
The Wire
Scandal
Empire

On Your Own

Practice brainstorming in the space below by listing your favorite television shows.

Mind mapping is a pre-writing technique that uses simple diagrams to show connections between key ideas.

Say that you've chosen to write about the show *Friends*; you can further develop your pre-writing by using mind-mapping to identify and group related ideas you might write about.

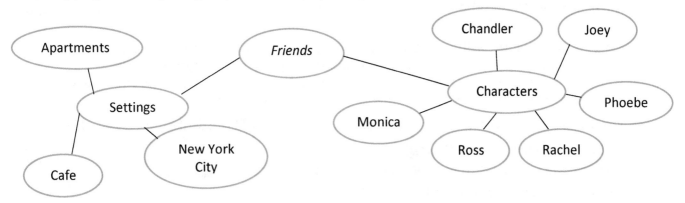

By sketching out the connections between related ideas, you can begin to identify what you know about your topic and visualize how different **main ideas** and **supporting details** relate to each other.

Learning Style Tip
Different types of learners might prefer different pre-writing styles or techniques.

- Visual learners might find mapping helpful because it illustrates a visible connection between ideas.
- Verbal learners might find it helpful to record themselves brainstorming out loud.
- Active learners might find it useful to handwrite, rather than type, their pre-writing exercises so that they feel more engaged in the pre-writing process.

Free-writing and focused free-writing are two closely related approaches to pre-writing that can be especially helpful if you are having a hard time getting started on a writing project.

When **free-writing,** simply write down whatever comes to mind for a set period of time. Don't try to edit your ideas as you free-write; wait until you're finished to review what you've written and see what ideas you've discovered. To focus your free-writing, begin by thinking about a specific topic.

Take a look at the following example of a free-write on the topic "People I Admire." The highlighted ideas might serve as a good starting point for a paper.

> Who do I admire? It's hard to say. My family members: Mom, Dad, my sister but I guess she's younger than me so maybe I don't exactly "admire" her? But anyway, what about other people? There are great leaders who I really look up to, but I don't exactly know why. Barack Obama is certainly inspirational; he managed to remain positive despite lots of opposition during his time in office. And what about other people? Anyone who has overcome obstacles to achieve great

things. I feel like I have a lot to learn from them. Lady Gaga? Beyoncé? J.K. Rowling? I don't know much about their stories, but I admire them; maybe I'd like to learn more.

> Although the writer begins this exercise uncertain of who or what to write about, he or she ultimately comes up with several ideas that could serve as good starting points for additional pre-writing (and ultimately the writing assignment).

Group Activity

Who do you admire? Set a timer for five minutes and conduct a free-writing session on this question. When you're finished, re-read what you've written and share some of your favorite ideas with the group. Then, discuss how each person's free-write led him or her to different ways of thinking about the question.

Questioning is a style of pre-writing that helps you consider a topic from all angles so that you can determine what you need to learn about a subject. Questioning is a helpful starting point for research-driven projects because the questions you come up with can help you shape your research. Questioning also helps you make sure you are thoroughly **analyzing** a subject.

Here are examples of pre-writing questions for an essay analyzing William Shakespeare's play *Hamlet*:

> Who are the characters in *Hamlet*?
>
> What are the central themes of *Hamlet*?
>
> When and where does *Hamlet* take place?
>
> Why did Shakespeare write *Hamlet*?
>
> Why is *Hamlet* considered such a great play?
>
> How does Hamlet avenge his father?

Notice that some of these questions could be answered by carefully reading the play while others would need to be answered through outside research.

As you narrow your topic, the questions you ask will become more complex, helping you think more deeply about your subject.

Writing Environment: Academic

Pre-writing can help you in all kinds of writing situations, not just when you're writing essays. Here are some examples:

- o   Use mind mapping to help you visualize the relationships between different components of a complex or multifaceted system. This could be a great way to help you review body systems for biology or country locations for geography.
- o   Use free-writing to test yourself on what you know about a subject. If you've been studying for a test and you feel like you're not remembering anything, free-writing can be a kind of "information unload." You might discover that you know a lot more than you think you do!
- o   Use questioning to help you actively read textbooks. First, look over the chapter. Then, come up with a list of questions about the main topics it covers. Looking for the answers to these questions as you read will help you stay engaged with the material.

Keep in mind that you can use pre-writing exercises like brainstorming, mapping, free-writing, and questioning in combination with each other. Doing so will ensure that you're thinking about your subject from every angle and coming up with lots of ideas to work with as you transition into the next phases of the writing process.

Now that we've reviewed techniques for pre-writing, let's take a look at how outlining helps you transition from pre-writing to drafting.

How to Transition from Pre-Writing to Drafting

Outlines help you make sure that you have done two things:

- Identified all the information you need to include in a writing project
- Organized that information in the best way possible

Depending on your reason for writing, you can use two different kinds of outlines to help you transition from pre-writing to **drafting**: working outlines and detailed outlines.

A **working outline** is relatively short, with no special formatting or structure; it typically includes the following information:

- A working **thesis**
- Main ideas
- An overview of your supporting ideas

Working outlines can be written quickly, so they are helpful when you have to write a lot in a short period of time.

Writing Environment: Everyday

Feeling overwhelmed? Brainstorming a to-do list before you go to bed at night or first thing in the morning can help you feel more in control of your day. Here are some tips for creating to-do lists:

- If you have a smartphone or tablet, create your to-do list in a notes app. That way, the list is always nearby, and you can easily refer to or edit it.
- Instead of deleting finished items, put a star or special symbol next to them. When you review your completed to-do list at the end of the day, you will feel a great sense of accomplishment.
- Prioritize by moving the most important tasks to the top of the list. Organizing your tasks makes your list a working outline for your day. Try to complete the tasks at the top of your list first.

A **detailed outline** is considerably longer than a working outline. It typically includes the following parts:

- A working thesis
- Main ideas
- All of your supporting ideas
- Research you plan to include in your writing

The more thorough your detailed outline is, the easier it will be for you to write a **first draft**. A fully detailed outline should be about as long as you intend your draft to be. If you've outlined well, all you have to do is turn the information from your outline into complete sentences!

Helpful Hint

Use a working outline to keep track of your research and writing process. Once you've done some pre-writing, create a working outline that includes your working thesis and main ideas. As you continue to research and develop your ideas, you can add supporting details and questions you plan to answer in your essay. Gradually, you will build a detailed outline that is well on its way to becoming a draft!

On Your Own

Read the following outlines and identify which one is a detailed outline.

Outline A

I.   Introduction

    A. Listening to and reading reports on Google's self-driving car project makes it seem like the future has arrived

        a. Would make driving easier for people of all ages and abilities

        b. Would allow for greater productivity: multitasking on the road

        c. Would prevent accidents and deaths by reducing human error ("Why Self-Driving Cars Matter," https://www.google.com/selfdrivingcar/)

    B. But ongoing tests of self-driving cars have demonstrated that this new technology is not yet perfect

        a. Importantly, an accident occurred on February 14, 2016. Google admitted that the self-driving car was partially at fault; the first time the company admitted shared responsibility (Shepardson, http://www.reuters.com/article/us-google-selfdrivingcar-idUSKCN0W22DG)

        b. Incidents like this suggest a need for ongoing testing and development of the cars themselves

        c. Also suggest the need for a new level of awareness among drivers who share the road with self-driving cars

    C. Working thesis: While self-driving cars have the potential to be safe and convenient modes of transportation, neither roads nor drivers in the United States are prepared for the widespread implementation of this new technology.

Outline B

I.   Intro

    A. Working Thesis: Self-driving cars have a lot of potential but aren't yet ready for widespread use.

II.   Explanation of self-driving cars

    A. Discussion of benefits

    B. Discussion of risks

III. What needs to change in order for self-driving cars to become a widespread mode of transportation?

IV.   Conclusion

Note that the excerpt from a detailed outline presents an overview of just one paragraph. Because it is so thoroughly prepared, however, it would be easy for the author to turn that outline into an introduction for a rough draft. In contrast, the working outline provides an overview of the shape of the argument, which makes it more useful early in the writing process.

Lesson Wrap-up

Key Terms

Academic Writing Process: a strategy that breaks up a writing assignment into five stages: pre-writing, drafting, revising, editing, and submitting

Analyze: to understand something by looking at its parts

Brainstorming: exploring and developing ideas

Detailed Outline: an outline that organizes most or all of the ideas and research that will be included in a first draft

Drafting: a stage of writing that involves writing out ideas and supporting/concluding sentences

First Draft: the first version of a text

Free-writing: writing any words, phrases, or ideas that come to mind during a set period of time

Main Idea: the statement or argument that an author tries to communicate

Mind mapping: a method for making visual connections between topics

Outline: a tool developed during pre-writing that provides a visual of a paper's organization and ideas

Pre-writing: a stage of writing that involves making decisions, planning ideas, and identifying assignment guidelines

Questioning: using questions to consider a topic from diverse angles and perspectives

Supporting Detail: a piece of information, also called evidence, that is used to support a main idea

Thesis Statement: a sentence that expresses the main idea of a longer work

Topic: the general subject of a text

Working Outline: an informal outline with no special formatting or structure

Writing Application: Pre-Writing

The following samples demonstrate the pre-writing process through brainstorming and outlining. Then, those ideas transition into a first draft.

Brainstorm

Disney on Broadway: what shows?

Beauty and the Beast: first show

The Lion King: creative staging; different from the movie in a lot of ways

Aida: not based on a movie

Mary Poppins: more like the book than the movie?

Tarzan: almost forgot about this one!

Little Mermaid: it's weird that this show didn't stay open longer

Aladdin: running now

Newsies: closed recently

In this brainstorm, the author has come up with a list of topics relating to the main idea. There is no need to edit or censor a brainstorm or another type of pre-writing.

What Disney films have been adapted into Broadway musicals?

When did each of the musicals open on Broadway?

Where are the musicals performed (what theaters)?

Who have been some of the major creative forces behind these musical adaptations?

How long has each show's Broadway run lasted?

What has critical reception to the shows been? How have audiences responded?

Why did Disney decide to adapt animated films into Broadway musicals?

What impact have Disney musicals had on Broadway? New York City?

This example of questioning helps the author prepare research and consider the subject from multiple angles. While the author may not answer every question in the essay, it helps him or her gather information that will shape the argument.

Detailed Outline

I. Introduction

    A. Disney on Broadway today

          1. Advertising and merchandise everywhere

          2. Current shows: *Aladdin, The Lion King*

    B. Working thesis: Over recent decades, Disney Theatrical Productions has made NYC a destination for Disney fans.

Conclusions and introductions can be difficult to write until the end of the drafting process. Sometimes, it is enough to include a placeholder in your outline. You can then develop an introductory paragraph later.

II. First Broadway show: *Beauty and the Beast* (1994)

    A. Film adapted into musical three years after movie was released

    B. Some new songs by Alan Menken

    C. Costumes, sets, effects focused on bringing movie to life

    D. Mixed reviews of show: quote *New York Times* review

          1. David Richards wrote "the astonishments rarely cease...nothing is left to the imagination"

          2. Nothing especially new about musical version

    E. Show was huge commercial success: ran for 13 years

Incorporating the quote and author's name in the outline means that the author won't have to look for it when drafting.

III. Second Broadway Show: *The Lion King* (1997)

    A. More creative than *Beauty and the Beast* in the way it adapted the film

        1. Used masks and puppetry

        2. New material incorporated African music and language

        3. Deeper symbolism added to the plot/themes of the film

    B. More successful

        1. Won six Tony Awards, including Best Musical

    C. Still running on Broadway

        1. Currently fourth-longest running show ("*The Lion King*")

IV. Disney has maintained presence in New York

    A. Some shows have been successful, others haven't

        1. *Aida* (first musical not based on a film) ran for over four years

        2. *Tarzan* and *The Little Mermaid* flopped

    B. Overall, Disney has had a success rate of over 70% (compared to 20% for other Broadway producers) (Rosenberg and Pereira)

V. Conclusion

    A. Critics worry Disney puts too much emphasis on spectacle

    B. Disney has brought about lasting changes

        1. Renovation of New Amsterdam Theatre

        2. Made Broadway family-friendly

    C. Hopefully will turn Disney lovers into Broadway lovers.

> Each point doesn't have to be written in complete sentences. Pieces of information that are only a few words long will make this outline easier to refer to while the author is drafting.

> Since this is a detailed outline, the author has used a formal numbering system to organize points as they will appear in each section of the essay. This makes it easier to keep track of the information that will be included in the body of the essay.

Draft

Visit Times Square today, and it's no surprise to see Disney's presence everywhere. Billboards, taxis, and gift shops advertise familiar Disney titles, like *Aladdin* and *The Lion King*, that have been adapted into Broadway musicals. <u>Over the past few decades, the establishment and growth of Disney Theatrical Productions as a major production company has helped make New York City another destination for Disney fans from all over the world.</u>

In 1994, *Beauty and the Beast* became the first Disney film to be adapted into a Broadway musical. Premiering three years after the film was released, the show featured new songs by Alan Menken and a parade of costumes and special effects that brought the film to life. The

> This is a more polished version of the working thesis presented in the detailed outline.

musical received mixed reviews. David Richards of the *New York Times* observed that while "the astonishments rarely cease . . . nothing is left to the imagination," arguing that the musical added no new depth to the story told by its animated predecessor. Audiences, however, flocked to the musical, which ran for thirteen years.

Disney's next stage production challenged critics' concerns that Disney's Broadway ventures would do little more than turn successful animated films into live-action spectacles like the ones found at Disney theme parks. *The Lion King*, which opened in 1997, incorporated masks and puppetry as well as African-influenced music and language. These elements brought new layers of symbolic depth to the story's *Hamlet*-inspired plot. *The Lion King* won six Tony Awards, including one for Best Musical, and is currently fourth on the list of longest-running musicals on Broadway ("The Lion King").

Since the success of Disney's first two Broadway musicals, Disney Theatrical Productions has maintained a continual presence in New York. *Aida*, the first Disney musical not based on a previous film, ran for more than four years. At times, film adaptations that seemed sure to be successful—such as *Tarzan* and *The Little Mermaid*—flopped. Nevertheless, after over twenty years on Broadway, Disney's productions have had a success rate of more than 70%. Other producers have success rates closer to 20% (Rosenberg and Pereira).

While some theatre-goers continue to worry that Disney's presence on Broadway emphasizes the "spectacle" of theatre (visually stunning sets, costumes, and lights) at the expense of thought-provoking or innovative elements, it is hard to deny that Disney's presence has brought about some important lasting changes. Prior to Disney's renovation of the New Amsterdam Theatre in the early 1990s, families would not often be seen on 42nd Street. Today, families come to New York because of their love of Disney, and they may keep coming back because of their new love for Broadway.

Works Cited

"The Lion King." *Internet Broadway Database*, The Broadway League, 20 Mar. 2016.

Richards, David. "Beauty and the Beast; Disney Does Broadway, Dancing Spoons and All." *The New York Times*, 19 Apr. 1994.

Rosenberg, Scott A., and Ivan Pereira. "Twenty Years of Disney on Broadway: A Transformative Force." *AMNewYork*. Newsday, 27 Mar. 2014.

The author's choice to include this quote in her outline makes it easy to incorporate it into the draft of the essay.

Notice how each paragraph lines up with the structure of the detailed outline.

Instead of discussing all the shows Disney has produced, the author emphasizes a few musicals that help her shape her argument.

The author's choice to incorporate this information and to cite this source in her outline makes this evidence easier to include in the draft.

To create a stronger conclusion, the author has revised the final point she introduced in her outline.

Lesson 3.2
Drafting

Drafting is the second step of the **academic writing process**. It involves figuring out how to communicate the ideas you came up with in the **pre-writing** stage.

> *"I hate first drafts, and it never gets easier. People always wonder what kind of superhero power they'd like to have. I wanted the ability for someone to just open up my brain and take out the entire first draft and lay it down in front of me so I can just focus on the second, third and fourth drafts." -Judy Blume*

Although staring at a blank page can be intimidating, this lesson will help you think about drafting as a set of small steps. During the drafting phase, you will start adding some structure to your thoughts by crafting a **thesis statement,** or a sentence that expresses the **main idea** of a longer work (if you didn't already during pre-writing). You will also work with **supporting details,** which are important pieces of information or evidence that support your thesis.

In this lesson, you will learn the following aspects of drafting:

Key Elements of Drafting
Getting Started
What to Consider While Drafting

Drafting tends to be more important in **academic writing** and **professional writing** than **everyday writing.** When was the last time you used the writing process to write a text message? Probably never, right? But drafting in business and academic writing is important. In those environments, you want to make sure your message comes across in a coherent, intelligent way. For most of us, that requires writing one or more drafts.

Key Elements of Drafting

While drafting may look different from person to person, and even from assignment to assignment, there are some key things to know about the process.

Drafting Relies Heavily on Pre-writing

Know that you're not done with the work you did during pre-writing. While you were researching and taking notes during pre-writing, you probably weren't too focused on one main idea for your writing. As a result, when it's time to draft, you'll need to go back to your notes to come up with your thesis statement.

Writers Use Drafting to Work Through Ideas

After all the research you've done, you have a lot of ideas swirling around in your brain. It's not unusual for writers to start drafting about one **topic** only to veer off in a totally new direction. Drafting allows you to think through all of those opinions, positions, and thoughts and begin to make sense of them.

For example, this is a totally acceptable paragraph to have in a first draft:

> While the author's stance that vegetarianism is beneficial to the environment seems to be based on credible science, I wonder how credible the author is himself. He seems to assert himself as an authority in food science, but when doing additional internet research, I don't find much

information supporting that claim. I do wonder about how vegans get enough protein. I can see not eating meat a few days a week; it's clearly good for your body and the environment. But how do you get enough nutrients when you don't eat any animal products at all? Selective vegetarianism, or "meatless Mondays" as people sometime call it, is not the only way to help the environment. Eating fresh, seasonal foods from local farms has an even bigger impact because food doesn't travel as far, so less gas emissions.

The author of the above paragraph is working through some different claims and theories as he or she figures out what the paper's direction will be.

Reflection Questions

Can you remember a time you when made a decision only to change your mind later? The drafting process is all about making decisions and knowing they might change in the future.

Late-Stage Drafting Relies Heavily on Revision

First drafts, or the first version of a text, are also called "rough drafts" or "sloppy copies." They are the somewhat messy, disorganized first passes you make at writing down your ideas.

After you finish drafting, you revise. During **revision,** you think about how all the parts of your draft work together.

To guide the revision process, ask yourself these questions:

- Does your thesis still make sense?
- Did you support your thesis clearly?
- Is the information well-organized?
- What further research needs to be done?
- How well does your conclusion tie together your arguments?

After considering these questions, you may find that you need to rewrite some sections of your paper. Conversely, you may find that you need to start writing a new draft. No one likes to rewrite papers over and over, but remember that late-stage drafts are usually more clearly aligned with the final vision for your writing.

To learn more about revising, see Lesson 3.3.

Drafting is Not About Perfection

The great thing about drafting is that you can be a little lazy. If you can't come up with just the right word, don't worry about it. You can come back to it during revision and fix it. Did you use too many clichés? Not a problem in a draft because, you guessed it, you can change it later!

Here are some examples of things *not* to worry about in your first draft:

- Using **clichés,** which are popular phrases that have lost their original impact due to overuse such as, "At the drop of a hat" or "The best of both worlds"
- Relying on **jargon,** which is overly technical language that is specific to a certain field. For example, acronyms like *POTUS* and *FLOTUS* are political jargon
- Introducing **slang,** which is casual language specific to a group of people such as *salty* or *GOAT*.
- Finding the right academic language
- Perfecting **tone,** which is the positive, negative, or neutral attitude that an author expresses about a topic

Writing Environment: Professional

Professional writing can include everything from résumés and cover letters to emails, white papers, and research reports. You should utilize the drafting process for every type of professional writing. Your professional persona is judged by how well you communicate with others. If you make a lot of errors in your writing and don't take the time to think through your message, you won't be taken seriously in the workplace.

Imagine you need to write a proposal for a new project that you believe will change the business landscape. When you write the draft, you will probably include a lot of informal, passionate language because you are so excited about it. However, you'll want to use the revision stage to go back through the draft and make sure it is professional enough to represent you and your ideas.

Getting Started

Here are some ways to dive into writing when you're faced with a blank page.

Write What You Know

One way to start drafting is to assess what you already know about your topic and the position you intend to take.

To do this, grab a piece of paper and a pen and start writing everything that comes to mind about your topic. It doesn't have to be organized. You can journal about your thoughts on the topic, the research that stands out to you, your opinions, and your questions or concerns. Let your mind take you wherever it goes. Working through these thoughts will let you see what is most important and relevant from all of the research and pre-writing you've done.

Here's an example of what this might look like for a student writing about the rise of the middle class in England:

> The Victorian era was during Queen Victoria's reign of Great Britain. 1837-1901. There was a lot of political reform. Taxes were low and government was less involved. (Still need to research what life was like before this era). People felt more free and there was a slightly smaller gap between the rich and the poor, but living conditions for working people and poor were still bad. Industrialism was BIG during this era. Lots more textiles and machinery. Great Britain increased its exports. Industry led to larger middle class. Middle class values changed family structures. People wanted more privacy and were less dependent on larger extended families. Rise in middle class also meant more outings and entertainment options. Seaside resorts sprang up all over England. People also liked sports and music.
>
> In the example above, the writer isn't including very specific details, just things he or she remembers from research and ideas that seem important. Later, the writer can incorporate specific details and shape this into a piece that flows like an actual paper.

Group Activity

Talking to a friend or peer about your topic is another great way to uncover what's on your mind. If you enjoy explaining things to people, this method is even better than journaling. Working with one or two other students, choose one person to go first. That person should explain what he or she is writing about and what seems most important about the topic. Partners can ask these questions:

- Why is this important?
- How is this different from what other people think?
- What do your sources say about it?
- What questions do you still have about the topic?
- What additional research do you need to do?

Use Your Pre-writing Materials

If you completed pre-writing, you've probably already figured out the important details and focus of your text.

Go back to what you developed in the pre-writing stage. The **mind maps** you created to make visual connections between topics or the **outline** you created to group information into topics and subtopics will now help you start writing about that information.

Use your notes from pre-writing as the basis of the draft. Connect those ideas using the information you know about the topic.

For example, take a look at this outline and the following paragraph:

I.   Introduction
II.   History of radios
    a. Instruments before the radio
    b. Invention
        i.   1846: electromagnetic waves (Maxwell)
        ii. 1888: Hertz proves electromagnetism
        iii. 1894: Marconi wireless telegraphy system
    c. Early uses of the radio
        i.   News
        ii. College football
        iii. Aircraft

> The theory of electromagnetism was developed by James Maxwell in 1846. At the time, he wasn't able to physically prove the energy waves, but his mathematical theory showed that these waves could be transmitted through the air. In 1888, Heinrich Hertz proved Maxwell's theory by creating instruments that could transmit and receive radio waves. The electrical term "hertz" is named after him. Italian inventor Guglielmo Marconi built a wireless telegraphy system to transmit communication signals. His early prototypes transmitted signals only a half-mile. Eventually, he improved the system and it was credited with saving the 700 people who survived the sinking of the Titanic.

Divide the Draft into Manageable Chunks

You don't have to write the entire draft in one sitting. If you try, you might burn yourself out.

Instead, return to your pre-writing materials and figure out the sections you need to include in your draft. For example, if it's a typical five-paragraph essay, plan on writing each of the five sections over the course of five days: one paragraph per day.

You may want to power through and just write the whole thing at once, but it's better to give yourself plenty of time. Getting some distance from the writing will help you think of better ideas and new ways to approach the topic.

On Your Own

Identify the best drafting schedule for a paper that will contain three sections.

- ☐ Write it all over the course of three hours in one morning.
- ☐ Write one section a day for three days.
- ☐ Write it the night before it's due.

Forget About the Introduction . . . For Now

The **introduction,** which is the paragraph used to introduce the main idea at the beginning of a paper, needs to both engage your reader and set the stage for the rest of the paper.

While it may provide some background information, it shouldn't expand too much on it. That being said, save writing the introduction until you're done writing the body of the work. You'll know what important points to hit and how to entice the reader to stay with you through the duration of the text.

Keep Away from Distractions

It can be easy to procrastinate when it comes to drafting. There's something about the blank page that seems to say, "Don't worry about it. You can fill it in later." However, the only way to start writing is to put something down on paper. This is nearly impossible if you allow distractions.

To stay focused, try these strategies:

- Work in a quiet place, like the library
- Turn off your phone off so you don't get notifications
- Ask friends not to bother you during your designated writing time
- Write somewhere other than home. Laundry will get done, bills will be paid, and ovens will be cleaned before papers are written. It's amazing how clean and organized writers' houses are when a deadline is looming.

> Further Resources
>
> Websites, social media, and email are sometimes the worse distractions. You think you're just going to read a quick social media post, and suddenly you've spent an hour watching videos. Try installing a productivity app that temporarily blocks websites while you're writing. Check out SelfControl (https://selfcontrolapp.com/) or Cold Turkey (https://getcoldturkey.com/) to get started.

Be Willing to Write Poorly

Remember, a draft is usually not the final product. You'll revise, re-draft, revise again, and **edit**, all before writing the final paper.

Drafting is just one part of a process, and the rest of that process is about making the draft better. That means the draft can be terrible. In fact, most first drafts are. To get to a better version of your work, you have to start somewhere.

One way to just get started is to choose a word and start every sentence with that word. Here's an example:

> Chalk is a sedimentary rock. Chalk is a form of limestone. Chalk is soft and porous. Chalk makes up the White Cliffs of Dover. Chalk is used for writing. Chalk can be used in agriculture. Chalk raises pH in soil that is too acidic. Chalk is an ingredient in certain types of toothpaste. Chalk is used to draw hopscotch boundaries.
>
> This paragraph shouldn't be submitted for a grade, but it helped the author start writing about his or her topic.

Writing Environment: Academic

Your professors expect you to use drafts to organize and refine your work. Some classes even require drafts to be handed in several weeks before final papers are due. Take advantage of the writing process in academic settings. It gives you time to formulate new thoughts and opinions (a skill that is highly valued in the workplace).

For example, imagine you have to write a paper comparing and contrasting two major archaeological sites in the southwestern United States. You'll start pre-writing, maybe using some kind of graphic organizer to show what the sites have in common and how they differ. Then, you'll need to take that information and compose a draft. You won't hand in that first draft because you'll need to continue refining your ideas and editing your work. Your professor is an expert in the topic and will know if you've actually put time and effort into the paper.

What to Consider While Drafting

Once you've finally gotten all your thoughts on paper, the drafting phase of the writing process should go pretty smoothly. You have lots of ideas and some wind under your sails. Here are a few things you'll want to keep in mind while you're completing your draft.

Don't Be Afraid of Reorganization

It's possible that once you start writing your draft, you'll realize that your original structure no longer works. Maybe you didn't consider how to address all the facts, details, and reasons in the most logical way, or maybe you didn't plan an organizational structure to begin with. Either way, as you're writing, be open to changing the structure of your paper. Your organizational structure should serve the content by making it easy for readers to follow a coherent path through your ideas.

To learn more about organizational patterns, see Lessons 4.1 and 5.3.

Keep Content Unified

Many errors can be fixed during revision and editing. However, there are certain things that are more difficult to change, so keep them in mind while drafting.

Your work needs to be organized in paragraphs, and those paragraphs need to include topic sentences, supporting sentences, and details. Your topic sentence should relay the main idea of that paragraph to the reader while the supporting sentences include supporting details:

- **Anecdote:** a long example told as a story
- **Expert Analysis**: an opinion or statement shared by someone who is knowledgeable about a topic
- **Description:** a passage that explains the appearance of someone or something using words that appeal to the senses
- **Example:** a specific instance or illustration that demonstrates a point
- **Fact:** a piece of information that most people generally agree to be true
- **Reflection:** the thoughts or feelings of the author

Both paragraphs and sentences should be connected with **transitions** that show the reader how ideas are related. Here are some examples of transitions:

Therefore

Also

In addition

However

For instance

Decide on tone and style. Your author's voice should help convey your message. A few ways to develop an interesting style are to use techniques such as **repetition** or **parallelism** (a method for showing a relationship between ideas by using similarly structured words, phrases, or clauses).

On Your Own

Read the paragraph below and identify the sentence that uses a transition word or phrase.

> In the early 1500s, Spain had already conquered South and Central America, so it set its sights on exploring North America. King Charles I sent Hernando de Soto to seize Florida and discover the Seven Cities of Cibola. However, instead of finding these cities of gold, de Soto systematically destroyed the Apalachee tribe. He continued to war with the Choctaw, Cherokee, and Creek tribes throughout his exploration of the southeastern parts of North America.

Know What You Don't Know

As you write your draft, you'll likely realize you don't have all the information you need to fully support your thesis. When this happens, don't stop your drafting to start researching. Instead, write comments to yourself as you go along.

In these comments, remind yourself what you need to find out and what needs to be added. When your draft is complete, go back to the research and add the necessary information.

Silence Your Inner Critic

Even the best writers hear an inner voice telling them that what they've written is bad, that it doesn't make any sense, or that they're failing. But, like prolific writer Stephen King said, "Writers are often the worst judges of what they have written." While you're drafting, learn to silence the negative thoughts that come to mind and just focus on the task at hand: writing an organized and coherent version of your ideas.

Remember, the first draft isn't meant to be perfect; it's meant to be a vessel holding together your great ideas. As you continue working through the writing process, those ideas will become clearer, more precise, and more attuned to your intended **audience.**

Writing Environment: Everyday

When was the last time you drafted a text to your roommate or composed a draft of a grocery list? More often, we just write our thoughts quickly and without care for grammar, organization, and cohesion because we just want our messages received and understood.

For example, texting your uncle, "Thx 4 the b-day card," lets him know you received the card and appreciate it. It doesn't require you to collect several ideas, make judgment calls, and organize information in a specific way.

Actually, the way we write in everyday life is a good example of how to think about drafting in academic and professional environments. First, just focus on getting your message across. Then, you can worry about making it sound better later.

Lesson Wrap-up

Key Terms

Academic Writing: a text intended for instructors or students and often directed by specific prompts and requirements

Academic Writing Process: a strategy that breaks up a writing assignment into five stages: pre-writing, drafting, revising, editing, and submitting

Anecdote: a long example told as a story

Audience: the person or people who read or interpret a text

Cliché: a popular phrase that has lost its original impact due to overuse

Description: a passage that explains the appearance of someone or something using words that appeal to the senses

Drafting: a stage of writing that involves writing out ideas and supporting/concluding sentences

Editing: a stage of writing that involves reconsidering and rewriting grammar, style, and spelling

Everyday Writing: personal and/or informal texts intended for anyone

Example: a specific instance or illustration that demonstrates a point

Expert Analysis: an opinion or statement shared by someone who is knowledgeable about a topic

Fact: a piece of information that most people generally agree to be true

First Draft: the first version of a text

Introduction: the paragraph used to introduce the main idea at the beginning of a paper, also called an introductory paragraph

Jargon: overly technical language

Main Idea: the statement or argument that an author tries to communicate

Mind Map: a graphic that allows writers to visualize and structure different types of essays

Outline: a tool developed during pre-writing that provides a visual of a paper's organization and ideas

Parallelism: a method for showing a relationship between ideas by using similarly structured words, phrases, or clauses

Pre-writing: a stage of writing that involves making decisions, planning ideas, and identifying assignment guidelines

Professional Writing: a text intended for managers, coworkers, or customers

Reflection: the thoughts or feelings of the author

Repetition: when a word, phrase, or sentence is repeated to stress meaning or create an engaging rhythm

Revision: a stage of writing that involves revising content and organization

Slang: casual words or expressions specific to a particular group of people

Supporting Detail: a piece of information, also called evidence, that is used to support a main idea

Thesis Statement: a concise sentence that expresses the main idea of a longer work

Tone: the positive, negative, or neutral attitude that an author expresses about a topic

Topic: the general subject of a text

Transition: a word, phrase, or sentence that shows a relationship between ideas

Writing Application: Drafting

Read the following draft of a cover letter. The annotations indicate places where the author can revise and strengthen his writing.

Hi Hiring Manager,

My name is Gregory Holmes, and I am writing to you to apply for the entry-level marketing assistant position I saw advertised on your website.

> In a draft, this is an acceptable placeholder for a more professional greeting.

I just graduated from the University of Florida (Go Gators!) with a degree in marketing and advertising. My résumé is attached. You will see that I have not had a lot of experience in paid marketing positions, but I have volunteered alot. I also urge you to look at the continuing education section. Even though I was enrolled in school full-time, I also took classes through community organizations so that I could better understand marketing in the real world.

> The author will need to revise the draft and remove typos and casual language.

The entry-level position at your company would allow me to utilize the skills I do have and grow as a marketer. I want to continue to build my portfolio to show that I have a lot of experience in many different areas. Some of the skills I do have are: copywriting, proofreading, analytics, and basic HTML. Tbh, I'm not very good at writing for radio, yet. It's something I'm working on, though.

> This statement needs more explanation, which the author can add later.

> The informal abbreviation *tbh*, for "to be honest," will need to be removed or revised.

I am sure my skills and abilities will be an asset to your company. I am willing to work diligently for you and learn as much as I can.

I look forward to hearing from you and appreciate your willingness to read through this cover letter.

This cover letter isn't perfect, but it's a solid first draft.

Thanks for the consideration.

Sincerely,

Gregory Holmes

Lesson 3.3
Revision

Like referees watching an instant replay during a basketball game, reviewing your writing in "slow motion" can help you clearly understand the choices you make while writing and the effects your writing choices have on readers. After seeing your work from a variety of angles, you can determine if you've made the right call.

Reviewing your writing helps you become a better writer and a better reader.

This process is called revision. **Revision** is a stage of writing that involves reconsidering and rewriting content and organization. During the revision process, writers consider broad concerns such as their overall claim or organization. Revision is an ongoing process, and effective revision will result in stronger writing that's more accurate, thorough, and cohesive.

In this lesson, you will learn about the following topics:

The Difference Between Revision and Editing

Key Elements of Revision

Important Areas to Revise

Methods of Revising

The Difference Between Revision and Editing

Before we look too far into what revising is, let's make sure we understand what it is *not*. Revising and editing may seem like the same process, but they're actually very different. Revision is about strengthening your big ideas and supporting them with strong content whereas **editing** is about fixing errors.

Revision generally works at a broader level and considers a paper's overall strengths and weaknesses as well as how it accomplishes this.

Editing, on the other hand, is a stage of writing that comes *after* revision. It involves more specific elements like grammar, style, and spelling. Consider the following comparison of revising and editing.

Revision assesses . . .	**Editing assesses. . .**
Overall strengths and weaknesses	Specific elements
Focus	Transitions
Organization	Punctuation
Tone	Word choice
Evidence	Grammar

Generally, it's better to revise thoroughly before editing because revision can lead you to reconsider major sections of an essay or even your overall thesis. It would be a waste of time to edit a sentence or paragraph that you might end up changing or deleting during revision.

> **Helpful Hint**
>
> If the guidelines of an assignment allow it, be flexible with the message of your writing. Often, the revision process can help you refine your thesis or **main idea,** but this can also mean you end up writing a very different essay than you originally expected.

Key Elements of Revision

> *I'm not a very good writer, but I'm an excellent re-writer." James Michener*

A good revision process does not assume that your first draft is the best version. Instead, it enables you to see your writing with fresh eyes. Revision is conducted at a general level that will probably lead you to do any of the following things:

- Move, delete, or add entire paragraphs
- Expand or contract (narrow) points
- Completely rewrite awkward or confusing passages

Revising the ideas in your work involves two main areas: focus and development. A **focused** text clearly communicates and supports your main idea. It uses every paragraph to support and expand your **thesis statement.** As you revise for focus, you may need to modify information to stay on topic.

A **developed** text presents information in an effective way and includes plenty of details to support its thesis statement. While revising for development, you may need to expand or add information to strengthen your ideas.

During revision, you're continually responding to these basic questions and using your responses to write new drafts:

- What do I want my essay to say?
- How is my essay communicating this effectively? Where is it ineffective?

Another good idea is to ask "what if?" questions to consider new possibilities:

- What if I narrow my **argument** or my thesis more?
- What if I move a certain paragraph?
- What if I start or end a paragraph in a new place?
- What if I explain my point more and provide extra **evidence**?

Asking questions and then thinking through your responses can help you understand the results of the decisions you're making as a writer and equip you to revise well.

Revision can feel risky. As you question whether or not an entire paragraph is worth keeping, you risk letting go of the material that you worked so hard to develop. But take courage: taking this risk is critical to creating something great, and it's practiced by even the most accomplished writers.

Helpful Hint

To reduce some of the risk involved with revising, save multiple drafts. Then, you can go back to previous versions and recover what you wrote if you change your mind during revision.

Writing Environment: Everyday

We're always revising: we revise what we say, what we think, and how we approach certain situations and relationships. For example, you might already think that fruits and vegetables are good for you, but if you spent time reading about the vitamins and minerals they provide or about how some types of vegetables are better for you than others, you would probably revise your opinions about healthy eating and how you express those opinions.

Important Areas to Revise

As you revise, focus on each element of your writing. For example, you may spend time only revising the evidence or the organization. Here are some questions to ask yourself as you focus on each part of your draft.

Focus, Thesis, and Style

- Is your thesis clear, narrow, and arguable?
- Is your thesis stated explicitly?
- Does the reader have adequate information for understanding your thesis?
- Does your thesis remain consistent throughout your essay?
- Is all information in the draft relevant to your thesis?
- Have you chosen a style that fits the purpose and audience?

Structure/Organization

- Does the **introduction** use a **hook** to engage the reader?
- Does your essay develop in a logical progression?
- Does each paragraph have a clear connection to the thesis?
- Have you arranged paragraphs intentionally?
- Does each paragraph develop and maintain a clear main idea?
- Does the conclusion summarize well and tie ideas together?

On Your Own

As an exercise in asking "what if?" in relation to an essay structure, complete the following exercise, basing your answers on an essay that you are currently working on.

1. Write an outline of your essay, listing as your headers the main idea of each paragraph.

2. Then, write a brief reflection on why you organized the essay this way.

3. Now, develop a second outline. This time, begin or end in a different place from your original outline, and then reorganize more as necessary. Be sure you still maintain a logical progression of ideas.

4. Finally, write a brief reflection on the different effects this second approach to organization may have on a reader.

Expand or Contract

- Given the thesis, what does the reader need to know?
- Does each point include explanation and evidence? What's missing?
- What opposing viewpoints do you need to anticipate and address with **counterarguments**?
- Are there sections or paragraphs that are irrelevant or do not support your thesis?

On Your Own

Read the passage below and identify the claim that requires further explanation or evidence.

Kettering is a dynamic neighborhood that has undergone a lot of change over the last four decades, most of which has been negative. Since 1976, the population has decreased from 4,899 to 2,019. The number of vacant or abandoned homes has more than doubled. The average median income has steadily gone down. Major businesses have viewed Kettering as a place that cannot support them. "There was no longer a viable workforce," said Samuel Horning of Jojo Corp, a manufacturer of kids' toys that recently moved its headquarters from Kettering to Cleveland, Ohio. "We'd put out a call for jobs and get very few qualified applicants." Meanwhile, "white flight" of the 1960s out of inner city neighborhoods laid the groundwork in Kettering for these failings.

Still, residents remain engaged and invested in their neighborhood. More than sixty people attended a recent community meeting, and half of those attending shared prepared statements. "We understand these problems are, in some ways, bigger than Kettering," said one resident. "They have to do with global markets and national problems. But my family has lived in Kettering for three generations, and we're not going anywhere." Most everyone in attendance applauded this last statement.

Clarity and Cohesion

- Does your essay maintain a consistent **tone** or are there shifts?
- Are all unfamiliar terms defined?
- Does each paragraph use **transitions**?
- Are your sentences wordy or concise?
- Does your sentence structure fit your purpose?

Helpful Hint

When using a grammar checker, keep in mind that only you can write in your particular style and voice and with your particular purposes in mind. While grammar checkers can identify blatant grammatical errors, they may not be able to identify creative approaches to word choice, sentence structure, and sentence variety.

Methods of Revising

During the revision process, there are several steps you can take to make it worthwhile.

Place

Sometimes, it helps to write in a quiet space. On other days, you might find that a public space enables you to write, think, and feel differently about a draft. Try changing your writing location to see what works best. You may find yourself writing and seeing your work in new ways.

Medium

Similar to place, vary the way you write. Some people type everything on a laptop. Others write in a notebook and then revise their essay while typing on a computer. Some people type a paper but print out a hard copy to revise with a pen or pencil. Try a few different mediums and see what works best for you.

Writing Environment: Professional

Editors and other communications professionals often develop their own marks for revision and editing. Some companies even have their own style guides for how they wish to format reports and other company publications. Be sure you understand your job's expectations for any revision that happens among colleagues.

Peer Review

In a **peer review**, a partner reads your work and makes note of what is working in your essay and what could use improvement. Ask a friend or classmate to peer review your draft and tell you the effects of the writing choices you've made. Ask them to point out anything they find confusing or incomplete.

To learn more about the peer review process, see Lesson 3.4.

Reading Aloud

You can also revise your essay by treating it like an audible text. Reading your work aloud, or asking someone else to read it to you, can help you spot awkward wording or undeveloped ideas. As you listen to your essay, jot down ideas or possible changes; then, go back and work those ideas into the next draft.

Time

As you write and rewrite, take a break between drafts. This will help you see your work with fresh eyes. Depending on your time constraints, this break could be fifteen minutes or a few days. Either way, let your mind rest before starting a new draft.

Helpful Hint

When planning your **writing process**, try starting with the final deadline. Then, work your way backwards to ensure that you allow adequate time for each step in the writing process.

Lesson Wrap-up

Key Terms

Academic Writing Process: a strategy that breaks up a writing assignment into five stages: pre-writing, drafting, revising, editing, and submitting

Argument: a reason why you should think or act a certain way

Counterargument: when an author anticipates objections from the audience and refutes them with logic

Development: effective presentation of information and inclusion of sufficient supporting details

Editing: a stage of writing that involves correcting grammar, style, and spelling mistakes

Evidence: the available body of facts or information indicating whether a belief or proposition is true or valid

Focus: clear communication and support of a main idea

Hook: the first sentence or two in a piece of writing that aims to immediately engage the reader

Introduction: the paragraph used to introduce the main idea at the beginning of a paper, also called an introductory paragraph

Main Idea: the statement or argument that an author tries to communicate

Peer Review: working with a classmate to give feedback on each other's papers

Revision: a stage of writing that involves reconsidering and rewriting content and organization

Thesis Statement: a concise statement that expresses the main idea of a longer work

Tone: the positive, negative, or neutral attitude that an author expresses about a topic

Transition: a word, phrase, or sentence that shows a relationship between ideas

Writing Application: Revision

Read the following samples that demonstrate the revision process. In the first draft, the author has used the questions in the lesson to identify areas that need to be revised. The second draft implements those revisions. Although the essay may contain grammar and spelling areas, the author will address those later during the editing phase.

Sample 1: Before Revision

Wendell Berry's Use of Word Choice and Structure in "The Pleasures of Eating"

The author Wendell Berry, in the essay "The Pleasure of Eating," wants readers to understand that today's food is more an industry than it is agriculture. He does this through the way he structures his essay and his word choice.

This introduction isn't very clear; I probably need to make my argument more obvious.

A strongly worded passage in Berry's essay is as follows:

> The passive American consumer, sitting down to a meal of pre-prepared or fast food, confronts a platter covered with inert, anonymous substances that have been processed, dyed, breaded, sauced, gravied, ground, pulped, strained, blended, prettified, and sanitized beyond resemblance to any part of any creature that ever lived (148).

The reader may read this list and get the impression that food is not food at all.

Need to expand this idea.

Berry started with an anecdote about his experience speaking on the subject to audiences and how listeners will ask him, "What can city people do?" In short, he says, they can "eat responsibly." He then describes today's agriculture, and does so by bringing in a variety of images and words that readers may not usually associate with food such as "industrial eater" and "politics of food" (147). Berry compares the food industry to the entertainment industry. He describes restaurants as "filling stations" and compares homes to motels. He writes with sarcasm when he describes advertisements in the food industry as possessing "virgin purity." Berry then goes on to tell readers what they can do about these terrible images of food.

Move this so that it's the second paragraph in the essay? Organization of my essay prob. needs to follow structure of Berry's essay.

More positive word choices describe traditional farming in Berry's essay. He says he knows of vegetables and fruits that have "lived happily and healthily in good soil," as if we know such plants to have emotions (151). He says animals that have been grown for meat that live a "pleasant, uncrowded life outdoors, on bountiful pasture" are the kinds of animals we should eat. These are more positive word choices. By using them, Berry has set up traditional farming opposite industrial farming.

In addition to showing readers what industrial food is like, he also describes farming practices behind the food industry and the fact that the overriding motivation for consumers is "volume and price" rather than "quality and health." After this, he uses a list of directions on what one can do to "eat responsibly." The list relies upon commanding verbs—or the imperative tense—which gives the reader the sense that action can be taken. This is a structural choice to make a list. It's also about the word choice in that these imperative verbs engage the reader pretty directly: "Participate in food production"; "Prepare your own food"; "Learn what is involved." By using this imperative tense, Berry is able to effectively address the readers directly and put them in the place of acting on the issues being raised. These specific actions might also give readers hope that a solution is possible.

This transition is good.

This list also builds Berry's authority because the reader understands that he shows that he knows of so many possible means of action. The numbered list also helps readers follow along from one point to point, providing easy transitions between ideas. Readers are able to work their way through this series of commands in a quicker fashion, and do just before the essay ends. This is a matter of structure and organization; after putting forth the problem and then outlining his overall solution to the problem, this list gives Berry an opportunity to leave the reader with a way forward and reasons for hope, and also his choice to put this list late in the organization of his essay is strategic.

May need to "contract"/shorten this paragraph. It doesn't really support my thesis.

Throughout the essay, Berry also uses italics to mark off certain word choices and to emphasize them in readers' minds. For example, on page 151, he italicizes "extensive" pleasure as a way to visually show readers the importance of this word.

Finally, Berry's structural choices enable him to build toward his list, which is full of key word choices in the form of directions for action. Up to this point, he uses words to describe industrial food that might disgust readers. Meanwhile, he uses very pleasant descriptors for food that is more connected to traditional agriculture. His goal for the essay is to persuade readers to avoid industrial food at this point, and his structure and word choices help him develop this argument.

Revise conclusion so that it talks about how Berry's approach would benefit my audience.

Sample 2: After Revision

Wendell Berry's Use of Word Choice and Structure in "The Pleasures of Eating"

In the essay "The Pleasure of Eating," Wendell Berry effectively uses thoughtful word choice as a tool of persuasion as he argues that readers should regain awareness of their agricultural sources of food. His specific word choices make industrial food seem negative and food produced by traditional agriculture positive, an approach that helps him argue his point more effectively.

The introduction has been clarified to focus on the main idea of word choice. Also, it has an arguable claim about the effects of the author's approach to word choice.

Berry starts with an anecdote about his experience speaking on the subject to audiences and how listeners will ask him, "What can city people do?" In short, he says quite directly that they can "eat responsibly." He then describes today's agriculture by bringing in a variety of images and words that readers may not usually associate with food such as "industrial eater" and "politics of food" (147). Berry compares the food industry to the entertainment industry. He also describes restaurants as "filling stations" and compares homes to motels. Berry writes with sarcasm when he describes advertisements in the food industry as possessing "virgin purity." Berry then goes on to tell readers what they can do about these terrible images of food.

This paragraph has been moved to an earlier place in the essay, which improves the structure of the essay.

These word choices and images leave readers associating industrial food with negative things.

A particularly strongly worded passage in Berry's essay is as follows:

> The passive American consumer, sitting down to a meal of pre-prepared or fast food, confronts a platter covered with inert, anonymous substances that have been processed, dyed, breaded, sauced, gravied, ground, pulped, strained, blended, prettified, and sanitized beyond resemblance to any part of any creature that ever lived (148).

The reader may read this list and get the impression that food is not food at all; Berry uses words like "processed," "dyed," "prettified," and "sanitized," words that people do not usually want to associate with food. Also, by providing such a thorough list of action words to describe food production, Berry reveals how complex food processing can be, and therefore, how far food travels from its natural state.

More positive word choices describe traditional farming in Berry's essay. He says he knows of vegetables and fruits that have "lived happily and healthily in good soil," as if we know such plants to have emotions (151). He says animals that have been grown for meat but live a "pleasant, uncrowded life outdoors, on bountiful pasture" are the kinds of animals we should eat. These are more positive word choices: "pleasant," "bountiful," "happily," and "healthily." By using these kinds of word choices, Berry has set up traditional farming opposite industrial farming.

In addition to showing readers what industrial food is like, he also describes farming practices behind the food industry and the fact that the overriding motivation for consumers is "volume and price" rather than "quality and health." After this, he uses a list of directions on what one can to "eat responsibly." The list relies upon commanding verbs—or the imperative tense—which give the reader the sense that action can be taken. These imperative verbs engage the reader directly: "Participate in food production"; "Prepare your own food"; "Learn what is involved." By using the imperative tense, Berry is able to effectively address readers directly. Berry gives readers the responsibility to act on the issues being raised. These specific action words also give readers hope that a solution is possible.

Throughout the essay, Berry also uses italics to emphasize them in readers' minds. For example, on page 151 he italicizes "*extensive* pleasure" as a way to visually show readers the importance of this word. Similarly, early in the essay Berry describes "*mere* consumers" to emphasize the meaning as "only," before going on to elaborate that these consumers are "passive, uncritical, and dependent" (146). Here

Here, the author has explained his/her reasoning much more thoroughly than in the previous draft.

The paragraph that originally came after this one has been taken out because it did not support the thesis.

again, he italicizes simple words to create emphasis and expand upon their meaning.

Berry's structural choices enable him to build toward a list full of key word choices in the form of directions for action. Up to this point, he has used words to describe industrial food that disgust readers. In contrast, he has used pleasant descriptors for food that is connected to traditional agriculture. His goal for the essay is to persuade readers to avoid industrial food, and his word choices help him develop this argument. In order to effectively convey this message, Berry uses a variety of examples and evidence, but just as important is *how* he conveys this support for his claim. Berry shows readers and writers alike that strategic word choice is critical for effectively convincing readers of a certain point of view.

The essay now ends with a summary of both Berry's approach as well as what it means for the audience's writing.

Lesson 3.4
Peer Review

You've brainstormed, organized, **drafted,** and **revised** your paper. You've looked at it so many times that you need a break. Now what?

This is a great time to include someone else. At some point in school or at work, you may want to ask a friend, colleague, or classmate to read over your writing. Conversely, you may have been asked to read someone else's work and give them verbal or written feedback. This process is called **peer review.**

There are two main advantages of peer reviewing. First, as a writer, peer reviews help you strengthen content and fix errors in your own writing. Second, as a reviewer, this process exposes you to a variety of writing styles and can offer tips on smart writing techniques. These advantages strengthen both your writing and **editing** skills and those of your peer review partner.

In this lesson, you will learn about the following aspects of peer reviewing:

How to Give Constructive Feedback

How to Receive Feedback

Reflection Questions

If you've participated in a peer review before, did you enjoy it? Why or why not? What helpful information were you able to take away from the experience?

How to Give Constructive Feedback

All peer reviews are not created equal. To give your peer the best possible feedback, you must actively read the text and keep your suggestions clear and organized. Keep the following guidelines in mind as you work.

Be Focused

As you peer review, stay focused on the most important issues in the text. This means giving suggestions about the **thesis statement**, organization, main points, and **supporting details**, not getting side-tracked by grammar and spelling issues. If the author has asked you to evaluate certain areas of the text, make sure that you take the time to do so.

Staying focused also means keeping your feedback manageable. Leaving comments on every single problem might be overwhelming to the author. Instead, try to keep your suggestions focused on the most critical areas of weakness.

Writing Environment: Academic

Many of your courses will require projects that would benefit from a strong peer review. Here are some examples:

- **Science**: projects, lab reports, experiments, or research plans
- **Psychology**: research papers, personal reflections, or case studies
- **History**: reports, response papers, or annotated bibliographies
- **Math**: projects, creating your own problems, or computer-based demonstrations
- **Art**: drawings, paintings, sculptures, or papers on art history

Be Honest

The whole purpose of reviewing a text is helping the author see areas of weakness that he or she previously overlooked. Sharing only positive feedback will actually hurt the author in the long run. Remember that no one is a perfect writer; everyone can benefit from a second opinion.

Be Specific

The more specific information you can give, the easier it will be for the author to make changes later. Take a look at these examples of a helpful and unhelpful comment:

Unhelpful	This paragraph doesn't work.
Helpful	You should consider making this paragraph more supportive of your thesis. The evidence you include in the paragraph focuses on the business side of *minor* league baseball, but your thesis is focused on the business aspects of the *major* leagues.

Another aspect of making your comments more specific is adding suggestions for improvement. Instead of focusing on just the negative, share specific ways that the author can make changes. This is known as **constructive criticism** because it helps the author build on your feedback.

Be Professional

As you review, keep your comments respectful and straightforward. You should avoid using any language that might hurt or offend the author. When possible, share positive comments in addition to your constructive criticism.

Further Resources

A Japanese scientist has theorized that positive and negative words can impact water's molecular structure. To read more, check out this article (http://www.huffingtonpost.com/mehdi-toozhy/the-effects-of-your-posit_b_9557912.html) from *Huffington Post*.

Be Thorough

Being thorough means reading your peer's paper carefully so that you can leave clear, thoughtful feedback. Simply skimming the text is not enough. You will not be able to evaluate the most important issues in the text if you don't read and reflect on the information.

Learning Style Tip

If you are not a verbal learner, you may struggle to read someone else's paper silently. Find a place where you can read the paper out loud. Alternatively, ask someone to read the paper to you and take notes while they read. After that, you can visually check the paper for any spelling or grammar mistakes.

As you read through the text, try asking yourself questions to stay focused on the most important issues. Here are a few examples:

Introduction

- Does the **introduction** grab your attention?
- Is the thesis statement of the paper clear and interesting?
- Does the organization of the main points make sense?

Body Paragraphs

- Does each **body paragraph** start with a clear **topic sentence**?
- Are all of the main points well supported with **evidence**?
- Do all of the main points support the main point of the paper?
- Which main point is the strongest?
- Which main point is the weakest?

Conclusion

- Does the author restate the thesis at the beginning of the **conclusion**?
- Does the conclusion tie together the entire paper?

Helpful Hint

Because writing is often a creative and experimental act, the previous questions will not be relevant to all assignments. If you're not sure which questions apply to the paper you're reviewing, check with your instructor or partner.

On Your Own

Read the ineffective feedback below. In the second column, practice turning it into constructive criticism.

Ineffective Feedback	Constructive Criticism
Not a very good ending.	
Great argument!	
This paragraph is in the wrong spot.	
Ehh. I don't like this.	
This needs to be changed.	

Writing Environment: Everyday

Below are some everyday situations that would benefit from asking a peer to review your writing:

- Maintaining your personal blog
- Petitioning for some sort of local or national change
- Writing a thoughtful post on social media
- Writing content for a website
- Filling out a job application or writing a cover letter
- Writing a personal advertisement
- Writing a letter to the editor of your local newspaper

How to Receive Feedback

As an author, there are steps you should take both before and after the peer review to benefit your writing. Think about these four guidelines:

Come Prepared

The more material you bring to a peer review, the more feedback you will receive. If your draft is missing key points or pieces of evidence, you reviewer may not understand important aspects of your **main idea.** You should also consider preparing a brief list of problem areas. This will help your reviewer stay focused on the items that are most important to you.

Keep an Open Mind

Be open to your reviewer's feedback since that person represents your intended **audience.** The feedback you receive is not intended to be a personal attack. You reviewer has invested time into helping you become a better writer, so resist the urge to become defensive or argumentative.

Writing Environment: Professional

When you apply for a job, consider asking someone you trust to look over your résumé and/or cover letter. Ask your reviewer to consider the following questions when they provide feedback:

- Upon first glance, what stands out the most? Does this feel appropriate?

- What is the strongest part of the résumé?
- Is the layout easy to read, or is there too much going on? How can it be adjusted?
- Do you notice any spelling or format consistency errors?
- Based on this, would you say I'm worthy of the position? If not, is there something I can expand on?

Ask for Clarification

If you don't understand a comment, follow up with the reviewer for more clarification. Talking through an issue will give you a better understanding of how to fix it.

Filter the Feedback

You should thoughtfully consider all the feedback you receive from your reviewer. However, remember that the final decision rests with you. Once you've determined which suggestions you want to take, start revising and editing your draft.

Here are some final questions you should consider when deciding what feedback to use after a peer review:

Do I think these suggestions will improve my grade?

Will making all of the corrections improve my assignment as a whole?

Do I understand all of the comments and why they were made?

Do I agree with the corrections made to spelling and grammar?

Do I need to speak with the teacher about any corrections?

Lesson Wrap-up

Key Terms

Audience: the person or people who read your writing
Body Paragraphs: the paragraphs that contain the main points of a paper and use supporting details
Conclusion: a paragraph that ties together the ideas in a paper and summarizes the main points, also called a concluding paragraph
Constructive Criticism: suggestions of specific ways that an author can improve his or her work
Drafting: a stage of writing that involves writing out ideas and supporting/concluding sentences
Editing: a stage of writing that involves proofreading for style, grammar, and spelling errors
Evidence: a piece of information, also called a supporting detail, that is used to support a main idea
Introduction: the paragraph used to introduce the main idea at the beginning of a paper, also called an introductory paragraph
Main Idea: the statement or argument that an author tries to communicate
Peer Review: working with a classmate to give feedback on each other's papers
Revision: a stage of writing that involves revising for focus and development
Supporting Detail: a piece of information, also called evidence, that is used to support a main idea
Thesis Statement: a sentence that expresses the main idea of a longer work
Topic Sentence: a sentence that states the main point of a paragraph

Writing Application: Peer Review

Read the following paper that demonstrates the peer review process. The peer reviewer has left comments and constructive criticism on the essay.

Whatcha Gonna Watch? *Ghostbusters*!

Ghostbusters is a movie that was released in 1984. The whole family can enjoy it, as it is considered by many to be a classic. It features stars who had successful careers in the '80s and are still active today. *Ghostbusters* is worth watching because it is a great movie.

> I like this movie a lot too! You should include the main ideas you are going to cover in your thesis to make it more specific.

One of the things that makes *Ghostbusters* a great movie is the characters. There are well-known actors, including Bill Murray, Dan Akroyd, and Sigourney Weaver. It also has actors who are lesser-known but still comedic, such as Harold Ramis, Ernie Hudson, Rick Moranis, and Annie Potts. All of these characters are entertaining to watch, and the faces Bill Murray makes are hysterical. It also has ghost characters, including a green slimy blob made of ectoplasm, called Slimer, and a giant marshmallow man called Stay Puft. These ghosts add humor to the movie instead of scaring the audience.

> I looked up this name, and it says the correct spelling is "Aykroyd."

> You should think about adding a transition sentence to the end of the second paragraph that connects the characters to the plot.

Another great thing about *Ghostbusters* is the plot. The story follows a group of eccentric men who go after ghosts haunting the city. They were once professors, so their knowledge of the paranormal enables them to make high-tech equipment to help them find the supernatural. One of the men meets a woman he likes who is being haunted, and he has to save her from the spirits. While the Ghostbusters are on their quest, they run into trouble, not only from the ghosts, but from people who are sceptical of their business. They have to prove their worth and save the whole city from a serious supernatural problem, but they show us that this does not have to happen without humor.

> *sceptical* should be spelled *skeptical*.

Ghostbusters is also great because it is so funny. As mentioned before, Bill Murray and the ghosts add a humorous element to the story. Murray's character, Venkman, fights with an extremely nerdy man over a woman who needs the Ghostbusters' help The Ghostbusters themselves talk back and forth in rapid-fire, amusing conversations that contain silly allusions. They also have a secretary with a funny voice who is great at sarcastic comments. Even fighting the ghosts is funny in this movie.

> This sentence needs a period at the end.

If you're looking for an interesting comedy to watch, you should check out the 1984 classic *Ghostbusters* because it has great characters, an interesting plot, and lots of comedy throughout.

> The conclusion is pretty short; you might want to add some sentences restating the main arguments you've made.

Lesson 3.5
Editing

You may have heard the saying, "Don't miss the forest for the trees." In other words, don't miss the big picture by getting caught up in details. If **revision** is an examination of your writing's big picture (the forest), then editing is tending to the details (the trees).

Think of the details in your writing like the trees in a forest.

To learn more about revising, see Lesson 3.3.

Tending to the details means closely examining the paragraphs, sentences, and words that form your writing. More specifically, editing entails working your way through an essay paragraph by paragraph, line by line, looking for opportunities to make improvements and fix mistakes.

In this lesson, you will learn about the following aspects of editing:

Key Elements of Editing
Important Areas to Edit

Key Elements of Editing

Editing is a stage of writing that involves reconsidering and rewriting grammar, style, and spelling. When we edit, we refine what's already been **drafted** and thoroughly revised. Below are some broad elements to keep in mind when editing:

- Know your **audience**
- Identify patterns

Know Your Audience

Whether you're working on paragraph organization or sentence-level clarity, you will improve your writing if you can anticipate the needs of your audience. Ask yourself the following questions:

What does the reader need in order to fully understand what I am saying?

How much does the reader already know about my topic?

Will the meaning be clear and logical to the reader?

Writing Environment: Professional

Workplace projects often require each person on a team to make contributions. Before you edit a group project, be sure each part is in place and that it is thoroughly revised. Only then can you effectively edit. Otherwise, additions or revisions that come in late could undermine the editing process.

Identify Patterns

You may discover certain patterns or tendencies in your work. Rather than just correcting individual mistakes, identify and record these patterns. This will help you focus on improving specific aspects of your writing. For instance, you may use fused sentences or comma splices frequently, which can cause confusion. Some other common mistakes include the ones below:

- A paragraph without a clear **main idea**
- Unclear or missing transitions
- Sentence fragments
- Run-on sentences
- Clutter or wordiness
- Weak verbs
- Dangling or misplaced modifiers
- Disagreement between a pronoun and its antecedent
- Misuse of adjectives as adverbs

Having identified these patterns, you can then learn strategies for addressing and improving upon confusing sentence structures.

Writing Environment: Everyday

Ever notice that certain friends or family members have distinctive speech patterns? Some people speak in long, rambling sentences. Some say little. Others repeat particular phrases. As an exercise in identifying patterns in sentences, record an everyday conversation. Then, go back and transcribe the conversation, jotting down everything word for word. Notice any patterns?

You may find that certain settings or relationships lend themselves to informal language, including fragments and run-on sentences, that are less acceptable in academic or professional settings. Regardless, by learning to identify such patterns, you can also learn to edit your writing.

Learning Style Tip

If you're a visual learner, try editing your next essay by color-coding. Edit on a paper copy and use a different color for each type of mistake. For example, you might mark misspelled words with green, misused verbs with red, and incorrect punctuation with blue. This colorful approach to editing may help you see your writing in a new way and identify patterns more effectively.

Important Areas to Edit

Transitions Between and Within Paragraphs

Transitions are words, phrases, or sentences that show relationships between ideas. Here are some questions to ask yourself when editing transitions:

> What is the logical connection between each idea?
>
> Is the general organization of these ideas logical?
>
> Would a different transition be more effective?

Read the following paragraph, noting the effective use of transitional words and phrases.

> William Langewiesche's choice to report in the first person contributes to the success of his writing. His personal testimony gives the account an immediacy that is often absent in other reports. Through Langewiesche's point of view, the audience can connect to the experience of a terrorist attack. Also, his relationships with other characters allow him to highlight each person's complexities. For example, Frank Lombardi, the Port Authority's chief engineer, swings between "can-do confidence" and "persistent fatigue, a vagueness" (63). As a result of including these details, Langewiesche's accounts have lasting value and help people understand history in new ways.

To learn more about transitions, see Lesson 4.5.

Fragments

In order to check your work for **fragments**—sentences that don't express a complete thought—re-read each line of your essay and consider these questions:

> What is the subject of this sentence?
>
> What is the verb?
>
> Does this sentence express a complete thought?

On Your Own

Read the sentences below and identify the fragment.

> The impression I got from reading the introduction to this short story was that many people dislike Carver's style of writing because it is not convincing enough. However, I found "Cathedral" very convincing because of the plain style of writing. How an ordinary person would talk. In fact, the dialogue reminds me of a script for a play, with fragmented sentences and odd structure that are much more normal in speech than in writing.

Clutter and Run-on Sentences

> *"Look for the clutter in your writing and prune it ruthlessly. Be grateful for everything you can throw away. Re-examine each sentence you put on your paper. Is every word doing new work? Can any thought be expressed with more economy?"*
>
> *On Writing Well by William Zinsser*

In other words, simplify. As you look for clutter, ask yourself these questions:

- Is the meaning of each sentence clear?
- Could I clarify by dividing long sentences into two or more sentences?
- Are there any short and choppy sentences that could be combined?
- If I remove this word or phrase, will the reader still be able to understand my point?
- Has this idea already been stated in a different sentence?

On Your Own

Read the sentence below and identify the word groups that can be deleted without changing the meaning.

Currently in the tennis match, I am sweating down so much sweat that it's more than I ever have even though we're playing doubles and not singles.

Dangling Modifiers

As you edit, watch for common modifier mistakes. When a modifier has no word in the sentence to modify, it's a **dangling modifier.** Here's an example:

After finding the DVD remote between the couch cushions, the movie gave us a chance to relax for the evening.

The modifier error makes it sound like the *movie* found the DVD remote, which of course doesn't make sense. In fact, the author does not actually tell us who found the remote. Here's a corrected version:

After finding the DVD remote between the couch cushions, we had a chance to watch the movie and relax for the evening.

Now it's clear that the speaker(s) found the remote and watched the movie.

Misuse of Adjectives as Adverbs

Also watch for this common mistake as you edit:

The janitor washed the sink out quick.

Quick is an **adjective**, a word that describes a noun. Here, it is incorrectly used to modify *washed*, a verb. Remember, only **adverbs** modify verbs. Here's a corrected version:

The janitor washed the sink out quickly.

Verbs

Verbs can take on a variety of tenses. Because of this, it's important to pay attention to them while you edit. Using the wrong form of a verb can confuse your audience and cause you to lose credibility as a writer.

To learn more about verbs, see Lesson 9.1 and 10.2.

To examine verbs while you edit, look for verb trends in your writing. Some people frequently use a certain tense (past, present, future) regardless of an assignment's guidelines or purposes. Other writers find it difficult to use action verbs. Look for these tendencies in your own work so that you can address them effectively throughout your writing.

As you edit, ask yourself these questions:

Does each verb agree in number with its subject?

Do I maintain consistent verb tense?

Does my tense fit assignment requirements?

Do I use strong action verbs?

Helpful Hint

Go through one to two paragraphs of your essay and circle each verb. Then, go back and look for error patterns. Knowing your tendencies will help you edit your writing more efficiently moving forward.

Pronoun-Antecedent Agreement

A **pronoun** stands in for a noun, also called an **antecedent.** As you edit, be sure you can clearly determine the antecedent each pronoun refers to. Additionally, make sure they agree in number and gender.

On Your Own

Read the sentence below and identify which pronoun should go in the blank.

While some people like coffee and tea late at night, *[blank]* makes Sam and Liz unable to sleep.

☐ she
☐ it
☐ they

Comma Splices

A **comma splice,** the result of using only a comma to join two complete sentences, is a common error that can cause confusion. Let's take a look at an example.

The soccer player ran toward the ball, he was not even expecting to play in the game.

To fix a comma splice, you can divide the sentences.

The soccer player ran toward the ball. He was not even expecting to play in the game.

Conversely, you could join them with a **coordinating conjunction** such as *or*, *and*, or *but*.

> The soccer player ran toward the ball, but he was not even expecting to play in the game.

You might also choose to rework the sentences altogether in order to create one full sentence or independent clause.

> Though he'd not even expected to play in the game, the soccer player ran toward the ball.

Writing Environment: Academic

Comma rules can vary depending on the context. For example, when listing a series of more than two items, academic assignments may require you to use a comma before the coordinating conjunction, but this comma is not required in other settings. Be sure you understand punctuation standards for your particular assignment or project. Here's an example to consider:

> In his memoir *Brown*, Richard Rodriguez grounds the narrative in the opera house, the library, the Chinese restaurant, Yale University, and Stanford University.

> In his memoir *Brown*, Richard Rodriguez grounds the narrative in the opera house, the library, the Chinese restaurant, Yale University and Stanford University.

To learn more about commas, see Lesson 9.3.

Semicolons

Remember that **semicolons** are punctuation marks used to combine two independent clauses and separate long list items. Writers often make the mistake of using semicolons to connect fragments or two sentences that are unrelated. Below is an example:

Incorrect	Each year, it rains in Springtown, Florida, for about 182 days; this year I am planning to visit several amusement parks on my trip to Texas.
Correct	Each year, it rains in Springtown, Florida, for about 182 days; this high amount of precipitation, along with plenty of sunshine, allows many plants to grow.

Lesson Wrap-up

Key Terms

Adjective: a word that describes a noun or pronoun

Adverb: a word that describes a verb, adjective, or another adverb

Antecedent: the word that a pronoun renames

Audience: the person or people who read your writing

Comma Splice: a sentence error made when two independent clauses are combined with a comma but no conjunction

Coordinating Conjunction: a conjunction that joins similar words or groups of words

Dangling Modifier: a modifier that has no word to modify

Drafting: a stage of writing that involves writing out ideas and supporting/concluding sentences

Editing: a stage of writing that involves proofreading for style, grammar, and spelling errors

Fragment: a sentence, without a subject or verb, which does not express a complete thought

Main Idea: the statement or argument that an author tries to communicate

Pronoun: a word that takes the place of a noun in a sentence

Revision: a stage of writing that involves revising for focus and development

Semicolon: a punctuation mark used to combine two independent clauses and separate long list items

Transition: a word, phrase, or sentence that shows a relationship between ideas

Writing Application: Editing

Read the following paper that demonstrates the editing process. The first essay has not been edited, and the author has used annotations to identify areas that need to be fixed. The second essay implements those corrections.

Sample 1: Before Editing

Wendell Berry's Use of Word Choice and Structure in "The Pleasures of Eating"

In the essay "The Pleasure of Eating," Wendell Berry effectively uses thoughtful word choice as a literary tool of persuasion as he argues that they should regain awareness of their agricultural sources of food. His specific word choices make industrial food seem negative and food produced by traditional agriculture positively, an approach that helps him argue his point more effectively.

> *They* does not have an antecedent.

> *Positively* is an adverb, so it cannot modify the noun, *food*.

Berry starts with an anecdote about his experience speaking on the subject to audiences and how listeners will ask him "What can city people do?" In short, he says quite directly that they can "eat responsibly." He then describes today's agriculture by using a variety of images and words that readers may not usually associate with food, such as "industrial eater" and "politics of food" (147). Berry compares the food industry to the entertainment industry. Berry describes restaurants as "filling stations." Berry wrote with sarcasm when he described advertisements in the food industry as possessing "virgin purity." Berry then tells readers what they can do about these terrible images of food. These word choices and images leave readers associating industrial food with negative things.

> The phrase *on the subject to audiences* is wordy.

> In academic writing, the present tense should be used to discuss texts.

A particularly strongly worded passage in Berry's essay is as follows:

> Re-wording this sentence with a strong action verb would make it less confusing.

> "The passive American consumer, sitting down to a meal of pre-prepared or fast food, confronts a platter covered with inert, anonymous substances that have been processed, dyed, breaded, sauced, gravied, ground, pulped, strained, blended, prettified, and sanitized beyond resemblance to any part of any creature that ever lived" (148).

This list gives the impression that food is not food at all; Berry utilizes such words as "processed," "dyed," "prettified," and "sanitized," which people do not usually want to associate with food. Also, by providing such a thorough list of action words to describe food production, Berry reveals how complex food processing can be, and therefore how far food travels from its natural state.

More positive word choices describe traditional farming as well in Berry's essay. He says he knows of vegetables and fruits that have "lived happily and healthily in good soil," as if we know such plants to have emotions (151). He says animals that have been grown for meat that live a "pleasant, uncrowded life outdoors, on bountiful pasture" are the kinds of animals we should eat. These are more positive word choices: "pleasant," "bountiful," "happily," and "healthily." By using these kinds of word choices, Berry has set traditional farming opposite industrial farming.

The phrase as well in Berry's essay *is wordy; it's already clear that the author is analyzing this text.*

In addition to showing readers what industrial food is like, he also describes farming practices behind the food industry and the fact that the overriding motivation for consumers is "volume and price," rather than "quality and health." Last, he uses a list of directions on what one can do to "eat responsibly." The list relies upon commanding verbs—or the imperative tense—which gives the reader the sense that action can be taken. This is a structural choice to make a list. It's also about the word choice in that these imperative verbs engage the reader pretty directly: "Participate in food production"; "Prepare your own food"; "Learn what is involved." By using this imperative tense, Berry is able to effectively address the reader directly. Berry puts the reader in the position of acting on the issues being raised. These specific actions also give readers hope that a solution is possible.

Gives, the verb, does not agree in number with *verbs,* the subject.

By using specific, vivid words to contrast traditional farming and food with industrial farming and food, Berry shocks his audience into regaining awareness of their eating habits. He emphasizes the artificiality of industrial food, idealizes the purity of traditional farming, and urges readers to be more intentional about their food. Berry's skillful word choice strengthens his argument and leaves a lasting impression on the audience.

Sample 2: After Editing

Wendell Berry's Use of Word Choice and Structure in "The Pleasures of Eating"

In the essay "The Pleasure of Eating," Wendell Berry effectively uses thoughtful word choice as a literary tool of persuasion as he argues that readers should regain awareness of their agricultural sources of food. His specific word choices make industrial food seem negative and food produced by traditional agriculture positive, an approach that helps him argue his point more effectively.

They has been replaced with *readers* and *positively* with *positive*.

Berry starts with an anecdote about his experience speaking about food and how listeners will ask him, "What can city people do?" In short, he says quite directly that they can "eat responsibly." He then describes today's agriculture by using a variety of images and words that readers may not usually associate with food, such as "industrial eater" and "politics of food" (147). Berry compares the food industry to the entertainment industry and describes restaurants as "filling stations." Berry writes with sarcasm when he describes advertisements in the food industry as possessing "virgin purity." He then tells readers what they can do about these terrible images of food. These word choices and images leave readers associating industrial food with negative things.

The wordy phrase *on the subject to audiences* has been changed to *about food*.

The incorrect past tense verbs have been replaced with present tense.

Berry develops a particularly strongly worded passage:

> "The passive American consumer, sitting down to a meal of pre-prepared or fast food, confronts a platter covered with inert, anonymous substances that have been processed, dyed, breaded, sauced, gravied, ground, pulped, strained, blended, prettified, and sanitized beyond resemblance to any part of any creature that ever lived" (148).

This sentence has been restructured in order to utilize a more active verb.

This list gives the impression that food is not food at all; Berry utilizes such words as "processed," "dyed," "prettified," and "sanitized," words that people do not usually want to associate with food. Meanwhile, by providing such a thorough list of action words to describe food production, Berry reveals how complex food processing can be, as if so many steps in the process shows us just how far food travels from its natural state.

Conversely, more positive word choices describe traditional farming. He says he knows of vegetables and fruits that have "lived happily and healthily in good soil," as if we know such plants to have emotions (151). He says animals that have been grown for meat that live a "pleasant, uncrowded life outdoors, on bountiful pasture" are the kinds of animals we should eat. These are more positive word choices: "pleasant," "bountiful," "happily," and "healthily." By using these

The wordy phrase *as well in Berry's essay* has been deleted.

kinds of words, Berry has set traditional farming opposite industrial farming.

In addition to showing readers what industrial food is like, he also describes farming practices behind the food industry and the fact that the overriding motivation for consumers is "volume and price" rather than "quality and health." Last, he uses a list of directions on what one can do to "eat responsibly." The list relies upon commanding verbs— or the imperative tense—which give the reader the sense that action can be taken. This choice to use imperative verbs enables Berry to engage the reader directly: "Participate in food production"; "Prepare your own food"; "Learn what is involved." Berry puts the reader in the position of acting on the issues being raised. These specific actions also give readers hope that a solution is possible.

Gives has been changed to *give* so that it agrees in number with the subject.

By using specific, vivid words to contrast traditional farming and food with industrial farming and food, Berry shocks his audience into regaining awareness of their eating habits. He emphasizes the artificiality of industrial food, idealizes the purity of traditional farming, and urges readers to be more intentional about their food. Berry's skillful word choice strengthens his argument and leaves a lasting impression on the audience.

Lesson 3.6
The Final Draft

Polishing and **submitting** your final draft is a great feeling. You've worked hard throughout the entire **writing process**, and now, you finally have the opportunity to share your ideas with your **audience.**

The final version of your text might be a paper, blog post, book, video, or presentation. However, regardless of the **format** you choose, your work isn't quite done. You must make a few important decisions before finalizing and submitting the finished version of your work.

In this lesson, you will learn four steps of submitting a longer text:

Reflect on the Goals of a Writing Assignment
Choose a Layout and Design
Add Visuals
Print or Upload Your Work

Helpful Hint
Before submitting a text for school or work, be sure to review any specific guidelines from your instructor or supervisor.

Reflect on the Goals of a Writing Assignment

In school, you receive writing assignments from your instructors all the time. At work, you might be asked by your manager to draft an important email or memo. One of the most important questions you can ask yourself is, "What is my overall goal in writing this document?" Without a goal, your writing may become disorganized and leave your audience confused.

In general, your goal will be provided by your instructor in school or your manager at work. By the time you are ready to finalize your draft, you need to make sure you have addressed everything expected of you.

You will usually find the goals of an academic task on the syllabus, a course website, or a specific assignment handout. Here's an example:

> Please write a detailed analysis of the most prominent themes in the novel *Catch-22*. When analyzing, break down parts of the text to examine how they interact with each other.

Writing Environment: Academic

By the time you are ready to submit your work to an instructor, you have probably gone through multiple drafts. Take a look at these two drafts on classroom resources and compare their readiness for submission.

Draft 1:

> When reviewing classrom materials to be used by an instructor I saw that there are different things that can be used. Software and hardware, for example. If teachers could have their own website to post valuable information, it might help they're students. I found a web page for the Florida Community College. Their information is informative. They talk about what works and what doesn't work in the classroom. Websites are a different story. It seems like most of them are designed poorly and not very user friendly.

Draft 2:

> When reviewing feasible materials and resources for teachers to use in the classroom, technology should always be considered. Overhead projectors and MS Office software—namely Word, Excel, and PowerPoint—are materials that can be used effectively. Florida Community College provided a very informative web page discussing what works and what doesn't work in the classroom. Class websites are ideal because instructors would be able to post assignments and grades for students to easily access. However, finding a good platform can be difficult. Personal websites are rarely both user-friendly and robust enough for the instructor yet easy to navigate for students.

On Your Own

Based on the previous passages, which draft has not been polished? Check the box next to your answer.

☐ Draft 1
☐ Draft 2

Choose a Layout and Design

The first step of submitting a longer text is choosing a layout and design. **Layout** refers to the way your writing is arranged on the page or the screen. **Design** refers to the colors, **fonts**, and images that you select.

Genre often determines the layout and design of your finished work. For example, an academic text like a research paper will probably be plainer than a personal text like a blog post. **Academic writing** may also require a specific format such as **MLA** style, which has a set of layout and design rules.

> To learn more about using MLA style, see Lesson 7.8.

In other projects, you may have more control over the final format of your writing. If so, use this as an opportunity to strengthen your writing through good layout and design choices. A well-designed document is more interesting, readable, and meaningful to the audience.

Imagine a science textbook filled only with tiny black and white text. You would probably struggle to read the pages or understand complex topics. This is because textbooks are designed to make the information as clear as possible. The images, fonts, and colors in textbooks aren't chosen just to look good. They are there to explain confusing concepts and to highlight important ideas.

As you think about the layout and design of your finished text, consider the acronym **ACE**:

> A: Are the layout and design **appealing**?
> C: Are the layout and design **consistent**?
> E: Are the layout and design **easy to read**?

First, your design should be *appealing* to your audience. For a paper, this may simply mean that your pages are free of stains or marks. You might also decide to include a cover page or to place the finished document in a plastic folder. When submitting a more creative work, you should use colors and fonts that are attractive to your audience.

You work should also have a consistent *appearance*. If you use certain fonts or colors at the beginning, continue using these so that the entire work looks neat and unified. Using consistent design and layout not only makes your work more attractive, it also helps your audience understand the information better.

For example, if you have centered headings at the beginning of each section, you audience will always know when a new section starts. If you switch to left-aligned headings halfway through, your audience may think these sections are somehow different.

Finally, make sure that your work is *easy to read*. If your audience can't read the message of your text, then you haven't truly accomplished your **purpose.** An easy-to-read text uses clear fonts with a reasonable amount of spacing between lines and paragraphs. Your page or screen should also be free from clutter or distractions.

Reflection Questions

The format of your work can affect your design choices. What are some of the differences between print and electronic formats? Why do you think these differences exist?

Group Activity

As a group, find five examples of well-designed texts. Create a presentation that discusses how each one uses good layout and design to communicate its message. Share your presentation with the class. (Be sure to follow the layout and design guidelines for your work!)

Add Visuals

Using visuals in a text engages the audience and can communicate your ideas more clearly. Think about the advertisements, documents, books, and posters you encounter in your everyday life. Most likely, those texts include images.

To ensure that you are using the best possible visuals for your writing, think about these three areas:

- Purpose
- Genre
- Design

Think About Your Purpose

Before you add an image, think about your purpose for using visuals in the text. For example, advertisements often use images to show the design and features of a product while presentations use images to catch the audience's attention and emphasize important points. Once you've determined your purpose, use it to evaluate any potential images. If an image doesn't help you meet your goals, think twice before including it.

Think About the Genre

The genre of your published work will determine the types of images that you are able to include. For example, if you are submitting an article to a magazine, that publication will have specific rules about the types of images that can be used. If you are giving a speech, you may not have access to a projector or computer to display visuals.

Think About Your Design

Always think about the layout and design of your text before adding visuals. Images should follow the same design guidelines as the rest of the text. A visual should be appealing to your audience, consistent with the overall design, and easy to see and understand. You may need to adjust the position or size of the image to ensure that it fits into your work properly.

Writing Environment: Professional

Depending on where you work, you may be asked to give a formal presentation. If so, consider the ways you've designed and implemented images. Visuals should not be merely decorative; this can appear unprofessional and distracting. To evaluate the images in your presentation, ask these questions:

- Do these images all serve a purpose?
- How do these images support my **main idea**?
- Are these images appropriate for the intended audience?

Print or Upload

The last step of submitting a text is actually printing or uploading the final copy. Even though this step is small, it's important. Always schedule yourself extra time in case of printer or computer problems. You don't want to realize that your printer is out of ink right before class.

You should also double-check your work once it's been printed or published. For example, if you accidentally left the last page of your document in the printer tray, you want to notice this before submitting your work to your instructor or manager.

In some situations, submitting isn't the last step. You may be turning in your work for instructor or **peer review.** Afterward, you will use this feedback to continue improving and polishing your work. In other cases, however, this is the final step in the writing process. Either way, take a moment to congratulate yourself on a wonderful accomplishment.

Lesson Wrap-up

Key Terms

Academic Writing: a text intended for instructors or students and often directed by specific prompts and requirements

Academic Writing Process: a strategy that breaks up a writing assignment into five stages: pre-writing, drafting, revising, editing, and submitting

ACE: an acronym (Appealing, Consistent, Easy to read) for thinking about the layout and design of a text

Audience: the people who read your writing

Design: colors, fonts, and images included in a text

Font: the size and style of letters

Format: the style and arrangement of a text

Genre: a type of writing

Layout: the way text and images are arranged on a page or screen

Main Idea: the statement or argument that an author tries to communicate

MLA: the Modern Language Association is a group of scholars dedicated to research in modern languages

Peer Review: working with another person in order to give feedback on each other's papers

Purpose: the goal of a text

Submitting: a stage of writing that involves formatting a text and sharing it with its audience

Writing Application: The Final Draft

Read the following letter written to an appeals board. The layout and design are appropriate for the audience, purpose, and genre.

June 17, 2015

Financial Aid Appeals

Re: Doris Hannekin

Student ID: 208N672

This letter is formatted according to the standards of the Financial Aid Appeals office.

Dear Appeals Board:

Several years ago, I was diagnosed with post-traumatic stress disorder (PTSD), but only recently have I sought treatment. The treatment plan includes weekly Eye Movement Desensitization and Reprocessing (EMDR) sessions and counseling sessions. EMDR has been proven successful in alleviating PTSD in veterans as well as victims of trauma. When I first started therapy, I was progressing well. Unfortunately, about halfway through my first class in SWI, my daughter called to let me know that due to losing her job, she was facing eviction, losing her car, and other complications. Even though I am living on a fixed income, I found a way to help her. However, the situation exacerbated the stress that I was already beginning to feel from my therapy. Fortunately, I was able to successfully complete that class.

The author provides background information first.

I was ready to take my second class in SWI, namely, ADET 622 (the class I withdrew from). However, I noticed after the third week of the course that symptoms of my stress were growing stronger each time I had to turn in an assignment. In addition, I received another call from my daughter to inform me that her car had been repossessed. Only the day before, I had gone through an especially difficult EMDR session. Between the PTSD and dealing with my daughter's chaotic life, I could barely function.

As expected at this stage in the writing process, this letter is well-organized and contains no spelling, grammar, or punctuation errors.

The good news is that through my therapy, I am learning how to prioritize. My main priority is school. Not only am I learning to focus on balancing my needs, but I am also learning how to circumvent potentially stressful events altogether or to return to my grounded state of being in order to finish the task at hand.

With the help of my therapist, I am in a position to move forward with my studies. I feel confident that I will be able to complete my courses. My academic history at Regis reflects a 3.79 GPA and induction into the Jesuit Honor Society (Alpha Sigma Nu). If you review my records, you will see that I'm not in the habit of withdrawing from courses.

This is the first and last appeal I ever expect to write.

I humbly ask that you reinstate my financial aid so that I am able to continue my education. Once reinstated, I will be able to successfully complete my courses. Thank you.

Sincerely,

Janet Miller

This sentence sums up the goal of the text.

Depending on the audience, *respectfully* would also be an acceptable closing.

Chapter 4
Parts of the Essay

Lesson 4.1
Common Essay Structures

In the field of architectural design, you'll often hear people say, "Form follows function." What they mean is that you should always think about the purpose of a building before you build it.

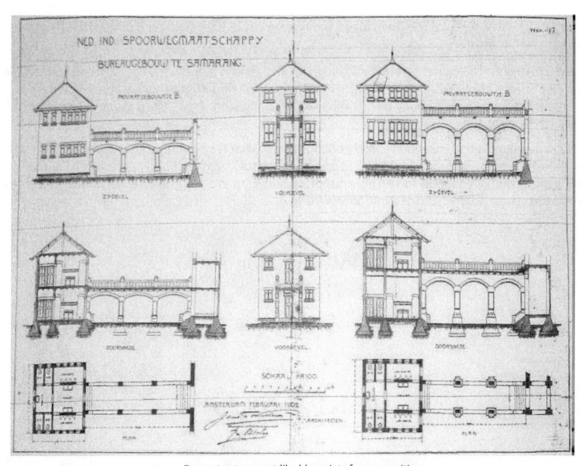

Essay structures act like blueprints for your writing.

Although all buildings share common elements like walls, a floor, and a roof, we expect the form and features of the structure to vary according to purpose. In other words, a hospital does not look like a sports arena or a movie theater.

This is equally true for writing. It's no accident that the word *structure* is borrowed from architecture. Not all writing is "constructed" in the same way, and its forms reflect those differences. Knowing how to choose and use a variety of essay structures will help you achieve your writing purpose and meet your readers' expectations.

> In this lesson, you will learn about essay structures:
>
> Essential Essay Components
> Adapting Essay Structures to Modes of Writing
> Choosing an Essay Structure

Essential Essay Components

The Standard Essay Form

A well-built essay helps people know what to expect before they enter a building. It also helps them find what they need once they walk inside. A well-constructed essay accomplishes three similar goals:

- It quickly lets the reader know the **topic** and purpose of the essay.
- It helps the reader access and use the essay's information by presenting it in a logical and organized way.
- It concludes with a recap of the **main ideas**, leaving no doubt in the reader's mind what the essay is trying to communicate.

Essays are constructed using paragraphs. Although no two essays are exactly the same, readers have certain expectations about what kinds of information they will find in each paragraph. Most essays include an introduction, a set of body paragraphs, and a conclusion. **Transitions** guide readers from one paragraph to the next.

Especially in academic contexts, you've likely encountered what is commonly known as the 5-paragraph essay model. This model includes 1 introductory paragraph followed by 3 body paragraphs and 1 concluding paragraph. While this model may not often suit your writing goals, its general structure is usually expected in academic and professional writing.

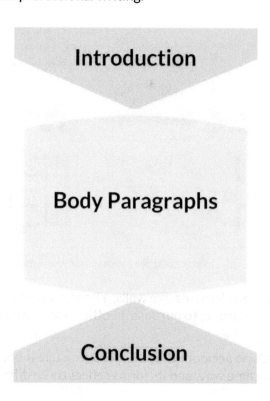

Introduction

The **introduction** is the first paragraph of an essay. It presents the topic, provides necessary background information, and states the **thesis**, a sentence that expresses the main idea of a longer work. It lets the reader know the overall **purpose** of the essay.

Body Paragraphs

Each **body paragraph** explores, explains, and/or proves one idea related to the thesis. For example, in an academic essay about the causes of World War I, each body paragraph would discuss or explain a different cause. In a professional context, a proposal recommending new software would include a paragraph for each reason.

Conclusion

The **conclusion** restates the main idea and reviews or summarizes the key arguments, ideas, reasons, and/or other elements of the body paragraphs. In some cases, the conclusion also asks the reader to change his/her views and/or take a specific action. For example, a letter from a political candidate might ask readers to vote or donate to the campaign.

On Your Own

Take a look at the following paragraphs. One is a body paragraph from a narrative essay, and the other is an introduction for an academic essay. Which is which, and how do you know? Consider the apparent purpose of each piece and its structure.

Ten miles southwest of the Skagway airstrip, the tourists fall silent. Until that moment, the half-dozen passengers had been chattering excitedly, pointing to the bald eagles wheeling above the snowy walls of the fjord. For the first twenty minutes of the flight, the wide channel beneath them had been glassy, the smooth surface broken only by the arched backs of orcas slicing upward and then disappearing. But even before State Street's candy-colored storefronts appear off the nose of the single-engine plane, the fjord narrows and the winds awaken. The captain, a red-haired bush pilot named Ray, glances back from the cockpit and catches the eyes of Joanne, an apple-cheeked Tlingit homemaker returning from her weekly shopping run to Juneau. Ray and the woman share a conspiratorial smile and glance at the tourists. The smile means, "Just wait."

In the lower forty-eight states, we leave the gate only to sit for hours on the hot tarmac, endure invasive searches with sweaty shoes in hand, and cram our three-ounce shampoo bottles into plastic bags. The boredom, inane rules, and indignities of commercial flight have extinguished the glamor and adventure of air travel. We've lost the sense of wonder that aviation once held. We find no delight in the skies, and even our children are too jaded to marvel that tons of metal can rise up from the earth and soar. But here it is different. To fly over glaciers and desolate mountains is to feel both powerful and small. To fly in this place is to feel alive but afraid. This place is Alaska, where harsh landscapes, violent weather conditions, and vast distances without radio communication make aviation more exciting and deadly than anywhere else in the United States.

Helpful Hint

Authentic writing in academic, professional, and everyday situations doesn't always conform to a neat structure of three body paragraphs. What if you perceive four significant causes of infections in hospitals? What if you have only two compelling reasons why your customers should choose your product? Let your purpose have the final say in your essay's structure, not the other way around.

Adapting Essay Structures to Modes of Writing

Writing Modes

Different writing tasks will require you to consider different structures. The structure of a text refers to how the parts of the essay are organized to serve the writer's purpose.

There are four main modes of writing: **descriptive**, **narrative**, **expository**, and **persuasive**. Generally, expository and persuasive writing are the most common modes of writing in academic and professional settings. For this reason, this lesson will emphasize essay structures for writing primarily within these two modes.

To learn more about the four writing modes, see Lessons 2.1-2.4.

Review the key similarities and differences between the writing modes below:

	Description/Narration	Expository/Persuasive
Purpose	To recount and/or and describe a person, place, event, or experience (real or imagined) so that the reader can picture it	To convey information so that the reader will learn something new or adopt a new way of thinking or acting
Content	Based on memory or imagination and often emphasizes creativity more than literal truth	Features verifiable **facts**, **examples**, and **evidence**, often based on research
Focus	Beauty of expression and vividness	Clarity of ideas and **arguments**
Structure	Often uses a variety of paragraphs and paragraph lengths, usually presented in a chronological pattern of organization	Employs a clear, straightforward, and/or formal essay structure based on a logical progression of ideas

Reflection Questions

Why do you think expository and persuasive writing are the most common modes in academic and professional settings? Consider the functions of writing in those settings; why might the essay structure be a good fit?

The essay form is flexible, and it can be adapted for each of these modes. However, description and narration often adopt unique, creative structures.

The standard introduction-body-conclusion structure works equally well with expository and persuasive modes of writing.

Adapting the Essay Structure to Expository Writing

Building on the previous professional example, here is how an expository essay on different fundraising methods might be structured:

1. Introductory paragraph

    a. Thesis: "The top fundraising techniques for schools include grants, direct appeals to individuals, and corporate sponsorships."

2. First body paragraph

    a. Grants: what they are, how they work, and examples of available grants and/or organizations that offer them.

3. Second body paragraph

    a. Direct appeals: what they are, whom to ask and how, and ways to show appreciation to donors.

4. Third body paragraph

    a. Corporate sponsorships: what they are, how to find them, levels of sponsorship, and what businesses expect in return.

5. Conclusion

    a. Synthesizes and provides an overview of the various fundraising options.

Adapting the Essay Structure to Persuasive Writing

Now, here's how a persuasive essay might be structured:

1. Introductory paragraph

    a. Statement of position: "Corporate sponsorships are not an appropriate fundraising source for the new school gym."

2. First body paragraph

    a. Reason #1: "Students are already bombarded with advertising."

    b. Evidence

3. Second body paragraph

    a. Reason #2: "Corporate sponsorships rarely generate as much money as they claim."

    b. Evidence

4. Third body paragraph

    a. Reason #3: "Propaganda undermines critical thinking."

    b. Evidence

5. Conclusion

    a. Call to action: "Vote against using corporate sponsorships to raise the money for the new gym."

Writing Environment: Professional

Many careers require expository and persuasive writing. Consider these writing tasks for a fundraising specialist charged with raising money for a new school gym.

- A report explaining top fundraising techniques, including grants, direct appeals to individuals, and corporate sponsorships
- A letter to the school board arguing against corporate sponsorship and explaining why it is not an appropriate fundraising strategy for a school

The first task is expository. The writer's job is to present and explain all the options without expressing a position for or against any of them. The second example is persuasive because the writer is arguing against a particular fundraising method and providing reasons for that opinion.

On Your Own

Use the following image as inspiration to generate at least four essay ideas: two for an expository essay and two for a persuasive essay.

Using one of your four ideas, fill in the following template. Make sure you include the appropriate kind of thesis, body paragraph approach, and conclusion for the essay's purpose: to inform or persuade.

Thesis Statement	
Body Paragraph 1	
Body Paragraph 2	
Body Paragraph 3	
Concluding Statement	

Essay Structures for Specialized Purposes

Throughout your academic and professional career, as well as in daily life, you will encounter many different writing tasks.

Although most writing aligns (for the most part) with one of the four modes of writing, a text can incorporate a variety of different purposes from one paragraph to the next. For example, although expository writing is used primarily to inform readers, it can incorporate a variety of writing purposes. Likewise, good persuasive writing often seeks not only to convince, but also to *inform* readers about a certain position, idea, or course of action.

Based on your specialized purpose, your writing might be best structured in one of the following ways:

- Definition
- How-To/Process
- Cause and Effect
- Compare and Contrast

The basic essay components (introduction/thesis statement, body paragraphs, and conclusion) are the same for writing that takes on each of these structures. It's what you *say* in your thesis and what you *do* with your body paragraphs that will vary according to the task.

Helpful Hint

You may notice that some of these essay structures are also described as "**organizational patterns**" in other contexts. Though related, essay structures and organizational patterns are (respectively) unique considerations. Recall that essay structures work like blueprints for your paper. These structures are the foundation for your overall approach to an essay. They determine how you will present your ideas based on your specific purpose(s), and they may even impact the details you choose to include or exclude. Organizational patterns are more specifically focused on the order of ideas. They determine the order of sentences within a paragraph and/or the order of paragraphs within an essay.

To learn more about organizational patterns, see Lesson 5.3.

Definition

From a one-sentence definition of a term in your science notes to a multi-page essay on "the meaning of moral courage," **definition essays** define, describe, and/or explain a person, place, thing, event, or idea. You probably do this kind of writing quite often in your daily life without even noticing.

Writing Environment: Everyday

Consider this excerpt from an email. The writer, who is planning to move into a cohousing community, explains what cohousing is to a friend.

> Cohousing isn't actually a new idea. It's been around since the 1960s, but it hasn't caught on in the U.S. until just recently, so I'm not surprised you haven't heard about it. Cohousing is a cross between a regular neighborhood and a '60s-style commune. All of us will have our own houses, but they are small. We'll have all the basic stuff in a regular house, like a kitchen, bathrooms, and bedrooms. But there's also a park in the middle with a building called a common house. It has a huge kitchen, a dining

> room, a laundry room, a workshop, and a gym that the whole neighborhood share. The idea is that not every family needs a home theater or all those tools that you have in your garage. By sharing the things we don't use all the time, we can save money. It's also greener, which is part of the reason it's becoming more popular. Plus, we know some of the other couples in the neighborhood. It'll be nice to hang out with friends and not have to drive to see them.

Though only a paragraph long and written in an informal style, this email is clearly defining a concept. It also includes a variety of defining techniques that could be developed into body paragraphs for a full-length essay on the topic.

The introduction of a definition essay always identifies the person, place, thing, event, or idea that will be defined. Typically, the thesis statement also indicates which unique or significant features of the topic will be addressed in the body of the essay. For example, here is a thesis statement for an extended definition essay on this topic: "What is a good teacher?"

> A good teacher is an expert in the subject, explains the subject clearly, and uses flexible methods.

Many writers find it helpful to visualize a definition essay using a mind map like this one. A **mind map** is a graphic that allows writers to visualize and structure different types of essays.

The topic is in the center circle with the attributes or features of the topic in the surrounding circles. Each circle represents one paragraph in the essay. The introduction and conclusion will discuss the main topic: good teachers and teaching. Each body paragraph will present and explain one important characteristic that defines the topic.

A mind map works well for a definition essay because all body paragraphs relate to the topic in the same way. You can present the body paragraphs in any order that makes sense to you. If you want to discuss a fourth feature, you can simply add another circle to the web and build a paragraph on that idea.

> **Helpful Hint**
>
> Once you've decided on the order of your body paragraphs, go back and check your thesis statement. Readers will expect the essay to discuss the defining features of your topic in the same order as you listed them in the thesis.

Process

Another widely used essay type is the process essay, sometimes called a "how-to" essay. A **process essay** explains how to do something or how something happens. In everyday life, we encounter process writing every time we open up a cookbook or read the instructions for a new gadget.

> **Reflection Question**
>
> Based on your own experiences as a reader and consumer, what makes a set of instructions easy to understand? What makes instructions hard to follow?

In academic and professional settings, process essays are generally longer and more developed than a simple recipe or list of instructions. For example, a process essay might explain how a scientific process like cellular mitosis occurs or provide detailed instructions on how to prepare an end-of-month financial statement for a large corporation.

Similar to the other essay types we've looked at so far, the process essay structure includes an introduction, body paragraphs, and a conclusion. The introduction presents the process and why it is important. The body paragraphs identify and explain each step. The conclusion recaps the main steps, describes the finished product, and/or explains how to use it.

Unlike some other essay types, in process writing the order of the body paragraphs is critical. Your process will only make sense to the reader if you present each step chronologically: first step, second step, etc. For that reason, writers often visualize the structure of a how-to essay like this:

Introduction
→ Step 1 → Step 2 → Step 3
Conclusion

This structure requires you to think sequentially about your topic before you start writing. Many processes require more than just three steps, so you can always add boxes to accommodate extra body paragraphs.

> Group Activity
>
> In a small group, choose an everyday process like assembling a taco, backing into a parking space, or creating a playlist. Using the previous mind map as a model, work individually to write out the steps along with a concluding statement that describes the final product. What will it look like if you follow the process correctly? Compare maps with the others in your group. Did you place them in the same order?

Cause and Effect

We make logical connections between causes and effects every day. Even as a child, you quickly discovered a causal link between events like forgetting your mittens and having cold hands or doing your homework and getting better grades. That kind of thinking forms the foundation for writing a **cause and effect essay**. This essay type explores causal links between events, decisions, or situations, and their consequences.

Writing Environment: Academic

Consider this introductory paragraph from an essay for a health policy and management course.

> Ever since Alexander Fleming discovered penicillin in 1928, antibiotics have saved countless lives. Before the advent of these drugs, diseases like bacterial meningitis killed 90% of the children who contracted it. Common infectious diseases like strep throat could be deadly, and even a simple ear infection could spread to the brain and cause permanent damage. In spite of these benefits, the use—or overuse, some would argue—of antibiotics has led to unintended and undesirable consequences. Chief among these are resistant strains of bacteria (often called "super-bugs"), rising hospital costs, and an increase in fatal cases of diarrhea among children.

Note how the introduction begins with general background information on the topic: antibiotics. In the second half of the paragraph, the writer establishes a cause-and-effect connection between antibiotics (the cause) and several consequences (effects). The rest of the essay would devote one body paragraph to each of these effects.

With a few easy changes, the basic mind map we used for the definition essay can be adapted to visualize and structure a cause and effect essay. Here, all the circles are placed to the right of the "cause" square, with arrows pointing to each one. This serves as a visual reminder of the essay's purpose: to point out, explain, and/or prove the link between the cause and each effect.

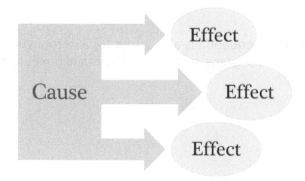

In your introduction, present the topic, or "cause." The thesis statement should express the link between that cause and all the effects the essay will explore. Each body paragraph should then discuss one effect in greater detail and explain or prove how the cause leads to that effect.

The conclusion paragraph always restates the thesis, but it often does more than that. For example, some writers conclude their essays with recommendations or **proposals** for how to address the cause, minimize negative effects, or increase positive effects.

To learn more about writing to propose, see Lesson 1.4.

On Your Own

Read the following concluding paragraph from a cause and effect essay and identify the sentence that restates the thesis.

> Childhood obesity is a complicated and sensitive issue, one that will take years of effort to remedy. However, it is clear that we must address it. Obesity in childhood has both short-term and lifelong consequences: social stigma and low self-esteem, diabetes, and higher risk for many types of cancer. Lifestyle changes like diet and exercise can combat obesity and improve health at any point in a person's life, but childhood intervention would yield the greatest benefits.

Compare and Contrast

A **compare and contrast essay** discusses similarities and differences between multiple people, places, things, events, or ideas. Consider how often you explain something new by comparing it to something familiar. Here are some examples:

> A calzone is like a pizza but with the dough rolled up and the toppings inside.

> The modern dictator has similar powers to an absolute monarch of earlier times. However, a dictator is more likely to seize power through military means rather than inherit the position.

A useful visual for this essay structure is a **matrix**, a table used to organize compare and contrast essays for a point-by-point discussion of similarities and differences. It organizes each body paragraph around a single point of comparison. The first step of creating a matrix is writing a list of possible points of comparison. Here are some examples:

- Physical properties: size, shape, color, age
- Components: what it is made up of
- Purpose: what it is for/how it works
- Cost: in time, money, effort
- Source: where or how you get it

Helpful Hint

You can choose to devote more paragraphs to similarities than differences. However, most employers and professors will expect a mix of comparisons and contrasts. If the items are either identical (all "compare") or different in *every* way (all "contrast"), you may want to consider another structure.

Once you've chosen your points of comparison, filling out a matrix will help you organize your ideas into body paragraphs:

Introduction: Presents each item to be compared and contrasted. Ends with a thesis statement that tells what is similar and what is different about each.

Body Paragraph 1	The two items are similar in this way	The first item is like this	The second item is the same because
Body Paragraph 2	The two items are different in this way	The first item is like this	The second item is different because
Body Paragraph 3	The two items are also different in this way	The first item is like this	The second item is different because

Conclusion: Always restates the thesis. Often includes some kind evaluation (which one of the two is better) or recommendation (when to choose one over the other).

Group Activity

With a partner, choose a pair of items to compare. Select your points of comparison and create your own matrix showing what you would discuss in each paragraph of a compare and contrast essay. Here are some possible topics:

- Watching movies at home vs. at the theater
- Scripted vs. reality TV shows
- Peer vs. parent influence
- Dogs vs. cats as pets

Choosing an Essay Structure

Knowing the essay structures presented in this lesson will not help you be a more effective writer if you don't know which essay is right for the job.

The first step in any writing task is to determine the purpose. To do this, closely examine the task and look for key words that indicate what kind of writing is expected. The following table lists common terms and sample questions, along with the essay structure that matches each task.

Key Words/Phrases	Sample Topic	Essay Structure
Define, describe, components, features, provide main characteristics, meaning of, what is?	What is a true friend?	Definition
Trace, list (in order), *steps, process, become, develop, explain how, give instructions, provide sequence*	Trace the development of the internet from the ARPANET in the 1960s to what it has become in the 21st century.	Process
Causes, reasons (for), *origins, source, trigger, initiate, effects, consequences, results, outcomes, lead to*	Discuss the laws and policies that have led to the current high levels of incarceration in U.S. prisons.	Cause and Effect
Compare, similarities, alike, same, contrast, differences, dissimilar, different, unalike	Identify key similarities and differences between our product and the one produced by our closest competitor.	Compare and Contrast

On Your Own

Read the following writing prompt; then, determine the best essay structure to use. Check the box next to your answer.

> Identify and discuss three changes in the roles of women in American society that came about as a result of World War II.

☐ Compare and Contrast
☐ Process
☐ Cause and Effect
☐ Definition

Helpful Hint

Another way to check that you are using the most appropriate structure is by using the "one-sentence answer" method. Try responding to an assignment prompt with a one-sentence answer that closely matches one of the essay structures above.

For example, if the prompt asks, "What are the main reasons for car accidents?" you might answer, "The main *causes* of car accidents are fatigue, distraction, and impairment due to alcohol or drugs." The word *cause* clearly shows your intention to use the cause and effect structure.

If your one-sentence answer makes sense with the prompt, you can feel confident you have chosen the best essay structure for your purpose. What's more, your sentence can act as a working thesis statement that you can build on to write the whole essay.

Lesson Wrap-up

Key Terms

Argument: a reason why you should think or act a certain way

Body Paragraphs: the paragraphs between the introduction and conclusion of an essay that use supporting details to explore, explain, and/or prove the main idea(s)

Cause and Effect Essay: an essay type that explores causal links between events, decisions, or situations and their consequences

Chronological Order: an organizational pattern that arranges ideas or events in the order that they occur (also known as sequential order)

Compare and Contrast Essay: an essay type that discusses similarities and differences between multiple people, places, things, events, or ideas

Conclusion: a paragraph that ties together the ideas in a paper and summarizes the main points, also called a concluding paragraph

Definition Essay: a type of essay that defines, describes, and/or explains a person, place, thing, event, or idea

Descriptive Writing: writing that communicates the characteristics or qualities of a thing or event

Evidence: a piece of information, also called a supporting detail, that is used to support a main idea

Example: a specific instance or illustration that demonstrates a point

Expository Writing: writing that uses evidence to support a main idea

Fact: a piece of information that can be proven true or false

Introduction: the paragraph used to introduce the main idea at the beginning of a paper, also called an introductory paragraph

Main Idea: the statement or argument that an author tries to communicate

Matrix: a table used to organize compare/contrast essays for a point-by-point discussion of similarities and differences

Mind Map: a graphic organizer that uses shapes to illustrate connections between ideas

Narrative Writing: writing that conveys events that happen during a defined period of time

Outline: a tool developed during pre-writing that provides a visual of a paper's organization and ideas

Persuasive Writing: writing that uses argument to influence someone's beliefs and/or actions

Process Essay: an essay that explains how to do something or how something happens

Purpose: the goal of a text

Thesis Statement: the concise sentence or group of sentences that expresses the main idea of a longer work

Topic: the general subject of a text

Writing Application: Common Essay Structures

Read the following essay, paying attention to how it's organized. What is its structure, and how does this fit the purpose and topic?

Training for Your First 5K Race

If you are like me, running has always been something other people do. When friends asked me, "Want to go for a run?" I'd ask, "Why?" Well, here I am, eating my words and lacing up my running shoes. What changed? I could point to the physical benefits—cardiovascular health, stronger muscles and bones, weight loss—but the real breakthrough was discovering a way to train that was actually fun and

The opening hook establishes a connection between the reader and writer.

made me feel great after every workout, starting on day one. Let me take you step by step from being a non-runner to finishing your first 5K race in twelve weeks.

The first step is to sign up for a 5K in your area. Human development and psychology experts Steven Covey and Brian Tracy tell us we need a specific goal we can work toward. No matter how much you might value something like getting fit, it's just an idea. It won't lead to sustained action or a new habit until you set a specific goal and work toward it. Find a race about three months from now and send in your registration fee.

The second step is to carve out some time. If you want running to become a habit, you'll need to do it habitually. Obvious, I know, but it's easy for a new activity to just drop out of your schedule if you don't dedicate regular time to it. Set aside about an hour, two to three times a week, between today and your race date. Be self-aware. If you are a morning person who tends to crash by late afternoon, don't schedule your runs for after work. If you like to take walks in the woods, replace some walks with trail running. Just having a schedule makes it more likely you'll follow it.

Next comes a major step: the actual running. Think of your training routine as three stages rather than as a precise timetable. Everyone is different, so even though I'll talk about each phase as approximately four weeks long, use your own fitness and comfort level as a guide. The three stages are below:

Stage	Starting Point	Goal/Ending Point
1: Walking & Running	Walking with 60-second bursts of running	Alternating 5 minutes of walking with 5 of running
2: Picking up Speed	Half walking and half running for 20 minutes	25 minutes of running without stopping
3: Endurance & Distance	About 2 ¼ miles of steady running	Race day: 5K (3.1 miles) of running

Stage 1

The first few weeks involve a significant amount of walking with short bursts of jogging or running. This slow entry gives you time to work on regulating your breathing and finding the right pace. The purpose of this week is to show you how easy and pleasant running can be. After a five-minute warm-up of quick walking, alternate between sixty seconds of running and ninety seconds of walking. Do this for twenty

The thesis makes it clear that this is a process or "how-to" essay.

Even if an essay's style is informal, it should still use accurate information.

Each main idea gets its own body paragraph, and the body paragraphs are presented in chronological order.

Process essays use transitions of time (*first, second, next*) to introduce each step.

Process writing is often made more "considerate" (easy for a reader to follow) by using lists, tables, or other graphics.

minutes. Then, walk for another five minutes and follow up with stretching.

Over the next three weeks, very gradually increase the time for both walking and running. In the second week, you could run for ninety seconds and walk for two minutes, then run for two minutes and walk for three. Your goal for the end of Stage 1 is to be running for half of the twenty minutes in five minute segments.

Stage 2

The middle phase of the training will add some distance and take you from half-walking/half-running to all running. Some increase in distance just happens naturally as you add more running into the mix. It's very likely you were already running more than a mile at the end of Stage 1. The end goal for this part of the training is to cover about two and a half miles or run for twenty-five minutes without stopping, whichever is shorter. In the first week, start very close to where you ended Stage 1: run for five minutes, but this time only walk for four minutes. Repeat for twenty minutes and then walk and stretch.

For the next two weeks, gradually increase the time you spend running until you can run ten minutes without stopping. At the same time, decrease your walking time in-between runs from three minutes to two. In the final weeks of Stage 2, phase out walking entirely and slowly add time until you can run twenty-five minutes without stopping. Pause here to celebrate. You are probably running well over two miles now!

Stage 3

These last few weeks can be very helpful for preparing your body and mind for race day. Your running goal in this phase is distance: reaching 5K and covering at least that distance every time you run. At this place in my training, I found a three-mile trail near my house. With a clear distance goal, you no longer have to count minutes while you run. When you reach the goal, the run is over. This frees up more space in your mind for thinking about your pace and concentrating on keeping your breathing steady. You can look around, enjoy your surroundings, and feel more and more like a "real" runner every time you train.

Come race day, you should feel strong, confident, and completely ready for the challenge that once seemed impossible. Enjoy the cheering crowds, take pride in your accomplishment, and do not measure yourself against others. If you started this process as a non-runner and you're now completing your first 5K, you've already succeeded.

Subheadings can also signal major steps in a process.

Providing a rationale for steps in a process gives the writer credibility.

Process writing often concludes with some description of the "finished product," in this case the satisfaction of reaching the goal to run the 5K race.

Lesson 4.2
The Introduction

Imagine that you walk into history class and your teacher says this:

> "In the year 1775, the Revolutionary War began. This war created turmoil all over the country and elicited many debates about the purpose of taxes."

Your friend's professor is also teaching about the Revolutionary War, but she starts class by saying this:

> "Imagine it's a dark night, and you're leading a troop of soldiers through a murky river to attack your enemies. What do you say to keep your soldiers feeling confident and prepared?"

How do these introductions compare? Which class would you want to take?

You likely found the second introduction more interesting. Although both instructors are introducing the same subject, your friend's instructor has hooked her **audience** by starting with a creative and thought-provoking prompt.

Just like the first words of an in-class presentation or conversation, the first words and sentences of a text also matter. This is your chance to draw in your audience and explain why they should care about what you have to say.

For many writers, the introduction is the most difficult part of an essay. Have you ever sat down to start working on a writing assignment, and the next thing you know you've wasted time staring at a blank screen just hoping for the perfect words to arise? This kind of experience is counterproductive, and it can leave you feeling frustrated and unmotivated.

Introductions can be frustrating, but they don't have to be.

Learning Style Tip
For many learners, particularly global learners who prefer looking at the "big picture," it can be helpful to hold off on writing the introduction until after the rest of the essay is finished. If you take this approach, however, you should come up with your **main idea** or thesis statement beforehand so that you have direction as you build your **body paragraphs**.

Luckily, there are several things you can do to create an effective introductory paragraph. The **introduction** should present your **topic** and its importance, explain your focus or **argument**, and engage your readers.

In this lesson, you will learn to create a strong introduction using the following strategies:

Understand the Role of the Introduction

Hook Your Audience

Get to the Point

Further Resources

As you've probably experienced when meeting someone for the first time, introductions in everyday life are also important. Read or listen to the National Public Radio article, "You Had Me at Hello: The Science Behind First Impressions," (http://www.npr.org/sections/health-shots/2014/05/05/308349318/you-had-me-at-hello-the-science-behind-first-impressions) to learn more.

Understand the Role of the Introduction

Introductions appear at the very beginning of your paper. They are like roadmaps for the rest of your work, providing a starting point for your readers. While every assignment is different, most introductions seek to achieve three main goals:

- Engage the audience's attention
- Present the focus or argument of the text
- Explain why the topic is important and worth reading about

Helpful Hint

Introductions vary in length and structure based on the type of writing. For example, some longer writing assignments like research papers might include multi-paragraph introductions. Always consult your syllabus and the assignment details to make sure you're aware of the expectations.

Introductions include general information about a topic. This might be background information or important terms and definitions. All of this information should slowly build toward the main idea of your paper, which is stated in your thesis statement.

Although you should save the specifics for later, don't be *too* general in your introduction. You should share background information or terms as they relate to your topic. Look at how these examples differ in their approaches:

Many people feel frustrated with the political system in America.

Frustration with the American political system has increased due to more political scandals and untrustworthy politicians making empty promises.

▸ Both sentences use general information to introduce the audience to the topic of the essay. However, the first example is too vague. The second sentence is a much better example of how to use general information that still relates to the topic.

Here's another example:

Strong	My internship at the Digital Corridor was an eye-opening experience that helped me discover my passion for writing.
Weak	Internships can help students discover their goals.

Organizing the Introduction

The introductory paragraph should be organized in a clear, easy-to-follow manner. Usually, introductions can be broken down into these parts:

- An attention-grabbing hook
- A concise introduction to the topic and its relevance to the audience
- A thesis statement

Think of your introduction like an upside-down triangle. Start broadly with your hook and work toward the narrow, focused argument in your thesis statement.

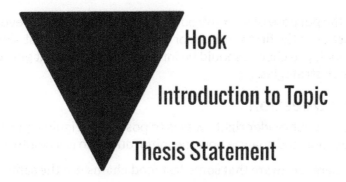

Hook

Introduction to Topic

Thesis Statement

> **Helpful Hint**
> Writing is a creative act. Therefore, not all introductions will require this standard structure. Generally, the triangle pattern works best for **descriptive** and **persuasive writing**. If you're not sure if your writing assignment would fit this method, check with your instructor.

Writing Environment: Academic

Usually, the introduction of an academic essay should be at least three sentences long and end in a thesis or **purpose statement**. The introduction will also present as much relevant background information as possible. Take a look at this introductory paragraph for a short paper on post-traumatic stress disorder in children:

> Although the medical community studies post-traumatic stress disorder (PTSD) extensively in adults, psychiatrists conduct significantly less research to determine the way the disorder affects children. In fact, only during the last twenty years have psychiatrists noticed the growing prevalence of PTSD in individuals under the age of eighteen. On the *Anxiety Disorders Association of America* website, Stephanie Sampson notes that children develop post-traumatic stress disorder much more

easily than adults because of children's "limited coping and communication skills, the powerful influence of media exposure such as television, and the often insufficient attention focused on early identification and intervention." Other than psychiatrists and other medical professionals, most people know little about the causes of the disorder. Additionally, many parents are unaware of the effects of trauma on their children. The ignorance surrounding post-traumatic stress disorder demonstrates how much more research and awareness is needed by psychiatrists to prevent misdiagnosing children.

Group Activity

With a partner, make a list of the strengths and weaknesses of this introduction and discuss them when you're finished. Consider what features might be worth replicating in your own writing.

Hook Your Audience

Once you've determined the **purpose** of your introduction, you can begin to develop those first words. The **hook** of your introduction is the first sentence or two in your writing that aims to immediately engage your reader. The type of hook you choose should be influenced by your text **genre**, audience, and purpose. Consider the following hook strategies.

Pose an Interesting Question

One effective way to engage your reader right away is to pose an intriguing question worth pondering. Read the following introduction and analyze how the initial question is a helpful connection to the topic.

How many consumers are aware that some fast food chains use the same ingredients in their food that are used in cement, Silly Putty, and soap? Many fast food chains use whatever ingredients necessary to create products that are cheap and easy to make. It is important to be aware of what we put into our bodies that could impact our health and well-being. We should avoid eating fast food on a regular basis because it is detrimental to our physical health, mental state, and medical future.

Group Activity

As a group, brainstorm other strong questions that could take the place of the one in this paragraph.

Start with a Strong Quote

Relevant and interesting **quotes** add style and validity to your writing. Try to find quotes that appeal to your intended audience and transition well into your topic. Read the following introductory paragraph:

"When they said, 'Sit down,' I stood up," sings legendary musician Bruce Springsteen on his track "Growin' Up." The ability to live for oneself and not for the appeasement of others can be a difficult task. Some people lead their entire lives this way, realizing only when it's too late that they never pursued their own dreams. Luckily, Bruce Springsteen is not one of those people.

Now read the same introduction without the quote. Which introduction is more effective?

> The ability to live for oneself and not for the appeasement of others can be a difficult task. Some people lead their entire lives this way, realizing only when it's too late that they never pursued their own dreams. Luckily, Bruce Springsteen is not one of those people.

Helpful Hint

When using a quotation as a hook, try to make it something new to your audience. Avoid overused quotes or **clichés**, which are popular phrases that have lost their original impact due to overuse.

On Your Own

Read the sentences below and identify the one that is a more appealing hook.

> "Time flies when you're having fun."

> "You're only given a little spark of madness. You mustn't lose it," said the late Robin Williams.

Provide a Relevant Anecdote or Example

Sometimes, your introduction can be best served by a brief story, or **anecdote**, that is noteworthy and applicable to your topic. This can be a personal anecdote or a retelling of someone else's story. Take a look at the following example and pay attention to the effectiveness of incorporating a personal story.

> Decades ago, my grandfather came to America from Mexico. Like many immigrants, he came to the United States to search for opportunities that his native country lacked. He remained driven by the American Dream. In the best of these tales, immigrants succeed through hard work, dedication, and a little luck. However, for *mi abuelo* the road to change was paved with many hardships. He faced unplanned financial setbacks, prejudice, and, worst of all, the loss of loved ones. I have been fortunate to hear his stories; at the heart of each one lies the resilience of the human spirit. His example has had an impact on my personal beliefs and goals and how I approach my own life.

Group Activity

Discuss the introduction above. What sort of paper does it introduce? Come up with an informal outline listing the topics that would make up the rest of this paper. Then, brainstorm other ideas for anecdotes or **examples** that connect to these topics.

Use a Proclamation

If using a quote or question feels forced, consider using a **proclamation**, which is a strong declaration of an opinion or fact. Take a look at the following example and consider how the first sentence impacts the rest of the paragraph.

> People have become so dependent on cell phones that they rarely realize how disruptive they are in public places. A recent survey suggests that 80% of Americans have felt frustrated in the last month alone by strangers' overuse of technology in public spaces. It's vital for people to change

this behavior. Limiting cell phone use in public will preserve peace, maintain socialization and human connection, and prevent careless accidents.

Writing Environment: Everyday

If you've used a social media app like Instagram, Facebook, or Twitter, you've probably written a short "bio" or "about me" section. This is like a personal introduction for everyone who views your profile. Most people want this short piece of writing to reflect their personality and stand out from the crowd. Take a look at this example of a social media user's "about me" introduction:

> Pancakes or waffles?
> I'm a journalist from Omaha, Nebraska who's asking the tough questions. Currently, I'm writing a column for the *Global Report* and doing unofficial research on how many TV show episodes I can watch in one weekend.

Reflection Questions

Consider the strategies we've discussed for starting an introduction. Are some of these strategies more appropriate than others for certain writing assignments?

Get to the Point

For many people, the first words of a paper are the most challenging. Once you've accomplished this goal and hooked your audience, where do you go from here? The rest of your introduction should prove that you have a strong and important topic worth reading about.

Introduce the Topic and Its Relevance

If your readers feel no connection with or responsibility for your topic, they are likely to ignore it. Therefore, once you've gotten their attention with your hook, it's time to explain your topic and why it should matter to your audience. Read the following excerpts from two introductions on the same topic, noting the differences between them.

> Public education has been fighting a battle for adequate funding for decades. Provided with an increase in funding and resources, schools will develop academically, artistically, and athletically.

> Public education has been fighting a battle for adequate funding for decades. Provided with an increase in funding and resources, schools will develop academically, artistically, and athletically. Because schools represent the foundation and future of their communities, this growth will affect not only in students but the surrounding area as well.

> ▸ In the second example, the writer speaks to both students and community members, convincing both groups to feel compelled that higher funding for their schools will lead to positive change for all people.

On Your Own

Read the following introductory paragraph. In what sentence(s) does the author present the topic and its relevance to the audience?

> Danny Muntz spent five years robbing small convenience stores, citing lack of financial opportunity for his family as the cause. After three years in jail and rehabilitation programs that focused on personal responsibility and steps toward active change, Muntz came out of prison to open a restaurant that employs residents in low-income areas. Danny Muntz represents thousands of people who flood our prison systems all over the country, but not all inmates are lucky enough to be offered a chance for rehabilitation. A prison system that focuses on personal growth and not confined punishment would assist inmates who are willing to change and create room for those who deserve longer sentences. Ultimately, more public funding and energy should be directed towards our prison rehabilitation programs. These programs provide opportunities for inmate development as well as the chance to save taxpayer money by releasing prisoners after they complete a rehabilitation program.

Sum It All Up in a Thesis Statement

A **thesis statement** expresses the main idea of a longer work. After hooking your audience and explaining your topic's importance, it's time to focus in on exactly what you want to argue.

An effective thesis statement makes it clear to your audience what your main idea is and how you plan to support it. Consider the following examples and note their differences:

> Cancer research has made massive progress in the past ten years, and many things have improved to make this happen.

> Cancer research has made massive progress in the past ten years as a result of increased financial support, better training for doctors and nurses, and improvements in technological and medical equipment.

> ▸ Both statements introduce the topic: cancer research. However, the second thesis also introduces the key arguments that will support this topic.

To learn more about thesis statements, see Lesson 4.3.

Let's consider an introduction that puts all these pieces together.

> When Maci Chapman was a freshman at Oak City College, her best friend begged her to come to a meeting for the school newspaper, *The Branch and Herald.* Maci had hated her required extracurricular activities in high school, but she reluctantly attended the meeting (mostly to oblige her friend). As she slumped in a chair in the student union, she realized that everyone on the newspaper's staff was also a student. She had biology class with the sports writer, and she had seen the photographer walking around campus the day before. No one had

The hook of this introduction is a brief anecdote.

forced them to sign up; they actually cared about creating a great newspaper for the school. At the end of the meeting, she was surprised to find herself signing up to work as a copy editor two nights a week. By her junior year, she was the editor-in-chief of *The Branch and Herald*, and by the time she graduated, she had job offers from major newspapers all over the state. Maci would have never discovered her passion for journalism if the newspaper had been managed by faculty members. The board of directors at our school, Oak City College, is discussing whether or not to hire staff from outside the student body to supervise student media. This would be a mistake. Students should continue to have complete control of media outlets on campus—the newspaper, magazine, and radio—because this responsibility encourages creativity, fosters independence and self-discovery, and teaches important life skills.

> The author then explains the topic (students managing campus media) and why it should matter to readers.
>
> Last is the thesis statement; the author provides a clear argument and three supporting points.

Helpful Hint

Once you've built your introduction, you'll want to consider how to move from your introductory paragraph to your first body paragraph with a transition. **Transitions** show relationships between ideas.

To learn more about transitions, see Lesson 4.5.

Writing Environment: Professional

Most companies request that applicants include a personal introduction along with their resume. Sometimes, this is called a "cover letter," which is similar to a formal letter. It could also be a "summary of qualifications," which is short and direct. Either way, this piece of writing introduces you and explains your skills and interests. Take a look at this example of a summary of qualifications:

> Passionate literacy professional with seven years of experience as a public-school educator and fifteen years of leadership experience at a nonprofit organization. Specialize in volunteer project management and program training. Ability to adapt and thrive as a team leader in a collaborative, supportive environment. Exceptional interpersonal skills, both written and verbal. Master's degree.

Lesson Wrap-up

Key Terms

Anecdote: a long example told as a story

Argument: a reason why you should think or act a certain way

Audience: the person or people meant to read and interpret a text

Body Paragraphs: the paragraphs between the introduction and conclusion of an essay that use supporting details to explore, explain, and/or prove the main idea(s)

Cliché: a popular phrase that has lost its original impact due to overuse

Descriptive Writing: writing that communicates the characteristics or qualities of a thing or event

Example: a specific instance or illustration that demonstrates a point

Genre: a type of writing

Hook: the first sentence or two in a piece of writing that aims to immediately engage the reader

Introduction: the paragraph used to introduce the main idea at the beginning of a paper, also called an introductory paragraph

Main Idea: the statement or argument that an author tries to communicate

Persuasive Writing: writing that uses argument to influence someone's beliefs and/or actions

Proclamation: a strong declaration of an opinion or fact

Purpose: the goal of a text

Purpose Statement: a sentence that tells the audience exactly what points will be covered in a longer text

Quote: someone's exact words

Thesis Statement: the concise sentence or group of sentences that expresses the main idea of a longer work

Topic: the general subject of a text

Transition: a word, phrase, or sentence that shows a relationship between ideas

Writing Application: The Introduction

Read the following persuasive essay, paying special attention to the introduction. How does it get the audience's attention, provide background information, and state the main idea? How does the structure in the introduction guide the rest of the essay?

The Privilege of Thinking

French philosopher Voltaire said, "Think for yourselves and let others enjoy the privilege to do so, too." *The Giver*, a well-known novel by Lois Lowry, portrays a futuristic society in which no one thinks for themselves. There are no choices, nor is there color, pain, or emotion. Memories of these things are entrusted to only one person in the community: the Giver. When Jonas, a young boy, is chosen to be the new Giver, he receives these memories, and they change his life dramatically. The 2014 movie adaptation of *The Giver* does some things well. The film celebrates diversity by including images from multiple cultures in the memories passed from the Giver to his protégé Jonas. It also effectively portrays Jonas' gradual ability to see colors and his changing perspective of the community's highly structured society. However, two aspects of the film deprive the viewers the privilege of thinking for themselves. The short, written explanation at the beginning of the movie and the explanatory voice-overs throughout the film provide so much explanation that the movie ends up mimicking the repressive community it portrays.

The first way that the movie adaptation of The Giver prevents the audience from thinking is by including an explanation of the film's

This introduction begins with a strong quote used as a hook.

The author then introduces the audience to the topic.

The last sentence is the thesis, which summarizes the author's argument. Readers can expect the body paragraphs to discuss two points: the written explanation and the explanatory voice-overs.

The first sentence of this paragraph introduces the topic as it was mentioned in the thesis: the written explanation.

context. Before the first scene, a short paragraph appears on a dark background for a minute or two. It explains the major plot points. *The Giver* take places in the future, perhaps in the United States, although the exact location is unknown. In this version of the future, people live in "Communities," which are overseen by the "Elders." All the worst parts of life on earth have been eliminated from the Communities: war, poverty, discrimination, natural disasters, disease, and violence. The only person who remembers these things is the Giver. The Elders control every aspect of every Community-dweller's life: whom they marry, which children they are assigned, what career they have, and even what they wear. When the Elders choose Jonas to be the next Giver and receive the current Giver's memories, Jonas slowly realizes that some of the best parts of life have also been eliminated from the Communities: love, free will, adventure, and even color. In the book, these things are slowly revealed both to Jonas and the reader. However, the movie explains most of this before the film even begins. The filmmakers may have been attempting to provide context for people who had never read the book so that they wouldn't be confused. However, the movie itself shows what Communities are like and how they function. Even if the audience was confused at first, this temporary disconnection would only add to the impact of Jonas' discovery. Additionally, the history of the Communities is explained by the Giver later in the movie, when the audience is familiar with the setting, so it's unnecessary to explain it to the audience at the beginning of the film. Finally, the explanation robs movie-goers of the opportunity to draw their own conclusions. It tells the audience exactly what to think, much like the Elders of the Community.

An alternative to beginning each body paragraph with the next point in the thesis is to transition from the last sentence of the previous paragraph.

One particular way that the Elders enforce their control over the people is through a type of loudspeaker that is audible to the entire Community. Through the loudspeaker, the Elders admonish rule-breakers, give daily schedules, and make announcements. At the beginning of the book, when the people in the Community are startled by an unexpected aircraft flying overhead, "adults, as well as children—stop what they [are] doing and wait, confused, for an explanation" to come from the loudspeaker (Lowry 2). The movie adaptation of *The Giver* has its own version of the loudspeaker: voice-overs from Jonas, the main character, explaining his thoughts and feelings. However, like the written explanation, the voice-overs are unnecessary. The very nature of a movie is that the acting, script, and visuals provide enough information for the audience. The voice-overs also give the audience a ready-made interpretation of the characters' actions, removing any opportunity for movie-goers to interpret the performances. This type of filmmaking only reinforces an environment in which people wait to be given an explanation instead of thinking critically for themselves.

The movie adaptation of *The Giver* has positive features, like its inclusive message. However, the written explanation at the beginning of the movie and the explanatory voice-overs actually defeat the purpose of the story. By providing too much explanation to the audience, the movie imitates the controlling environment of the Communities and deprives people the privilege of thinking for themselves.

Because the introduction provided enough explanation, the conclusion is a short restatement of the essay's main argument and thesis.

Lesson 4.3
Thesis and Purpose Statements

Before a road trip, you check the weather and pack the car, eagerly anticipating your adventures, but do you just take off? Before you leave, shouldn't you first decide where to go? Then you can calculate the best route and know what to expect along the way.

Thesis statements act like road maps for your writing.

Like a road trip, reading and writing will be more productive with a clear plan. A well-written thesis statement serves as a map for your writing, announcing the goals and expectations for a text.

In this lesson, you will learn about the following aspects of thesis and purpose statements:

The Basics of a Thesis
Creating a Thesis Statement
Supporting a Thesis

The Basics of a Thesis

What Is a Thesis Statement, Anyway?

A **thesis statement** is a sentence that expresses the **main idea** of a longer work. Generally, a thesis presents an **argument**, or a reason why you should think or act a certain way. If it is possible to disagree with a statement, it's probably an argument.

For example, these statements are arguable:

> Basketball is America's best sport.

> Cities should not enforce curfews on teenagers.

If you can explain *how* and *why* you feel these statements are true, you make them even stronger. Your thesis statement includes your main argument along with your *how* and your *why*.

A thesis statement accomplishes all of these goals:

- Explains the author's position or perspective
- Functions like a scientific hypothesis (a theory to prove)
- Sets expectations for the audience
- Demonstrates a relationship between concepts or events
- Provides an organizational path for the author

The thesis is often included near the end of the **introduction** and provides a foundation for the rest of the paper. The **body paragraphs** reference the thesis and follow its order. These references are like road signs on a highway that remind the reader of your plan and confirm that you are on track. After the body paragraphs, the **conclusion** often restates or paraphrases the thesis. Repeating your perspective reminds the **audience** that you have covered the information you set out to discuss, and it also brings your argument full circle.

Here are some guidelines to remember as you draft a thesis:

A thesis should be . . .	A thesis should not be . . .
An authoritative position statement	A broad or oversimplified topic sentence
A complex sentence	A theme
Arguable (someone may disagree)	A direct quotation
Answering the question *why* and/or *how*	A statement of fact
Relevant	A personal preference

Helpful Hint

Like most rules in writing, thesis statements have exceptions. Some essays work toward a thesis statement at the end of a paper. Others include a thesis in the second or third paragraph (or not at all). In some texts, the thesis statement is actually made up of multiple sentences or even a paragraph.

Some experimental writing genres might include their main argument in alternate ways. If you're not sure if experimenting is wise, think about what makes the most sense for your audience, **purpose**, and **genre**.

Before we break down the components of a thesis statement, let's first consider two examples.

Weak Thesis

> *Harry Potter* is the greatest young adult book series of all time.
>
> How? Why? This statement is too short, and it's just an opinion, so it's not arguable.

Strong Thesis

> To create a modern classic, J.K. Rowling modeled the *Harry Potter* series on elements of classic myth: an unlikely protagonist of enchanted origins with mystical guides and a universal message.
>
> This statement has an arguable claim, layered connection, and provided support.

Writing Environment: Everyday

Sometimes, it's necessary to write a complaint letter. Whether you want a refund or replacement, providing a thesis statement is professional and persuasive. A strong thesis statement focuses on the facts. This is more likely to produce results than emotional language or accusations.

> I have always been pleased with your products, but after careful consideration, I'm requesting a full refund based on late delivery, damaged condition, and visual misrepresentation on your website.

The body of the letter will add details that support the reasoning in this thesis.

Is a Thesis Always Essential?

Narrative and **descriptive writing** don't always require a thesis. Since a thesis tells the reader exactly what to expect, a good narrative could be ruined by telling the audience what's going to happen. Also, a thesis generally eliminates surprise and suspense, which is good for persuasion but disappointing in a story.

> To learn more about descriptive writing, see Lesson 2.1.

> To learn more about narrative writing, see Lesson 2.2.

An informed and organized thesis is essential in **expository** and **persuasive writing**.

On Your Own

In the blank spaces, briefly describe a situation in which each of these tasks might be required. Consider professional, academic, and everyday settings. The first is offered as an example.

Take a side	Make a vacation recommendation
A political stance supporting your candidate	

Support your argument	Provide evidence to support a value/belief
Analyze a film	Evaluate a historical claim
Research a new apartment/house	Compare dining options

Writing Environment: Professional

In the corporate world, a thesis is vital for sales pitches, memos, business plans, proposals, and even cover letters. If you do use a thesis in a cover letter, position it at the end of the introduction and support it with brief paragraphs that illustrate each of your strengths with an anecdote, or a long example told as a story. This directs your audience's attention to key points quickly and concisely. Take a look at this example of a thesis statement from a cover letter:

> My combination of communications skills, facility with social media, and passion for marketing makes me a great addition to your team.

Creating a Thesis Statement

A strong thesis doesn't usually spring from your head fully-formed. Depending on your research task, writing one may take hours or even weeks. Give yourself time for the process. A strong thesis will evolve as you read, think, and generate ideas, so be open to changing it as your ideas develop.

During this time, you will have a working thesis. A **working thesis** is a thesis statement in progress. Like a scientific hypothesis, it changes according to the data you collect. Start broad and expect your thesis to become more specific. As you read and research, use the following questions to look for ideas or patterns that can help you form your core argument:

Is there an arguable cause and effect?

Do I strongly agree with anything I have read?

What may have influenced the author to write this piece?

Do any experts suggest perspectives I haven't considered?

Is there anything controversial or intriguing to investigate?

Are there unusual similarities or connections to other events?

Writing Environment: Academic

Sometimes, your instructors will ask you to complete a writing task that you're not interested in or comfortable with. For example, your English professor might ask you to write a literary analysis of *Macbeth* even though you're more interested in history than literature. In a case like this, try combining your interests with the assignment. *Macbeth* is based on a historical event, so you can use that to create a strong thesis that analyzes the historical aspects of the play.

Making Your Thesis Complex

As your thesis evolves, it should naturally become more complex with multiple connections to other ideas. **Complexity** depends on developing and supporting these ideas and connections.

When you have written what you believe is a strong thesis, apply these simple "tests." If the thesis fails any of these tests, you may want to consider adding complexity to your writing.

Thesis Test Checklist

☐ Will anyone disagree with it (is it arguable)?

☐ Does it answer a *how* or *why* question? (complexity indicator #1)

☐ Does it show a relationship between concepts or events? (complexity indicator #2)

☐ Does you claim add value or a new perspective?

Putting Your Thesis Components Together

Let's review the components of a strong thesis statement:

- An authoritative, arguable position statement
- Your *how* and/or *why* as support
- A complex idea
- A relevant topic

Now, let's break down the following example:

> **Topic:** Should college tuition be adjusted?
>
> **Argument:** College should be free for all students who volunteer.
>
> **How:** More government funding + higher taxes on the wealthy
>
> **Why:** College is expensive + student loan debt is crippling
>
> **Thesis Statement:** Due to increased tuition and an overwhelming amount of student loan debt, college should be offered as free to all students; funding can occur through increased taxes on the wealthy and larger contributions of government aid.

This thesis statement contains four components. It is also complex in the way that it connects multiple ideas to one broad argument.

> Helpful Hint
>
> Not all thesis statements need both the *how* and the *why*. Don't force anything that isn't natural or that you don't plan to support later in your writing.

The previous thesis was a working thesis. The author has a direction in mind. However, let's assume that during the research process, he or she finds an article about the positive effect that volunteering has on communities. Is this another answer to the *why* question that could strengthen the argument? Something clicks, and the author revises the thesis:

> Due to increased tuition prices and an overwhelming amount of student loan debt, college should be offered as free to all students who give back to their communities by volunteering. This can be achieved by raising taxes on the wealthy and increasing government funding.
>
> This is a strong thesis; it has an arguable position. It's also complex, relevant, and answers *why* students should attend college for free. It's intriguing for the author and the audience.

Purpose Statements

In some settings, it may be more appropriate to draft a purpose statement as opposed to a thesis statement. A **purpose statement** tells the audience exactly what points will be covered in a longer text. While they are similar to thesis statements, purpose statements are more commonly used in professional settings. Often, they deal with business plans, proposals, and new ideas as opposed to academic analysis.

Writing Environment: Professional

In business, making arguable recommendations is crucial. If you were a finance director for a major company, which of the following purpose statements would you find most useful?

> Our firm's financial situation requires drastic budget cuts.

> Analysis of our second quarter financial statements makes it clear that our firm must reduce spending by 15% in the areas of employee vacation packages, relocation allowances, and client gift baskets.

The first purpose statement merely states a fact without providing answers for how to cut the budget or why the cuts are necessary. Because the author hasn't recommended specific solutions, the first statement doesn't demonstrate that the author has given much thought to the problem.

However, financial statements have clearly driven the decisions in the second purpose statement. If anyone complains, the statistics support the analysis. The author of this thesis has made practical and specific recommendations, which the report will explore in detail.

Supporting a Thesis

Once you've drafted a thesis statement, you want to be sure that it remains fully supported throughout your writing. In this section, consider these strategies for organization and support.

> **Helpful Hint**
>
> Your busy manager, CEO, or supervisor will appreciate a paper with high "skim factor." Visual and verbal cues allow the reader to quickly "skim" your proposal, report, or email to determine its readability and relevance. High skim factor adds value to your writing and shows respect for your reader's time.

The Three-Part Thesis

Like the tip of an iceberg, the thesis is a preview of what the body paragraphs cover.

One easy organization model is the "three-part thesis." This strategy approaches the thesis like an iceberg: a preview in the introduction with a powerful supporting base in the body paragraphs. It's not always necessary to have a three-part thesis, but it's an easy method for making sure your thesis is complex.

Imagine you're assigned to evaluate the causes of the Great Depression. You don't have the space to write about *all* the causes. However, some causes probably had more impact than others.

Use the following questions to consider how these connections add depth, focus, and complexity:

- Which factors were most damaging?
- Most financial impact?
- Most social impact?
- Most long-term impact?
- Most familiar to you?
- Most globally significant?

Weak	While the Great Depression was caused by many factors, some were more influential than others.
Strong	While many factors contributed to the Great Depression of the 1930s, the most damaging effects were widespread drought, bank failures, and the stock market crash.

The strong three-part thesis tells the reader that the paper will list and explain the impact of the interdependent causes and how they contributed to the Great Depression. It also answers a *how* or *why* question and promises the reader enough depth to consider the argument. As a bonus, it provides an outline for writing the paper!

The Minto Pyramid

The **Minto Pyramid** is a visual organizer used for structuring from the top down; it provides a framework of balanced support for each section. This strategy is often used in business writing to organize the three-part thesis. Depending on your purpose and argument, your pyramid may require more than three sections.

> **Learning Style Tip**
> For visual and active learners, the Minto pyramid is a great visual organizer to structure your paper. Construct a sticky note "triangle" on a door, window, or wall. Center your thesis at the top with your main argument sections (thesis parts) on separate notes in a row directly beneath the thesis. Write each quote you're considering on a separate sticky note and place it beneath the argument you believe it supports. You may move each sticky note several times before you arrive at a working order.

Balance Your Subheadings

If your paper is lengthy, you may want to consider using subheadings. Subheadings are visual clues signaling the reader that a new topic or section is beginning. They make it easy to review or relocate an especially interesting or provocative point.

Subheadings are most effective when they are short and consistent. Each subheading should highlight a section of special interest that relates to your thesis. A sentence-long subheading may be confusing and distracting.

Use Transitions

Make sure any transitions you use in the thesis statement signal appropriate shifts. **Transitions** are words, phrases, or clauses that show a relationship between ideas. If no causal relationship is being argued, words like *therefore* or *consequently* are not logical. Take a look at this example:

> The whale-watching tours provide a fun, unique experience for travelers of all ages. Therefore, the tour guides often have a marine science background.

> Using the signal word *therefore* in this example doesn't make sense. The unique experience of the whale-watching tours does not cause the tour guides to have a certain background. *First, second, additionally*, or *equally important* would be more logical.

To learn more about transitions, see Lesson 4.5.

Lesson Wrap-up

Key Terms

Argument: a reason why you should think or act a certain way

Audience: the person or people meant to read and interpret a text

Body Paragraphs: the paragraphs between the introduction and conclusion of an essay that use supporting details to explore, explain, and/or prove the main idea(s)

Complexity: an essential component of a thesis that depends on developing and supporting ideas or connections

Conclusion: a paragraph that ties together the ideas in a paper and summarizes the main points, also called a concluding paragraph

Descriptive Writing: writing that communicates the characteristics or qualities of a thing or event

Expository Writing: writing that uses evidence to support a main idea

Genre: a type of writing

Introduction: the paragraph used to introduce the main idea at the beginning of a paper, also called an introductory paragraph

Main Idea: the statement or argument that an author tries to communicate

Minto Pyramid: a graphic organizer used for structuring a three-part argument from the top down

Narrative Writing: writing that conveys events that happen during a defined period of time

Persuasive Writing: writing that uses argument to influence someone's beliefs and/or actions

Purpose: the goal of a text

Purpose Statement: a sentence that tells the audience exactly what points will be covered in a longer text

Thesis Statement: the concise sentence or group of sentences that expresses the main idea of a longer work

Transition: a word, phrase, or sentence that shows a relationship between ideas

Working Thesis: a thesis statement that is in progress and likely to change

Writing Application: Thesis and Purpose Statements

Read the following essay about *Beowulf* and note how the thesis statement is structured. How does the thesis statement act like a roadmap for the rest of the essay?

The Purpose of Monsters in Medieval Literature

If you've ever watched a bad horror film, you probably laughed at the irrational choices of the characters and at the chaos they created. However, in medieval Europe, chaos was no laughing matter. After the Roman Empire collapsed, cities were sacked and laws were unenforceable. As a fragile order began to re-emerge, citizens were wary of anarchy. Survival was a full-time job, violence was rampant, and fear was easy to leverage for control. Bards, who were the medieval equivalent of professional storytellers, created monsters and rampant beasts to instill a fear of chaos in medieval audiences. In *Beowulf,* the monster Grendel, Grendel's mother, and the dragon represent imminent threats to societal order when individuals succumb to isolation, vengefulness, and greed.

The three-part thesis statement is arguable, answers how and why questions, connects ideas, and addresses a relevant topic.

Early Anglo-Saxons valued order because it was essential for survival against the constant danger of Viking raids. According to John Earle, "mutual dependence was the law of human society" for the Anglo-Saxons (57). This is evident in their hierarchy of thanes serving a common liege, who in turn rewarded them with gold, rings, mead, and protection. The *comitatus,* or warrior band, shared an allegiance that bound them by honor to protect each other, their community, and their lord. This common unifying purpose held society together. It offered a sense of identity based on belonging to the community.

This sentence expands on societal order, which was mentioned in the thesis.

In the late 6th century, Christian missionaries arrived in England and began to record the Anglo-Saxon oral story of Beowulf, a warrior hero who leads the war band to defeat evil creatures. One of these evil creatures, Grendel, is the epitome of isolation and exile, opposing the Anglo-Saxon ideals of community and allegiance that gave them cohesion. "Grendel . . . made his home in a hell not hell but earth . . . shut away from men" (*Beowulf* 6). Grendel is shunned by a society that values order and connection, and as a result, he attacks the king's hall for the next twelve years. With no relationships or allegiance to a *comitatus*, he lacks identity and purpose. His vicious power enables him to tear down iron-bound doors with little effort (724-725). Grendel's overwhelming anger and jealousy are believed to be the result of his exile, reminding the Anglo-Saxons that self-destruction and chaos are imminent without close adhesion to the group. Grendel's attacks induce the thanes to run away, which brands them as cowards and erodes their own vows of allegiance to the lord. This is a clear reminder that an individual's isolation can have a monstrous influence, causing cowardice, anarchy, and a defenseless society.

This paragraph discusses the first part of the thesis: Grendel.

In this sentence, the reader connects the paragraph's focus back to the thesis.

A second monster, Grendel's mother, represents further erosive behaviors. When Beowulf kills her son, the mother comes to retrieve Grendel's arm, which Beowulf has kept as a trophy. Her attempts to avenge her son by killing a Danish warrior initiates another battle. This clearly cautions Anglo-Saxons against the urge to become vengeful because it leads to unnecessary violence and risks more lives. Critic Andy Orchard suggests that the monsters are "closely connected not simply by the family relationship . . . but by their cannibalistic acts and their shared dwelling" (92). Grendel's mother has been with him in exile, and while her desire for revenge may seem natural, cannibalism is the ultimate inhuman act. This suggests that a society bent on revenge risks consuming itself as a result.

This paragraph discusses the second part of the thesis: Grendel's mother.

In his final moments, Beowulf fights and kills a dragon, which ultimately leads to his own death. The dragon is guarding an underground treasure. This evil creature is believed to represent the dangers of greed. J.R.R. Tolkien believed that "the dragon is a contrast to Beowulf's heroic character, especially his generosity" (16). In Anglo-Saxon society, warriors were rewarded with gold and baubles for their service to their lord. The dragon's desperate hoarding of treasure (and fighting for it to the death) serves as a further caution for Anglo-Saxons, who valued their gold and other war prizes. Losing a valiant leader like Beowulf after a fight over gold suggests that wealth itself is not worth the risk. Additionally, it warns that even the strongest and best of men are vulnerable to this weakness. The Anglo-Saxons later bury the treasure with Beowulf's body as a further precaution against the divisive power of greed. "They let the ground keep that ancestral

Here, the author provides more support from an expert.

treasure, gold under gravel, gone to earth, as useless to men now as it
ever was" (*Beowulf* 3166-3168).

Each of Beowulf's opponents represent a palpable threat to
community, especially one as tenuous as that of the Anglo-Saxons.
Isolation, vengefulness, and greed are human weaknesses that may
corrupt anyone, triggering moral depravity and excesses that destroy
order in society from the inside out. Medieval bards and storytellers
wanted to remind their audiences of these human struggles. In stories
such as *Beowulf,* fantastical monsters were an effective way to
represent real dangers, stirring the fear of humans' self-destructive
potential and the chaos this might ultimately produce.

> The inclusion of this textual evidence balances the expert analysis.

> In this sentence, the writer paraphrases the thesis, reminding the reader of the essay's focus.

Lesson 4.4
Body Paragraphs

When you write, you want to provide your readers with information to help them understand your
purpose. After you present your **thesis statement** in an **introduction**, you then have to consistently
support and develop your **main idea** throughout your writing. Writers do this in their body paragraphs. A
body paragraph contains the main points of a paper and uses supporting details.

> To learn more about thesis statements, see Lesson 4.3.

Read the following example of a body paragraph:

> Evan had heard the shouts and the sound of breaking glass, but it wasn't until the next morning
> that he learned what had happened. Miranda, as revealed by a distinctive stiletto shoeprint, had
> climbed the fence by the toolshed shortly after midnight and made her way across the lawn. She
> must have only made it part of the way before the sprinkler system turned on, catching her off-
> guard. Her cry of surprise alerted James, who rushed outside without his glasses, wielding a
> baseball bat and shouting incoherently at the suspected intruder. It was he who broke the kitchen
> window, mistaking a small, crooked tree for a man with a knife. After that, all was quiet. James
> had checked on Miranda before he went to bed. She was sleeping peacefully in her room, but a
> soaked evening gown, a pair of muddy heels, and some clumsy smudges on her windowpane
> provided more evidence that she was the culprit. Half-embarrassed, half-enraged, James
> recounted this story to Evan and fumed over his coffee, waiting for his daughter to wake up.

While this paragraph describes a particular event, you can tell that it's not the beginning or the end of this
particular story. You probably have a number of questions after reading the passage:

- Who is Evan?
- Why was Miranda sneaking across the lawn at midnight?
- What is going to happen to Miranda when she wakes up?

The details included in this part of the story are presented in a way that helps the reader understand some
key information. The information is organized, specific, and uses transitions that illustrate the
connections between ideas.

In this lesson, you will learn the steps of creating strong body paragraphs:

Organize the Components
Select Content
Create Strong Transitions

Organize the Components

Typically, body paragraphs include the following parts:

- A **topic sentence** that establishes the main idea of the paragraph
- **Supporting details**, also called evidence, that are used to support a main idea
- A **concluding sentence** that sums up the paragraph, serves as a transition to the next paragraph, and/or connects the main idea of the paragraph to the thesis

---

Helpful Hint

When you read, you'll likely encounter body paragraphs that don't seem to have clear topic sentences or that establish the purpose of the paragraph later in the essay. These can be effective strategies. However, if you're new to writing body paragraphs, putting the topic sentence first can help you ensure that the paragraph's focus is clear.

On Your Own

Read the following paragraph and identify the sentences that provide supporting details.

> While making a loaf of homemade bread can be time-consuming or complicated, the right tool can simplify the process for home bakers. A bread machine fully automates bread-making. Once you add the ingredients in the amounts and order specified by the manufacturer, the bread machine will mix and knead the dough. Then, it will allow the dough to rise at an ideal temperature and even bake the loaf. This entire process can take as little as an hour. Alternatively, some recipes require almost no preparation time. For so-called "no-knead" bread, a few ingredients— flour, water, salt, and yeast—are stirred together with a spoon or mixer and allowed to slowly rise over several hours or even a couple of days before it is baked. This results in a crusty, rustic loaf. Both of these methods provide great options for new or experienced cooks who are interested in making fresh bread on a regular basis.

Helpful Hint

Keep in mind that you should choose an **organizational pattern** for your supporting details that allows you to present your ideas as clearly as possible. In **narrative writing**, for example, the supporting details might be listed in **chronological order** (the order in which they happened). In other paragraphs, you might choose another organizational pattern for your details, such as **order of importance** (ranging from least to most or most to least important) or **compare and contrast** (highlighting similarities or differences between subjects).

To learn more about organizational patterns, see Lesson 5.3.

You may notice that a body paragraph has a similar structure to an essay: the topic sentence is like the introduction to the paragraph because it establishes the main idea. The supporting details are like the body of the essay: they provide evidence and context to support the main purpose. The concluding sentence is like a **conclusion**: it ties the ideas together but also prepares or challenges the reader to think about what comes next.

Writing Environment: Professional

When potential employers look at application materials, they read cover letters and résumés quickly. Organizing each paragraph of a cover letter as clearly as possible will make it easier for an employer to learn about you and your skills in just a few seconds. Take a look at the following versions of the same paragraph. Which is easier to read? Why?

Version 1

> My professional experiences have prepared me for a career with Pup Patrol Dog Walkers. Most recently, I have worked as a certified trainer for dogs of all sizes and ages with Pets 'N' More. In this position, I assessed and addressed the individual needs of up to twelve dogs in a single class, using positive reinforcement to encourage healthy relationships between dogs and their owners. Additionally, I have owned and operated Go Dog Go, an award-winning private dog-walking business, since 2010. My work with dogs is rooted in my deep love and respect for them. While I am equally comfortable working with a single dog or a whole pack, I make it a point to get to know each dog's needs, preferences, and personality. This allows me to ensure that all of my clients receive optimal care.

Version 2

> My work with dogs is rooted in my deep love and respect for them. Additionally, I have owned and operated Go Dog Go, an award-winning private dog-walking business, since 2010. Most recently, I have worked as a certified trainer for dogs of all sizes and ages with Pets 'N' More. While I am equally comfortable working with a single dog or a whole pack, I make it a point to get to know each dog's needs, preferences, and personality. In this position, I have had to assess and address the individual needs of as many as twelve dogs in a single class, using positive reinforcement to encourage healthy relationships between dogs and their owners. Consequently, individualized care is a hallmark of my professional philosophy.

You've probably determined that Version 1 is much easier to read than Version 2 because it follows the typical organization for a body paragraph: a topic sentence, followed by supporting details, followed by a concluding sentence that reinforces the main point of the paragraph.

Select Content

One of the biggest challenges of writing a body paragraph can be choosing which information to include.

First, you need to determine the purpose of the paragraph. To do this, ask yourself the following questions:

> What is the main point I want to make in this paragraph?
>
> Is the scope of this main point too broad or too narrow?
>
> Do I have sufficient details to support this main point?
>
> How will this paragraph support and develop my thesis?

As you determine your main idea, you might find it helpful to map out the two parts of your topic sentence: the **topic**, or the subject of your paragraph, and the **controlling idea**, which focuses and guides how you will write about your subject. Just as a thesis statement provides a framework for an entire essay, a topic sentence provides a framework for a paragraph. Once you have a topic sentence, you can evaluate information to determine whether or not it belongs in the paragraph.

Look at the following brief outline of a review of a Mediterranean cruise.

1. Introduction

    a. Thesis: A Mediterranean cruise to Athens, Santorini, and Rhodes is a worthwhile experience because it is a great way to experience diverse historical sites and cultures.

2. Body Paragraph #1: Athens

3. Body Paragraph #2: Santorini

4. Body Paragraph #3: Rhodes

5. Conclusion

The thesis in this outline establishes a clear focus for this essay: the places typically visited on a Mediterranean cruise. The topic of each paragraph is apparent, and each one will describe or review a particular port commonly visited on the cruise. However, without a controlling idea, it might be hard for the author to determine exactly what she wants to say about each port.

To narrow the scope and identify the purpose of the second body paragraph, the author might add the following controlling idea:

> Santorini: as beautiful as it is in pictures but even more exciting to visit.

A controlling idea gives each body paragraph a clear focus.

Once you have determined your main idea, you can begin selecting the supporting details that belong in your paragraph. Remember that your supporting details should clearly relate to and develop the controlling idea introduced in the topic sentence.

Group Activity

As a group, choose a topic from the following list:

- Roller coasters
- Flying on planes
- Horror movies
- Mountain climbing
- Deep sea diving

Individually, write a sentence that establishes how you personally feel about the topic your group has chosen. Then, create a list of reasons (or controlling ideas) for why you feel this way about the topic. Share and compare your list with your group members. Consider the following questions:

- How did your controlling ideas differ?
- How would the ideas influence the details in a paragraph about the topic?

The types of details you include in a body paragraph will vary depending on the **genre** of your writing. Here are some examples:

- A narrative paragraph will likely include details pertaining to one particular event or part of an event.
- A compare and contrast paragraph will likely present similarities or differences between two subjects.
- A **persuasive** paragraph might present facts, examples, or professional opinions.

On Your Own

Read the following topic sentence.

> The Greek island of Santorini is as beautiful as it is in pictures but even more exciting to visit.

Review the following list of supporting details and identify the ones you think should be included in a paragraph that has this topic sentence.

> To get from the cruise ship to the island, visitors have the option of taking a gondola ride with soaring views, a rustic mule ride, or a rugged switchback hike up the side of an extinct volcano.

> The gondola ride is terrifying because it feels like the cable could snap at any moment.

> At the top of the cliff, the bustling port town of Skala boasts numerous shops and restaurants.

> Skala is really crowded and feels like a tourist trap.

> For an afternoon of sand and surf, travel to one of Santorini's famous red or black sand beaches.

To experience Santorini at its very finest, travel by bus to Oia, the famous blue and white town built high above the sea, where you can enjoy *al fresco* dining overlooking the rooftops, meet local artisans, and experience a typical day on the island.

Helpful Hint

If you find that you have a lot of information in your essay, it's okay to break that information into multiple paragraphs. Look for shifts in the kinds of information you're presenting; often these breaks occur naturally. If you have a hard time identifying the shifts between ideas, try reading your paragraph out loud to yourself or a friend.

Writing Environment: Everyday

We often have to make decisions about which details we should or shouldn't include when we speak or write. Consider the following situations:

You're asking a family member to pick you up at the airport. What details do you need to give them?

You are late for an appointment. How might you explain your lateness if you overslept or had car trouble?

Create Strong Transitions

Once you've selected and organized the information you're including in a body paragraph, you might think you're done. However, within and between paragraphs, you also need to illustrate connections between ideas. This can be done with **transitions**, which are words, phrases, or sentences that show a relationship between ideas.

Take a look at the following example that uses good transitions:

To avoid additional pre-race stress, you can take several steps to prepare the night before your first marathon. First, lay out your race outfit. Knowing exactly what you'll wear—from your hat to your shoes—can give you peace of mind, allowing you to rest easier and preventing indecision on the morning of the race. Second, make sure that your race bib and timing chip are attached to your shirt and, when applicable, your shoe. Third, pack a bag with all of the items you plan to take with you to the race. Fourth, plan and prepare your breakfast, even if it just involves putting a banana and a granola bar on the counter. Finally, hydrate well and go to bed as early as possible so that you feel refreshed when you wake up. These evening preparations will help you feel in control, relaxed, and confident as you head to the starting line.

Note that the topic sentence of this paragraph establishes that it will review a process: the steps a runner can take the night before a marathon. Consequently, the transitions—*first, second, third, fourth,* and *finally*—highlight the order of ideas throughout the paragraph.

Let's look at an effective follow-up paragraph. Note how the topic sentence here also serves as a transition from the previous paragraph.

Although it may be harder to manage your anxiety the next morning, the following strategies can keep you feeling excited for your race. Wake up early so that you have plenty of time to eat and get dressed before you go to the race location. Give yourself extra time for travel in case you run into delays. Warm up for the race with a light jog or stretching as well as some deep breathing. If you're running alone, recruit a friend or family member to go with you to the race so that you don't have to wait by yourself for the race to begin.

The highlighted sentence creates an effective transition between the two paragraphs. The phrase *the next morning* reminds the reader that the previous paragraph discussed the night before a race, and the phrase *the following strategies* reminds readers that they are still learning about ways to prepare for a marathon.

Writing Environment: Academic

Transitions appear in writing from all kinds of disciplines. Take a look at the following passage from a biology textbook. What words and phrases in the passage show how each idea builds on the one that comes before it?

"Organisms are highly organized structures that consist of one or more cells. Even very simple, single-celled organisms are remarkably complex. Inside each cell, atoms make up molecules. These in turn make up cell components. Multicellular organisms, which may consist of millions of individual cells, have an advantage over single-celled organisms in that their cells can be specialized to perform specific functions and even sacrificed in certain situations for the good of the organism as a whole. How these specialized cells come together to form organs such as the heart, lung, or skin in organisms ... will be discussed later."

Adapted from: Openstax. *Concepts of Biology.* Openstax CNX. March 22, 2016.
http://cnx.org/contents/b3c1e1d2-839c-42b0-a314-e119a8aafbdd@9.6.]

To learn more about transitions, see Lesson 4.5.

Lesson Wrap-up

Key Terms

Body Paragraphs: the paragraphs between the introduction and conclusion of an essay that use supporting details to explore, explain, and/or prove the main idea(s)

Chronological Order: an organizational pattern that arranges ideas or events in the order that they occur (also known as sequential order)

Compare and Contrast: an organizational pattern used to show the similarities and differences between two topics

Concluding Sentence: a sentence that ends a paragraph by reviewing the ideas just discussed

Conclusion: a paragraph that ties together the ideas in a paper and summarizes the main points, also called a concluding paragraph

Controlling Idea: an idea that focuses and guides what an author wants to say about a topic

Genre: a type of writing

Introduction: the paragraph used to introduce the main idea at the beginning of a paper, also called an introductory paragraph

Main Idea: the statement or argument that an author tries to communicate

Narrative Writing: writing that conveys events that happen during a defined period of time

Order of Importance: an organizational pattern that arranges ideas from least to most significant, or vice versa

Organizational Pattern: the structure of a written text, used to arrange the main points of a work

Persuasive Writing: writing that uses argument to influence someone's beliefs and/or actions

Purpose: the goal of a text

Spatial Order: an organizational pattern used to describe a subject's physical characteristics, usually from top to bottom, left to right, or front to back

Supporting Detail: a piece of information, also called evidence, that is used to support a main idea

Thesis Statement: the concise sentence or group of sentences that expresses the main idea of a longer work

Topic: the general subject of a text

Topic Sentence: a sentence that states the main point of a paragraph

Transition: a word, phrase, or sentence that shows a relationship between ideas

Writing Application: Body Paragraphs

Read the following essay and pay close attention to the body paragraphs. How do they use supporting details, and how is each paragraph structured?

The Mediterranean: Luxury and History

For travelers planning the trip of a lifetime, it can be hard to choose the perfect vacation. Some destinations promise relaxation and amenities while others guarantee cultural immersion. A Mediterranean cruise offers a combination of these experiences: it provides luxury accommodations on a ship that travels to a different site almost every day. Each port gives visitors an opportunity to experience a unique, beautiful, and historic location.

The thesis alerts the reader that the essay will describe diverse Mediterranean cruise ports.

A common stop on many Mediterranean cruises is the city of Athens, a modern metropolis abundant with striking monuments from ancient civilizations. The city is just a short metro or taxi ride from the port of Piraeus. History lovers can spend a morning exploring the Acropolis, which includes the ruins of the Parthenon and the theatre of Dionysus; visitors can also enjoy breathtaking panoramic views of the city and surrounding countryside. At the foot of the monument, local shops and restaurants stand just outside the ancient agora, or marketplace, which travelers can explore on foot. Perhaps more than in any other Mediterranean port, past and present are visibly and inseparably intertwined in Athens.

This topic sentence includes a topic, Athens, and a controlling idea about that topic.

The details in this paragraph support the controlling idea that Athens is both modern and full of history.

Another common cruise port is the Greek island of Santorini, which is as beautiful as it is in pictures but even more exciting to visit. To get from the cruise ship to the island, visitors have the option of taking a gondola ride with soaring views, a rustic mule ride, or a rugged switchback hike up the side of an extinct volcano. At the top of the

*The details of this paragraph are organized using **spatial** organization, moving from what visitors first see when they leave the cruise ship to the town on the far side of the island.*

cliff, the port town of Skala boasts numerous shops and restaurants. For an afternoon of sand and surf, guests can travel to one of Santorini's famous red or black sand beaches. To experience Santorini at its very finest, visitors can travel by bus to Oia, the famous blue and white town built high above the sea, where they can enjoy *al fresco* dining overlooking the rooftops, meet local artisans, and experience a typical day on the island.

If Santorini is striking because of its beauty, Rhodes is striking because of its diverse architecture and rich history. The stone-cobbled Street of the Knights leads to the impressive Palace of the Grandmaster, a huge medieval castle. Elsewhere on the island, excavation sites feature ruins from ancient civilizations. While the famous bronze Colossus of Rhodes—one of the seven wonders of the ancient world—no longer stands astride the island's harbor, Rhodes continues to boast many marvelous examples of the diverse populations that have inhabited the island since the Stone Age.

This sentence uses a point of contrast to create a transition from the previous paragraph.

Mykonos, Crete, Sicily, Rome, Venice, the list of incredible places tourists can visit in a single Mediterranean cruise goes on. Each port promises a new cultural experience; each night aboard the ship ensures fine dining, nightlife, and a new destination in the morning. A Mediterranean cruise just might be the perfect vacation for the adventurous traveler.

The first two sentences of the conclusion restate the essay's purpose and support the idea that a Mediterranean cruise combines culture and luxury.

Lesson 4.5
Transitions

If you've ever been kayaking or white-water rafting, you know about following the current. You see the turns ahead and work with the natural course of the water to maneuver your raft. Paying attention to the river's flow is important if you want to avoid running ashore or getting stuck.

Transitions prevent your writing from running aground.

The same concept of flow also applies to your writing. If your instructor says that your writing didn't flow well or that your changes were abrupt or hard to follow, your transitions probably need work.

> In this lesson, you will learn about transitions:
>
> Using Transitions in Various Writing Situations
> Transitions for Different Organizational Patterns
> Commonly Confused Transitions

Using Transitions in Various Writing Situations

Clues in a text help readers know when to shift their focus from one idea to the next. These clues are called transitions. **Transitions** are words, phrases, or sentences that show a relationship between ideas.

Sometimes, transition words are called "signpost" words because they guide the reader through the text like road signs guide drivers.

Sentence Transitions

As you develop your writing, you will often build upon your ideas. Transitions help you to build these connections smoothly among sentences.

Often, transitions have a direct connection to a text's **organizational pattern**. The next section will explore these patterns in more detail.

On Your Own

In the following table, create two simple sentences and use the provided transition word or phrase to connect them.

Transition	Sentences
Later	
As a result	
On the other hand	
Meanwhile	
However	

Paragraph Transitions

Similar to sentence transitions, paragraph transitions connect key points. For example, in a five-paragraph essay, a signpost phrase or sentence should appear at the beginning of each paragraph to link it with the information in the previous paragraph. Sometimes, it's also effective to include a transition at the end of a long paragraph for extra emphasis.

In the following example, the highlighted transitions at the beginning and end of the paragraph give clues about the order of events.

> Initially, Hitler was admired as a charismatic leader. He restored belief in German values and unified the people under a renewed sense of national pride. Losses after World War I had been devastating, and the country needed a confidence boost. Hitler rewarded the working class with tax breaks and state-supported benefits. He promised prosperity and provided perks for military men and their families. The honeymoon phase didn't last, however.
> By 1936, restrictive Gestapo Law began to hint at inequitable treatment.
>
> Given these transition phrases, you can expect the rest of this paper to proceed chronologically. The last sentence of the first paragraph indicates that a change is coming up.

Helpful Hint

When you use chronological order to discuss a series of events, try to avoid transitions like *first*, *second*, and *third*. These transitions indicate a list of points and are better suited to a procedural or "how-to" writing task.

Transitions may also appear *within* paragraphs for the following purposes:

- To shift from one supporting detail to the next:

   "Dr. Connor's argument is further reinforced by the results of this recent study from…"

- To draw contrasts between what is and what might be:

   "Although current monthly growth is estimated at 15%, we can improve this by…"

- To elaborate upon supporting details:

  "In fact, these statistics are confirmed in a similar scenario…"

- To introduce support sources:

  "One nationally renowned expert indicates…"

- To acknowledge opposition:

  "Some may suggest these statistics are skewed, but…"

Group Activity

With your group, brainstorm three **topics** for a research paper arranged in chronological order. What events might be included in each topic, and how would you introduce each event? Choose strong transition words to generate a **topic sentence** for each paragraph.

Introduction and First Body Paragraph

Often, the **introduction** of an essay is useful for summing up facts or background information. For example, if you're writing a literary analysis, you might summarize the author's background or cultural influences on the work. For a history course, you might describe a political scenario or establish some key facts about people involved.

Once you've accomplished your goals for the introduction, consider how to use a transition to segue into your first **body paragraph**. Here are some common transitions for this purpose:

As we all know	Given that	Undeniably
Clearly	In light of the facts	You may be aware
For most of us	Obviously	You may remember

Conclusion

Conclusions indicate finality and use **evidence** from the body paragraphs to reassert the author's authority. The following transitions can begin a conclusion.

All in all	For the most part	It should be clear that
As we have seen	In conclusion	Obviously
As you can see	In general	The facts indicate
Clearly	In the final analysis	Therefore
Finally	It's evident that	To sum up

Acknowledging the Opposition

It can be effective to acknowledge points of view that oppose your own. This is called **counterargument**, which means anticipating an opposing perspective and refuting it. This is another scenario when effective transitions are important.

Here are some words and phrases that you can use to transition into acknowledging opposing perspectives.

Although	In contrast	There is room for dispute
At the same time	On the contrary	Whereas
Conversely	On the other hand	While some will argue that
However	Some might believe	While this is true

Take a look at this example that uses transitions to introduce an opposing perspective to the author's **argument**:

> Originally, GMO foods were engineered to produce higher-yield crops with more resistance to insects and disease, reducing the need for insecticides and other environmental hazards. In recent years, however, it has become clear that many GMO foods are unnatural and may contribute to health problems including cancer and obesity. These concerns have made it necessary to require warning labels on GMO products.
>
> While some will argue that we don't have sufficient evidence of a connection between GMO products and cancer, most of us agree that the possibility is enough to warrant labeling. Why risk poisoning ourselves with unnatural food?
>
> In this sample, the author includes the opposition's viewpoint to demonstrate his or her awareness of the argument. Then, the author dismisses the argument as invalid.

Using Evidence

Supporting details, or evidence, should also be announced with transitions. You shouldn't include evidence and assume that the audience knows how it connects to your other ideas.

The following transitions will help you connect your argument to supporting details from other sources.

According to (name)	A renowned theorist suggests	One critic claims
A noted professor, (name), indicates	Data suggests that	Scholars contend that
A recent study concluded	Leading authorities agree	Some experts insist

---

Helpful Hint

When introducing a **quote**, transitions help you explain the quote instead of leaving it isolated. As an author, you need to make the significance of the quotation clear to your audience.

Transitions for Different Organizational Patterns

While it's important to understand when to use transitions, you also want to be aware of how different organizational patterns can dictate appropriate types of transitions. Let's review some suggestions for using transitions with common organizational patterns.

Cause and Effect

For writing organized by **cause and effect**, you're probably arguing one of the following points:

- one event led to or caused another event
- an individual was responsible for an event or series of events
- a group of events or actions produced a particular result

Here are some transitions that emphasize *cause.*

Because of	If ... then	Since
Due to	Owing to	Thanks to

These transitions emphasize *effect*:

Accordingly	For this reason	So
As a result	Hence	Therefore
As expected	Inevitably	Thus
Consequently	Not surprisingly	Understandably

Writing Environment: Professional

In business, it's essential to find ways to cut costs and improve profitability for your company or your clients. Financial analysis examines profits and losses over a period of time. A cause and effect organizational pattern is ideal for financial analysis to demonstrate a connection between strategic spending and returns on investment.

On Your Own

Read the passage below, looking for the four cause and effect transitions. Once you've located them, write them in the table.

> Because of falling commodity prices, we are seeing a stock market slump. Due to the extended price drop in oil, natural gas, and copper, this may also indicate surplus supply and lowered demand. If key U.S. companies don't reach growth expectations, then the global economy will slow down as well. Consequently, many investment experts are expecting a recession.

Order of Importance

Here are some examples of effective transition words and phrases to establish the most important point in writing organized by **order of importance**.

A primary factor	Most importantly	The best evidence of this
As expected	Most notably	The chief reason
Certainly	Most significantly	The key reason

The following transitions could be used to discuss points that are less important:

Additionally	A secondary reason	It may help to consider
An additional reason	Equally important	No less important
A secondary concern	Furthermore	On a related note

> Helpful Hint
>
> Remember, when using the order of importance pattern, you may use a "top-down" method to rank items from most important to least important. However, if you want to build your argument's intensity, save the most important point for last.

Chronological Order

When your writing is organized **chronologically**, your transitions should reflect this order. Here are some chronological transition words and phrases for your first body paragraph:

At the beginning	It started with	Suddenly
Early in [date]	On Sunday	To begin with
Initially	Originally	The inciting incident
In the first place	Starting with	The trigger event

Use the following transitions for the rest of your paragraphs:

Afterward	Later	Not long after
At this point	Meanwhile	Over time
Equally	Moreover	Previously
Eventually	Moving forward	Subsequently
In the meantime	Next	While

> **Group Activity**
> Make a list of five topics that could use a chronological organizational pattern.

Sequential transitions, though similar to chronological transitions, are recommended for listing steps in a process or items in a list. Here are some examples of sequential transitions.

Finally	Last but not least	Second
First	Meanwhile	Then
In sequence	Next	Third
Last	Previously	To finish

Spatial

Spatial order is a less common organizational pattern in academic writing, but it's helpful for giving directions, assigning seats for an event, or describing a product, building, or landscape. The following transitions indicate a spatial pattern.

Above	Close by	Nearby
Adjacent to	Inside	Over
Below	In front	Throughout
Beside	In the distance	To the far right
Beyond	Midway through	To the side

Spatial transitions are common in travelogues, tour manuals, real estate listings, and descriptions of a work of art. In creative writing, spatial order develops the setting. Take a look at the example below.

> Beyond Audubon Park, in the heart of the Garden district, stands a crumbling two story Greek Revival-style house. In front is a long portico with a rusty old porch swing and a view of the river. Nearby is a majestic grove of old-growth oak trees. Midway through the house is an open courtyard with a moss-covered fountain.

Compare and Contrast

Compare and contrast is a pattern that is used to discuss similarities and/or differences between ideas. Here are transitions that indicate *comparison*:

By the same token	In the same fashion	Likewise
In a like manner	In this way	Similarly

Here are some transitions that indicate *contrast*:

But	In contrast	On the other hand
Conversely	Instead	Otherwise
However	Nevertheless	Whereas

On Your Own

Imagine you are writing an article about each of the following topics. For each topic, choose the best organizational pattern and transitions and write them in the space provided.

Topics	Organizational Pattern and Transitions
Magazine article about three fashion labels at three different price points	
Five major battles of the Vietnam War	
Accomplishments of the Lincoln administration	
Strategy to generate sales leads	
Ground plan for a new concert venue	

Commonly Confused Transitions

Transitions serve distinct purposes, but it's a common mistake to misuse them. Using the wrong transition can interrupt the flow of your argument, confuse your audience, and even change the meaning of your statement.

Consistency is Key

To indicate a progression, transitions throughout your writing must "match" each other. For instance, if you begin your first body paragraph with *most significantly*, your second paragraph should begin with a transition like *also important to consider* or *in addition*.

No matter which organizational pattern you use, your transitions should reflect that order consistently throughout your writing. Otherwise, your signposts will contradict each other.

The following transitions are frequently misused and misunderstood. Using these transitions incorrectly can create the impression that you don't understand the information you're presenting.

If they're not used carefully, transitions can confuse readers instead of guiding them.

Although and *However*

Both *although* and *however* indicate contrast. *However* is a synonym for *but* and can stand alone (followed by a comma). *Although* means "in spite of the fact," and it must be attached to a longer phrase. It should *not* be followed by a comma. For examples of correct use, take a look at the following sentences:

> Many politicians are corrupt. However, some are sincere and well-intentioned.

> Although Louisa Adams, the wife of John Quincy Adams, was frequently ill, she was also surprisingly resilient.

Consequently and *Subsequently*

Consequently means "as a result," so it should only be used if the information is truly a consequence or result of something. *Subsequently* simply indicates that an event happens next, not necessarily as a result of what came before. The examples below use these words correctly.

> The Department of Transportation was re-paving the main highway. Consequently, rush-hour traffic was even worse than usual.

> The Civil War was fought in the United States in the 1860s, and the Boer War was fought in Africa in the 1890s. Subsequently, World War I was fought in Europe in the early 1900s.

Helpful Hint

When referring to your support sources, it's usually inaccurate to use the transition *this proves* unless you have concrete, definitive evidence. It's often more accurate to say *this indicates*, *this suggests*, or *this aligns with*.

On Your Own

Read the following sentences and identify the transition that is used incorrectly.

> Last night's football game was especially tense. The opposition's defense was very strong, although we managed to outscore them. Subsequently, our coach took us out to celebrate!

Lesson Wrap-up

Key Terms

Argument: a reason why you should think or act a certain way

Body Paragraphs: the paragraphs between the introduction and conclusion of an essay that use supporting details to explore, explain, and/or prove the main idea(s)

Cause and Effect: an organizational pattern used to explore events, decisions, or situations and their consequences

Chronological Order: an organizational pattern that arranges ideas or events in the order that they occur (also known as sequential order)

Compare and Contrast: an organizational pattern that discusses similarities and differences between multiple topics

Conclusion: a paragraph that ties together the ideas in a paper and summarizes the main points, also called a concluding paragraph

Counterargument: anticipating objections and refuting them with logic supported by evidence

Evidence: a piece of information, also called a supporting detail, that is used to support a main idea

Introduction: the paragraph used to introduce the main idea at the beginning of a paper, also called an introductory paragraph

Order of Importance: an organizational pattern that arranges ideas from least to most significant, or vice versa

Organizational Pattern: the structure of a written text, used to arrange the main points of a work

Quote: someone's exact words

Sequential Order: an organizational pattern that arranges ideas or events in the order that they occur (also known as chronological order)

Spatial Order: an organizational pattern used to describe a subject's physical characteristics, usually from top to bottom, left to right, or front to back

Supporting Detail: a piece of information, also called evidence, that is used to support a main idea

Topic: the general subject of a text

Topic Sentence: a sentence that states the main point of a paragraph

Transition: a word, phrase, or sentence that shows a relationship between ideas

Writing Application: Transitions

Consider the transitions in the following essay. Do they make sense for the organizational pattern? Do they "match" each other and make the writing flow from one idea to another?

Hospital or Home?

In the next fifteen years, 20% of Americans will be over the age of sixty-five as Baby Boomers become senior citizens with special care needs. Many of these senior citizens and their families will rely on medical facilities to provide this care. However, hospitals and nursing facilities operate in a flawed system. Most healthcare providers don't have the time, resources, or opportunities to acquaint themselves with each patient in the ways that would be most meaningful and conducive to recovery. Acknowledging and respecting individuality, privacy, and personal space are pivotal facets of healing. In this regard, home-based health services can offer what hospitals cannot: personalized patient convenience, comfort, and affordability.

> The thesis statement indicates that this paper will compare and contrast hospitals with home-based health services based on three factors: convenience, comfort, and affordability.

Most agree that hospitals can be sterile and detached. Many patients struggle to adapt to the scent of industrial antiseptic, the glare of fluorescent lights, and the buzz of noisy equipment. Medical research says that healing depends on rest and sleep, but ironically, many hospitalized patients don't sleep well in such a stark and stressful environment.

> This sentence uses the transition *most agree that* to establish common knowledge.

One cause for patients' insomnia may be the cost of hospitalization. A survey published in Becker's Hospital Review estimates the national average cost for *one day* in a public hospital is $1,878 (1).

Further patient stress stems from the fact that hospitals are often a breeding ground for health care-associated infections (HAIs), including staph infections and other diseases. A recent study from the Centers for Disease Control (CDC) indicates that "in 2011 alone, there were roughly 722,000 cases of HAIs in U.S. hospitals, and about 75,000 of those patients died during hospitalization" (2). While elderly patients may be hospitalized for a simple treatment, they often develop a more serious condition as a result of unsterile equipment or airborne viruses.

> The next three paragraphs are organized by order of importance, which is indicated by transitions like *one, further,* and *perhaps most prevalent.*

Perhaps most prevalent is the senior patient's vulnerability to emotional and psychological stress. Depression is often a side effect of medication, reduced mobility, feelings of isolation, or a lack of purpose. According to one study, rates for depression among the elderly "rise dramatically with the loss of independence. Fourteen percent of those receiving home care have depression, whereas twenty-nine to fifty-two percent of elderly people living in nursing homes suffer from depression" (3).

Conversely, home health care plans are highly adaptable to the patient's individual needs and preferences. For seniors who don't require around-the-clock medical care, intermittent treatment in the comfort of a familiar space is infinitely more convenient. Home health care plans are highly adaptable to the patient's individual needs and preferences.

Conversely shows a contrast is coming; we can expect to learn the benefits of home health care after reading about the flaws of hospital care.

Even more comforting is the familiarity of personal space. Many seniors have spent their adult lives buying or building a home. Being relegated to a nursing home or assisted care facility is disruptive and often triggers depression and despondency. For patients with life-threatening illnesses, home care options are overwhelmingly preferred. As a matter of fact, the National Hospice and Palliative Care Organization claims, "Ninety percent of Americans prefer to spend their final time at home. If they don't express this, however, they are more likely to die in a facility instead" (4).

Best of all, Medicare and private insurance plans cover most medical services, including skilled nursing services; physical, occupational, or speech therapists; medication; medical equipment; and supplies. As an added perk, doctor recommendations may include the services of a home health aide. These services are not always covered by Medicare but are usually available at the rate of $10-20 per hour. Companionship and conversation provide opportunities for the elderly patient to enjoy personalized interaction.

To parallel the previous three paragraphs about hospitals, the paragraphs about home health services also use order of importance.

Home-based care is a far more attractive choice than hospitalization because it allows more comfort for many senior patients. The familiar environment of a home may speed the healing process and trim costs. Also, those facing terminal illness often prefer to be at home. Honoring their wishes to remain at home allows patients peace and dignity. There's no need for anyone to endure the displacement that can result from hospitalization. Home health care allows affordable, personal choices and respect for elderly patients as individuals.

The final sentences sum up and restate the thesis.

Lesson 4.6
The Conclusion

As you finish an essay, you may feel like you've been on a journey. Step by step, you have put words, sentences, and paragraphs together to explore a topic. Just like a literal journey, writing a strong essay also involves considering the destination: the conclusion.

> *"The Road goes ever on and on*
> *Down from the door where it began.*
> *Now far ahead the Road has gone,*
> *And I must follow, if I can."*
> *J.R.R. Tolkien*

Once you've drafted all other components of your essay, it's time to finish the journey and conclude your writing. There's no single way to conclude properly, but this lesson explores some useful approaches for doing so.

In writing, conclusions signal the end of the journey.

In this lesson, you will learn about the following aspects of the conclusion:

A Conclusion's Place in the Writing Process
Conclusion Strategies

A Conclusion's Place in the Writing Process

Writing a strong essay requires a lot of time and effort. Your conclusion should reflect that work just as much as the rest of the essay. The **conclusion** is the final paragraph of an essay that restates the main point and reviews the key arguments, ideas, reasons, and/or elements of the **body paragraphs**.

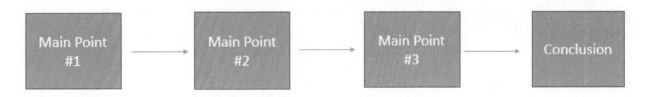

Of course, the first purpose of a conclusion is to tell the reader that the essay is complete. However, a conclusion should also leave the reader with a single clear idea or argument.

Before concluding your essay, be sure you've developed it adequately and that, given what you've written so far, it's ready to end. If not, you may need to return to the **drafting** or **revision** stages.

Test your work by answering the following questions and proceeding accordingly:

Question	If the answer is "no" or you're uncertain . . .	If the answer is "yes" . . .
Is my **thesis** adequately supported with **evidence**?	Return to your essay and revise it until you can reasonably say that readers would be thoroughly informed and convinced.	If you feel you have no new **supporting details** to share, you've clearly argued your **claim**, and you've anticipated opposing viewpoints, you're ready to wrap up the essay.
What do I want my reader to be thinking or feeling at this point?	If you or your reader are confused, or if you're unsure what the reader would be thinking at this point in the essay, then it's likely you need to do more revision.	If you can confidently say that your readers have followed your reasoning clearly, then they will be wondering about the essay's takeaway. Remember to address it in your conclusion.
What matters most to my reader?	If you haven't tried to make your readers care about your message, then you probably need to revise. If your **audience** doesn't know why your **topic** is important, they're not going to care much about the conclusion.	If your **main idea** is clear and you've convinced your reader that your topic and thesis are relevant and important, then you're ready to conclude.

Effective writing leaves your audience with a strong, provocative thought that they may not have considered before. As you read over your essay, ask yourself the following questions:

> Can I empathize with my readers and see the essay through their eyes?
>
> Can I pinpoint the single most important thing I want readers to know
>
> after reading my essay?
>
> Is there a powerful story or fact that will effectively end the essay?

If you can answer these questions with positive, developed responses, you're prepared to create a conclusion that brings an adequate sense of closure to your claim or argument. This may mean re-summarizing your thesis and supporting details. It may mean leaving the reader with a single, lasting image, detail, or piece of data. Regardless, consider something that has the power stay with a reader.

Helpful Hint

Your approach to the ending should make sense to the reader and be consistent with the **genre**. For some essays, this may call for a summary paragraph. However, don't be afraid to choose a more creative route.

Group Activity

Tell a partner a story about something that happened to you today. As you tell your story, consider how you can use a focused idea to create the conclusion, and try to leave your listener with a meaningful idea or thought.

Conclusion Strategies

Once you've determined that you're ready to draft your conclusion, consider how to approach this important task. Depending on the **purpose**, audience, and genre of your writing, you may choose different paths for your conclusion.

> **Helpful Hint**
>
> If you're feeling exhausted from writing your paper, come back to the conclusion later. Avoid throwing something together just for the sake of being done. Instead, take a break or write it the next day. However, when you do sit down to draft the conclusion, read over the entire essay so your main points are fresh in your mind.

Much like an **introduction**, you want the conclusion to be engaging, powerful, and audience-appropriate. Here are some useful approaches for ending an essay.

- Summarize your main argument or claim
- Present a climactic moment or lesson learned
- Use a powerful **quote**
- End with a surprising **statistic**
- Include a narrative or vivid **example**
- Present a call to action
- Connect your topic to the future
- Pose a meaningful question

Summarize Your Main Argument or Claim

One of the most common concluding methods is to summarize your thesis and main points before leaving the reader with a final thought. This approach ensures that you've clarified the basic point of the essay.

A downside of this approach is that if readers recognize ideas and repeated language, they may skim over the conclusion without giving it much thought.

Consider this concluding paragraph:

> Again, concerns about foreign media ownership will only grow as America becomes more connected to foreign economies and changes due to demographic shifts. A more diverse public will seek more diverse broadcasting. For these and other reasons, most experts recommend loosening regulations. Since banning foreign companies could cause other countries to fight back with the same strategy, such regulations are no longer necessary.
>
> Here, the writer has summarized his or her point and then finished with a simple concluding sentence.

> **Helpful Hint**
>
> What you don't want to do in a conclusion is *only* summarize. The audience will sense that they have little reason to read the end of the essay if it's too obvious.

Writing Environment: Academic

Essays for college courses will often require a summary of the thesis statement and major details. However, some assignments may require you to work more creatively and go beyond this formula for essay writing. Be sure you know the expectations of each instructor, course, and assignment.

Present A Climactic Moment or Lesson Learned

To determine the main point of an essay that's more exploratory or driven by discussion, the audience may need to add up all the details to draw a conclusion. For an essay like this, your conclusion can lead up to a climactic moment or present a lesson learned.

> To learn more about climactic moments in narratives, see Lesson 2.2.

The following excerpt ends an essay called "On Dumpster Diving." Up to this point, the author, Lars Eighner, has defined his topic and walked readers through the process of "diving" into dumpsters on a daily basis for food and other goods. Then, he finishes by reflecting on the things he found and what they meant to others. The piece concludes with a simple but pointed paragraph.

> "Anyway, I find my desire to grab for the gaudy bauble has been largely sated. I think this is an attitude I share with the very wealthy—we both know there is plenty more where what we have came from. Between us are the rat-race millions who nightly scavenge the cable channels looking for they know not what. I am sorry for them."

> **Helpful Hint**
>
> Avoid adding a lot of new information to your conclusion. If you find yourself thinking of points you still need to make or evidence that would strengthen your claims, you may need to revisit the body of your essay.

Use a Powerful Quote

A quote can help you say a lot quickly and in a creative way. At times, someone else's words might capture something that you can't communicate as well through your own words. Maya Angelou ends her brief essay, "The Sweetness of Charity," with a quote from the Bible about love. This quote makes her final line even more convincing than if she'd used her own words.

> "If we change the way we think of charity, our personal lives will be richer, the larger world will be improved. When we give cheerfully and accept gratefully, everyone is blessed. "Charity . . . is kind . . . envieth not . . . vaunteth not itself, is not puffed up."

End with a Surprising Statistic

A particularly relevant statistic can provide hard evidence to end an essay. Objective data will leave the reader with convincing proof for your claim.

> The value of natural gas fracking may be debatable. As this essay has noted, environmental impacts must be weighed against the economic gains. What is not debatable is that natural gas has, in recent years, become a major force in the energy sector, and trends tell us the industry is only going to keep growing in the United States. By 2015, fracking had, for the first time ever, accounted for more than half of all natural gas output in this country.

> Here, the writer emphasizes the point that regardless of fracking being positive, the presence of fracking as an industry is undeniable. This enables the writer to end on a fact that cannot be argued, thus providing the reader with a single piece of memorable information.

Writing Environment: Professional

In professional settings, how you conclude may depend upon the purpose of a text. If you're providing a report with a lot of research, finishing the report with a key statistic might make a lot of sense. If you're evaluating courses of action that your company might take, you might end with a call to action.

To learn more about purpose, see Lesson 5.4.

Include a Narrative or Vivid Example

A concluding story or strong image can spark a reader's imagination while also expressing the main idea of the writing.

> There I was, sitting with my brother during his final moments on earth. It was just us in that room; the doctors and nurses were giving us our space. I knew the moment had been coming, and I had rehearsed it a thousand times in my head. I had the perfect words planned, the right expression practiced, and the tears tucked far, far away. But when Eddie looked at me with a nod that said, "It's time for me to go," I only managed to choke out, "Say hello to Dad."

> In this conclusion, the author includes a somber moment between brothers. The narrative encourages the audience to keep reading by building up to the last line of dialogue.

Writing Environment: Everyday

We're constantly exposed to advertisements that finish with a vivid image, like friends clinking glasses or a happy family driving to the beach. These images express the argument of the ad: the reason why the ad wants you to think or act a certain way. As you go about your day, watch for these concluding images in the media.

Create a Call to Action

If you're challenging readers to support a certain candidate for public office, you might finish by encouraging them to vote. If you're persuading readers to save energy and cause less pollution by driving less, you might suggest alternative means of transportation. After convincing your audience of the validity of your thesis, you need to encourage them to act upon what you've stated.

> Obviously, the school board has not kept its budget for the last twelve years. Meanwhile, the school system is shrinking as people move away from our city. At this point, the only fiscally responsible approach to our situation would be to combine two of the high schools and sell one of the buildings. I urge readers to contact school board members and encourage them to take this difficult but important action.

Connect Your Topic to the Future

When a piece of writing serves as a warning or message for future generations, the conclusion can be a smart place to emphasize the topic's connection to the future.

> The battle of climate change will not directly impact the Baby Boomer generation. However, their children's generation will face a grim future if people don't fight this issue *now*. Contact your local

government, educate yourself, and take a stand. We share this world with millions of others—past, present, and future—so we must preserve it with loyalty, intelligence, and care.

Pose a Meaningful Question

You may wish to use a question to get the reader's attention as an essay ends. A question could either summarize what's already been said or look ahead to a new issue.

> It seems that every day the media barrages us with images of African tragedy and loss, giving viewers, readers, and listeners the sense that all African nations are constantly struggling. However, these images and stories lack context. According to Nobel Peace Prize winner Wangari Maathai, "Perhaps it is playing on human nature: when Africa is projected as negatively as possible, it makes others elsewhere feel better and overlook the economic and political policies of their own countries, many of which are responsible for the situations they see on television." Given this, how might we, as consumers of such media, educate ourselves about what life is really like on Africa's diverse continent?

Helpful Hint

While **transitions** can be helpful in showing the relationship between ideas and paragraphs, predictable transition phrases like *in conclusion*, *therefore*, and *in summary* can feel stiff.

Similarly, avoid **clichés**. Overused phrases don't leave the reader with a memorable image or idea because they rely on something so familiar that the reader isn't moved.

On Your Own

Fill in the table below with examples of writing tasks that would use each conclusion strategy.

Strategy	Writing Task
Summarize your main argument or claim	
Present a climactic moment or lesson learned	
Use a powerful quote	
End with a surprising statistic	
Include a narrative or vivid example	
Create a call to action	
Connect your topic to the future	
Pose a meaningful question	

Lesson Wrap-up

Key Terms

Argument: a reason why you should think or act a certain way

Audience: the person or people meant to read and interpret a text

Body Paragraphs: the paragraphs between the introduction and conclusion of an essay that use supporting details to explore, explain, and/or prove the main idea(s)

Claim: a writer's opinion or position on an issue

Cliché: a popular phrase that has lost its original impact due to overuse

Conclusion: a paragraph that ties together the ideas in a paper and summarizes the main points, also called a concluding paragraph

Drafting: a stage of writing that involves writing out ideas and supporting/concluding sentences

Evidence: a piece of information, also called a supporting detail, that is used to support a main idea

Example: a specific instance or illustration that demonstrates a point

Genre: a type of writing

Introduction: the first paragraph of an essay that presents the topic, provides necessary background information, and states the thesis

Main Idea: the statement or argument that an author tries to communicate

Purpose: the goal of a text

Quote: someone's exact words

Revision: a stage of writing that involves reconsidering and rewriting content and organization

Statistic: a number or percentage based on a collection of data

Supporting Detail: a piece of information, also called evidence, that is used to support a main idea

Transition: a word, phrase, or sentence that shows a relationship between ideas

Thesis Statement: the concise sentence or group of sentences that expresses the main idea of a longer work

Topic: the general subject of a text

Writing Application: The Conclusion

Read the following essay and consider how the conclusion restates the main idea and ties the entire text together.

A Child's Experience Divided: The Narrative Voice of *Cracking India*

"Having polio in infancy is like being born under a lucky star. It has many advantages—it permits me access to my mother's bed in the middle of the night" (Sidhwa 20). *Cracking India* is uniquely written as a child's narrative of the Indian partition. This story juxtaposes curious purity and vile destruction as it raises a sad and probing question: what is a child's experience growing and coming of age during a period of turmoil, and how does it shape a child's sense of past, present, and future?

Like other youthful voices in postcolonial literature, Lenny walks the reader through her understanding of the world around her. Seeing her worldview shaken, beaten up, and held under violent scrutiny reminds the readers that children participate in these events much in

Just like a conclusion, the introduction is often well-served by a strong quote.

The author presents the focus of the writing here; this is referenced in the conclusion.

the same way that adults do. They sense a shift in loyalties, they overhear hushed conversations between family members, and most scarring, they see. They see dead bodies in the street. They see men in trucks patrolling roads with loaded guns. They see women exploited and shamed. For Lenny, there is no sense of a childhood or a land before this. Several characters in *Cracking India* reference a simpler, calmer world. However, for characters like Lenny, the devastating acts are etched in their realities and ingrained in their nature. It is not only an external observation but also an internal experience of confusion, guilt, and isolation.

Specific details like this support the author's main points.

In addition to the violence children like Lenny are forced to witness and encounter, there is also a destructive blow to the sense of self. In many novels about colonization and postcolonial environments, identity pervades characters' internal conflicts. Arguably, this reflects the experience of real individuals who are natives of colonized lands. Like Lenny, the children are culturally divided from their older family members and ancestors. Consequently, one could claim that children suffer the most from colonialism because they are forced to grow up in a world that teaches them not only violence and loss but also confusion and uncertainty.

As Lenny admires multiple characters in her family, she is also forced to watch them shift loyalties, change behaviors, or, most commonly, submit to the demands of those in power. For many children, the experiences of growing up in a violent, divided warzone have had lasting impacts on who they are and what becomes of them. These experiences will always be scarred in their memories and imprinted on their hearts. It is the child's experience which highlights the true tragedy of postcolonialism: a questionable future, an empty present, and, someday, a confused sense of the past. Is this what we want for our children's future?

Here, the author sums up the actions of the main character.

Then, the author broadens the conclusion to reach a wider audience.

The author ends with a question, leaving the readers with a lasting thought.

Chapter 5
Reading Critically

Lesson 5.1
Taking Notes and Annotating Texts

Good note-taking skills are essential for active listening and engaged reading in both academics and the workplace.

Experienced readers do more than view the words on a page; they practice reading strategies that keep them engaged and ensure reading comprehension. Similarly, active listeners use note-taking methods to engage in lectures, discussions, and presentations. By noting important ideas, you not only prevent your mind from wandering but also create a study resource that can be referenced in the future.

Listening and note-taking are just as important in most workplace settings. Throughout your week, you participate in training demonstrations, job interviews, medical appointments, and personal conversations. Just like in class, your success in these activities relies on your ability to pay close attention and keep track of key details.

In this lesson, you will learn about the following aspects of taking notes and annotating texts:

Note-taking Strategies
Note-taking Methods
Annotating Texts

Group Activity

As a group, search for a YouTube video about a topic you are currently studying. Watch the video and take notes on the presentation. Compare your notes and discuss any helpful strategies.

Note-taking Strategies

As you take notes in any scenario, keep the following guidelines in mind:

- **Use neat handwriting.** You can't study from notes that you can't read. If you know that your handwriting will be difficult to decipher later, consider typing your notes on a computer instead.

- **Use abbreviations and phrases.** While recording information word-for-word might reinforce the ideas in your mind, you will quickly feel overwhelmed by the amount of material you are recording. Furthermore, the density of your notes will make reviewing the information difficult.

- **Use your own words.** Remember that your notes are your own personal study resources. You must be able to understand the information when you review it later. Don't be afraid to use acronyms, examples, or even drawings to explain the concepts in the clearest possible way.

- **Summarize important ideas.** A **summary** is a brief overview of main ideas or key information.

Writing Environment: Professional

Accurate summarizing is important in any profession. Good managers are often good listeners; they can summarize what someone said before responding to it, a trait that many questioners appreciate because they know they are at least being heard. Being able to take good notes at a meeting may seem like a thankless job, but it can also lead to recognition of your aptitude for managerial duties like writing reports and proposals.

Taking Notes on Lectures or Presentations

Taking notes on the right information can be tricky. Here are a few considerations to keep in mind when taking notes during a lecture or presentation:

Main Idea vs. Supporting Details

Taking class notes involves filtering out the less important information and staying focused on the more important information. Don't let yourself get bogged down by recording every single detail. Instead, save the most explanation for **main ideas** and use less explanation for **supporting details**.

Screen vs. Speaker

Have you ever tried to write down everything on a PowerPoint slide only to find that you've accidentally ignored everything your professor just said? If possible, download a copy of the slides before class so that you can follow along and take notes without having to record every single detail from the presentation. Even if you don't have access to the slides, treat the presentation just like you would a normal lecture. Write down important concepts in your own words using abbreviations and phrases.

Presentation vs. Analysis

Don't assume that the most important concepts in a lecture are included on the PowerPoint presentation. Often, these slides are used to outline the basic structure of the information. The analysis provided by your instructor and class discussions is just as valuable as the definitions and facts included on the slides.

Taking Notes on Readings

While reading a complex text, you should keep track of important concepts and key terms. Writing down this information gives you an opportunity to explain the ideas in your own words and organize your thoughts on the topic. Taking notes also helps you retain information longer by forcing you to focus on the ideas twice: once while reading and once while writing them down.

When taking notes on readings, focus on locating and recording the following information:

Note-taking Checklist: Taking Notes on Readings

☐ **Main Ideas and Supporting Details:** what are the most general ideas and topics discussed in the text? What are the specific types of evidence the writer uses?

☐ **Key Vocabulary:** what language is used in the text? Are there any words you don't understand? Are there context clues or examples that can help you define the unfamiliar terms?

☐ **Visual Clues:** what visuals does the text include? Are there graphs or charts that serve as supporting details? Are there illustrations that serve to leave a strong impression on the audience?

☐ **Organization:** how is the text structured? Why might it be organized this way?

Summarizing Readings

If you're reading a longer essay or report, your notes should include a summary of each paragraph or section. Consider the following excerpt:

> *Franklin D. Roosevelt's "Four Freedoms" speech*
> *Annual Message to Congress on the State of the Union 1/06/1941 (excerpt)*
>
> In the future days, which we seek to make secure, we look forward to a world founded upon four essential human freedoms. The first is freedom of speech and expression—everywhere in the world. The second is freedom of every person to worship God in his own way—everywhere in the world. The third is freedom from want—which, translated into world terms, means economic understandings which will secure to every nation a healthy peacetime life for its inhabitants—everywhere in the world. The fourth is freedom from fear—which, translated into world terms, means a world-wide reduction of armaments to such a point and in such a thorough fashion that no nation will be in a position to commit an act of physical aggression against any neighbor—anywhere in the world.

Here's a summary of the excerpt:

> In his "Four Freedoms" speech, Franklin Delano Roosevelt explained that freedom of speech and worship and freedom from want and fear are the four freedoms essential for democracy.
>
> The excerpt from FDR's nine-page speech is fairly brief itself, so the summary is even shorter, yet comprehensive.

On Your Own

Read the following passage and summarize its most important idea in the space provided.

> The settlement of the United States happened through the processes of encroachment, expansion, and acquisition. Encroachment began with individual colonists who extended their fence lines into native territory, lopping off a few square feet or an acre here and there. Later, when treaties set the boundaries of Native American lands, prospectors and settlers would flock to mineral strikes, as in California, Colorado, the Dakotas, and Nevada. Though rarely, if ever, used as a deliberate strategy, disease also enabled encroachment. Sometimes, especially along the Eastern seaboard, whole villages were decimated as contact with Europeans spread smallpox and other fatal diseases among Native Americans. There may have been as many as 24 million natives in the Americas before 1492. However, by the time the frontier disappeared with the 1890 census, perhaps 1% of that number remained in the confines of the United States, the last few being killed or forced onto reservations by the so-called "Indian Wars," especially after the American Civil War.

Note-Taking Methods

There are several well-known ways to structure notes. Some of the most popular are outlines, the Cornell Method, and graphic organizers like mind maps. Don't be afraid to try all three until you find a system that works the best for you.

Outlines

Many students record class notes in outline form, writing down short phrases for each concept and using numbering or bullet points to show the relationships between ideas. Outlining class lectures helps you understand the way a topic is structured by grouping all the information into topics and subtopics.

Consider the following example:

Life Cycle of a Star (Feb. 19 lecture)

A. *Stardust*
- *Stellar nurseries*
  - *Eagle Nebula's Pillars of Creation*
- *Accretion disk: dense enough for gravity to condense*
  - *If "blobs" of Hubble images look 3D, why become flat disks with an ecliptic?*

B. *"Birth"*
- *Cloud of dust and gas condenses enough to ignite & glow*
- *Solar wind blows out lightest materials away from center*
- *Heavier materials "agglutinate" to "sweep" up the rest of materials in their orbital area.*

C. *"Life"*
- *Planets can "adjust" their orbits around the star.*
  - *In our solar system, Jupiter catches a lot of stuff that might fall back in toward the Sun.*

D. *"Death"*
- *Death method and result depends on a star's size in life.*
  - *Supernova - Where fits gamma ray bursts?*
  - *Pulsar dwarf stars?*
- *Result scatters heavy elements around its galactic neighborhood.*

E. *Population 1 vs. Population 2*
- *When is Population 3?*

▹ Notice that this example also includes questions that the student will need to research. Don't be afraid to annotate your notes and review them later. In fact, adding additional notes and annotations after class will help reinforce the concepts in your mind and allow you to identify any questions you should bring up during the next class meeting.

Learning Style Tip
Outlines are useful tools for **global** learners. If you are a global learner, you can use an outline to see the relationships between ideas and understand how those ideas connect to the big picture.

Further Resources

Take a look at this YouTube video (https://www.youtube.com/watch?v=AffuwyJZTQQ) that uses classic video game characters to explain different note-taking methods.

Cornell Notes

Another method for taking notes is the **Cornell Method**, a strategy first created by Dr. Walter Pauk at Cornell University. To take Cornell notes, divide your paper into four sections:

- Section 1 is the top of the page. Use this space to list the class information, date, and lecture topic.

- Section 2 is for taking notes during class. Instead of complete sentences, use lists or clusters of words, phrases, or even abbreviations. Feel free to color-code or highlight your notes.

- Section 3 is for after class. Make a list of new or important terms from the session. Then, come up with questions. Some of these questions can be reflective, helping you think more about what you learned in class. Others should be questions that you still have about what was covered. Consider these action items for preparing for your next class or your next test.

- Finally, when you finish reviewing your notes, write a brief summary of the topic in Section 4. This summary should boil down the main point of the lecture in fewer than five sentences.

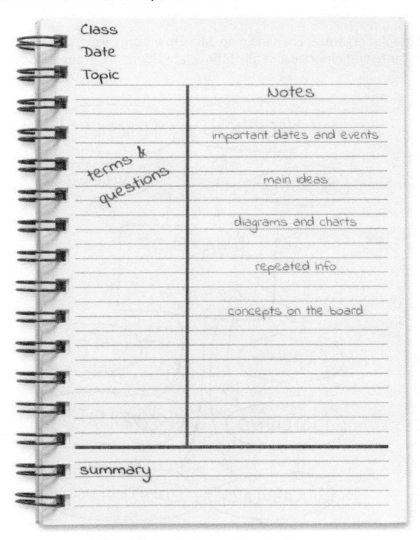

Here are some questions you might want to include in Section 3 of your notes:

> How is this related to other topics?
> Why is this important?
> Do I have any follow-up questions about these concepts?
> Do I understand what the instructor emphasized most?
> What exam questions might I anticipate based on what we learned today?

Further Resources

To learn more about Cornell Notes, watch this brief introductory video: https://www.youtube.com/watch?v=HJCnqj7j7rU.

Graphic Organizers

A **graphic organizer** is a note-taking template for visually demonstrating relationships between ideas. The layout of a graphic organizer could include shapes, charts, timelines, diagrams, or drawings. Filling out a graphic organizer can be a very useful method for not only reviewing notes, but also summarizing texts and brainstorming for writing assignments.

Mind Maps

One popular type of graphic organizer is a mind map. **Mind maps** organize the main points of a topic visually. They are similar to outlining because all of the related ideas are grouped together.

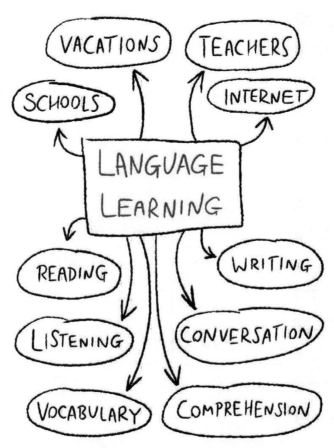

Mind maps make it easy to visualize information.

The main concept goes in the center of the mind map. Any important topics are connected to the main concept by lines. These topics can then be connected to subtopics that are even more specific.

This format is a visual representation of the material that allows you to quickly see connections between ideas. Just like with outlining, you may not be able to group everything together perfectly the first time. Don't be afraid to take down regular notes during class and create a graphic organizer when you review your notes later.

On Your Own

In addition to mind mapping, try out some other types of graphic organizers to prepare for an upcoming class or assignment. Use the following examples as worksheets or as ideas for your own creations.

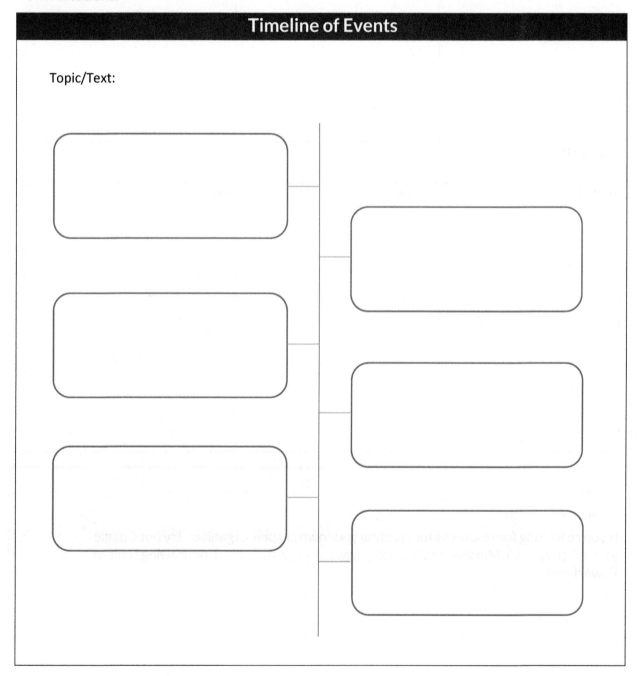

Timeline of Events

Topic/Text:

Ideas and Details		
Topic/Text:		
Big Idea:		
Detail:	Detail:	Detail:
Big Idea:		
Detail:	Detail:	Detail:

Further Resources

If you're looking for resources for creating your own graphic organizer, try out Coggle (https://coggle.it/), Mindmeister (https://www.mindmeister.com/), or drawing tools in PowerPoint.

Annotating Texts

Annotating is a note-taking method for pointing out key information within a text. Annotations can include underlining, highlighting, phrases, words, or symbols (any type of mark that helps you easily locate and understand the information later).

As a college student, you read a large amount of information for your classes. Annotating helps you stay focused. Additionally, an annotated text is a valuable study resource. When you are reviewing the information for a test or a project, you can use your notes to quickly locate and understand important details.

Before annotating a reading assignment or research source, carefully read through the entire text once. This will give you a chance to focus on the information without any extra distractions. Once you've finished, review the material again. This time, mark up any important or unfamiliar portions of the text.

Mark Important In-text Words and Ideas

Start by highlighting, underlining, circling, or labeling important words and word groups within the text. Look for key vocabulary, main ideas, and major details.

Mark only the most helpful or important portions of the text. If every single sentence is highlighted or underlined, it will be difficult to distinguish the important concepts from the less important ones.

Consider the following examples. Which one does a better job of highlighting only the key information?

Paragraph 1

Expansion and acquisition often overlapped. Expansion was sometimes accomplished by giving away land. Once the 13 colonies were free of England, for example, determination arose to settle the Ohio Valley and the lands south of the Great Lakes. The Northwest Ordinance of 1787 provided homesteaders with acres of free lands if settlers would simply build there, preferably living there and working the land. Similarly, the Homestead Act of 1862 looked ahead to a time after the Civil War when families might move westward; again, free land was available for homesteaders. The Oklahoma Land Rush of the 1880s was the last great land giveaway for homesteading, though homestead grants were given until 1915. Settlers went not only to Oklahoma but also the Pacific Northwest.

Paragraph 2

Expansion and acquisition often overlapped. Expansion was sometimes accomplished by giving away land. Once the 13 colonies were free of England, for example, determination arose to settle the Ohio Valley and the lands south of the Great Lakes. The Northwest Ordinance of 1787 provided homesteaders with acres of free lands if settlers would simply build there, preferably living there and working the land. Similarly, the Homestead Act of 1862 looked ahead to a time after the Civil War when families might move westward; again, free land was available for homesteaders. The Oklahoma Land Rush of the 1880s was the last great land giveaway for homesteading, though homestead grants were given until 1915. Settlers went not only to Oklahoma but also the Pacific Northwest.

As you can see, the second paragraph does a much better job keeping the annotations focused on the key portions of the text. If you needed to review this text later, you would easily be able to find the information you need.

Add Notes in the Margins

An annotated text also includes notes in the margins of the document. Write notes that add meaning to the highlighted or underlined portions of the text. Use the following strategies:

Note-taking Checklist: Annotations

☐ **Define** concepts, technical terms, and unfamiliar vocabulary.

☐ **Summarize** ideas that seem well-supported and logical.

☐ **Challenge** ideas that seem incorrect or poorly supported.

☐ **Respond** to any ideas that spark an emotional reaction.

☐ **Question** yourself about areas for further research.

Remember that annotations do not require any specific type of markup. You can use sticky notes, pens, and highlighters to annotate a text. Try adding special colors or symbols for different types of information. For example, questions could be in pink with a question mark, and definitions could appear in blue.

Expansion and acquisition often overlapped. Expansion was sometimes accomplished by giving away land. Once the 13 colonies were free of England, for example, determination arose to settle the Ohio Valley and the lands south of the Great Lakes. The Northwest Ordinance of 1787 provided homesteaders with acres of free lands if settlers would simply build there, preferably living there and working the land. Similarly, the Homestead Act of 1862 looked ahead to a time after the Civil War when families might move westward; again, free land was available for homesteaders. The Oklahoma Land Rush of the 1880s was the last great land giveaway for homesteading, though homestead grants were given up to 1915. Settlers went not only to Oklahoma, for a large influx also settled the Pacific Northwest.

Define:
So expansion means populating and acquisition means getting more land?

Challenge:
Did anybody stop to say, "Doesn't that land belong to the Native Americans?"

Question:
Why stop after 1915?

Helpful Hint

Remember that any element of the text, including visuals, can be annotated. Your job as a reader is to integrate the visual content with the surrounding text to understand how the graphics illustrate and support the ongoing narrative in the text.

Helpful Hint

There's not one right way to take notes. Instead, it's important to find a system that works for you. Some people prefer to create **outlines**, which use numbering and indents to show the relationships between ideas. Others prefer to color-code or highlight key ideas in their notes. Regardless of the system you prefer, use the strategies that work best for you.

Lesson Wrap-Up

Key Terms

Annotating: a note-taking method for pointing out key information within a text

Cornell Method: a note-taking tool that divides a page of notes into four sections

Main Idea: the overarching statement or argument that a text communicates about its topic

Outline: a note-taking tool for sorting information in multi-level lists

Summary: a brief, generalized overview of a larger amount of information

Supporting Detail: a piece of information, also called evidence, that is used to support a main idea

Writing Application: Taking Notes and Annotating Texts

Read the following passage from a history textbook. Note the underlined information and read the corresponding student annotations.

Disappearance of the Frontier

The settlement of the United States happened through the processes of encroachment, expansion, and acquisition. Encroachment began with individual colonists who extended their fence lines into native territory, lopping off a few square feet or an acre here and there. Later, when treaties set the boundaries of Native American lands, prospectors and settlers would flock to mineral strikes, as in California and Colorado, the Dakotas, and Nevada.

Though rarely, if ever, used as a deliberate strategy, disease also enabled encroachment. Sometimes, especially along the Eastern seaboard, whole villages were decimated as contact with Europeans smallpox and other fatal diseases among Native Americans. Though there may have been as many as 24 million natives in the Americas before 1492, by the time the frontier disappeared with the 1890 census, perhaps 1% of that number remained in the confines of the United States, the last few being killed or forced onto reservations by the so-called "Indian Wars," especially after the American Civil War.

Expansion and acquisition often overlapped. Expansion was sometimes accomplished by giving away land. Once the 13 colonies were free of England, for example, determination arose to settle the Ohio Valley and the lands south of the Great Lakes. The Northwest Ordinance of 1787 provided homesteaders with acres of free lands if settlers would simply build there, preferably living there and working the land. Similarly, the Homestead Act of 1862 looked ahead to a time after the Civil War when families might move westward; again, free land was available for homesteaders. The Oklahoma Land Rush of the 1880s was the last great land giveaway for

So expansion means populating and acquisition means getting more land?

Did anybody stop to say, "Doesn't that land belong to the Native Americans?"

homesteading, though homestead grants were given until 1915. *Why stop after 1915?*
Settlers went not only to Oklahoma but also the Pacific Northwest.

The land for most of this homesteading was acquired via the Louisiana Purchase of 1803. Most of what is now the Midwestern United States saw only a few European trappers until that time. Once Jefferson had purchased the land, doubling the area of the United States, settlement proceeded gradually. Before the Civil War, people usually went no *Why did people stop at the Mississippi River?* further than the Mississippi River, though routes to the West Coast were explored as early as 1836. The most famous came to be known as *Is this really where the trail began?* the Oregon Trail and went from the Missouri River to the Willamette Valley, Oregon's rich farmland.

War, of course, played a part in acquisition. The American Southwest now holds states that were all acquired by war. In Texas, though, European settlers had come in the early part of the 19th century. As the numbers of these "Texicans" grew, their patience with being governed from Mexico City decreased until a war for independence made Texas *What else did Polk do that affected this shift?* its own nation for a few years. After some negotiation, this free nation became a U.S. state. The other Southwestern states were acquired about a decade after the Texican war as President Polk's forces defeated Mexican forces in 1846. Since he was already fighting one war, however, Polk was more wary of setting the northern U.S. border. He negotiated the Oregon Treaty with the British, who probably didn't *What were the terms of the Oregon Treaty?* want a third war with the Americans, anyway.

By 1892, the U.S. census showed an average of one American per acre in the Western United States, and the frontier line had disappeared after making its way from the Appalachians (after the War for Independence) to roughly the Mississippi by the Civil War and into the West after that.

Lesson 5.2
Identifying the Main Idea and Supporting Details

Reading is not a passive activity; it is a conversation between you (the reader) and the author of the text. When you understand the author's main idea and supporting details, you can translate the words on the page into a language that you understand. This is an essential step of reading critically. Before you can identify bias or distinguish between opinion and facts, you need to understand the text's argument.

Imagine that your friend missed class and asked you to tell her what she missed. You probably wouldn't tell her only about the little details—the outfit you wore to class, the students who participated, the squirrel you noticed outside the window—because this wouldn't be very helpful information. Instead, you would provide some sort of a summary, explaining only the most important and big-picture information.

In a similar way, comprehending and responding to a text requires first understanding the different components of a **paragraph**. Before you can think critically about an argument in a piece of writing, you should be able to locate the main idea(s). Then, you can evaluate the details used to support those ideas. Although this might sound like an overwhelming task, you can use strategies to break down the parts of a paragraph one step at a time.

In this lesson, you will learn how to deconstruct the components of a text using these strategies:

Understand the Parts of a Text
Locate the Topic and Main Idea
Break Down the Supporting Details
Consider the Purpose

Understand the Parts of a Text

Distinguish Between General and Specific Information

The first step to finding the main idea of a text is to understand differences between general and specific information.

General information can include a word, phrase, or idea that shapes the scope and overall point of a text. **Specific information** can include a word, phrase, or idea with a narrowed focus on a single piece of a text.

Reflection Questions
Think about how you would describe your personality to someone. What are your general characteristics? What are the specific features that are unique to who you are?

Simply put, general is broad while specific is narrow. Specific words and ideas can fit into general categories. Here are some examples:

General	Specific
School Supplies	pens notebooks textbooks highlighters
Engineering	Civil Engineering Mechanical Engineering Chemical Engineering Electrical Engineering Geotechnical Engineering
Living Expenses	rent cable water electric

When you can distinguish between general and specific information, you can more easily locate the major components of a text.

Topic

The **topic**, or subject, of a text is the most general component of a text. It may or may not be explicitly identified. Think of the topic as an umbrella. In a text containing multiple paragraphs, the main idea of each paragraph fits under that umbrella.

Main Idea

The **main idea** is the statement or argument that a text communicates about its topic. Each paragraph in a text should contain a main idea. Texts with multiple paragraphs usually include multiple, related ideas that contribute to a bigger idea about the topic.

Supporting Details

Finally, the **supporting details** in a paragraph serve to support or describe the main idea with more specific information. Supporting details can be broken down into two levels: major details and minor details. Minor details are more specific than major details.

Remember that these components can be listed in order from general to specific information so that you can more easily locate them as you read a text. Recognizing each of these components is key not only for reading comprehension but also for effective writing.

Locate the Topic and Main Idea

The main idea is the statement or argument that a text communicates about its topic. Both paragraphs and essays contain main ideas.

In a paragraph, the main idea is often stated in a **topic sentence**.

> To learn more about topic sentences, see Lesson 4.4.

In an essay, the main idea is often stated in a thesis or purpose statement. Then, each body paragraph covers a unique subtopic to support or build upon the author's main point.

> To learn more about thesis and purpose statements, see Lesson 4.3.

To determine the main idea of a text, you should consider these questions:

- What is the general topic of the text? (This can usually be summed up in one or two words.)
- What is the author saying about the topic?

Recognize the General Topic

The **topic** is a general word or phrase that tells you who or what a passage is about. It is very much like a title or heading; in fact, the topic is often used in the title or heading of a piece of writing. The topic is typically a word or phrase. To determine the topic, ask yourself these questions:

- What words are repeated in this text? (Be sure to note repeated pronouns that refer to repeated subjects.)
- What is the broad subject of this text? What topic could act as an umbrella that houses all of the sentences or paragraphs in this text?

> **Helpful Hint**
> Keep in mind that various topics can apply to a text.

Locate the Main Idea

The main idea of a text answers these questions:

- What big-picture message is the author communicating in this text?
- What idea or statement is supported by the evidence or details?

The main idea is closely related to the author's **purpose**, or goal, for writing. Consider these examples:

Topic	Purpose	Main Idea
Hurricanes	to inform the audience about what causes hurricanes	Hurricanes are caused by water vapor and warm air.

College Experience	to reflect on the difficulties the author faced when she returned to school	Returning to school was difficult for the author because of financial and emotional reasons.
Smoking	to persuade the audience to quit smoking	Smoking is a dangerous and costly addiction.
Family	to entertain the audience with a funny story about the author's family	The author's family ran into a number of strange situations during their last family vacation.

On Your Own

As you read the following passage, consider its topics and main idea. Then, answer the following question.

> The Standard American Diet (SAD) is a common source of debate in today's society. Due to unwise food choices, many American citizens struggle to maintain a healthy weight. Then, they turn to pharmaceuticals and diet programs to fix the problems caused by unhealthy eating. One reason people may struggle to maintain their weight is, surprisingly, from eating too little food. Believe it or not, skipping breakfast can actually cause people to gain weight. Not feeding the body after the fast that happens during sleep deprives it of nutrients and sugars that it needs to jump-start the metabolism. Additionally, skipping breakfast can make people eat more food throughout the day or turn to a "quick fix" snack that is high in sugar and empty calories. These options will spike the blood sugar and give people an initial burst of energy, but they do not provide the nourishment the body needs. Ironically, once people do eat, their bodies may decide to store those calories as fat. Therefore, by skipping meals, people will ultimately gain weight instead of losing it.

Which of the following statements are supported in this paragraph? Identify all that apply.

- ☐ Skipping breakfast can cause people to gain weight.
- ☐ The Standard American Diet is too carbohydrate-heavy.
- ☐ Skipping breakfast is bad for people's health.
- ☐ Skipping breakfast causes people to eat more.

What does this tell you about the main idea of the text? Where is the most emphasis placed?

Writing Environment: Professional

One of the most prevalent types of writing you will encounter in the workplace is written correspondence. Often, email is used as a substitute for face-to-face meetings. Therefore, you will need to locate the main ideas and objectives in the email.

Consider the following email sent to the employees of a small dog-grooming company:

> Hello all,
>
> Thank you for your outstanding work last month; we gained more new clients in four weeks than in the last six months combined! Now, the bar is set even higher. One new incentive that we will be implementing this month is the Ruff-errals Program.

For every "ruff-erral" you receive in the month of May, your name will be entered in a drawing to receive a $500 bonus. Your name can be entered into the drawing an unlimited number of times. The groomer who receives the most "ruff-errals" between May 1st and May 31st will win the bonus. However, we will also do two random drawings at the end of the month, and each winner will receive a $50 giftcard.

Thanks again for all of your hard work! I look forward to seeing who my "ruff-erral" rockstars will be this month!

Best,

Bob Riordan, CEO

To locate the main idea in this email, we must ask ourselves the two questions mentioned earlier:

- What is the topic?
    o "Ruff-errals" contest

- What is the author saying about the topic?
    o How an employee can win the contest

Break Down the Supporting Details

After determining the topic and main idea, you need to ascertain how the author supported that main idea. Anyone can state an idea, but what makes that idea stronger are the details that support it. Understanding the supporting details is the next step of understanding the entire text.

Supporting details often make up the bulk of a paragraph. For example, in a paragraph about the importance of budgeting, supporting details might include statistics about how much you could save in a year with proper budgeting tools.

Supporting details come in different forms and categories.

Here are the types of information you (or an author) might use as evidence:

Anecdote: a long example told as a story

Description: words that appeal to the senses to explain the appearance of someone or something

Example: a specific instance or illustration that demonstrates a point

Expert Analysis: an opinion or statement shared by someone who is knowledgeable about a topic

Fact: a piece of information that most people generally agree to be true

Reflection: the thoughts and feelings of the author

Statistic: a number or percentage that represents research data

There are two categories of supporting details: major and minor. **Major details** support and prove the main idea. **Minor details** support the major details.

Major Details

When locating major details, look for number words like these:

Another	Next
First, Second…	One, Two…
Last	Several

Also look for **transition** phrases that introduce evidence. Here are some examples:

One reason this occurs…	The effects are…
Several factors contribute to…	The first cause is…
The advantages are…	There are various ways…

Minor Details

Minor details give more specific information about the major details and often include examples and/or explanations.

When locating minor details, look for transition phrases like these:

Example	For instance
Specifically	To illustrate

Remember that the main idea and major details make up the framework of the writing, while the minor details give the reader more information to assist in understanding.

Group Activity

As a class, brainstorm a few topics based on current events or personal experiences and choose one. Then, in your group, write a main idea based on the topic and come up with at least three supporting details. Present them to the class and discuss which details were strongest and why.

Consider the Purpose

Why is it even important to know the author's main idea? The main idea is closely related to the author's purpose, or goal, for writing. In order to translate a text into your own language, you need to understand *why* the text was written in the first place.

Consider these examples (and remember that often, texts have more than one purpose):

Topic	Main Idea	Purpose
Hurricanes	Hurricanes are caused by water vapor and warm air.	To inform the audience about what causes hurricanes (writing to summarize)
College Experience	Returning to school was difficult for the author for financial and emotional reasons.	To review the difficulties the author faced when she returned to school (writing to discuss)
Smoking	Smoking is a dangerous and costly addiction.	To persuade the audience to quit smoking (writing to argue)

Families in *East of Eden*	The families in *East of Eden* gave the author a new perspective on what "family" means.	To reflect on the author's reaction to the families in *East of Eden* (writing to respond)

Once you identify the purpose, you need to anticipate your response. The questions in the table below can help you get started, but don't limit yourself to just those two.

Purpose	Main Idea	Response
Summarize	Hurricanes are caused by water vapor and warm air.	Is this information consistent with my prior knowledge about the topic? Is the evidence factual or based on opinion?
Discuss	Returning to school was difficult for the author for financial and emotional reasons.	Does the author help me understand the topic? Is the author unbiased?
Argue	Smoking is a dangerous and costly addiction.	Does the author strongly support his/her point? Do I agree or disagree with the author? Why?
Respond	The families in East of Eden gave the author a new perspective on what "family" means.	Does the author compare multiple things or ideas? Does the author **critique** the topic?

Once you have identified the topic, main idea, supporting details, and purpose of a text, test your knowledge by answering the questions below. If you can't answer one of them, you may need to review the text again.

- **Topic:** who/what is the author discussing?
- **Main Idea:** What is the most important thing the author is saying about the topic?
- **Supporting Details:** What reasons does the author provide to support the main idea?
- **Purpose:** Why does the main idea matter?

Lesson Wrap-up

Key Terms

Critique: a critical analysis of a subject's components

General Information: a word or word group that can be linked to a broad range of specific ideas and details

Main Idea: the statement or argument that an author tries to communicate

Major Detail: a detail that supports and proves the main idea of a paragraph

Minor Detail: a detail that with specific information that supports a major detail in a paragraph

Paragraph: a short piece of writing that focuses on one main idea

Purpose: the goal of a text

Signal/Signpost Word: a word that makes transitions between ideas by showing order or making connections

Specific Information: a word or idea with a narrow focus

Supporting Detail: a piece of information, also called evidence, that is used to support a main idea

Topic: the general subject of a text

Topic Sentence: a sentence that states the main idea of a paragraph

Writing Application: Identifying the Main Idea and Supporting Details

Read the following persuasive essay and pay special attention to the main idea. How does the author support his or her argument?

Fake and Plastic: Not Fantastic

A wild duck entangled in six-pack plastic rings; garbage littering the sides of highways; dead fish floating in an oily spill. All three of these images can be traced back to plastic: that non-biodegradable material that takes from one hundred to one thousand years to deteriorate and is filling our landfills and roadsides in ever-increasing amounts. This is a huge global problem with a rather simple solution. In order to prevent harm to wildlife, save landfill space, and preserve our natural resources, the world populace needs to recycle plastic.

The topic of this essay is plastic.

This thesis states the main idea and the supporting details.

Videos abound on the internet that display the volume of garbage swirling around in the ocean. Eighty percent of that garbage is made up of plastic. Sea life and waterfowl often mistake these items for food, ingest them, and sicken or die. Land animals are also in danger of mistaking plastic for food or trying to eat leftovers from a plastic container. It might look funny to see an animal struggle to remove a peanut butter jar from its muzzle, but the animal could be unable to breathe or defend itself. Endangering animals, especially the ones people rely on as a food source, is irresponsible. Human beings are at the top of a food chain that could collapse if a species on a lower level is eliminated. Saving the earth's wildlife is one important reason to recycle.

This paragraph provides minor details that support the major detail: plastic harms wildlife.

Sometimes, it's acceptable to place a paragraph's topic sentence at the end instead of the beginning.

An equally important reason to recycle is to reduce the amount of garbage dumped into our landfills and oceans. One ton of plastic takes up 7.5 cubic yards of space, and hundreds of tons are being disposed of every day. Where is it going? It is going into landfills. While some landfills layer garbage on top of plastic to prevent soil pollution, they still require a huge amount of space. For instance, one landfill in Los Angeles covers 700 acres and is five hundred feet high. According to How Stuff Works, a landfill can hold the equivalent length of 82,000 football fields of trash buried thirty feet deep. Consider how many landfills are needed to service all the cities in the United States alone. Landfills take up an enormous amount of land that could otherwise be used for growing crops, building recreational areas, or left natural for humans and wildlife to enjoy. What is even more distressing about landfills is that they can accept garbage for only about fifty years before another one needs to take its place.

The transition for instance indicates a minor detail.

A third reason to recycle plastic is to preserve the earth's natural, non-renewable resources. Plastic is made from petroleum, a fossil fuel that is also used to make gasoline. Recycling plastic saves about two thousand pounds of petroleum. In addition, according to Plastic-Recyclers, "recycling one ton of plastic results in saving the energy used by two humans in a year and the water required by a person for two months." Recycled plastic can be sorted according to the Resin Identification Code (RIC) printed on the bottoms of bottles and containers. These plastics can then be ground or shredded, re-melted, and formed into new products. For example, plastic #2 is used to make milk jugs and, when recycled, can be turned into picnic tables and benches. Recycling is a wiser alternative to throwing plastic into a landfill and then pumping more oil to make new plastic. We cannot continue to use the earth's resources irresponsibly. Recycling adds resources rather than exhausting them, and it saves the energy that would otherwise be expended to extract and refine new materials.

> This is the topic sentence. It states the third major detail: recycling preserves natural resources.

> The transition phrase *in addition* indicates a minor detail that supports the major detail.

> What is the purpose of this essay? Based on that purpose, how should you respond?

Throwing away plastic items is unhealthy for wildlife, uses valuable land, and forces the plastics industry to deplete the earth's natural resources. Society needs to become more aware of the how harmful plastic can be, more conscientious of where it ends up, and more diligent to recycle it. Many people know about recycling, but few understand its importance or the consequences of not recycling. When we think about what can be saved by recycling—wildlife, land, and natural resources—we realize that it does not make sense not to recycle.

> The conclusion restates the main idea and sums up the major supporting details.

Lesson 5.3
Identifying Organizational Patterns

Have you ever been lost in a new city? Maybe you were trying to find a specific place but had no idea how to get there. You consulted the road signs, checked the map app on your phone, and asked someone for directions, but you received a different route every time. Which one was the best choice? Eventually, you realized that all three were correct; there were just multiple ways to get to your destination.

This principle also applies to organizing essays. Writers can utilize different **organizational patterns** to describe the same idea or topic. That said, an essay's organization should always align with the **purpose**, or goal, of the text.

Learning to identify organizational patterns will help you comprehend information and understand the author's purpose. You will also feel more comfortable using these patterns in your own writing.

This lesson will discuss the following aspects of organizational patterns:

Considering the Order of Ideas
Cause and Effect

Chronological Order
Compare and Contrast
Order of Importance
Spatial Order
Topical Order

Considering the Order of Ideas

Authors use organizational patterns to emphasize certain ideas that help them achieve their purposes, or goals for writing.

For example, an author might want to write about the positive effects that nature can have on people living in urban areas. However, he or she wants to focus most on trees and how planting more of them can lead to improved health. Here's how the outline for that essay might look:

1. Introduction
    a. Thesis: Incorporating nature into urban areas will improve the quality of life for residents.
2. Body Paragraph 1
    a. Trees, flowers, and shrubs will beautify urban areas.
3. Body Paragraph 2
    a. Spending time in nature can improve people's moods.
4. Body Paragraph 3
    a. Planting more trees will purify the air and can even prevent depression and homicide.
5. Conclusion

All three body paragraphs support the **thesis**, but Body Paragraph 3 addresses the author's focus and provides the most compelling reasons for incorporating nature into city plans. Placing this information last makes it stand out to the audience. The author is using an organizational pattern (order of importance) in harmony with his or her purpose: to persuade the audience that planting trees will improve people's quality of life.

Outlines clearly illustrate an essay's organization and ideas, so they're an ideal way to identify organizational patterns. You can create an outline of any text you read or write by following these steps:

Step-by-Step Checklist: Outlining a Text

☐ | 1. Identify the implicit or explicit thesis on the top level of your outline.

☐ | 2. Summarize the body paragraphs to determine the main idea of each.

☐ | 3. Use the main ideas as headings in your outline.

☐ | 4. Review the supporting details to determine where the author has placed emphasis.

☐ | 5. Add brief descriptions of the supporting details as subtopics in your outline.

Helpful Hint

The organizational patterns in this lesson represent the most basic structures that many writers use. As you deconstruct and outline texts, you may discover patterns that don't match up perfectly with a single approach. Use the patterns in this lesson as a general set of considerations, not a rigid set of templates.

After you've created your outline, review the order of the information, considering both main ideas and supporting details. Also look for transitions as indicators of organization. **Transitions** are words, phrases, or sentences that show relationships between ideas.

Determining the organizational pattern(s) used in a text will help you think critically about an author's explicit and implicit intentions.

Cause and Effect

A paper organized according to cause and effect shows the reader how one idea results in or leads to another idea. This essay pattern provides a snapshot of the beginning or present circumstances and then walks the reader through the steps that lead to what comes next.

A **cause and effect** paper might be organized in the following order:

1. Introduction
2. Cause or initial circumstances
3. Effect or results
4. Further explanation
5. Conclusion

To identify this organizational pattern, watch for language describing circumstances or factors that then lead to a change or to new circumstances. If you sense that an author is trying to explain how something happened or came into being, he or she may be utilizing a cause and effect structure.

> **Helpful Hint**
>
> Think of cause and effect like dominos. Tipping over the first domino could cause the entire line to fall. Similarly, one action, event, or decision leads to multiple effects.

A text using a cause and effect organizational pattern may use the following transitions to organize its main points:

Accordingly	Because	Due to
As a result	Consequently	Therefore

On Your Own

Practice identifying causes and effects in the following sentences.

> According to research conducted by behavioral scientist Roger S. Ulrich, the presence of nature can lead to positive health outcomes among hospital patients.

> Ulrich's work has led architects to design hospitals with more green space in the form of trees, bushes, and other plants.

Chronological Order

An essay organized **chronologically** generally describes a progression of events over time. Step-by-step instructions are written this way; they describe the actions that readers should take sequentially, one after the next. Personal stories or narratives are also often written in this way as action unfolds from one moment to the next.

Chronological papers often follow this type of outline:

1. Introduction
2. First event
3. Second event
4. Third event
5. Fourth event
6. Conclusion

Usually, a chronological organizational pattern will utilize transitions that help the reader follow the sequence of events or ideas. Here are a few common examples:

After	Furthermore	Next
Finally	Immediately	Second
First	Later	Then

When you are trying to identify a chronological organizational pattern, watch for the basic elements of **narrative writing,** such as **setting** and **characters.** Personal reflections, historical accounts, and news reports are just a few examples of texts that often use chronological order.

Group Activity
With a partner, discuss the routine you do every morning to get ready for the day. Describe your actions chronologically, and use transitions to help your partner follow along.

Compare and Contrast

When you compare two or more ideas, you describe their similarities; when you contrast these ideas, you point out the differences. As an organizational pattern, **compare and contrast** involves describing Idea A and comparing or contrasting it with Idea B.

A compare and contrast paper may be structured like this:

1. Introduction
2. Description of Idea A
3. Description of Idea B
4. Differences between Idea A and Idea B
5. Conclusion

In a longer paper, the writer may want to examine Idea A and Idea B together in relation to various sub-topics:

1. Introduction
2. Idea A and Idea B compared to Idea C
3. Idea A and Idea B contrasted with Idea C
4. Conclusion

Using compare and contrast helps readers understand ideas in relation to each other. When reading these types of texts, you may feel like you're watching a tennis match. The repeated movement between two or more compared or contrasted ideas resembles a ball being hit back and forth between players.

Texts with a compare and contrast organizational pattern may contain the following transitions:

However	In the same way	On the other hand
In contrast	Likewise	Similarly

Writing Environment: Everyday

You're constantly comparing and contrasting as you make personal decisions. Should I take this job or that job? Should I attend this school or that school? Note the tennis-match pattern of the following paragraph about choosing a car. It relies on a compare and contrast organizational pattern to organize its supporting details:

> The KIA Optima gets about 35 miles to the gallon, whereas the KIA Sorento, a bigger vehicle, only gets about 30. According to reviews, the Optima is less likely to need replacement parts than the Sorento. On the other hand, I do like how high up you sit in the Sorento compared to the Optima, which is a sedan. However, I'm not sure that'd be practical for my elderly father, who rides with me often. The Sorento engine is going to have a lot more power than the Optima; whether or not I actually need that power, though, would be another important point. In the end, I'm not sure which of these options would be best.

Order of Importance

In some texts, authors begin with the most important point and then build upon it with minor relevant points. In other cases, the writer may choose to do the opposite, starting with the minor points and building to the most important idea.

Order of importance papers may follow one of these two patterns:

1. Introduction
2. Idea A: Most important point
3. Idea B: Minor point
4. Idea C: Minor point
5. Conclusion

1. Introduction
2. Idea A: Minor point
3. Idea B: Minor point
4. Idea C: Most important point
5. Conclusion

Writers show importance with the following transitions:

Best of all	Foremost	Less importantly
Critically	Key	Most importantly

Helpful Hint

Organizational patterns can be applicable to an entire paper or even just to a single paragraph. In either case, clear organization helps the reader understand your ideas more easily.

Spatial Order

Spatial order is generally used for describing something by moving from one point to the next. For example, if an author is describing a city park, he or she might "walk" readers along a central path and describe what the audience would see along the way.

Another approach would be to describe a scene from left to right, beginning with a grassy sitting area on the left, a gazebo in the center, and a flower bed on the right.

A spatial text can be organized in any direction: top to bottom, left to right, in a circle. Here's an example of a spatial outline:

1. Introduction
2. Item at the top
3. Item in the middle
4. Item on the bottom
5. Conclusion

Descriptive writing that guides your senses from one location to the next likely uses spatial order. You might also identify a spatial organizational pattern if you see these transitions:

Above/below	Next to	To the right/left
Near	On the opposite side	Under/over

Topical Order

Texts organized **topically** are fairly common. A writer will develop a list of supporting details or points in support of the main idea of the paper. In relation to one another, these points are equally important.

A paper organized in topical order might look like this:

1. Introduction
2. Idea A
3. Idea B
4. Idea C
5. Conclusion

In these types of texts, the points will frequently use transition words or phrases to refer back to the author's main idea, keeping the discussion focused:

For example	For instance
To illustrate	Another way

> **Helpful Hint**
>
> While the topical organizational pattern is one of the most common essay structures, a good writer uses a variety of organizational patterns to support his or her purpose and main idea. When reading, don't assume the author is using topical organization.

Writing Environment: Academic

Imagine a student in a natural biology class is describing how well certain tree species thrive in different settings. Either of the following topical organizational patterns would be appropriate:

1. Sycamore
2. London Planetree
3. Oak

1. Crowded cities
2. Rural areas
3. Forests

Writing Environment: Academic

Topical organization is sometimes known as **support organization** when the main points of a paper are arguments or support for the main idea. This is the most typical approach to writing in introductory English classes.

Lesson Wrap-up

On Your Own

Which organizational pattern do the following outlines use? Check the box next to your answer

1. Outline:
   i. Introduction
   ii. Cause or initial circumstances
   iii. Effect or results
   iv. Further explanation
   v. Conclusion

   Organizational Pattern:
   ☐ Topical
   ☐ Cause and Effect
   ☐ Order of Importance
   ☐ Spatial

2. Outline:
   i. Introduction
   ii. Item on the left
   iii. Item in the center
   iv. Item on the right
   v. Conclusion

   Organizational Pattern:
   ☐ Topical
   ☐ Cause and Effect
   ☐ Order of Importance
   ☐ Spatial
   ☐

3. Outline:
   i. Introduction
   ii. Idea A – Most important point
   iii. Idea B – Minor point
   iv. Idea C – Minor point
   v. Conclusion

   Organizational Pattern:
   ☐ Topical
   ☐ Cause and Effect
   ☐ Order of Importance
   ☐ Spatial

4. Outline:
   i. Introduction
   ii. Idea A
   iii. Idea B
   iv. Idea C
   v. Conclusion

   Organizational Pattern:
   ☐ Topical
   ☐ Cause and Effect
   ☐ Order of Importance
   ☐ Spatial

Key Terms

Audience: the person or people who read or interpret a text

Character: a person or thing imagined or invented by an author for a story

Cause and Effect Organization: an organizational pattern that shows causal relationships between ideas

Chronological Organization: an organizational pattern that shows a sequence of events

Compare and Contrast Organization: an organizational pattern that shows similarities and differences between ideas

Descriptive Writing: a writing mode used to communicate the characteristics or qualities of a thing or event

Narrative Writing: a writing mode used to tell a detailed story about a sequence of events or experiences that occur during a defined period of time

Order of Importance Organization: an organizational pattern the presents the most or least important information first

Organizational Pattern: the order of ideas within a text

Purpose: the author's goal for writing

Setting: the time and place in which a story takes place

Spatial Organization: an organizational pattern that presents physical characteristics in a logical progression

Support Organization: another name for topical organization when the main points of a paper are arguments or support for the main idea

Thesis Statement: a sentence or multiple sentences that express the main idea of a paper

Topical Organization: an organizational pattern that lists equally important main points

Transition: a word, phrase, or sentence that shows a relationship between ideas

Writing Application: Identifying Organizational Patterns

Read the following essay that summarizes and responds to a publication about international women with low economic and social status. What organizational pattern does it use? Does this pattern work well with the topic?

The Effects of Poverty on International Women

In many nations across the globe, poor women face social structures that foster inequality: work-related roles, political participation, marital practices, and cultural assumptions that men may and even must dominate women, even if by force. Still, according to *Voices of the Poor: From Many Lands*, a publication of the World Bank, "There are now formal laws in all countries that, to varying degrees, legally safeguard women's interests when their husbands die or abandon them" (Narayan 482). But *Voices of the Poor* also notes that many women must forego these rights and follow customary practices.

> This introduction does not provide many clues about the organizational pattern of the essay.

In some parts of Nigeria, poorer women frequently hold low-status positions in organizations. Thus, even though they're able to take part in the work of local institutions, they have little voice. Males make most of the decisions and "women continue to be excluded from civic and religious forums" (96). At the "Court Hall," women must sit outside. Additionally, only men may enter mosques—which provide "religious and moral direction to the community"—to worship.

> The phrase *In [location]* is repeated throughout the essay to lead the audience from one idea to the next. This indicates spatial order.

In Bangladesh, the marital tradition of dowry puts pressure on poor families to gather vast amounts of money for their daughters' marriages. As a result, daughters may have little choice in the process, and they may marry younger than usual or else families run "a very high risk of being stigmatized and their daughters risk being sexually violated" (128). Many families will even reduce their own consumption or fall into debt due to dowries.

The transition *as a result* indicates a cause and effect relationship even though the entire essay is not organized this way.

Even when "securely" married, many women experience injustice. In Argentina, social norms sanction domestic violence against women, thus highlighting another structure that nurtures inequality, the belief that men must subdue women: "Sons beat their mothers" and husbands "teach their sons to beat women up" (343). Such abuse occurs in many nations, though to various degrees and the problem is on the wane in some places.

This essay also uses topical order. Each country's practices are discussed as equally important points.

In these and other nations, cultural norms and tradition have generally dictated that women not work outside of the home. Rather, their role is to tend to family and domestic needs. While this is in fact an important role, it leaves women dependent upon men for economic survival. This also means that men make most all decisions for, as one Brazilian discussion group of women notes, "whoever has the money controls the situation" (372).

Clearly injustice and inequality continue to characterize many women's lives around the world. Even though many legal protections are in place, such laws are often not enforced. Government bodies and non-governmental organizations must enact awareness campaigns that champion women's rights and work to enforce these laws if equality is ever to be a reality in throughout the world.

Overall, this essay used both spatial and topical order to discuss the inequality that faces women of low economic status.

Works Cited

Narayan, Deepa, and Patti Petesch. *Voices of the Poor: From Many Lands*. World Bank, 2002.

Lesson 5.4
Purpose, Audience, and Tone

William Shakespeare famously wrote, "All the world's a stage, and all the men and women merely players." All of life, he seems to be saying, is a performance. Similarly, all writing is a performance, a writer working "on stage" for others to see and experience his or her work.

Like any theatrical or musical performance, writing can be driven by a variety of **purposes** and can be intended for a variety of **audiences**. Writing is also going to *sound* specific to its author.

To learn more about various purposes for writing, see Chapter 1.

Consider the differences between the sounds of an opera and those of a rock concert. The opera's sound is likely produced by a full orchestra, whereas a rock concert's sound is likely created by drums, guitars, and keyboards. Likewise, the texts you read are going to sound very different, or express a very different tone, from one performance to the next. **Tone** is the positive, negative, or neutral attitude that an author expresses about the topic of a text.

Although it's important for authors to convey their own attitudes toward a topic, they must also consider the perspectives of their audiences. Imagine how audience members would react if they paid for and expected the sounds of an orchestra but instead observed a rock concert.

Good authors write with their intended audiences in mind as they work toward an intended purpose. When you're a part of that audience, it's important to think critically about the text to uncover the author's intended meaning and evaluate his or her claims accordingly.

In this lesson, you will learn to approach reading critically with three main skills:

Analyzing an Author's Intended Purpose
Considering an Author's Expected Audience
Recognizing an Author's Tone

Analyzing an Author's Intended Purpose

In order to best understand an essay and analyze it critically, you have to understand the writer's **purpose** for writing it in the first place. Determine this and you can then begin to determine the writer's motives for making certain choices within the writing.

Some texts seek to entertain; some are intended only to inform. One author might want to convince you to adopt a new belief, while another aims to discuss a complex issue *without* trying to convince you to think one way or another about it. Many—if not most—texts you'll encounter throughout your college and professional career will seek to achieve a variety of combined purposes.

On Your Own

See if you can match each of the following purposes with its corresponding writing passage.

A. Writing to Describe   B. Writing to Propose
C. Writing to Argue   D. Writing to Analyze

1. Purpose: _____

   > The rows of books revealed him to be quite the reader. Jack's study had bookshelves, end tables, crates, and boxes, all of them covered with books. Even the posters, with platitudes like "Read on!" and quotes from William Wordsworth, indicated that Jack was truly a bibliophile, a lover of books.

2. Purpose: _____

   > Research has found that sexual assault on college campuses has increased dramatically over the last several years, yet too many students also say they don't know how to define "assault." We need more effective awareness programs that both educate students and inform them of steps they can take to prevent sexual assault.

3. Purpose: _____

   > In 1528, Martin Luther wrote *Liber Vagatorum* ("The Book of Vagabonds and Beggars"), in which he described a "community chest" of food and supplies for the poor. The chest was funded by a tax on all citizens. Luther's approach inspired the social service networks that exist today.

4. Purpose: _____

   > Examining U.S. aid over the last two decades will reveal how much war, U.S. domestic and international priorities, NGOs (non-governmental organizations), IGOs (international governmental organizations), and media coverage have all influenced American foreign-aid policy.

Context

Purpose is heavily determined by **context**, or how and when information is presented.

- How long or short is the piece of writing?

- What is its format? For example, is it a book, magazine article, or short essay?

- Does it appear online or in print?

- Does it use visuals?

- When was it written?

- What do you know about the author?

- If an essay or article appears within a publication, consider the purposes of that particular publication. How might those purposes influence the specific piece of writing?

Consider the following introductory paragraph. It appears on the website for a local news station. In this context, the writer doesn't have space to develop long, detailed passages full of descriptive writing or analysis. Rather, s/he must be direct and to the point, and the essay will be fairly short:

> The school board must pass a balanced budget that empowers teachers and students with vital resources. For too long, our school system has overspent while neglecting the technological resources necessary for today's classrooms. Without these resources, teachers can't fully prepare students. If this board cannot show progress this year, it's time for a re-election.

Limitations

As you read, analyze, and discuss writing, keep these questions in mind:

- If an assignment or publication requires only short essays, is it fair to criticize an essay for not elaborating every point thoroughly?

- If an essay is intended for a formal, academic audience, can you fault it for not entertaining you enough?

- If an article is written by a humorist, must the article use formal and complicated word choice?

If you evaluate a text without making these considerations, you ignore context and may not read accurately or with full knowledge of a writer's purposes. In fact, to do so might even be unfair to the author.

Writing Environment: Academic

When reading and analyzing essays for class, be sure you apply these same questions, but also be sure you consider the purposes of a particular class or assignment, as well. Your instructor may want you to read for content and keep track of what a piece of writing *says*. But he or she may also want you to consider *how* something is written so you can understand writing as a craft. Read assignment instructions and prompts very closely. These are your guides for how to understand the *purpose* of a text, as well as the *purpose* of your assignment.

Group Activity

Spend a few minutes comparing two very different magazines or online publications, such as a sports magazine and a current events journal, or a travel magazine and a trade publication. As you do, consider these questions for discussion:
- How long are the articles in each publication?
- Do they use a lot of images?
- Are the paragraphs long or short, or a mix of the two?
- How would you describe the word choices? Are the words simple or complex in meaning? Do you know the meaning of most of the words?

Now, consider the differences between these publications and consider why their creators may have taken different approaches to the writing.

Recognizing an Author's Intended Audience

Unless we're writing in a private journal or some other personal format, we're *always* writing for an audience other than ourselves, even if we're not always thinking of that audience as we write.

To learn more about writing to a target audience, see Lesson 6.2.

Once you determine an author's purpose, within his or her particular context, you can then determine who they're writing for. This is the writer's **audience**. This audience might be generalized, or it might be a very specialized group. An audience might be rather large and diverse, or else it might be confined to a specific, uniform group of people. Note that even though you are reading a particular text, this doesn't necessarily mean that an author intended that text to be directed at *you* or even some group that you're part of.

Writing Environment: Everyday Situations

Think about purpose, audience, and tone as you read the following passage:

> If you're like me, and you really like living in this neighborhood, then you'll also care about this traffic problem. Almost every day I find myself dodging vehicles that refuse to stop at the four-way intersection at the heart of our neighborhood. And almost every day I see kids getting off of school buses needing to be walked across the street by the crossing guard with such caution and concern because she, too, has seen how drivers passing through our neighborhood aren't concerned about the problems they might cause.

In this passage, the writer addresses her neighbors in a way that is warm and personable because her readers are likely allies to her cause. Her audience includes friends and people who will likely share her concerns, so she uses the second person *you*, thereby addressing them directly. She also tries to relate to the readers' experiences in an informal way (*If you're like me*). Finally, she provides evidence that her readers will care about: children's safety.

Analyzing Audience Expectations and Limitations

When considering audience in your analysis of a text, think about the following questions:

What kinds of readers would find the writing interesting?

An essay analyzing character development in a theatrical script by Henrik Ibsen may not, for example, be appealing to a broad audience. Whereas general audiences might find an informative piece about the job market to be pretty relevant.

What do readers already know? What do they need to know?

If an article describes a game won by a local sports team, then an audience of local readers likely does not need a lot of background information on the team. On the other hand, a detailed statistical analysis of that team's season may, for that same local audience, require further explanation because not everyone understands sports stats.

How invested are they already in the topic? Do they need to be convinced that the topic is significant or important?

If readers already believe in the importance of a cause or topic, they may need less explanation or background on why it's being written about. If the topic is new to readers or they may not readily see the significance of a topic, then a writer may need to provide deeper explanation.

What is the relationship between author and audience?

If the writer and his audience members are likely in disagreement on an issue, then he will need to justify and explain his thinking more thoroughly. If the relationship between writer and readers is more agreeable, then the writer's tone will likely be more welcoming and kind.

Writing Environment: Professional

Here's another question for consideration when it comes to audience: What are readers' expectations for a text? On the job, a clear understanding of the purpose of a report or other text will enable you to have clear expectations when reading. For example, if a report is intended to simply inform its readers about a topic, then you can read that report to gather information. But if its purpose is to analyze a method or product, then you'll need to read more critically and piece together various concepts to determine what you think about the report. In each case, you can expect purpose to influence your expectations about content.

Group Activity

With a small group, study the following image and discuss how you might describe it for two different audiences: (1) a group of tourists, and then (2) a group of engineers and architects.

An engineer's view of a bridge would be different from that of a non-engineer.

Recognizing an Author's Tone

You can determine an author's tone by considering how the word choices and sentences "sound" as you read them, considering the emotions (or lack of emotions) that they convey.

Tone is influenced by purpose and audience, and a writer's chosen tone should help advance the writer's goals for a piece. For example, an essay with a playful attitude or tone might be fitting for a reflective essay about memorable childhood experiences. On the other hand, a playful tone would be inappropriate—and even insensitive—for an essay about the problem of childhood illiteracy.

As you read, consider the author's choice of words and the reactions they evoke. Do the words sound harsh? Does the word order de-emphasize important factors? You can use a wide variety of adjectives to describe the tone of a text. Here are some examples:

Joyful

A writer may want to sound cheerful or happy about his or her topic.

Angry

Anger can help readers understand the severity or significance of a topic.

Reflective

A reflective tone shows the writer to be absorbed in thought.

Sarcastic

A sarcastic tone points creatively and even humorously to ironic, hypocritical, or generally concerning aspects of a topic.

Distanced

A distanced tone remains objective in relation to its subject matter, and the author may avoid asserting his personal opinion.

Word choice can be a very powerful tool. Consider the following sentence:

> The mayor is being ridiculously stubborn and I, too, refuse to budge on the issue.

> Note the assertiveness of this statement. These words indicate opposition toward the subject.

On Your Own

See if you can match each excerpt with its tone.

Example 1:

> "The next president could get together with the leaders of both parties in Congress and say: "We're going to change the way we do business in Washington. We're going to deliberate and negotiate. We'll disagree and wrangle, but we will not treat this as good-versus-evil blood sport." That kind of leadership might trickle down.
> But it's increasingly clear that the roots of political dysfunction lie deep in society. If there's truly going to be improvement, there has to be improvement in the social context politics is embedded in."
> - David Brooks, *New York Times* columnist

Tone:
- ☐ Friendly
- ☐ Sarcastic
- ☐ Nostalgic
- ☐ Argumentative

Example 2:

> Well, I guess you never do know how a dog is going to act when it's cornered, do
> you? I'd not hold it against that old pooch of mine if he did defend himself, if he did
> growl and snap and even lunge. (How is he supposed to know what you intend to do
> if you're a stranger and standing over him?) Nope, can't say I'd blame him one bit.

Tone:

- ☐ Friendly
- ☐ Sarcastic
- ☐ Nostalgic
- ☐ Argumentative

Example 3:

> "Sure, I'd go with them into those dark woods – as soon as I transformed into a ninja
> warrior and grew four more limbs, the better to fight with. Because, yeah, I'm always
> looking for a good scare and a chance to narrowly escape danger. The old Windsor
> place had, supposedly, been host to murders, fires, natural catastrophes, and ghost
> sightings, dating all the way back to the Civil War. So I was delighted the group
> asked me to join them on this ill-advised venture to explore."

Tone:

- ☐ Friendly
- ☐ Sarcastic
- ☐ Nostalgic
- ☐ Argumentative

Example 4:

> "I took along my son [to the lake], who had never had any fresh water up his nose
> and who had seen lily pads only from train windows. One the journey over to the
> lake I began to wonder what it would be like. I wondered how time would have
> married this unique, this holy spot – the coves and streams, the hills that the sun set
> behind, the camps and the paths behind the camps. I was sure that the tarred road
> would have found it out, and I wondered in what other ways it would be desolated. It
> is strange how much you can remember about places like that once you allow your
> mind to return to grooves that lead back."
> – E.B. White, from "Once More to the Lake"

Tone:

- ☐ Friendly
- ☐ Sarcastic
- ☐ Nostalgic
- ☐ Argumentative

Lesson Wrap-up

Key Terms

Audience: the person or people who read or interpret an author's message

Context: how and when information is presented

Evidence: the specific information an author uses to illustrate or prove a claim

Irony: a literary technique in which meaning is expressed through language that usually indicates an opposite meaning

Purpose: the goal an author seeks to achieve in writing a text

Slang: casual words or expressions specific to a particular group of people, like teenagers or sports fans

Supporting Details: a piece of information, also called evidence, that is used to support a main idea

Tone: the positive, negative, or neutral attitude that an author expresses about a topic

Writing Application: Purpose, Audience, and Tone

The following excerpts both examine famine in 1980s Ethiopia. Consider the influence of each author's unique purpose, audience, and tone you read each excerpt:

1. Author: a student completing an academic assignment

I'm interested in the images and stereotypes that Americans have of Ethiopia as a political state but even more so of Ethiopians as a people. Any mention of Ethiopia to many Americans will conjure recollections of famine, starving children, and bands playing in Live Aid to raise emergency funds. Some may note the proliferation of marathon runners coming from that region. Others may be aware of Ethiopia's Christian Orthodox history, the nation's more recent Communist history, or even the rule and grandeur of Haile Selassie. But generally speaking, starvation is the prism through which most Americans view Ethiopia. And yet, of course, these stereotypes don't account for much.

> The tone of this text is formal and informational.

Today, Ethiopia has a growing export market, in particular in leather, livestock, and hydropower as the government has successfully created electricity-producing plants on its major rivers. The country also has its own commodity exchange, which enables farmers to effectively sell their crops, including sesame, corn, and coffee. While Ethiopia still experiences severe famine at times, this East African nation is not defined solely but such famine. Ethiopia has also made great strides to establish economic stability.

> The author provides evidence to support her claim that Ethiopia is not defined by only famine.

2. Author: a journalist discussing her career

I distinctly remember seeing that footage from Ethiopia for the first time, those newscasts in the 1980s from the BBC. They showed people that didn't even look like people; they were so frighteningly thin and frail, so much so you could almost count their tired bones. I know that's a cliché, and maybe even hard to believe, but in this case, I swear

> This author uses informal language and powerful, descriptive words to paint a picture for the audience.

to you it's true. Viewers could see and study them as skeletons more than live and healthy humans.

And the people moved so slowly, through the food lines, to the medical clinic, to their cots. They had so little energy, it seemed. Parents could barely hold onto their kids' hands as they shuffled along so silently. Just so slowly. So, so slowly.

I knew then that I had to dedicate my life to preventing this from ever happening again. As a writer, as a storyteller, I knew that such tragedy would become the subject of my work. In the end, not a whole lot else mattered.

Lesson 5.5
Recognizing Rhetorical Appeals

Before an election, politicians use carefully crafted persuasion to sway voter opinion. Through speeches, ads, and debates, the candidates emphasize their qualifications and electability. Many politicians use biased, misleading information to promote their platforms. Others resort to exaggerated slander against their competition, hoping to make themselves look good by comparison.

Rhetoric—language designed to persuade or impress an audience—is a key element in political campaigns. Campaign rhetoric is extreme, but rhetoric itself is not inherently negative. It is simply persuasive speech. You encounter rhetoric every day in advertising, news, social media, speeches, screenplays, and more.

While an advertisement or an opinion article is clearly pushing you to buy a specific product or believe a certain way, other texts are intended to persuade their audiences in more subtle ways. Imagine that you are reading an article about the history of the telephone. The author's main purpose is to inform. Whether the author realizes it, however, s/he is also trying to convince you that his or her article is true and reliable.

Argumentation strategies are used in a variety of contexts outside of academics.

Learning to recognize the rhetoric around you will help you strengthen your skills as both a reader and a writer.

In this lesson, you will learn more about rhetoric through the following topics:

The Basics of Rhetoric

The Rhetorical Appeals

Group Activity

As a group, make a list of three to four commercials you've seen on TV. What memorable features do you recall about each ad? What aspects of the ad were convincing? Which aspects were annoying? What aspects piqued your interest?

The Basics of Rhetoric

Most texts include an element of persuasion, even if the author is simply convincing the audience to accept his or her perspective. A strong writer wants readers to recognize the time, research, and thought spent on the topic so that they conclude that the information is valid and reliable.

Rhetoric is an effective approach for persuasion because it involves appealing to an audience using three complementary appeals: *ethos*, *pathos*, and *logos*.

Ethos, *pathos*, and *logos* are the cornerstones of a triangle, and authors use these strategies to form a convincing argument.

- *Ethos*: an appeal to ethics

- *Pathos*: an appeal to emotion

- *Logos:* an appeal to logic

Consider the chart below for examples of how the medical community might use these different strategies to appeal to an audience:

ETHOS	PATHOS	LOGOS
The audience's need to trust the speaker	The audience's emotional responses	The audience's intellectual, logical responses
"In my 10 years as a pediatrician, I've treated over 400 ear infections."	"As a parent, it hurts to see your precious little ones in pain."	"In 9 out of 10 clinical trials, EarEase reduced swelling and inflammation within 24 hours"
Establishes the speaker as a doctor, an authority figure with credible experience	Triggers empathy, reminding the audience of feelings associated with ear infections	Includes numbers and statistics that suggest proof of the product's effectiveness

A strong persuasive argument uses a balance of all three elements.

Unfortunately, media companies and advertisers often attempt to manipulate people through the use of flawed rhetoric, also called **logical fallacies.** One example is false authority, which is the claim that fame makes a person an expert.

To learn more about logical fallacies, see Lesson 5.8.

The Rhetorical Appeals

Ethos

Ethos is an appeal to ethics. When evaluating this type of appeal, you'll want to determine whether or not to trust the information in a text. You'll consider **credibility**: what makes someone or something believable. An effective text will use the opinions of experts to argue its points.

> Reflection Questions
>
> Think about the type of people you would consider experts. What kinds of qualifications do they have?

One type of *ethos* is a person's professional credentials. An article about weight loss would be more reliable if it included information from doctors or medical researchers. Similarly, a manual on construction site safety would be considered more trustworthy if it were written by a construction supervisor.

You should also consider personal experience. For example, a prize-winning home gardener would be considered credible even though he doesn't have formal education in gardening. Instead, he has years of personal experience that make him a knowledgeable and reliable source of information.

Finally, *ethos* can be based on someone's trustworthiness. The way that a person has acted in the past will affect his current credibility. You probably remember the old fable about the boy who cried *wolf*. Because he had a history of lying, the villagers considered him an unreliable source of information.

When faced with new information, make sure to always check the source of the information. First, look at the author of the text and any sources within the text. Are these people credible based on their credentials, experience, or trustworthiness?

You should also look at the arguments that the authors are making. Their credentials, experience, and trustworthiness should fit the purpose of the text. For example, a doctor who specializes in lung disease might not be the best source for information about car maintenance. A college athlete would likely know more about college sports than about the NFL.

Keep in mind that *ethos* does not guarantee that an argument is valid. Plenty of experts within the same field disagree or even contradict each other. A good argument will use a balance of *ethos*, *logos*, and *pathos* to prove its point.

Logos

A **logical argument** makes a reasonable claim using facts and statistics. **Facts** can be verified and are accepted by the majority of experts in the field. **Statistics** represent data from research studies, and they are most accurate when gathered from a wide range of research methods and samples. To locate this sort of **evidence**, look for statements like this: "Experts agree that 25% of Americans think cats are better than dogs."

To learn more about types of supporting details, see Lesson 5.2.

Not all facts and statistics are reliable. Always be on the lookout for clues that a source might be untrustworthy or biased, as these factors could impact the validity of the information.

When possible, also investigate how the information was gathered. A survey of only five people would not be as reliable as a survey of over five hundred. The sample size should be large and the research methods should be appropriate for a well-constructed, valid research study.

A logical argument must also be reasonable. The author's **conclusions** should match the types of facts and statistics included in the text. Look at this example:

> Cars are dangerous. Every year, the National Highway Traffic Safety Administration reports that thousands of people have been killed in car accidents. In 2012, over 33,000 people died in the United States alone ("Traffic Safety Facts" 1). This is 32,980 more fatalities than airline travel, one of the most commonly feared modes of transportation (Locsin). In response to these statistics, state and federal lawmakers have passed legislation to increase driver awareness and vehicle safety. To reduce the number of fatal car accidents, the federal should lower the maximum speed limit on highways to 65 miles per hour.

> In this paragraph, the author uses good facts and statistics to make her point. The conclusion that she makes at the end of the paragraph, however, doesn't make sense. None of the information she shared would be a logical argument for speed limits.

Pathos

The final argumentation strategy is *pathos*, an appeal to emotion. Human emotions are strong. If an argument makes you feel emotional about a topic, you will probably act on those emotions.

An author can use *pathos* by choosing words that appeal to the audience's emotion. Read the following sentences, carefully considering the emotional impact of each.

> The results of the drought were bad for the town.

> The results of the drought were devastating for the citizens of Claremont Valley.

> ▶ Which one is the most expressive and powerful? While both sentences suggest that the impact of the drought was negative, using the word *devastating* and sharing the name of the town is more likely to spark an emotional response from the reader.

Emotions can also be communicated through the **anecdotes** or **examples** that an author chooses to include in a text. These stories help the audience personally relate to the logical information being presented. For example, charities often use anecdotes to encourage donations. Once you hear the stories of real people who have been impacted by a charity, you are more likely to donate your time and money.

Finally, one of the most effective ways to communicate emotions is through the use of images. A picture or a video can trigger emotions in mere seconds, even without any words or text. Think about the commercials and advertisements you see every day. Many of them use images of happy families, funny animals, or beautiful scenery to make an emotional impact on their audiences.

While pathos can be an effective tool for making an argument, emotions can also be potentially misleading. Have you ever heard of "making an emotional decision"? This phrase means that you were so caught up in your emotions, you didn't stop to think through the facts. A reliable text will use emotion to support its argument, not to manipulate its audience.

Reflection Questions

An argument that uses too much *pathos* can quickly become cheesy or melodramatic. When have you experienced this in the past? What was your reaction?

Writing Environment: Professional

Cover letters often use rhetorical appeals to convince an employer that you are qualified for a position. An effective letter will acknowledge the needs of the prospective employer (*pathos*), indicate your experience and skills (*ethos*), and demonstrate your experience and training as proof of your qualifications (*logos*).

Writing Environment: Everyday

Many political leaders and visionaries have used rhetoric to unify people and offer hope. Dr. Martin Luther King, Jr. was a master of rhetoric. Dr. King's famous "I Have a Dream" speech contains many examples of the three rhetorical appeals working together.

> "Five score years ago, a great American, in whose symbolic shadow we stand today, signed the Emancipation Proclamation."

> King's references to President Lincoln and the Lincoln Memorial (where he gave the speech) appeal to *ethos*. He even hints at the language of the Gettysburg Address with "five score." Establishing common ground with Lincoln suggests, "Those who admire Lincoln will trust me."

"Many of our white brothers, as evidenced by their presence here today, have come to realize that their destiny is tied up with our destiny . . . their freedom is inextricably bound to our freedom. We cannot walk alone."

References to growing white support for the Civil Rights movement appeal to *pathos* by creating feelings of unity, freedom, and brotherhood.

"America has given the Negro people a bad check, a check which has come back marked 'insufficient funds.' And so we have come to cash this check."

King's "bad check" analogy is a logos-based appeal that helps the audience understand the disadvantages African Americans faced in society.

Lesson Wrap-up

Key Terms

Anecdote: a long example told as a story

Argument: a reason why you should think or act a certain way

Conclusion: the result of a logical argument

Credibility: what makes someone or something believable

Ethos: an argument based on a person's credibility

Evidence: the specific information an author uses to illustrate or prove a claim

Example: a specific instance or illustration that demonstrates a point

Fact: a piece of information that most people generally agree to be true

Informative Text: a text that gives the audience information about a topic

Logical Argument: an argument that makes a reasonable claim, usually using facts and statistics

Logos: an argument based on logic

Paragraph: a short piece of writing that focuses on one main idea

Pathos: an argument based on emotion

Persuasive Text: a text that convinces its audience to adopt a belief or take an action

Purpose: the goal of a text

Statistic: a number or percentage that represents research data

Supporting Detail: a piece of information, also called evidence, that is used to support a main idea

---

Group Activity

As a group, choose an article from the *New York Times* Opinion website (http://www.nytimes.com/pages/opinion/). Read the article and discuss the *ethos*, *logos*, and *pathos* being used by the author.

Writing Application: Recognizing Rhetorical Appeals

Campaign Speech – Karen Burrows for Ohio State Senator, District 22

Good afternoon, Sunnyvalers! I'm Karen Burrows, and I'm running for State Senate. Sunnyvale has enjoyed longstanding status as a leader and risk-taker in our district, but we can't afford to rest on reputation. I want to see us reach our potential, push forward, and take Ohio with us! District 22 needs leaders who aren't afraid to tackle Ohio's toughest challenges and create solutions.

In this introduction, note the use of we and our. These are appeals to ethos, establishing common ground with the audience.

That has been my policy as a leader in Sunnyvale. That has been my policy in my law practice. That will be my policy as your state senator.

I grew up right here in this neighborhood. I went to school down the street at Arden Elementary. Stingray blood runs through my veins. In high school, I spent my Friday nights as the "Dancing Stingray" mascot at football games. I'm a Sunnyvale girl who wants to continue to serve my city and take the next step to serve my state.

This is where I learned that accomplishment and service are more important than who you know and what you own. I learned to listen, to negotiate, and to keep an eye on the bigger picture. I also learned that I can't walk away from a tough battle if I expect to change my world and improve the lives of people around me.

My late father, Dr. Dale Burrows, served Sunnyvale as a pediatrician for almost 40 years. He taught me that serving people and listening to people is the most important work you can do. Now, it's my turn to serve and to continue his legacy of service.

As councilwoman, I served Sunnyvale for two terms before my current role as City Attorney. The past 8 years have been very busy and offered me invaluable preparation to serve in the state senate. I have worked to re-route commercial traffic to keep our residential areas safe. I'm very proud of our new women's shelter and of the state initiatives against domestic violence that I've supported. Later this month, I look forward to cutting the ribbon at the groundbreaking ceremony for the new "Senior Care" wing at the Sunnyvale Hospital.

Here, the author appeals to logos, emphasizing her proven success with evidence.

My hometown is near and dear to me, but I believe I have more work to do. I want to see higher levels of cooperation between police officers and citizens. I propose improved training for law enforcement personnel and higher standards for citizens to hold our public servants accountable for their actions, including my own!

As Sunnyvale moves forward through these trying times, many of our citizens are concerned about jobs continuing to disappear, forcing them into Cleveland and other urban areas. I will be a senator who pushes for job creation and renewed commerce in mid-sized cities like Sunnyvale.

It's time for leadership with a local perspective to operate at the state level. We have to represent community interests on a statewide scale. As your senator, I will work tirelessly to protect the rights of small business owners, the stability of family farms, and the quality of life for everyday Ohioans.

Recently, I worked to prevent state confiscation of a local dairy farm. I'm pleased to say that legislation is now being considered to reform the process of agricultural foreclosures. I recognize the struggles of local farmers and the need to give longstanding local businesses every opportunity for success. I believe that's what the constituents of District 22 want, and that's what I intend to give you.

Sunnyvale is my home, where my family has lived for generations and where my son plays baseball for the Sunnyvale Sluggers. Like so many of you, I learned to swim out there in Wheeler Creek. I'd love to see it cleaned up and restored so that future generations can enjoy it as much as we did.

Here, the author makes an appeal to *pathos* with a nostalgic tone and emphasis on personal feelings and experiences.

I believe my experience is a proven scaffold to build upon for Sunnyvale, for District 22, and for Ohio. I know Sunnyvale, I love Sunnyvale, and I believe in all Sunnyvale can become. I want the opportunity to serve you and to serve our district. When you go to the polls, I'm asking you to check "Karen Burrows for District 22." Thank you!

Lesson 5.6
Analyzing Word Choice

As a reading audience, we are often constrained by a lack of knowledge about the author and his or her intentions. Thus, as *responsible* readers, we must think critically about the word choices an author incorporates into a text. What do these specific word choices tell us about the true, intended meaning an author hopes to convey?

In this lesson, you will learn how to recognize and think critically about the following:

Tone
Details
Bias

Tone

Authors are always attempting to achieve a goal, whether it's helping you understand a topic better or convincing you to take action. Identifying that goal is the first step in understanding the meaning of a text. Then, you consider the audience, which includes you, the reader. To achieve his or her purpose and reach the target audience, the author employs tone.

Tone is the attitude expressed about the topic of the text. Tone is usually described using adjectives that are positive, negative, or neutral.

Positive	Negative	Neutral
excited	angry	objective
encouraging	disapproving	straightforward
confident	critical	direct

In most cases, tone is not stated outright; instead, the reader has to read between the lines to determine how the author feels about the topic.

If you notice that many of the words have negative meanings, the tone is likely critical, sarcastic, or skeptical. Likewise, if many of the words have positive meanings, the tone may be optimistic, encouraging, or confident.

Using completely neutral language is difficult, but a text that uses words without any strongly positive or negative meanings is trying to be as objective and unbiased as possible.

Details

In addition to the vocabulary an author uses, pay attention to the details emphasized in the author's word choice. Keep in mind that writing always involves choices. Two authors writing about the exact same topic might end up using completely different tones simply because they included different words and details.

Think about these questions:

> What details does the author choose to include?
>
> Why does the author feel it is important to include these details?
>
> What details has the author chosen to ignore or exclude?
>
> Why does the author feel these details are unimportant?

If the author includes mainly negative details about the topic, he may want to achieve a negative tone. Likewise, if he includes mainly positive details about a topic, he probably wants to use a positive tone. A mix of positive and negative details would indicate a neutral tone.

Read through these examples:

Negative

> This was the worst tornado to come through the town in over fifty years. Entire neighborhoods were damaged or destroyed, and many of the survivors were struggling to find food and shelter.

Positive

> After the tornado swept through the town, the community immediately supported everyone who had suffered losses. Friends, neighbors, and strangers united in a way that transformed the entire area.

Neutral

> The aftermath of the tornado resulted in several million dollars of damage. However, local outreach groups provided free food and supplies to those in need.

Purpose and tone are closely related. An author may use tone to make an argument more persuasive or to help the audience relate to the topic. If the tone doesn't support this purpose, the author's writing will be unsuccessful.

Helpful Hint

Thinking critically about an author's purpose and tone can help you enhance your own writing skills.

On Your Own

Read the following online review, paying close attention to the emphasized words and details. What is the overall tone of this review? Check the box that contains your answer.

> My husband and I visited Marion Diner on the recommendation of a friend who is also a local food blogger. As we were walking into the restaurant, we were greeted with the delicious scent of sautéed garlic and rosemary. The waiter was friendly and knowledgeable about the menu. She even recommended her personal favorites. The menu itself was not lengthy at all. Clearly, this restaurant focuses on a few key specialties and customer favorites. I was surprised to see the blend of fresh, healthy ingredients incorporated into traditional "diner food."
>
> I ordered the Bleu Ribbon Burger with baked onion straws, and my husband had the Grandstand Salad. My burger was cooked perfectly, although the onion straws were more seasoned than I would have preferred. I'm not a salad fan, but even I had to admit that my husband's meal looked great.
>
> Overall, I would definitely recommend Marion to anyone who's looking for a fresh twist on well-loved diner favorites.

☐ Negative   ☐ Neutral   ☐ Positive

Reflection Questions

In a text message or social media post, it's impossible to see a person's body language or hear his or her voice inflection. This can lead to awkward mix-ups when tone is misunderstood. How do you communicate tone in a text message or tweet? Is this method effective?

Bias

All authors have personal experiences and beliefs that influence the way they write about specific issues. For instance, someone who rides the train to work every day may have a strong opinion about the importance of public transportation. He would be more likely to write a letter to city hall arguing against a proposal to reduce funding for the train system.

Everyone is influenced by their personal beliefs.

Bias is a term used to describe a person's personal experience and preferences.

Think about how word choice and tone can indicate bias. Selecting extremely positive or negative words often signals that the author is trying to manipulate the audience.

Look at these examples:

Unbiased

> The investigation revealed that the café manager had caused the fire by leaving a pot of boiling water unattended.

Biased

> The investigation revealed that the negligent café manager must have thought talking on the phone was more important than monitoring the safety of his kitchen.

> ▸ Do you notice the difference? The first sentence focuses on giving the reader information, while the second sentence uses negative words to make the manager seem like a villain. Unless the manager is an actual supervillain, the author should make his point using supporting **evidence**, not emotional language.

Spin

Authors sometimes use **spin** to put a topic in a more positive light. Here's an example:

> This quarter, profits stayed slightly below average. One possible factor may have been customer satisfaction. While customer complaints were not as low as expected, over 23% of customers stated that they were satisfied with the support they received.
>
> In this example, the author uses an extremely positive tone to describe a situation that is actually negative.

Exclusive Language

One final way that word choice indicates bias is the use of stereotypes or **exclusive language** about a person's age, ethnicity, gender, or religion. This is almost always an indication that the piece of writing contains bias against certain groups of people. Look at the following examples:

> The high number of accidents involving female drivers this year gives credibility to the saying that women can't drive.

> The accident was caused when the driver, a woman, grazed the side of the car next to her.

> ▷ Both of these sentences show bias by using exclusive language. In the first sentence, the author uses a clear stereotype about women. The bias in the second sentence, however, is a little harder to detect. In this example, the author uses exclusive language by choosing to include the driver's gender, even though this information is unnecessary to the meaning of the sentence.

When evaluating the reliability of a text, remember to ask yourself these questions:

> Does the author use an extremely negative tone?
>
> Does the author use a positive tone to spin information?
>
> Does the author use stereotypes or exclusive language?

Lesson Wrap-up

Key Terms

Agenda: an author's hidden motive

Argument: an author's presentation of reasons why you should think or act a certain way

Bias: a person's opinions and preferences

Conflict of Interest: when an author has a personal stake in a topic that affects their purpose

Evidence: a piece of information, also called a supporting detail, that is used to support a main idea

Example: a specific instance or illustration that demonstrates a point

Exclusive Language: disrespectful language that refers to a person's gender, ethnicity or culture, physical or mental ability, or sexual orientation

Fact: a piece of information that most people generally agree to be true

Informative Text: a text that gives the audience information about a topic

Paragraph: a short piece of writing that focuses on one main idea

Persuasive Text: a text that convinces its audience to adopt a belief or take an action

Purpose: the author's goal in writing a text

Spin: making a topic seem more positive than it actually is

Supporting Detail: a piece of information, also called evidence, that is used to support a main idea

Tone: the positive, negative, or neutral attitude that an author expresses about a topic

Writing Application: Analyzing Word Choice

Review the following blog post. What can you learn about word choice from the author's choice in language?

Yesterday, I went skydiving for the first time. It was incredible and much less expensive than expected! When we arrived, we got into our jumpsuits and harnesses, but it didn't feel real until we got in that airplane. The closer we got to the clouds, the more real it felt. My palms started to sweat. My heart raced feverishly. When the first diver took her jump, I thought I would bail out! I had volunteered to go last, but I started thinking that was a mistake.

> This descriptive sentence sets an exciting tone for the text by using positive wording.

> These details shift the tone from positive to anxious.

Ultimately, I decided not to overthink it. The next thing I knew, I was flying. Even though I was plummeting toward the ground, I felt still. The ground looked like it was rising to meet me. My face, apparently, was not as still—in the pictures I saw later, it was flapping in the breeze like a bulldog.

> The writer uses both creative and humorous details to reflect on their personal experience.

I'll never forget the landing. It was like abruptly waking up from a dream. But, there *was* something comforting about feeling my feet back on the ground. I took a few deep breaths, scanned the open field around me, and enjoyed the rush of the experience. In all, it was an unforgettable day. I would recommend it if you're feeling adventurous or you want to feel alive!

> Although the writer is recommending the experience, her purpose is not persuasive. Instead, she is entertaining her audience and reflecting on her experience.

I'm ready to go again.

Lesson 5.7

Understanding the Basics of Logic

Every day, you are confronted with conflicting opinions in news articles, social media posts, and online discussions. In these situations, logical thinking will help you determine which opinions are more believable.

Logic involves using critical thinking to reach a **reasonable conclusion.** One of the most well-known examples of logic is the fictional detective Sherlock Holmes. Holmes famously solves crimes by using both inductive and deductive logic to consider all the evidence and reach the most logical conclusion. He notices the tiny details that everyone else overlooks and refuses to let emotion cloud his judgement.

Logic is what makes Sherlock Holmes a great detective.

Understanding the basics of logic will help you use critical thinking to become a better reader and writer.

This lesson will help you learn the basics of logic:

Premises and Conclusions
Deductive and Inductive Reasoning
Evaluating Logic in a Text

Reflection Question
Failing to think about a situation logically can result in jumping to the wrong conclusions. Think about the last time you made an incorrect assumption. What prevented you from thinking through the situation more carefully?

Premises and Conclusions

In its most basic form, a **logical argument** is made up of two main components: premises and conclusions. **Premises** are the statements that an author uses to make an argument. These premises should lead to logical conclusions.

The history of logic actually goes back much further than Sherlock Holmes. One of the most famous examples of premises and a conclusion was created by the philosopher Aristotle in Ancient Greece:

Premise 1: All men are mortal.
Premise 2: Socrates is a man.
Conclusion: Therefore, Socrates is mortal.

The first premise in this argument is that all men are mortal, a **fact** that everyone agrees is true. The second premise states that Socrates is a man, another fact that everyone agrees is true. Therefore, if all men are mortal and if Socrates is a man, then the logical and true conclusion is that Socrates is mortal.

> Helpful Hint
> Think of premises and conclusions like the parts of an essay. Just as a main idea must be supported by evidence, a logical conclusion must be supported by its premises.

On Your Own

Read the following argument and identify the premises.

> Some frogs are poisonous.
> Frogs are amphibians.
> Therefore, some amphibians are poisonous.

Deductive and Inductive Reasoning

There are two main types of logical reasoning: deductive and inductive.

Deductive Reasoning
Deductive reasoning starts with a general premise and works toward a specific conclusion.

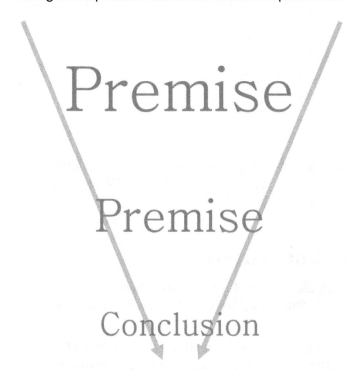

Consider this example:

> **Premise 1**: All full-time employees at my company receive ten paid vacation days.
> **Premise 2**: Kenna is a full-time employee.
> **Conclusion**: Therefore, Kenna has received ten paid vacation days.
>
> The argument in this example starts with a general statement about all full-time employees. The second premise is more specific, and the conclusion is the most specific. Since Kenna is a full-time employee, she receives a certain number of paid vacation days.

Because deductive arguments are concerned with reaching true conclusions, they must be valid and sound. For a deductive argument to be **valid,** the conclusion must be supported by the premises.

Consider this example:

> **Premise 1**: All men are mortal.
>
> **Premise 2**: Socrates is a man.
>
> **Conclusion**: Therefore, Socrates is mortal.
>
> In this example, the conclusion, *Socrates is mortal*, is supported by the premises, so the argument is valid.

Once you've determined that an argument is valid, the next step is to determine if it's sound. A **sound** argument is not just valid; it also has true premises. The premises in the previous example are true: all men are mortal, and Socrates was a man. Therefore, the argument is sound.

Now that we've determined that the argument is both valid and sound, we can confidently say that the conclusion is true.

If a deductive argument is valid but one or more of the premises is false, the argument is unsound.

Think about this example:

> **Premise 1**: All men are American.
>
> **Premise 2**: Socrates is a man.
>
> **Conclusion**: Therefore, Socrates is American.
>
> This argument is valid because the conclusion is supported by the premises. If all men are American, and Socrates is a man, then it would make sense that Socrates is American. However, the conclusion is obviously false: Socrates wasn't American; he was Greek. What went wrong? The first premise is false: all men are not American. Therefore, the argument is unsound.

Helpful Hint

You can think of of *valid* as a synonym for "logical" and *sound* as a synonym for "true." However, as the previous example demonstrated, an argument could follow logical reasoning and still be false. As you analyze arguments and create your own, remember that the deductive arguments should not just be logical; they should also lead to true conclusions.

Use the flowchart below to test deductive arguments and determine if their conclusions are true.

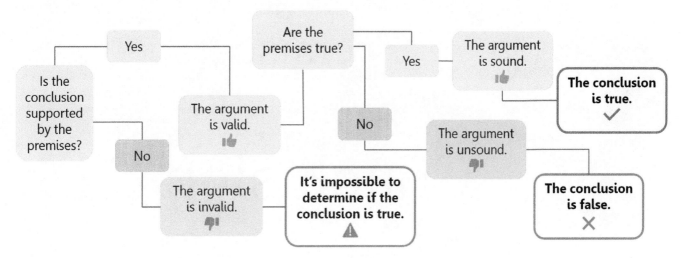

Think about the following example:

> **Premise 1:** Full-time city bus drivers make less than $20,000 a year.
>
> **Premise 2:** Amanda is a full-time city bus driver.
>
> **Conclusion:** Therefore, the city should raise minimum wage to $15 an hour.
>
> In this example, the premises are true and closely related. However, the argument is **invalid** because the conclusion introduces new information that is not supported by the premises. To make this argument valid, you must revise either the premises or the conclusion so that new ideas aren't introduced in the conclusion.

On Your Own

Complete the deductive arguments below by adding a second premise and conclusion to each.

Premise 1	Premise 2	Conclusion
All birds have four-chambered hearts.		
All U.S. citizens have social security numbers.		

Inductive Reasoning

Deductive reasoning is rare in the real world because there are very few arguments with general premises that are considered 100% true, or valid. Instead, you're more likely to encounter inductive reasoning. **Inductive reasoning** uses specific premises to reach a general conclusion.

Premise

Premise

Conclusion

A common example of inductive reasoning is political polling. Obviously, interviewing every voter in the United States would be impossible. Instead, polling organizations interview a limited number of people and use those results to predict the behavior of all voters in general.

Because inductive arguments use specific examples to make general conclusions, they can never claim that a conclusion is *absolutely* true or valid, unlike deductive arguments.

Here's an example:

Premise 1: Every tornado I have seen in Kansas has rotated counterclockwise.

Premise 2: The tornado that hit Kansas last night rotated counterclockwise.

Conclusion: Therefore, all tornadoes rotate counterclockwise.

Both premises in this argument are true. However, they are based on very specific pieces of information. The general conclusion that all tornadoes rotate counterclockwise cannot be made with such a limited amount of evidence.

An argument that uses inductive reasoning can only claim that a conclusion is *probably* true. Therefore, a better conclusion might look something like this:

Conclusion: Therefore, the tornado predicted to hit Kansas tomorrow will probably rotate counterclockwise.

The more evidence included in an inductive argument, the more logical its conclusion. By adding a third premise to the previous example, the inductive reasoning becomes even stronger.

Premise 1: Every tornado I have seen in Kansas has rotated counterclockwise.

Premise 2: The tornado that hit Kansas last night rotated counterclockwise.

Premise 3: The last ten tornadoes in Kansas have rotated counterclockwise.

Conclusion: Therefore, the tornado predicted to hit Kansas tomorrow will probably rotate counterclockwise.

On Your Own

Complete each inductive logic statement with an additional premise and a reasonable conclusion.

Premise 1	Premise 2	Conclusion
Marcella Rogers is a professional cyclist.		
The sun rose at 6:35 a.m. this morning.		

Evaluating Logic in a Text

Understanding logic is a useful skill for both authors and audiences in most writing situations. It will help you identify and evaluate the credibility of other writing. You're less likely to be fooled by faulty or weak arguments if you know how to analyze the reasoning behind them. Likewise, knowing the characteristics of a well-developed logical argument enables you to construct stronger arguments of your own.

Most texts do not have clearly labeled premises and conclusions. Before you can evaluate an argument's logic, you must be able to identify the parts of the argument in the text.

Consider the following example:

> Many people fear certain kinds of technology, such as robots or automated interfaces. They believe that using this technology in everyday life will lead to more errors or accidents in the workplace and will alienate humans from the each other. However, using robotics in healthcare actually does just the opposite: it allows for more consistently accurate medical procedures and more interpersonal, empathetic care. For one, robot surgeons have proven to be much more precise than human doctors when making incisions, and they are not prone to fatigue or mood swings. Moreover, the use of automated devices for simple medical tasks allows nurses to better attend to patients' emotional needs and check on them more frequently since they don't have to worry about menial chores.

If you were to unpack the logic of this paragraph, it would look something like this:

> **Premise 1**: Accurate medical procedures and empathetic emotional care are desirable for the healthcare system.
> **Premise 2**: Robots and automated interfaces allow for accuracy and increased empathetic care.
> **Conclusion**: Robots and automated interfaces are desirable for the healthcare system.

Once you've identified the author's premises and conclusion, you can determine whether or not you believe the argument is logical and believable.

Inductive reasoning is the most commonly used type of logic in writing. When an author includes facts, **statistics**, **examples**, and other types of **supporting details**, he or she is laying the groundwork for a logical conclusion.

Helpful Hint

In many essays, the order of the logical argument is reversed: the conclusion comes first and the premises come second. This is because the introduction usually contains the logical conclusion while the body paragraphs contain the premises.

Some texts use both inductive and deductive reasoning to make an argument. For instance, if an author is arguing that the city should pursue a major-league sports franchise, he or she might use inductive reasoning to persuade the city to take action. However, the author is also making a deductive argument about major league sports.

Inductive Logic

> **Premise 1**: A major-league sports franchise will bring jobs to the city.
> **Premise 2**: A major-league sports franchise will bring positive media coverage to the city.
> **Premise 3**: A major-league sports franchise will bring a sense of community spirit to the city.
> **Conclusion**: The city should pursue a major-league sports franchise.

Deductive Logic

> **Premise 1**: Jobs, community spirit, and media coverage are good for the city.
> **Premise 2**: A major-league sports franchise offers jobs, community spirit, and media coverage.

Conclusion: A major-league sports franchise is good for the city.

> The deductive logic here is *valid*; however, it's debatable if Premise #1 is *sound*. Some people might want their town to remain small and don't like community gatherings or media attention.

Now that we've discussed logic, you will begin to notice that the assumptions a writer makes are often based on implied deductive premises.

Writing Environment: Everyday

The following short paragraph is based on inductive reasoning. Note that the conclusion appears early in the writing to clarify the overall point the author is trying to make. Is there an unspoken deductive argument here as well?

I fell in love with North Beach as soon as I moved here three months ago. However, I have one major problem with our town: it doesn't have any bike paths! <u>I think adding some paths would really improve our quality of life.</u> For one, <u>biking is a very healthy activity, and bike paths would encourage more people to get outside and exercise.</u> Second, <u>since we have so many local businesses that are easily accessible to residents, many of us don't need to drive our cars to get to them.</u> If we had more bike paths leading to Smith Street where so many of these businesses are located, we could cut down on traffic and perhaps even encourage more support for our local entrepreneurs! <u>Finally, bike paths could help cut down on accidents. I've seen two bikers get run off the road over the last two weeks, and one of my friends was grazed by a car when she was riding down Fresna Street last Friday.</u> Let's keep our biking neighbors safe and encourage more people to ride by adding some paths— then our wonderful neighborhood will be even better!

The first underlined sentence is the writer's logical conclusion. Then, the author presents the first two premises.

Here, the author presents the final premise.

Lesson Wrap-up

Key Terms

Deductive Reasoning: a type of logical reasoning that starts with a general premise and argues toward a specific conclusion

Example: a specific instance or illustration that demonstrates a point

Fact: a piece of information that can be proven and/or most people generally agree to be true

Inductive Reasoning: a type of logical reasoning that uses specific premises to reach a general conclusion

Invalid Argument: a deductive argument with a conclusion that is not supported by its premises

Logic: a way of thinking with a focus on finding or building reasonable claims

Logical Argument: an argument that makes a reasonable claim, usually using facts and statistics

Logical Conclusion: the proper, accurate result of a relationship between two or more premises that are valid and sound

Premises: a set of two or more pieces of evidence used to support a logical argument

Sound Argument: a deductive argument that is valid and has true premises

Statistic: a number or percentage that represents research data

Supporting Detail: the specific information, also called evidence, used to support a main idea in an argument

Unsound Argument: a deductive argument that is valid but has false premises

Valid Argument: a deductive argument with a conclusion that is supported by its premises

Writing Application: Understanding the Basics of Logic

The below essay uses the following logical argument to oppose the elimination of school sports programs.

Premise #1:

High schools should support activities that build character and discipline and provide a means for students to succeed in college.

Premise #2:

Sports programs build character and discipline and provide a means for students to succeed in college.

Conclusion:

High schools should support sports programs.

Based on the specific premises and general conclusion, this argument uses inductive reasoning.

Eliminating Sports in Schools is a Bad Idea

Organized school sports are being targeted in our area as a result of a million-dollar budget crisis. Many believe such cuts are feasible because sports are "extracurricular" and primarily a source of entertainment. On the contrary, sports programs build character, teach discipline, and increase the chances for many students to further their education and go to college. Eliminating sports will have a negative impact on our student athletes, so we need to continue supporting sports programs.

The thesis states the author's logical conclusion.

As a former high school athlete, I know just how important sports programs can be. Playing sports helped me stay out of trouble by forcing me to be accountable for my grades. Instead of getting into trouble with my friends, I focused on my homework to make sure I was eligible to play in each and every game. In addition, baseball and football gave me a sense of commitment. Before I started playing high school sports, my grades were low, and I would often skip school. However, when I tried out for football, I found out that I would not be able to participate if my grades fell below a certain level or I missed too many classes. I studied hard and only missed class if I got sick. My perseverance paid off, and I graduated tenth in my class out of two hundred students. Without sports, at-risk students like me may lose

Here is a reiteration of the first half of premise #2. The previous sentences attempt to prove that the premise is true.

focus or become vulnerable to destructive behaviors because they don't have a clear set of goals to work toward every day.

Moreover, sports programs provide a way for some teenagers to realize their college dreams. If schools don't budget for sports, many potential college graduates won't get a chance to go to school because they won't be able to earn scholarships. One of my best friends went to university on a football scholarship, but if he didn't have that kind of financial aid, he could not have attended due to his family's economic situation. He is currently studying to be an engineer. What would he be doing right now without that scholarship?

Cutting money out of sports programs will do far more harm than good. Students with solid family support and the means to go to college may be relatively unaffected by such cuts. However, those of us who aren't so lucky stand to lose opportunities and motivations for success if our community doesn't budget for these programs. If you agree with keeping sports in school, let your voices be heard; many of our students' futures may depend on it.

> Here is a reiteration of the second half of premise #2. The sentences after it attempt to prove that the premise is true.

> This is the essay's conclusion, which reiterates the writer's logical conclusion and calls readers to action.

Lesson 5.8
Recognizing Logical Fallacies

Have you ever seen a commercial like this?

> The whole neighborhood is gathered for a big barbeque. There is plenty of food, the sun is shining, and all the guests are beautiful and happy. Then, the scene cuts to a man sitting alone in his house watching TV. He doesn't want to leave because he doesn't have the right sneakers for the occasion. When a sneaker commercial plays on TV, he's inspired to run out and buy them. He laces them up and heads to the barbeque. By the end of the commercial, he's become the life of the party.

Hundreds of commercials use this tactic to argue that if you buy a certain product, you will become a prettier, smarter, or more interesting person. Obviously, this **argument** doesn't make sense. Simply buying one brand of deodorant or body spray will not make you instantly sexy.

However, companies continue to make these commercials because they are effective. Viewers do not always take the time to look beneath the surface and think critically about what a commercial is claiming.

Group Activity
Choose two popular commercials to re-watch on YouTube. As a group, discuss the argument that each commercial is making. How are they different or similar?

A **logical fallacy** is a faulty or incorrect argument. When discovered, fallacies always make a text or presentation weaker. All too often, however, fallacies appear so logical and persuasive that the audience accepts them as fact. This is the goal of a fallacy: to convince a reader or viewer to react before thinking critically.

Many commercials use logical fallacies to sell a product.

Writing Environment: Everyday

Personal beliefs can make a person more likely to accept certain fallacies. If you love chocolate, you would be happy to find an article claiming that because dark chocolate has health benefits, you should eat two pounds of chocolate every day. Obviously, this argument sounds questionable. However, your love for chocolate may lead you to accept the claim of the article without any further investigation or research.

Not all fallacies are intentional. Sometimes, a topic is so personal or emotional that authors or speakers do not take the time to think through their arguments fully. The audience may feel the same way, leading them to accept a faulty argument at face value. While these situations are understandable, they are dangerous because fallacies can lead people to make poor decisions.

> Reflection Questions
> Have you ever made a purchase that you regretted later? What caused you to buy the product in the first place?

This lesson will help you accomplish the following goals:

Recognize Common Logical Fallacies

Find Fallacies in Texts

You can then use this knowledge to become a more critical thinker, reader, and writer.

Reflection Questions

Think about news websites that you consider would consider trustworthy or untrustworthy. Why do you think of these sources in this way?

Recognize Common Logical Fallacies

To find logical fallacies in an argument, you need to become familiar with what they look like. Don't feel overwhelmed by terms that may seem unfamiliar or complicated. Memorizing the names of the fallacies is not as important as knowing their characteristics.

Remember that statements of opinions are not necessarily logical fallacies. However, authors can use logical fallacies in an attempt to support those opinions.

Ad Hominem

Ad hominem arguments attack a person's character or reputation instead of examining his or her actual position. Look at this statement:

> This author has admitted to smoking marijuana in the past, so her new book about climate change must be completely unreliable.
>
> In this example, the author's personal decisions about marijuana do not affect her ability to research and write a book about climate change.

Helpful Hint

Many people are naturally suspicious of advertisements selling a product or service. Recognizing fallacies from a more "trustworthy" source, however, can be difficult. News reports, books, and research studies can all contain fallacies, both intentional and accidental. To avoid being manipulated by false information, don't allow the author or publishing organization to influence your opinion of the author's argument.

Appeal to Tradition

An **appeal to tradition** argues that something is right simply because it has always been done that way. Think about how this fallacy has been used historically to argue for injustices like Jim Crow laws in the American South. Many people claimed that discrimination against people of African descent was acceptable because different ethnic groups had always been kept separate in the U.S.

Bandwagon

A **bandwagon** fallacy claims that something is true because many people are doing it. If you ever tried using this fallacy as a child, your parents probably responded by saying, "If everyone were jumping off a cliff, would you jump too?"

Devil Words

Devil words are terms that stir up negative emotions in an audience. You've seen examples of these in political speeches and advertisements. Think about the words *liberal, conservative, socialism,* and *fundamentalism.* Because people often react strongly to these terms, devil words can label someone or something as negative before the audience has had a chance to think through all the evidence.

Further Resources

This lesson focuses on eight common fallacies. To learn more about these fallacies and others, you can check out this infographic from *Information Is Beautiful*: http://www.informationisbeautiful.net/visualizations/rhetological-fallacies/ or this video series from PBS: https://www.youtube.com/playlist?list=PLtHP6qx8VF7dPql3ll1To4i6vEIPt0kV5.

False Authority

False authority claims that a person's fame gives them authority on a topic, even if the discussion is completely unrelated to their area of expertise. This fallacy is commonly used to sell products that have been endorsed by celebrities. For example, an actor may write a diet book that becomes a best-seller even though that actor has no medical training or experience.

Hasty Generalization

A **hasty generalization** bases an argument about a large group on evidence from a small group. The more subjects that you include in a study, the stronger your argument becomes. This is why companies spend large amounts money on consumer testing before they release a new product. Conducting a survey of five thousand people will give them more reliable information than a survey of only fifty people.

Post Hoc

The Latin phrase *post hoc ergo propter hoc* means "after this, therefore caused by this." A *post hoc* fallacy assumes that one event caused a second, completely unrelated event. Here's an example:

> I passed an orange cat on my way to school this morning, and then I flunked my biology exam. If I want to do well in class, I should avoid all orange cats.

Straw Man

A **straw man** fallacy changes an opponent's argument to make it easier to attack. If a research study concludes that eating large amounts of sugar can lead to childhood obesity, the food industry may claim that these researchers want to make all sugar consumption illegal. By making the researchers' argument sound more extreme, the food industry can convince the public to ignore the findings of the study.

On Your Own

Review the list of logical fallacies and try to come up with your own example for each one.

Logical Fallacy	Example
Ad Hominem	
Appeal to Tradition	
Bandwagon	
Devil Words	
False Authority	

Hasty Generalization	
Post Hoc	
Straw Man	

Group Activity

As a group, write a 1-2 minute commercial that uses a fallacy to argue its point. Try to be as convincing as possible. Share your commercial with the class.

Find Fallacies in Texts

To find potential fallacies in a text or presentation, you must first carefully study the author's argument. Try using the following questions:

What is the author's main idea?

What evidence does the author use to support the main idea?

What is the author's **purpose**?

How does the author want me to respond?

Once you've thought through these questions, you can start looking for possible fallacies in the author's argument.

To learn more about the basics of logic, see Lesson 5.7.

Learning Style Tip

If you're a global learner, you learn best when you understand the big picture. When you are analyzing an argument, read through the entire text first to give you an idea of the overall structure. Then, go back and re-read the information, looking specifically for fallacies.

Writing Environment: Professional

When you are interviewing for jobs, you want to avoid using logical fallacies that your potential employers can see through. Don't answer questions by attacking other candidates (devil words). Also, be careful of false authority, such as claiming to be an expert chef just because your résumé includes the three-months you were a waiter at a local diner.

Another common rule to avoid is making hasty generalizations. For example, the fact that you've led a small team of five individuals is great, but it does not necessarily mean that you have the necessary experience to lead a team of one hundred. You may be capable of this, but find another way to support the question!

On Your Own

Read the following essay and identify the logical fallacies.

> The impersonal nature of the internet could be one major cause of cyber-bullying. When communicating online, many people are more comfortable than they would be in a face-to-face conversation. Research by psychologist Rhonda Peters shows that "typing words on a keyboard feels very different than actually saying them to someone's face" (54). This leads young people to write cruel things online that they would never say in person.
>
> Helping teenagers think about the person "behind the screen" can teach them that their words have hurtful, often tragic consequences. According to a survey of thirteen students at McKinley High School, discussing real-life stories of cyber-bullying makes young people less likely to post cruel comments about others online. The results of this survey show that using a similar strategy would greatly reduce cyber-bullying at schools across America.

Further Resources

Choose an opinion article from the *New York Times* website (http://www.nytimes.com/pages/opinion/index.html). Read the article carefully, thinking through the following questions:
- What is the author's main idea?
- What evidence does the author use to support the main idea?
- What is the author's purpose?
- How does the author want me to respond?

Lesson Wrap-up

Key Terms

Ad Hominem: an attack against a person's character

Appeal to Tradition: an argument that something is right because it has always been done that way

Argument: a reason why you should think or act a certain way

Bandwagon: an argument that something is right because everyone is doing it

Devil Words: terms that stir up negative emotions in an audience

False Authority: an argument that claims a person's fame makes them an expert on a topic

Hasty Generalization: an argument about a large group based on a small amount of evidence

Logical Fallacy: a faulty, or incorrect, argument that appears logical and persuasive

Post Hoc: the assumption that one event caused a second, unrelated event

Purpose: the goal of a text

Straw Man: changing an opponent's argument to make it easier to attack

Writing Application: Recognizing Logical Fallacies

Read the following transcript of a speech given by someone running for governor. Think about the logical fallacies it uses. How effective are they, and have you heard them **before in a similar setting?**

Speech #4 – Town Hall Meeting

In case we haven't had the pleasure of meeting yet, my name is Marcus Wentworth, and I hope to have the honor of being mayor.

> The speaker makes his/her purpose clear.

I need your vote to make this town blossom again. The Wentworths have had a long tradition of leadership in Hartville, and I want to breathe new life into that legacy. I will make this city proud with my ideas for reform and improvement. Recently, I've spent the last three months as a volunteer fireman, which has given me valuable insight into what low-income families experience. I will fight to meet these families' needs. I will boost our economy, lower taxes, and increase high school graduation numbers. I will also add jobs to this town and keep crime at an all-time low.

> This statement is an appeal to tradition.

> This statement claims false authority because three months as a volunteer fireman would not give someone adequate insight into the low-income family experience.

If you've considered voting for my opponent, Mary Swanson, I urge you to reconsider; do you really want a fundamentalist as your next mayor? Let's not forget the fire that burned down half of Tate Middle School when Mary was in office two years ago. Vote Wentworth and keep our schools safe!

> This is an emotionally charged word making this a devil words fallacy.

> This example is a *post hoc* fallacy. One event did not cause the other.

My opponent also says she wants to improve the city's infrastructure, but aren't taxes high enough? I promise that I will never take hard-earned money out of your pocket.

> This is a straw man fallacy as the speaker attacks his or her opponent by changing the argument.

I believe in you, and I believe in Hartville. When you go out and vote next month, remember, vote Marcus Wentworth for mayor! You won't be sorry.

Lesson 5.9

Evaluating Evidence

The Loch Ness Monster is one of the most famous urban legends in the world. According to the stories, this mythical creature has lived in a Scottish lake for hundreds, if not thousands, of years. While some supporters of the Loch Ness legend have produced **evidence** to support their claims, most experts agree that these descriptions, photos, and videos are probably fake.

While you probably don't encounter urban legends in your everyday life, you do come across news reports, articles, books, and emails. All of these texts use **supporting details**, or evidence, to strengthen their **conclusions.** You must learn to evaluate this evidence so that you can decide if a text is trustworthy or not.

This lesson will help you evaluate evidence based on three conditions:

Accuracy

Credibility

Relevance

Sometimes, evidence that seems convincing is actually false.

Reflection Questions

How has the internet made it easier to create and share false evidence?

Depending on the purpose of a text, an author can choose from the following types of evidence:

Anecdote: a long example told as a story

Description: words that appeal to the senses to explain the appearance of someone or something

Example: a specific instance or illustration that demonstrates a point

Expert Analysis: an opinion or statement shared by someone who is knowledgeable about a topic

Fact: a piece of information that most people generally agree to be true

Reflection: the thoughts and feelings of the author

Statistic: a number or percentage that represents research data

Accuracy

The first step in examining evidence is checking for **accuracy.** If the author uses information that is incorrect, the text itself is not reliable. Carefully review each supporting detail and ask yourself the following questions:

> Does this information seem logical?
> How much detail does the author give?
> Are there any other sources that agree?
> Do the results seem consistent?

In extreme cases, an author makes up a piece of evidence. While rare, this does happen. Even well-known writers and researchers have confessed to using false information. Usually, however, inaccurate evidence isn't completely fake. The author might just be careless or unaware.

Evidence based on research, such as facts and statistics, should be clearly explained by the authors or researchers. Look for information about the research methods and calculations. Be cautious of any facts or statistics that use words like *always*, *never*, or *every*. Most studies aren't large enough to make those kinds of claims.

Writing Environment: Academic

In academic writing, peer-reviewed sources are usually a good source of accurate information. A peer-reviewed source has been edited and revised by experts in that topic, and most scholarly articles must go through this process before they're published.

When you are evaluating evidence based on personal experience, like anecdotes or reflections, make sure that the author has shared specific details about the story. If the information is vague or generic, the evidence is probably not trustworthy. Also, watch out for evidence that seems to be overly emotional or manipulative.

> ### Helpful Hint
>
> If authors are doing ground-breaking research or arguing an unpopular opinion, there may not be other sources who agree with their findings. This doesn't necessarily mean that a source is inaccurate. Make sure that authors give clear explanations for these differences and pay close attention the way they come to their conclusions.

Credibility

To prove that the evidence in a text is trustworthy, the author must demonstrate that the information comes from a **credible** source.

Credible evidence comes from an expert in the field. In many cases, the authors or researchers have education and professional training that gives them authority on a topic. Of course, the background and credentials of an expert source should match the evidence. A literature professor would not be as knowledgeable about sports-related concussions as a doctor or trainer would be.

Non-expert evidence is acceptable as long as the source has relevant experience in the topic. For example, someone who runs an eBay business out of his home could be an expert in online selling. This person would probably be a good source for a description of the auction process, not for a statistic about eBay market share.

If the evidence is produced by an organization, that organization should be well-respected and recognizable. Sources that have a personal stake in the information, such as corporations or political parties, are not the best sources of information. Usually, these organizations publish information that upholds their public image and supports their opinions.

You can still use information from these sources; just make sure you acknowledge and explain possible bias. **Bias** is a person's personal opinions and preferences.

Reading Application: Evaluating Evidence

Consider the credibility of the article below. Read the provided notes and add some of your own.

Do Vaccines Cause Autism?

Thousands of individuals across the United States believe that vaccines are a cause of autism. Many parents have delayed or prevented their children from receiving vaccines for diseases like measles or Rubella. Sander Van der Linden, a psychologist from Princeton University's Global Health Program, writes that "a recent study found that although outright refusal is still relatively uncommon, in a typical month, over 90% of surveyed US physicians receive requests to delay childhood vaccines" (119). This has sparked a nationwide debate about the ethics of denying these vaccines. Many parents are terrified that their children will acquire illnesses from non-vaccinated children, particularly those too young to be vaccinated or whose immune systems are especially weakened by other illnesses. This leads to two relevant questions: how did this debate begin, and which side does the medical world support?

> Pay attention to the credentials of the person giving the information. Make sure they are credible, like the one described here.

According to Paul Offit and Susan Coffin, researchers at the Children's Hospital of Philadelphia, it began in 1998 when a study in the UK "published a report of eight children …with… autism following receipt of the MMR vaccine. As a consequence of media coverage of this report, MMR-immunization rates in England fell from 94% to 75% and cases of measles increased" (1). These concerns quickly spread to the United States. There are a few items that are significant about this. First, a study made up of only eight participants cannot be considered credible. Most medical studies are completed over many years with hundreds of participants. When there are more participants, the results are more accurate. Secondly, the study does not address whether the vaccines caused autism. It only claims that children with autism were all given this vaccine. It does not mention that many children without autism were also given this vaccine. Even though there are clear problems with this study, the media spread perpetrated this connection.

> When authors include quotes from reliable sources, you can assume the information is accurate and relevant.

> The word *most* shows the author of this essay making a generalization without evidence. Be careful of these types of statements.

"Over 90% of doctors agree that adults and children should receive all recommended vaccines" (Van der Linden 1). Medical experts deserve the nation's trust far beyond the media, who often spread fear-based rumors while researchers use statistics and evidence. Paul Offit agrees when he cites studies by other doctors: "the hypothesis that the MMR vaccine causes autism has been evaluated now in six separate studies … [that] reached the same conclusion—when autism followed receipt of MMR vaccine, it occurred at a rate that would have been predicted by chance alone" (3). So, there is a correlation between the vaccine and autism, but autism is not caused by the vaccine. The connection is purely coincidental.

Doctors are experts in the medical field. They are credible and reliable sources.

People need to stop spreading the idea that vaccines cause autism. This false belief is based on an unreliable study that was later disproven, and those who spread it are putting children in danger. When parents do not vaccinate their own child, they also put their child at risk for a deadly illness. It's time to act based off fact, not media frenzy.

Overall, this reads as a credible source. However, since this essay is trying to convince you of something, there is some bias here.

Offit, Paul A., and Susan E. Coffin. "Communicating science to the public: MMR vaccine and Autism." *Vaccine* 22.1 (2003): 1-6.

Van der Linden, Sander. "Why doctors should convey the medical consensus on vaccine safety." *Evidence Based Medicine* 21.3 (2016): 119-119.

On Your Own

For each of the following topics, decide if the suggested source is a credible place to find information. Feel free to look up each source if any are unfamiliar.

Topic	Source	Credibility
Ways to avoid cancer	The Phillip-Morris Company	
Best practices for the classroom	Pinterest	
Finding help for depression	American Psychology Association	
Learning to care for horses	American Rodeo Association	
How to choose a college	Facebook	

Relevance

Finally, the evidence used in a text must be **relevant** to the author's main idea. If an author is writing on the ethics of circuses, she should include facts and statistics that clearly relate to this topic. Using irrelevant or out-of-context information is a sign of an untrustworthy text.

Writing Environment: Everyday

Relevant information also applies to practical situations. Imagine you need to buy a new fan belt for your car, a 2008 Toyota Camry. You go to the auto parts store and ask the sales associate for help. However, instead of telling you the types of fan belts available and the prices of each, he tells you that they're having a sale this week on tires. This might be helpful information for someone else, but it's not relevant to your goal.

Certain types of evidence are more relevant to some topics than others. A text on a scientific or technical topic should include more expert analysis, statistics, and facts. On the other hand, a text on a personal topic should include anecdotes, reflections, and examples.

Relevant evidence is also current. Usually, research from fifty years ago is no longer the best source of information. This is especially important in the fields of technology, science, and medicine. In these cases, evidence from only one or two years ago may already be outdated. In a field like history or literature, however, dates are much less important.

Helpful Hint

A copyright year is always listed on one of the first few pages in a book. Use this date as you determine the book's relevance.

To evaluate a source's relevance, consider the following questions:

Does the information relate directly to my topic?
Who is the intended audience?
When was the information published or posted?
Has the information been revised or updated?

Group Activity

Discuss possible research topics you could use in your classes. How current should your sources be for these topics? Can you use information that's fifty years old or older, or should you use recent information? Consider the following topics:

Medical history
Best treatments for diabetes
Christmas stories
Efficient computer software
Excel spreadsheets
Jazz
Clothing in the '90s
Drug culture

Lesson Wrap-up

Key Terms

Accuracy: when information is as correct and unbiased as possible

Anecdote: a long example told as a story

Bias: the personal backgrounds and opinions that authors and their audiences bring to a writing situation

Logical Conclusion: the result of a logical argument

Credibility: what makes someone or something believable

Evidence: a piece of information, also called a supporting detail, which is used to support a main idea

Example: a specific instance or illustration that demonstrates a point

Expert Analysis: an opinion or statement shared by someone who is knowledgeable about a topic

Fact: a piece of information that most people generally agree to be true

Reflection: the thoughts or feelings of the author

Relevance: when information is clearly related to the text around it

Statistic: a number or percentage that represents research data

Supporting Detail: a piece of information, also called evidence, that is used to support a main idea

Writing Application: Evaluating Evidence

Read the following essay about video games and use what you learned in the lesson to evaluate the evidence it uses.

Game On!

People love games. Humans play games as simple as hide 'n seek and tug of war and as complicated as *Dungeons and Dragons* and *Risk.* There are athletic games, like baseball and football; humorous games, like *Apples to Apples*; and cerebral games, like chess and *Scrabble.* How many different ways has humanity found to play? In today's society, however, the word "gamer" almost always indicates a person who plays video games. How did this world-wide phenomenon begin, and where is it headed?

Video games "officially" began with *Tennis for Two* in 1958. The concept of the game was simple: hitting a ball between two controllers (much akin to *Pong,* which would come later). However, coding the game for computers at that time was complicated: a nuclear physicist wrote the programming. The graphics were basically non-existent, and the screen was a simple grid, but people lined up for days to try it ("The First"). Why? The novelty was definitely a factor, but something appealed to gamers at a deeper level as well. Video games introduced a new environment in which people could compete against not only the game but against others, too. This particularly appealed to people who didn't enjoy or excel in traditional games. At an even deeper level, games provide a world where people can escape their problems: "Whatever is on my mind . . .

This information was originally posted on a national scientific site sponsored by the federal government, making it credible.

begins to withdraw. My attention focuses on the relatively simple virtual world . . . nothing in the real world matters right then" (Highland 6). As the industry advanced, gaming arcades proliferated and became a major pastime for millions. People would spend rolls and rolls of quarters as they tried to best others' scores on games like *Pac-Man*, *Galaga*, and *Centipede*.

Michael Highland is a game designer and an expert in his field (the psychology of gaming), so this evidence is credible.

Games advanced from the simpler titles of arcade games to more varied console games. According to *Time*, the first console was created in 1967. However, consoles didn't hit their stride until a few decades later when Nintendo and PlayStation hit the mainstream market. With these consoles, introduced in 1985 and 1995 respectively, gaming saw a huge shift. Instead of players going out and spending tons of change at the arcade, kids and adults alike could play to their heart's content in the comfort of their own homes ("A History"). It was during this period that massive franchises like *Mario*, *Zelda*, and *Final Fantasy* were born.

Dates are important when discussing history; this evidence is relevant to the topic.

This article was published by *Time*, a reputable magazine, so the evidence is trustworthy.

Microsoft joined the mix in 2001 with its Xbox system and again in 2005 with the Xbox 360 (Gross). Microsoft also introduced the achievement system and live online play, ushering in a new era of gaming in which gamers no longer played just for fun but to hear the magical "pop" of an achievement being gained. This proved so wildly popular that other gaming behemoths, like Sony and Steam, followed suit. This made gamers anxious for gaming accomplishments. Being able to challenge friends or strangers online also proved enormously successful.

Michael Gross is a writer on a technology site. The evidence from his writing is up-to-date and credible.

The latest generation of gaming consoles, such as the Xbox One and the PS4, have evolved breathtakingly from their humble beginnings. First-generation games like *Final Fantasy VII* are still classics in their own right, but their graphics pale in comparison to today's offerings. The voice, music, and visual quality of recent games like *Forza 6* or *Halo 5* are photographically realistic as players hit the race track in the rain or fiercely battle The Covenant. It would be easy to believe that there's nowhere else to go from here, but that's far from true. Gaming is now headed into the new territory of virtual reality.

Known by differing names—such as Oculus Rift, HTC Vive, and Sony VR, depending on the parent company—virtual reality devices are the next big innovation headed to PC and console gaming. By wearing a helmet-like visor, the gamer is immersed in the game in a new way. Virtual reality is comparable to 3D glasses but on a much more sophisticated scale. It remains to be seen how many gamers choose to dive this deeply into their games (and their wallets), but it's clear that the gaming industry continues to evolve at a breakneck pace. The Sony VR, for example, launched in October of 2016 (Wright). The idea of

The *Daily Star* is a paper based in the UK. The article is in an academic database, so the evidence is probably credible.

people actually becoming part of the games they're playing to the point that they can feel pain or die has long been a staple of science fiction, but after the introduction of virtual reality, perhaps this concept isn't out of reach.

Works Cited

"The First Video Game?" *Brookhaven National Laboratory.* Brookhaven Science Associates.

Gross, Patrick. "Ten Years of Xbox: a brief history." *TechRadar: The Home of Technology.* Future plc, 15 November 2011.

Highland, Michael. "Breaking Realities: A Subjective Account of Gaming as a Catalyst for the Development of Consciousness." *Video Game Play and Consciousness.* Ed. Jayne Gackenbach. New York: Nova Science Publishers, 2012. 3-12.

"A History of Video Game Consoles." *Time.* Time, Inc., 2016.

Wright, James. "PlayStation VR price and launch date finally revealed." *Daily Star,* 15 Mar. 2016. *ProQuest Central.*

Lesson 5.10
Analyzing Visuals

Every day, you encounter hundreds of images on billboards, commercials, websites, and magazines. You see so many that you probably don't even notice half of them.

Images are powerful tools for communicating ideas. They can influence what you buy, how you vote, and even whom you date. Not all images, however, are trustworthy. Just like a book or document can mislead its audience, an image can manipulate or deceive its viewers.

Learning to evaluate images is an essential critical thinking skill. Once you are able to interpret the meaning of a photo or video, you can decide how you want to respond.

In this lesson, you will learn how to evaluate three aspects of images:

Purpose
Composition
Argument

It's become normal to see hundreds of images every day.

Learning Style Tip
If you're a verbal leaner, you may be tempted to ignore images. Remember that both text and images are valuable resources for any type of learner.

Purpose

To start analyzing an image, you must first think about its **purpose**, or goal. Just like texts, images can achieve many purposes, such as discussing, arguing, responding, and describing.

Reflection Questions
Do paintings or sculptures have a specific purpose? Why or why not?

The purpose of some images is easy to determine. Print advertisements and commercials are usually trying to persuade you to purchase a particular product. Finding the purpose of other types of images, however, may be more difficult.

Often, the purpose of an image is made clear through **context:** how and when the image is presented to the viewer. For example, think about the following photograph. How could context help you determine the purpose of the following image?

The context of an image provides clues about its purpose.

Depending on the context, the previous photograph might communicate any of the following purposes:

Context	Purpose
A scientific magazine	To discuss the physical characteristics of yaks
A travel blog	To argue that Nepal is an excellent tourist destination
A social media post	To respond to the photographer's recent trip to Nepal
A memoir	To describe drinking yak milk for the first time

Keep in mind that the actual purpose of an image may be different from the stated purpose. For example, companies sometimes include photos of military veterans in their advertisements. As a viewer, you have to decide if the purpose of these images is to honor veterans or to sell a product.

Writing Environment: Academic

Textbooks for scientific or technical disciplines usually have specific purposes for any images they include. For example, consider this photo (https://apod.nasa.gov/apod/ap130306.html). To "read" an instructional photograph, you need to move beyond your initial reaction and use critical thinking to analyze it. When you first saw the photo, you may have felt disgusted, shocked, or fascinated. However, did you read the text underneath the image? What did you learn? Did you look at the photo more closely? What did you observe?

Composition

Once you've determined the purpose of an image, you should carefully consider its **composition:** how the contents of an image have been selected and arranged. When creating an image, the artist or designer makes decisions about which details to include and which ones to exclude.

Think about the following example:

Composition involves details that are both included in and excluded from an image.

This image includes seven racehorses and their jockeys. Other details, such as the crowd watching the race or the racing facilities, are excluded. Leaving out these details changes the meaning of the image.

In some instances, composition choices are used to manipulate or mislead. For example, a dishonest real estate agent might create a photo slideshow of a house that excludes important details, such as rotting floorboards or a collapsing roof. When you arrive at the house for a showing, you'll see all of the information that was excluded from the photos.

Artists and designers also use composition to emphasize or deemphasize details. When an item is larger or brighter than the rest of the image, your focus stays on that particular item the longest. In contrast, items that are smaller or lighter are easily overlooked.

Emphasizing or including certain details isn't necessarily dishonest. It's important to remember, however, that images are not "photographic truth." Any time you analyze photos or videos, you need to consider how composition affects the way you interpret their meaning.

Writing Environment: Everyday

Photo-sharing apps and phones with built-in cameras make it easy for anyone to create visuals. Think about the purpose and composition of the pictures you take. For instance, when you use Snapchat to take photos, your purpose might be to entertain your friends or inform them about what you're doing. When you take a selfie, you might arrange the composition by carefully choosing the most flattering angle, lighting, and background.

Argument

The final step of analyzing an image is reflecting on the argumentation strategies it uses to communicate ideas. All images make some kind of **argument**. Even informative photos and videos must argue for your attention and trust.

Arguments often use **rhetorical appeals,** which are divided into three categories: *ethos*, *logos*, and *pathos*.

To learn more about rhetorical appeals, see Lesson 5.5.

Ethos

The first rhetorical appeal is *ethos*, an argument based on **credibility.** Images often include experts to build credibility with viewers. For example, a toothpaste commercial might feature a dentist, while a shoe commercial might feature an athlete.

Images can also be used to add credibility to a text. If an author is writing about the time she spent working for the Red Cross, including images of her travels and experiences would strengthen her *ethos*.

Logos

Logos is an argument based on logic. Advertisements often use before-and-after photos to prove that a certain product will result in weight loss or stain removal.

Logos can also be established by showing just the results of an action or event. For example, an educational video on the dangers of drunk driving might include images of car accidents. The logic is that if someone else got into an accident because of drunk driving, the same thing could happen to you.

> Helpful Hint
>
> Most images don't use just one rhetorical appeal, so make sure you look for all three: *pathos*, *logos*, and *ethos*. For example, a commercial for face wash that features before-and-after pictures of a celebrity is appealing to both *logos* and *ethos*.

Pathos

Finally, *pathos* is an argument based on emotion. Images are often the easiest way to touch the emotions of viewers. For example, a documentary might include images of people living in shelters to help you make a human connection to the problem of homelessness. However, images that rely only on *pathos* can become emotionally manipulative.

Once you've thought carefully about the *ethos*, *logos*, and *pathos* in an image, you can evaluate the strength of the argument itself.

Try asking yourself some of these questions:

Does the image use a legitimate expert to establish *ethos*?

Does the *logos* of the image make sense?

Does the image rely too heavily on *pathos*?

Do the argumentation strategies fit the purpose of the image?

> Group Activity
>
> As a group, choose one advertisement or commercial to analyze. Look for the way that *ethos*, *logos*, and *pathos* are used in the image. Present your findings to the class.

Reading Application: Analyzing Visuals

Spend a few minutes studying the following image. What can you note about purpose, composition, and argument of the billboard?

Photo Courtesy of Wikimedia Commons

Now, read this visual analysis. Pay attention to how the author analyzes these elements within the billboard.

Across the street from my old middle school, there is a billboard advertising for Apple's iPod. This location is deliberate—a space where young people see it regularly. The color scheme is bright and eye-catching, with shades corresponding to choices for an iPod. While the background of the ad is colorful, the people in the ad are featured in silhouette, leaving them ambiguous in their representation, but also standing out amongst the vibrant background.

> The location of this billboard, *near a local middle school*, provides context.

The people in the ad appear energetic, youthful, and fit: one woman is in a bathing suit while another is wearing schoolbag straps. A shirtless man wears a hat while another sports spiky hair. The ad repeats these same four images, each one in a differently-colored tile. Additionally, they all are dancing while wearing earbuds and holding iPods. While each person is featured in his or her own separate tile, the tiles are placed deliberately to make it appear like they are dancing together.

> This image is composed specifically with a youthful audience in mind. Here, the writer provides details that support that analysis.

When I first saw this billboard, I felt confident knowing that I already had the product that the billboard advertises. It made me feel funky and hip, dancing in my own color tile. It was strange reflecting on billboards like this, part of my everyday visual landscape, and how they could have affected me in the past. Moving forward, I'll be sure to not only see the images around me but also hear what they are saying.

According to the author, the advertisement uses *pathos* to inspire people like herself to feel young and have fun by owning an iPod.

Lesson Wrap-up

On Your Own

Think about the photograph below. How do purpose, composition, and argument affect the way you understand and interpret this image? Then, in the following space, write your interpretation of the image and which argumentation strategies you think it uses.

Key Terms

Argument: a reason why you should think or act a certain way

Composition: how the contents of an image have been selected and arranged

Context: how and when information is presented in a text

Credibility: what makes someone or something believable

Ethos: an appeal to ethics in a piece of writing

Logos: an appeal to logic in a piece of writing

Pathos: an appeal to emotion in a piece of writing

Purpose: the overall message an author seeks to convey in a text or image

Rhetorical Appeal: an approach to argumentation based on ethics, logic, or emotion

Reading Application: Analyzing Visuals

Examine the following photograph. Likely, you've seen an image like this before in an ad or online posting. Though it appears ordinary, note how the writer analyzes details, purpose, and composition to better understanding the image's meaning.

The purpose of this photo is to persuade viewers that the organization it represents, Carrier Networking, is professional, accomplished, and creative. The context is established through the office setting and professional clothing of the four figures. It is also important to notice what is not in the picture. The desk surface is clean and without clutter, and there are no coffee cups, snacks, or stacks of paper that would distract viewers or suggest the space is disorganized.

The position of the participants' hands indicates their role in the meeting. In the background, the woman's hands are folded as she listens to her coworker. The man stretches his left arm toward the computer, his finger pointing to the computer screen. He appears to be commenting on what is being shown. The man and woman in the foreground are focused on the laptop screen. Their heads are turned toward their screen and away from the man and woman in the

The purpose of the photograph is explained by analyzing its context: the details about the people and office setting.

Notice how the author points out *why* these items are intentionally left out of the photo, and how it adds to the overall meaning.

Here, the photo's composition is being analyzed as the author includes details about the people's gestures.

background. This suggests that they are not a part of the meeting and are working on something else.

Chapter 6
Writing Critically

Lesson 6.1
Understanding an Argument

Arguments are all around us. Some are **explicit**, or obvious, like when you try to convince a friend to agree with you or when a lawyer defends her client in a courtroom. Other arguments are **implicit**; they convey a message without directly stating a claim.

Arguments are especially important in academic writing. An academic argument requires that you use research to stake a claim, typically in the form of a **thesis statement**.

Arguments are what move disciplines like the sciences or humanities forward. Arguments don't always mean that researchers are angry at each other because an academic argument is not the same as an everyday argument. Academic arguments seek to keep their discipline current, pure, and accurate. In whatever major you choose, you'll encounter differing positions on even the oldest and most important topics of that field.

> In this lesson, you will learn about the following considerations for constructing an effective argument:
>
> Altercation vs Argument
> Evidence
> Occasion
> Goals of Argument

Altercation vs. Argument

The word *argument* is often used negatively as a synonym for *altercation*, but an altercation and an argument are different in key ways. When you have an **altercation** with a parent, significant other, or friend, it's more like bickering without a real purpose. An **argument**, however, involves an evenhanded discussion of two or more sides of an issue.

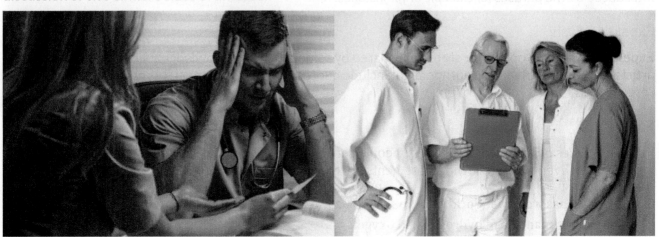

Altercation	Argument
Often occurring spontaneously and during moments of frustration	Fair-minded, pre-planned discussion of a debatable issue
Highly emotional with very little discussion of reasons or evidence, mainly opinion	May involve emotions, but balanced with logical reasoning and evidence

The key difference to remember is that an argument involves a discussion of *reasons* and *evidence*, not just opinion or emotion. **Evidence** is the specific information—statistics, examples, definitions, direct quotes, anecdotes—an author uses to support the main claim in an argument.

Evidence

There are many types of evidence to use, and you'll want to think about what is most appropriate and effective for your argument.

Anecdotes

Anecdotes are long examples told as a story. In an essay on breast cancer, for example, the author might include a personal story about how a friend or family member was affected by this disease.

Author Analysis

Author analysis is an opinion or explanation in the author's own words. This information is used to show how other types of supporting details relate to the main ideas of the text.

Descriptions

Descriptions are passages that explain the appearance of someone or something using words that appeal to the senses. Here's an example:

> Randolph was a short, stocky man with a permanent scowl on his face. My sister Kezia always called him "the bulldog," and after meeting him for the first time, I immediately saw the resemblance. Despite his intimidating appearance, there was something kind about the corners of his eyes. Every so often, they would crinkle with humor, contradicting the frown just a few features below.

Examples

Examples are specific instances or illustrations that demonstrate a point. These details are often introduced by the phrases *for example* or *for instance*.

Expert Analysis

Expert analysis is an opinion or statement shared by someone who is knowledgeable about a topic. In an article about space travel, the author might include quotes from former astronauts and NASA researchers.

Facts

Facts are pieces of information that most people generally agree to be true, such as scientific principles and historical events. The following statements are examples or facts:

> Brazil has won five World Cups in 1958, 1962, 1970, 1994, and 2002.
> Water is made up of hydrogen and oxygen.

Reflections

Reflections are the thoughts and feelings of the author. They are often stated using first-person pronouns such as *I* or *me*.

Statistics

Statistics are numbers that represent research data. For example, a survey may find that 75% of cable TV users think their service is too expensive. This statistic represents all of the people who participated in the survey.

Helpful Hint

If you get stuck writing your argument (e.g., in a thesis statement) or you're unsure if it's truly an argument yet, try using a *because* clause. Add the word *because* to the end of your statement and list out your reasons.

Writing Environment: Everyday

We make arguments all of the time, but we don't always approach them as such since the process is so ingrained. Think about the last time you and a group of friends decided on what to do for the weekend or the last time you planned a vacation with your family. Did you discuss alternatives and list out reasons and evidence for determining a solution? Which version of the examples below best represents your conversations?

> "Laura, do you want to grab a bite to eat?"
>
> "Sure, how does Thai food sound?"
>
> "I've had Thai this week, so I don't feel like eating that again so soon. I'd like something healthy."
>
> "OK, how about the new place up the road? They have salads and low-calorie options."

Notice the reasoning and evidence that goes into this decision-making process. An option is presented and then refuted (or countered) with reasons before a choice is made with evidence to support choosing it.

Of course, decision-making conversations don't always go this well. An example of decision that lacks reasons and evidence might sound more like this:

> "Where do you want to go to eat?"
>
> "I don't care."
>
> "Fine, we'll go to a fast food restaurant."

Although a decision was made in this example, no reasons or evidence was discussed.

When evaluating research for your own argument, consider what the goals of the author might be. Look at the sponsoring organization, the writer's affiliations, and the balance of evidence for all sides. This is one reason academic libraries are so helpful during the research process; they work hard to make sure you're getting a fair point of view.

Occasion

In addition to reasons and evidence, an argument involves a specific **occasion**. You can make arguments about the past, present, or future. As the occasions change, so will certain aspects of your argument.

The ancient Greek philosopher and teacher Aristotle developed three branches of argument that he labeled forensic (past), deliberative (future), and ceremonial (present). Depending on the occasion of the argument, the purposes and topics change.

An argument about the *past* would be considered a **forensic** argument. You've probably seen criminal investigation television shows that mention forensics. This is because they are making arguments about something that has happened in the past. The term forensics is also associated with a courtroom, since arguments that occur in a courtroom are about proving or disproving that something happened in the past.

An argument about the *future* is **deliberative** because options are weighed and a decision about the future is made. The legislative branch of the government engages in deliberative arguments as they make arguments about future courses of action.

Finally, an argument about the *present* is called **ceremonial**. Arguments about the present typically reinforce an idea or value rather than debate what has happened or should happen. A wedding toast, a eulogy, and a sermon are all generally arguments about the present that reinforce currently held ideas or values.

Goals of Argument

We argue with many different goals in mind. Sometimes the goal is to persuade at all costs. For example, **propaganda** uses biased arguments that rely on faulty reasoning or emotion without examining all sides. False advertisements would fall on this part of the continuum.

Writing Environments: Everyday

During elections, politicians often use propaganda to increase support or recruitment without involving a discussion of all sides of the issue. This is one reason "fact checks" have become an important part of journalism during campaign seasons. One candidate might report that another candidate voted to cut spending on a hot-button issue, but he may not reveal that the spending cut was hidden in an amendment or that he advocated for fewer cuts than the previous version of the bill.

A non-partisan organization might create a truth-seeking argument by identifying all of the positions of each candidate without slanting the language or evidence for any particular person. For example, some sites identify all candidates' tax plans and implications of those plans without offering support to any of them.

In a debate, a politician may actually make an academic argument by laying out his or her plans as compared to the opponent's position using logical evidence and reasons. A candidate may share her plan for reducing spending in one area and use the published plans of her opponents to discuss how they aren't cutting spending in that area. In a debate, the opponents have the opportunity to offer their side, too, to keep the argument as honest as possible.

Writing Environment: Professional

A committee is one of the main places that arguments are used in the workplace. At some point, your supervisor will likely task you and a group of colleagues to make a tough decision. In committees, you'll be required to examine all sides of the issue and determine a plan of action. As you consider the following scenario, remember the elements of an argument and note that this type of argument is deliberative (about the future).

The Scenario:
The store manager asks you and a group of colleagues to review the résumés and references of a few candidates he likes. He gives you the criteria for the job and tasks your group with making a recommendation for an assistant manager role. In this case, you might consider questions like those below. Although they may reference past experience, they are deliberating about the future.

> Did her past experience and education prepare her for the role she would have in the company?

> Did her references say she was supportive and fair to her employees?

> Did her references give good reasons for why we she would be a good fit for our organization?

Group Activity

Imagine you are on the academic complaints and appeals committee at your school. A fifty-year-old student scheduled to graduate at the end of the semester has written a letter to your committee asking for his English literature course requirement to be waived. If he has to take the course, he would not be able to graduate on time. He notes that he has earned an A in each of his first-year writing courses, so he says he does not need the writing aspect of the course. He also notes that he has traveled extensively and has taken history courses, so he says he doesn't need the cultural awareness aspect either.

Form small committees and take about ten to fifteen minutes to discuss the student's proposal and weigh the evidence. Then, take a vote and give your individual reasons for your decision.

Key Terms

Altercation: bickering without a real purpose
Argument: a reason why you should think or act a certain way
Deliberative: an argument about the future
Epideictic/Ceremonial Argument: an argument about the present, reaffirming current values or ideas
Evidence: the specific details an author uses to support or prove a claim
Explicit: something that is directly stated
Forensic/Judicial: an argument concerning the past
Implicit: something that is not stated directly
Point of Contention: certain aspects of your argument
Propaganda: a biased argument seeking to persuade without giving all information
Stasis Theory: a process to determine the central issue of an argument
Thesis Statement: a sentence that expresses the main idea of a longer work

Writing Application: Understanding an Argument

Most citizens do not think about the men and women behind the walls of prison systems, and they think much less about what is happening in the prisons. Because of the lack of interest in prison policies, the system in effect in many penitentiaries today is not as effective as it could be. There are many ideas for how prisons should function, but a process needs to be enforced that is productive not only for prisoners but society as well. The high rate of recidivism, or relapses, that results in overpopulated prisons has the potential to be lower. Rehabilitating prisoners is the key to a more productive change in the prison systems because it takes into account the prisoner's background and individuality and benefits both society and prisoners. When compared with other alternatives for prisons, the rehabilitation process actually changes the lives of prisoners, thus making it the best choice.

An academic argument often makes a claim amidst differing points of view. This thesis statement is an example of a deliberative argument since it is about the future.

When a prisoner is released back into society, he or she must learn how to thrive without reverting back to old behaviors that in some instances have become second nature. Violators can either change in the prison system or remain in a career of crime. Because of the unlikelihood of changing themselves without help, inmates will most likely be put back into an overcrowded prison system in which they learn even more about breaking the law through collaboration with others who have committed similar offenses. Offenders need to be put into a situation where the ability to change is present. The best way to help prisoners change "is to make [change] accessible" (Lewin 202).

In this paragraph, the writer identifies lines of reasoning and makes use of evidence to support the argument, separating it from just an opinion piece.

Although there are many benefits to helping prisoners, not all views on prison reformation concur with the idea of rehabilitation. Some people think that inmates do not need a second chance. Without change for prisons, society is affected by more crime and more money spent on housing for repeat offenders. It is easy to see that "punishment is one thing, but our current incarceration policies are wasteful and should be changed" (qtd. in Biskup 33). Some boldly state that a massive overhaul would have to take place in the prison systems for this new method. It is true that many prison officials would need to be trained for such a program and many changes would have to take place, but one source states that "the costs of action are substantial. But the costs of inaction are immensely greater" (Felkenes 293).

An academic argument is fair in its examination of all sides of an issue but offers counterpoints to those perspectives since the goal is to prove the thesis.

Inmates should not be treated as if they are completely different from the rest of society. It only takes one wrong turn for an individual to spiral into a criminal lifestyle. Rehabilitation does not undermine the punitive means behind prison, but offenders can be helped, which in turn helps society. Rehabilitating offenders puts civilization in a better place and allows a change for those offenders. While there may be some work required to put the rehabilitation into effect in prisons, the benefits far outweigh the cost.

The goal of an argument is made clear throughout the essay and reiterated at the end. Here, the reader is reminded that the argument is deliberative in its occasion and an issue of policy.

Works Cited

Biskup, Michael D., ed. *Criminal Justice: Opposing Viewpoints*. San Diego: Greenhaven, 1993. Print.

Felkenes, George T. *The Criminal Justice System: Its Function and Personnel*. Englewood Cliffs, New Jersey: Prentice Hall, 1973. Print.

Lewin, Stephen, ed. *Crime and Its Prevention*. New York: H.W. Wilson, 1968. Print.

Lesson 6.2
Considering Purpose and Audience

Everyone has a sense of style that's unique. When you wear clothing that fits your personality, you feel like yourself. If you've ever found yourself wearing an outfit that wasn't your style, you probably remember how uncomfortable and awkward you felt.

Just like your clothing choices, your writing also has a specific style that fits your personality. You sound more natural when you are comfortable with the words and structures in your text. As a writer, you must learn to adapt to your motive or writing assignment while still being true to your own unique voice.

In this lesson, you will learn about the following:

Writer's Purpose
Writer's Audience
Balancing Purpose and Audience with your Personal Writing Style

Reflection Questions
Think about your own writing habits and tendencies. How does your writing reflect specific aspects of your personality? What makes your writing style unique?

Purpose

Most writing is driven by some combination of several purposes, or goals of writing, that serve to express, communicate, inform, or entertain. Here are some common purposes that can work together to achieve a bigger writing goal:

- **Writing to Discuss**: presents issues or interprets something you have read or studied
- **Writing to Respond**: expresses your reaction, thoughts, and opinions about something you have read or studied
- **Writing to Summarize**: uses a few phrases or sentences to summarize a large piece of information
- **Writing to Describe**: explains the appearance of someone or something using words that appeal to the senses
- **Writing to Argue**: convinces the audience to adopt a belief or take an action
- **Writing to Propose**: gives suggestions and solutions to an issue or problem
- **Writing to Analyze**: examines and evaluates, or thinks critically, about something you have read or studied
- **Writing to Evaluate**: creates criteria and then judges or comments on something you have read or studied

Keep in mind that you should not view these purposes as a defined list of standalone writing strategies. Instead, consider this list a toolbox that you should consult before you write and as you build your writing.

Writing Environment: Academic

Be on the lookout for indicators of purpose in essay prompts and assignment details. Look for key words in the below examples.

> Write a 5-paragraph response to the novel *White Oleander*. Summarize the major themes and discuss how they affect your perspective.

> As you explore Chapter 7 of your textbook, evaluate the approaches to sustainable natural-gas drilling. Do further research and choose one approach you think is most sustainable and economic. Write a proposal for enforcing that approach to decision-makers in your state. Use your research as evidence to support your argument.

When you're writing for school or work, your purpose is often determined by instructions from your professor or supervisor. For example, if your instructor wants you to write a research paper on education reform, your purpose is probably to inform. If your boss wants you to submit a business proposal to a client, your purpose is probably two-fold: to inform and to persuade.

Establishing Context

Imagine the open-ended writing assignment described in the introduction. To start moving forward on that project, you'll want to think carefully about your context. These may seem like simple questions, but the answers have big implications on the effectiveness of your communication. The items below are starting points for identifying what makes up context and why it matters. Each of these impacts your communication choices:

- Who is my audience? Knowing this will have a significant impact on your communication. This is a key one that we'll discuss in the section below, including depth of discussion, vocabulary, and examples.

- What level of formality is expected? Knowing this will impact your word choice, tone, and style.
- How will this be delivered (e.g., online, on paper, in a speech)? Knowing this will impact decisions about what can or cannot be used.

Audience

Once you've decided your purpose for writing, you need to consider your audience. Your **audience** is made up of the people who will read your writing. This might include your professor, your classmates, your coworkers, your friends, or even strangers. The **tone**, or attitude, you express in your writing should be appropriate for both your purpose and audience.

Here's an example. Which of the following sentences would best fit a paper with an informative purpose and an audience of film studies students?

> People praised the film, but I hated every minute of it.

> People praised the film, but I found it disappointing.

> The tone of the first sentence is too negative for a scholarly paper. The second sentence is more appropriate for the audience and purpose.

Meeting Audience Needs

Have you ever heard the advice of imagining your audience in their underwear? While this might calm your nerves in public speaking, in reality, you don't want to ignore your audience's individual characteristics. Knowing your audience is just as important as knowing your purpose because it will shape how you get your point across.

There is no "generic audience" that reaches everyone, so you'll always want to know the particular people to whom you'll be writing or speaking. Ask yourself these questions about your audience when developing your writing project:

- Why does my audience care about this topic?
- What medium or delivery method is my audience most interested in receiving this information?
- From which sector(s) of the population are my audience members?

> **Reflection Questions**
> Who are some of the possible audiences of an email? How would the style of your writing change based on the audience?

Balancing Purpose and Audience with Your Personal Style

The more you gear your writing toward your specific purpose and audience, you write with increasingly narrowed goals in mind. However, it's important to make sure that this stylistic approach still incorporates your personal writing style.

Considerations for your personal writing style include the following:

- Formality
- Complexity

Formality

Formality, the way a text conforms to certain standards, is another factor that affects your writing style. Some **genres**, or types of writing, require a more formal writing style than others. For example, an article for your campus newspaper would probably sound very different from an email to your best friend. Both might use a positive, enthusiastic tone. However, the email would most likely sound more casual than the article. Here are some examples of texts that use different levels of formality:

Formal	Informal
Academic research paper	Personal narrative
Business proposal	Blog post
Cover letter	Text message

Informal writing usually uses first-person and second-person **pronouns** such as *I, me*, and *you*. For example, in an online review of a local restaurant, you would use first-person pronouns to describe your experience:

> I stopped at the Sesame Bakery this morning to pick up a doughnut. The clerk was very rude. Not only did she ignore me for over five minutes, but she also looked extremely annoyed when I asked for assistance. I will not be returning to this restaurant again.

You use informal writing in your everyday life for emails, Amazon reviews, text messages, and Facebook posts. When you communicate with your circle of friends, you can use verbal shortcuts because you know that your audience will understand.

Helpful Hint

If you are writing a more formal text, using an informal sentence will stand out as awkward. Look for slang terms or contractions that aren't consistent with the rest of your writing.

Formal writing is required for many professional or academic genres. In these situations, you use more complex sentence structure and technical terms, and you will rarely use personal pronouns. Even for a formal text, however, you must write in a way that's natural to you. Don't make your writing complicated just to sound fancy.

Formal writing also follows the rules and conventions of Standard English. All of the text should be free of sentence, punctuation, and spelling errors.

The following types of language may be common in informal writing, but they should be avoided in formal writing:

- **Contractions**: shortened versions of words and phrases such as *can't* and *isn't*
- **Slang**: casual words or expressions specific to a particular group of people such as *salty* or *GOAT*
- **Clichés**: popular phrases that have been overused such as, "The early bird gets the worm"
- **Idioms**: phrases—unique to a certain language—that have become clichés such as, "It costs an arm and a leg"
- **Textspeak**: abbreviations, emoticons, and other phrases used in text messages or social media such as *bae* and *ttyl*

> **Helpful Hint**
>
> Many people use multiple end punctuation points in informal writing. Remember, multiple exclamation points, question marks, or a mixture of the two is not considered formal writing.

Remember that your unique writer's voice can come out even in formal writing assignments. Think about the last time you dressed up for a special occasion. Even though your clothing was more formal than usual, it still reflected your individual personality. Your writing should do the same thing. Just because you can't use contractions or slang doesn't mean that you have to sound like a robot.

Complexity

Another factor in writing style is the complexity of your words and sentences. Complexity doesn't have to mean "complicated." Instead, **complexity** just means that your writing has many connected parts.

Sometimes, complicated words are unavoidable. If you're writing about a topic that involves technical or academic terms, you will probably need to use terms that are unfamiliar. However, these words are there for a purpose. Don't use complicated words just because they seem "smarter." Your writing will end up clunky or incorrect.

> **Helpful Hint**
>
> Using a thesaurus while writing is a great way to add complexity to your language. However, pay attention to the meanings of the words. Just because two words are synonyms, it doesn't guarantee that their meaning and connotation are the same. For example, even if *essay* and *dictionary* are listed in a thesaurus as synonyms, most everyone would agree that they are actually very different.

Before you substitute a more complex word, ask yourself the following questions:

> Would I ever use this word in normal conversation?
>
> Do I understand exactly what this word means?
>
> Does this word seem consistent with the rest of my writing?

If the answer to all of these questions is *no*, then you should probably use a different word.

In a similar way, overly-complex sentences can make a text awkward or difficult for your reader to follow. Complicated sentences can be caused by any of the following reasons:

Prepositional Phrases

A **prepositional phrase** is a group of words that starts with a **preposition** and ends with a noun or pronoun.

To learn more about prepositions, see Lesson 9.1.

If you add too many prepositional phrases to a sentence, the reader might have a difficult time finding the **main idea**. Look at this example:

> In situations like the one that the committee of impartial voters selected, the choice between right and wrong becomes complicated by the opinions and suggestions of parties that are outside of the committee's control.

The **subject** and **verb** in this sentence are both buried under all of the prepositional phrases. If all of this information is truly necessary, consider breaking up the sentence into two separate sentences.

Dependent Clauses

Dependent clauses are groups of related words that contain a subject and verb, but do not express a complete thought. Just like prepositional phrases, too many dependent clauses can get in the way of your meaning. Think about the following example:

> Although the position seemed like a good fit, I was nervous because the job that I had before was in a completely different field that I didn't know very well.

To learn more about dependent clauses, see Lesson 9.2.

Passive Voice

In **passive voice**, the subject of the sentence is receiving the action of the verb. In **active voice**, the subject is doing the action of the verb. Sentences using active voice are more direct than sentences using passive voice. Look at these two examples:

Active   The county sheriff filed a report with the court clerk.

Passive   The report was filed with the court clerk by the country sheriff.

Both of these sentences have the same basic meaning. However, the sentence in passive voice seems to be talking around the subject rather than clearly stating its point.

To learn more about active and passive voice, see Lesson 10.6.

Remember that *complicated* doesn't necessarily equal *good*. The best writing can take a confusing topic and make it understandable to the audience.

To make sure your sentences are clear, read your text out loud and mark any areas that are difficult to read. If you find yourself running out of breath or stumbling over your words, this may be a good area to revise.

> **Helpful Hint**
> Many people tend to speak more directly than they write. If you are having a difficult time changing an overly complicated sentence, consider recording yourself explaining the information out loud.

Writing Environment: Professional

Your audience and purpose should influence our organizational pattern. This is important in the workplace, where reports and other documents can have very different organizational patterns. Ask yourself what your readers need. Do they need instructions for how to do something? If so, you might use chronological order. Do they need to understand why a decision was made? You might use order of importance to present each reason.

Lesson Wrap-up

Key Terms

Active Voice: when a sentence is written so that the subject is performing an action

Audience: the people who read your writing

Cliché: a popular phrase that has been overused

Complexity: when a text has many connected parts

Contraction: a phrase that has been shortened into one word

Dependent Clause: a group of words with a subject and a verb that does not express a complete thought

Formality: the way a text conforms to certain standards

Genres: a type of writing

Idioms: a phrase—unique to a certain language—that has become a cliché

Main Idea: the statement or argument that an author tries to communicate

Passive Voice: when a sentence is written so that the subject is receiving an action

Preposition: a word that shows a relationship among people, places, things, events, and ideas

Prepositional Phrase: a group of related words that starts with a preposition and ends with a noun or pronoun

Slang: casual words or expressions specific to a particular group of people

Subject: the person, place, thing, event, or idea a sentence is about

Textspeak: abbreviations, emoticons, and other phrases used in text messages or social media

Tone: the positive, negative, or neutral attitude that an author expresses about a topic

Verb: a word that represents an action, relationship, or state of being

Writing to Analyze: a writing purpose achieved by examining something you have read or studied

Writing to Argue: a writing purpose that convinces the audience to adopt a belief or take an action

Writing to Describe: a writing purpose that explains the appearance of someone or something using words that appeal to the senses

Writing to Discuss: a writing purpose that presents issues or interprets something you have read or studied

Writing to Evaluate: a writing purpose achieved by creating criteria for judging something you have read or studied

Writing to Propose: a writing purpose achieved by giving suggestions and solutions to an issue or problem

Writing to Respond: a writing purpose that expresses personal thoughts and opinions about a text

Writing to Summarize: a writing purpose that presents a small, generalized overview of a larger amount of information

Writing Application: Considering Purpose and Audience

Read the following persuasive letter and consider how language creates a strong tone and clear bias toward one side of the argument.

Dear Mr. Senator,

As an art teacher, I am shocked by your heartless plan to remove national funding for arts programs.

I teach for a program that is partly funded by the National Endowment for the Arts, and I have enjoyed watching my students grow and learn. They and many others benefit from having dynamic, free art programs in their communities that promote creativity and inspire the pursuit of inventive careers and new interests.

The tone here is positive and confident, favoring arts programs.

Since my program is partially funded by the endowment, funding cuts would put the entire program and its staff members in jeopardy. It would also rob students of educational and creative experiences.

Here, emotionally-charged negative words shows bias and create an adverse tone.

In 2016, The National Endowment paid $149.7 million for arts programs in nearly 16,000 communities across the country. These programs include music, theater, creative writing, dance class, and more. The funding also pays the instructors, who purchase art supplies, costumes, and even pencils.

Mr. Senator, you say removing the National Endowment for the Arts would save the country money. You say that private organizations could instead raise money for arts programs. However, putting pressure on organizations to raise tens of thousands of dollars each year will bring their resources and energy away from teaching and creating art, thereby lowering the quality of the programs. Additionally, many arts programs serve low-income areas where communities do not have the finances to run these programs alone.

The author uses clear language to establish a firm and demanding tone.

The National Endowment for the Arts makes up .004 percent of the national budget. That's a nominal cost when you consider that these programs reach millions of Americans in important and meaningful ways.

I am saddened that we have a senator who does not understand the benefit of funding arts programs in schools and neighborhoods. I urge you to reconsider funding this highly important program.

Here, the author recaps the purpose of the text and create a strong, determined tone.

Sincerely,

Jane Woo

Art Educator

Lesson 6.3
Recognizing Your Constraints

Communicating involves making a lot of choices, the number of which sometimes can be overwhelming.

Knowing your **audience**, **purpose**, and context gives you much clearer direction for those choices. Your particular situation will also reduce the number of choices. In all writing and communication contexts, there will be some constraints, or limits, to what you're able to accomplish.

Have you ever tried to communicate an unfamiliar concept to someone older or younger than you? Have you had to explain an idea or process through texting that would have been easier to explain in person? If so, you're already familiar with constraints.

In this lesson, you will learn about the following aspects of recognizing constraints:

Recognize Audience Constraints
Adapt to Situational Constraints
Adjust to Delivery Constraints
Identify Genre Constraints

Recognize Audience Constraints

Knowing your audience can help you meet their needs. However, your audience also puts constraints on your writing. You must consider these limitations so that your communication can be as effective as possible.

Audience constraints will affect *what* you communicate and *how* you communicate it.

You will need to make some practical, content-related decisions based on your audience. Use these questions as a guide:

- What level of expertise or familiarity does my audience have with this topic?
    - Knowing this will impact the depth of your discussion, your vocabulary choices, and how much you explain evidence.
- What type of life experiences has my audience had?
    - Knowing this will impact your examples and illustrations.

To learn more about considering purpose and audience, see Lesson 6.2.

On Your Own

Imagine that you're a salesperson for a company that offers three services: landline phones, cable television, and broadband internet. You have meetings with decision-makers at a retirement community, a research university, and a daycare. Considering the previous questions, how would you adjust your presentation for each audience?

Audience	Presentation
Retirement community	

Research university	
Daycare	

Adapt to Situational Constraints

Kairos is an ancient Greek term that refers to appropriateness and timeliness. Similar to audience constraints, there are also some situational constraints that impact your communication. When considering these situational constraints, ask yourself the following questions:

> Are there any cultural differences, such as language,
>
> customs, or norms?
>
> Why is the audience present?
>
> Why are you communicating?
>
> What is the current overall attitude about the topic?

These situational constraints may impact the content of your message as well as the style in which it is delivered.

Cultural Differences

Cultural differences don't just occur between people from two different countries; they can affect people from two different neighborhoods. Most of us aren't even aware of the customs and norms in which we're participating, which can make effective communication even more challenging.

Differences in language, cultural norms, and customs all play a role in our communication. If they're not carefully considered and addressed, they can become a barrier. Make sure you're aware of cultural differences; then, use them to tailor your writing and speaking.

For example, some cultures value showing emotion while others value hiding emotion. If you're communicating with someone in a culture that values hiding emotion, you could alter your **tone** so that it is neutral and use a statement like, "You've missed the deadline and have violated our contract."

In contrast, if you're communicating with someone in a culture that values showing emotion, you might be a bit more animated and say something like, "You've made my clients wait too long for this. We're growing impatient!"

To learn more about tone, see Lesson 6.5.

Why the Audience is Present

Two more situational constraints on communication are the audience's choice to be an audience and your choice to be a writer.

Have you ever not wanted to read something simply because you "have" to? Keep in mind that your audience will often respond based on whether they had a choice to read your work. Make sure you attempt to engage them early and often.

Think about the times you had to sit through a boring lecture or presentation. What would you have changed to make that experience more valuable? Similarly, when you're writing something that's required, try to find personal value in it. If you're interested in your topic, your communication will be more interesting.

Current Attitude about the Topic

The more controversial a topic, the more carefully you need to approach it. For example, if you discuss a divisive political issue during election season, you will need to consider current events and people's emotions during that time.

Remember *kairos*, which indicates timeliness. Depending on what's going on in society (whether that means your school or the whole country), it may be an inappropriate time or a perfect time to address that topic. For example, a funeral is probably not the best time to tell jokes or to start critiquing the deceased person. Similarly, trying to sell bathing suits in the middle of winter would probably be unsuccessful.

Situational appropriateness is applicable to your coursework, too. You need to be aware of current debates surrounding a topic. This will help you decide whether the best time has passed or if you're ahead of the game. This doesn't mean you can't address it, but you may need to explain your timing.

> Group Activity
>
> In small groups, identify two or three significant events in American history. Use those events as keywords in the search engine at http://archives.org and find related documents. Note the date of the document in relation to the event, and determine how *kairos* works in each document. How does timeliness or appropriateness play a role in the document? Would the document look different today?

Adjust to Delivery Constraints

Communication can also be constrained by how it will be delivered to the audience. You'll need to adjust the content and delivery of your message based on those limitations. In academic situations, some of these constraints, like page or time limit, may be provided by your instructor.

When you have a message that you're ready to communicate, use the following questions to consider possible delivery constraints:

- Is there a minimum or maximum length requirement?
    - Knowing this will impact the depth of your discussion.
- If it's a writing project, where will it be submitted and in what format?
    - Knowing this will impact program and printing choices.
- If it's a speech project, where will this be presented and what equipment is available?
    - Knowing this will impact your visual aids, notes, and speaking preparation.

Delivery constraints may seem trivial, but they actually have a significant impact on the effectiveness of your communication.

Writing Environment: Professional

In advertising, delivery constraints play a major part. For example, marketing departments must consider how to tailor ads based on whether they appear in emails, on TV, or online. In journalism, newspaper and magazine editors have to limit content based on the page size.

On Your Own

In the table below, brainstorm the potential constraints of each medium.

Medium	Possible Constraints
Podcast	
Video	
Website	
Printed essay	
Presentation with slides	

Identify Genre Constraints

Similar to delivery constraints, the specific **genre**, or category, in which you'll be communicating also places limitations on your writing. These considerations include formatting requirements and other expectations of written, oral, and visual communication. As with other constraints, some of these may be provided for you.

While most people value creative expression, there are certain expectations for every category in which you may be asked to communicate. Most of these expectations are there for good reasons, so don't ignore them. Staying within these constraints is important for both clear communication and **credibility** (what makes you believable).

Reflection Questions

Think of some conventions that you encounter in everyday life. Why do those conventions exist? Can you think of logical reasons for them?

Any time you are given an assignment, note the expected genre and ask yourself these questions:

- How am I supposed to cite my references?
    - Knowing this will impact whether you cite in the text (or speech), at the end of the text (or speech), or in another location.
- Will multimedia be incorporated?
    - Knowing this will impact how you integrate multimedia into your project and make it accessible to everyone in the audience.
- Are there special formatting expectations?
    - Knowing this can impact anything from margin size to binding.

Writing Environment: Professional

Professional communication has multiple genres, including memos, letters, reports, and emails. Each is used in a specific situation for different purposes and audiences. A memo is generally concise and to-the-point without all of the conventions of a letter. A report is longer and more detailed than a letter. An email is similar to a memo but less formal. In the following situations, which genre of communication do you think works best and why? For the genres you didn't use, what scenarios do you think would work well for them?

Letting an employee know that his idea is going to be rejected.

Pitching an idea for the company website.

Informing employees about new office hours.

Group Activity

In pairs, use a **Venn diagram** (a chart that uses overlapping circles to illustrate similarities and differences) to compare and contrast oral presentations and written papers. Then, brainstorm ways that you would adapt a written paper to a presentation and a presentation to a written paper.

Lesson Wrap-Up

Key Terms

Audience: the person or people meant to read and interpret a text

Credibility: what makes someone or something believable

Genre: a type of writing

Kairos: a term derived from ancient Greek that refers to an argument's appropriateness and timeliness

Purpose: the goal of a text

Tone: the positive, negative, or neutral attitude that an author expresses about a topic

Venn Diagram: a chart that uses overlapping circles to illustrate similarities and differences between two or more things

Writing Application: Recognizing Your Constraints

Read the following brief article from a fictitious, printed newspaper. How has the author considered audience, situational, delivery, and genre constraints?

National News Section

Poll shows voters choose Mickey Mouse

In a recent national poll of 1,000 voters, participants chose Mickey Mouse as their preferred presidential candidate over all others. Mickey Mouse's approval ratings have risen steadily for the past five weeks. Experts say that the beloved cartoon is on track to win the presidential election in November.

As the heated race to the White House continues, voters are growing weary of candidates in both major parties. According to political analyst Robin Brady, "Given how quickly Mickey took the lead, we can't take the poll for granted. It's possible that someone else could rise to the top just as quickly if Mickey falls out of favor." Brady also noted, "This is a national poll, which doesn't give us a full picture of the delegate count. As we've seen before, a candidate can win the popular vote of all Americans but still lose the election."

Additional polling will continue for the next three weeks.

Note the constraint of "National News" that is placed on this particular section.

The content is constrained by length requirement, so details for the candidates are excluded.

The expert analysis notes the situational constraint of a national poll as opposed to state polls.

Candidates

▪ Mickey Mouse   ▪ All others

The choice of a single graph is a function of a genre and delivery constraint.

Lesson 6.4
Employing Rhetorical Appeals

> "This car gets great gas mileage, and it's designed to keep your family safe. Think of all the fun times you'll have in it! Come see us, the number one dealer in town for forty years."

This commercial is appealing to the viewers' logic and emotions, as well as to the car dealership's credibility and ethics. The Greek philosopher and teacher Aristotle identified these appeals as *logos*, *pathos*, and *ethos*.

Advertisements are one of the best ways to see these three appeals at work, but *logos, pathos, and ethos* are in every type of communication. They just reveal themselves in different ways depending on the context, or the setting and circumstances.

In this lesson, you will learn how to make effective arguments with the following appeals:

Logos

Pathos

Ethos

Logic and Reasoning (*Logos*)

At the core of most of your communication will be an appeal to logic, or *logos*. For example, most academic arguments are based on evidence, such as facts or statistics. Even the specific formatting requirements in academic writing and in other environments is an appeal to *logos*. In a professional environment, too, the emphasis of a text will be on clear and coherent information.

Here are some strategies to use in your writing to appeal to your audience's sense of *logos*:

- State your claim and premise clearly
- Incorporate reliable sources
- Include a logical line of reasoning

State Your Claim Clearly

One of the most important ways to appeal to *logos* is to state your claim clearly. There should be no confusion for the reader about your main idea; otherwise, your audience might assume that you don't fully understand the issue.

> **Weak**: The Electoral College is not a great system for electing a president.

> **Strong**: The Electoral College process is not fair to all voters because it does not always correlate to the popular vote.

Incorporate Reliable Sources

Using sources strengthens your argument in several ways. Instead of asking your readers to simply trust you, include evidence you found during research to support your claim. Whether you agree or disagree with your sources in your project, they show that the conversation you're joining is a legitimate one, and they show that you've spent time getting to know all sides of the issue.

To learn more about the research process, see Chapter 7.

> **Weak**: Everybody has a mobile device these days, and the capabilities continue to grow.

> **Strong**: According to the Pew Research Center, over 60% of Americans own a mobile device, and almost 75% of those devices are smartphones, which allow for internet browsing, checking email, using apps, and much more.

Helpful Hint

When you're working on a paper, always check the resources at your school's library. Librarians spend a lot of time and money to ensure you have reliable resources to use.

Include a Logical Line of Reasoning

While including research in your project strengthens your appeal to *logos*, analyze your evidence and connect it to your claim. This involves a clear line of reasoning, or sequence of ideas. Essentially, readers should be able to follow your thought process and understand how all of the elements connect.

> In a democracy, everyone's vote should count. The Electoral College does not ensure that every vote matters because if a candidate were to win the vote of the majority of American voters, she could still lose because of the way delegates are assigned to each state. This is unfair; America should change to a direct voting system.

Emotions and Values (*Pathos*)

While we would like to think we make logical decisions all the time, the truth is that we make *a lot* of decisions based on our emotions or values. Have you ever gotten angry and done or said something that you regretted later?

Although academic writing most often uses *logos*, appeals to *pathos* do have their place. People are moved by their emotions, so finding the ways your argument aligns with your audience's emotions and values will make your writing more persuasive.

Below are three strategies for appealing to *pathos*:

- Acknowledge your audience's feelings and values
- Use examples that appeal to emotions or values
- Consider tone and personality

Acknowledge Your Audience's Feelings and Values

Have you ever heard someone described as "out of touch?" That person was probably uninformed about something. To avoid being an out-of-touch communicator, make sure you know your audience well enough to assess their emotions and values. This doesn't mean that you need to pander to their emotions or values, but that you will adjust what or how you say something depending on their anticipated reactions.

For example, if you were a fire safety officer, you would teach kindergarteners differently than adults. You would teach kindergarteners safety strategies in a way that is easy to understand and fun (hence the use of fire safety mascots in some departments). For adults, you would note that they value time and efficiency, so your training would be different (and probably would not involve a mascot).

Ethics and Credibility (*Ethos*)

Have you ever agreed with someone just because you trusted them? This could be the result of an appeal to *ethos*.

> **Helpful Hint**
>
> An easy way to remember *ethos* is to think about the word *ethics*. An ethical person does what is considered right and good and could thus be called reliable and credible.

Second to *logos*, academic writing values appeals to *ethos*. Below are three strategies for using *ethos*:

- Convey knowledgeability
- Demonstrate fair judgment
- Recognize the complexity of an issue

Conveying Knowledgeability

One of the key ways to appeal to *ethos* is to show that you've done your research. Including sources increases your credibility, but it's not enough. You need to show your audience that you understand the sources and the implications for your argument.

Academic writers can lose credibility in this area if they haven't researched thoroughly enough, or they don't use a variety of different sources.

Note in the example below how the writer demonstrates a comprehensive view of technology, conveying knowledgeability and thus credibility.

> Many thinkers have debated the impact that technology is having on our lives. People have been skeptical of new devices, from handwriting to the typewriter to smart phones. Some, like Mark Bauerlein, suggest that technology makes us dumber, but others, like Greg Ulmer, argue that digital tools present a new method for thinking and creating that does not compare to older methods. We need boundaries when it comes to using technology, but being fearful of it or avoiding it altogether should not be our response.

Demonstrating Fair Judgment

One way to demonstrate that you're not out for your own good, but for the good of your readers too, is showing them that you've evaluated all sides of an issue and can be fair in your discussion of their points of view.

In academic writing, you'll probably be making an argument that you hope to convince readers to agree with or act upon. Include counterarguments either after you present your own argument or woven throughout the essay.

Counterarguments are claims that contradict your own; including them in your paper shows your readers that you are aware of other perspectives. You can use the counterargument section to discuss why you agree and/or disagree with different perspectives.

Recognize the Complexity of an Issue

Similar to conveying knowledgeability and demonstrating fair judgment, you want readers to know that you see the whole picture and recognize all of the parts. While it's tempting to frame an issue as simple and straightforward, this is usually just a way to avoid doing the hard work of recognizing that there are many layers and perspectives.

> **Weak**: If we just cut taxes, everybody will have more money.

> **Strong**: Setting tax rates is a detailed, tedious process that lawmakers, the IRS, and state governments have to agree upon. They must make sure that there is enough money to cover the roads and to account for the subsidies included in university tuition, among numerous other programs and services that enhance everyday life. Cutting taxes in one area means sacrificing services that people rely upon. We need to eliminate services that have the fewest users and cut

taxes in a way that benefits a large number of people. This paper will discuss those services that will need to be removed in order to establish a tax cut for even more people.

Just as there are fallacies of *logos* and *pathos*, there can be fallacies of *ethos*, too. Fallacies of *ethos* include appealing to someone's fame as credible even though they have no expertise in that area. Always make sure that the sources you cite are unbiased and have legitimate credentials.

Lesson Wrap-up

Key Terms

Counterargument: recognition of opposing viewpoints on an issue

Ethos: an appeal to ethics

Fallacy: a faulty or incorrect approach

Logos: an appeal to logic

Pathos: an appeal to emotion

Propaganda: a biased argument seeking to persuade without giving all information

Writing Application: Employing Rhetorical Appeals

Read the following letter that incorporates all three argumentation strategies. Using the annotations as help, consider how the author deliberately appeals to her audience.

Dear Members of City Council:

It has come to my attention that the city has been gifted a piece of property by a local business and that you are currently deciding what will come of the land. I have lived in Greenville my entire life, and I've seen a lot of changes. What was once open space has been replaced with strip malls, condominiums, and chain stores. When I was young, I had five parks I would regularly visit. Now, there are fewer green spaces for my own children to play. If you're considering selling this land to developers for financial gain, also consider what stands to be lost.

> The writer establishes *ethos*, or credibility, as a life-long resident of the city.

> This sentence indicates that this letter is persuasive, asking the reader to adopt a belief or take action.

According to city records, ten new neighborhoods, each with over fifty homes, have been built within city limits in the past seven years. Five big retailers, three new strip malls, and four grocery stores have opened in the past three years. In that time, the city has contributed zero new parks or green spaces. In fact, several commonly used green spaces were sold to allow for construction. Yesterday, I put my dog in the car and drove to our favorite walking trail by the lake. As we got out of the car, we were greeted by a new fence and a "Private Property" sign. Walking back to the car, both of us disappointed, I noticed another sign closer to the road: "Coming Soon: Luxury Condominiums by the Lake!"

> Here, the writer is using *logos*, a logical argument based on facts and statistics from a reputable source: the city's own records.

My uncle is a mayor in Pennsylvania. He began an initiative to designate a certain amount of green space per capita, so that as the town grew, the green space would not decrease. While the residents may not have as many shopping options, they have plenty of outdoor opportunities. Furthermore, the city saw better jobs and higher economic growth due to the high quality of living, according to the latest census.

The inherited property is large enough to contain bike and walking trails, a dog park, basketball and tennis courts, and more. There is even enough space for a musical stage. This is a great way to enhance art, entertainment, and culture in the area. The space can also be used for special events like festivals, farmers markets, charity events, birthday parties, and weddings. Having more spaces like this would not only increase the quality of life in our city but also provide potential for generating revenue.

> Offering suggestions and solutions is a way to exercise *logos* and to strengthen the persuasiveness of an argument.

It's wonderful that our town is growing and expanding, and we do need places for people to live, work, and shop. But we also need space for play, fun, and exercise. When you imagine yourself having fun as a child, what are you doing? Does the supermarket or department store come to mind? My most cherished memories are riding bikes down dirt trails, lying in the grass playing with my dog, and having family picnics for my birthday. When voting on how this land will be used, please consider not only economic growth but also the growth and happiness of our people. Thank you for your time and consideration in this matter.

> Finally, the writer drives home the argument by using *pathos*, or appealing to the reader's emotions.

Sincerely,

Sonia Knope

> After reading this letter, do you think Sonia will be successful in her appeal to City Council? Why or why not?

Lesson 6.5
Using Consistent Tone

Think of a time when you had to give a friend or family member bad news. In addition to choosing your words carefully, you probably used your voice inflections, facial expressions, and hand gestures to show your sympathy. Now imagine that you had to share that same news in a letter. How would you communicate your feelings in words only?

Because you can't use gestures or facial expressions when you write, you have to use tone to communicate a positive or negative attitude about a topic. **Tone** is the positive, negative, or neutral attitude that your writing expresses about a topic.

This lesson will discuss three ways to communicate tone in your writing:

Word Choice
Details
Inconsistent Tone

> Helpful Hint
> Remember that your tone should always fit the purpose and audience of your writing. A text message to a friend would use a very different tone from an email to a hiring manager.

> Reflection Questions
> Have you ever talked to someone whose tone didn't match what they were actually saying? How did this affect the interaction?

Word Choice

The first way to communicate tone is through word choice. All words have positive, negative, or neutral feelings attached to them. Think about these examples:

The parents' visit was spontaneous.

The parents' visit was uninvited.

The parents' visit was unexpected.

▸ In these sentences, the word *spontaneous* sounds more positive than the word *uninvited*, although the definitions of both words are similar. The last sentence uses the word *unexpected*, which sounds neutral.

As you write, you must carefully select words that will accurately reflect the tone you want to communicate. An essay on the benefits of organic produce should use a positive and confident tone. On the other hand, a research paper on the health risks of secondhand smoke should use a more serious tone. If the purpose of your writing is to **inform**, a neutral and objective tone is usually best.

Be careful not to use words that communicate extremely positive or negative feelings, as this is usually a sign that you are a biased or an overly emotional author.

Read through the following paragraphs. Which one seems more reliable?

> *Looking Backward* is a misogynistic book that fails to represent women. The only time the author even discusses women's roles in modern society occurs during one minuscule chapter. Before this, no one knows anything about Edith other than her looks. Typically, the ladies are pushed out, leaving the big strong men to discuss important matters by themselves (79, 128). Conditions for the women in Bellamy's vision of the year 2000 are just as bad as in 1887.

> *Looking Backward* represents women unfairly by failing to represent them at all. The only full examination of women's roles in modern society occurs during one short chapter. Before this, little is known about Edith beyond her physical beauty. Just as in the nineteenth century, the ladies retire early, leaving the men to discuss important matters by themselves (79, 128). Conditions for the women in Bellamy's vision of the year 2000 remain almost unchanged from those of 1887.

▷ In the first paragraph, the author chooses words that communicate an aggressive and disapproving tone. Not only does this type of writing hurt the **credibility** of the author, it could also anger the audience. The second paragraph does a much better job of communicating its message in a specific, yet reasonable way.

Group Activity

As a group, discuss the tone of the following words. What similar words would convey the same meaning with a different tone?

chat

quirky

walk

cautious

lengthy

nosy

On Your Own

Read through the following paragraph and underline or highlight the sentence that does not use the best tone.

> The leadership meeting tomorrow is mandatory. Many of the company's executives will be in attendance, so please be prompt. Also, ensure you have your laptops and up-to-date weekly reports when you arrive. The really early meeting tomorrow in the AM will be an awesome chance for us to chat about the looming lay-offs. Thank you in advance for keeping your schedule flexible.

Details

The second way to convey tone is through the details that you choose to include in or exclude from your writing. Every time you write, you make choices about what you want to communicate. Your job as an author is to select the information that will fulfill your purpose both honestly and effectively.

If you include mainly negative details about a topic, the tone of your writing will be more negative. If you include mainly positive details, the tone of your writing will be more positive. Think about these examples:

> My son-in-law Paul just became an astrophysicist at MIT, one of the most prestigious schools in the country.

> My son-in-law Paul just started an entry-level position at a school on the East Coast.

> My son-in-law Paul just became an assistant professor of astrophysics at MIT.

> ▶ The first example sentence includes a number of details that are intended to impress the audience, while the second sentence excludes details to make Paul's job seem less important. The third sentence seems to strike a good balance between the two.

Reflection Questions
How is tone expressed in an image? How is this different from or similar to the tone of a text?

Inconsistent Tone

Writing that is inconsistent in tone can come across as awkward. Think about the tone of the following example:

> Arthur Young's essay "The Example of France, a Warning to Britain" expresses both the author's original admiration of the French Revolution and his subsequent disappointment in what the revolt became. Young remarks that by overthrowing their government, the French embraced chaos and mob rule. According to Young, the people of England need to learn from France's example in order to prevent similar tragedies. Obviously, Young is completely wrong because the citizens of a country shouldn't have to support a corrupt government that ignores the problems of common people.

> The overall tone of this paragraph could be described as neutral. However, the last sentence includes words and details that are very negative. This passage sounds awkward because the last sentence doesn't match the tone used throughout the rest of the paragraph.

To identify a shift in tone, follow these steps:

Checklist for Tone Consistency

☐ Read the text out loud to yourself.

☐ Decide if the overall tone is positive, negative, or neutral.

☐ Identify sentences that don't match the tone of the text.

☐ Look for words or details that could be altered or eliminated.

On Your Own

Read through the following paragraph and use the steps above to underline or highlight the sentence with inconsistent tone.

> Student teaching was a positive and rewarding experience. The students I taught were able to teach me so much more than I could teach them. Being in such a supportive school with hands-on parents made the semester move quickly. My principal critiqued me every single time she came into my room, which forced me to learn how to ignore negative leaders and press on. Student teaching showed me that I can imagine myself in no other profession, and I will be happy to one day have a classroom of my own.

Lesson Wrap-up

Key Terms

Audience: the people who read your writing
Credibility: what makes someone or something believable
Informative Text: a text that gives the audience information about a topic
Paragraph: a short piece of writing that focuses on one main idea
Purpose: the goal of a text
Tone: the positive, negative, or neutral attitude that an author expresses about a topic

Writing Application: Using Consistent Tone

Now, read the following letter written by a concerned community member. How do the tone and purpose of this writing compare to the one above? How does the author use similar strategies to achieve a different purpose?

To Whom It May Concern:

Cyberbullying is a growing problem in America and schools should do more to combat the epidemic. According to a 2016 report by the Cyberbullying Research Center, almost one-third of students aged 12-17 have been victims of cyberbullying. As an educator, I am deeply concerned about this issue. I have seen its consequences in the eyes of victimized students tortured by online bullies using online communication like weapons. Schools have a responsibility to teach students how to be good digital citizens, but they can't fight cyberbullying alone. This war needs to start at home.

This indicates the author's main topic: the rise of cyberbullying.

The word *war* has strong connotations. It suggests the author feels this is a serious issue.

Many instances of cyberbullying can be prevented by vigilant parents who know the signs and who are willing to address these issues. Parents often point the finger at schools to address cyberbullying. However, by the time schools are notified of a problem, it's often too late. Bullied students have already been victimized, and the digital traces can leave emotional scars. Furthermore, cyberbullying disrupts the learning environment. Schools are forced to divert time and resources away from the educational process to handle problems that take place outside of the classroom. Parents can help with early detection and alleviate this burden from school personnel.

> The tone here is sympathetic toward schools, further supporting his purpose.

Another thing parents can do is monitor their teen's online activity. Computers and laptops can be housed in public places in the home to discourage poor online behavior, and kids can be monitored. If parents allow their children to have smartphones and tablets, there should reasonable limits placed on their use. Kids with unlimited access to these devices have unlimited ways of getting into trouble.

> The word *can* indicates the author is making a suggestion instead of a demand.

Teens shouldn't be the only people educated about cyberbullying. Parents should educate themselves on virtual slang that their kids may use. This allows parents to better identify cyberbullying when it starts. Parents can review their teens' profile pages and monitor their activity. Kids might complain about invasion of privacy, but they're also less likely to participate in cyberbullying.

> The author is making a persuasive recommendation, again supporting his purpose.

Enacting these measures can prevent cyberbullying. Unfortunately, this harassment takes place both inside and outside the classroom, so schools need help monitoring these behaviors. By adopting common-sense rules for online use, parents can help put an end to this torture.

> The author's overall purpose is to get the reader to adopt these recommendations.

Warmly,

Jonathan Campbell

Lesson 6.6
Choosing the Right Words

Telling an interesting story is difficult. To make a situation as exciting as possible, you have to include vivid descriptions and fascinating details. However, language that is too flowery or complicated might distract your audience from the **main idea**. Balancing these two extremes is essential for becoming a good storyteller.

In writing, you have to find a similar balance between keeping your readers interested and expressing your ideas clearly. Read through the following examples:

Preparing a culinary entrée such as elbow pasta noodles and melted cheddar cheese, of the boxed variation, can be an enjoyable and tranquil undertaking if one is cognizant of the most vital procedures. First, fill a pot with an abundance of temperate water and gently situate it on the cooking apparatus, or stove, the dial of which should be directed to a temperature of great warmth. The liquid will presently begin to bubble and yield steam, at which juncture the foodstuffs, or elbow noodles, should be incorporated. When they are tender and delectable, sprinkle in the cheese mixture and blend judiciously.

To make macaroni and cheese from a box, put water in a pot. Turn on the stove to high heat and place the pot on top. Soon, the water will boil; when it does, add the noodles. When they are fully cooked, stir in the cheese.

▷ In the first example, the author uses descriptive, vivid language. However, the paragraph is so complicated, it's almost impossible to follow the author's train of thought. The second example has the opposite problem. While the information is straightforward, the paragraph itself is bland and boring.

Thinking about your audience and purpose will help you determine how descriptive you should be. Word choice is also an important part of drafting and revising.

In this lesson, you will learn how to effectively communicate meaning with the following word choices:

Clear Words
Concise Words
Vivid Words

Clear Words

Strong writing is clear and easy to understand. Don't be tempted to use complicated language just because it sounds "smarter." While academic and professional documents may be **formal**, they should not be confusing.

Think about the following sentences:

This stratagem will advocate tandem techniques to diminish building perpetuation expenditures.

This proposal will suggest two ways to reduce building maintenance costs.

▷ While both of these examples have the same basic meaning, the second sentence is much clearer than the first.

> Helpful Hint
> Be careful when using **synonyms** to make your writing more interesting or academic. Some of these words have slightly different definitions that will change the meaning of a sentence.

One specific type of unclear language is **jargon**, or overly technical terms. Here's an example:

The nomenclature of the *Acer rubrum* is derived from the visual perceptual property of the principal lateral appendages of its stems during the temperate season of autumn.

Can you tell what this sentence says? It's explaining that red maples get their name from their leaves, which turn red in the fall. However, figuring this out is difficult because of scientific jargon like *Acer rubrum* and *principal lateral appendages*.

Generally, you should avoid jargon unless you are specifically writing for a technical **audience**. If you need to use unfamiliar terms, always include clear definitions.

Consider your purpose and audience before you use jargon in writing.

Concise Words

Concise word choice eliminates unnecessary language from your writing. Consider the following paragraph:

I wanted to see if you would be willing to meet with me for just a couple minutes tomorrow in the afternoon at 2:15 or sometime around then. I would really appreciate being able to hear what you think about the progress I've made with the first draft of the paper that I've been writing. Due to the fact that I am having some trouble with organizing my paragraphs, I am hoping that you can help me. It would be great if I could come to your office after class tomorrow afternoon, but I can also meet at another time if it would work better for you.

This paragraph is wordy. The author circles around the meaning of each sentence, often using four or five words instead of one. Not only are these phrases difficult to read, they are also confusing.

A much more concise version of the paragraph might look like this:

Are you available for a brief meeting around 2:15 tomorrow afternoon? I would like to hear your feedback on my first draft of Essay #3. I am having trouble organizing my paragraphs and would appreciate your help. If another time would be better, please let me know.

▸ The basic meaning of both versions is the same; however, the revised version is easier to read.

On Your Own

In the table below, write a more concise version of the three wordy phrases from the previous passage.

WORDY	CONCISE
just a couple minutes tomorrow in the afternoon at 2:15 or sometime around then	
the first draft of the paper I've been writing	
Due to the fact that I am having some trouble with organizing my paragraphs	

Keep in mind that a concise sentence is not always short. You don't want to confuse your readers by eliminating important information from your writing. Instead, you should focus on using words that state exactly what you want to say.

Writing Environment: Professional

Effective word choice is critical in any context, and it can play an especially meaningful role when it comes to a job application. Are you using effective, meaningful power verbs in your résumé? These should be strong yet concise. Try to incorporate some of the following power verbs:

- administered
- authored
- built
- coached
- coordinated
- delegated
- designed
- developed
- directed
- executed
- expedited
- facilitated
- formulated
- founded
- initiated
- investigated
- launched
- operated
- orchestrated
- overhauled
- pioneered
- produced
- programmed
- resolved
- revitalized
- scheduled
- spearheaded
- supervised
- systematized

Wordy	Concise
the researchers who work at Columbia University	researchers at Columbia University
owing to the fact that	because
the type of material used for fuel purposes	used for fuel
Andrew Jackson was a man who served	Andrew Jackson served
a story that is strange	a strange story
situations that could be considered exceptions	exceptions
worked as a manager	managed

> **Helpful Hint**
>
> One way to make your writing more concise is to use active voice whenever possible. In **active voice**, the **subject** of a sentence is *doing* the action instead of *receiving* the action. Compare these examples:
>
> This hotel had been highly recommended by my brother.
>
> My brother highly recommended this hotel.

Vivid Words

The final aspect of word choice is using vivid language. When you are sharing information with your audience, you want your words to be interesting and precise.

Think about the following image. How would you describe it?

Vivid words will make your descriptions more effective.

While the contents of this image could be described with the words *bear* or *animal*, using *polar bear* helps your audience picture your words better.

Nouns and Action Verbs

To make your writing more vivid, use specific **nouns** and **action verbs**.

Vague	Vivid
girl	partner-in-crime
stuff	clutter
pet	iguana
show	*How I Met Your Mother*

Vague	Vivid
walking	striding
sat	slumped
found	discovered
going	traveling

Adjectives and Adverbs

Another way to write vividly is to use unique **adjectives** and **adverbs**. Words like *nice* and *good* are often overused. Finding a more original descriptive word will keep your writing fresh and interesting.

Vague	Vivid
nice	thoughtful
very	extremely
dark	pitch black
cold	frigid
really	undoubtedly

Use adjectives and adverbs carefully. Usually, a strong noun or **verb** alone is better than a weak noun or verb with an adjective or adverb.

> After the game, Andrew ~~slowly walked~~ home.

> After the game, Andrew trudged home.

Helpful Hint

Good writers will spend time finding the right word. As you write, take note of any words that you feel can be stronger or more vivid and revise them later.

Any type of writing can benefit from vivid language. While you may not use imaginative language in a research paper or resume, you should still choose words that are descriptive and accurate.

Vague	Vivid
a group of experts	researchers at Harvard Medical School
a source	*Forbes* magazine
quickly went	sprinted
said	accused
those affected by the flood	citizens of Lebanon Valley
people	psychologists
some	twenty-five

Group Activity

As a group, come up with a list of vivid words to replace the vague words below.

group of people   teachers   happy   hungry   fast   boring

Lesson Wrap-up

Key Terms

Action Verb: a verb that indicates a physical or mental action

Active Voice: when a sentence is written so that the subject is performing an action

Adjective: a word that describes a noun or pronoun

Adverb: a word that describes a verb, an adjective, or another adverb

Audience: the people who read your writing

Formality: the way a text conforms to certain standards

Jargon: overly technical language

Main Idea: the statement or argument that a text communicates about its topic

Noun: a word that represents a person, place, thing, event, or idea

Phrase: a word group that adds to the meaning of a sentence but does not express a complete thought and usually lacks a subject and verb

Subject: the person, place, thing, event, or idea a sentence is about

Synonym: a word that has the same meaning as another word

Verb: a word that represents an action, relationship, or state of being

Writing Application: Choosing the Right Words

Consider the impact of word choice in the following short story:

Bookends

Approximately thirty-six inches. That was the maximum amount of space between them that the bench would allow. At that moment, both occupants wished their dimensions smaller. It was old and rusty (the bench that is). The wood was a compilation of various brown shades mixed with stains and fading from years of service. A few tired nails poked through, and each of the seats inhabitants made a mental note of where to avoid shifting. Of course, they spoke nothing of it.

Neither of them knew exactly how to retrace the path that had led them to appear like unused bookends. Nonetheless, there they were on a sunny winter's afternoon, waiting for the one person that could help them reach a final resolution.

Perhaps it was the kids. Yes, they told themselves often, it was the kids. The demanding schedules and selfless daily habits allowed for no time to harness a marriage. How did people do it? Others seemed happy. But then, they'd think, it must be a façade! It was only in public that couples acted in such a customary fashion.

Other days, she'd blame it on his job. He'd blame it on her mother. But they both knew that it was not as easy as faulting one guilty party. The liability belonged to a parade of events and issues. All too exhausting to untangle anymore, they'd just decided it was unnecessary. After all, the circular conversations and personal attacks were getting old, and they no longer had the energy to keep them up.

It would be for the best, they thought. Take some time apart, maybe space will help, distant will provide clarity; they tried to fool themselves into thinking. This isn't permanent; it's a temporary solution, a means to an end. But, as they often did, they both possessed the knowledge and heartache that told them otherwise. Such is a curse of most writers. Too many years of observing human behavior, of standing at a distance just far enough to be acutely critical.

And, of course, that's how they met. Many moons ago, they were threadbare poets working multiple jobs and living in apartments that made the subway feel spacious. It's the life of the struggling writer in New York City, they'd declare many times. Standing in line at a book signing in Central Park, they had struck up a conversation.

"Yes, I am a huge fun of Updike. I've read everything he's written at least twice," he boasted proudly. "Perhaps we can grab a cup of coffee and discuss his latest short story compilation?"

She was slightly put off by the contrived way in which he spoke but half-heartedly said, "I don't see why not." She'd thought maybe he could provide her with some tips on getting her work published.

As they stood in the molasses-paced line, they spoke of commonalties, struggles, and upbringings until he started to worry about what else could be left to discuss on the first date. After their encounters at the front of the line, the conversation remained fluid (much to her surprise).

"Perhaps you'd like to grab that coffee now?" he asked bravely, only half-confident his advances would be well-received.

He was surprised as she took his hand, led him down the block, and said, "You read my mind."

…

As she sat on the bench, cozying up to the armrest, the remnants of her morning coffee had turned cold. The breeze was picking up and she saw, out of the corner of her eye, that he had since zipped up his coat and atop of his head perched a black snowcap.

"A bargain at ten dollars," she thought to herself, as she remembered the day she had purchased his hat. "I wonder if he remembers that I brought it home for him?" she continued to think, allowing herself to reminisce for a moment. She was well-trained by now in putting a stop to any warm memory, initially afraid it would cause sadness. But now, it was simply a force of habit. She had disciplined herself perhaps too well.

The silence between them was starting to become powerful. He always did let too much time pass without so much as a polite question or an attempt at small talk. He was a word man, this was his craft, but now he told himself dejectedly, "There's nothing left to say."

Sauntering through the park, finally, was their last hope at a peaceful resolution. Tall and dapper, he walked with a briefcase in one hand while the other was nestled in his pocket, keeping warm. He was the one person that had a sense of control over their current relationship, a fact of which she was very self-aware and almost resented. But then again, that was what they were paying him to do.

"Howdy," he proclaimed in a tone a bit too casual for the present situation.

"Hi there," they accidentally said in unison, caught off guard by the sound of their own voices together.

"The paperwork is all set, and at this point, all that is left is each of your signatures. Then, it's a done deal."

They were both secretly offended by his matter-of-fact tone, and he had to bite his lip so he wouldn't speak out of anger. She simply looked away, and he knew she was sharing a similar sentiment.

As the attorney drew the papers and handed each one a pen, they made eye contact for the first time. A half-smile parted his lips, an action she quickly mirrored, and a sense of calm pervaded the winter's day. For the first time in years, as they signed their names, they knew that they were agreeing on something.

After the ritual was over and the deed done, the man with the briefcase left. The pair stood up. He nodded, she smiled, and they turned their separate ways.

"Hey," he shouted suddenly as he cleared his throat and turned to face her. "Thanks for the hat."

She turned to him, nodding and smiling, the way someone might smile after finally accepting disappointing news. "I hope it keeps you warm."

A breeze blew softly as they walked away. She kept walking. He turned around only once, and found a young couple sitting on the bench, cuddled up, laughing and sharing a warm drink. He pursed his lips regretfully as he looked at them and continued on his path back home.

Sidebar notes:

Language and dialogue like this sets a tone of emptiness and abandon. These words also reflect the feelings the characters have toward one another.

The continued use of the pronouns *he* and *she* are deliberately chosen to help the characters feel relatable, as if they could be anyone.

This sentence uses a subordinating clause at the beginning, emphasizing the larger point at the end: the moment they finally make eye contact.

Lesson 6.7
Using Word and Sentence Variety

> **Group Activity**
>
> As a group, discuss the effect of engaging writing. Does it matter if a text is interesting to its readers?

Have you ever had trouble keeping yourself focused on reading a text? Read the following paragraph:

> Alyssa had a bad night. Her work shift ran late. Alyssa came home late at night. It was very dark. The front door was locked. Alyssa could not find her keys. It started to rain. She looked for the spare. She couldn't find it anywhere. She had to bang on the door. Her parents woke up. They were angry. Alyssa had missed her curfew.
>
> While the paragraph tells you what happened, it probably doesn't hold your interest because every sentence is short and simple; it sounds boring and choppy because each sentence is exactly the same.

Read this version of the same paragraph:

> Alyssa had a bad night after her work shift ran late. By the time she got home, it was dark outside, and the front door was locked. She was searching for her keys when it started to rain. Feeling scared and defeated, Alyssa banged on the door. When her parents woke up, they were angry. Alyssa had missed her curfew.
>
> Even though both examples contain essentially the same sentences, the second paragraph uses a variety of words and sentence structures to keep the reader engaged.

As a writer, one of your goals should always be to hold the attention of your readers. Even if the material isn't exciting, you can still find ways to make your writing interesting and engaging for your readers.

In this lesson, you will learn how to introduce more variety into the following areas:

Words
Word Groups and Clauses
Sentences

Words

English has been influenced by many other languages, including German, Latin, French, Spanish, Arabic, and Sanskrit. This diverse influence gives you a wealth of words to choose from, and it's wise to explore these options in your writing.

Repeating the same word can indicate a writer who is not an expert on a topic or uncomfortable with the language. Strong, varied, and specific language makes your message powerful and keeps your **audience** focused. By using terms that resonate with your readers, you will be more likely to reach them. The best way to do this is to have a well-rounded vocabulary.

> **Helpful Hint**
>
> If you say a word, such as *bubble*, twenty times in a row, it sounds meaningless and feels ridiculous. Similarly, reading the same word or phrase over and over has a numbing effect on the reader. The word loses its meaning and impact, and your message is lost.

To avoid repetition in your writing, you should substitute words with pronouns and synonyms.

Pronouns are words that replace **nouns**. Using pronouns can help you avoid repeating the same noun over and over again. Consider this sentence:

> Sally snapped the leash on Sally's dog, and then Sally walked the dog to the park.
>
> To make this sentence more interesting and less repetitive, use pronouns as a substitute for the word *Sally*.
>
> Sally snapped the leash on her dog, and then she walked the dog to the park.

> To learn more about using pronouns to replace nouns, see Lesson 10.3.

Another strategy for introducing new words into your writing is using synonyms. **Synonyms** are words that share the same meaning as another word. For example, the word *vehicle* is a synonym for *automobile* or *car*. Synonyms are a useful tool for adding variety to your writing because they help you avoid repeating nouns and pronouns.

Here are some commonly used words and their synonyms.

Job	Tired	Happy
• Occupation	• Exhausted	• Joyful
• Employment	• Fatigued	• Blissful
• Position	• Sleepy	• Delighted
• Duty	• Worn out	• Pleased

Read the following passage:

> Janice has always wanted to own a home of her own. When she was fifteen, her father lost his job and her parents were unable to make payments on the family's home. As a result, Janice found herself staying in the homes of other relatives, moving from home to home every few weeks. To Janice, a home is more than a building: it's a symbol of security and safety.
>
> In the paragraph above, the word *home* is repeated six times in only four sentences. This repetition makes the paragraph sound repetitive and choppy. Here's an improved version of that same paragraph:
>
> Janice has always wanted to own a home of her own. When she was seven, her father lost his job and her parents were unable to make payments on the family's house. As a result, Janice found herself staying in the apartments of other relatives, moving from residence to residence every few weeks. To Janice, a home is more than a building: it's a symbol of security and safety.

On Your Own

Look back at these paragraphs. What synonyms are used for the word *home*? Are there any others you can think of? Write them in the following table.

Synonyms for *home*

Helpful Hint
Although using synonyms is a quick and easy way to add variety to your writing, don't try to replace every word with a synonym. Sometimes, there is no good substitute for a word. This is especially true when you are writing about a subject with technical terms and definitions.

As you search for synonyms to use in your own writing, notice how a synonym may have a slightly different meaning from one of its other synonyms. For example, you could be *hungry*, but not necessarily *starving*. Be sure to choose a synonym that fits best with the meaning of your sentences. This concept is related to denotative and connotative meaning.

Denotative Meaning: the literal, dictionary definition of a word

Connotative Meaning: the positive, negative, or neutral undertones of a word

Most people can agree on a word's denotative meaning, but connotative meanings are tied to emotions and experiences that result from cultural or regional differences, age, upbringing, and/or occupation. For instance, the denotative meaning of *shark* is, "a type of fish." However, for some people, the connotative meaning of *shark* is, "a dangerous and frightening creature."

Writing Environment: Academic

Research, procedural, and technical writing depend on objective facts, so the denotative meanings of words are most important. For narrative and descriptive writing, it's important to choose words based on their connotative meanings and how you expect your audience to respond.

One final way to add interesting words to your sentences is to add **adjectives** that end in *-ed* or **adverbs** that end in *-ly* to the beginning of the sentence. Look at these examples:

> Unfortunately, Samantha didn't get the job.

> Exhausted, the foreman collapsed into bed after working an eighteen-hour shift.

Group Activity
As a group, think of some adjectives or adverbs that could be added to the beginnings of the following sentences.

The ballerina twirled across the stage with almost no effort.

Seth corrected the mistake before his boss found it.

Professor Wilson rushed into the room holding a huge box.

Word Groups and Clauses

Another strategy for using variety in your writing is replacing single words with descriptive word groups. Read this example:

> The town watchman patrolled the same route every evening. At exactly 9:30 p.m., you would see the old man shuffling down Main Street. Although I never spoke to him directly, I can still picture his stooped form making its way through the streets of the town.
>
> In this paragraph, *old man* and *his stooped form* refer to a single person: the watchman. These phrases serve two purposes. First, they prevent the repetitive use of *watchman*. Second, they paint a vivid and memorable picture of what happened in the story.

Be cautious about adding descriptions to your writing. Too many can be confusing and wordy. When you do use an extra word group, make sure that it is adding meaning to the sentence, not just increasing the word count. Look at the following example:

> A large, cylindrical container that is filled with oil fell off of a truck and stopped traffic for five hours.
>
> This example uses a lot of words to say very little. In this case, it would be better to use the descriptive noun phrase *oil barrel* instead of *a large cylindrical container that is filled with oil*.

Writing Environment: Professional

In professional writing, it's wise to keep paragraphs and sentences short. This increases readability and clarity. Most managers are busy and don't have time to re-read long, complicated sentences. However, don't confuse *complicated* with *complex*. Even in the business world, effective writing uses multiple sentence types. Limiting your writing to use only simple sentence structure becomes boring and makes the message seem choppy or robotic.

You can also add **dependent clauses** and **prepositional phrases** to the beginning of a sentence to add variety and interest. Here are a few examples:

> During the drought last summer, the flower garden withered and died.

> To find the best deal on a new car, Hannah visited several dealerships.

Remember that any time you add a dependent clause or long prepositional phrase to the beginning of a sentence, you must follow it with a **comma**.

> Group Activity
>
> Think about the sentences you modified with adjectives and adverbs. Now, add phrases to the beginnings instead of words.
>
> > The ballerina twirled and twirled with almost no effort.
> >
> > Seth corrected the mistake before his boss found it.
> >
> > Professor Wilson rushed into the room holding a huge box.
>
> Discuss with your group whether the sentences sound better with a single word or a phrase. Which phrases serve a purpose and which are just adding unnecessary words?

Sentences

A final way that you can add interest to your writing is varying the structures of your sentences.

Independent clauses are complete sentences that stand on their own.

> Jing was studying to be a special education teacher.

It's fine for some of your sentences to be short and simple. However, for more variety, you can join two independent clauses.

For instance, read these two sentences:

> Danielle wanted to go to the movies. She planned to go with her roommate.
>
> You can combine these sentences using a comma and a **coordinating conjunction**.
>
> Danielle wanted to go to the movies, and she planned to go with her roommate.
>
> In this example, the coordinating conjunction *and* joins two simple sentences together into a compound sentence.

When you join sentences, make sure that they are closely related. Combining two completely unrelated sentences will be confusing to your readers.

Helpful Hint

To remember the seven coordinating conjunctions, use the acronym FANBOYS.

For
And
Nor
But
Or
Yet
So

Another way to combine these sentences is by using a semicolon. **Semicolons** can be used to combine two related, independent clauses.

> Danielle wanted to go to the movies; she planned to go with her roommate.

To add more variety, you can also combine two sentences by making one a dependent clause. To make a dependent clause, add a **subordinating conjunction** like *although* or *because* to the beginning of a sentence.

Consider the following example:

> Shauna paid her cell phone bill late. Her service was disconnected.
>
> Because Shauna paid her cell phone bill late, her service was disconnected.
>
> ▶ Combining these sentences makes the message clearer. The subordinating conjunction *because* shows the relationship between the two ideas.

Dependent clauses can also be placed at the end of a sentence. Here's an example:

> Carson never liked children. Once he had a child of his own, he did like children.
>
> Carson never liked children until he had a child of his own.

Notice that you won't use a comma to separate the two clauses if the dependent clause comes after the independent clause.

Helpful Hint

Here are some of the most common subordination conjunctions.

after	although	because	before
even if	once	provided that	rather than
since	unless	until	when
where	whether	while	

To learn more about coordination and subordination, see Lesson 10.8.

On Your Own

Read the following paragraph and look for ways to add word and sentence variety. Then, use the table below to rewrite the paragraph with your changes.

> The most significant result of the Boston Tea Party and the Intolerable Acts was the formation of the Continental Congress. In 1774, fifty-five men met in Philadelphia, PA, to discuss the Boston Tea Party and the Intolerable Acts. Some of the notable men were Samuel Adams, George Washington, and Patrick Henry. The men met for seven weeks. John Adams convinced the men of the need for a confederation. He stressed, above all, unification of purpose within the colonies. The first Continental Congress did not directly support a revolution. The Continental Congress laid the framework for a revolution by unifying the colonies. The Continental Congress also drew up documents such as the Declaration of Rights.

Lesson Wrap-up

Key Terms

Adjective: a word that describes a noun or pronoun

Adverb: a word that describes a verb, adjective, or another adverb

Audience: the person or people meant to read and interpret a text

Comma: a punctuation mark used to separate items in a list; join compound sentences; mark introductory words, phrases, and clauses; add extra or unnecessary details to a sentence; and separate similar adjectives

Compound Sentence: two independent clauses joined by a semicolon or a comma and conjunction

Connotative Meaning: the positive, negative, or neutral undertones of a word

Coordinating Conjunction: a conjunction that joins similar words or groups of words together

Denotative Meaning: the literal, dictionary definition of a word

Dependent Clause: a group of words with a subject and a verb that does not express a complete thought

Descriptive Writing: writing that communicates the characteristics or qualities of a thing or event

Independent Clause: a group of words with a subject and a verb that expresses a complete thought

Narrative Writing: writing that conveys events that happen during a defined period of time

Noun: a word that represents a person, place, thing, event, or idea

Prepositional Phrase: a group of related words that starts with a preposition and ends with a noun or pronoun

Pronoun: a word that takes the place of a noun in a sentence

Semicolon: a punctuation mark used to combine two independent clauses and separate long list items

Subordinating Conjunction: a conjunction that introduces a dependent clause

Synonym: a word that has the same meaning as another word

Writing Application: Using Word and Sentence Variety

Read the following essay about *The Canterbury Tales* by Geoffrey Chaucer, paying attention to how it uses word, clause, and sentence variety.

Chaucer: The Great Equalizer

Today, we mock people and make fun of things freely. If there's trouble on Capitol Hill, it'll be ridiculed on Reddit soon after. Modern comedians like Jon Stewart, Stephen Colbert, and John Oliver have built their careers on satire. Mocking our political, economic, moral, and social weaknesses is an enjoyable way to vent frustrations and suggest better alternatives. However, in fourteenth-century England, direct criticism of the ruling class and social structure was dangerous. In *The Canterbury Tales,* Geoffrey Chaucer's carefully constructed satire exposes hypocrisy, greed, and duplicity at all levels of society, with equal reproach for those superstitious enough to be duped.

> In the introduction, note the variety of sentence lengths and types.

The Catholic Church controlled Europe in the fourteenth century, and not merely as a spiritual force. The popes used political power to make the church wealthy at the commoners' expense. While each of Chaucer's pilgrims in *The Canterbury Tales* belongs to a specific subclass, the clergy is indistinguishable from the upper class because of their acquired wealth and elitism. Several of the traveling pilgrims represent the church: the Prioress, the Pardoner, the Monk, the Nun's Priest, the Friar, and the Limiter. These supposedly pious, religious people are actually greedy and deceitful.

> Notice the variety of synonyms for money, wealth, and greed.

One such character is the Prioress. In the general prologue, this high-ranking nun appears pure and tender-hearted, feeding little dogs from the table. Her tale begins with a prayer to the Virgin Mary and focuses on the purity and innocence of a martyred child. Ironically, the tale reveals a deep-seated prejudice toward the Jews, finding them guilty without trial and recommending violent death. "He had them drawn by horses, then he saw that they be hanged according to the law" (Chaucer 633-34). Despite her position of reverence and pretenses of charity, this deeply religious woman is selfish, mean-spirited, and lacks human compassion. Through "The Prioress' Tale," Chaucer condemns the church for its persecution of Jews.

Another clergyman, the Pardoner, is obsessed with money. He profits from allowing people—who hope to receive healing or blessings—to touch phony relics for an exorbitant price. After confessing his own greed, the Pardoner's tale condemns this quality in others. Chaucer exposes a moral double standard: one for the congregation and another for its leaders. Although each of the gold-hungry drunkards in "The Pardoner's Tale" receives his deadly comeuppance, the Pardoner flaunts his false piety with the mantra, "money is the root of all evil," and mocks his parishioners for their gullibility.

Each of these "holy" characters is also comically selfish. Chaucer exaggerates these specific flaws to accent the egregious (but legal) excesses of the church as a whole. However, duplicity and fraud are common in the upper and middle-class characters too, who are clearly obsessed with status and the outward appearance of wealth. Hypocrisy and duplicity know no class or gender.

Perhaps Chaucer's most subtle commentary is found in "The Miller's Tale." This is a popular tale known for its bawdy humor and crude language. A foolish, elderly carpenter marries an attractive young woman without considering the consequences. Furthermore, he falls for an outrageous rumor and an even more outrageous plan. Absalom the priest and Nicolas the clerk shamelessly pursue the married woman instead of observing the chivalrous ideal of defending her honor. In the end, the carpenter, the corrupt priest, and the dishonest clerk are justly rewarded with humiliation.

"The Miller's Tale" is a vulgar situation comedy, but given Chaucer's shrewd sense of irony, the vulgarity is likely subterfuge for a far more serious message. Chaucer is calling for society to be honest with themselves. The tale exposes the shams of "courtly love" and other idealistic moral traditions. One critic indicates that Chaucer saw "the values of an 'old' world eroded by those of the new" (Thompson 47). Although Chaucer certainly blames the church, the aristocracy and the rising bourgeoisie, his "Miller's Tale" also reprimands the lower

Note the variety of terms referring to the Prioress. Each reinforces and defines her position, giving the reader a clear picture of her status.

In these two paragraphs, the sentence structures vary, which reinforces the ideas and extends the foolishness of the carpenter.

classes that must be held responsible for their superstition and ignorance.

Ultimately, Chaucer's world revolved around a complex social hierarchy. Corruption flourished under a moral code that was impossible to uphold or enforce, with leaders who set no good example. Immorality simply awaited opportunity. Chaucer recognized that all levels of society shared the responsibility for its corruption. In *The Canterbury Tales*, the pretentious pilgrims make it very clear that ego is the great human equalizer, rendering us all susceptible to selfishness and deceit.

This simple, four-word sentence provides a short break for the reader before restating the thesis in the last two sentences of the essay.

Lesson 6.8
Polishing an Argument

Polishing the style of your argument is like the icing on a cake. You already have a grammatically solid sentence, but a little more style could make it even better.

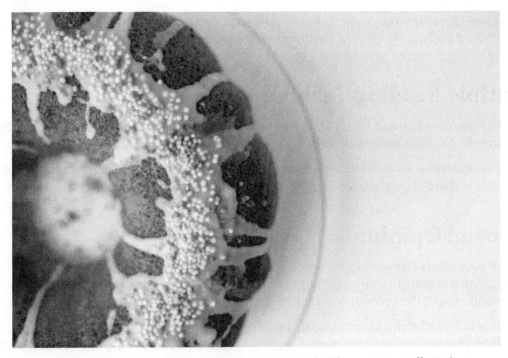

Sentence style is something extra to help you express your ideas even more effectively.

That extra polish might be just what you need to earn a higher grade, impress a hiring manager, or convince a skeptical audience.

In this lesson, you will learn how to proofread a text for style issues.

Proofreading is much easier when you have a strategy in place. Proof the style of your writing with the following steps:

Review Writing Style Guidelines

Review the characteristics of good style to guide your focus as you proofread. Here are some of the most important considerations:

Proofreading Checklist: Sentence Style
☐ **Meaning:** clear words, concise words, vivid words, appropriate tone, inclusive language
☐ **Delivery:** modifiers, parallelism, coordination, subordination
☐ **Consistency:** consistent tone, appropriate usage of active and passive voice, consistent verb tense, consistent point of view

Think back to the papers you've written in previous classes. What kind of suggestions did your teachers usually give you? If you tend to struggle in a specific area, spend extra time reviewing information about that particular style issue.

Proofread in Stages

Proofreading in stages will help you make specific, meaningful improvements to your writing. During each stage, focus on just one style issue at a time. For example, you might start by making sure all of your **verb tenses** are consistent; then, you might look for opportunities to use more **active voice**.

> Learning Style Tip
> If you're a **sequential** learner, make a checklist of each stage in the proofreading process. Use this list as a guide as you check your writing for style issues.

Try Multiple Reading Techniques

One of the best ways to proofread for style is reading your work aloud to yourself. Actually listening to your words can help you hear confusing sentences, **parallelism** problems, and inconsistent tone.

Reading aloud also forces your brain to slow down and pay attention. When you read to yourself, it's easy to scan the words instead of actually reading them.

Get a Second Opinion

When you read your own writing multiple times, you will slowly get used to the structure and sound of your sentences. Ask a friend or family member to review your text and give you feedback. This is the perfect opportunity to get the opinion of an actual **audience** member.

If your friend doesn't mind, consider making an audio recording of him or her reading your paper aloud. You can then listen for sentences that sound awkward or confusing. Anytime your friend stumbles over words or runs out of breath, double-check those sentences for possible style issues.

> Further Resources
> NaturalReader (http://www.naturalreaders.com/index.html) or another text-to-speech service could be a helpful resource when you are proofreading your sentences for style.

Take Frequent Breaks

Taking a break from your paper is essential when proofreading for style. When you read your paragraph or document multiple times, everything will start sounding the same after a while.

To make sure that you have enough time to review your work thoroughly, schedule proofreading time in your planner. You should spread these times across multiple days. Splitting up your proofreading time will give you the fresh eyes you need.

> **Helpful Hint**
>
> Some writing programs, like Microsoft Word, offer automatic writing style suggestions. Carefully review any advice before making changes. The style suggestions are generally less reliable than the spelling suggestions.

Lesson Wrap-up

Key Terms

Active Voice: when a sentence is written so that the subject is performing an action

Audience: the people who read your writing

Awkward Writing: writing that comes across as unnatural because of errors in style

Parallelism: a method for clarifying the relationship between ideas by presenting them in similarly-structured words, phrases, or clauses

Sequential Learning: learning information through a step-by-step process

Tense: how a verb indicates when it took place: past, present, or future

Verb: a word that represents an action, relationship, or state of being

Chapter 7
Research

Understanding the Research Paper

Research is required for many academic and professional tasks, but it is also something we do regularly in our daily lives. Have you ever been in a situation with a group of people, and you started debating about a particular topic? Maybe you felt differently than someone else did. How did you support your argument? Today, you'd likely turn to the internet for clarity and evidence.

Researching is all about finding information to explore ideas and ultimately make arguments. Research is a critical tool for finding sources of information that support your claim. However, you must be careful when you use these research sources. There are several important considerations you must make in research writing.

Most importantly, whenever you are using borrowed ideas to build your own authored text—whether it be a piece of music, art, or writing—it's vital that you provide proper credit to those who helped shape your final product. If you pass off borrowed information as your own, you are committing plagiarism.

Additionally, many research assignments will have very specific requirements. In academic settings, especially, you will likely be asked to write a research paper using a particular research style. Some of the most common research styles include MLA, APA, and Chicago style. Although many of the concepts in this chapter will apply for a broad range of these styles, the examples you'll encounter are formatted specifically in MLA style.

> In this lesson, you will learn about the following:
>
> The Role of Sources in Research Writing
> Integrating Source Information
> Recognizing the Basics of Research Styles

The Role of Sources

Research is primarily concerned with finding the right sources. Sources can include many forms of texts—artwork, speeches, recordings, movies, articles, etc.—that provide information relevant to a particular goal of research.

Some sources are more formal than others. For example, if you're using a Yelp! review as a basis for finding a good doctor in your neighborhood, you're consulting a common, informal source of information. If, however, you've found the doctor credited in a scholarly article, you have located a formal, academic source.

Depending on your task, you may be required to use only academic sources. You may also need to use a variety of sources from different places.

In academic writing, citing reliable sources is not only required, but it's necessary if you want to establish yourself as a reliable writer. You can use expert opinions and statistics to show your audience that your argument is well-informed and supported by current research.

The goal of academic research is to locate credible information that can be used to support your claim. Using research to explore the right sources has a number of advantages:

- Strengthens your opinion about a topic by supporting it with fact, details, and evidence
- Offers powerful anecdotes, or long examples told as stories, to highlight your main arguments
- Adds validity to your writing by linking your own claims to experts within your field of study
- Provides timely and relevant information that will advance the education of your audience
- Informs your audience where they can find further information regarding your topic

Read and evaluate the below paragraphs. Which sounds more convincing? If you were trying to make the case against eating celery, which paragraph would you use in your own writing? Why?

Paragraph 1

> Perhaps one of humankind's most valued senses is the sense of taste. This sense helps to weed out those foods that humans don't enjoy. At the top of this list is the celery stalk. Celery is disliked by many people, in many parts of the country. So, it shouldn't be of any real surprise to hear someone complain about the taste.

Paragraph 2

> In a recent study conducted at Yale University, "The most valued human sense is the sense of taste." This sense helps to weed out those foods that humans don't enjoy. At the top of this list is the celery stalk. According to esteemed researcher Kenneth Braymer, celery has the "lowest success rate in initial taste tests of any food" (96). So, it shouldn't be of any real surprise to hear someone say that "celery tastes like dirt." According to Dr. Kane of the Harvard University Research Team, tree bark actually has more nutritional benefit than the celery stalk (34).

Integrating Source Information

Once you've worked your way through the selecting your research, you'll want to consider how to actually utilize your sources within your writing. There are three main ways to integrate sources into your writing:

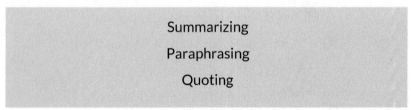

Summarizing

Paraphrasing

Quoting

Summarizing

A **summary** is a few sentences that explain a large amount of information. Using summaries makes the most sense when your readers need a broad overview of a topic but not specific details. Because summaries are general, they should only be used when you need to inform your audience about important background information on a topic.

Take a look at this example:

> In his novel, *Things Fall Apart*, on the rise of colonialism in Nigeria, author Chinua Achebe follows the story of Okonkwo, a tribal leader who has risen from very little and has maintained a

power and dominance amongst his clan and his family. As colonists begin to invade Okonkwo's land, culture, and traditions, he struggles to fight against the forces that threaten all he knows.

In this brief summary, the author highlights important components of the story in his own words, conveying broad ideas and major conflict.

Paraphrasing

When you paraphrase, you explain someone's words or sentences using your own words. This helps to explain the text's purpose or to add clarity to the author's argument. You can paraphrase anything from a single sentence to a complex idea. Consider the example below.

Original sentence:

"Female elephants are pregnant for a longer period of time than any other mammal, keeping their child with them for an average of twenty-two months" (Johnson 63).

Paraphrase:

Shockingly, elephants carry their babies for close to two years; this is longer than any other mammal (Johnson 63).

Quoting

Quotations are the direct words of a source. Quotes should be reserved for instances when the author's language is powerful or unique and supportive of your claim. Otherwise, you should paraphrase the borrowed language.

Here's an example:

Eleanor Roosevelt famously said, "You must do the things you think you cannot do."

Using Appropriate Research Styles

In your academic and professional experiences, depending on your task and your audience, you may be asked to work with multiple formatting styles. These styles require differences in basic formatting rules as well as in-text citations and works cited/reference pages.

Let's review four of the most common styles that are used today:

MLA (Modern Language Association)

APA (American Psychological Association)

CMS (Chicago Manual of Style)

CSE (Council of Science Editors)

MLA

The MLA format is the formatting style guide created by a group of scholars dedicated to research in modern languages. It is used most frequently by professionals and students of English and foreign language. However, it is also commonly used in the study of communications, religion, and philosophy.

MLA recommends utilizing the "Think, Select, Organize" process, which requires you to think about what type of sources are relevant to your research, select appropriate sources and source information, and organize your citations in a clear manner.

Additionally, when drafting your works-cited page, MLA asks you to consider using the 9 MLA Core Elements, which are guidelines to assist writers in forming thorough and organized citations. You will need the following information to compile these elements:

- Author
- Title of Source
- Title of Container
- Other Contributors
- Version
- Number
- Publisher
- Publication Date
- Location

To learn more about applying MLA standards, see Lesson 7.8.

APA

APA format is a research style guide created by psychologists used for academic documents such as journal articles and books. It is used in a great number of academic disciplines, so learning its general rules is a good idea for just about every student. In particular, courses in the social sciences (like psychology and sociology), nursing, journalism, and business typically use the APA style.

As a general rule, APA papers are written with a very formal tone, which means they strive to sound as objective or unbiased as possible. For this reason, writers using the APA style are usually expected to avoid first-person (*I, me, we, us, my, mine, our*) and second-person (*you, your*) pronouns and to steer clear of contractions and slang. Also, since APA is often used when writing about research and experiments, writers are asked the keep the following guidelines in mind when choosing their language:

APA Checklist: Writing Style

☐ Be as specific as possible

☐ Be sensitive to labeling and unintentional prejudice

☐ When writing about people, write about them as active participants, not passive components

CMS

Although not as popular in academia as MLA or APA formats, occasionally a professor will ask you to compose and cite in Chicago Manual of Style, or CMS. CMS is a formatting style guide published by the University of Chicago Press. Often preferred by publishers, CMS is the most comprehensive option for citing books, magazines, and journals.

Some disciplines that commonly use CMS are the arts, computer science, criminology, and history.

As opposed to the previously mentioned formats, CMS offers two ways of citing research sources:

Notes-and-Bibliography Method

The Notes-and-Bibliography Method is preferred by the humanities because it allows for easy reference of sources and the insertion of additional information.

Parentheses-and-Reference-List Method

The Parentheses-and-Reference-List Method is often preferred by science departments because it references the date of research within the body of a paper.

CSE

CSE is not quite as common as the three previous styles, but it has its place. CSE is the formatting style guide created by the Council of Science editors. This format is most commonly used for the sciences, particularly the natural and physical sciences.

CSE provides three different methods for documenting sources. Each method includes a series of in-text markers that show when a source has been used, and a corresponding list of sources, typically titled "References," that appears at the end of the document. The three methods are known as:

- Citation-Sequence
- Citation-Name
- Name-Year

The citation-sequence system organizes sources at the end of the paper according to the order that they appear in the text.

In the citation-name system, each source used in the paper is assigned a number, which is used to refer to that source throughout the document. However, the list of sources at the end of the paper are arranged and numbered according to alphabetical order rather than the order that they appear in the document.

The name-year system uses in-text citations that include the last name of the author or authors as well as the year of publication.

> **Further Resources**
>
> The Online Writing Lab (OWL) developed by Purdue University provides ample information about how to cite sources and format papers in different styles. Visit this website for an in-depth explanation of each.

Lesson Wrap-up

Key Terms

Academic Source: a source that has been peer-reviewed by other experts in the author's field

Anecdote: a long example told as a story

APA (American Psychological Association) Style: the research style guide created by psychologists used for academic documents such as journal articles and books

Audience: the people who read your writing

Claim: an argument or statement, usually supported by evidence

CMS (Chicago Manual of Style): a research style guide published by the University of Chicago Press

CSE (Council of Science Editors) Style: a research style created by the Council of Science Editors

In-text Citation: a note in a paragraph that tells the reader which words and ideas come from a source

Main Idea: the statement or argument that an author makes about a topic

MLA (Modern Language Association) Style: the research style guide created by a group of scholars dedicated to research in modern languages

Page Number: a way to help the audience find information in a text

Paraphrase: rewording the words of another person in order to explain the text's purpose or to add clarity to the author's argument

Lesson 7.2
Planning and Tracking Your Research

When searching the internet for a simple piece of information, it's easy to be distracted. How often have you found yourself clicking through photos or reading articles only to realize that an hour has gone by and you can't remember what you needed in the first place?

Misguided research can consume hours of time and leave you sorting through material that may be interesting but not necessarily relevant to your purpose. This strategy may work when you have plenty of time on your hands, but tackling a research paper for class requires a more efficient approach. Fortunately, you can streamline the research process through thoughtful preliminary work and planning.

In this lesson, you will learn important concepts of planning and tracking your research:

Preliminary Research
Types of Information
Sources of Information
A Research Timeline

Writing Environment: Professional

Planning and tracking your research is an important skill not just in school but for the workplace as well. When you and your colleagues start a new project, you may be asked to conduct market research on customer demand, pricing, or competitors. If you don't carefully organize your findings, you may get bogged down in the preliminary stages of the project. Careful planning at the beginning will ensure that you stay on track.

Preliminary Research

A research plan must begin with a clearly stated and focused subject, or **narrowed topic.** Even if you have an assigned topic, you must come up with specific aspects of the topic to research and discuss. For example, let's assume that you have been assigned the topic of gun control. A simple internet search using this phrase will result in millions of articles. This is a clear indication that your topic is too broad.

During the writing process, you may use **brainstorming** or other techniques to narrow down your topic. Conducting **preliminary research** can also be an effective way to explore a topic and identify the specific aspects you want to discuss. Think about the previous example. While searching for the topic "gun control" may result in far too much information, scanning a few articles or websites may introduce you to interesting aspects of the topic. You can then conduct further research into those ideas until you decide on the narrowed topic you want to explore further.

Additionally, preliminary research will provide helpful background information. Even if you are already familiar with a topic, you can always learn more about key events and ideas or discover recent developments.

One of the easiest ways to start researching is simply to use an online search engine like Google. Glance through the top five or ten sites that pop up in your search results. These will give you a quick idea of the type of source material you can expect to find during your research.

You should also do a quick search of your library's catalog to see the sources that they have available. Consider discussing your paper ideas with a librarian to get additional research ideas.

Writing Environment: Academic

Brainstorming to develop your ideas makes your preliminary research even more effective. As you learn about your topic, take a few moments to brainstorm additional ideas or questions you have. You may generate new ideas that you'll want to explore further through research.

Imagine that your research topic is single-gender education. Your preliminary research activities might look something like this:

- Search the internet using the phrase "single-gender education." Then, locate the following:
  - a dictionary definition of the phrase
  - newspaper and magazine articles debating the pros and cons of single-gender education
  - professional organizations providing information about single-gender education in the U.S.
  - relevant social media discussions about the subject
- Conduct a basic search of library materials using the phrase "single-gender education." Consider the following sources:
  - encyclopedia articles that include key players and early experimentation with single-gender education
  - scholarly articles discussing the psychological effects of single-gender education
  - interviews with teachers and/or students at these institutions

An added benefit of preliminary research is identifying topics that are too narrow. If you are having difficulty finding information on a narrowed topic, you may need to make your ideas slightly broader. For example, the topic "single-gender education in New York charter schools" is very specific. Preliminary research will reveal whether you're able to find sources on this topic. You may find that the topic "single-gender education in the U.S." yields more results.

Approaching preliminary research in a casual, information–seeking manner will reduce your research anxiety and boost your interest in the topic. Before you know it, you will be unearthing information that will help you define a clear and focused topic for your research.

Helpful Hint

Discovering specific terminology associated with your topic is another helpful result of preliminary research. For example, a preliminary search would indicate that single-gender education is also referred to as "single-sex education," "all-girls education," "gender segregation," and "same-gender schools." When using less intuitive searching tools, such as research databases or online scholarly article collections, knowing alternate terminology can be crucial in finding results.

Further Resources

If you can't come up with any keywords or search terms that are related to your topic, try a keyword generator like this one: http://www.lib.utexas.edu/keywords/index.php. This tool creates a list of keywords about your topic that you can use to search for sources.

Types of Information

Once you have a narrowed research topic, you must identify what types of information will work best for your paper. **Primary sources** are first-hand accounts such as interviews, photographs, and research studies. Using primary sources builds the **credibility** of your argument and is especially important for scientific or historical topics. **Secondary sources,** on the other hand, are texts that discuss a primary source. For example, an article about the findings of a research study or a review of a book would be considered secondary sources.

Academic writing often includes a third type of source: scholarly sources. **Scholarly sources** are **peer-reviewed,** which means that the information was reviewed by experts in the field before it was published. Scholarly articles are usually accessible in **online databases** made available by the library; scholarly books are usually published by university presses. Because scholarly sources are reviewed before publication, they usually contain more reliable information than typical news or magazine articles. However, they are often more densely packed with information and written at a rigorous reading level.

> To learn more about the different types of sources, see Lesson 7.3.

Writing Environment: Everyday

Another way to think about primary and secondary sources is to think about getting information directly from the source or getting it secondhand. If your manager sent out an important memo about company goals for the month and you missed it, what would be the best thing to do? Getting a copy of the original document is better than asking a co-worker to sum it up because then you know exactly what your manager said.

Sources of Information

Now that you know what types of sources you need, it's time to identify the best places to find those sources of information. Some of the most common places to conduct research are the following:

- The internet
- Online research databases
- The library
- People
- **Field research**

Your narrowed topic will determine the type of information you need, which will ultimately determine where you should look for it. Here are a few examples:

How do people feel about banning guns from college campuses?

This is an opinion question, so a good source of answers would be field research. To gather this information, you might want to take a poll of your classmates, check newspaper editorials, or search the internet for debate websites. You might also find similar studies or survey results from scholarly sources.

Benefits of single-gender education

This topic requires facts backed by data obtained through scholarly research. You will need to conduct a thorough search of your library's online databases. One of the oldest and most comprehensive educational databases is the Educational Resources Information Center (ERIC).

The role of social media in political elections

This topic involves social media and current events, two areas that you are most likely to find discussed online. Keep in mind that information on the internet is not always reliable. Look for credible, well-known news sources as you conduct your research. There may also be scholarly sources available. Check your library's online databases to see if any studies have been done in the last few years.

A Research Timeline

Once you've narrowed down your topic and considered the type of research you need, the next step is to create a **research timeline,** which is a mapping of your research tasks and when you plan to accomplish them. Use your class deadlines to structure your research plan. For example, if your narrowed topic is due in two weeks, you need to complete your preliminary research before then. Setting aside time in your planner or calendar will help you stick to your schedule and complete your research on time.

Your research timeline might look like this:

> November 12: Start preliminary research
> November 18: Final topic due
> November 19: Identify list of possible sources
> November 21: Visit library to learn more about research database searches
> November 22: Find 2 good sources
> November 24: Find 2 more good sources
> November 28: Finalize all sources
> November 30: Bibliography due
> December 10: Finish research
> December 15: First draft due

The most important aspect of a research timeline is adhering to your goals. Hold yourself accountable to your deadlines and don't forget to reward yourself when you accomplish them.

Writing Environment: Everyday

Visual tools like tables, maps, and calendars can be very helpful in getting you started on projects that seem overwhelming. Organizing your thoughts with the help of these tools can make even large tasks seem more manageable.

Lesson Wrap-up

Key Terms

Academic Writing: a more formal style of writing used to analyze a topic
Brainstorming: exploring and developing ideas
Credibility: the trustworthiness of an author
Field Research: personally collecting information through interviews and surveys
Online Database: an online collection of scholarly and non-scholarly sources
Narrowed Topic: a clearly stated and focused subject
Peer Review: working with a classmate to give feedback on each other's papers
Preliminary Research: the general research writers use to narrow a topic and generate ideas
Primary Source: a first-hand account such as an interview, photograph, or research study
Research Timeline: a mapping of your research tasks and when you plan to accomplish them
Secondary Source: a text that discusses a primary source
Scholarly Source: a source that has been peer-reviewed before it was published

Writing Application: Planning and Tracking Your Research

Consider the following notes from a student who is starting a research paper on the legal drinking age.

Research notes for topic: the legal drinking age

Conduct preliminary research.

Searched the internet using the phrase "the legal drinking age"

The legal drinking age by country: Wikipedia

Pros and cons of lowering drinking age, public opinion: www.drinkingage.procon.org

Professional organization: MADD, www.madd.org: information about why the drinking age was changed and how many lives it has saved.

Facebook: Soldiers can serve the country but not buy a drink

Alternate search terms: "legal drinking," "buying alcohol," "underage drinking"

Conduct a basic search of library reference materials for the legal drinking age.

Book series: Opposing Viewpoints in Context

Scholarly articles on effects of lowering the minimum legal drinking age (ex: *American Journal of Public Health*)

The minimum drinking age of 21 and traffic safety (National Highway Traffic Safety Administration)

Consider different types of sources.

Primary sources, such as interviews, diaries, and photographs. Poll college students: What would be the effects of lowering the drinking age?

Scholarly sources, including articles from medical journals and professional organizations. What has been the effect on car accidents, alcoholism, and accidental death by raising the drinking age? How many underage drinkers were there before the legal age was raised to 21, and how many are there since they raised the drinking age?

Articles from newspapers, magazines, and other types of secondary sources. Local news reports of underage drinking and driving

Lesson 7.3

Identifying Different Types of Sources

It's easy for us to instantly find information. If you need to check a fact or find a definition, you can go online and find an answer within seconds. Online searches may be convenient, but they don't always provide the most reliable information. As you conduct research, it's important to know the different types of sources that are available and the best ways to use them.

One source isn't automatically better than another. For example, a paper on the causes of the Boston Tea Party requires very different sources than a paper about cyberbullying. You want to choose the types of sources that contain reliable information relevant to your topic. This doesn't mean that you should use just one type of source. On the contrary, including a combination of sources will ensure that you have a variety of opinions and perspectives.

In this lesson, you will learn about different types of sources:

Print Sources
Online Sources
Multimedia Sources
Personal Sources

Print Sources

Print sources include any materials originally printed on paper. Books are the most common form of print sources as they're useful for almost any topic imaginable. Keep in mind, however, that books are not always revised and reprinted as new discoveries and innovations are made. If you are writing a paper about science or technology, make sure you are using a text that was published recently. Conversely, the date of publication may not be as important for topics involving history or literature.

Further Resources

If you need a book that your library doesn't carry, you can often request a copy through **interlibrary loan**. This program allows libraries throughout the U.S. to share resources. A librarian can help you find the book you need and place your request. Check out the link below to explore this resource:
https://www.loc.gov/rr/loan/.

Other common types of print resources are magazine and newspaper articles. These are often called **periodicals** because they come out periodically at certain times during the year. In addition to physical print copies, the library often has access to thousands of periodicals in **online databases.** Many of these periodicals are **scholarly sources** that have been **peer-reviewed** by experts in a particular field.

While scholarly sources are reliable, they are not always as easy to find as other types of articles. This is especially true if your topic involves current events or popular culture. Don't be afraid to use regular magazine and newspaper articles as long as they come from reputable organizations.

Further Resources

In the past, libraries stored vast archives of print articles. Storing and accessing this information was tedious, and many libraries eventually moved to microfilm, a technology that allowed them to reproduce text on special film that could be viewed using a microfilm machine. While microfilm took up less space than print copies, the film still had to be stored and manually indexed. Today, most articles that were originally printed can now be accessed online, where the text can be easily searched and saved. To learn more about the history of microfilm, read this article from *Atlas Obscura*: (http://www.atlasobscura.com/articles/the-strange-history-of-microfilm-which-will-be-with-us-for-centuries)

Online Sources

If used correctly, the internet is a valuable tool for research. Not only can you find information about almost any topic online, but also you can access information that can't be found elsewhere. Remember that not all sources are created equal. A general rule to use when looking for reliable sites is to check the URL; *.edu*, and *.gov* addresses are generally considered reliable. Exercise caution with *.com* and *.org* sites because their primary purpose is commercial (to sell a product or service).

Searching online is one of the easiest ways to conduct research, but don't limit yourself to the websites that show up in your Google results. There's a wealth of information available in other formats that will complement your online resources.

> To learn more about properly evaluating online sources, see Lesson 7.4.

Periodicals in online databases could be considered print or online resources. However, as the internet becomes cheaper and more accessible, many organizations are starting to publish their articles online. Online news sites are constantly posting articles, and even traditional newspapers and magazines often publish online-only content.

Writing Environment: Professional

Not all online databases are general information sites; many are specific to a particular field. For instance, BioMed Central is a small database that specializes in biology and medicine, and the Gale Reference Library is a collection of reference books: encyclopedias, dictionaries, and historical documents. These specialized databases are available for almost every field of study, and they're excellent resources for your professional career.

Ebooks are another type of **online source.** These may be electronic versions of printed material or electronic-only books. An advantage of ebooks is that they are easy to search and don't need to be carried around. Be careful if you copy and paste information from ebooks into your research notes; you don't want to accidentally **plagiarize** the content.

Group Activity

In pairs, search your school's databases for ebooks and ebook collections. Roughly how many books are available this way? Notice how many reprints of paper versions are available. Remember, this is a great way to find books when you can't get to the library.

Further Resources

Project Gutenberg (https://www.gutenberg.org/) is a non-profit organization that converts out-of-copyright books into ebooks and makes them available for free online. If you are writing about a classic novel or historical document, consider searching the site to see if any useful books are available to you.

Multimedia Sources

Multimedia sources involve media other than the written word and include films, recordings, television episodes, and photographs. These sources could be excellent additions to your print and online research. In addition to quoting the material, consider including images or videos in your research paper when possible. Visuals can spark your audience's interest and make your writing even more powerful.

For example, while researching the philosophies of Martin Luther King, Jr. and Malcolm X, you will come across a number of recorded speeches. Not only will these sources help you understand their different approaches to civil rights, but also an audio or video clip could support the argument you're making in your research paper.

As with any other source, you should carefully evaluate each one to ensure the information is trustworthy. For example, YouTube contains billions of videos, many of which are created by people with an amateur interest in a topic. Look for videos published by well-known organizations that feature experts in a field.

Group Activity

Do a quick search on YouTube for one of the following topics:

- The Maillard reaction
- Unconscious bias
- Occam's razor
- The prisoners' dilemma
- The rule of thirds

As a group, try to identify one video that could be useful for a research project. What makes that video a trustworthy source?

Writing Environment: Everyday

People share multimedia resources regularly with friends and family. Think about the last time you sent or received a link to a humorous photo or a powerful video. In these situations, it's not as vital to validate the credibility of your source since the resource isn't serving an academic or professional purpose.

Personal Sources

Personal sources are people, usually experts, who share information in an interview or conversation. Occasionally, you may find yourself writing about a topic that is so specific or personal, sources are difficult to find. In these instances, interviewing someone with experience or education in a topic is an excellent option. Interviews can be conducted in person, by phone, or by email.

For example, imagine your aunt was working at Three Mile Island during the infamous nuclear disaster. She would be an excellent personal source on a research paper about the dangers of nuclear energy or the shortcomings of disaster relief.

A personal source would be considered a **primary source** because it is a first-hand account or opinion. While you may not have access to personal sources for every research paper, look for opportunities to include this type of research when possible.

> Group Activity
>
> Think about someone you know who has experienced something unique or interesting. With a group, have each person share a brief summary of this individual's experience and discuss how he or she might be used as a personal source in a research paper.

On Your Own

Evaluate the following sources and determine if they are print, online, multimedia, or personal sources.

Source	Type
A news report about a local charity event	
A website article discussing the origins of Memorial Day	
An interview with a friend who volunteered with the Peace Corps	
An encyclopedia entry on xenophobia	
A documentary about illegal dolphin fishing	

Lesson Wrap-up

Key Terms

Ebook: a type of online resource that includes electronic versions of printed material or electronic-only books

Interlibrary Loan: a program that allows libraries to share resources

Multimedia Source: a source that involved media other than the written word such as a film or a photo

Online Database: an online collection of scholarly and non-scholarly sources

Online Source: a source available through the internet

Peer Review: a review by experts in the field before

Periodical: a magazine or newspaper published periodically throughout the year

Personal Source: a person who shares information in an interview or conversation

Plagiarism: the act of using someone else's words or ideas without giving credit to the original source

Print Source: a source originally printed on paper

Primary Source: a first-hand account such as an interview, photograph, or research study

Scholarly Source: a source that has been peer-reviewed by an expert in the field before it was published

Writing Application: Identifying Different Types of Sources

Read the following essay and consider how it has used multiple types of research sources to support its argument.

Love Spans Time

According to the famous song of the same name, "love is a many splendored thing." However, the splendors of love go back much further than Frank Sinatra. The earliest known love poem was written about 4,000 years ago (Mark). Do humans still love the way they used to? Are the glories of love the same as they once were? While our culture has transformed, and the language of love has evolved, our emotions have remained mostly unchanged.

Here, you'll find a citation from a printed encyclopedia.

The oldest known love poem was written on a small clay tablet and discovered in what is now modern-day Iraq. The poem is Sumerian and dates back 4,000 years. Sumerian culture revolved around fertility, and their beliefs centered around the life that sensuality brings. Ancient historian Joshua Mark explains that this poem was written by a high priestess to the king, with whom she slept with once a year to ensure the fertility of their people and crops. By sleeping with the priestess, King Shu-Sin symbolically slept with the goddess Inanna, who then blessed them. A section of "The Lovesong of Shu-Sin" reads:

The source of this information is a professor of ancient history and philosophy, so it's trustworthy.

> You have captivated me, let me stand tremblingly before you.
>
> Bridegroom, I would be taken by you to the bedchamber,
>
> You have captivated me, let me stand tremblingly before you.
>
> Lion, I would be taken by you to the bedchamber. ("Lovesong" 5-9)

The author uses a secondary source for the poem because the primary source is in ancient Sumerian, a language in which few scholars are trained.

Two thousand years later, Rome was the greatest power on the planet. Unlike the fertility culture of the Sumerians, the Romans were known as masters of war. Yet, here too love shines. Catullus' "Poem 109" sings the wonders of being in love.

> Joy of my life! You tell me this-
>
> That nothing can possibly break this love of ours for each other.
>
> God let her mean what she says,
>
> From a candid heart,
>
> That our two lives may be in linked in their length

Day to day,

    Each to each,

In a bond of sacred fidelity. (line 221)

The speaker is deeply in love and prays that his lover is telling him the truth when she says they will be together always.

England's Elizabethan Age, named after Queen Elizabeth I, had a culture quite different from the Romans and Sumerians. England had long been at war with other countries over its religion since Elizabeth's father, Henry VIII, rebelled against the Pope to create the Church of England. Both Anglican and Catholic leaders advocated strict rules surrounding love and romance. However, William Shakespeare (among many other great poets) lived during this era and wrote prodigiously about love and desire in much the same way as Catullus. For example, he explores his love's beauty in "Sonnet 18": "Shall I compare thee to a summer's day? / Thou art more lovely and more temperate" (lines 1-2).

> The author of this essay is an English major who has studied the Elizabethan Age, so she doesn't need to cite a source for this information.

> This quote came from a book of Shakespeare's poems at the college library, a print source.

The 21st century also has numerous examples of love poetry. Below is an excerpt from Dorothea Lasky's poem "The Wall Hanging I Never Noticed":

> Until I noticed you I could not help it
>
> Until you made the red flowers alive again
>
> Until the blue branches
>
> The lemons you loved, but also the way you loved me, too
>
> Until all of this I never noticed you
>
> But once I did
>
> I never minded noticing
>
> I never stopped noticing (lines 11-18)

> This quote found at *poets.org*, a reputable website sponsored by the Academy of American Poets.

> Again, this is the original poem (a primary source).

The author is so in love that she's seeing things as if for the first time. She never noticed how red the flowers were in the picture hanging on the wall until she fell in love; now she's seeing everything in bright colors. She's seeing with the eyes of one mesmerized by her emotions.

Despite the thousands of years between each of these poems, love has remained constant. No matter the language, the country, the culture, or the people, love is love. From the ancient Sumerians to modern Americans, emotions of love, desire, and romance have remained unchanged.

Works Cited

Catullus, Gaius Valerius. "Poem 109." *The Poems of Cantullus*,
translated by Peter Wingham, Berkeley: U of California P, 1969.

Lasky, Dorothea. "The Wall Hanging I Never Noticed." *Poets*, Academy
of American Poets, 2014, www.poets.org/poetsorg/poem/wall-
hanging-i-never-noticed.

Mark, Joshua J. "The World's Oldest Love Poem." *Ancient History
Encyclopedia*, Ancient History Encyclopedia. Ltd., 2014.

Shakespeare, William. "Sonnet 18." *William Shakespeare: Complete
Poems*, edited by Christopher More, Avenel: Gramercy Books,
1993.

Lesson 7.4
Evaluating the Credibility of Sources

One of the main reasons for using research sources is to support your conclusions. If your sources aren't **credible,** your **audience** will have no reason to believe your claims. To make your writing as effective as possible, use sources that are trustworthy and relevant to your purpose.

Imagine that your Constitutional Law instructor has assigned a group project to research the history of the Pledge of Allegiance and its recitation in public schools. During your first meeting, a fellow group member claims that it is now illegal for students to recite the Pledge in their classrooms, and she produces an article she found on a website to support her claim. You are suspicious of this assertion, but you need more than your opinion to convince the other students. How do you demonstrate to your group that this assertion may be untrue?

Part of what makes research challenging is that not all information is trustworthy. In fact, a large amount of the information you encounter every day is unreliable. Learning to distinguish between fact and fiction is an essential skill for your academic career and beyond.

Read the following paragraphs. Which one would you be more likely to trust?

Paragraph 1

> Because of the confusion regarding the symptoms of post-traumatic stress disorder, physicians often misdiagnose PTSD in children. A few common misdiagnoses are depression, hyperactivity, and Attention Deficit Disorder (ADD). Because these conditions all share common symptoms, professionals have trouble differentiating between them. In many cases, anxiety disorders overlap, or an individual may be suffering from more than one condition at a time. The *KidsHealth* website lists physical complaints and low academic performance as potential symptoms of PTSD in children. In addition, traumatized children often develop legitimate learning disabilities and problems with attention and memory. Some teachers at Pickens County Middle School say that children with post-traumatic stress disorder are more likely to need remedial classes.

Paragraph #2

> Because of the confusion regarding the symptoms of post-traumatic stress disorder, physicians often misdiagnose PTSD in children. A few common misdiagnoses are depression, hyperactivity, and Attention Deficit Disorder (ADD). Because these conditions all share common symptoms, professionals have trouble differentiating between them. In many cases, anxiety disorders overlap, and an individual may be suffering from more than one condition at a time. An article by Yale Medical Professor Kevin D. Marshall notes that children with PTSD may vocalize physical complaints, such as stomachaches or headaches, with no medical basis. He also observes that the child's performance in school usually lowers significantly. In addition, traumatized children often develop legitimate learning disabilities and problems with attention and memory. Research conducted by medical scientist Mary McLaughlin indicates that children with post-traumatic stress disorder are more likely to need remedial classes.

▷ In the first example, the author uses information from sources that seem questionable. Even though both paragraphs share similar information, the sources mentioned in the second example seem much more trustworthy.

This lesson will discuss four steps of identifying a credible research source:

Look for Potential Bias
Evaluate the Relevance
Check the Credentials
Research the Source Material

Reflection Questions

When you are trying to make an important decision, whom do you usually ask for advice? What makes this person trustworthy?

Further Resources

The Onion is a humorous website that uses outrageous fake stories to comment on current events. Occasionally, journalists and politicians cite false information from *The Onion* without truly evaluating the site's credibility. Read this article to learn more about these embarrassing mistakes: http://www.thedailybeast.com/articles/2012/09/29/fooled-by-the-onion-8-most-embarrassing-fails.html.

Look for Potential Bias

To begin evaluating the credibility of a source, search the text for signs of bias. **Bias** is a term used to describe a person's opinions and preferences. Although all authors have some amount of bias, a credible author will work to keep his or her writing as straightforward and honest as possible.

As you check for credibility, think about the author's **purpose.** In a biased text, the author may have a stated purpose that is different from the true purpose. Imagine that you are reading an article about the health benefits of exercise. The purpose of the text is **informative,** but the author spends most of the article promoting a particular brand of energy bar. This text is not credible because the author has hidden his or her true purpose.

A research source may also be biased if the author is associated with a specific organization or **agenda.** For example, a commercial produced by a political party will contain information that supports that party's positions. This commercial would not be considered a credible source for most papers.

One final sign of bias is extremely positive or negative language. If the author uses an angry, sarcastic tone or disrespectful language, the text almost certainly contains bias. Overly positive or optimistic language can also indicate bias.

Read the following paragraph. Can you detect the sentence that indicates bias?

> I don't remember a day of my schooling that did not begin with the Pledge of Allegiance. We all said it, regardless of our political beliefs. There was no hidden meaning or agenda that we could see; it was simply a signal that the school day was about to begin. Today, those simple words in honor of the American flag have come to represent much more to a generation of faithless and unpatriotic students and their parents (McHugh 34).
>
> In this paragraph, the first three sentences reflect on the author's experience as a child in school. However, in the last sentence, he or she uses negative language and generalizations, which indicates bias.

Writing Environment: Everyday

How many times have you passed along unproven, biased, or false information via social media? Many of us have been guilty of this at some point. However, being a responsible researcher means evaluating all sources for accuracy and truth before passing them along.

To learn more about different types of bias and methods for finding bias in a text, see Lesson 5.6

Helpful Hint

Using a questionable source in an essay or research paper can be acceptable in some situations. If you are discussing the stance of an organization, for instance, you might use the organization's website as a source. However, you would not want to use this information to support the **argument** of your paper.

Reflection Questions

Think about a time when you had to mediate a conflict. Did you have to convey different sides of a story to each party? If so, did you notice how each person's account of what happened differed? How did each person's bias affect the situation? Was there value in investigating each person's bias when trying to understand what actually occurred?

Evaluate the Relevance

The second step in evaluating the credibility of a source is checking for **relevance.** A relevant source will help you **develop** the ideas in your paper by providing specific, **focused** information about a topic. If a text is full of general information that anyone could have written, it's probably not a credible research source.

Relevant sources are also current. For most topics, it's advantageous to use sources that have been published or updated in the last five years. Topics that change rapidly, such as technology or science, may require sources from the last twelve months.

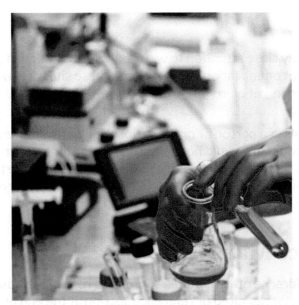

Technology develops quickly, so you must be diligent in selecting sources.

Ask yourself the following questions:

> Is the topic of the source focused or general?
> Is the information in the source current?
> Can it directly support one of my claims?

Read the following excerpt and ask yourself if each sentence is relevant to the purpose presented in the topic sentence.

> Great white sharks are one of the most dangerous species to encounter. One bite can be life-threatening or fatal. Great whites can grow to 15-20 feet and weigh more than 5,000 pounds. Some species of sharks are not very dangerous and actually enjoy interacting with humans. Though it's highly unlikely, if you are ever attacked by a great white shark, stun it by hitting it on the nose as hard as possible and quickly swim to safety.
>
> In the paragraph above, the purpose is to inform the reader about the dangers of the great white shark. While most sentences support this purpose, re-read the fourth sentence:
>
> Some species of sharks are not very dangerous and actually enjoy interacting with humans.
>
> This sentence, while accurate, does not relate to the overall goal of the paragraph. Therefore, it is irrelevant.

Check the Credentials

The credibility of a research source can also be affected by the author's professional credentials. An expert will have extensive education and training in a topic. Think about the level of respect that this person would receive from other authors and researchers in a particular field.

Sometimes, personal experience is more important than professional credentials. For example, a famous artist would be considered an authority on art even if he or she had no formal training. In these cases, make sure that the area of experience closely matches the topic of the paper.

If you are evaluating a document or website, research the organization that published the information. A document authored by a government office or university is more likely to be credible than one authored by a for-profit company.

> **Helpful Hint**
>
> As you evaluate websites, pay close attention to web addresses that end in *.gov* or *.edu*; they belong to official government or educational institutions. These sites are usually more credible than other websites that end in *.net* or *.com*.

As you investigate the credentials of a person or organization, be aware of potential **conflicts of interest**. For example, a pharmaceutical company would not be a good source for a paper on contaminated prescription drugs. Even though this organization is closely associated with the topic, the company's main goal is making money. This conflict of interest could lead them to omit any information that might damage the reputation of their company.

Research the Source Material

Finally, a credible source will reference other credible sources. In research studies and articles, the authors will list their sources in a **works-cited** or reference section at the end of the text. On a website, the author may include hyperlinks to sources. Skim through any source material to make sure that the information seems valid and credible.

When an author uses information from other persons or organizations, that material must be cited properly. If a text does not include a list of sources, the information may be plagiarized or unreliable.

A lack of sources might also indicate that the information is so general that no sources are needed. In this case, look for a better source with more specific, relevant information.

> **Helpful Hint**
>
> Sources that contain entirely original information, such as a first-hand account, do not require sources. The author is the only source for these types of texts.

Lesson Wrap-up

Key Terms

Agenda: a person's hidden motive

Argument: a reason why you should think or act a certain way

Audience: the people who read your writing

Bias: a person's opinions and preferences

Conflict of Interest: when an author has a personal stake in a topic that affects their purpose

Credibility: what makes someone or something believable

Development: effective presentation of information and inclusion of supporting details

Focus: clear communication and support of a main idea

Informative Text: a text that gives the audience information about a topic

Purpose: the goal of a text

Relevance: when information is clearly related to the text around it

Works Cited: a page at the end of your research paper that includes full bibliographic citations of each source in your essay

Lesson 7.5

Understanding and Avoiding Plagiarism

Imagine you've been working on a marketing idea that you want to propose to your boss. You show your notes to your coworker for feedback, and the next thing you know, that coworker is presenting your idea to your supervisor. His words are his own, but the ideas are yours.

Clearly, your coworker was wrong to present your work as his own. For the same reason, when you use words or ideas from an outside source without crediting the author, you commit **plagiarism.** Most colleges take this issue seriously; one major offense is often grounds for serious punishment.

In this lesson, you will learn the following about how to avoid plagiarism:

Track Your Sources
Use In-text Citations

Some forms of plagiarism are much more obvious than others. For example, you know that it's wrong to purchase an essay online and pass it off as your own. Similarly, you probably know not to copy and paste text from an outside source and claim authorship.

However, other common forms of plagiarism are not as obvious, and students sometimes plagiarize unintentionally. For example, if you've conducted a lot of research on a topic, you may end up writing about someone else's ideas without even realizing it. If you don't cite the source, or cite it incorrectly, you are committing plagiarism.

> Helpful Hint
>
> Many schools define their policies and procedures for plagiarism in a few different places. Try looking in a course syllabus, a college handbook, or your library website for more information specific to your school.

Track Your Sources

Research writing requires a large amount of time and materials. As you gather **source** material, it's important to keep track of where the information came from. Otherwise, you might end up citing a source incorrectly or forgetting to cite it at all.

To avoid accidental plagiarism, use a notebook or digital file to keep track of your research. The key is to immediately catalog material you think you might use in your paper. As you read a text, take note of any facts or ideas that connect to your topic.

Some students like taking notes on index cards while others prefer copying and pasting the text into a document. Either method is fine as long as you carefully record the following source details:

Type of Source

Title

Author

Year of Publication

Any time you copy down ideas from your research, place **quotation marks** around **direct quotes.** This will help you remember that the information is not your own.

Note-taking will also help you focus on reading the text closely and ensure that you understand the ideas and words that you borrow. A common mistake students make in the research process is to get impatient and skim through texts instead of reading them. If you **paraphrase** a text that you don't understand, you'll likely mislead the reader.

Writing Environment: Professional

Plagiarism can have serious consequences for your professional life as well. There are numerous stories of authors, journalists, musicians, and others who have been caught plagiarizing someone else's work. In these situations, the person committing plagiarism not only faces legal action but also loses credibility in their field.

Group Activity

Plagiarism in music is difficult to prove because the similarities between songs can be subjective. Throughout the years, multiple artists have been accused of stealing melodies from other artists. As a group, think of a famous example and find clips of both songs online. Discuss whether or not you think one of the songs was plagiarized.

Use In-Text Citations

When writing with sources, you must give credit to other authors using **in-text citations,** which are notes in a paragraph that tell the reader which words and ideas come from a source.

Your reader should be able to distinguish between your original work and that of your sources. To avoid plagiarism, you must use correct in-text citations and signal phrases for any content that is **summarized,** paraphrased, or directly **quoted. Signal phrases** are phrases used to identify source information—like the title and author—within a sentence.

Because the English discipline most commonly uses **MLA** formatting, the examples below follow MLA guidelines. If you are unsure which **research style** to follow, always check with your instructor.

- According to [Author's Last Name] ...

  > According the NFL commissioner Roger Goodell, "I don't expect to try to get people to like everything I do. I want them to respect what I do."

- In his/her book, [Title of Book], [Author's Last Name] discusses ...

  > In her article, "The High Price of Diamonds," Jenny Reed argues that the majority of people who wear diamond jewelry are unaware of the consequences to mining for this rock.

If you do not identify the author's name in the paragraph, remember to include it in an in-text citation at the end of the summary. This citation will let your readers know exactly what information you've borrowed from the source.

Don't forget to include a works-cited page even if your summarized source is the only source you've used. The **works-cited page** lists the sources used in a text.

Direct quotes are the exact words of outside sources. You must put all direct quotes in quotation marks. These might be individual words, sentences, or groups of sentences.

Citations for direct quotes also require extra details. In addition to the author, you should always add an in-text citation that includes the page number. If you are unable to fit the author's name in the sentence itself, add the author's last name to the citation.

> In *Jesse James: American Antihero*, professor Lawrence Bruce explains that the American public "imagined Jesse James as Robin Hood of the Wild West" (20).

> The imagery that Matthew Arnold uses in this poem "represents the author's longing for a literal and emotional home" (Edahl 33).

By including the author and title of the source, you are clearly signaling to the reader that the words in quotation marks are not your own.

On Your Own

Read the following excerpts and identify the one that does not need a citation.

> Although on the surface *The Bicycle Thief* seems to support an underlying misogynistic agenda, the main character, Antonio Ricci, contradicts his utterances about male superiority through his actions.

> Both Antonio and Baiocco chide Maria for revealing her emotions publicly. When Maria confronts the two men about Antonio's stolen bicycle, Antonio says, "Don't start crying here."

> Film critic Bosley Crawther explains that the film is a beautiful interpretation of Italian city life.

Writing Environment: Everyday

While many books, photos, and films are protected by copyright laws, more artists and authors are choosing to release their works under a creative commons license. This type of license gives others permission to use the document or image for personal and, in some cases, commercial use. As free content is shared over the internet, creative commons licensing is becoming more popular.

Use the following checklist to double-check for possible plagiarism:

Plagiarism Checklist

- ☐ Do all direct quotations have quotation marks and citation information?
- ☐ Do all paraphrases and summaries have citation information?
- ☐ Is it clear where each of my paraphrases and summaries end and where my words begin?
- ☐ Are all sources listed on a works-cited page?

> **Further Resources**
> In U.S. copyright law, the concept of Fair Use allows you to use limited amounts of material without permission from the original source. For a brief overview of Fair Use, read this summary provided by Stanford University: http://fairuse.stanford.edu/overview/fair-use/what-is-fair-use/. Are the sources in a research paper covered under Fair Use? Why or why not?

Lesson Wrap-up

Key Terms

Direct Quotes: quotes that take words and phrases directly from the original source

In-text Citation: a note in a paragraph that tells the reader which words and ideas come from a source

MLA (Modern Language Association) Style: the research style guide created by a group of scholars dedicated to research in modern languages

Paraphrase: the ideas of an outside source presented in an author's original writing

Plagiarism: the act of using borrowed words or ideas without giving credit to the author

Quotation Marks: a pair of punctuation marks used to repeat someone else's words

Quote: a reference to direct words from a source

Research Style: a set of standards used for research writing within a particular discipline

Research Writing: the process of conducting research and using sources to compose arguments

Signal Phrase: a phrase used to identify source information—like the title and author—within a sentence

Source: an original document or first-hand account that a writer consults for research

Summary: a few sentences that explain a large amount of information

Works Cited: a list of sources at the end of an MLA-styled text

Writing Application: Understanding and Avoiding Plagiarism

Read the following essay and pay special attention to how it cites outside information.

The Inability to see Humanity's Duality: The Downfall of Hawthorne's "Young Goodman Brown"

When asked, many people say they are inherently good, but what does this mean? Nathaniel Hawthorne's short story "Young Goodman Brown" explores the notion of good and evil. Through the events of the story, Hawthorne explores the dangers of holding an overly simplistic view of human morality. Young Goodman Brown fails to recognize his own duality and this duality in other townsfolk; this results in a loss of faith and self-imposed isolation.

Because this is the author's own analysis, it does not require a citation.

Young Goodman Brown reacts with pessimism when seeing the village people in the forest, which was generally associated with chaos and darkness. His view of the villagers changes from good to evil. The first person Brown sees is Goody Hoyse; he is shocked because she was the one "who had taught him his catechism" (454). The following morning, when Young Goodman Brown sees her in the village "catechizing a little girl, [he] [snatches] away the child, as from the grasp of the fiend [Devil] himself" (460). This response shows Brown's inability to accept that Goody Hoyse is a good person; in his eyes, she has become all evil. This idea is reaffirmed by Paul J. Hurley in his article "Evil Wherever He Looks." Hurley notes how Brown sees only evil in the village people now that he has allowed their capacity for sin to replace any goodness they may have (466). Brown only sees the evil in his cohabitants, thus destroying his relationships with them. His failure to recognize that people are both good and evil results in his loss of faith in people and leads him to an isolated, lonely life.

Direct quotes must be cited.

The author uses a signal phrase to cite the author and source of this paraphrase.

Hawthorne also uses symbolism to convey the importance of duality. Browns' wife, Faith, as well as the pink ribbon she wears, are symbols of duality. Faith is aptly named because she is symbolic of Brown's initial faith in people and God. Because of his experience in the forest, he loses his Faith and his faith. Hawthorne demonstrates this loss when Brown encounters Faith after his night in the forest:

> Turning the corner by the meeting-house, he spied the head of Faith, with the pink ribbons gazing forth, and bursting into such joy at the sight of him, that she skipped along the street, and almost kissed her husband before the whole village. But, Goodman Brown looked sternly and sadly into her face, and passed on without a greeting. (Hawthorne 460)

The author uses a block quote to support his or her argument.

His faith is weak and subsequently lost because he cannot understand that faith in God requires recognizing that man is both sinful and worth saving. The pink ribbons Faith wears confirm this idea. Pink is a combination of white (signifying purity and innocence) and red (signifying passion and experience). The fact that Faith wears pink supports Hawthorne's claim that duality in faith is necessary and that without this recognition, Young Goodman Brown's "dying hour was gloom" (460).

The quotation marks indicate which information came from the primary source and which came from the essay's author.

Hawthorne's "Young Goodman Brown" causes the reader to question, and ultimately recognize, the duality of good and evil in people and in themselves. This concept is vital to the Puritan faith, yet Young Goodman Brown cannot accept it. After seeing the people of the village seemingly engage in sinful activity, he no longer sees any good in them. Young Goodman Brown's failure to accept humanity's duality results in a loss of faith and self-imposed isolation.

Works Cited

Hawthorne, Nathaniel. "Young Goodman Brown." *Literature: An Introduction to Fiction, Poetry, Drama, and Writing*, edited by X.J. Kennedy and Dana Gioia, 13th ed., Pearson, 452-460.

Both sources cited in the essay are listed under Works Cited.

Hurley, Paul. "Evil Wherever He Looks." *Literature: An Introduction to Fiction, Poetry, Drama, and Writing*, edited by X.J. Kennedy and Dana Gioia, 13th ed., Pearson, 456-466.

Lesson 7.6
Integrating Sources into Your Writing

Once you've worked your way through the selecting your research, you'll want to consider how to actually utilize your sources within your writing. There are three main ways to integrate sources into your writing.

In this lesson, you will learn about these three ways to integrate sources:

Summarizing
Paraphrasing
Quoting

Summarizing

A **summary** is a small, generalized overview of a larger amount of information. Instead of recreating the entire incident, summary captures the point—the gist—with only the most relevant and important details.

Using summaries makes the most sense when your readers need a broad overview of a topic, but not specific details. Because summaries are general, they should only be used when you need to inform your audience about important background information on a topic.

Take a look at this example:

> In his novel, *Things Fall Apart*, on the rise of colonialism in Nigeria, author Chinua Achebe follows the story of Okonkwo, a tribal leader who has risen from very little and has maintained a power and dominance amongst his clan and his family. As colonists begin to invade Okonkwo's land, culture, and traditions, he struggles to fight against the forces that threaten all he knows.
>
> In this brief summary, the author highlights important components of the story in his own words, conveying broad ideas and major conflict.

Paraphrasing

When you **paraphrase**, you explain someone's words or sentences using your own words. This helps to explain the text's purpose or to add clarity to the author's argument. You can paraphrase anything from a single sentence to a complex idea. Consider the example below.

Original sentence

> "Female elephants are pregnant for a longer period of time than any other mammal, keeping their child with them for an average of twenty-two months" (Johnson 63).

Paraphrase

> Shockingly, elephants carry their babies for close to two years; this is longer than any other mammal (Johnson 63).

Quoting

Quotations are the direct words of a source. Quotes should be reserved for instances when the author's language is powerful or unique. Otherwise, you should paraphrase the borrowed language.

Here's an example:

> Eleanor Roosevelt famously said, "You must do the things you think you cannot do."

If possible, you should use a signal phrase to identify the original author of a quote. Place the quoted words inside of quotation marks so that your audience knows exactly where the quotation begins and ends. When you use direct language from a source, you must always include an in-text citation immediately following the quote. Here's an example:

> As Alfred Mac Adam emphasizes in his introduction to *Northanger Abbey*, the "fate of women was more fixed than that of men: They could not hope for careers in trade or in the military; their educational opportunities were few ..." (xxvi).
>
> In this example, the author's name is introduced in the signal phrase, so it does not need to be repeated in the parenthetical citation. Also notice that the page numbers are written differently because they are from the book's introduction. Here is the corresponding work-cited entry:
>
> Adam, Alfred Mac. "Introduction." *Northanger Abbey*, by Jane Austen. Barnes & Noble Classics, 2005, pp. xiii - xxvii.

Lesson Wrap-up

Key Terms

In-text Citation: a note in a paragraph that tells the reader which words and ideas come from a source

MLA (Modern Language Association) Style: the research style guide created by a group of scholars dedicated to research in modern languages

Paraphrase: the ideas of an outside source presented in an author's original writing

Plagiarism: the act of using borrowed words or ideas without giving credit to the author

Quotation Marks: a pair of punctuation marks used to repeat someone else's words

Quote: a reference to direct words from a source

Research Style: a set of standards used for research writing within a particular discipline

Research Writing: the process of conducting research and using sources to compose arguments

Signal Phrase: a phrase used to identify source information—like the title and author—within a sentence

Source: an original document or first-hand account that a writer consults for research

Summary: a few sentences that explain a large amount of information

Works Cited: a list of sources at the end of an MLA-styled text

Lesson 7.7
The Annotated Bibliography

Just as a building requires a strong foundation to support its weight, a research paper must be based on strong support. Locating valuable sources is an essential part of writing a **research paper.** The validity of your argument is based on the strength of your sources just as much as the quality of your words. Without **credible** evidence, the argument of your paper will fall flat.

An **annotated bibliography** is one way to highlight your sources' validity. This document lists your sources and includes brief annotations and publication information for each one. This information helps other writers consider the depth and quality of their sources as they develop supporting evidence for their position.

Writing Environment: Academic

Annotated bibliographies are also common in **scholarly articles** or books because the audiences of these texts are most likely interested in researching the topic further. As you conduct your own research, use the annotated bibliographies of your sources to identify other possible sources of information.

In this lesson, you will learn more about annotated bibliographies by exploring the following topics:

Structuring an Annotated Bibliography
Writing a Strong Annotation

Structuring an Annotated Bibliography

An annotated bibliography goes a step beyond a **works-cited** or **bibliography** page because, in addition to listing publication information, it includes a short annotation for each source. An **annotation** is made up of one to two paragraphs of information.

> Helpful Hint
> Your instructor may have specific length requirements for your annotations. Be sure to reference your syllabus or project guide before starting an annotated bibliography.

Strong annotations include two key components: a description and an evaluation of each source.

Description: This section tells the reader what type of information the source material contains, how the information is expressed, and what the author argues or explains. Details such as the format of the text or the publishing organization may also be included if they are important.

Evaluation: This section explains whether or not the content of the source is valid based on the author's evidence. Usually, evaluating a source involves not only explaining the importance of the information but also how the content is relevant to the paper's argument.

In addition to demonstrating the strength of source material, annotated bibliographies help readers determine if a text is relevant to their own research. Annotated bibliographies are also useful to you as an author. They help you catalog the resources you find during your research and remind you of important sources during the writing process. Even if you are not required to submit an annotated bibliography for an assignment, writing one from your own research notes can prevent you from overlooking important information.

Writing Environment: Everyday

An annotated bibliography is similar to the back cover of a book. When browsing at a bookstore, how do you choose what to read? You might read the description on the back to decide if you would like to read the entire text. Likewise, a person who wants to learn about a particular subject or make a decision about a controversial topic may read an annotated bibliography to determine if reading the entire text would be useful.

Each entry in an annotated bibliography always includes the publication information of the source. This information is formatted according to a standard style—such as **MLA, APA, CMS,** or **CSE**—and includes the author's name, the title of the work, and the publication information. Given these facts, the reader should be able to easily locate the source.

To learn more about formatting and citation styles, see Lessons 7.8-7.11.

Here's an example of an annotated bibliography entry in MLA format:

> Rose, Gillian. *Visual Methodologies: An Introduction to the Interpretation of Visual Materials.* London Thousand Oaks, CA: SAGE Publications, 2007.
>
> This book analyzes the way audiences read and understand visual materials. The author focuses on the different ways people interact with images, ranging from the physical act of looking to emotional and psychological responses. Additionally, the book explores how culture, environment, and ideology affect a person's understanding of an image.
>
> The specific topics covered by the author provide strong support for the arguments she is making. While the book covers a broad range of topics, there are enough source materials and examples to keep the discussion focused. This book is also an excellent guide to key theories of visual analysis. The bibliography at the end of the book has a number of research sources that provide further useful information.

Group Activity

As a group, select an article online that is an appropriate source for a research paper. Try brainstorming topics together or choosing a topic someone is currently researching. Read the article and work together to create an annotated bibliography entry.

Writing Environment: Everyday

Writing annotations is not just limited to your academic career. In your everyday life, you will encounter opportunities to annotate recipes, articles, movies, and objects. What are some examples of times you've been asked to briefly describe and evaluate something for an audience? Consider the following product review that combines description and evaluation:

> The seat cushion arrived about a week after I ordered it. The box was a little battered, but the product itself was fine. The cushion had a slight chemical smell, but it went away quickly. The color is a nice neutral gray, and it fits perfectly in my office chair. Since getting this cushion, I hardly ever have pain in my lower back and tailbone. Whether you need better support for medical reasons or just for comfort, I highly recommend buying this seat cushion!

Writing a Strong Annotation

Writing specific annotations for each of your research sources is not always easy. The information should be detailed but brief so that someone unfamiliar with the text can understand it easily and absorb it quickly. Use the following process to ensure that your annotations clearly communicate the right details about your source.

Step 1: Describe the Content

Before you start writing an annotation, you need to read most or all of the source material you are describing. The length of the text and the due date of your annotated bibliography will often dictate how much you are able to review in advance. Even if you are unable to read the whole source, make sure that you have read enough to understand its purpose and main points. Once you've had a chance to read the information in more detail, you can update your annotation as needed.

As you read each source, ask yourself the following questions:

> What is the author's purpose?
>
> What is the main argument or thesis of the text?
>
> What types of supporting evidence does the author use to
>
> argue his or her conclusions?
>
> What information from this text will be useful for my paper?

Once you've identified the answers to these questions, you can use the information you've gathered to describe the source. Let's break down the annotation from earlier in the lesson. Here's the first part:

> This book analyzes the way audiences read and understand visual materials. The author focuses on the different ways people interact with images, ranging from the physical act of looking to emotional and psychological responses. Additionally, the book explores how culture, environment, and ideology affect a person's understanding of an image.
>
> This description is brief; just three sentences. However, the writer does a good job of summarizing the author's purpose. Even if readers are unfamiliar with the source, they can understand the general content of the book.

Group Activity

As a group, choose a book or movie that everyone has read or seen. Individually, write a brief (3-5 sentence) description, using the following questions as a guide:

- What is the author's purpose?
- What is the main argument or thesis of the text?
- What types of supporting evidence does the author use to argue his or her conclusions?
- What information from this text will be useful for my paper?

Compare your descriptions and discuss the strengths and weaknesses of each person's description.

Step 2: Evaluate the Content

Once you've given the audience a general idea of the text's content, show them why the source is relevant either to your own research or a field of study in general. Giving clear justification for your choice will help establish your *ethos* as an author and reassure your readers that you've carefully evaluated the source.

If you're planning to use the sources in your own paper, sharing the reasons behind your decision to include them also gives you an opportunity to explain unexpected or potentially confusing sources.

For example, imagine that you are writing a paper on LGBT discrimination in fraternities. To support your argument, you decide to use an article from a local campus newsletter. While this source may not be academic, you believe it clearly reflects the attitudes and opinions of a college student who has experienced this type of discrimination personally. The annotated bibliography gives you a chance to explain to your readers why this particular article is a valuable source for your topic.

As you evaluate your sources, think about the following questions:

Why is the source credible?

How does the source support my research paper?

Why is this source better than others?

What should the audience know about this source?

Consider the way the author evaluates the source material in the second half of the annotation from earlier in the lesson:

> The specific topics covered by the author provide strong support for the arguments she is making. While the book covers a broad range of topics, there are enough source materials and examples to keep the discussion focused. This book is also an excellent guide to key theories of visual analysis. The bibliography at the end of the book has a number of research sources that provide further useful information.

This evaluation not only touches on the strengths of the text but also explains specific ways that the information is useful to the author.

On Your Own

Choose an article and practice writing a description and evaluation of its major points.

Description	Evaluation

Writing Environment: Professional

While you may not write a formal annotated bibliography in the workplace, you may find yourself describing and evaluating resources and presenting this information to colleagues. For example, you might give a PowerPoint presentation on a topic and include annotated source information on the last slide. Your boss will likely find it helpful to gauge the validity and relevance of your sources and may even be impressed with your thoroughness. What are some other situations where you might annotate research?

Lesson Wrap-up

Key Terms

Annotated Bibliography: a list of sources that includes brief annotations for each source along with the publication information

Annotation: additional information that often describes and evaluates

APA Format: a citation and documentation style published by the American Psychological Association

Bibliography: a list of sources used in a paper

CMS Format: a citation and documentation style known as the Chicago Manual of Style

Credibility: the trustworthiness of an author

CSE Format: a citation and documentation style published by the Council of Science Editors

Ethos: the credibility of an author based on education or experience

MLA Format: a citation and documentation style published by the Modern Language Association

Research Paper: an academic paper that incorporates material from multiple sources

Scholarly Article: a source that has been peer-reviewed before it was published

Works Cited: a list of sources used in a paper

Writing Application: The Annotated Bibliography

Read the following annotated bibliography for sources about genetically modified organisms. How does the author combine description and evaluation to summarize each source?

Genetically Modified Organisms: Friend or Foe?

Fagan, J. (2014). "GMO Myths and Truths: An evidence-based examination of the claims made for the safety and efficacy of genetically modified crops and foods." London: Earth Open Source.

This 330-page document introduces 38 myths that are proposed by the proponents of GMO foods. It further divides these myths into categories, such as myths about the technique of making GMOs, scientific regulation of GM crops, health hazards (such as Roundup), impacts on the environment, and the fallacy that GM crops will help us feed the world. The author brings to light many facts related to controversial genetically modified crops and includes nearly 300 peer-reviewed papers to support his or her myth vs. truth discussion.

While format requirements vary, it's recommended that you give your annotated bibliography a title.

This sentence begins the descriptive portion of the annotated bibliography.

The author further describes and evaluates the content by including this detail.

It is clear from the first lines of the introduction that the author of this book is quite passionate about debunking the myths associated with the growing number of GM foods on the market today. This is the second edition of the text, and it has been attacked for its boldness in discussing the topic. This discussion is valuable in that it clearly and overwhelmingly represents the position of the anti-GMO movement.

This language is evaluative; it is analyzing the author's meaning and intention.

National Academies of Sciences, Engineering, and Medicine. (2016). Genetically Engineered Crops: Experiences and Prospects. Washington, DC: The National Academies Press.

In this recent 408-page report, the National Academies of Sciences discusses the claims made by the GE (genetically engineered) food lobbyists. After concluding its research, the NAS judged GMOs as completely safe. However, it also mentions that some of the claims made by manufacturers of GM foods have no basis in fact, such as the likelihood that GM crops will help to feed the world by producing a higher yield. The report also considers other topics such as how GM crops affect the economy, nutrition, and the environment.

The author starts with a clear description of the source.

The authors of the report view the topic through a scientific lens. Contrary to other publications related to the GMO debate, the findings of this publication are based only on scientific research. Rather than combining research with individuals' personal opinions about the topic, the contributions take on a truth-seeking role and are willing to criticize either side of the GMO argument. Therefore, this report is important to consider when evaluating the potential benefits.

Since this sentence analyzes the perspective of the paper, it is evaluation.

The author ends by explaining the source's relevance to his or her argument.

Lesson 7.8
Basics of MLA

Research sources support the **main idea** of your paper and give you **credibility** as an author. If you properly acknowledge your sources and format your papers consistently, you writing will be even stronger. In the English discipline, you will often be required to use the **Modern Language Association (MLA)** guidelines to cite and format your essays.

> Helpful Hint
> Keep in mind that there are citation guidelines other than those offered by MLA. For example, a psychology professor may require American Psychological Association (APA) style. Always check with your professor to ensure that you are using the correct research style in your writing.

When creating your citations, MLA recommends utilizing the "Think, Select, Organize" process, which requires you to *think* about what type of sources are relevant to your research, *select* appropriate sources and source information, and *organize* your citations in a clear manner.

In this lesson, you will learn how to:

Format Your Research Paper
Integrate Borrowed Ideas
Create a Works-Cited Page

Format Your Research Paper

When writing a research paper, it is important to use consistent formatting throughout the entire paper. Format involves things like margins, fonts, and headers. MLA style addresses two categories of formatting rules:

- Page layout guidelines
- In-text formatting

When you set up your page layout, follow these settings:

MLA Checklist: Page Layout
☐ Use one-inch margins
☐ Choose an easy-to-read font with differentiated italicized and plain text options (like Times New Roman), size 12
☐ Use left-aligned text and begin each paragraph with a .5-inch indentation
☐ Center the title of your paper; do not **italicize**, underline, put in quotation marks, or bold
☐ Include a **running head** .5 inches from the top right corner of each page with your last name and **page number**

Additionally, you need to add a heading in the top left corner of the first page of your paper. It should be double-spaced and follow this template:

- Your name
- Your instructor's name
- Course name and number
- Date

Moreover, there are guidelines for formatting in-text elements, such as numbers, names, and dates:

- Typically spell out numbers less than one hundred unless frequently used in the paper
- Choose a consistent time format for the entire paper (either 12- or 24-hour)
- When introducing the name of a person for the first time in your paper, provide the person's first *and* last name
- Italicize book titles and titles of longer works; put the titles of shorter or contained works in quotation marks

> Helpful Hint
>
> MLA also offers rules regarding the capitalization of words in titles and subtitles:
>
> **Capitalize:** nouns, pronouns, verbs, adjectives, adverbs, subordinating conjunctions
> **Do Not Capitalize:** articles, prepositions, coordinating conjunctions, *to* infinitives

Integrate Borrowed Ideas

Your reader should be able to distinguish between your original work and that of your sources. You must give credit to other authors using both in-text citations and a list of works cited. Throughout your paragraphs, **in-text citations** tell the reader which specific words and ideas come from each source. A **works-cited** page tells the reader what sources you've used in a straightforward list at the end of the paper.

To avoid **plagiarism**, you must use correct in-text citations for summarized, paraphrased, and quoted text. You can also use **signal phrases** to introduce source information, like the title and author, within a sentence.

Here are some examples:

> According to [Author's Name], …

> In his article ["Title of Article,"] [Author's Name] argues …

> [Author's Name] illustrates this concept in [Title of Book].

In-Text Citations

In-text citations provide source information in **parentheses** at the end of a sentence. These parenthetical citations allow your reader to see exactly which words and ideas you've borrowed from a particular source. In-text citations follow an author-page format. Here are a few examples of common in-text citations:

Citation with one author and single page	(Greene 79)
Citation with one author and multiple pages	(Brady 122-131)
Citation with two authors	(Jackson and Brown 85)
Citation with two separate sources	(Jackson 55; Brown 67)
Citation with three or more authors	(Jackson et al. 155)

Helpful Hint

If you are citing a source in your text that does not provide page numbers, like a movie or an episode in a TV series, include information on the time within the source that contains the information you are citing.

(*30 Rock* 00:03:1-30)

Take a look at the following paragraph. It includes two in-text citations.

> The most effective way to learn a foreign language is frequently debated by language instructors and language learners alike. According to a 2011 study by linguist Chris Jackson, "the best way to learn a language is through early exposure; in other words, the acquisition of a foreign language is easiest at a young age" (3). In a recent documentary on language learning, scholars discuss the ease of acquiring the ability to form new sounds at a younger age, citing the challenges associated with learning tonal languages such as Chinese later in life (Thevos 01:20:20-55). Clearly, learning languages at a young age is a widely accepted method for mastering a language quickly and with ease.

The in-text citation should be as specific as possible. If you're summarizing a section of a longer text, include the page range of the borrowed information. If, however, you're summarizing an entire text, you need to identify only the author's last name.

Summaries

A **summary** explains a large amount of information in a few sentences. Using summaries makes the most sense when your readers need a broad overview of a topic but not specific details. Because summaries are general, they should only be used when you need to inform your **audience** about important background information on a topic.

Even though a summary uses completely original wording to explain the source information, you still need to credit the author using signal words and in-text citations. Keep these MLA rules in mind:

- If you're summarizing one section of a longer text, you must include an in-text citation in parentheses at the end of the final sentence. If you already identified the author in a signal phrase, you only need to include the page range.

> In her discussion on human rights in China, analyst Aliya Dumas suggests that there is room for improvement. In particular, Dumas notes that the treatment of women in society, policies regulating the number of children a family can have, and economic disparity between urban and rural areas are all facets of Chinese society that need to be addressed within the context of human rights. However, Dumas does note that China's economy has the potential for a more active working class and consumer rights (15-21).

- If you're summarizing the entire text, you do not need to include page numbers in the in-text citation. Instead, you can simply identify the last name(s) of the author(s) in a signal phrase or in-text citation. The following example summarizes relevant events from a novel:

> In George Eliot's novel *Middlemarch,* the restriction in Casaubon's will and societal expectations keep Dorothea and Will apart before they realize their love for each other. Later, even after they acknowledge their mutual affection, their individual ideals of honor and morality prevent them from marrying. Only after both Dorothea's and Will's sensitive consciences are assuaged do they finally agree to give up their inheritances in order to be together.

Helpful Hint

Whether or not you include an in-text citation for summaries, you will always need to include a complete and accurate bibliographic citation on the works-cited page.

Writing Environment: Professional

There may be times at work when your manager asks you to summarize research you've completed. You might be describing a competitor, a controversial new theory, or a new and interesting insight in your field. No matter what you summarize, correctly cite your sources. This ensures that your audience can locate the original sources and validate your findings.

Paraphrases

When you **paraphrase,** you present ideas from a source using your own words. Paraphrases are more in-depth than summaries. You should paraphrase when the source material contains important details or facts that support your main idea. Additionally, if you feel the author's language is confusing or challenging, it may be best to simplify it using your own words.

Any time you paraphrase, introduce and explain the information in language that makes sense to you. This is especially important for clarifying what makes the information relevant to your topic. Even though the language is yours, you still need to include an in-text citation because the ideas are not your own. Simply changing one or two words is not enough. The following sentences are examples of good and bad paraphrasing:

Original

From early adolescence (11-12 years), children's thinking becomes more multidimensional, involving abstract as well as concrete thought. Adolescents still can be persuaded by the emotive messages of advertising, which play into their developmental concerns related to appearance, self-identity, belonging, and sexuality.

Plagiarism

Even beyond childhood, adolescents can still be persuaded by messages that play into their developmental concerns related to appearance, self-identity, sexuality, and belonging.

Correct Paraphrase

Many food advertisements target children who do not yet understand the negative, long-term consequences of eating unhealthy foods. These advertisements also influence adolescents by playing into common developmental concerns to spark emotional responses (Story and French 3).

▸ In the first paraphrase, the author uses the same sentence structure as the source material. Only a few words have been changed. This is not an acceptable paraphrase. The second example expresses the same ideas as the source material but uses completely different language relevant to the borrower's topic.

On Your Own

In the space provided, paraphrase the information in the "Original Text" below.

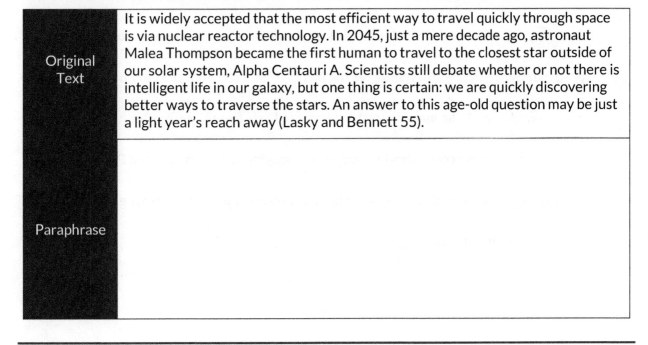

Original Text	It is widely accepted that the most efficient way to travel quickly through space is via nuclear reactor technology. In 2045, just a mere decade ago, astronaut Malea Thompson became the first human to travel to the closest star outside of our solar system, Alpha Centauri A. Scientists still debate whether or not there is intelligent life in our galaxy, but one thing is certain: we are quickly discovering better ways to traverse the stars. An answer to this age-old question may be just a light year's reach away (Lasky and Bennett 55).
Paraphrase	

Quotations

Quotations are the direct words of a source. Quotes should be reserved for instances when the author's language is powerful or unique and supports your claim. Otherwise, you should paraphrase the borrowed language.

If possible, use a signal phrase to identify the original author of a quote. Place the quoted words inside **quotation marks** so that your audience knows exactly where the quotation begins and ends. When you use direct language from a source, always include an in-text citation immediately following the quote. Here's an example:

> As Alfred Mac Adam emphasizes in his introduction to *Northanger Abbey*, the "fate of women was more fixed than that of men: They could not hope for careers in trade or in the military; their educational opportunities were few ..." (xxvi).
>
> In this example, the author's name is introduced in the signal phrase, so it does not need to be repeated in the parenthetical citation. Also notice that the page numbers are written differently because they are from the book's introduction. Here is the corresponding work-cited entry:
>
> Adam, Alfred Mac. "Introduction." *Northanger Abbey*, by Jane Austen. Barnes & Noble Classics, 2005, pp. xiii-xxvii.

If you are directly quoting prose and the quote exceeds four lines within your essay, you will need to use a **block quote**. A **block quote** is a special type of direct quote that indents the entirety of the quote and does not require the use of quotation marks. Moreover, you will place the period at the end of the quote which will be immediately followed by the in-text, parenthetical citation. Always double-space this quote.

Here's an example of a block quote within an essay:

In a literary critique of Markus Zusak's *The Book Thief*, Dr. Alex Jones explains:

> Contrary to many other pieces of literature focusing on the Holocaust, *The Book Thief* by Markus Zusak investigates the lives of ordinary Germans while the Nazis held control over Germany. Moreover, while Zusak touches on the persecution and oppression of Jewish people in Germany, he also reinforces the fact that Jews were not the only persecuted group. For instance, Liesel, the main character, is adopted by a foster family after her mother is presumably sent to a concentration camp for belonging to the Communist Party. Zusak portrays an under-represented side of the Holocaust that prompts sincere grief and shock within the audience. (14)

> ▸ Since a signal phrase is used to introduce the quote, it suffices to place the page number in the parenthetical citation directly after the quote.

Keep in mind that the function of block quotes is not to simply take up space. It is always a good practice to limit the amount of text you take from any source. Use block quotes only when they support your claim in a way that other types of quotes do not.

Whether you are incorporating regular quotes or block quotes in your research paper, make sure you have properly explained and contextualized your quote. Simply placing a quote in your paper without introducing or explaining it will confuse your audience. Always be sure to include your own thoughts, questions, explanations, or analyses before or after quotes.

> **Helpful Hint**
>
> Any time you adjust the wording of a quotation, be careful not to distort or change the author's ideas.

Create a Works Cited Page

The last page of your research paper should be a list of the sources you used. This is your works-cited page. This list provides more information about each source cited in your writing.

Generally, works-cited entries follow this structure:

[Author Name]. [Title of Source]. [Title of Container], [Other Contributors], [Version], [Number], [Publisher], [Publication Date], [Location].

The following example includes two entries:

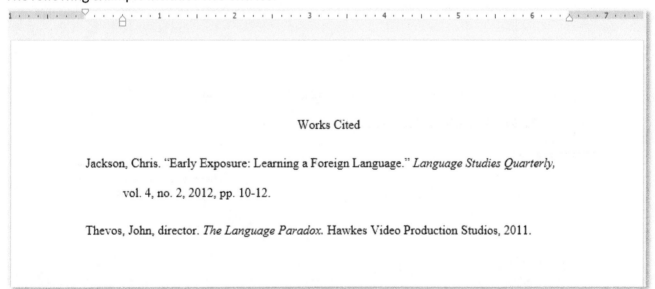

Two works-cited entries are written in a similar structure though they reference different source types.

Notice that these entries are formatted in a similar order even though they reference two different types of sources: a journal article and a documentary.

> **Helpful Hint**
>
> A source may have a **container,** which is a larger work that holds or contains your source. For example, if you are citing the chapter of a book, the container would be the book. If you are citing an episode of a television show, the television show would be the container.

Here are some key rules for proper formatting of a works-cited page:

MLA Works-Cited Checklist

☐ Continue the running head that you started at the beginning of the paper

☐ Enter the heading, "Works Cited," on the first line of the page. It should be centered and one inch from the top of the page

☐ Double-space between the title and the first entry in your list

☐ Double-space and alphabetize each entry in your list. If a source doesn't have an author, alphabetize according to the first letter of the title

☐ Left-align the first line of each entry. If the entry exceeds one line, the subsequent lines should be indented

For sources with more than one author, you should only use the *Last Name, First Name* format for the first author listed. Identify all subsequent authors starting with the first name. Here's an example:

> King, Stephen, and Peter Straub. *The Talisman.* Random House, 2001.

Here's an example of a properly formatted works-cited page.

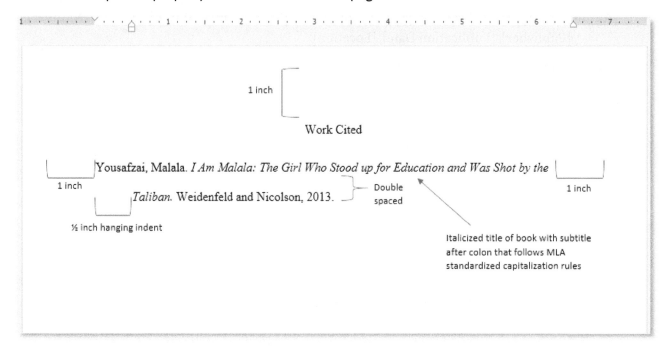

Lesson Wrap-up

Key Terms

Audience: the people who read your writing

Block Quote: a special type of direct quote that indents the entirety of the quote and does not require the use of quotation marks

Container: the larger work that holds or contains your source

Credibility: what makes someone or something believable

In-text Citation: a note in a paragraph that tells the reader which words and ideas come from a source

Italics: slanted letters most often used to set apart titles of longer works, important words, and foreign terms

Main Idea: the statement or argument that an author tries to communicate

MLA: style guidelines created by the Modern Language Association, a group of scholars dedicated to research in modern languages

Page Number: a way to help the audience find information in a text

Paraphrase: rewording the words of another person in order to explain the text's purpose or to add clarity to the author's argument

Parentheses: a pair of punctuation marks used to add extra information to a sentence or introduce an abbreviation

Plagiarism: using the words or ideas of a source without giving credit to the author

Quotation Marks: a pair of punctuation marks most commonly used to repeat someone else's words

Quotations: the direct words of a source

Running Head: information, including a page number, that goes at the top of a page

Signal Phrase: a phrase used to introduce source information—like the title and author—within a sentence

Summary: writing that explains a large amount of information in a few sentences

Works Cited: a list of sources at the end of an MLA-styled text

Writing Application: Basics of MLA

As you read the sample research paper in the following pages, note the source integration and formatting the author has used to meet research-style guidelines.

Anna Ingle

Professor Roberts

ENGL 432

3 November 2014

In Our Hands: Responsibility, Gender, and the Holocaust in Young Adult Fiction

In My Hands is the memoir of Irene Opdyke, a young Polish woman who witnesses and

experiences great cruelty during World War II, yet develops compassion and strength. Woven

throughout the story of her extraordinary life are issues with which many young adults grapple,

like agency, purpose, and responsibility. *In My Hands* is an excellent addition to a syllabus for

young adult literature course for several reasons. In simple but beautiful language, it combines

history and personal memory to create a unique yet familiar perspective. Additionally, it

consciously engages the topic of the Holocaust in four primary ways to explore its historical

implications and to provoke vital questions about the nature of evil and personal responsibility.

In "A New Algorithm of Evil," Elizabeth Baer discusses how to select books about the

Holocaust. Though Baer's article primarily addresses how to identify the "usefulness and

effectiveness" of Holocaust literature for children, the principles are the same for readers of all

ages (384). She proposes four criteria for addressing broader and more philosophical issues in

Holocaust narratives. The first condition is that these books "must grapple directly with the evil

of the Holocaust" (383). People often state, correctly, that the Holocaust and its evil must be remembered in order to prevent it from recurring. However, Baer points out that most young

readers are learning about the Holocaust for the first time, "and indeed, as more time elapses

between the Holocaust and the present, this will be true of all readers" (380). *In My Hands* is not

gratuitous in its depiction of the horrors of World War II, but it also does not omit or sidestep it.

Opdyke describes how she and her family endured occupation by the Nazis, who despised Polish

people. They were forced from their homes, separated from their families, and forced to work for

the Nazis. Their food was rationed severely, and they were under constant threat of physical

harm or even death. Irene discovers that the Jews are experiencing persecution on an even larger

scale and to a more extreme extent. While she is visiting friends in a Jewish ghetto, Nazis raid

the houses and take many of the residents to labor camps. Irene herself grapples with the evil she

witnesses. As she hides in an abandoned home, she watches an officer throw into the air and

shoot what at first appears to be a bird until she realizes "it was not a bird," but a child (Opdyke

and Armstrong 117). Several times throughout the book, Opdyke alludes to this tragic scene and

the "bird," at first unable to admit what she really saw. However, she eventually allows herself to

confront reality. Irene's innocence and gradual exposure parallels the realizations of young adult

readers who learn about the evil of the Holocaust.

The second criterion that Baer suggests is that a Holocaust narrative should not be over-

simplified; instead it should ask "difficult questions for which there are no formulaic answers"

(384). Opdyke's narrative captures this complexity, particularly as she forms relationships. After

she is beaten and assaulted by Russian soldiers, she is take under the wing of a kindly Russian

doctor, Dr. Olga Pavlovskaya. Later, she works under Herr Schulz, a German cook who feeds

and cares for Irene and her sister. Eventually, when Irene begins undermining the Nazis and sheltering Jews, he looks the other way. However, she struggles to resolve his kindness with the cruelty of every other German she has encountered: "he made hating the Germans a complex matter, when it should have been such a straight-forward one" (134). Opdyke's recollections of cruelty and kindness from people who should have been her enemies are thought-provoking for readers because they don't allow simple and stark categorization.

Baer's third criterion is broad, and probably one of the most obvious things that is to be expected in this genre of literature, but nonetheless important: Holocaust narratives must strongly caution against "racism," "anti-Semitism," and "complacency" (385). Baer does not elaborate any further on this point, but it is the baseline requirement that an educator, parent, or publisher should consider when evaluating a book about the Holocaust. Opdyke recounts her confusion as to why the Nazis specifically targeted the Jews: "It had never occurred to me to distinguish between people based on their religion" (18). Her statements apply to the senseless nature, not just of anti-Semitism, but prejudice in general. Poland, with its own rich culture and history, was reduced by the Nazis to "a land of Slavic brutes, fit only for labor" (18). Irene's narrative demonstrates the ripple effect of prejudice, racism, and genocide. It raises questions for young readers about where the stopping point is if cruelty is allowable based only on what makes one person different from another.

In My Hands is also uniquely suited to Baer's fourth consideration for Holocaust literature because it encourages "a sense of personal responsibility" (385). Opdyke's first-person narrative draws the reader into her perspective as she develops her own sense of responsibility for the Jews' suffering. At first, she feels helpless and swept along by forces greater than herself. However, after witnessing the cruelty of the Nazis, she quickly develops a feeling of personal

Ingle 4

responsibility and empathy for what is happening. When she witnesses Nazis shoot an elderly

Jewish man, she "felt a scream rising . . . as though I had been shot myself" (102). This moment

is a turning point for Irene; immediately afterwards, she steals food from the hotel kitchen where

she works and leaves it outside a Jewish ghetto. Irene's story proves that even a young female in

a seemingly helpless position can exert agency and subvert corrupt powers. Louise O. Vasvári

writes that this area of literature "still tends to privilege the Holocaust experience of men as

universal" (1).

At the beginning of her story, Irene is young and female, and therefore vulnerable both in

her own eyes and the eyes of society: "I was only a girl, alone among the enemy. What could I

do?" (121). However, as her resistance efforts continue, she takes ownership of her femininity,

so that her "weakness" becomes her "advantage" (124). She spies on German officers and passes

along information to the ghetto, supports a group of Jewish workers, and eventually hides them

in the basement of a Nazi major's villa. Later, she joins a Polish partisan group that sabotages

and undermines the Nazis, all the while escaping detection by using gender stereotypes to her

advantage. Her reputation as a resistance fighter spreads until she is suspected by the enemy to

be the rebels' leader. The phrase "only a girl" echoes throughout her narrative, becoming an

ironic mantra as she flouts what her enemies expect of a young female. Opdyke's unique

perspective is vital for both male and female young adult readers because she took action instead

of complying with cultural and societal expectations.

In My Hands addresses issues facing young adults, like identity, responsibility, and

agency while providing a compelling and thought-provoking depiction of the Holocaust.

Opdyke's willingness to recount her experiences allows others to grapple with the complexity of evil and personal responsibility. Her personal growth as an adolescent woman and her unique

perspective as a female during the occupation of Poland is inspiring to men and women alike.

The novel's simple and expressive language makes it an ideal literary, as well as historical and

philosophical, addition not just to Holocaust literature, but literature in general.

Ingle 6

Works Cited

Baer, Elizabeth Roberts. "A New Algorithm in Evil: Children's Literature in a Post-Holocaust

World." *The Lion and the Unicorn*, vol. 24, no. 3, September 2000, pp. 378-401. *Project

Muse*. http://muse.jhu.edu/article/35480.

Opdyke, Irene Gut, and Jennifer Armstrong. *In My Hands: Memories of a Holocaust Rescuer*.

New York: Dell Laurel-Leaf, 1999.

Vasvári, Louise O. "Bibliography of Central European Women's Holocaust Life Writing in

English." *Library Series, CLCWeb: Comparative Literature and Culture*, Purdue UP,

2012, http://docs.lib.purdue.edu/clcweblibrary/vasvariceushoahbib/.

Lesson 7.9
Basics of APA

American Psychological Association (APA) style is a set of formatting and citation guidelines. APA style is used in academic disciplines like business, nursing, psychology, and sociology. Gaining a basic understanding of these standards will help you incorporate sources into your paper correctly and ethically.

In this lesson, you will learn about APA style by exploring the following topics:

APA Paper Format
APA In-Text Citations
APA References

> **Further Resources**
> If you have questions about APA style or need an in-depth overview of its rules, you can go to the official APA website (www.apastyle.org).

APA Paper Format

APA style uses a strict set of page formatting requirements. Before you start your paper, use the following guidelines to set up your document:

Page size	8.5" x 11"
Page margins	1" on all sides
Font	12-point Times New Roman or Arial
Alignment	Left
Spacing	Double

At the top of each page except the title page, insert a **running head** that includes a shortened version of the paper title (shorter than 50 characters, including punctuation and spaces) and the page number. The page number should appear in the top-right corner of the paper, and the shortened title should appear in the top-left corner in all capital letters.

> **Helpful Hint**
> Pay careful attention to the requirements of every assignment. Some instructors may have specific requirements for assignments.

A paper in APA style includes four sections:

- The title page
- The abstract
- The body of the paper
- The references page

Title Page

On the **title page,** you need to include a special version of the running head. Simply add the words "Running head:" before the title. It will look like this:

> Running head: BRAND COMMUNITY SEEN IN FISKATEERS

The page number should still be in the top-right corner of the title page.

The actual title of the paper should be centered in the upper half of the title page. It should be one or two lines long and free of abbreviations. Unlike in the running head, the main title should be in normal title case, meaning the first letter of all words except articles and prepositions are capitalized. (Remember to capitalize the first word of the title no matter what.)

Underneath the title, type your full name and the name of your college or university, all centered and double-spaced.

Abstract

After the title page, you need to include an abstract. An **abstract** is a 150 to 200-word summary of your paper. This summary is provided to pique the interest of a prospective reader. Make sure to only include the most important ideas from your paper, including the original research question, your basic findings, and your conclusion. Do not include anything in the abstract that isn't covered within the essay itself.

Consider the following abstract from a paper for an education class:

> This essay examines factors leading to student anxiety in college English composition courses across the United States in order to determine best practices for minimizing student discomfort while maximizing learning opportunities. Survey data is discussed alongside expert opinion from psychologists and education specialists. Writing prompts, oral presentation assignments, group activities, reading assignments, grammar lessons, and peer review sessions are among the various

factors under review. Types of faculty feedback and opportunities for revision are considered; in addition, contemporary treatments for anxiety and their effects on student attention, writing ability, interpersonal relations, and reading comprehension are discussed. Finally, a brief analysis of current trends in student disability services is provided in order to determine the most effective ways for staff and faculty to cooperate and provide optimal experiences for students prone to anxiety related to reading and writing assignments.

The abstract will include a running head and page number at the top of the page just like the rest of the paper. On the first line of the page, center the word "Abstract." You do not need to indent the first sentence of the abstract and make sure the entire abstract is double-spaced.

Body

In the body of the paper, you will continue using the same page format you previously set up. Remember to include the running head on each page, without the words "Running Head." Before starting your text, add your full title, centered at the top of the page. You do not need to add any special text formatting such as italics or underlining to the title.

References

The **references** page is always at the very end of an APA style paper. Start a new page and add the word "References" centered on the first line. On the next line, you will begin listing the sources you used in your paper. These entries are all double-spaced and sorted alphabetically; you do not need to use numbers or bullets.

Use **hanging indents** for each entry. If an entry is more than one line long, each line except the first is indented half an inch from the left margin.

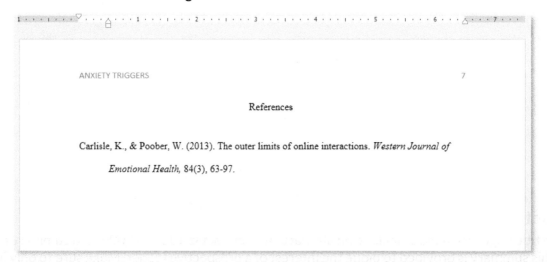

Writing Environment: Academic

APA style can be difficult to master because it has so many formatting rules. However, its purpose is to ensure that researchers are accountable for the information they present. This accountability is important for all disciplines, but especially in the sciences, where primary research and experimental data are key. Why are formatting styles important for the intellectual community? What is the risk of loosening standards?

APA In-Text Citations

Giving proper credit to the sources you use in your research paper is one of the most important functions of any documentation style, including APA. Much like **MLA**, APA style uses in-text citations.

Each **in-text citation** lets the reader know which source you are using; a curious reader can then flip to the references page for relevant information about that source. While the references page has more information about the source, the in-text citations show the reader exactly where each source is used throughout the text.

There are two kinds of in-text citations in APA style: signal phrases and parenthetical citations.

Signal phrases are short groups of words that explicitly announce the use of a source inside the sentence. Consider the following example:

> Smith (2016) argues that insistence on optimistic outlooks is actually damaging to neurotic patients.

> The signal phrase here is at the front of the sentence: *Smith (2016) argues that*. These words act as a signal to the reader that the writer is citing the source on the references page written by an author whose last name is Smith and whose work was published in 2016. Since sources on the references page are listed alphabetically, a reader could easily find this source.

For simple sources with single authors, signal phrases consist of the author's last name and the source's publication date in parentheses right after the author's name.

You'll notice that in the example above there are no quotation marks around any of the words. That's because the writer of the sentence has not **directly quoted** Smith; instead, he or she has **paraphrased** Smith's idea.

According to APA style, when you paraphrase or **summarize** a source, you do not need to include page numbers; you only have to list the author's name and the publication date in either a signal phrase or a parenthetical citation.

However, when you directly **quote** a source, you also need to include a parenthetical citation with a page or paragraph number along with a signal phrase.

Here's an example:

> Smith (2016) counters that "undue optimism leads to a more profound depressive spiral during the patient's next manic episode" (p. 245).

> In this sentence, a parenthetical citation appears after the quotation marks but before the period. The information in this citation signals to the reader that the quotation can be found in the original source material on page 245.

Notice that when you list a page number in an in-text citation, you precede it with the abbreviation *p.*

If you quote a website or online article without page numbers, APA style mandates that if the paragraphs are numbered, you should provide the paragraph number preceded by *para.*:

> Vazquez (2014) maintains that "many neurotic patients are seeking truth, not platitudes" (para. 14).

If no paragraph numbers are provided, find the nearest heading and count the paragraphs. List the heading in the parenthetical citation, separated from the paragraph number by a comma.

> Herbert (2016) says "treatment is not necessarily a means to truth" ("Life in Exile" section, para. 3).

When a sentence that uses source material does not include a signal phrase, all the citation information should be included in the parenthetical citation.

If the material is a paraphrase or summary, the **parenthetical citation** will include the author's last name and the publication date with commas separating each item in the citation.

> She also insists that being depressed is like being exposed to an overwhelming reality (Vazquez, 2014).

If the material is a quote, the citation must include the page number (or paragraph).

> He goes on to argue that "truth claims can in fact disrupt a patient's recovery" (Morton, 2013, p.74).

APA style uses slightly different in-text citations for the following special situations:

Indirect Citations

If you are citing information from another source, you should include a signal phrase with the original author's name and include the parenthetical citation for where you found the information.

> Jones explains that "facing negative ideas directly can be a source of empowerment" (as cited in Perkins, 2013, p.45).

> This indirect citation cites information from Jones that was included in Perkins's book.

Sources with No Author

If no author is listed, use the title of the work instead.

> "Disturbing the Depths" (2016) presents an interesting case of a neurotic who found peace after binge-watching horror films.

> Another source contends that "depictions of death or destruction have proven to be cathartic in several clinical studies" ("Cinematic Therapy," 2015, para. 12).

Sources with Multiple Authors

If a work has two authors, all the authors' last names should be mentioned the first time they are used.

> Smith and Harris (2005) argue that profane expressions can have a therapeutic effect.

When a work with two authors is used in a parenthetical citation an ampersand (&) is used instead of the word *and*. This is also the case for citations on the references page.

> They also cite violent video games as having "a surprisingly cathartic effect on withdrawn patients" (Smith & Harris, 2005, p. 123).

If a work has three to five authors, all the authors' names should be listed in the first citation. After that, you can use the abbreviation *et al.* along with the first author's name.

> Rodriguez et al. (2012) explained how regression therapy can be unreliable.

> Regression therapy can be unreliable if use improperly (Rodriguez et al., 2012).

A quote with 40 words or more is considered a **block quote**, and the following rules apply:

- The block quote should start on a new line.
- The entire block quote should be indented half an inch from the left margin.
- The block quote should not use quotation marks.
- The block quote should be double-spaced.
- If a block quote requires a parenthetical citation, the parentheses should start after quotation's last punctuation mark.

On Your Own

Create APA style in-text citations for each of the following situations:

A direct quote from page 45 of Sally Northrup and Kevin Dawson's 2010 book *Monster Monster*:

> Sometimes the depiction of a monster can even be reassuring to a child, especially when the figure in question is presented as vulnerable or unsure despite its frightening visage.

A paraphrase of the 2016 online article "Reaching Bottom to Breathe."

> In case after case, patients reported fewer anxiety attacks when they were encouraged to disparage the self-help gurus who insisted on pressing the point that happiness was inevitable and pessimism was a false perspective.

An indirect quotation from paragraph 17 of Nancy Burba's 2014 article "Reason to Doubt."

> Dr. Gilbert insists that watching professional wrestling is actually an effective means for cathartic release, especially matches involving masked wrestlers. "These muscular avatars effectively incarnate their fans' deepest desires," he explains, "and they can thus virtually embody the sorts of extreme successes on a public stage that many of us will never experience in real life."

APA References

Every time research is used within an APA style paper, the original source is credited in two ways: in an in-text citation and on the references page. Each source used in the paper is included as a separate entry on this page.

> **Helpful Hint**
>
> If you found a source during research but didn't actually use it in your paper, you do not need to include this source in your references page.

The most basic type of reference is a book with one author:

> Last Name, Initials. (Year). Title of the work. City, Abbreviated State: Publisher.

References always begin with the author's last name followed by the author's first and middle initials, when available. Notice that only the first word of a title is capitalized in an APA reference. Titles are capitalized like normal everywhere else in the paper. Remember that titles of major works are italicized, and the titles of shorter works, like chapters and articles, are put in quotation marks. For state abbreviations, always use the two-letter postal code.

> **Helpful Hint**
>
> In titles, always capitalize these words:
>
> The word at the beginning of the work's title
> Proper names
> Words directly after colons and dashes

Here are some common types of references:

Book with Two Authors

> Last Name, Initials & Last Name, Initials. (Year). Title of the work. City, Abbreviated State: Publisher.

Book with Three to Seven Authors

> Last Name, Initials, Last Name, Initials, & Last Name, Initials. (Year). Title of the work. City, Abbreviated State: Publisher.

Website

> Last Name, Initials. (Year, Month Day). Title of the page. Retrieved from http://www.URL.com.

Magazine Article

> Last Name, Initials. (Year, Month Day). Title of the work. Magazine, Volume, Pages.

Online Journal Article

> Last Name, Initials. (Year, Month Day). Title of the work. Journal Name, Volume. Retrieved from http://www.URL.com.

On Your Own

Using APA style, create references for the following sources (make sure to account for the hanging indent):

A print book called *All the Mighty Fall* by Gwendoline Ravine. It was published in 2012 by Redd and Fickle Press, which is located in Atlanta, Georgia.

The article "End of the Line for Southwest Gardens." It was published in the journal *Black Swan Digest* in 2014, volume 4, number 5, on pages 7-10.

Brian Palmer's article "Would a World without Bees be a World without Us?" published on May 18th of 2015 on NRDC.org. This is the hyperlink: (https://www.nrdc.org/onearth/would-world-without-bees-be-world-without-us); imagine that you retrieved it today.

Lesson Wrap-up

Key Terms

Abstract: a brief summary of a paper

APA Format: a citation and documentation style published by the American Psychological Association

Block Quote: a special type of direct quote that indents the entirety of the quote and does not require the use of quotation marks

Direct Quotation: using words and phrases directly from the original source enclosed in quotation marks

In-Text Citation: source information included in a text

Hanging Indent: a style that left-aligns the first line of an item and indents all subsequent lines

MLA Format: a citation and documentation style published by the Modern Language Association

Paraphrase: using your own words to explain a sentence or paragraph written by someone else

Parenthetical Citation: an in-text citation in parentheses

Quote: using the exact words from a source

References Page: a list of sources used in a paper

Running Head: a heading that includes a shortened version of the paper's title and the page number

Signal Phrase: a phrase that introduces another piece of information

Summary: using your own words to condense large amounts of information into 1-2 sentences

Title Page: the first page in a paper that contains author information and the title of the paper

Writing Application: Basics of APA

As you read the sample research paper in the following pages, note the source integration and formatting the author has used to meet research-style guidelines.

Self-Help and the Optimism Bias

Cindy Carrington

The University of the Southeast

Self-Help and the Optimism Bias

Many self-help gurus turn to notions of self-empowerment and willfulness to encourage depressed individuals to engage the world. However, this sort of instruction ignores what many contemporary scientists and philosophers know: a person's ability to control his or her own thoughts is extremely limited. Burton (2008) explains that "lower-level brain modules can profoundly affect not only our ordinary sensory perceptions but also how we experience abstract symbols" (p. 65). He goes on to explain that these lower-level processes actually precede feelings of certainty when people make decisions, so unconscious thinking, not willful intentions, actually underwrite human actions (Burton, 2008). Thus, it is not at all clear that positive thinking is within a person's control or, at the very least, functions the way traditional notions of self-empowerment assume.

Sharot (2011) examines the illusory nature of optimism itself when it comes to positive perspectives on the world. She calls the "optimism bias" a built-in response that "protects us from accurately perceiving the pain and difficulties the future holds, and it may defend us from viewing our options in life as somewhat limited" (p. xvi). Though she attributes many positive outcomes to this bias, she also links it to the economic recession in the mid-2000s when "the relatively small biases of different individuals . . . combine[d] to create a much larger illusion" which led to economic disaster (Sharot, 2011, p. 209). In other words, people who are determined to look on the bright side of things may themselves be engaging in destructive behavior, regardless of whether such an attitude helps them to feel better about themselves.

OPTIMISM BIAS   3

In fact, it may be that depression is a rational response to an environment that is at best

indifferent to the human species. As Thacker (2011) notes, "the world is increasingly

unthinkable—a world of planetary disasters, emerging pandemics, tectonic shifts, strange

weather, oil-drenched seascapes, and the furtive, always-looming threat of extinction" (p. 1). He

goes on to say that the expanse of these incomprehensibly dangerous forces make it

"increasingly difficult to comprehend the world in which we live and of which we are a part"

(Thacker, 2011, p.1). Zizek (2010) argues that our impossible position in relation to the

impending disasters around us, such as the threat of a nuclear attack, lead many people to "live in

a state of collective fetishistic disavowal: we know very well that this [kind of disaster] will

happen at some point, but nevertheless cannot bring ourselves to really believe it will" (p. xi).

Perhaps depressed individuals are incapable of this sort of dismissive gesture, but that certainly

doesn't mean they aren't rational; on the contrary, perhaps they are too rational for their own

good.

References

Burton, R.A. (2008). *On being certain: Believing you are right even when you're not.* New York, NY: St. Martin's Press.

Sharot, T. (2011). *The optimism bias: A tour of the irrationally positive brain.* New York, NY: Pantheon Books.

Thacker, E. (2011). *In the dust of this planet.* Hants, UK: Zero Books.

Zizek, S. (2010). *Living in the end times.* New York, NY: Verso.

Lesson 7.10
Basics of CMS

Chicago Manual of Style, or CMS, is the most comprehensive documentation style. Publishers often prefer this style guide.

Helpful Hint

In 2007, author Kate Turabian published *A Manual for Writers of Research Papers, Theses, and Dissertations* based on the Chicago Manual of Style. Her text is geared toward academic student writing. After the publication of Turabian's book, Chicago Manual of Style has also been referred to as Turabian Style. Keep in mind that these two styles are essentially the same.

Writing Environment: Everyday

Did you know that Chicago Manual of Style is the preferred style guide of most large publishing houses? The style guide dictates how the table of contents, headings and page numbers, and copyright page are arranged. When you pick up your favorite book to read—maybe it's *Harry Potter and the Sorcerer's Stone* or *The Hunger Games*—chances are the book is formatted based on CMS.

In this lesson, you will learn more about CMS:

CMS Paper Format
CMS Notes-and-Bibliography Method
CMS Parentheses-and-Reference-List Method

Further Resources

The Online Writing Lab (OWL) (https://owl.english.purdue.edu/owl/resource/717/01/) developed by Purdue University provides ample information about how to cite sources and format papers in **MLA** style, **APA** style, and CMS.

CMS Paper Format

When setting up a paper in CMS, follow the guidelines below:

Page Size	8.5" x 11"
Page Margins	1" on all sides
Font	12-point Times New Roman or Palatino
Alignment	Left
Spacing	Double

On Your Own

Which font wouldn't you find in a CMS paper? Check the box next to your answer.

- ☐ Arial, 12-Point Font
- ☐ Times New Roman, 12-Point Font
- ☐ Palatino, 12-Point Font

Papers formatted with CMS should include a **title page.** Center the title in all capital letters in the top third of the page. Center your name, the course name, and the date in the bottom third of the page.

Page numbers should be placed in the top-right corner of every page except the title page, half an inch from the top and right margins. Start the page numbers at 1.

JANE EYRE AND THE MOTHER ARCHETYPE: A JUNGIAN PERSPECTIVE

Claire Epps
English 201: Psychology and Fiction
March 7, 2016

Writing Environment: Academic

Formatting a paper properly is the easiest way to avoid point deductions. Make sure that you purchase or borrow a copy of the style guide your professor would like you to use and format your paper exactly according to the guide's specifications. There's no reason to miss a point or two for failing to include a cover page or using the wrong font.

CMS Notes-and-Bibliography Method

Citing your research is extremely important in any paper. Without citations, you are at risk of plagiarizing. To avoid **plagiarism** and give credit to those who helped inform your argument, all style guides require a method of citation.

CMS offers two methods of documenting sources. The first is the **Notes-and-Bibliography Method**, which utilizes footnotes or endnotes and a **bibliography**.

First, consult your professor to confirm which method he or she prefers. Next, if you're using the Notes-and-Bibliography method, determine if you'd like to use footnotes or endnotes (either method is acceptable).

Footnotes are listed on the same page as the source material, separated from the main text by a line. **Endnotes** are similar to footnotes except they appear on a separate page at the end of the paper. Footnotes and endnotes in CMS should adhere to the following guidelines:

Font	10-point Times New Roman or Palatino
Alignment	Left
Spacing	Single, with an extra space between each note

Whether you're using footnotes or endnotes, when you use source information within your paper, it should be cited with a superscript number that corresponds to either the endnote or footnote. The superscript number should be at the end of the sentence that uses source material, after the ending punctuation mark. Then, you'll compose a bibliography for the end of your paper.

> Wolf says that to create meaning out of a musical, one must consider the "meaning triangle," which consists of historical "context," the "spectators" viewpoints, and the actual text itself.[1]

The number should coincide with a numbered note at the bottom of the page or on the endnotes page. For the first occurrence of a source, the footnote or endnote should include the author's name, the source title, the publishing location, the publisher, the date, and the page numbers. Here's an example:

> 1. Stacy Wolf, *A Problem Like Maria* [Ann Arbor: University of Michigan Press, 2002], 4-5.

If you use a source multiple times in a row, replace all the information except the page numbers with "Ibid.," an abbreviation for the Latin term *ibidem*, meaning "in the same place." You can use this form of shortening a note only when the note in question comes from the same source as the previous note.

> 1. C.G. Jung, *The Archetypes and the Collective Unconscious* [Princeton: Princeton University Press, 1968], 5.
>
> 2. Ibid., 81.
>
> Note 1 contains the full citation. Note 2 indicates that the quote or reference came from the same source as the first note.

Helpful Hint

Keep in mind that if you use a source repeatedly but also use other sources in-between, you can't use *Ibid.* in the footnote or endnote. You must write out the full citation if it is not from the same source as the one listed above it.

Any sources that you cite in-text should be added to your bibliography page, which comes at the very end of your paper. The bibliography page should use the same page format as the rest of the paper, with the word "Bibliography" centered on the first line.

All sources should be listed in alphabetical order by the author's last name. If you are citing multiple works by the same author, use five dashes in a row instead of repeating the author's name. Like other formatting styles, CMS uses a **hanging indent** for each bibliography entry. This means that every line in an entry except the first should be indented half an inch.

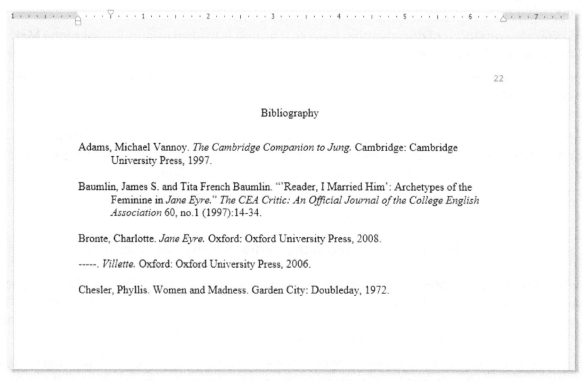

Writing Environment: Academic

The Chicago Manual of Style requires that online citations include either a URL or a DOI. A URL is a Uniform Resource Locator. It is essentially a web address that begins with "http://www." At minimum, CMS requires that you use a URL in your citations. However, since URLs change frequently and pages can be updated regularly, CMS prefers that you use a more reliable DOI, or Digital Object Identifier. This can be found on the front page of a journal article online, in the copyright information, or on a reference page from an online database. It is a series of numbers that looks like this: 10.1037/1528-3542.8.4.494.

Here are some common types of sources formatted with the notes-and-bibliography method.

Book with One Author

Bibliography

Last Name, First Name. Title. Location: Publisher, Year.

Footnotes or Endnotes

First Name and Last Name, Title. [Location: Publisher, Year], Pages.

Book by Multiple Authors

Bibliography

Last Name, First Name and First Name Last Name. Title. Location: Publisher, Year.

Footnotes or Endnotes

> First Name and Last Name and First Name and Last Name, Title. [Location: Publisher, Year], Pages.

Journal Article

Bibliography

> Last Name, First Name. "Title of the Work." Journal Title Volume.Issue [Year]: Pages.

Footnotes or Endnotes

> First Name Last Name, "Title of the Work" [Journal Title Volume.Issue, Year], Pages.

Journal Article from an Online Database

Bibliography

> Last Name, First Name. "Title of the Work." Journal Title Volume.Issue [Year]: Pages, http://www.URL.com (accessed Date).

Footnotes or Endnotes

> First Name Last Name, "Title of the Work" [Journal Title Volume.Issue, Year]: Pages, http://www.URL.com (accessed Date).

Website with No Author

Bibliography

> Website Name. "Page/Article Name." Organization. http://www.URL.com [accessed Date].

Footnotes or Endnotes

> Website Name, "Page/Article Name," Organization, http://www.URL.com [accessed Date].

Website with an Author

Bibliography

> Last Name, First Name. Website Name. "Page/Article Name." Organization. http://www.URL.com [accessed Date].

Footnotes or Endnotes

> First Name Last Name, "Page/Article Name," Organization, http://www.URL.com [accessed Date].

On Your Own

Identify the piece of the following bibliographic citation that references the publishing company.

> Brontë, Charlotte. *Jane Eyre*, 2nd ed. South Bend, IN: Infomotions, 2001. http://site.ebrary.com/lib/charlesouth/detail.action?docID=5000558 [Accessed May 5, 2016].

CMS Parentheses-and-Reference-List Method

The CMS **Parentheses-and-Reference-List Method** provides another variation of citing your sources. This method is sometimes known as the Reference List Style.

In the Parentheses-and-Reference-List Method, sources are cited **in-text** with parentheses that include the author's last name, the date, and the page number. If the author is unknown, use the title of the work instead.

> Sheldon Patinkin, in his history of American musical theater, describes *The Sound of Music* as a "bittersweet" musical set in 1938 in which "an unharmonious Austrian family learn[s] to harmonize literally and figuratively" (2008, 342).
>
> Since the author, Sheldon Patinkin, is mentioned in the sentence, there's no need to include his name in the parenthetical citation.

CMS citations appear directly after the quoted or paraphrased source material, even in the middle of a sentence.

> Katherine Creedy, a microbiology professor Southern State University, concludes that "the amount of time it would take for the bacteria to grow is negligible compared to inoculation time" (2012, 445) and warns that panic would only increase the outbreak rate.

At the end of the paper, a **reference list** provides full citations for each source. The reference list is organized in alphabetical order by the author's last name. If you are citing two sources by the same author, use five dashes in a row instead of repeating the author's name. This method also uses a hanging indent for each bibliography entry. This means that every line in an entry except the first should be indented by half an inch.

> Patinkin, Sheldon. 2008. *No Legs, No Jokes, No Chance.* Evanston, IL: Northwestern University
>   Press.

References in the Parentheses-and-Reference-List Method are single-spaced with an extra space between each entry. The word "References" is centered on the first line of the page.

Here are some common types of sources with citations and reference examples:

Book by a Single Author

Reference List

> Last Name, First Name. Year. Title. Location: Publisher.

Parenthetical Citation

> (Last Name Year, Page)

Book by Multiple Authors

Reference List

> Last Name, First Name and First Name Last Name. Year. Title. Location: Publisher.

Parenthetical Citation

> (Last Name Year, Page)

Journal Article

Reference List

Last Name, First Name. Year. "Title of the Work" Journal Name Volume.Issue [Date]: Pages.

Parenthetical Citation

(Last Name Year, Page)

Journal Article from an Online Database

Reference List

Last Name, First Name. Year. "Title of the Work" Journal Name Volume.Issue [Date]: Pages, http://www.URL.com (accessed Date).

Parenthetical Citation

(Last Name Year, Page)

Website

Reference List

Last Name, First Name. Year. "Page/Article Title" Journal Name Volume.Issue [Date]: Pages, http://www.URL.com (accessed Date).

Parenthetical Citation

(Last Name Year)

Lesson Wrap-up

Key Terms

APA Format: a citation and documentation style published by the American Psychological Association

Bibliography: a list of sources used in a paper

CMS Format: a citation and documentation style known as the Chicago Manual of Style

Endnotes: a numbered in-text citation that appears on a separate page

Footnotes: a numbered in-text citation that appears on the same page as the source material

Hanging Indent: a style that left-aligns the first line of an item and indents all subsequent lines

In-Text Citation: source information included in a text

MLA Format: a citation and documentation style published by the Modern Language Association

Notes-and-Bibliography Method: a CMS documentation method that uses footnotes or endnotes and a bibliography

Parentheses-and-Reference-List: a CMS documentation method that uses parenthetical citations and a references list

Plagiarism: using someone else's words or ideas without giving credit to the original source

Reference List: a list of sources used in a paper

Title Page: the first page in a paper that contains author information and the title of the paper

Writing Application: Basics of CMS

As you read the sample research paper in the following pages, note the source integration and formatting the author has used to meet research-style guidelines.

ABU HAMID AL-GHAZALI AND MYSTIC EXPRESSION:

AN ANALYSIS OF HIS LIFE AND WORKS

Katelyn Clarke

REL 405

April 26, 2016

Abu Hamid al-Ghazali was one of the most influential writers on mystic expression.[1] He was acclaimed as the Proof of Islam, the Ornament of Faith, and the Renewer of Religion.[2] As a mystic of Sunni Islam, he was confronted with contradictions between reason and revelation. He sought to resolve these contradictions for the sake of his followers as well as himself in *The Mysteries of the Human Soul (al-Madnun Bihl 'Ala Ghairi Ahlihi)*.[3] This short but comprehensive work describes al-Ghazali's psychological understanding of the soul, and through his understanding of the soul, his basic understanding of the world and religion.

Abu Hamid al-Ghazali was born in 1058 AD in Tabaran-Tus (modern-day Iran), where he received his early education. He went on to study with Ash'arite theologian al-Juwayni at Nizamiyya Madrasa in Nishapur. It was here that he became closely connected with the political elite, specifically the caliphal court in Baghdad. However, he realized that the "high ethical standards of a virtuous religious life [were] not compatible with being in the service of sultans, viziers, and caliphs" because "benefiting from the riches of the military and political elite implies complicity in their corrupt and oppressive rule and will jeopardize one's prospect of redemption in the afterlife."[4] It was this realization that caused him to leave Baghdad in 1095 and vow at the

---

1. Al-Ghazali, *The Mysteries of the Human Soul*, trans. 'Abdul Qayyum "Shafaq" Hazarvi [Lahore: Ashraf Printing Press, 1991], vii.

2. Muhammad Hozien, "A History of Muslim Philosophy," *ghazali.org*, www.Ghazali.org/articles/hmp-4-30.htm. [2016].

3. Frank Griffel, "Al-Ghazali," *Stanford Encyclopedia of Philosophy*, http://plato.stanford.edu/entries/al-ghazali/.[2016]; Ghazali, *The Mysteries of the Human Soul*, vii.

4. Griffel, "Al-Ghazali."

2

tomb of Abraham in Hebron to never serve political authorities or teach in state-sponsored schools again.

In 1096, shortly after a pilgrimage to Mecca, he founded a small private school and Sufi convent (*khanqah*). During this time, he continued writing. Many of his most influential writings were written during this time. Unfortunately, it did not last, and he broke his vow in 1106 to teach at Nizamiyya Madrasa in Nishapur, where he was once a student. He cited political pressure and theological conflicts for breaking his vow. He taught at small schools until 1111 when he died in Tus.

The Mysteries of the Human Soul, one of his most influential works on mystical expression, examines the intricacies of the soul and its connection to the body. Though the exact date is unknown, it was most likely written around 1096-1106 after al-Ghazali's revelation caused him to leave Baghdad. He spent the majority of his time during this period at his private school and Sufi convent in Tus. This work would certainly be useful for Sufi converts with its emphasis on emptying oneself of earthly desires and feelings to attain unification with God.[5]

Al-Ghazali's works were widespread and made their way from West Africa to Oceania. However, his teachings were not always readily accepted. His use of philosophical language, his mode of argument, and his preoccupation with Sufism led many to label him as "one of the misguided."[6] Qadi abu 'Abd Allah Muhammad ibn Hamdin of Cordova issued a decree *(fatwa)* against al-Ghazali's work and had it destroyed throughout Spain. Marrakush Sultan 'Ali ibn

---

5. Ghazali, *The Mysteries of the Human Soul,* 43.

6. Hozien, "A History of Muslim Philosophy," Influence.

3

Yusuf ibn Tashifin, an Almoravid ruler, also ordered the destruction of al-Ghazali's philosophical writings in North Africa during his reign in 1084-1142 C.E.[7]

Al-Ghazali lived in a post-golden age where exact sciences lost importance, and the caliphate that the Islamic state had grown into faced destruction as more provincial governors gained power. In fact, soon after al-Ghazali was born, the Sultan was forced on Baghdad and a split in power between the Sultan and the Caliph occurred. It was a time marked by wealth and power but separated from its roots. This resulted in a resurgence back to the roots of Islam where Sufism, the path that al-Ghazali followed, dominated.[8]

Sufism heavily influenced much of al-Ghazali's work as demonstrated by *The Mysteries of the Human Soul.* This work focuses on the soul and how it is the basic connection to God and mystical knowledge, the "highest thing to which a man can attain."[9] According to al-Ghazali, diving into the purity of the soul and separating oneself from the earthly desires and feelings is the only way to achieve one's purpose of returning the soul to its Creator.[10] *The Mysteries of the Human Soul* gives a comprehensive examination of the soul and its connection to all parts of life.

---

7. Hozien, "A History of Muslim Philosophy," Influence.; "Yusuf ibn Tashufin," *Encyclopaedia Britannica,* http://www.britannica.com/biography/Yusuf-ibn-Tashufin#10750.hook [2016].

8. Mustafa Abu Sway, "Muhammad al-Ghazali," *Center for Islamic Sciences,* www.cis-ca.org/voices/g/ghazali.htm. [2016].

9. Ghazali, *The Mysteries of the Human Soul,* 54.

10. Ibid., 80, 44.

4

Bibliography

Abu Sway, Mustafa. "Muhammad al-Ghazali." *Center for Islamic Sciences.* 2001.
    www.cisca.org/voices/g/ghazali.htm.

Al-Ghazali. *The Mysteries of the Human Soul.* Translated by 'Abdul Qayyum "Shafaq" Hazarvi.
    Lahore: Ashraf Printing Press, 1991.

Encyclopaedia Britannica. "Yusuf ibn Tashufin." 2016.
    http://www.britannica.com/biography/Yusuf-ibn-Tashufin#10750.hook.

Griffel, Frank. "Al-Ghazali." *Stanford Encyclopedia of Philosophy.* 2007.
    http://plato.stanford.edu/entries/al-ghazali/.

Hozien, Muhammad. "A History of Muslim Philosophy." *ghazali.org.* 2015.
    www.Ghazali.org/articles/hmp-4-30.htm.

Lesson 7.11
Basics of CSE

The **Council of Science Editors**, or CSE, is a documentation style used for scientific papers. CSE provides three different methods for documenting sources. Each method requires a series of in-text citations and a corresponding list of **references** that appears at the end of the document.

This lesson will discuss the three citation systems used in CSE style:

Citation-Sequence
Citation-Name
Name-Year

Helpful Hint

While this lesson provides an overview of CSE systems for citations, advanced students and scholars in the sciences will need to become familiar with all the rules for formatting and writing in accordance with CSE guidelines. The comprehensive CSE manual is *Scientific Style and Format,* which is currently in its 8th edition. More information about this resource can be found on the CSE website (http://www.scientificstyleandformat.org/Home.html).

Writing Environment: Professional

CSE, APA, MLA, CMS. All these acronyms may seem confusing, but each citation style is carefully formulated to meet the needs of professionals within a particular discipline, helping them track sources accurately and alert other scholars to important information. Scholars and researchers interested in publishing articles must pay careful attention to the "house style" used by the publication to which they are submitting their manuscript.

You may be thinking, "Why should I care about that?" Citations are a great way to practice providing appropriate detail and careful organization, and that kind of attention can make you stand out in professional settings.

CSE essays should begin with a title page that includes the title of the essay, the author's name, the class name, the instructor's name, and the date. All this information should be center-aligned in the middle of the page.

The title page does not need headers, footers, or page numbers. However, the rest of the paper should have a header on all pages. The header is right-aligned and includes the paper title and the current page number, starting at 2. All text is double-spaced with one-inch margins.

The references page at the end of the essay begins on a new page. It too is double-spaced with no extra spaces between citations. The page is titled "References," which is centered at the top of the page.

CSE has three different ways of documenting sources. Check with your instructor to make sure you are using the most preferred method for that assignment.

- Citation-sequence
- Citation-name
- Name-year

Citation-Sequence

The first citation system used by CSE is Citation-Sequence. The **Citation-Sequence** system organizes sources at the end of the paper according to the order that they appear in the text.

A superscript number is used to refer to each source. Once a number is assigned to a source, the same number is used to refer to that source throughout the document. The superscript number will always appear before ending punctuation. Take a look at how Citation-Sequence organization is used in the following example:

A number of backyard bugs look threatening but are harmless to humans and actually help keep other pests in check. For example, the ominously-named assassin bug kills large prey[1], while ground beetles help to keep insects that live in the soil under control[2].

References

1. Cranshaw W. Garden insects of North America: the ultimate guide to backyard bugs. Princeton (NJ): Princeton University Press; 2004.

2. Penn State Extension: Attracting beneficial insects. University Park (PA): Penn State College of Agricultural Sciences; 2015 Jul 30 [accessed 2016 May 10]. http://extension.psu.edu/.

Now that these two sources have been cited once, they will be cited with the same number throughout the rest of the paper.

Consider the following guidelines when you create your references in CSE style:

- References entries are typically formatted using a hanging indent, meaning that every line but the first is indented half an inch.
- Author names are given in the format "Last Name Initials." No punctuation separates the parts of an individual name. Commas are used to separate the names of multiple authors:

    Smith SC, Martin L, Press JM

- No italics or quotation marks are used in CSE reference entries unless specified by submission guidelines provided by a teacher or publication.
- In article and book titles, only the first word and proper nouns are capitalized.
- In journal, newspaper, and magazine titles, all key words capitalized. Journal titles are abbreviated according to a standard system.

Further Resources

Lists of journal title abbreviations can be found here:
http://www.wsl.ch/dienstleistungen/publikationen/office/abk_EN.

In CSE, the references list should always begin at the top of the page that immediately follows the end of your paper. If your paper ends on page five, your references list will begin on page six.

The following examples show how to cite some commonly used types of sources in CSE when following the Citation-Sequence system:

Book

> Last Name Initials. Title. Edition (if applicable). Location: Publisher; Date.

Book with Multiple Authors

> Last Name Initials, Last Name Initials, Last Name Initials. Title. Edition (if applicable). Location: Publisher; Date.

Journal Article

> Last Name Initials. Article title. Journal title. Date; Volume(Issue): Location.

Online Journal Article

> Last Name Initials. Article title. Journal title. Date [Date Updated; Date Accessed]; Volume(Issue): Location. http://www.URL.com. DOI.

Citing websites in CSE can be difficult because formatting varies depending on what information is available about the source you are citing. Make sure you look carefully at the website or webpage you are using, as well as the website homepage, to make sure you find all the necessary information.

Website without an Author

> Title of homepage. Location: Publisher; Publication Date [Date Updated; Date Accessed]. http://www.URL.com.

Website with an Author

> Last Name Initials. Title of homepage. Location: Publisher; Publication Date [Date Updated; Date Accessed]. http://www.URL.com.

Newspaper Article

> Last Name Initials. Title of article. Title of Newspaper [Edition]. Date; Section: First Page (Column Number).

Online Newspaper Article

> Last Name Initials. Title of article. Title of Newspaper [Edition]. Date; Section: First Page. [Date Accessed]. http://www.URL.com.

You will, of course, come across other kinds of sources that you will need to cite in CSE. If you're unsure how to format a citation, reference an online citation website or ask a librarian.

Writing Environment: Everyday

Imagine that you want to recommend an article you read online to a friend. What information would help them find the article? How does that information correspond to the information in a citation?

Citation-Name

The second citation system used by CSE is **Citation-Name.** Like Citation-Sequence papers, each source used in the paper is assigned a number, which is used to refer to that paper throughout the document. However, the list of sources at the end of the paper is arranged and numbered according to alphabetical order (rather than the order the sources appeared in the document).

Now, let's take a look at a brief example passage and reference list:

Golden rice was developed in the late 1990s in order to address health problems in developing countries[1-3].

References

1. Dubock A. The politics of golden rice. GM Crops & Food. 2014 [accessed 2016 May 18]; 5(3): 210-222. http://www.ebscohost.com. doi: 10.4161/21645698.2014.967570

2. Golden rice project. [Location unknown]: Golden Rice Humanitarian Board; c 2005-2015 [accessed 17 May 2016]. http://www.goldenrice.org/.

3. Johnson S. Genetically modified food: a golden opportunity? Sustainable Development Law & Policy. 2014 [accessed 2016 May 18]: 14(1): 34-70. http://www.ebscohost.com.

In this example, the list *1-3* is referring to the sources by Dubock, Golden Rice Project, and Johnson. The hyphen between 1 and 3 indicates that all three sources include this information.

Remember, in the Citation-Name system, the sources are alphabetized and then numbered accordingly. Otherwise, the references are identical to those you would use in the Citation-Sequence system. To see examples of reference list entries, refer to the section on the Citation-Sequence system.

Writing Environment: Academic

For another example of the Citation-Name system, consider the following sample:

Golden rice was developed in the late 1990s in order to address health problems in developing countries[1-3]. The DNA of golden rice plants has been altered so that the grains of rice contain beta-carotene, a form of vitamin A[2]. When this vitamin is missing from the diet of malnourished children, which is often the case, it can result in blindness and eventually death[1,2]. The creators of and advocates for the widespread distribution of golden rice argue that making Vitamin A more readily available to people in developing countries could prevent approximately one-third of deaths in children under age five[2]. However, critics argue that the safety of GMOs has not been sufficiently demonstrated and that the widespread distribution of golden rice would allow biotech companies to increase GMO production and distribution without evidence that the crops bring the promised benefits[3].

References

1. Dubock A. The politics of golden rice. GM Crops & Food. 2014 [accessed 2016 May 18]; 5(3): 210-222. http://www.ebscohost.com. doi: 10.4161/21645698.2014.967570

2. Golden rice project. [Location unknown]: Golden Rice Humanitarian Board; c 2005-2015 [accessed 17 May 2016]. http://www.goldenrice.org/.

3. Johnson S. Genetically modified food: a golden opportunity? Sustainable Development Law & Policy. 2014 [accessed 2016 May 18]: 14(1): 34-70. http://www.ebscohost.com.

Name-Year

The third citation system used by CSE is Name-Year. The **Name-Year** system uses **in-text citations** that include the last name of the author or authors as well as the year of publication. Let's take a look at some examples:

> (Smith 2014)
> (Lee and Jones 2010)
> (Marks et al. 2015)

Note that if a source has two authors, both of their last names are given in text. For sources with three or more authors, only the first author's surname is provided, followed by the phrase *et al.*

Benjamin Franklin's invention of the lightning rod was a direct result of his first experiment. In this experiment, he hypothesized that lightning is a source of electricity and intended to prove it by creating a spark (Allison 1982). Franklin took his kite out during a storm, and lightning hit the kite, catching the contraption on fire. The lightning rod was then conceived to keep houses from being struck by lightning (Walter 2003). The rods were placed on the roofs of houses and fashioned so the end point struck the ground, rather than the house itself (Franklin 1996).

Reference

Allison, A. 1982. The real Benjamin Franklin. 1. Malta, ID. National Center for Constitutional Studies. 504 pp.

Franklin, B. 1996. The autobiography of Benjamin Franklin. 1. Mineola, NY. Dover Publications. 144 pp.

Walter, I. 2003. Benjamin Franklin: an American life. 1. New York, NY. Simon & Schuster. 586 pp.

Organizations can also be listed as authors. In those instances, an abbreviation of the organization's name is usually created in order to prevent the in-text reference from interrupting the flow of reading.

In-text citation

(WHO 2016)

Reference

[WHO] World Health Organization. Year. Title of article. Location: Publisher; [Date Accessed]. http://www.URL.com.

If a work does not specify a personal or organizational author, begin the in-text citation with the first word or first several words of the title, followed by an **ellipsis**, as in the following example:

In-text citation

(Zero . . . 2016)

Reference

The Zero Dilemma. Date. Location: Title of article: [Date Accessed]. http://www.URL.com.

You may notice that the end references used in the Name-Year system differ slightly from those used by the Citation-Sequence and Citation-Name systems. Because an increased emphasis is placed upon the date of publication, that information is moved closer to the beginning of the end reference, immediately following the author (or the title of the work if no author is given).

Here are a number of references formatted according to the specifications of the Name-Year system:

Book

Last Name Initials. Date. Title. Edition (if applicable). Location: Publisher.

Print Journal Article

Last Name Initials. Date. Article title. Journal Title. Volume(Issue): Pages.

Online Journal Article

Last Name Initials. Date. Article title. Journal Title [Date Updated; Date Accessed]; Volume(Issue): Pages. http://www.URL.com. DOI.

Website

Title of homepage. Date. Location: Publisher; [Date Updated; Date Accessed]. http://www.URL.com.

Newspaper Article

Last Name Initials. Date. Title of article. Title of Newspaper (Edition). Section: First Page (Column Number).

Online Newspaper Article

Last Name Initials. Date. Title of article. Title of Newspaper (Edition); [Date Accessed]. http://www.URL.com.

Group Activity

Select a science-related topic that is interesting to the members of your group. Each person should then find one source about that topic. Agree on a CSE citation system to use, and work together to create a references list for the sources you have found.

Writing Environment: Academic

Which CSE system might allow you to best organize your research in the following academic writing situations?

- You are writing a history of the discovery of supermassive black holes; you want to present the research chronologically.
- You are evaluating the potential benefits and risks of a new water conservation program that draws upon a number of existing programs and policies.
- You are writing a literature review that introduces the key ideas on which you have built your own original study, which will be the main focus of your paper.

Lesson Wrap-up

Key Terms

CSE Format: a citation and documentation style published by the Council of Science Editors

Citation-Sequence: a type of CSE format that organizes sources at the end of the paper according to the order that they appear in the text

Citation-Name: a type of CSE format that organizes sources at the end of the paper alphabetically

Ellipsis: a punctuation mark made up of three periods that indicates excluded words

Name-Year: a type of CSE format that uses in-text citations

In-Text Citation: source information included in a text

References List: a list of sources used in a paper

Writing Application: Basics of CSE

As you read the sample research paper in the following pages, note the source integration and formatting the author has used to meet research-style guidelines.

Hunting Mechanisms of Komodo Dragons

Barry Wilmington

SCI 506

Dr. McKiney

April 17th, 2016

Hunting Mechanisms of Komodo Dragons

Komodo dragons, *Varanus komodensis*, may not breathe fire, but how exactly do they capture their prey? The answer to this question has been the subject of some debate and mystery as scientists have worked to understand the world's largest living lizard.

Investigating Komodo dragons' hunting methods is difficult in part because they are found on only a few remote Indonesian islands[4,6]. Once researchers reach these islands, they have to carry their equipment over uneven terrain shaped by volcanic activity in order to reach the lizards' habitats. Then, large traps must be set up every few miles, and the traps must be checked every day for Komodo dragons. However, the traps often remain empty because Komodo dragons resist the temptation of the fresh meat used as bait. When a Komodo dragon is trapped, it is quickly evaluated and tagged before being released back into the wild[4].

Scientists have also studied Komodo dragons in captivity, but while American zoos have housed Komodo dragons for over a century, the lizards have not always readily adapted to their non-native environment. For many years, Komodo dragons in American zoos did not live more than five years[3], much fewer than the 30 years they may live in the wild[6]. It was not until 1992 that captive Komodo dragons were successfully bred in the United States[4,6].

As efforts to understand Komodo dragons—in particular, their eating habits—have paid off, researchers have made some surprising, and at times seemingly contradictory, discoveries. There has been some uncertainty as to whether Komodo dragons are predators or scavengers. Evidence now indicates that Komodo dragons both hunt prey and feed on the carcasses of already dead animals. Due to their large size and the infrequency with which they eat—adult

2

Komodo dragons may eat only once every two months[5]—Komodo dragons take advantages of the meals that are most readily available. Even young Komodo dragons are not off-limits to hungry adults; the young spend their first year in trees to avoid being cannibalized[3].

When Komodo dragons do hunt, they have several attack methods that may contribute to their capture of prey. Komodo dragons are stealthy and surprisingly fast, able to sneak up on and ambush weak or wounded deer, water buffalo, and other animals[5,6]. Originally, researchers believed that prey were killed by a Komodo dragon's powerful bite. Additional evidence now demonstrates that the Komodo dragons' prey often suffers a slow death, for one of two possible reasons[1]. A wild Komodo dragon's mouth teems with septic bacteria that can infect and eventually kill other animals[1,6]; Komodo dragons also have venomous saliva that prevents blood clotting and causes the prey to go into shock[5,6]. Once an animal has been bitten, a Komodo dragon will wait patiently until the prey is fully incapacitated. Then it will be joined by other Komodo dragons in the area, which will eat the prey--hooves, fur, and all[5].

Although Komodo dragons are considered a national treasure in Indonesia[3] and their habitat in Komodo National Park has been preserved[3,4], they are considered an endangered species, and their population appears to have declined over the past several decades[4]. While Komodo dragons have not historically shown aggression towards humans, some recent attacks suggest that the increased human presence in the Komodo dragons' habitat has caused the lizards to feel threatened[4]. Researchers advocate ongoing conservation efforts involving collaboration with environmentalists, national authorities, and community members in order to effectively monitor and ensure the continued protection of Komodo dragons[1].

References

1. Ainsworth C. How to train your dragon. New Scientist. 2013 [accessed 2016 May 16];

   220(2948): 56-58. http://www.ebscohost.com.

2. Ariefiandy A, Purwandana D, Natali C, Imansyah MJ, Surahman M, Jessop TS, Ciofi C.

   Conservation of Komodo dragons Varanus komodoensis in the Wae Wuul nature reserve,

   Flores, Indonesia: a multidisciplinary approach. Int Zoo Yearb. 2015 [accessed 2016 May

   16]; 49(1): 67-80. http://www.ebscohost.com. doi: 10.1111/izy.12072.

3. Cohn JP. Indonesian treasure has a Jurassic appeal. Bioscience. 1994 [accessed 2016 May 16];

   44(1): 4-7. http://www.ebscohost.com.

4. Holland JS. Once upon a dragon. National Geographic [Internet]. 2014 January [accessed

   2016 May 16]. http://ngm.nationalgeographic.com/2014/01/komodo-dragon/holland-text.

5. How a dragon kills [video]. Venom islands. Smithsonian Channel. 2014 Mar 25, 3:59.

   [accessed 2016 May 19]. http://www.smithsonianchannel.com/videos/how-a-dragon-

   kills/18873,

6. Smithsonian national zoological park. Komodo dragon fact sheet: [Date unknown; accessed 19

   May 2016].

   https://nationalzoo.si.edu/Animals/ReptilesAmphibians/Facts/FactSheets/Komododragon.

   cfm.

Chapter 8
Unique Forms of Writing

Lesson 8.1
Writing Across the Disciplines

All your body's systems (circulatory, respiratory, digestive, etc.) depend on each other for optimal function. The body can't work effectively without cooperation among these vital operations; each uniquely supports the others.

The same applies to the college curriculum; all disciplines are interdependent. In particular, English courses emphasize writing because it's is a vital function present in all other courses. Even if you're not an English major, your success in other courses depends, in part, on strong writing skills.

Both in school and at work, instructors and supervisors will require a variety of written texts that have unique **purposes**. While a lab report, a business proposal, and a literary analysis are vastly different in purpose, they share common key features.

In this lesson, you will learn about the following aspects of writing across the curriculum:

English in Other Disciplines
Writing Expectations across Disciplines
Writing Tasks across Disciplines

English in Other Disciplines

Before you write anything, for any course, you must be clear on your purpose for writing. Here's a list of some common writing purposes.

- **Responding**
- **Proposing**
- **Describing**
- **Analyzing**

- **Summarizing**
- **Discussing**
- **Arguing**
- **Evaluating**

To learn more about these writing purposes, see Chapter 1.

Writing Environment: Academic

In your English courses, you will be assigned writing tasks that emphasize purposes and sometimes combine them. For instance, analyzing and evaluating are often used together in a literary analysis. English courses help you practice and refine these writing skill sets so that you can apply them in other situations.

Reflection Question
What types of writing tasks and purposes would you expect to encounter in the following courses?
- Business administration
- Psychology
- Engineering
- History
- Chemistry

Instructors and employers across the spectrum agree that these writing skills are essential:

- Write coherently, clearly, and concisely
- Observe the conventions of written language
- Analyze and evaluate data and other field-specific content
- Develop thesis and purpose statements
- Form compelling arguments and support them
- Organize ideas strategically
- Cite sources appropriately

Common Writing Assignments

Let's start by examining some of the common writing assignments in an English course.

On Your Own

For each of the following common English writing tasks, add another discipline in which this writing skill/purpose may be useful. The first one is done for you.

Task	Purpose	Other Discipline
Argument/Persuasion	Make a claim and defend it	History
Evaluation	Follow criteria to make a value or merit-based judgment	
Comparison	Examine similarities/differences between two or more things	
Narrative	Tell a story (fiction or non-fiction)	
Proposal	Explore a problem and recommend a solution	
Annotated Bibliography	Evaluate and cite sources	

Each of these processes and writing tasks is intended to develop thinking and writing skills that apply to other disciplines.

> Group Activity
>
> With your group, make a list of the courses you have taken that required written assignments. Which assignments were similar to the ones above? How were the requirements different for that course, and how did you approach the writing task?

Writing Expectations Across Disciplines

Each academic field and professional industry involves unique tasks and purposes. For instance, business writing often involves sales and promotion, writing for engineering is more technically focused, and writing for psychology often involves making recommendations based on interpretation of data.

However, strong organization, well-supported claims, and logical reasoning are important features of writing for any discipline or professional setting. Additionally, many of the skills required in each discipline overlap.

> Reflection Question
>
> Consider the day-to-day activities of your anticipated career. What do you believe are some necessities for writing in that field? What happens to communication when these features are missing?

Business

Whether you own a small business or work for a large corporation, and whether you're communicating with a client, superior, or members of your own team, it's important to be clear, focused, and considerate of your **audience's** time. A lengthy or unfocused memo or proposal can result in missed opportunities.

The following skills are essential in most professional writing:

- Include a clear purpose statement or thesis near the end of your introduction
- Use organization and **transitions**
- Use subheadings for sections
- Keep paragraphs at 250 words or fewer
- Keep sentences under 35 words
- Make sure your argument is focused
- Support your claims with case studies and data

History

Historians must be vigilant about comparing and evaluating reliable sources. Bias must be recognized and reported clearly. Additionally, mastering cause and effect, comparison, and accurate citation are imperative. Law and political science have similar expectations.

Writing skills required in history courses often include the following:

- Be thorough and consistent
- Use a focused topic and argument
- Critically analyze sources
- Master the factual material
- Use correct grammar, spelling, and organization
- Have original ideas regarding research and analysis
- Utilize **primary** and **secondary sources**
- Document all sources

Engineering

By nature, engineering is a highly technical field, so it's not surprising that engineering requires highly technical writing.

The following skills are needed in most engineering courses:

- Interpret figures and diagrams
- Use concise and precise language
- Write in complete sentences
- Follow logical thought sequences toward solutions
- Provide a clear course of action for readers
- Use terms correctly and consistently
- Provide valid evidence to support claims
- Identify unfamiliar terms and concepts
- Use standard conventions for presenting figures and appendices

Writing Environment: Professional

Speaking or presenting a paper at an engineering conference is a great opportunity for an engineer to be acknowledged as an industry leader. A highly specific, multi-page submissions template is required just to be considered for this honor. The entire application template can be accessed at www.ieee.org.

Psychology

Much of the writing in psychology involves analyzing the results of research and case studies and making supportable recommendations based on those results.

These writing skills are necessities:

- Develop logical arguments
- Support arguments with scientific sources
- Write clearly
- Use good organization and grammar
- Properly cite sources
- Present ideas and arguments concisely
- Interpret and utilize evidence from experimental research

Sciences

Lab sciences and medical studies require accurate recording and observation of data and processes. Interpretations of the data must also be well-documented and supported.

Instructors expect these skills:

- Write strong, focused description of content
- Understand the scientific process
- Clearly state the scientific question
- Thoroughly describe methods of study and results
- Provide context before introducing new information
- Use correct grammar and spelling
- Use simple, clear sentences
- Utilize strong transitions

Writing Tasks across Disciplines

Business

Most jobs require some type of writing, so we'll start by examining common business writing tasks. Often, the goal of professional writing is to sell a product, improve quality of life, or propose solutions to problems. Every business has its own frequently used documents, such as quarterly financial reports, proposals, marketing plans, and memos. Each of these has its own purpose and audience.

Business depends on profits. Making sales is key, and because selling requires persuasion, many business tasks include elements of **rhetoric**, which is persuasive language that appeals to *ethos* (trustworthiness), *pathos* (emotion), and *logos* (logic).

To learn more about rhetorical appeals, see Lesson 6.4.

On Your Own

For the following list of professional writing tasks, write *yes* or *no* in the far-right column when you suspect rhetoric would be part of the writing strategy.

Text	Purpose	Use of Rhetoric?
Cover letter and résumé	Gain an interview or job.	
Blog post	Promote your business.	
Memo/email	Inform your colleagues of recent research.	
Proposal	Recommend action.	
Marketing plan	Make a case for a new campaign.	

Business writing tasks may *appear* straightforward and informative, but rhetoric almost always plays a part. Every business is promoting something.

Writing Environment: Professional

A press release informs potential clients about events or recent accomplishments, but it also subtly reminds your audience of what your business has accomplished, how you've helped the community, and what you can offer the reader. Notice the promotional phrasing in this example:

FOR IMMEDIATE RELEASE

Contact: Lorne Hapley, Services Director

Phone: 238-234-2688

Email: lhapley@care4you.com

Care4You Announces New Website

Improved access to customized, home health care options for the elderly

Atlanta, GA (2/1/15) – Care4You, a senior home health service, has announced the deployment of a new website, Care4You.com. The Atlanta-based home health provider offers a comprehensive menu of medical and non-medical assistance for homebound and disabled seniors that make care and recuperation more comfortable. The new site features easy access to a menu of care services and contact points.

Services Director Lorne Hapley commented, "We're very proud of our new web presence. We expect this to build awareness of the convenience and affordability of senior home care options." Hapley further indicated that often, an aging parent or loved one needs companionship and safety supervision more than they require medical services. "Care4You offers both types of services, and we can easily customize a plan to meet all the client's needs, for comfort, convenience and peace of mind."

The citation format for business courses may be **APA**, **CMS**, **CSE**, or **MLA**. If the preferred format is not indicated on your assignment or course syllabus, be sure to ask your professor.

> To learn more about the basics of MLA, APA, CMS and CSE, see Lessons 7.8-7.11.

> Group Activity
>
> With your group, discuss which professional writing tasks you expect to use in your chosen career paths. How will these texts be different for each career? Which purposes will be most and least applicable for your field?

History

History is not an objective field of study; **bias** is common. As a result, history instructors place special emphasis on evaluating the **credibility** of sources. Being able to explain why a source is reliable is extremely important in this field, especially with all the sources available.

Reading historical sources critically requires recognizing similarities and differences between multiple sources that focus on one event. Historical writing is also detail-oriented and relies heavily on evaluation and analysis.

Here are some common texts and purposes in history courses:

Text	Purpose
Research paper	Provide reliable information and comparison of sources.
Biographical analysis	Research and assess the life and impact of a historical figure.
Document analysis	Critically evaluate and analyze a **primary source**.
Annotated bibliography	Assess and summarize sources and content.

History courses often adhere to CMS guidelines. Consult your syllabus or assignment requirements, and if no preference is indicated, ask your professor which is appropriate.

Engineering/Technology

The technical report is one of the most common texts for engineers. Technical reports can have many parts, including a letter of transmittal, an abstract, an executive summary, the report body, diagrams, figures, tables, and floor plans. It is usually submitted as a plan or proposal for a specific building or improvement project. While figures and data are presented in many forms, the report body interprets the data and proposes the plan as a solution for a problem. Technical justification and results provide support.

In any engineering text, the language should be simple and straightforward, detailing each segment of the project as specifically as possible.

Text	Purpose
Technical report	Analyze and describe a problem; then, prescribe a solution.
Article critique	Critically analyze and evaluate a design while writing with sources.
Process manual	Describe procedures or other how-to sequences in a user-friendly way.
Journal article	Present findings, including analysis, procedure, and recommendation. Conform to regulated submission requirements.

For engineering courses, refer to the IEEE Citation guidelines. For some technology related coursework, the Mayfield Guide may be preferred. Check your assignment or syllabus to determine which applies, or ask your instructor for clarification.

> Reflection Question
>
> You may have encountered technical writing in a user manual while trying to install an appliance, repair an electronic device, or assemble furniture. If so, you've read a simplified version of the style of writing engineers do. What did you find frustrating about reading this type of text? What do you think would be most challenging about writing in this format?

Psychology

Psychological studies are based on observation, empirical evidence, and lab results. Psychologists often write for journals and publications, and they also **summarize** their findings with individual clients.

The writing assignments for this field often summarize, analyze, and evaluate clinical reports for the purpose of recommending treatment. In addition to the texts listed below, psychologists also write research proposals and request grants for funding.

Text	Purpose
Case study	Provide in-depth analysis of human subject, diagnosis, and intervention.
Lab report	Record details, processes, and results of an experiment.
Psychological evaluation	Analyze data from formal assessment and recommend treatment.
Position paper	Take a position on a topic: analyze, argue, and defend with evidence.

APA citation format is usually required in psychology coursework and other social sciences like sociology and anthropology.

Other Sciences

While scientific writing may appear to be factual, objective, and data-driven, it's important to remember that the data acquired in any scientific study must be interpreted by humans. As a result, there is always room for bias, error, and misapplied conclusions.

Writing to interpret data is often analytical, persuasive, and argumentative. It uses *logos* to argue for certain interpretations of data.

On Your Own

For the following list of scientific writing tasks, write *yes* or *no* in the far-right column when you suspect rhetoric would be part of the writing strategy.

Writing Task	Purpose	Use of Rhetoric?
Research paper	Read, analyze, and present conclusions with reliable support.	
Case study	Report research, interpret results, and provide a recommendation.	
Lab report	Document procedures and results of experiments.	
Journal article	Defend a new theory based on results of research.	

Some sciences require APA style while others expect CMS. Chemistry requires ACS (American Chemical Society) style. Consult with your instructor or your syllabus to be clear.

Lesson Wrap-up

Key Terms

Analyze: the process of breaking something into parts and using inferences to interpret it

APA Style: a citation and documentation style published by the American Psychological Association

Argument: a reason why you should think or act a certain way

Audience: the person or people meant to read and interpret a text

Bias: a person's opinions and preferences

CMS: a citation and documentation style known as the Chicago Manual of Style

Credibility: what makes something or someone believable

CSE Style: a citation and documentation style published by the Council of Science Editors

Ethos: an argument based on the speaker's authority, credibility, or trustworthiness

Evaluate: the process of judging something based on a set of criteria

Logos: an argument based on logic

MLA Style: the research style guide created by the Modern Language Association

Pathos: an argument based on emotion

Primary Source: a first-hand account such as an interview, photograph, or research study

Purpose: the goal of a text

Purpose Statement: a sentence that tells the audience exactly what points will be covered in a longer text

Rhetoric: persuasive writing or reasoning with appeals to *ethos, pathos,* and *logos*

Secondary Source: a text that discusses a primary source

Summary: a small, generalized overview of a larger amount of information

Thesis Statement: the concise sentence or group of sentences that expresses the main idea of a longer work

Transition: a word, phrase, or sentence that shows a relationship between ideas

Writing to Analyze: a writing purpose achieved by examining something you have read or studied

Writing to Argue: a writing purpose that convinces the audience to adopt a belief or take an action

Writing to Describe: a writing purpose that explains the appearance of someone or something using words that appeal to the senses

Writing to Discuss: a writing purpose that presents issues or interprets something you have read or studied

Writing to Evaluate: a writing purpose achieved by creating for judging something you have read or studied

Writing to Propose: a writing purpose achieved by giving suggestions and solutions to an issue or problem

Writing to Respond: a writing purpose that expresses personal thoughts and opinions about a text

Writing to Summarize: a writing purpose that presents a small, generalized overview of a larger amount of information

Writing Application: Writing Across the Disciplines

The following is an annotated bibliography for an American history class. It analyzes multiple issues of a newspaper originally printed in 1759.

Sample 1: History

Newspaper Bibliography

Title: New York Gazette (1759)

Editor: appears to be W. Weyman (also the printer)

Place of publication: New York

Frequency of publication: weekly (every Monday)

Special issues: No self-contained special issues, but occasional postscripts of about two pages added to the end of a regular paper.

This assignment relies heavily on analysis to evaluate the credibility of a primary source.

Format:

Every issue has, on average, four pages with three columns on each page. Generally, foreign news is listed first, local news second, and advertisements last. However, this system is not consistent for every issue; advertisements or notices are sometimes scattered among articles. Bold, large typeface is used to set off advertisements, locations of news sources, and key words or phrases. Italics are also used to indicate news from different dates. Except for the emblem in the masthead, the royal coat of arms of England, there are no illustrations.

Content:

The news content, as well as the ads, for the most part seem tailored to middle-aged men in the middle- to upper- class. However, it is easy to imagine these men taking note of important information to share with their families or reading the newspaper out loud to others. Women have no voice and very little presence in the Gazette aside from a small advertisement for a wet nurse.

There is no statement that clarifies what information is reprinted from other sources, but letters from all parts of the world seem to be a major source of news.

Four-Month Sample Percentage:

Foreign news: 50%

Advertising: 40%

Local news: 8%

Literary & cultural submissions: 1%

Religious material: 1%

Public documents: 1%

Three Most Historically Significant Events:

July 30, 1759: "London, May 9 - The Pope has issued a decree, allowing the bible [sic] to be translated into the language of all the catholic [sic] countries."

June 4, 1759: "Philadelphia, May 31." This small section mentions a treaty between Sir William Johnson, presumably a colonial authority figure, and an unspecified Indian nation. Among the prisoners they returned was a five-year-old girl. This short interlude provides a look into the hardships induced by the French & Indian War.

June 4, 1759: "London, March 3." Describes the investigation into the attempted assassination attempt by the Jesuits of the Portuguese king.

The bibliography begins by explaining the newspaper's basic characteristics. The author paid close attention to the details.

The author uses inference to draw conclusions about the source's intended audience.

Selecting specific stories to analyze requires thoroughly reading the entire source.

According to letters from Lisbon, over five hundred people were imprisoned.

Other Interesting/Unusual/Significant Items:

July 30, 1759: "Since our last we have received the following Letter, being as circumstantial of the Affair at Oswego the 7th and 6th Instant as need be, and is far more particular than any yet received." A grueling firsthand account of the conflicts between colonists and the American Indians/French.

June 11, 1759: "London, March 13 - A matter of a vessel lately arrived from North America, is taken up on suspicion of having been the death of a young Lad, who had shipp'd himself on board in order to return to his Parents in London, from whence he went some time ago." This bit of news is mysterious. The fate of the man, and his original purpose in America, is unconfirmed. It's possible that he was a former convict trying to return home after fulfilling his time of indentured servitude.

June 18, 1759: "Run away last Tuesday, from John Rikor, of Horseneck, a Mulatto Woman, named, Sarah Street, very much pock-marked, has long curled Hair, and a Piece of her Ear cut off. Whoever takes up and secures the said Mulatto, so that the said Rickor [sic] may have her again, shall haoe zos [sic] Reward, and all reasonable Charges paid by John Welch, in Beaver-Street, New York, or by the said Rikor in Horseneck." This ad raises some interesting questions. Considering the status of multi-ethnic people in early America, what relationship did Sarah have with Rikor, why did she run away, and why is he so eager to regain her? What happened to her ear? It's very possible that she ran away to escape abuse.

The author asks questions, considers possible bias, and makes historical connections.

June 18, 1759: "Annapolis (in Maryland) June 7, 1759." Describes a runaway "Convict Servant Man," who had a surprisingly high set of skills: jewelling, engraving, and writing.

July 2, 1759: "Charlestown, in South-Carolina, May 12." Describes violence between Indian tribes, particularly the Chickasaw and Shawnee. In an attempt to draw out the Shawnee for a fight, the Chickasaw even tied a Shawnee prisoner woman to a stake and set her on fire.

July 2, 1759: "Charlestown, in South Carolina, June 9." Describes the booming "silk culture" in Georgia: "the raw silk exported from Georgia sells at London from Two to Three Shillings in the pound more than that bought from any other part of the world." It shows that the colonies were gaining attention for their commodities.

July 2, 1759: "Garrat Noel & Comp." A book, stationary, and magazine subscription store announces that it is merging with a coffee-house, demonstrating the relationship in the 18ᵗʰ century between coffee and news/information.

July 30, 1759: "London, March 13." Two rather humorous and odd accounts of men who died. One refused to shave his beard until he received his promised inheritance, and even on his deathbed refused to let anyone shave his beard or improve his personal hygiene. The second man, a reverend, owned fifty dogs and was presumably drowned in chest-height water when they converged on him. These anecdotes could be fictional, factual, or a mixture of both.

Here, the author once again evaluates the credibility of the source.

The following scientific paper uses technical language and chronological order to describe the process of crude oil refraction for an audience that may not be experts in this topic.

Sample 2: Science

Refining Crude Oil

Crude oil is a fossil fuel, which means that it is made up of long-ago fossilized plants and animals. This also means that there is a limited amount. Once oil is found and actually mined, it must be refined or else it is useless. Crude oil can be made into and used to make many products, like diesel fuel, tar and asphalt, naphta, lubricating oils, kerosene, paraffin wax, petroleum coke, fuel oils, gasoline, and liquid petroleum gas (LPG). The byproducts of refining are used to make plastics, detergents, and polyester.

This paper is objective and driven by data. It does not make an argument or attempt to persuade the audience.

Crude oil, or petroleum, is basically comprised of hydrocarbons, a compound of hydrogen and carbon atoms. There are many types of hydrocarbons that need to be separated, thus refining the oil. The most significant kinds of hydrocarbons are paraffins, aromatics, and napthenes. Crude oil also contains inorganic salts, water, suspended solids (particles suspended in water), and water-soluble trace metals (extremely small amounts of metals that can be dissolved in water). These must be taken out to prevent problems later on. There are several categories and descriptions of crude oil. "Light" means that it has low density, and "heavy" means it has high density. If oil is "sweet," it contains very little sulfur, while "sour" means there is a high sulfur count. One barrel of crude oil can make 19.5 gallons of gasoline, 9.2 gallons of distillate fuel oil, 4.1 gallons of jet fuel, 2.3 gallons of residual fuel oil, 1.9 gallons of liquefied refinery gases, 1.8 gallons of coke, 1.3 gallons of asphalt and road oil, 1.2 gallons of petrochemical feedstocks, 0.5 gallons of lubricants, 0.2 gallons of kerosene, and 0.3 gallons of other (*Texas Oil & Gas Association*).

Even though this paper does not make an argument, it still analyzes a process and organizes it clearly.

There are several crude oil refining methods. The first step is fractional distillation. First, the mixture is heated using highly pressurized steam. The temperatures can reach 1112° Fahrenheit. When the mixture boils, the vapors rise into the fractional distillation column filled with trays. These trays have holes that allow the vapor to pass through and collect the liquid at different heights. When the gas reaches a point in the column where the column is the same temperature as a material's boiling point, it condenses into a liquid, which is collected by one of the trays (a fraction). Once the liquid is collected, it will go to a storage tank to cool more or move on to finish being refined.

The second step of refining is changing one "fraction" into another. This can be done in three ways: "breaking large hydrocarbons into smaller pieces (cracking), combining smaller pieces to make larger ones (unification), [or] rearranging various pieces to make desired hydrocarbons (alteration)" (Freudenrich). Cracking can be done two ways. The first way is thermally. Hydrocarbons are heated up until they break apart. For ethane, butane, and naptha, this can be done using steam. The end result is ethylene and benzene, which are used to make chemicals. A second way to crack hydrocarbons thermally is by visbreaking. Residue from the distillation tower is heated to 900° F, cooled using gasoline oil, and quickly burned, again in the distillation tower. This process reduces the thickness of heavy oils and makes tar. Finally, the third thermal cracking method is called coking. Residue from the distillation tower is heated above temperatures of 900° F until it cracks into gasoline, naptha, and heavy oil. Afterwards, a nearly purely carbon mixture is left (the coke) and sold. A second way of cracking is catalytic. This process uses a catalyst to speed up the cracking. Some catalysts are aluminum hydrosilicate, zeolite, silica-aluminum, and bauxite. Fluid catalytic cracking uses a hot liquid (up to 1000 ° F) that cracks heavy gas oils into gasoline and diesel oil. Hydrocracking is quite similar to fluid catalytic cracking but it uses higher pressure, lower temperatures, and different catalysts. Hydrogen gas is used to crack heavy oil into gas and kerosene (jet fuel). After this long process, the end products go through a second fractional distillation column to separate the different oils. The third step in crude oil fractionation is "unification."

Unification combines smaller hydrocarbons to make large ones. The most common way to do this is by catalytic reforming, which uses a platinum-rhenium mixture to make light naptha into aromatics. Those are then used in blending gas and making other chemicals. A significant by-product of catalytic reforming is hydrogen gas.

The third way to refine oil is by "alteration." Alteration basically means rearranging hydrocarbons into different pieces. This is usually done by alkylation. Compounds with a low molecular weight are

The author consistently uses chronological order to methodically break down and describe each process.

The author uses a balance of technical terms and explanation, so the intended audience probably isn't made up of experts on this topic.

mixed in the presence of a catalyst, which makes high octane hydrocarbons, which are then used in gasoline blends to prevent knocking in the engine. Finally, all the different products are treated to remove impurities, cooled, and mixed. Most refineries use large amounts of water to cool both equipment and oil. The oil is usually transported throughout the factory through metal pipelines as well.

Lesson 8.2

Visual and Digital Arguments

In today's everyday, professional, and academic environments, methods of communication have become increasingly diverse. **Arguments** can be made and supported with writing, pictures, memes, tweets, videos, and more.

While there are many ways to make an argument, the foundation is always **credibility:** what makes someone or something believable. Credibility is one of the three Cs of an argument:

1. Claim

2. Clarity

3. Credibility

The **claim** is the main position presented in the argument. **Clarity** is the clear presentation of information. Once you've got the three C's down, you'll need evidence to support it all. **Evidence** is the information used to support a main idea.

So, how do visual and digital arguments differ from one another and from other argument formats? Why would you consider presenting your argument in one of these formats? This lesson will provide answers to these questions.

> In this lesson, you will learn about the following aspects of visual and digital arguments:
>
> Four Types of Arguments
> Analyzing and Developing Visual Arguments
> Analyzing and Developing Digital Arguments

Four Types of Arguments

Throughout your life, you've already had extensive experience with arguments. You've probably utilized written and spoken arguments the most. However, there are two other argument types that were mentioned in the introduction: the visual argument and the digital argument.

A **visual argument** uses an image without extensive accompanying text to make a claim and support it with evidence. The purpose of the image is to persuade the viewer, and the impact of the visual is immediate.

A **digital argument** is a multimedia argument that includes many methods of presentation. A digital argument could include some or all of the following: text, photos, editorial cartoons, music, and sound effects.

Writing Environment: Professional

At work, you may be tasked with explaining why you or your team deserves more: more money, more time, or more responsibility. Imagine you work in the advertising department at a major company and have been asked to explain why you should be given greater responsibility. You are considering whether to use a visual or digital argument. How might these two formats differ? What would be the advantage of each?

As we've reviewed in the introduction, there are elements that all argument formats have in common, but there are also differences. Consider the chart below that compares and contrasts the four types of arguments.

Format	Use of Evidence + 3 Cs	Delivery
Visual Argument	Always	Primarily uses images
Digital Argument	Always	Uses images and text together
Written Argument	Always	Usually text only; occasionally will include images
Spoken Argument	Always	Oral communication; might include images

> **Helpful Hint**
> Regardless of the type of argument you're using, always deliver it with confidence. If you seem hesitant, you'll fail to establish credibility, and the audience will be less likely to believe your claim.

Analyzing and Developing Visual Arguments

What comes to mind when you think of the word *argument?* Perhaps it's one of these scenarios:

- students in a debate
- an editorial in a digital or print newspaper
- coworkers making a presentation

When it comes to arguments, people might think of something written or spoken, but it's less common for people to think of an image standing alone.

A visual argument uses an image to persuade the viewer. This may sound simple, but a strong visual argument is complex. Closer examination should reveal multiple layers of meaning.

This argument format is useful when there's a limited amount of space or time in which to make an argument.

On Your Own

Where do you expect to see visual arguments? Read the list below and add any more ideas you can come up with.

Advertisement
Magazine cover
Poster/flyer
Chart/graph
Editorial cartoon

Helpful Hint

When you evaluate a visual argument, avoid the temptation to take it at face value. The creator of a visual argument is trying to persuade you to believe a claim, but you are not required to agree with the claim(s) represented by the visual. You must carefully evaluate a visual argument just as you would any other type of argument.

At first, it can seem daunting to present a visual argument. However, it is possible! Use the questions below to **analyze** a visual argument and develop your own:

Does the visual have a title or caption? If so, how does it help you understand the visual?

Is there any text within the visual? How does it help you understand the visual?

Are there any characters in the visual? If so, who are they, and what are they doing?

What is the overall scene in the visual?

Are there symbols in the visual? What do they represent?

What part of the visual stands out most? Why?

Once you've gathered your responses to the previous questions, translate your analysis into meaning.

Here are some follow-up questions to ask yourself:

What is the subject of the visual?

What is the argument?

What claim does the visual assert about the argument?

How does the visual support this claim?

> **Helpful Hint**
> Although a visual argument doesn't have extensive accompanying text, it might have some text within the visual, a title, and/or a caption.

Let's take a look at an example of an analyzed visual argument.

If you don't vote . . .

Initial Questions:

Does the visual have a title or caption? Yes

If so, how does it help you understand the visual? I can tell the visual relates to voting.

Is there any text within the visual? No

Are there any characters in the visual? No

What is the overall scene in the visual? The U.S. flag appears to be unraveling.

Are there symbols in the visual? The symbol is the flag.

What does the symbol represent? The flag represents the United States.

Follow-up Questions:

What is the subject of the visual? Voting in the United States

What is the purpose of the argument? To persuade people that voting is important

What claim does the visual assert about the argument? If people don't vote, the country will unravel.

How does the visual support this claim? The visual shows that the flag is unraveling, which represents the country unraveling and falling apart.

Group Activity

As a group, take a look at this editorial cartoon (http://www.loc.gov/pictures/item/2008661753/). In 1832, U.S. President Andrew Jackson vetoed a bill passed by Congress. The bill related to the re-charter of the Bank of the United States. Using the previous sets of questions, analyze the cartoon as a group.

Writing Environment: Everyday

Commercials are one example of a common visual argument. Recall the times you've see an ad for a hair product, and the model's hair looks flawless. Did you immediately assume that the hair product being advertised was the best on the market? Did you question if it would work well for *you*? Always evaluate any type of argument through a critical lens.

Analyzing and Developing Digital Arguments

Because technology has developed so rapidly, digital arguments are still a relatively new form. Remember, a digital argument is a multimedia argument that includes multiple methods of presentation. It does not rely solely on text, speech, or images. Instead, it can draw from many resources. This makes it easier to collect powerful evidence that supports your claim. This also means that digital arguments are useful for presenting complex information.

Here are some of the resource types for a digital argument:

Resources for Digital Arguments	Examples
Text	a list of crime statistics
Videos	a video of an investigation at a crime scene
Photos	photos from a crime scene
Editorial cartoons	an editorial cartoon focused on insufficient punishment for convicted criminals
Sketches	a sketch depicting criminals walking out of a courtroom and smiling
Music	a melancholy song
Recorded speech	a judge announcing a light sentence for a criminal

Use the following questions to analyze digital arguments and develop your own.

What is the topic of the digital argument?

What is the argument's claim?

What types of resources are used in the digital argument?

How does each resource provide evidence that supports the claim and persuades the audience?

Which resources are most effective? Why?

Which resources are least effective? Why?

How are the resources combined to create a cohesive argument?

Helpful Hint

Because digital arguments have multiple components, it's difficult to notice and understand them all at once. If possible, review digital arguments several times. For example, if you're analyzing a commercial, watch it once and pay attention to the words only. Then, watch it again and pay attention to the images only. You may notice things on the third or fourth viewing that you hadn't noticed before.

Group Activity

With members of your group, search online to locate a digital argument that you consider strong. Then, use the previous questions to analyze the argument as a group. Discuss how and why this activity showed you the power of an effective digital argument.

Writing Environment: Academic

Imagine you are taking a marketing class, and you're asked to advertise a fundraiser. You can create a digital argument that uses emotional music and captivating photos to get your audience's attention. There are many effective uses for digital arguments in the classroom. Next time you have the option to choose an assignment's format, consider how a digital argument could enhance your purpose.

Helpful Hint

While digital arguments allow for a variety of resource types, refrain from including a resource just to increase the number you're using. For example, if music doesn't enhance the mood, support your claim, and effectively persuade your audience, you don't have to include it. All parts of a digital argument should clearly support your claim and work well together.

Lesson Wrap Up

Key Terms

Analyze: the process of breaking something into parts and using inferences to interpret it

Argument: a reason why you should think or act a certain way

Credibility: what makes something or someone believable

Claim: the writer's position or opinion of an issue

Clarity: the clear presentation of information

Digital Argument: an argument that uses many methods of presentation to make a claim and support it with evidence

Evidence: a piece of information, also called a supporting detail, that is used to support a main idea

Visual Argument: an argument that uses one or more visuals without extensive accompanying text to make a claim and support it with evidence

Writing Application: Visual & Digital Arguments

Visual Arguments

Take a look at these visual arguments. What claims are they making? What causes do they seem to support? Use the questions from the lesson to analyze each visual. Then, compare your answers to the ones below each image.

Visual Argument 1

Initial Questions:

Does the visual have a title or caption? *No*

Is there any text within the visual? *No*

Are there any characters in the visual? *Yes, a person wearing what looks like army fatigues*

What is the overall scene in the visual? *Someone with his or her back to the camera is saluting the American flag.*

Are there symbols in the visual? *The flag could be a symbol; the action of saluting and the soldier could also be symbols.*

What does the symbol represent? *The flag probably represents the United States and patriotism. The soldier represents America's military personnel, and the salute represents respect.*

Follow-up Questions:

What is the subject of the visual? *It seems like the subject is the military and patriotism.*

What is the purpose of the argument? *To persuade people to respect the U.S. military*

What claim does the visual assert about the argument? *The U.S. military is vital to being an American.*

How does the visual support this claim? *The visual shows a saluting soldier in front of the American flag, which communicates a feeling of patriotism. It honors both America and the military.*

Visual Argument 2

Initial Questions:

Does the visual have a title or caption? *No*

Is there any text within the visual? *Yes, it says, "Say no to war."*

Are there any characters in the visual? *No*

What is the overall scene in the visual? *A mushroom cloud rises into the sky.*

Are there symbols in the visual? *The mushroom cloud could be a symbol.*

What does the symbol represent? *Nuclear warfare or warfare in general.*

Follow-up Questions:

What is the subject of the visual? *War*

What is the purpose of the argument? *To persuade people not to engage in warfare.*

What claim does the visual assert about the argument? *War is violent, so people should not fight.*

How does the visual support this claim? *The visual uses a red mushroom cloud to indicate violence and destruction. It uses large, blocky font to emphasize the words* no *and* war.

Digital Arguments

Follow the links to view two digital arguments. What claims are they making? What causes do they seem to support? Use the questions from the lesson to analyze each one. Then, compare your answers to the ones below each link.

Digital Argument 1

Link: https://www.youtube.com/watch?v=ye8QpjSlfYo

What is the topic of the digital argument? *A specific type of beer*

What is the argument's claim? *The voice-over claims that Miller Lite is the original light beer and tastes best. The images seem to claim that if you drink Miller Lite, you'll have a good time.*

What types of resources are used in the digital argument? *Voice-over narration, video/images, and music.*

How does each resource provide evidence that supports the claim and persuades the audience? *The voice-over supports the claim by describing Miller Lite. The person speaking has a decisive voice that is persuasive. The accompanying video is of young, attractive people talking and laughing around a bonfire. This is persuasive because it implies that you might encounter this situation if you drink the beer. The music is catchy and includes clapping, which suggests a feeling of community and excitement.*

Which resources are most effective? Why? *I think the video is most effective, followed by the voice-over.*

Which resources are least effective? Why? *I think all the resources are effective, but removing the music probably wouldn't change the commercial's persuasiveness.*

How are the resources combined to create a cohesive argument? *They are all played at one time to create a single commercial. The music is timed to sync with the images in the video, but the narration is slightly louder than the music.*

Digital Argument 2

Link: https://www.youtube.com/watch?v=bR7nLertwFk

What is the topic of the digital argument? *A particular type of alcohol and drinking in general*

What is the argument's claim? *Excessive drinking can lead to child neglect, violence, and addiction.*

What types of resources are used in the digital argument? *Voice-over narration, a narrative video, statistics and facts about alcoholism in Sweden, and music*

How does each resource provide evidence that supports the claim and persuades the audience? *The voice-over narration supports the claim by stating the facts and statistics about drinking. The music, which at first sounds peaceful, becomes melancholy later in the ad. The video supports the narration by depicting a child, a bar scuffle, and police officers entering the bar. All of these things persuade the audience that drinking leads to negative outcomes.*

Which resources are most effective? Why? *I think the all parts of the argument are effective.*

Which resources are least effective? Why? *None; they all work together to create a strong argument.*

How are the resources combined to create a cohesive argument? *They are all played at once; however, the narration, video, and music all begin on a positive note and then become negative at the same time. This creates a surprising twist that catches the audience off-guard and strengthens the argument. The sudden change in the commercial's tone could parallel the sudden consequences of drinking too much.*

Lesson 8.3

Oral Presentations

TED talks are entertaining, informative, and inspiring. These short presentations from international leaders and innovators focus on research and discoveries in technology, education, and design. The speakers' passion and confidence are infectious!

Public speaking is a valuable way to spread information and ideas. Image courtesy of Wikimedia Commons.

Some people make public speaking look easy. However, just like written texts, a successful presentation takes many hours of preparation.

Many people fear public speaking because of the potential for humiliation or embarrassment. There's a lot of pressure. What if you mispronounce words, get off track, run out of time, or look foolish? Don't panic! Organization, preparation, and practice can help you avoid these obstacles.

This lesson will teach you the following strategies:

How to Develop a Compelling Oral Presentation
How to Use Visual Aids and Nonverbal Signals
How Overcome Presentation Anxiety

How to Develop a Compelling Oral Presentation

Oral presentations are common in college courses because giving them is an essential skill in the professional world. Of course, job interviews are one form of oral presentation, but even after you've secured a position, you'll need to share information with colleagues or clients. In many ways, an effective oral presentation is similar to writing a compelling essay. Each of the following elements is essential:

- ✓ Clear, strategic organization
- ✓ Clear, well-defined **purpose**
- ✓ Clear transitions between points

- ✓ Strong **supporting details**
- ✓ Awareness and inclusion of your **audience**
- ✓ Rhetorical appeals (*ethos, pathos* and **logos**)

To learn more about rhetorical appeals, see Lesson 5.5.

Create Effective Introductions

Written essays begin with a compelling introduction that acknowledges the audience and establishes a clear purpose. In oral presentations, the introduction is even more important because people tend to remember beginnings and endings most clearly. Additionally, you must clearly state your purpose because your audience can't go back and re-read your **thesis** like they could when reading a paper.

On Your Own

Many strong presentation introductions include the following components. Read through and write in your own ideas.

Greeting and recognition of your audience	Your name and credentials
Topic and its relevance to the audience	What to expect: the order of your information
How long you'll be speaking	A hook or engaging activity

One purpose of the **introduction** is to set the audience's expectations. First, greet them and briefly tell them who you are. Use *ethos* (the appeal to credibility) to help the audience accept your authority. You can also use *pathos* (the appeal to emotion) to show that you understand the audience and their needs.

Second, remember that your audience probably isn't as familiar with the topic as you are, so provide the necessary background information.

Let's take a look at the example below; every word serves an important purpose:

> "Good afternoon, ladies and gentlemen, fellow clinicians and care providers. I'm Dr. Claire Pendleton from the Telfair Institute. I've been invited to share some of the findings of my research on autism. For the next fifteen minutes, we'll be discussing some of the suspected causes of autism, current treatment options, and initiatives for advancing the research."

This introduction accomplishes the following purposes:

- Greets and acknowledges audience (establishes *pathos*)
- Introduces the speaker and her background (establishes *ethos*)
- Explains the purpose of the presentation
- Gives the audience a time frame

Another important purpose of your introduction is engaging your audience. Oral presentations offer a unique opportunity for interaction. No one likes to sit and be "talked at." They'll appreciate your efforts to facilitate a conversation rather than simply make a speech. However, this must be tailored for the audience. What works in one situation may be wasted in another environment. Here are some possible ideas:

- Poll the audience for their opinions
- Ask a probing question
- Ask someone to summarize what you've said
- Use movement (audience stands or sits to show agreement)
- Divide into groups for commonality
- Ask them to participate

Let's consider an example.

> "Good afternoon, everyone, and thanks for joining us. This afternoon we'll spend about thirty minutes discussing some of the zoning issues in our community and how they influence us. I'm Tami Shelton. I've served on the city council for two years, and I'm working toward a zoning plan we can all live with. How many of you drove here this afternoon? If you took the bus, may I ask why you chose public transportation? Can anybody share?"

Here, the speaker accomplishes the following goals:

- Introduces the topic
- Introduces herself and briefly shares her background
- Asks a question that involves the audience and makes it personal
- Asks for personal testimony about public transportation, validating audience experiences

---

Reflection Question

Think about the last presentation you participated in, such as an in-class lecture, training, or sales presentation. What do you remember about it? Was there anything that stood out to you? How did the speaker begin, get your attention, keep your attention, or lose your attention?

On Your Own

Based on the audience descriptions in the left column, brainstorm appropriate engagement activities in the right column.

Audience	Engagement Activities
A high school assembly of 300 students	
A fraternity fundraising committee	
A women's motivational conference	
A college course on business economics	
A training session for new sales associates	

Create an Outline

Similar to essay outlines, a **presentation outline** creates and guides the organization, depth, and sequence of the information.

> **Helpful Hint**
>
> Before you give a speech, plan and practice any interaction or questions you're planning to use. You could even test them on your friends or family members. You can't always predict what answers the real audience will give, but you can plan how you'll react and refocus the interaction to move the presentation forward.

Consider this scenario:

> David is sharing a new marketing plan for his company. He wants to involve other members of the department, so he begins with this question: "What would you say are the major problems we've encountered with our current marketing strategy?" Of course, answers will vary. David gathers this information and refers to it later as he outlines his proposal. He knows his key points, he anticipates the responses to his question, and he refers to them later.

Structuring your introduction can ensure that there's no time wasted and no crucial information missing. The same is true for outlining your content.

In this example, the speaker will be introducing sources of common minerals. After a simple introduction, he structures his presentation with the following outline. Pay attention to the notes he's written for himself in parentheses.

Outline for Eric's Presentation

1. **Igneous**: 2 types, formation process (spend 4-5 min. on this section)
   a. **Volcanic Igneous**: formed above the surface from cooling lava
      i. Obsidian, basalt, silica (point to images on slide)
      ii. (Share obsidian chunk and pass around to audience)
      iii. **Extrusive**: above the earth, less dense, smaller crystals
   b. **Plutonic Igneous**: formed from magma below the surface
      i. Granite, quartz (display images, explain)
      ii. **Intrusive**: formed inside the earth, denser, larger crystals
   c. Transition: "We'll come back to igneous rocks, but for now, let's look at another type."
2. **Sedimentary**: solidification of sediment; organic or from other rocks
   a. Formed from particles, shells, deposits, fossils (spend about 3 min. on this section)
      i. Shale, sandstone, limestone (point to images, explain properties and uses)
         1. Less dense, rougher, and may crumble more easily
   b. Transition: "While igneous and sedimentary are most common, both may be transformed."
3. **Metamorphic**: intense pressure and heat transform 2 types above, make denser
   a. **Contact metamorphism**: temperature-driven, partially melt from magma
      i. Compression diagram, slides with images of metamorphic stones (time: about 5 min.)
   b. **Regional metamorphism**: pressure-driven change deep inside earth
      i. Differences between shale and slate, limestone and marble
   c. (Review key terms)
   d. Transition: "It should be clear by now that . . . (prep for conclusion, collect rock samples)

This outline contains a breakdown of Eric's ideas at the topic, point, and example levels. The topic and point indicate key information, while examples include details and other supporting information.

On Your Own

The previous outline organized the content by rock type. What might be an appropriate organization strategy for the following topics? Brainstorm your ideas in the table below.

Topic	Organization
A new marketing plan for a public relations company	
The causes of global warming/climate change	
Reasons to vote for a political candidate	

Events leading up to the Vietnam War	
The development of smart phone technology	

Use Notecards

Notecards break your outline into manageable pieces. Use words, short statements, or phrases: just enough information to jog your memory. They should also serve as reminders of talking points, **anecdotes**, and key ideas.

Quickly refer to your notes, but don't read from them. Glance down quickly, recover your place, and move forward. The following is an example of a useful notecard. Notice the concise language, clear labeling, and prompts for gesturing. Of course, the speaker will go into more detail; the notecard simply reminds him or her what to cover.

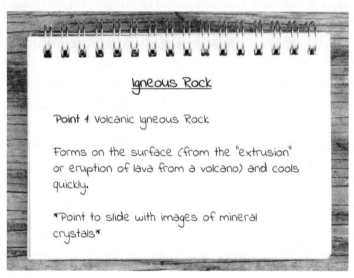

Helpful Hint

Color is another helpful cue. You can use color-coding to organize your cards at the topic/detail level or use a different color for each topic.

Notecards can also remind you of time limits. Include time limit notes for yourself, such as "be brief" or "two-minute max." Label any "extra" information—like anecdotes, data, or questions—on a back-up notecard to be used only if time allows.

Use Transitions

In oral presentations, transitions are very important. **Transitions** are words, phrases, or sentences that show relationships between ideas. Without clear transitions, your audience may become confused about how each of your topics relate to each other.

Consider the following common transitions you might use in a presentation:

- Similar to
- Next
- Additionally
- However
- First
- In contrast

To learn more about transitions, see Lesson 4.5.

In Eric's geological presentation, his outline and notecards remind him to transition between topics, sum up previous sections, and explain what to expect in the next section.

> **Helpful Hint**
>
> Pause 3-5 seconds before transitioning. You can even include this on your notecards as a reminder. Pausing emphasizes the separation between ideas and gives you time to take a breath. It also allows your audience to process the information you've just shared.

Writing Environment: Professional

Communication and cooperation are essential in every sector of the professional world. A confident, personable presenter is a valuable asset to a team. For example, you may be expected to give regular progress reports on a project or review plans for the upcoming quarter. You could be presenting to prospective clients, a classroom full of students, a board of investors and directors, or the state legislature. In any professional scenario, organization, planning, and practice are key for success.

> **Helpful Hint**
>
> Use technology to practice and improve your speech. Record yourself speaking, or even better, take a video. As you watch or listen to yourself, look for distracting habits like looking down, using filler words (*uh, ok, so, like*), or fidgeting. This strategy can help you develop your strengths and improve when necessary.

How to Use Visual Aids and Nonverbal Signals

There are some crucial differences between listening to information and reading words. Oral presentations have a few more moving parts to be aware of. Here, we'll focus on two important categories: visual aids and nonverbal signals.

Visual Aids

Visual aids can include any of the following things:

- Slide shows
- Graphics
- Charts and tables
- Videos
- Posters

- Handouts
- Props
- Demonstrations
- Dramatizations

Visuals should support your point but not *be* your point. Overly-elaborate slide shows or videos can end up dominating the presentation and confusing the audience.

Additionally, nothing says "unprepared" like reading your visual aids. Refer to them or point to them while looking at the audience. Don't turn your back and read from the screen. This suggests that you don't know what it says or that you've lost your place.

Finally, practice using your visual aids. For example, if you include charts and graphs in a slide show, rehearse how you'll explain them while pointing to the relevant data. Stand to the side to avoid blocking the audience's view.

Here are some tips for using different aids:

- If your presentation is instructional, consider a demonstration or how-to sequence
- Distributing copies of a one-page infographic may reinforce some of your key points
- A video of a relevant celebrity discussing your topic may generate interest
- Real items passed around for examination engage the audience
- Dramatization can infuse humor and make literary or historical topics more relatable

Writing Environment: Academic

Group presentations can provide great support because you're not up there alone. Here are some tips to consider when working with a group:

- Be sure everyone takes responsibility for some portion of the presentation.
- Practice together. Don't wait until the due date and assume that everyone has prepared. Schedule a group work session to rehearse at least twice before the presentation day, and rehearse your own portion alone outside of class too.
- Rehearse transitions carefully to introduce the next section and the next speaker.
- When you're not speaking, remain calm and focus on the colleague who is speaking. This subtly cues the audience to do the same.

Nonverbal Signals

During oral presentations, your movement, gestures, and facial expressions are visible to the audience, and they can affect your message whether you want them to or not. Subconscious tics, like rocking back and forth or crossing your arms, are distracting and may hurt your credibility.

Channel that nervous energy into gestures that express and emphasize your ideas. Consider the following commonly recognized gestures that reinforce communication.

Common Gesture	Suggests
Counting gestures: one, two, three fingers up	Listing reasons, items, or examples
Move hands to opposite sides	Showing opposing ideas or contrast
Pointing one finger up	This is an important point to remember

Both hands, palms together, vertically "slicing"	Showing order or sequence
Sweeping one hand out across the crowd	Communicates *everyone, all of you, most of you*
Placing one hand on the chest or heart	Communicates *for me personally, my own experience*
Open hands, palms up, out to sides	Openness, humility, and trustworthiness

On Your Own

Think of five gestures not listed in the previous table. What do they suggest, and when might you use them? Record your ideas in the table below.

Gesture	Suggests

How to Overcome Presentation Anxiety

Vocal Placement

Some people don't like the sound of their own voice, and nerves don't help because they make your throat tense and constricted. However, conscious relaxation can help tremendously; stage actors and singers use this technique. Breathe deeply to control the release of air from your lungs. This relaxes your nerves, lowers your heart rate, expands your lungs, and relaxes the tension in your vocal chords, making it easier for you to speak. Also, consider a vocal warm-up. This may involve humming, yawning, and/or tongue-twisters.

Further Resources

For more information on voice techniques and breathing exercises, check out this PDF from Toastmasters.
http://www.toastmasters.org/~/media/B7D5C3F93FC3439589BCBF5DBF521132.ashx

Eye Contact

Looking out at your audience conveys confidence. However, you may feel uncomfortable making direct eye contact with the audience. If so, at least look in the audience's direction frequently, not at the ceiling or floor.

Try directing your gaze to the left; then, look slightly to the right a few comments later. Choose another point toward the center of the crowd. Plan and mark your gestures, movements, and shifts of focus; your audience won't know it's planned.

Glance occasionally at someone you know and feel comfortable with. If you don't know anyone in the crowd, glance toward a particular spot in the room: a plant, an empty chair, or even the shoulder of a random audience member.

Smile

You don't have to be bubbly or make jokes. In fact, depending on the context, this may be inappropriate or seem unnatural. However, find times to smile occasionally. It helps your audience recognize you as approachable and genuine. Smiling also conveys confidence and helps you calm yourself. If your audience believes you're confident and calm, they feel comfortable and eager to trust you.

> **Helpful Hint**
>
> Dress professionally but comfortably. Avoid items like new shoes and unprofessional clothing, which can be distracting for you and the audience. You don't want anything pulling your focus from your message or hampering your ability to stay calm and in control.

Speech Set-up

Some factors are beyond your control. However, use this checklist to prepare for your presentation:

Presentation Checklist

Arrive early to check the sound and test technology.

Neatly arrange any printed materials or handouts.

Eat something beforehand that will give you energy and not weigh you down.

Have a bottle of water sitting nearby.

Arrange any cords safely and securely.

Writing Environment: Everyday

An oral presentation isn't always formal. Additionally, you may be asked to speak with little time to prepare. Even if you're only talking to friends or family members, organization strategies and rhetorical appeals can help you to feel more confident and comfortable sharing your ideas or persuading others to act on your recommendations. You may not use a slide show to convince your parents to fund a trip to Europe, but it helps to have a plan with a clear introduction and purpose and a confident, reasonable tone!

Lesson Wrap Up

Key Terms

Anecdote: a long example told as a story

Audience: the person or people who read or interpret a text

Ethos: an argument based on a person's credibility

Logos: an argument based on logic

Oral Introduction: the first part of an oral presentation and the speaker's opportunity to set expectations, provide background information, and engage the audience

Pathos: an argument based on emotion

Presentation Outline: a tool that organizes topic information and guides the speaker during an oral presentation

Purpose: the goal of a text

Rhetoric: the art of speaking effectively

Supporting Detail: a piece of information, also called evidence, that is used to support a main idea

Thesis Statement: the concise sentence or group of sentences that expresses the main idea of a longer work

Tone: the positive, negative, or neutral attitude that an author expresses about a topic

Transition: a word, phrase, or sentence that shows a relationship between ideas

Writing Application: Oral Presentations

Read the following presentation outline, example notecard, and speaker notes for a presentation on SCUBA certification.

Introduction

Good morning, everyone! I'm delighted that so many of you are starting your SCUBA certification training! I'm Alexis Carlson. I'm a certified SCUBA instructor and I've been diving for fifteen years. I've enjoyed some fascinating exploration and rescue missions. I also work with the Nature Conservancy to protect the coral reefs. Tell me, what do you find most appealing about SCUBA diving? (Note to self: Answers vary. Acknowledge and remember a few.) Today we're going to spend about twenty minutes focusing on adaptions for the aquatic environment. This will include vision, sound, tides and currents, and marine life.

In this brief introduction, Alexis' enthusiasm and personal passion helps to prompt her audience.

The information on this notecard corresponds to Topic 1 in the speaker's outline.

VISION ADAPTATIONS (4 min.)

Distortion: dive mask (demo and explain)
- Objects look closer *contrast slides*
- Objects appear 25% larger *show slides*
- Light changes color: red looks green
- Turbidity (murkiness) clouds visibility *share experiences off Bermuda*

Presentation Outline

Topic 1: Adapting to Visual Distortion

> **Point 1**: Objects appear closer and 25% larger than reality (indicate contrast slides)
>
> > Dive mask creates artificial air space that bends light and magnifies vision
>
> **Point 2**: Color is distorted. The deeper you go, the bluer things appear
>
> > At 30 meters, a red fish looks green (indicate contrast slides)
>
> **Point 3**: Turbidity or "murkiness" makes it difficult to see other divers, fish, coral, etc.
>
> > Water clarity affected by bottom composition or time of day

The speaker might demonstrate the dive mask in addition to showing slides of distorted underwater vision.

Topic 2: Adapting to Sound Distortion. "Someone said SCUBA diving looks peaceful and quiet; it's peaceful, but there are many sounds!"

> **Point 1**: Sound is magnified. Water conducts sound but distorts sense of distance/direction
>
> > You may overhear boat motors, voices, but how far away/what direction?
> >
> > Remember: don't return to the surface until sounds vanish completely
>
> **Point 2**: You may hear your own breathing louder/deeper than usual. Don't panic; that's just the water!
>
> **Point 3**: Fish and marine life make clicking, swishing noises that are also magnified (play audio clip)

The speaker is already incorporating her audience's feedback from the previous exchange in her intro. This shows them that she was listening.

In addition to using slides and images, the speaker has incorporated an audio clip to add variety.

Topic 3: Adapting to Tide and Currents. Motion/natural direction of the water varies with time of day and season

> **Point 1**: Check the tidal tables
>
> > In coastal areas, the current may be too strong to swim against
>
> **Point 2**: Two types of currents to recognize
>
> > **Longshore current**: strong waves approach shore at an angle and can sweep you into rip currents, piers, jetties, hazards (point to diagram at left and demonstrate proper responses)
> >
> > **Rip current**: Runs perpendicular to shore, quickly pulls you out to sea (point to diagram at right and demonstrate proper response)

Most of the speaker's slides will have only the basic information. This outline includes extra details that she will say and do.

Topic 4: Respecting Marine Life. "Someone mentioned sharks. Sharks encounters hit the media as a novelty, but humans aren't sharks' natural prey."

> Again, the speaker recalls her audience's comments and incorporates them in her presentation.

    Point 1: Most injuries come from jellyfish, sea urchins, and coral scrapes

    Point 2: These injuries can result in anaphylactic shock, infection, or paralysis

    Point 3: if you make contact with these marine creatures, return to the surface and apply vinegar or meat tenderizer until medical help arrives

        Remember: look but don't touch. (Point to slide: spectator sport.) These animals will defend themselves.

Conclusion: let's review

> This simple review is one strategy to get the audience involved.

    Can someone remember one of the three things to remember about underwater vision?

    Can anyone tell me how to respond when you hear boats overhead?

    What are the two types of currents? Can someone demonstrate how to respond to each?

    What's the most important thing to remember about marine life?

Lesson 8.4
Etiquette in Social Media

> You are required to participate in a discussion board for an online class. Not only do you have to post in response to your instructor, you also have to respond to your classmates. How can you get your ideas across and have a productive discussion with people you barely know?

> You log into Facebook one morning and a friend has posted comments that you disagree with. You don't want to lose your friend, but you also feel strongly about the issue. How do you respond?

> A friend tweets a photo of you that you don't want your coworkers to see. How can you address this problem?

Social media refers to any platform that individuals use to form online communities and share videos, photographs, personal messages, opinions, or ideas. Because this is a big part of our daily lives, it's important to learn how to navigate social media and communicate in a balanced and polite way.

In this lesson, you will learn about the following aspects of social media etiquette:

The Purposes of Social Media
How to Conduct Yourself on Social Media Platforms

Communicating on social media is relevant to academic, professional, and everyday life.

The Purposes of Social Media and Social Networking

Social media platforms allow individuals to communicate both in synchronous and asynchronous ways. **Synchronous communication** is communication occurring over social media at the same time but in a different place. This type of communication takes place on sites like Facebook, in chat rooms, and through instant messaging and texting. People write and respond in real time, similar to having an in-person conversation.

Writing Environment: Professional

In the workplace, webinars (aka "web seminars") are a common type of synchronous communication. For example, a department might offer a webinar to train staff. The webinar is synchronous because everyone receives the same information at the same time and can communicate via chat or by using a microphone and webcam.

Conversely, **asynchronous communication** is communication that occurs at different times. This type of communication can take place on platforms like Twitter, Instagram, and Blackboard. Conversations are not instantaneous, and participants expect to wait for responses from other participants.

Writing Environment: Academic

Imagine that your professor assigns a semester-long project that involves creating and maintaining a blog online. You post your thoughts each day on a chosen topic and wait for your audience to comment. This is an example of asynchronous communication.

On Your Own

In the following table, draft one synchronous and one asynchronous social media post for any social media platform.

Synchronous	Asynchronous

While some social media can be used purely for fun or for academics, there are other purposes, too. **Social networking** is the act of using social media to find and interact with individuals with similar interests or goals. One benefit of social networking is building connections that could benefit you either personally or professionally.

Here are some examples of social networking.

- Sending e-mails to your coworkers about a shared project
- Participating in a class discussion board
- Joining a group on Facebook that supports a specific cause
- Messaging a friend or acquaintance who has a resource or piece of information you need

When you participate in social networking, you are essentially presenting a version of yourself, or a **persona**, for others to see and interact with online. Often, people encounter your social media persona before they ever meet you in person. As a result, it's good to be aware of the ways you present yourself and the information you share on social media platforms.

> Further Resources
>
> Some social media sites, like LinkedIn, are dedicated to professional networking. Check out this infographic (https://www.entrepreneur.com/article/271919) about how to create a strong LinkedIn profile.

Part of creating your online persona should include an awareness of how your writing causes others to perceive you. As social media and networking have evolved, so has English. For instance, writing posts that are 140 characters or fewer has made some people streamline their writing by shortening words and using more abbreviations. While many believe that these streamlined words make reading easier, others believe that writing this way has lowered the integrity of the English language and is destroying standardized grammatical forms.

How to Conduct Yourself on Social Media Platforms

Imagine being in class and the professor opens a discussion about a controversial topic. As usual, different people, including the professor, have opinions about the topic. Suddenly, one student starts screaming his viewpoint and won't stop even after other students point out the errors in his reasoning.

As a participant in this discussion, how would you feel? This situation rarely happens in classes, primarily because most professors have rules (either stated or unstated) for how to behave.

Similarly, there are stated and unstated rules that guide our social interactions. These rules are called **etiquette**. We learn etiquette from a young age, and this allows us to navigate all the social interactions we encounter as human beings.

Social media etiquette isn't always taught, and many people are unprepared to navigate these interactions. As a result, they end up "screaming" their opinions on social media in a way that hurts their persona and alienates others.

Basic Social Media Etiquette

Be Kind

By following this one rule, you will gain respect in your online community. Consider this example:

> You are on a discussion board that asks you to explore how you feel about the candidates in an upcoming election. One of your classmates makes unflattering comments about a candidate you like. When you respond, she says rude things about you even though you have never met in person.

On Your Own

How should you respond? Check the box next to the best option.

- ☐ Call the classmate names and attempt to defend your candidate.
- ☐ Draw other classmates into the conversation so that you have support.
- ☐ Respond to the discussion question and ignore your classmate's statements.

Choose Your Community Carefully

We often don't know a lot about our coworkers or acquaintances. Consider what you want to see on your social media pages and how you want to engage with others, especially those you don't know well. Some people may not fit your social media goals, or their ideas may conflict with yours.

Think Before You Post

It's easy to share our thoughts on social media. However, it may not be wise to write a post fueled heavily by emotion. Be mindful that what you've posted could be detrimental to your reputation or could be hurtful to others.

Consider these examples:

Bad Idea	My boss treats me like trash! I hope he pays for this one day.
Better Idea	Don't post about this sort of thing at all. Call a friend to vent.

Bad Idea	You obviously have no idea what you're talking about when it comes to *Dracula*. Did you even read the book? Only an idiot would argue that Dracula was a force of good!
Better Idea	I disagree with your point about the goodness of Dracula. I'm curious about how you can support this thought.

Similarly, never post photos that may have a negative impact on yourself or others. More and more employers or potential employers use social media to learn about potential and current employees. Post photos only after asking permission of the people in the photo. Likewise, if a friend posts a photo of you without your permission, most social media platforms have an "un-tag" or "remove photo" feature.

Now that we have our etiquette basics, let's focus on some specific social media platforms.

Academic Discussion Boards

Professors often use discussion boards to continue discussions from class or allow students to explore concepts in their textbook. Along with the basic rules of etiquette, here are some things you need to keep in mind that are specific to this platform.

- Follow the instructions posted by the instructor. Your answers may be graded or evaluated. Additionally, by following the instructions, you will be able to interact with other students in ways that are inoffensive, meaningful, and topic-appropriate.
- Stay on topic.
- Check your grammar and spelling.
- View posting in the discussion board like being in class. Would you yell at your instructor or pick a fight with the girl who sits near the window? Probably not. Make sure this doesn't happen on the discussion board.

Helpful Hint

On many discussion boards, the instructions stay visible at the top of the posting area. Refer to the instructions several times as you write.

On Your Own

Read the following discussion board post and identify the sentence that violates etiquette for academic discussion boards.

Discussion Board Topic: Your Study Strategies
I usually snack while I study. I also study best when I play quiet music and don't turn on the television. I also re-write my notes because it helps me remember what was said in class. I think its stupid to not study, don't u angela? After I study, I play guitar or do something else that helps me relax.

Writing Environment: Academic

Read the following discussion board post. What parts could the author have made more understandable? Does the grammar affect how well you understand the author's ideas?

> I think personal communication is a trait that is dying a sudden death. Most people under the age of 35 don't know how to communicate. I lay the blame on the digital revolution. These people were basically born with a cell phone in their hands, and they don't use it as a phone. Instead, they use text messaging to communicate with others. I recently had a conversation with a friend whose job has taken him to Macon, GA, and he always texts me. I enjoy hearing from him but not by text. I told him I'd rather hear his voice than read an abbreviated version of what he was trying to "say." If I could hear his voice, I could understand his tone better. Some might say I'm just being old-fashioned, but I prefer the more traditional forms of communication. And there are certainly exceptions to that, too. If I'm in a situation where it is inappropriate to be on the phone (in a meeting) I don't mind a text, if it is necessary for that person to reach me. Other than that, I don't care for texting. I can say more in 2 minutes on the phone that I can by texting for an hour.
> Source: Chambers, Laura. "Examples of Good Discussion Posts." *Georgia Virtual Technical Connection*.
> <http://www.gvtc.org/Portals/34/Examples%20of%20Good%20Discussion%20Posts%20LChambers%20OTC.pdf>.

Facebook, Twitter, and Other Recreational Platforms

Here are some more guidelines that are vital when communicating on platforms like Facebook and Twitter.

- **Remember your audience.** Many social media platforms are public, and even the simplest post can be misunderstood.
- **Keep posts succinct.** Though this is easier with Twitter, which has a strict length requirement, most people will not read a post that is longer than a few sentences. Be brief if you want to be heard!
- **Don't harass.** Continuing to post in an argument or posting pictures, videos, or written material that you know is offending someone will not help any situation.
- **Write like you speak.** Remember that you are engaging in a conversation. Use words and phrases that show your personality.
- **Write clearly.** This helps people understand you and helps you avoid hurting anyone's feelings.
- **Respond in a timely fashion if a response is relevant.** If you are busy, consider explaining that and mention that you will respond more thoroughly at a later time.

Writing Environment: Personal

Sometimes, you may want to share thoughts about certain people or events without mentioning them directly. This is what some people call *vaguebooking*, It's often considered a passive-aggressive form of communication. Consider the following posts:

> It's so hard to stay positive at this moment with all that happened earlier...

> Maybe if a certain someone didn't speak to me today, I wouldn't be in such a bad mood.

What are these posts saying? Can you understand exactly what they are discussing?

Writing Environment: Professional

More and more companies are using in-house instant messaging systems to encourage conversation between co-workers and supervisors. Consider how you would message a coworker in the following situations:

- You need a quick answer to an important question.
- You made a decision with your superior and need to tell your coworker right away.

Further Resources

To explore how wording and tone affect social media posts, check out "Socially Awkward Media" (http://blogcenter.readingeagle.com/digital-watch-by-adam-richter/tag/social-media-fails/) on Adam Richter's blog *Digital Watch*.

Group Activity

Create a post for an academic discussion board on a piece of paper. Then, pass it around and allow each member of the group to write a response to the original post that follows the rules of social media etiquette.

Lesson Wrap Up

Key Terms

Asynchronous Communication: communication occurring over social media at different times but on the same platform

Etiquette: the stated and unstated rules that guide social interactions

Persona: the version of a person that is presented on social media platforms

Social Media: any platform that individuals use to form online communities and publicly or privately share information such as videos, photographs, personal messages, opinions, or ideas

Social Networking: the act of using social media to find and interact with other individuals with similar interests or goals

Synchronous Communication: communication occurring over social media at the same time but from different locations

Writing Application: Etiquette in Social Media

Read the following examples of effective posts on different social media platforms.

Discussion Board Post

Question: Describe your reactions to *Feed* by M.T. Anderson. Did you take away any lessons or ideas from the book?

Response: This book made me feel uncomfortable, but it also made me more aware of how our society interacts with technology. The lesions caused by the earth's toxic environment, Violet's tragic death, and Titus's inability to empathize were all disturbing. However, what made me the most uncomfortable was that the world Anderson portrays in the book doesn't seem so different from today. Advertisements on the internet are tailored for certain audiences depending on their browsing history. Technology is becoming increasingly personal and physical, from GPS to "smart glasses" to electronic tattoos. It's easy to imagine technology literally becoming a part of us. When Titus describes the original reasoning behind the feed, he says: "It was all . . . your child will have the advantage, encyclopedias at their fingertips, closer than their fingertips, etc." (p. 47). This stood out to me particularly because it's one of the justifications I've heard for children having cell phones or other similar devices. Access to information is an advantage that everyone should have, but both in reality and in *Feed*, this access is more often used to market and buy products or engage in virtual entertainment. In the book, the result is that the earth is neglected, people become slaves to their feed, and human relationships lose their value. Overall, I enjoyed reading *Feed*, but it made me feel disturbed and concerned. The world portrayed in the book sounds terrible but also similar to modern reality. I think this book has also made me think about the danger of valuing virtual experiences over real experiences.

Facebook

I want to wish my brother in Texas a happy birthday. He is a wonderful guy, and he's now thirty! Happy Birthday! I love you!

Twitter

Many thanks to @GrimmWriters for an excellent season of Grimm. #thankyou #Grimm

---

On academic discussion boards, there is usually a question or prompt that leads the students to answer or respond.

Just like a paragraph in an essay, discussion board posts should begin with a strong topic sentence. It should connect to the question or prompt clearly.

If relevant to the topic, including quotes and other supporting details will make the post stronger.

This post uses simple language but also utilizes correct grammar and spelling.

The post ends with concluding statements that reference the topic sentence.

A strong post uses complete sentences and gets the point quickly and understandably.

In the right context, using hashtags is perfectly acceptable.

Chapter 9
Basics of Grammar & Mechanics

Lesson 9.1
Parts of Speech

Clear communication is necessary in today's world. Consider the written communication you participate in every day: texting friends, posting on social media, emailing colleagues, and writing essays for instructors.

With all this communication, what can you do to make sure it's meaningful? The first step is to recognize how words relate to one another and put them together effectively. Categorizing words, or parts of speech, by their uses and functions helps you improve your reading and writing skills and communicate clearly.

In this lesson, you will review the functions, forms, and uses of the following parts of speech:

Nouns and Pronouns
Verbs
Adjectives and Adverbs
Prepositions
Conjunctions and Interjections

Nouns and Pronouns

A **noun** names a person, place, thing, event, or idea. Nouns can be specific or general. However, using too many nouns in one sentence or paragraph can sometimes feel awkward. An easy way to add clarity and variety to your writing is to use a pronoun instead. A **pronoun** is a word used as a substitute for a noun or another pronoun. Take a look at the nouns below and the pronouns that could be used as substitutes.

Nouns	Pronouns
Emily	She
Mount Everest	It
Civil rights leaders	They
Julius Erving	He
Gravity	It
School board meeting	It

Types of Nouns and Pronouns
Although there are many types of nouns, there are four common types you use every day. These nouns can be singular or plural.

Common nouns name general people, places, things, events, or ideas.

woman
town
month
cat

Proper nouns name specific people, places, things, events, or ideas.

Grand Canyon
July
France
President Obama

Concrete nouns name objects that occupy a physical space and/or can be recognized by our senses.

trombone
building
music
aroma

Abstract nouns name intangible ideas, qualities, or characteristics.

hope
mercy
power
courage

> Helpful Hint
> Some noun types overlap. For instance, *pizza* is both a common noun and a concrete noun. Depending on how it's used, *aunt* can be common ("She is an aunt") or proper ("My Aunt Kathy").

There are also four common types of pronouns.

Personal pronouns rename specific nouns.

my
I
they
he
it
us

> She ran out for milk.

Relative pronouns introduce dependent clauses.

that
which
whichever
who

> I had no idea that you wanted to see the movie so badly.

Demonstrative pronouns point to one or more specific nouns.

this

that

these

those

> These will make you sick if you eat too many.

Indefinite pronouns rename non-specific nouns.

all

many

anybody

few

something

> Anyone is welcome to the party!

On Your Own

Read the following sentence and identify all the nouns.

> Don, my boyfriend, does not want to go to dinner. He said he ate turkey right after he finished watching *Modern Family*.

Read the following sentence and identify all the pronouns.

> I told Dr. Lovell none of the answers were yours. He didn't believe me and said my homework needs to be re-done.

Functions of Nouns and Pronouns

A single word can function as different parts of speech depending on how it's used in a sentence. Consider the word *book*. Typically, our first reaction to the word *book* is to visualize a book that we can read, which is a noun. However, if I ask, "Would you please book my flight for me?" is *book* still a noun? No, in this sentence the function of *book* is a verb.

Let's examine some of the most common functions of nouns and pronouns.

Subject of a Sentence

The **subject** of a sentence is who or what the sentence is about.

> John went to the store yesterday.

> He went to the store yesterday.

Object of a Sentence

A **direct object** receives the action of a verb.

> Before she went out last night, Coco ate the chicken.

> Before she went out last night, Coco ate it.

An **indirect object** is a word that receives the direct object.

> Please give Heather your coat.

> Please give her your coat.

An **object of a preposition** is a word that completes the meaning of a prepositional phrase.

> I directed her toward the group.

> I directed her toward them.

Writing Environment: Professional

In most professional settings, you will be expected to know the basics of constructing a grammatically correct sentence. To do this, you need to understand parts of speech. This is especially important when communicating through writing. Always be sure to edit your emails, documents, and other items before passing them along to colleagues or managers.

Verbs

A **verb** is a word or a phrase that expresses an action, relationship, or state of being. Here are some examples:

> I jumped through the puddle during the rainstorm.

> She became despondent at the end of the vacation.

> Ken is aware of his actions and their pending consequences.

Types of Verbs

Verbs are the dynamic portion of a sentence; if there are no verbs, a sentence cannot go anywhere. There are many kinds of verbs, but let's review five of the most common types.

Action verbs indicate physical or mental actions.

> We slept all day.

Linking verbs link a subject to a description.

> Vanessa was my best friend in fourth grade.

Helping verbs change the form of main verbs so that they are grammatically correct.

> David has invited me to the party.

Transitive verbs need a direct object to be complete.

> Kara arranged the flowers.

Intransitive verbs do not need to be followed by a direct object.

> The baseball team played abysmally.

> **Helpful Hint**
>
> Be aware that it often sounds awkward when writers split infinitives. A **split infinitive** occurs when an adverb is inserted between *to* and the present form of the verb. Sometimes, writers add too much information between the *to* and the verb. Proofread to be sure a split infinitive is not confusing your readers.
>
> **Split Infinitive:** Michelle is the candidate to, whether you are conservative or liberal, vote for.
>
> **Corrected:** Whether you are conservative or liberal, Michelle is the candidate to vote for.

On Your Own

Read the following sentence and identify the verb.

> Sean became interested in art after his trip to New York.

Forms and Functions of Verbs

All verbs have four primary functions. You are probably familiar with the basic present-tense and past-tense forms of verb. Additionally, verbs can become participles. A **participle** is a word derived from a verb and used to describe a noun. Like regular verbs, participles can have tense.

BASIC FORM	PRESENT PARTICIPLE	PAST FORM	PAST PARTICIPLE
call	calling	called	called
roar	roaring	roared	roared

Regular verbs form their past-tense and past-participle forms by adding –*ed* to the basic form.

> Archaeologists have discovered the existence of music in ancient civilizations.

Irregular verbs form their past-tense and past-participle forms in other ways.

BASIC FORM	PAST FORM	PAST PARTICIPLE
be	was, were	been
drive	drove	driven
throw	threw	threw

> The pitcher threw the ball at ninety-two miles per hour!

Writing Environment: Academic

When you're editing academic writing, be sure that verb tenses do not shift or change when two or more events occur at the same time.

Incorrect: They wrote brochures and edit newspapers.

Correct: They wrote brochures and edited newspapers.

Adjectives and Adverbs

The primary purpose of both adjectives and adverbs is to describe. An **adjective** is a word that describes or modifies a noun or a pronoun. An **adverb** is a word that describes or modifies a verb, an adjective, or another adverb.

Adjectives

> The quiet girl slept near her cute puppy.

> The road was bumpy, but the trip was thrilling!

Adverbs

> I worked hard and got my promotion quickly.

> She was too sick to go to work, so I begrudgingly picked up her tasks.

Types of Adjectives and Adverbs

Adjectives

Descriptive adjectives name a quality or a characteristic of the noun they are modifying.

> rotten apples

> bright sky

Definite adjectives specify *which* or *how many*.

> this novel

> that piano

Indefinite adjectives are indefinite pronouns used to describe nouns or pronouns.

> some grapes

> which ones

Numerical adjectives express *how many* or *in which order*.

> four apples

> two zebras

> second place

Nouns and pronouns can also function as adjectives.

> Rebecca's coat

> Marcy's notebook

> my coat

> their house

Adverbs

Time

These adverbs answer, "When?"

> Let's go now.

Place

These adverbs answer, "Where?"

> They went inside.

Manner

These adverbs answer, "How?"

> Bob played the piano horribly.

Degree

These adverbs answer, "To what extent?"

> Susie is quite angry.

Miscellaneous

These adverbs may modify an entire statement, while others may provide a transition.

> Apparently, he missed the bus; therefore, he will have to take a taxi.

Helpful Hint

Be careful not to confuse adjectives and adverbs. First, find the nouns and pronouns. Then, see if there are any words modifying the nouns and pronouns; if so, those words are probably adjectives. Next, find the verbs. Then, see if there are any words modifying the verbs; if so, those words are probably adverbs.

Functions of Adjectives and Adverbs

Adjectives answer these questions:

- Which one?
- What kind?
- How many/much?

Take a look at the following examples:

> Those apple trees have grown quickly.

Those tells us which trees, and *apple* describes the type of tree.

> Both men ate steak.

Both describes how many men ate the steak.

On Your Own

Read the following sentence and identify the adjectives.

> The powerful thunderstorm provided a magnificent lightning show.

Adverbs answer these questions:

- How?
- Where?
- When?
- To what extent?

They can also strengthen or weaken the words they modify. Take a look at these sentences:

> Jen roughly washed the dirty plates.

Roughly modifies *washed* and indicates the way Jen washed the plates.

> The author briefly spoke at commencement.

Briefly modifies *spoke* and indicates how long the author spoke.

On Your Own

Read the following sentence and identify the adverb.

> Jim whistled loudly for the dog.

Prepositions

A **preposition** is a word that shows relationships among people, places, things, events, and ideas. Here are some examples:

> I left the plant on my shelf.

> My dog loves to sleep under the bed.

> Before dinner, I need to finish writing my paper.

Each of these sentences contains not only a preposition but also a **prepositional phrase**. This is a group of related words that starts with a preposition and ends with a noun or pronoun. Let's break down the sentences further. Here are the prepositional phrases from the previous sentences:

> on my shelf

> under the bed

> before dinner

Types of Prepositions

When you write, you will use two basic kinds of prepositions. The first are called simple prepositions, which were used in the previous examples. In addition, you will sometimes use **phrasal prepositions**, which are made up of at least two words.

SIMPLE PREPOSITIONS	PHRASAL PREPOSITIONS
above, at, behind, besides, for, from, in, of, on, over, through, to, under, up, with	according to, because of, by reason of, in regard to, with respect to

Structure of Prepositional Phrases

All prepositional phrases contain a preposition and an object of the preposition. Consider these examples:

> Tom was the leader of the motorcycle gang.

Of is the preposition, *of the motorcycle gang* is the prepositional phrase, and *gang* is the object of the preposition.

> She drove from Charleston to Cincinnati in one day.

There are three prepositional phrases in this sentence. In the first prepositional phrase, *from* is the preposition and *Charleston* is the object of the preposition. In the second, *to* is the preposition and *Cincinnati* is the object of the preposition. In the third, *in* is the preposition and *day* is the object of the preposition.

On Your Own

Read the following sentence and identify the prepositional phrases.

> Before the weekend, you should watch the movie I recommended during our meeting.

Conjunctions and Interjections

The last two parts of speech may seem small, but they have a big impact on clarity and emphasis.

Types and Functions of Conjunctions

A **conjunction** is a word that makes a connection between other words or a word groups. There are three basic types of conjunctions.

Coordinating conjunctions join similar words or word groups.

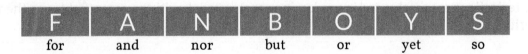

F	A	N	B	O	Y	S
for	and	nor	but	or	yet	so

> Don and I talked for three hours.

> I would go, but I have a sinus infection.

Subordinating conjunctions introduce dependent clauses.

SUBORDINATING CONJUNCTIONS		
after	if	when
as if	since	where
because	until	while

> We ate breakfast while Mary exercised.

> I will donate twenty-five dollars if you will.

Correlative conjunctions always appear in pairs and connect two or more similar ideas.

CORRELATIVE CONJUNCTIONS		
both/and	neither/nor	whether/or
either/or	not only/but also	if/then

> Savannah wants either a cat or a dog.

> If they don't arrive soon, then we'll have to eat without them.

Interjections

An **interjection** is an exclamatory word expressing strong emotion. Here are some examples:

wow	yikes
aha	whew
oh	ouch

Functions of Interjections

First, interjections are used as greetings in emails and letters:

> Good morning, all!

> Hi Emily

> Dear Mr. Russell

Second, you can also use interjections to emphasize words or feelings.

> Well, this is certainly a surprise.

> Wow! You definitely need to check out the new exhibit at the Museum of Modern Art.

Although interjections are rarely used in academic or professional writing, you probably use them often in personal writing.

Further Resources

Informal sound words like *ugh* and *um* are also considered interjections when they appear in a text. To learn more about the history of the word *meh*, check out this article (http://www.slate.com/blogs/lexicon_valley/2013/09/06/meh_etymology_tracing_the_yiddish_word_from_leo_rosten_to_auden_to_the_simpsons.html).

Writing Environment: Professional

Read the following memo and look for part-of-speech errors. Consider how the recipient of each email might view the person who wrote it.

Memo

TO: Bob Green, Vice President of Marketing

FROM: Joe Smith, Creative Support Team Member

To update you on the status of the marketing program.

Our team will begin meeting yesterday. We are planning to discussed ways to market this new product. We should been threw by 3:00 p.m. The Support Team is meeting in his office. The meeting will be conducted by Dave Hoffman. The meeting notes will be taken by Bill Vickers. Me will get the notes to you by tomorrow.

Thank them.

Corrected Memo

TO: Bob Green, Vice President of Marketing

FROM: Joe Smith, Creative Support Team

I would like to provide you with a status update on the program. Our team will meet today. We are planning to discuss ways to improve marketing strategies on this new product. Our meeting should be finished by 3:00 p.m. The Support Team will be meeting in Tammy Christa's office. Dave Hoffman will be conducting our meeting while Bill Vickers records the meeting notes. I will have the meeting notes on your desk tomorrow morning by 8:00 a.m.

Thank you.

Lesson Wrap-up

Key Terms

Abstract Noun: a noun that names ideas, qualities, or characteristics

Action Verb: a verb that indicates physical or mental action

Adjective: a word that describes or modifies a noun or a pronoun

Adverb: a word that describes or modifies a verb, an adjective, or another adverb

Common Noun: a noun that names a general person, place, thing, event, or idea

Concrete Noun: a noun that names an object that occupies a space or can be recognized by our senses

Conjunction: a word that makes a connection between other words or a group of words

Coordinating Conjunction: a conjunction that joins similar words or groups of words together

Correlative Conjunctions: conjunctions that always appear in pairs and connect two or more similar ideas

Definite Adjective: an adjective that specifies *which* or *how many*

Demonstrative Pronoun: a pronoun that points to one or more specific nouns

Descriptive Adjective: an adjective that names a quality or a characteristic of the noun it's modifying

Direct Object: a word that receives the action of the verb

Helping Verb: a verb that changes the form of the main verb so that it is grammatically correct in a sentence

Indefinite Adjective: an indefinite pronoun used to describe

Indefinite Pronoun: a pronoun that refers to nouns in a general way

Indirect Object: a word that receives the direct object

Interjection: an exclamatory word expressing strong emotion

Intransitive Verb: a verb that does not have an object to complete its meaning; is not followed by a direct object

Linking Verb: a verb that links or joins the subject of a sentence with an adjective, a noun, or a pronoun

Noun: a word that names a person, place, thing, event, or idea

Numerical Adjective: an adjective that expresses *how many* or *in which*

Object of the Preposition: a word that completes the meaning of a prepositional phrase

Participle: a word derived from a verb and used as an adjective modifying a noun

Personal Pronoun: a pronoun that renames a specific noun

Phrasal Prepositions: a preposition that is made up of at least two words

Preposition: a word that shows relationship among people, places, things, events, and ideas

Prepositional Phrase: the preposition with its object and any modifiers

Pronoun: a word used as a substitute for a noun

Proper Noun: a noun that name a specific person, place, thing, event, or idea

Relative Pronoun: a pronoun that introduces dependent clauses

Split Infinitive: occurs when an adverb is inserted between the "to" and the present form of the verb

Subject: who or what the sentence is about

Subordinating Conjunction: a conjunction that introduces a dependent clause

Transitive Verb: a verb that is followed by direct objects, usually nouns answering "what?" or "whom?" in a sentence

Verb: a word or a phrase that expresses an action, an occurrence, or a state of being

Writing Application: Parts of Speech

Read the following brief response essay about communication and consider how the words connect to form complete ideas. How many parts of speech can you identify in the passage?

Freedom Writing

I believe that writing is extraordinarily important because it is so versatile. It allows us to communicate on personal and professional levels, to be open and creative, and to be freed. Writing is also one of the most meaningful forms of communication because it can be saved and read repeatedly. Therefore, it's worth our time to perfect our writing instead of just getting by with poor grammar skills.

The adverb *extraordinarily* modifies the adjective *important*.

The adverb *repeatedly* modifies the verb *read*.

Writing is a wonderful avenue for creativity. There are so many different forms of writing that allow us to reveal our inner selves. We can write poetry, short stories, song lyrics, graphic novels, essays, or journal entries. To me, writing can provide freedom. I can write my thoughts without fear of anyone judging them. I can express myself openly and honestly. Of course, I can share my writing, but I can also keep my writing private. Writing is much more versatile than people realize.

Of writing is a prepositional phrase.

The nouns in the list are direct objects of the transitive verb *write*.

Lesson 9.2
The Characteristics of a Sentence

We communicate with others from the moment the day begins until it ends. From conversations, texts, and to-do lists to emails, presentations, and letters, communication forms so much of who we are as a society and as individuals.

Regardless of how or with whom we communicate, we all have to express our thoughts by putting together words to create a sentence.

Reflection Questions
Wilhelm von Humboldt, a German linguist in the 1800s, once said, "Language makes infinite use of finite means." What do you think this means? What implications does this have for writing?

In this lesson, you will learn about the following topics:

Required Components of a Sentence
Independent and Dependent Clauses
Types of Sentences

Required Components of a Sentence

There *are* situations in your life when complete sentences aren't a big deal. In a lab report for biology class, you might use a list of phrases to communicate your meaning. In a presentation, you might purposefully use an incomplete sentence for emphasis.

However, in other situations, like writing an essay or cover letter, complete sentences are expected because they make it easier for others to understand your message.

Consider the paragraph below. How does it use complete sentences to clearly communicate ideas?

> Adventure seekers and seasoned travelers from all over the world flock to Costa Rica every year to experience its vibrant culture and natural beauty. From surfers looking to catch their next wave off the Nicoya Peninsula to nature lovers seeking the lush environs of Monteverdi's cloud forests, Costa Rica has something for everyone. If you want to avoid the rainy season, December through the beginning of summer is the best time to visit. If you're on a budget and don't mind a little rain, late summer through late fall can't be beat. Whatever the season or activity, Costa Rica is a must for your next vacation!

Group Activity
After reading the previous paragraph, explore how these sentences are different and similar compared to one another. Discuss your thoughts with your group.

Before you can build a whole paragraph, you need to know how to construct a sentence. While sentences come in many lengths and forms, they all meet three basic standards:

- Begin with a capital letter and end with punctuation
- Include a subject and a verb
- Express a complete thought

Capitalization and Punctuation

Consider these sentences:

Whatever your life's work is, do it well. (Martin Luther King, Jr.)

Has the committee made a decision yet?

Don't lose your ticket!

▸ The first word of each sentence is capitalized. Additionally, each sentence ends with a period, question mark, or exclamation point.

Most of the time, the period is the most common ending punctuation mark. We use periods to share ideas and information that don't require the same level of excitement indicated by an exclamation point or the degree of uncertainty indicated by a question mark.

Here are some scenarios in which you will use periods more than other ending punctuation marks:

- You are writing a report on a South American country you researched for a Spanish course.
- You are drafting a proposal for a new construction project.
- You are writing a letter to the editor in favor of traffic remedies for a congested city street.

Make sure you use the right punctuation for **direct** and **indirect questions**. Use a question mark when you're asking your audience a direct question. However, use a period to tell the audience about a question.

Direct Question   How many reporters will be attending the game this afternoon?

Indirect Question   The coach wanted to know how many reporters are going to attend the game.

Using a Subject and Verb

Complete sentences always contain both a subject and a verb. A **subject** is who or what the sentence is about. A subject can be one word or a group of words.

Congress has been working for months to balance the budget.

In the middle of the Emmy awards, Aaron and I fell asleep on the couch.

On Your Own

Read the following sentences and identify the subject in each one.

A merchant ship finally rescued the survivors after six days at sea.

In laying the foundation of his essay, Bitzer makes a number of assumptions about rhetoric.

Burke was the author of the popular essay "Reflections on the Revolution in France."

Sentences that give the audience a command or request contain an **implied subject**. In these sentences, the speaker is talking to the audience directly.

(You) Get off of the grass!

(You) Please pass the salad.

Remember, a complete sentence also contains a verb. This can be in the form of an action verb, linking verb, or helping verb.

An **action verb** indicates a physical or mental action.

> During the rally, the crowd screamed in protest.

> The huge audience intimidated Bethany.

Linking verbs link the subject to a description.

> The conventional wisdom is often wrong. (Steven D. Levitt)

> The news was disappointing.

Like subjects, verbs can also be more than one word. **Helping verbs** are words that change the form of the main verb so that it grammatically fits the sentence.

> On your first day of work, you will complete the first two steps in the training manual.

> Because of the weather conditions, local families were forced to evacuate.

> The contestants are writing memoirs for this year's competition.

Finding the subject and verb in a sentence isn't always easy.

In most sentences in the English language, subjects come before verbs. Some sentences, however, place the subject after or inside the verb. This is especially common in questions. Look at the subject in this example sentence:

> Will you run in tomorrow's race?

In this sentence, the subject, *you*, appears inside the verb *will run*.

Both subjects and verbs can also be compound. For example, two people could be doing the same action, or one person could be doing two different actions. In these instances, the subjects and verbs are linked by conjunctions.

> *Horton Hears a Who!* and *The Cat in the Hat* are two famous books by Dr. Seuss.

> As volunteers, we prepared and packaged meals for families in need.

Writing Environment: Everyday

If you're writing a blog or communicating with friends, complete sentences are not common or necessary.

Lifestyle Blog

> "This is by far my favorite recipe for cheesecake. To. Die. For."

Text Message

> "K. Movie theater at 7:15."

Independent and Dependent Clauses

In addition to a subject and a verb, correct sentences always express a complete thought. This requires that the sentence include at least one **independent clause**: a word group that can stand alone as a complete sentence because it expresses a complete thought and includes a subject and a verb.

If a group of words contains a subject and a verb but does not express a complete thought, it is a **dependent clause**.

Read the following examples of dependent clauses:

> As Caitlin smiled at the crowd of friends and family members.

> When the pilot congratulated the crewmembers on their successful flight.

> That the florist added to the bouquet at the last minute.

Dependent clauses usually begin with a word that makes the rest of the sentence sound incomplete. Here are some examples of **subordinating conjunctions** that often make a clause dependent:

after	because	once	when
although	even though	since	while
as	if	until	

If this word is removed, the sentence expresses a complete thought.

> ~~As~~ Caitlin smiled at the crowd of friends and family members.

> ~~When~~ The pilot congratulated the crewmembers on their successful flight.

> ~~That~~ The florist added to the bouquet at the last minute.

> ▸ These examples are now complete sentences (independent clauses).

Even though they can leave you wondering, dependent clauses are not all bad. They can be combined with independent clauses to form complex sentences. Here are some examples:

> Even though it rained, we had a pretty good turnout for the chili bake-off.

> Sarah stayed up working on the project until she couldn't keep her eyes open any longer.

> Once the auditions are finished, we'll decide on the cast of the play.

On Your Own

Read the statements below and identify the dependent clause.

☐ Every student needs to study for midterm exams.
☐ Because grades are due by Friday.
☐ All assignments must be turned in by Wednesday.

Writing Environment: Academic

College-level writing should naturally be more complex than lower-level writing. One way to achieve this is by combining independent and dependent clauses. Consider the examples below:

History

> Throughout his life, Martin Luther King worked tirelessly for racial equality, always advocating peaceful progress rather than violence.

Biology

> Despite the ivory-billed woodpecker's reported extinction, a few wildlife biologists in Louisiana have reported hearing it's call, drawing bird-lovers from all over the world to the area.

Types of Sentences

Now that we have a complete sentence, we need to know the type of statement it makes. Sentences can usually be grouped into one of four types of statements:

- Declarative
- Interrogative
- Imperative
- Exclamatory

Declarative sentences make statements and end with periods. They provide facts, opinions, and information about a subject.

> The Golden Gate Bridge spans 1.2 miles across the San Francisco Bay. Although it's not the longest suspension bridge, the Golden Gate is one of the most recognizable.

Interrogative sentences are questions, so they end with question marks. Exams, applications, and surveys often use interrogative sentence. Consider the examples below.

> How many pounds are in one kilogram?

> Have you ever traveled to other countries?

Helpful Hint

When someone asks a question that doesn't require an answer, it's a rhetorical question. Often, writers and speakers ask rhetorical questions to make a point or encourage the reader to think about a topic. For instance, someone giving a presentation about social customs might say, "Do you judge people based on first impressions?" She doesn't expect someone to stand up and answer. Instead, she wants people to think about the question and come to a certain conclusion.

Imperative sentences are commands. They tell the implied subject (*you*) what to do. Sometimes, commands come in the form of instructions for a course project, work-related assignment, or assembly manual. Here are some examples:

> List three examples of metaphor in *The Tempest*.

> Attach the silver ground wire to the green screw.

Exclamatory sentences communicate something with strong emotion and end with exclamation points. Consider the examples below.

> I can't believe we won!

> Don't walk on the grass!

Helpful Hint

In informal writing, many people use multiple ending punctuation marks. However, remember that multiple exclamation points, question marks, or a mixture of the two is usually inappropriate for formal writing.

Lesson Wrap-up

Key Terms

Action Verb: a verb that indicates a physical or mental action

Declarative Sentence: a sentence that makes a statement

Dependent Clause: a group of words with a subject and verb that does not express a complete thought

Direct Question: a sentence that asks the audience a question and usually ends with a question mark

Exclamatory Sentence: a sentence that communicates strong emotion

Helping Verb: a word that changes the form of the main verb so that it grammatically fits the sentence

Imperative Sentence: a sentence that makes a command

Implied Subject: the subject of a sentence when the speaker is talking directly to the audience

Independent Clause: a group of words with a subject and verb that expresses a complete thought

Indirect Question: a sentence that tells the audience about a question and usually ends with a period

Interrogative Sentence: a sentence that asks a question

Linking Verb: a verb that links the subject to a description

Subject: who or what the sentence is about

Writing Application: The Characteristics of Sentences

Read the following letter to the editor arguing against local construction projects. It uses a mixture of independent and dependent clauses to create sentences that clearly communicate the author's thoughts.

Letter to the Editor

As a longtime resident of this town, I am saddened by the massive influx of development projects that have taken over Main Street. Not only are they inconsistent with the historical atmosphere of the community, these projects have introduced traffic, congestion, and noise pollution.

This dependent clause gives more information about the writer and his or her connection to the town.

Consider the new four-story apartment complex that towers over Main Street. The modern architecture looks out of place and gaudy. More importantly, its parking was poorly designed, forcing residents to park their cars on the streets of the nearby neighborhood. This

This sentence combines an independent and dependent clause.

complex, along with several others recently constructed in the vicinity of Main Street, bring hundreds of additional cars onto our primary thoroughfare on a daily basis.

In addition to the apartment complexes, the town has also approved the addition of several new restaurants and bars on Main Street. While I realize these establishments bring valuable revenue to our town, they also bring additional traffic to properties that are not large enough to support the necessary parking. This forces more people to park in nearby neighborhoods. Furthermore, the town has done very little to enforce the noise ordinance. While live music must end by 11:00 p.m., there's still the noise from many patrons sitting outside the restaurants and bars.

I truly love this town and have never considered living anywhere else, but my resolve is starting to dwindle. Do we really want to live in a place that devalues its history and longtime residents for the sake of being new and the trendy? Do we really want to live in a place that gives developers and business owners free reign? I hope your answer is no, and I hope the town will listen to its residents and take the necessary steps before it's too late!

These interrogative sentences are rhetorical questions. They're intended to point out negative aspects of the current situation.

The exclamatory sentence conveys the writer's emotion.

Lesson 9.3
Using Commas

Sometimes, a small punctuation mark can make a big difference.

Incorrect   Let's eat Grandpa.

Correct   Let's eat, Grandpa.

It's important to understand what **commas** can and cannot do. Like the previous example demonstrates, commas have the power to completely change the meaning of a sentence. Using them correctly shows that you are a competent communicator.

> Further Resources
> Check out this article (http://priceonomics.com/the-most-expensive-typo-in-legislative-history/) to read about the most expensive typo in history!

In this lesson, you will learn about commas:

The Purposes and Functions of Commas
Avoiding Unnecessary Commas

The Purposes and Functions of Commas

Commas are used in many ways. Let's take a look at how they function in different writing scenarios.

Helpful Hint

One common strategy for adding commas to a sentence is reading the sentence aloud and adding commas whenever your voice naturally pauses. While this will work in many cases, it's not a completely error-proof strategy. When you proofread, review the rules of commas to make sure that you catch as many errors as possible.

Lists

A list includes a series of three or more items in a sentence. The items may be single words, phrases, or clauses. Each item in the list, except the last one, is followed by a comma.

> My cousin traveled extensively in California, Texas, and Florida during his first year of retirement.

> This morning I woke up early, ate a big breakfast, and hurried to the university.

Further Resources

A comma used with a conjunction before the last item in a list is commonly known as the Oxford comma. To learn more about the history of the Oxford comma and the debate about its use, watch this video (https://www.youtube.com/watch?v=ptM7FzyjtRk&feature=youtu.be) from TED Education.

Compound Sentences

Compound sentences include two or more **independent clauses**, which express complete thoughts. These clauses can be joined by a comma and a **coordinating conjunction**, which joins similar words or a group of words. The pattern would look like this:

Independent Clause	Comma + Coordinating Conjunction	Independent Clause
Mary wants to see the new *Star Wars* film	, but	John wants to watch March Madness.
The new Fitbit includes GPS	, so	I plan to order one before I travel.

Helpful Hint

It's easy to make errors when writing a compound sentence. However, not using a comma in this type of sentence is incorrect because the coordinating conjunction is not strong enough to join the independent clauses.

Incorrect: My niece loves swimming and my nephew loves gymnastics.

Likewise, writing the sentence with only the comma and omitting the coordinating conjunction is a **comma splice** error.

Incorrect: My niece loves swimming, my nephew loves gymnastics.

When joining independent clauses, always include both the comma and the coordinating conjunction.

Introductory Elements

Using introductory elements at the beginnings of sentences creates variety. An introductory element could be a word, phrase, or clause. No matter what, introductory elements should be separated from the main sentence by a comma.

Introductory words	Unfortunately, the cold weather ruined our plans for a weekend trip to the beach.
Introductory phrases	During the hour-long layover, Savanna checked her email and texts.
Introductory clauses	After a blizzard closed the interstate around Denver, the weary travelers were forced to seek shelter at motels and rest stops.

To learn more about independent and dependent clauses, see Lesson 9.2.

On Your Own

For each type of introductory element, create your own example.

Introductory Type	Examples
Introductory word	
Introductory phrase	
Introductory clause	

Interrupting or Extra Elements

A sentence may be interrupted by nonessential information that adds detail but is not necessary to make the sentence complete. These elements can be words, phrases, or clauses. Interrupting elements must be surrounded by commas.

Sabrina, who recently moved here from San Francisco, hopes to apply for the Presidential Scholarship.

Extra information should be separated from essential information with a comma.

> The emotional ending of *Finding Dory* is heart-rending, making me cry each time I watch it.

Helpful Hint

By putting the interrupting element between commas, you indicate that the information may be omitted without changing the meaning of the main sentence. Think of the commas like "handles" that someone could use to lift the interrupting information out of the sentence.

On Your Own

How are commas used in the following sentences? Enter your answer in the right-hand column. The first one has been done for you.

Examples	Comma Use
If we plan carefully, we can afford to take a vacation next summer.	Introductory element
Fred, who has always lived in Michigan, plans to attend college in San Francisco.	
Watching sports on television is exciting, but participating in physical activities is healthier.	
Without a doubt, cell phones are an important part of communication.	
Popular social media sites include Facebook, Twitter, Instagram, and Pinterest.	

Quotations

Quoted material can usually be divided into two sections: a **signal phrase** and the actual **quote**. To separate these two sections, use a comma.

Signal Phrase	Quote
My friend exclaimed,	"Congratulations on the new job!"

The signal phrase may occur at the beginning, end, or middle of the sentence.

> The TSA officer said, "Please show me your boarding pass and driver's license."

> "Please show me your boarding pass and driver's license," the TSA officer said.

> "Please," said the TSA officer, "show me your boarding pass and driver's license."

To learn more about quotations, see Lesson 9.5.

Writing Environment: Professional

Comma rules vary depending on the context. For example, in Associated Press (AP) style, which is used by journalists, commas are not included before the conjunction in a simple series.

> The fire originated on Fifth Street and spread to the surrounding neighborhoods of Brickton, Granger and Trent.

Salutations and Closings

Personal letters often begin with a greeting, also called the **salutation**, which should be followed by a comma. Closings in personal and business letters also utilize commas.

Salutations/Greetings

> Dear Luca,

> Dear Professor Gates,

Closings

> Best wishes,

> Sincerely,

Writing Environment: Professional

When composing a business letter, the salutation ends with a colon rather than a comma.

> Research and Development:

> Mrs. Henderson:

Coordinate Adjectives

Coordinate adjectives, which are two **adjectives** of equal value that modify the same word, are separated by a comma. You can use two methods to determine whether or not two adjectives are coordinate.

- Can you reverse the order of the adjectives without changing the meaning?

> The slimy, odorous mud filled the low-lying neighborhoods in New Orleans after Hurricane Katrina.

> The odorous, slimy mud filled the low-lying neighborhoods in New Orleans after Hurricane Katrina.

- Can you insert the coordinating conjunction *and* between the two adjectives?

> The slimy, odorous mud filled the low-lying neighborhoods of New Orleans after Hurricane Katrina.

> The slimy and odorous mud filled the low-lying neighborhoods in New Orleans after Hurricane Katrina.

Miscellaneous Uses

Numbers

Facebook had 1,500, 000,000 active users in 2016.

Dates

On Tuesday, July 4, we will meet in Orlando for the family reunion.

Names and Titles

John Barrett, PhD, received his degree from Oxford University.

Locations and Addresses

Seattle, Washington, was rebuilt after the Great Fire of 1899, leaving remnants of the original city underground.

Avoiding Unnecessary Commas

Using commas incorrectly can alter your message and confuse your reader. Study these situations that use unnecessary commas so that you can avoid mistakes.

Lists with Two Items

A list must include at least three items to qualify as a series. A list with only two items does not qualify as a series, so a comma is not necessary.

Incorrect

Many college students survive on a diet of carry-out pizza, and Chinese noodle cups.

Clauses with Relative Pronouns

Clauses starting with the **relative pronoun** *that* should not be set off by a comma because the information is essential to the sentence.

Incorrect

I dislike pets, that are not housebroken.

Concluding Dependent Clauses

If a sentence concludes with a **dependent clause**, no comma is needed to separate the clauses.

Incorrect

Ella and Carson decided to go on a road trip, since they had Monday off.

On Your Own

Identify the sentence with a comma error.

- ☐ If you own a smart phone, downloading a weather alert app would be a wise investment in your safety.
- ☐ Jessie's plans for the weekend include binge watching *Downton Abbey*, and cleaning out her closet.
- ☐ Antique stores are filled with books, furniture, and trinkets.

Writing Environment: Everyday

Have you ever come across a punctuation mistake while reading a novel, magazine, or online article? How did it change your opinion of the author's credibility? Imagine you're reading a wildlife conservation article about baby seals and come across the following sentence:

> Stop clubbing, seals.

This sentence seems to reference seals dancing at a nightclub. Even if you realize that it's a comma error, you've already been distracted from the article's message.

Now consider the sentence without the comma error:

> Stop clubbing seals.

This sentence accurately states the intended message (stop killing seals) and does not have a distracting comma error.

Lesson Wrap-up

Key Terms

Adjective: a word that describes a noun or pronoun

Comma: a punctuation mark used to separate items in a list; join compound sentences; mark introductory words, phrases, and clauses; add extra or unnecessary details to a sentence; and separate similar adjectives

Comma Splice: a sentence error made when two independent clauses are combined with a comma but no conjunction

Compound Sentence: two independent clauses joined by a comma and a coordinating conjunction

Coordinate Adjectives: two adjectives of equal value that modify the same word

Coordinating Conjunction: a conjunction that joins similar words or a group of words together

Dependent Clause: a group of words with a subject and a verb that does not express a complete thought

Independent Clause: a group of words with a subject and a verb that expresses a complete thought

Quote: using the exact words from a source

Relative Pronoun: a pronoun used to introduce a dependent clause

Salutation: a phrase that greets the person or group receiving a letter

Signal Phrase: a phrase used to identify source information

Writing Application: Using Commas

Read the following cover letter and consider how it uses commas. In addition to the author's professional credentials, his correct use of commas also reinforces his credibility.

March 22, 2016

Dear Ms. Ellison,

As a recent graduate of Oregon State University, I am pleased to be considered for the teaching position with your school district. Pine Valley has a reputation as a progressive, challenging school, and I am looking forward to working there next year. My cooperating instructor, Dr. Jennifer Howard, told me, "Ms. Ellison will be glad to consider you for a position at Pine Valley Elementary School."

Overall, I am willing to teach any grade level since I am certified to teach kindergarten through eighth grade. All students inspire me to utilize my instructional skills in the classroom. The energetic, enthusiastic younger students inspire me; however, the older students challenge my creativity in the classroom

My college background includes minor studies in English, social studies, and business. These areas of skill would also enable me to be a flexible staff member.

I look forward to hearing from you at your earliest convenience regarding my status as a teacher candidate.

Sincerely,

Donald Wyman

Side notes:

The date and salutation both use commas.

The introductory dependent clause is followed by a comma.

The signal phrase and quote are separated by a comma.

Energetic and *enthusiastic* are coordinate adjectives that can be joined by a comma.

The closing also uses a comma.

Lesson 9.4

Using Semicolons and Colons

Whether you are writing for academic, professional, or personal reasons, variety is important. Imagine if the sentences in a book or article were always five words long and ended with a period. You would quickly become bored and confused.

How can you add variety to your writing? By simply using different punctuation marks, like semicolons and colons, you can increase the readability of your words and make subtle connections between ideas. Although often mistaken for each other, semicolons and colons play distinct roles.

In this lesson, you will learn about the following topics:

The Purposes and Functions of Semicolons
The Purposes and Functions of Colons
Common Misuses of Semicolons and Colons

The Purposes and Functions of Semicolons

Semicolons look like a period stacked on top of a comma.

Semicolons have two important uses:

- Joining related sentences
- Separating items in complicated lists

Related Sentences

Semicolons make it easy to join two independent clauses. An **independent clause** is a group of words that has a subject and verb and expresses a complete thought. Short, choppy sentences interrupt the flow of your words, making it more difficult for your reader to connect your ideas. Using semicolons to create compound sentences increases the readability of your essay.

Let's take a look at a sample paragraph filled with short, choppy sentences:

> Sarah wanted to go to the movie theater. She did not want to go alone. She thought about asking her friends to go. However, Sarah was afraid they would laugh at her choice of movie. She did not ask them. She spent the weekend catching up on homework.

Now, read the paragraph again now after the sentences have been joined by semicolons or commas and coordinating conjunctions. (**Coordinating conjunctions** join similar words or groups of words.)

> Sarah wanted to go to the movie theater, but she did not want to go alone. She thought about asking her friends to go; however, Sarah was afraid they would laugh at her choice of movie. She did not ask them, so she spent the weekend catching up on homework.

When you use a semicolon to join two related sentences, you are drawing a strong connection between them. Often, the second independent clause reinforces or elaborates on the first independent clause.

> Southern cuisine varies greatly; for example, Louisiana is famous for its Cajun and Creole dishes while Texas is famous for Tex-Mex and barbeque.

Helpful Hint

When you use a semicolon to separate two clauses, you can check it by replacing it with an imaginary period. Would the two clauses make sense as separate sentences? If so, using the semicolon is probably correct.

On Your Own

Re-write the following sentences so that the related independent clauses are joined with semicolons.

> Some college freshmen mistakenly believe that choosing a major is an irreversible decision. Most students will change their major an average of three times before graduating.

Complicated Lists

Another reason to use semicolons is to separate list items that already contain **commas**. For example, a list of cities and states would become too complicated and unclear with all the commas.

> Last year, we traveled to Dallas, Texas; Omaha, Nebraska; Tampa, Florida; and Chicago, Illinois.

> Thimphu, Bhutan; Maseru, Lesotho; and Porto-Novo, Benin are on my list of unusual places that I would like to visit.

A list of dates can also become confusing without semicolons to clearly group the month, day, and year.

> The plant manager announced that mandatory training would occur on November 15, 2015; December 17, 2015; January 11, 2016; and February 27, 2016.

You can also use semicolons in a list of nouns with multiple **adjectives** or a list containing **appositives** (descriptive phrases).

> College students on a tight budget can save money by purchasing current, used textbooks before the semester begins; finding a reliable, trustworthy roommate to split costs; and buying healthy, affordable groceries.

> The city council called an emergency meeting that included Pamela Black, the mayor; James Richardson, the city clerk; and Christina Waters, the city inspector.

On Your Own

Identify sentences in the following passage that should use semicolons.

> After nearly being hit by a car, the bicyclist decided it was time to stop at a restaurant and take a short break. Miguel had traveled through New Boston, Texas, Texarkana, Arkansas, and Idabel, Oklahoma in a single morning. However, he was not traveling alone. He was accompanied by Sayra, his mother, Alexandra, his sister, and Joseph, his father. As a family, they had bicycled across all 48 contiguous states, northern Mexico, and southern Canada. Miguel hoped to qualify to compete in the

2016 Summer Olympics. The qualifying dates for different bicycling events were March 27, 2016, September 19, 2017, and May 26, 2017.

As you can see, semicolons play an important role in your writing by adding variety to your sentence structure and style. Semicolons also add clarity to complicated lists that might otherwise confuse your audience. If you correctly use semicolons, your audience is more likely to understand your ideas.

The Purposes and Functions of Colons

Colons are also used frequently and not just in academic writing. They have several important functions.

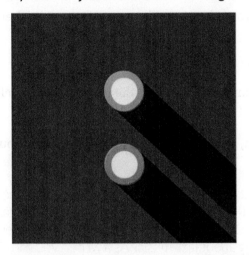

A colon looks like two periods stacked on top of each other.

Writing Environment: Everyday

Imagine that your credit card was charged for a purchase that you didn't make. You may have to submit a letter or email stating the facts. Whether you realize it or not, semicolons and colons will play an important role in your letter. Look for colons in the following example:

January 15, 2016
To the Dispute Department:
On my most recent statement dated January 10, I have a charge showing for January 2 at Betty's Baked Goods in the amount of $245.78. I have never purchased from this store. I called to receive a copy of the receipt, which I have included in this letter. According to the receipt, a wedding cake was purchased at 3:06 p.m. on January 2; the signature on the receipt is not even my name. Please consider this letter as a notice of the following two requests: an official dispute of this charge and a request to open an investigation into how my card was charged for someone else's purchase. Thank you,
Nathan Merit

The use of colons in this letter adds formality and clarifies what is required of the addressee.

Here are some specific functions of the **colon**:

- Setting off an important appositive or concluding explanation
- Introducing a list or quotation
- Listing two-part titles
- Writing business salutations
- Writing numbers

Appositives and Concluding Explanations

Sometimes, you may want part of a sentence to stand out. A colon can help you accomplish this because it indicates that whatever follows it is important.

The example below draws attention to an appositive by placing it after a colon at the end of the sentence.

> The teacher wanted us to understand two requirements for passing her class: attendance and participation.

Compare the following two sentences:

> One feature of the late 1940s stands out above all the rest: the introduction of the smooth, relaxed sounds of jazz music.

> The introduction of the smooth, relaxed sounds of jazz music stands out as one of the primary features of the late 1940s.

> ▶ Do you see the difference? Although we easily flipped the first sentence around to bring *jazz music* to the front, we have now lost the buildup, suspense, and attention attached to those words. The second sentence leaves the reader thinking about the 1940s. However, after reading the first sentence, the reader is thinking about jazz music. As a writer, you can choose how you want your readers to respond.

Group Activity

Working in a small group, make a list of circumstances when you would want to use a semicolon to join related ideas in your writing or a colon to set off something important. Provide specific examples.

Lists and Quotations

You can also use colons to introduce a list or **quotation**. However, the word group before the colon must be an independent clause.

> After taking a semester of English Composition, students should achieve the following goals: have a good grasp of grammatical rules, write a well-organized essay, and research a topic using reliable sources.

> John Wayne once made this inspiring declaration: "Courage is being scared to death but saddling up anyway."

Two-Part Titles

Colons are also useful when developing two-part titles. Generally, a two-part title begins with a general subject followed by the narrower topic.

> Climate Change: The Hidden Dangers of Nonnative Species
>
> The first part of this title, before the colon, tells the reader that the broad topic is climate change. The colon indicates a narrowed focus on the dangers of nonnative species. This title also tells the reader that the writer intends to make a connection between climate change and nonnative species.

Business Salutations

When writing a business letter, you should use a colon after your **salutation**. A business salutation is the introductory greeting at the beginning of the letter.

> Dear Jeremy:

Using a colon in a professional letter adds formality to your letter and can leave your reader with a better impression of you.

Writing Environment: Professional

At some point in your life, if you haven't already, you will have to apply for a job. Typically, part of the application process includes submitting a cover letter. A cover letter serves multiple purposes, including introducing yourself, pointing out highlights from your résumé, and making a connection to the hiring committee or department.

> February 18, 2016
> Hanna Clark:
> I would like to be considered for the position of 8th grade science teacher at Forrest Hills Middle School. My thorough training and extensive background in multiple sciences will facilitate my ability to teach students effectively.
> I have been a student teacher at Forrest Hills Middle School for the last five months. During my time here, I have coordinated the science club. I have also integrated as much technology in my classroom as possible to enhance my student's ability to comprehend and retain information so that they will be prepared for high school. Last, I have introduced students to laboratory experiments and hands-on projects; I am a firm believer in project-based learning.
> I would like to mention my most relevant qualifications:
>   1. State-certified educator, 2010
>   2. Graduated with a bachelor's degree in Education
>   3. Strong background in chemistry, biology, and earth science
> I look forward to meeting with you to discuss this position further.
> Sincerely,
> Janice Copelin

Colons play an important role in this letter by starting the letter with formality and respect. Later, the colon is used to introduce a short list of important qualifications. The semicolon also connects two related ideas: hands-on projects and project-based learning.

Numbers

Last, colons are used to show relationships between numbers.

Purpose	Examples
Volumes and issues of journals or magazines	*New England Journal of Medicine* 374:9 *Theoretical Criminology* 15:3
Parts of religious texts	Rig Veda 10:121:8 (book: hymn: stanza) John 3:16 (chapter: verse)
Ratios	20:1 5:8
Times	12:15 a.m. 6:38 p.m.

Writing Environment: Academic

Frequently, teachers will require you to write an analytical essay on a piece of literature. Using a mixture of punctuation adds sophistication to your writing. It shows your reader that you are comfortable with grammatical rules and have taken the time to link ideas in your writing. Your reader will be more engaged with your writing as well.

Common Misuses of Semicolons and Colons

Using semicolons and colons correctly in your writing shows that you have a firm grasp on their grammatical rules. However, because semicolons and colons look similar, they are often mistaken for each other.

Semicolons

A simple list does not require semicolons.

Incorrect   Some of the most common courses taken in college include biology; English composition; algebra; and psychology.

Corrected   Some of the most common courses taken in college include biology, English composition, algebra, and psychology.

Avoid joining an independent and dependent clause with a semicolon.

Incorrect   The boy threw the ball into the street; because he was angry at his brother.

Corrected   The boy threw the ball into the street because he was angry at his brother.

On Your Own

Identify the sentence that uses a semicolon correctly.

- ☐ My favorite band will be playing on March 30; April 12; and May 5.
- ☐ College students typically enjoy literature classes; because of the variety of stories they can read.

☐ Sarah performed well on her final exam; she had studied for it a few hours each day for two weeks.

☐ In the dark, murky waters of the lake; a school of fish surrounded a sunken boat.

Colons

The following example uses a colon incorrectly to introduce a quote.

> St. Augustine once said: "Patience is the companion of wisdom."

There are two easy ways to correct this error. Either make sure the word group before the colon is an independent clause, or replace the colon with a comma.

> St. Augustine once made the following statement: "Patience is the companion of wisdom."

> St. Augustine once said, "Patience is the companion of wisdom."

Though colons are used to emphasize appositives, they cannot set off a **direct object** or **object of a preposition**. **Prepositions** and **verbs** should not be separated from their objects.

Incorrect   A typical recipe for meatloaf calls for a variety of ingredients such as: pork, beef, crackers, bread crumbs, eggs, ketchup, tomato sauce, peppers, onions, and various seasonings.

Incorrect   Sammy wanted to buy: a soda.

In these cases, simply leave out the colon.

Correct   A typical recipe for meatloaf calls for a variety of ingredients such as pork, beef, crackers, bread crumbs, eggs, ketchup, tomato sauce, peppers, onions, and various seasonings.

Correct   Sammy wanted to buy a soda.

On Your Own

Identify the sentence that uses a colon correctly.

☐ Black holes exhibit a strong gravitational pull on: everything, even light.

☐ The edge of a black hole, the point where nothing can escape its gravitational pull, has an ominous name: the event horizon.

☐ In the 1970s, Stephen Hawking theorized that black holes released thermal radiation: this effect became known as Hawking radiation.

☐ Someone once said: "Black holes are where God divided by zero."

> **Helpful Hint**
> Be careful not to flood your writing with semicolons and colons. Remember that the ultimate goal is to use a variety of punctuation, not just colons and/or semicolons.

Lesson Wrap Up

Key Terms

Adjective: a word that describes a noun or pronoun

Appositive: a noun or noun phrase that describes something

Colon: a punctuation mark used to introduce a list or quotation, end a salutation, and join related numbers

Comma: a punctuation mark used to separate items in a list; join compound sentences; mark introductory words, phrase, and clauses; add extra or unnecessary details to a sentences; and separate simple adjectives

Coordinating Conjunction: a conjunction that joins similar words or a group of words together

Direct Object: a word that receives the action of a verb

Independent Clause: a group of words with a subject and verb that expresses a complete thought

Object of a Preposition: a word that completes the meaning of a prepositional phrase

Preposition: a word that completes the meaning of a preposition

Quote: someone's exact words

Salutation: a phrase that greets the person or group receiving the letter

Semicolon: a punctuation mark used to combine two independent clauses and separate long list items

Verb: a word that represents an action, relationship, or state of being

Writing Application: Using Semicolons and Colons

Consider how the following brief essay uses semicolons and colons to add variety to the sentences and create clear connections between ideas.

The Working Class: A Complicated Social Structure

In "The Old Nurse's Story," Elizabeth Gaskell gives the reader insight into the lives of servants in the mid-Victorian period. Unlike other authors of that time, Gaskell focuses on the working class, providing a deeper characterization of their lives. In fact, her primary character and narrator is a nurse-maid, Hester. Additional working-class characters include James, the footman; Dorothy, his wife and housekeeper; Agnes, James and Dorothy's own servant and manual laborer; and Mrs. Stark, Miss Grace Furnivall's life-long maid and companion. Using these five characters, Gaskell reveals a complex social hierarchy and intricate set of social rules among the servants.

The two-part title uses a colon to draw attention to the main point of the essay.

Instead of several short, choppy sentences about each character, semicolons create a clear, brief list.

Gaskell writes about two social classes: the nobles of the aristocracy and the servants of the working class. However, she focuses on the working class and reveals that it contains multiple sublevels. For example, early in the story Gaskell divulges that James, the footman, looks down upon his own wife "because, till he had married her, she had never lived in any but a farmer's household" (Gaskell 3). Since James has spent nearly his entire life as a servant in Lord Furnivall's home, he is in a higher social position than someone who merely worked in a farmer's home. No doubt, James believes that he is in one of the highest sub-levels of the working class. His position guarantees that he and his wife will always have a home, decent pay, food, and probably a position for any children. James and Dorothy even have their own servant, Agnes, who is at the bottom of the social ladder. They expect Agnes "to do all the rough work" (3).

Consequently, Hester, the nurse-maid, is in a unique position. She realizes her promotion in her social class even before leaving for Furnivall Manor. The reader catches a glimpse of this realization in Hester's statement: "I was well pleased that all the folks in the Dale should stare and admire, when they heard I was going to be young lady's maid at my Lord Furnivall's at Furnivall Manor" (1). She is not yet eighteen when she arrives at Furnivall Manor; however, she realizes her position as nurse-maid makes her equivalent in rank to James and Dorothy. "I had always held my head rather above [Agnes], as I was even to James and Dorothy, and she was little better than their servant" (4). Hester's statement reinforces the fact that there was a distinct separation between servants. It also indicates that the two ranks rarely intermingled. Hester can barely bring herself to ask Agnes about the ghosts, and when she does, it is as a last resort. However, one other servant holds herself above all the others, Mrs. Stark; she has been Miss Grace's maid and companion nearly her whole life. "[S]he seemed more like a friend than a servant" (3). The other servants look upon her as being nearly equivalent to Miss Grace. Due to Miss Grace's age and deafness, Mrs. Stark often takes charge.

In "The Old Nurse's Story," Elizabeth Gaskell creates an interesting snapshot of working-class society. Through the story's narration and dialogue, she preserves a picture of the hierarchy not just between the aristocracy and the servants but among the servants.

The colon in this sentence emphasizes the two social classes that Gaskell writes about.

Rather than repeating phrases like *Gaskell writes* or *Gaskell says*, using a colon changes up the way you can introduce a quote.

The semicolon in this sentence contrasts Hester's age with her rank.

Here, the semicolon connects two ideas. Mrs. Stark has the highest rank among the servants because she has been Miss Grace's maid and companion for many years.

Lesson 9.5
Using Quotation Marks, Parentheses, and Brackets

Sometimes, sentences contain information that is nonessential or is quoted from another source. If you don't visually separate this text from the rest of the sentence, your readers may become confused. Look at the following examples:

> The American Nutrition Association claims that it is vital to balance a healthy diet with exercise in order to increase optimal life expectancy.

> Last year's summer vacation was incredibly short three days so we're trying to convince my parents to take a week off this year.

> "It could be the best thing to ever happen to us!"

In the first example, it's unclear where the author's words end and the American Nutrition Association's claim begins. To make sure you are giving proper credit to your sources, you must use quotation marks.

> The American Nutrition Association claims that it is vital to balance "a healthy diet with exercise in order to increase optimal life expectancy."

The second sentence is difficult to read because there is extra information inserted right into the middle. Adding parentheses will make this sentence much clearer.

> Last year's summer vacation was incredibly short (three days) so we're trying to convince my parents to take a week off this year.

In the third sentence, there is no context provided for the reader; therefore, it's unclear what the word *it* refers to. To clarify your writing, use brackets to insert the meaning of unclear language.

> "[Spending a semester abroad in Italy] could be the best thing to ever happen to us!"

In this lesson, you will learn about the purposes of the following punctuation marks:

Quotation Marks
Parentheses
Brackets

Quotation Marks

Quotation marks are punctuation marks most commonly used to repeat someone else's words. Take a look at these examples:

> My favorite college professor was fond of saying, "The internet is an appendix for everything," right before he sent us searching for some odd piece of knowledge.

> "Many people will try to give you advice that they don't take themselves," my mom said. "Just think about what works best for you."

▸ In both of these examples, the exact words of a source are being repeated. The quotation marks clearly show which words belong to the author of the sentence and which ones belong to the person being quoted.

> **Reflection Questions**
>
> Think back to a time when a friend accidentally or purposefully misquoted you. What was that experience like? How does that situation relate to the use of quotation marks?

Quotes aren't limited to complete sentences. In some situations, you might quote just a small group of words to emphasize an important idea. Look at this sentence:

> Famous musician Buddy Collins once said that the best advice he can give new artists is "not to lose your voice."

Quotation marks are also used around titles of articles, short stories, poems, songs, and book chapters.

> Kate Chopin's "The Story of an Hour" is a short story that explores feminism in the 1800s.

> In Chapter 7, "Famous Battles of the Civil War," the author provides a detailed account of the First Battle of Bull Run.

Regardless of the purpose, quotation marks always come in pairs. This helps the reader know when a quotation or title begins and ends. Look at the following examples:

> "I've been busy baking my roommate, Julie, replied with a sigh.

> "I've been busy baking," my roommate, Julie, replied with a sigh.

> ▷ The first sentence does not use a pair of quotation marks, which makes the sentence confusing and even alters the meaning. Because the second sentence uses a pair of quotation marks, you can clearly see which words are quoted and which are not.

On Your Own

Read the sentence below and identify the word that should be followed by quotation marks.

> "It's important to learn to cook at a young age argued the chef.

Generally, periods, **commas**, exclamation points, and question marks that appear at the end of a quote should be placed inside the closing quotation mark.

> My professor always reminds us to "read the essays slowly so you catch every word."

> Portia asked, "Do you think you can meet this deadline by Thursday?"

> "I've decided to pursue my goal of becoming a lawyer," Eli explained.

> ▷ In the last sentence, note that a comma ends the sentence within the quotation while the period is used to end the entire sentence.

Question marks and exclamation points can sometimes be an exception to this rule. If the entire sentence is **interrogative** or **exclamatory**, put the punctuation mark outside of the quotation marks.

> Did anyone predict the ending of "The Legend of Sleepy Hollow"?

> I still cannot believe we have to read the entire article "In Search of Blood Diamonds"!

To learn more about interrogative and exclamatory sentences, see Lesson 9.2.

Occasionally, you might need to include a quote or title inside another quote. For these situations, use **single quotation marks**.

> The bystander explained, "I heard another customer scream, 'Emergency!' I had to stop what I was doing immediately."

> "Have you read 'The Yellow Wallpaper'? I think you would enjoy it," my English professor said.

Single quotations are always used inside regular quotation marks. They are never used alone.

Group Activity

Find a news article online, read it, and pay attention to how it uses quotations. Who is quoted? What is the content of each quotation? What lead-in and follow-up goes with each quotation, if any? How is the speaker of the quoted words acknowledged? Discuss your findings with your group.

Writing Environment: Professional

When you are drafting professional letters and emails, correctly using quotation marks can quickly communicate intelligence and a strong command of the English language.

Parentheses

Parentheses, like quotation marks, are always used in pairs. They are used to add extra information—like dates, examples, or comments—to a sentence or to introduce an abbreviation.

> William Shakespeare (1564-1616) is credited for writing almost forty plays during his lifetime.

> After my ancestors emigrated from Georgia (the country, not the state), they settled in West Virginia.

> The Super Bowl is a huge money maker for the National Football League (NFL).

> ▷ These sentences could be easily understood without the information inside the parentheses. However, the extra details, also called parenthetical information, are helpful to the reader.

Parenthetical information should always be placed *after* related words but *before* any punctuation marks.

Incorrect   After I signed the contract (and sent it back,) I knew the job was officially mine.

Correct   After I signed the contract (and sent it back), I knew the job was officially mine.

Incorrect   My favorite restaurant is Marco's Pizza. (in Greenville, SC)

Correct   My favorite restaurant is Marco's Pizza (in Greenville, SC).

Keep in mind that parenthetical information breaks the natural flow of a sentence. If you give your readers too many details, they may lose track of your main point. Consider the following example:

> Two years ago (when I had just graduated from medical school), I decided to work with Médecins Sans Frontières, (MSF, or Doctors Without Borders). It was a challenging (for financial, emotional, and physical reasons) yet fulfilling experience. I spent two weeks at headquarters (in Geneva, Switzerland) before being deployed to South Sudan (officially called the Republic of South Sudan).

The main point of this brief paragraph is that the author's experience with Doctors Without Borders was a "challenging yet fulfilling experience." However, all the parenthetical information makes it difficult to locate this idea.

On Your Own

Read the sentences below and identify the one that correctly uses parentheses.

> Even (if) I have to take my sister shopping, I'm still getting something for myself. I'll stop at my favorite store (Francesca's) to see if they have any new earrings.

Writing Environment: Academic

If you've ever written a research paper, you may recall that another use for parentheses is acknowledging the source of outside information. Take a look at this example that uses MLA style:

> Some people simply have more aptitude for learning a new language. However, children are the fastest learners by far. With each year after birth, it becomes slightly more difficult for humans to acquire language. Age thirteen is often said to be the cutoff point; from then onward, becoming perfectly fluent in a new language is nearly impossible (Richardson 45).

This passage uses parentheses to indicate that all or some of the information came from page forty-five of a source authored by someone with the last name Richardson.

To learn more about using parentheses to cite sources, see Lessons 7.8, 7.9, 7.10, or 7.11.

Brackets

Brackets are most commonly used inside parentheses or quotation marks to add minor details, explanations, or context.

If you want to add parenthetical information to text that is already inside parentheses, use brackets. Here's an example:

> My goal is to become a member of a scientific space team (particularly for the National Aeronautics and Space Administration [NASA]).
>
> Adding one set of parentheses inside another set of parentheses would be confusing, so brackets are used instead.

Writing Environment: Everyday

When we communicate with people informally, we tend to be much more relaxed about how we use punctuation. Take a look at this text conversation between friends:

Bryce: is Natalie coming to the party?
Hannah: who knows?!?
Bryce: hmm I may not go then . . .
Hannah: yah, me neither (ugh)

No one will grade your punctuation or spelling in a scenario like this (unless one of your friends is a stickler for grammar). However, even in texts or social media posts, it's still important to make sure your audience can understand you.

Brackets can also be used to insert missing text inside a quotation. Look at this quote:

Jayson said, "I love it."

The readers of this sentence don't know what the word *it* means. To make the quote clearer, the missing information is added using brackets.

Jayson said, "I love [my new job]."

Like single quotation marks, brackets are never used alone. They should only be used inside either quotation marks or parentheses.

On Your Own

Read the sentences below and identify the sentence that correctly uses brackets.

Original: George Wilson beamed at the crowd and said, "It is with profound gratitude that I accept this. I am humbled and will continue to work hard every day to make all of you proud!"

George Wilson beamed at the crowd and said, "It is with profound gratitude that I accept this [honorary award]. I am [humbled and will] continue to work hard every day to make all of you proud!"

Further Resources

For even more uses of parentheses and brackets, consult The Punctuation Guide (http://www.thepunctuationguide.com/index.html).

Lesson Wrap-up

Key Terms

Brackets: a pair of punctuation marks commonly used inside parentheses or quotation marks to add minor details to a sentence or insert missing text inside a quotation

Comma: a punctuation mark used to separate items in a list; join compound sentences; mark introductory words, phrases, and clauses; add extra or unnecessary details to a sentence; and separate similar adjectives

Exclamatory Sentence: a sentence that communicates a strong emotion

Interrogative Sentence: a sentence that asks a question

Parentheses: a pair of punctuation marks used to add extra information to a sentence or introduce an abbreviation

Quotation Marks: a pair of punctuation marks most commonly used to repeat someone else's words

Single Quotation Marks: punctuation marks used to mark a quote or title within a quote

Writing Application: Using Quotation Marks, Parentheses, and Brackets

Read the following paragraph and consider how it uses quotation marks, parentheses, and brackets. What would the paragraph be like without these punctuation marks?

Seeing is Believing

"Eureka!" cried Archimedes when he discovered the principle of displacement. Moments of insight like his are a reward of the creative, problem-solving process. For decades, psychologists have been analyzing how people immerse themselves in the process of creativity. Surprisingly, staring into space is one of the procedures that facilitates problem-solving and can prompt a eureka moment. Carola Salvi (Northwestern University and the Chicago Rehabilitation Institute) and Edward M. Bowden (University of Wisconsin) have been using eye-movement research to study how people manage their mental resources during creative acts. In their article, "Looking for Creativity: Where Do We Look When We Look for New Ideas," the authors note that people who are "looking at nothing" are actually shutting down external sensors in order to pay attention to internal (that is, mental) stimuli. They are "reducing the cognitive load and enhancing attention to internally evolving [mental processing]" (Salvi and Bowden). The next time you see someone staring into space (or catch yourself doing it), don't assume its idle daydreaming. He or she could be about to make an incredible new discovery!

The quoted word and exclamation point are inside quotation marks.

This sentence uses parentheses to add extra details about the researchers' credentials.

The article title is inside quotation marks.

The original quote used the word activation, *which has been replaced by a clearer phrase in brackets.*

Works Cited

Salvi, Carola, and Edward Bowden. "Looking for Creativity: Where Do We Look When We Look for New Ideas?" *Frontiers in Psychology*, 15 Feb. 2016. *ResearchGate*, doi: 10.3389/fpsyg.2016.00161.

Chapter 10
Grammatical Sentences

Lesson 10.1
Common Sentence Errors

Writing a basic sentence is fairly easy: all you need is a **subject**, a **verb**, and a complete thought. In some situations, however, these simple sentences aren't strong enough to communicate your ideas fully.

Imagine reading a book that contained only basic sentences. It might sound something like this:

> Mara woke up. She lay in her bed for a few minutes. She wondered about the day. What was going to happen? Worry began to pool in her stomach. Her alarm clock suddenly began ringing. She decided that she wasn't ready to wake up. She pulled a pillow over her head. She went back to sleep.
>
> Even though all the sentences in this paragraph are grammatically correct, they do not express the ideas in the most effective way. Combining some of this information into more complex sentences, as in the revised paragraph below, will help you demonstrate the relationships between ideas.
>
> Mara woke up. Lying in bed, she began to think about the day. What was going to happen? As worry began to pool in her stomach, her alarm clock suddenly began ringing. Not ready to wake up, she pulled a pillow over her head and went back to sleep.

While moving and combining information can help you write more effectively, these changes can also introduce errors into your writing. Being able to correct these mistakes will ensure that you are communicating your ideas in the best way possible.

Reflection Questions

How short can a sentence be? How long can a sentence be? What's the length of an average sentence?

This lesson will teach you to recognize and fix three types of sentence errors:

Fragments
Fused Sentences
Comma Splices

Fragments

A **fragment** is a sentence that does not express a complete thought.

> Behind the baseball field

> During the final moments of the hurricane

Some fragments are **phrases**, which are word groups that do not form a complete thought because they are missing a subject and/or verb. Look at the following examples:

> Was dreaming about life somewhere else

> One of the best sports arenas in the country, Camden Yards

> After painting with her sister

To correct these types of fragments, you can either add the missing subject and/or verb or combine the fragment with another sentence by using a **conjunction** and **comma**.

Add subject:

> I was dreaming about life somewhere else.

Add subject + verb:

> My father got to tour one of the best sports arenas in the country, Camden Yards.

Combine:

> After painting with her sister, Nicole took a walk through Central Park.

Helpful Hint

If you are having a hard time finding the subject and verb in a sentence, follow these steps:

1. First, put (parentheses) around any **prepositional phrases**.
2. Look for an **action verb** or **linking verb**.
3. Finally, ask yourself who or what is doing the action or being described.

Another type of fragment is a dependent clause. **Dependent clauses** have a subject and a verb, but they do not express a complete thought.

> Even though I exercised all summer

> Although my mother's apple pie did not win the county competition

Dependent clauses usually start with a word that makes the rest of the clause sound incomplete. Removing this word often creates a complete sentence.

> ~~Even though~~ I exercised all summer.

> ~~Although~~ My mother's apple pie did not win the county competition.

Dependent clauses can also be combined with an independent clause to show a relationship between two thoughts. An **independent clause** uses both a subject and a verb to express a complete thought. When combining an independent and dependent clause, make sure to adjust the punctuation and wording if necessary.

> I did not meet my weight-loss goal even though I exercised all summer.

> Although my mother's apple pie did not win the county competition, we thoroughly enjoyed eating it after dinner that evening.

> ▹ In these examples, the dependent clauses are combined with independent clauses to create complete sentences. Notice that if the dependent clause comes first, it's followed by a comma.

Sometimes, introducing supporting details can lead to accidentally using a fragment. Look at the example below:

> There are many career opportunities available for those with a degree in medicine. For example, pediatrics, a field of medical study that specializes in children's health.

Since the second sentence has no verb, it is incomplete. Look at the corrected version below.

> There are many career opportunities available for those with a degree in medicine. For example, pediatrics, a field of medical study that specializes in children's health, can provide a wonderfully fulfilling career.

In this sentence, the verb *can provide* completes the sentence.

Writing Environment: Everyday

In emails, blogs, and other casual communication, using a fragment is often not considered a serious error. In fact, some writers use fragments deliberately to give their writing style a breathless quality, to make a short punchline, or include a witty comment. However, when using fragments this way, be sure you are still clearly communicating your intended message.

On Your Own

Read the paragraph below and identify the fragments that need to be corrected.

> It's only a matter of time until environmental pollution catches up to us. Pollution, which has been a growing problem for decades now. There are numerous negative effects on our planet, including spreading disease among humans and animals, destroying plants and vegetation, and ruining beautiful scenery. To do your part to end pollution.

Fused Sentences

A **fused sentence**, sometimes called a "run-on" sentence, incorrectly joins two independent clauses without using a comma and conjunction.

> The delivery guy showed up thirty minutes late I convinced my friends that we should still tip him.

> My sunburn was really bad last weekend I need to be more careful in the future.

There are three ways to fix a fused sentence. The first way is to add the missing comma and **coordinating conjunction** so that the two related ideas are distinct.

> The delivery guy showed up thirty minutes late, but I convinced my friends that we should still tip him.

> My sunburn was really bad last weekend, so I need to be more careful in the future.

> **Helpful Hint**
>
> To remember the seven coordinating conjunctions, use the acronym FANBOYS.
>> For
>>
>> And
>>
>> Nor
>>
>> But
>>
>> Or
>>
>> Yet
>>
>> So

The second way to fix a fused sentence is to add a **semicolon** between the independent clauses.

> The delivery guy showed up thirty minutes late; I convinced my friends that we should still tip him.

> My sunburn was really bad last weekend; I need to be more careful in the future.

Because **compound sentences** are made up of two independent clauses, both halves of the sentence express a complete thought. Don't confuse a compound sentence with a compound subject or verb. In a sentence with a compound subject or verb, both of the subjects or both of the verbs are part of the same complete thought.

Compound Verb

> I ran and walked on my exercise route today.

Compound Subject

> My mother and father both attended my graduation ceremony.

Compound Sentence

> I can eat an entire calzone by myself, but I feel sick afterwards.

Writing Environment: Academic

At times, you may be asked to meet a minimum word or page length requirement for a piece of writing. Resist the temptation to fill up space with fused sentences. This tactic makes your writing difficult to read. Instead, fix sentence errors and consider how you can better support your main idea with more supporting details.

The third way to fix a fused sentence is to split it into two or more sentences.

> The delivery guy showed up thirty minutes late. I convinced my friends that we should still tip him.

> My sunburn was really bad last weekend. I need to be more careful in the future.

Comma Splices

The final type of sentence error is a comma splice. A **comma splice** incorrectly joins two independent clauses with just a comma.

> Our manager gets mad if she sees us on social media, Amanda got in trouble for it just last week.

> During the week before finals, the Cooper library was silent, all eight floors were full of students who were studying and writing.

Because comma splices and fused sentences are both compound sentence errors, they can be fixed in similar ways. The first way to fix a comma splice is to add the missing conjunction between the two independent clauses.

> Our manager gets mad if she sees us on social media, so Amanda got in trouble for it just last week.

> During the week before finals, the Cooper library was silent, and all eight floors were full of students studying and writing.

Helpful Hint

Coordinating conjunctions are not interchangeable. Choosing the right one is important because it could potentially change the meaning of your sentence. Think through the following examples. How does each conjunction affect the meaning?

The president conducted the meeting, and her assistants answered questions.
The president conducted the meeting, but her assistants answered questions.
The president conducted the meeting, for her assistants answered questions.
The president conducted the meeting, yet her assistants answered questions.
The president conducted the meeting, so her assistants answered questions.

The second way to fix a comma splice is to use a semicolon. The semicolon indicates a close relationship between the two ideas in the sentence.

> Our manager gets mad if she sees us on social media; Amanda got in trouble for it just last week.

> During the week before finals, the Cooper library was silent; all eight floors were full of students who were studying and writing.

The final way to fix a comma splice is to split the sentence into two separate sentences. This method works best for two sentences that aren't closely related. Remember to adjust the capitalization and punctuation.

> Our manager gets mad if she sees us on social media. Amanda got in trouble for it just last week.

> During the week before finals, the Cooper library was silent. All eight floors were full of students who were studying and writing.

On Your Own

Read the following sentences and identify the one that uses correct punctuation.

> Amanda and Justin just received news that their first baby is on the way, this has been extremely exciting for the couple. It came at a great time as they just lost their family dog and could use some positivity.

Writing Environment: Professional

Comma splices are a common grammatical mistake, but it's important to avoid them in the workplace. Most employers expect appropriate uses of basic punctuation, particularly commas and periods. Take a look at the examples below from a cover letter. Who would you hire?

> Thank you for your consideration in this matter, I look forward to hearing from you soon

> Thank you for your consideration in this matter. I look forward to hearing from you soon.

This simple change in punctuation communicates that the author has a stronger command of the English language.

On Your Own

Read the following paragraphs and identify all the examples of common sentence errors.

> Post-traumatic stress disorder, known as PTSD, affects millions of people each year. Individuals develop PTSD in response to experiencing some type of traumatic event. The most common forms of trauma include enduring physical or sexual abuse or experiencing the death of a close friend, witnessing wars or acts of terrorism can also cause PTSD. Although some people react to these events in a healthy manner, many find their grief or fear overwhelming.
>
> Psychiatry first recognized post-traumatic stress disorder over one hundred years ago. At the end of the Civil War, documented a condition named "Da Costa's Syndrome," which closely resembles PTSD. In subsequent years, people called the disorder combat fatigue or shell shock. However, only after the Vietnam War did the medical community begin to study post-traumatic stress disorder in earnest.

Lesson Wrap-up

Key Terms

Action Verb: a verb that indicates a physical or mental action

Comma: a punctuation mark used to separate items in a list; join compound sentences; mark introductory words, phrases, and clauses; add extra or unnecessary details to a sentence; and separate similar adjectives

Comma Splice: a sentence error made when two independent clauses are combined with a comma but no conjunction

Compound Sentence: two independent clauses joined by a comma and a conjunction

Conjunction: a word that makes a connection between other words or a group of words

Coordinating Conjunction: a conjunction that joins similar words or groups of words together

Dependent Clause: a group of words with a subject and a verb that does not express a complete thought

Fragment: a sentence that does not express a complete thought

Fused Sentence: a sentence error made when two independent clauses are combined without a comma and conjunction

Independent Clause: a group of words with a subject and a verb that expresses a complete thought

Linking Verb: a verb that links the subject to a description

Phrase: a word group that does not form a complete thought because it is missing a subject and/or verb

Prepositional Phrase: a group of related words that starts with a preposition and ends with a noun or pronoun

Semicolon: a punctuation mark used to combine two independent clauses and separate long list items

Subject: who or what a sentence is about

Verb: a word that represents an action, relationship, or state of being

Writing Application: Common Sentence Errors

Read the following brief paragraph and pay attention to how the sentences are formed.

The Dream Act Girl

When Daniella Zepeda first came to America, she snuck in with her father, who was an experienced field hand, carpenter, and roofer. She was five years old and ready to start school, so she stayed with her aunt in Bowie, Texas, where she could enroll. Eventually, Daniella graduated from high school; she then joined the navy because she had never seen the ocean. She qualified for training on radar and sonar as well as for electronics repair. She served the required four years, and then she headed for college to become an engineer. Using her GI benefits to pay tuition, she graduated in the class of 2012 and immediately filed for U.S. citizenship. A few years later, she finally reunited with her father, whom she had only seen when he occasionally came to visit between jobs. She eventually secured his green card, and he was able to openly live and work anywhere in America.

Lesson 10.2
Using Consistent Subjects and Verbs

Writing is a balancing act, and grammar often plays a big role in achieving this balance. This is particularly true for writing sentences.

A complete sentence always contains at least one **subject** and one **verb**. These subjects and verbs must match each other in number. **Number** refers to a way to divide words into two groups: singular and plural. Singular subjects are always used with singular verbs; plural subjects are always used with plural verbs. This consistency is known as **subject-verb agreement**.

Using consistent subjects and verbs gives your writing balance.

Subject-verb agreement has several benefits. It creates stability and rhythm in your writing, and it also allows your readers to better understand your main point without the obstacle of awkward language.

In this lesson, you will learn about the following aspects of using consistent subjects and verbs:

Recognizing Subject-Verb Agreement
Identifying Situations with Abnormal Subject-Verb Agreement

Recognizing Subject-Verb Agreement

All subjects and verbs are either singular or plural. Look at the following examples:

Charlie walks to school every day.

The students walk to school every day.

▶ In the first example, both the subject (*Charlie*) and the verb (*walks*) are singular. In the second example, both the subject (*students*) and the verb (*walk*) are plural.

Often, plural subjects are spelled with the letter *-s* while singular subjects are not. However, the spelling of singular and plural verbs appears reversed. Singular verbs usually end in the letter *-s*, while plural verbs do not.

Singular subjects are always paired with singular verbs, and plural subjects are always paired with plural verbs. Here are some additional examples:

Singular   The store owner rents a booth at the local flea market.

Plural   We rent a booth at the local flea market.

Singular   Mom is selling the house.

Plural   They are selling the house.

Identifying Situations with Abnormal Subject-Verb Agreement

While subject-verb agreement is fairly straightforward, these situations can complicate the sentence:

- Compound subjects
- Indefinite pronouns
- Collective nouns as subjects
- Distracting words and phrases
- Inverted word order

Compound Subjects

A **compound subject** is made up of two nouns or pronouns joined by a conjunction. Use the following special guidelines to decide if a compound subject is singular or plural.

If the sentence uses the **conjunctions** *and* or *both/and*, the subject is plural.

Myra and John answer questions at the end of each training session.

However, if the sentence uses any of the following conjunctions, use the subject closest to the verb to decide if the subject is singular or plural.

Nor   Neither/nor

Or   Either/or

Look at this example:

Either the bathroom or the kitchen is being remodeled this year.

This sentence uses the conjunction *either/or* to join a compound subject. The singular noun *kitchen* is closest to the verb, so the subject is considered singular.

Here's another example:

Amy or the twins are coming with us today.

In this sentence, the plural noun *twins* is closest to the verb, so the subject is considered plural. If the order were reversed, the subject would be singular since *Amy* is a singular noun:

The twins or Amy is coming with us today.

Indefinite Pronouns

Subject-verb agreement can become complicated when the sentence uses an indefinite pronoun as a subject. **Indefinite pronouns** refer to unnamed nouns. Some indefinite pronouns are always singular or plural while others change form depending on their use in a sentence.

SINGULAR		PLURAL	BOTH
anybody	nobody	both	all
anyone	no one	few	any
anything	nothing	many	most
each	somebody	several	none
everybody	someone		some
everyone	something		
everything			

To determine whether the words *all*, *any*, *most*, *none*, or *some* are plural, look at the meaning of the sentence.

Singular All of the cake has already been eaten.

Plural All of the orders have been filled on time.

Singular Most of the floor is covered by carpeting.

Plural Most of the apartments are carpeted.

Some indefinite pronouns are misleading when combined with a plural subject:

> Each of the cheerleaders has her own megaphone.

Although the word *cheerleaders* is plural, the true subject is *each*, which is singular. If we remove the prepositional phrase *of the cheerleaders*, the sentence clearly refers to individuals.

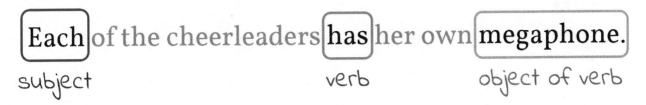

Simplifying the sentence to just the subject, verb, and object of the verb, as in the diagram above, is also a good test to see whether the verb should be singular.

Collective Nouns as Subjects

Collective nouns denote a group but are treated as **singular nouns**. Look at the following examples:

class	club	team	clique
family	band	congregation	faculty
company	choir	cast	department

Each of these collective nouns refers to a single group. Of course, the group is made up of many people, but the word itself is not plural.

Writing Environment: Academic

For a sociology or anthropology research paper, you may use collective nouns to refer to a nation, culture, or people group. It's important to recognize collective nouns and match them with the appropriate verbs.

the nation is
the Anasazi were
the human race is
members of the Mayan civilization were
The Inca were

Writing Environment: Professional

Business memos often address groups of people using collective nouns such as *marketing department*, *summit planning committee*, and *focus group*. Throughout the memo, you may refer to *committee* (singular); *committee members* (plural); or *each member of the committee* (singular), but be consistent in your application of appropriate verb forms each time you vary the noun.

On Your Own

For each of the following sentences, check the box next to the correct verb.

Our football team_____going to the state playoffs.
☐ is
☐ are

The entire cast_____offered free season tickets at the theatre.
☐ were
☐ was

Mr. Simpson's class_____in the library on Friday mornings.
☐ meet
☐ meets

Mount Bethel's choir_____at nursing homes every Sunday.
☐ sings
☐ sing

Distracting Words and Phrases

The more words and phrases that come between a subject and its verb, the more confusing a sentence can seem.

If there are words or phrases between the subject and the verb, make sure the verb agrees with the subject, not with any of the words that come between. Here is an example:

The people in the elevator is stuck between the third and fourth floors.

> The people in the elevator are stuck between the third and fourth floors.

▶ Which sentence is correct?

The subject of a sentence will never appear inside a **prepositional phrase**, a group of related words that starts with a preposition and ends with a noun or pronoun. First, put all the prepositional phrases in **parentheses**.

> The people (in the elevator) is stuck (between the third and fourth floors).

> The people (in the elevator) are stuck (between the third and fourth floors).

Once you've identified the true subject, you can make sure that you've used the correct type of verb.

> In this example, the second version of the sentence is correct. Both the subject and the verb are plural.

> The people in the elevator are stuck between the third and fourth floors.

Inverted Word Order

In a sentence with **regular word order**, the subject comes before the verb. However, sentences with **inverted word order** switch the locations of these sentence parts, so the verb comes before the subject. Look at the following example:

> Into the store walks three mysterious-looking men.

> Into the store walk three mysterious-looking men.

To decide if the subject and verb are singular or plural, you must identify the true subject of the sentence.

1. Mark prepositional phrases → **2. Identify the verb** → **3. Find the subject**

First, put parentheses around any prepositional phrases.

> (Into the store) walks three mysterious-looking men.

> (Into the store) walk three mysterious-looking men.

Next, identify your verb.

> (Into the store) walks three mysterious-looking men.

> (Into the store) walk three mysterious-looking men.

Finally, find your subject.

> (Into the store) walks three mysterious-looking men.

> (Into the store) walk three mysterious-looking men.

Once you've determined your subject and verb, you can decide if the verb should be singular or plural.

> (Into the store) walk three mysterious-looking men.

On Your Own

Read the following paragraph and identify the sentence with a subject and verb that do not agree in number.

> Photographs and video clips from the World Trade Center attacks on September 11, 2001, recall the fear and uncertainty that gripped the entire nation. Even for those who did not personally experience the loss of a loved one, images such as *The Falling Man* symbolizes the thousands of people killed on that day. This tragic yet simple news photograph and others like it have accumulated more meaning and significance than the photographers could have imagined.

Lesson Wrap-up

Key Terms

Collective Noun: a noun that denotes a group but is treated as a singular noun

Compound Subject: a subject made up of two nouns or pronouns usually joined by a conjunction

Conjunction: a word that makes a connection between other words or a group of words

Indefinite Pronoun: a pronoun that does not rename a specific noun

Inverted Word Order: when the verb comes before the subject in a sentence

Number: a way to divide words into two groups: singular and plural

Parentheses: a pair of punctuation marks used to add extra information to a sentence or introduce an abbreviation

Prepositional Phrase: a group of related words that starts with a preposition and ends with a noun or pronoun

Regular Word Order: when the subject comes before the verb in a sentence

Singular Noun: a noun that represents one person, place, thing, event, or idea

Subject: who or what a sentence is about

Subject-Verb Agreement: when a subject and verb used in a sentence are both singular or both plural

Verb: a word that represents an action, relationship, or state of being

Writing Application: Using Consistent Subjects and Verbs

Read the following brief paragraph and look for subject-verb agreement. Which sentences use indefinite pronouns? Which sentences include extra words between the main subject and verb?

George Orwell said, "History is written by the winners." He could not have been more accurate. Studying history can be frustrating, especially when we realize how much of it has been written from a biased perspective. It's difficult to determine the truth about the past. Many details are whitewashed or intentionally concealed. One example is the early settlement of North America. Everyone reads about the English colonists and their struggle for independence from England, and history textbooks mention the lost colonies of Roanoke and Croatoan. However, most schools don't mention the Spanish stronghold St. Elena even though it was established over thirty years before the fort at Jamestown. In fact, until the early 1990s, no one had thought much about St. Elena since its abandonment in 1587.

Lesson 10.3
Using Consistent Pronouns and Antecedents

Using pronouns correctly makes your writing smoother and less repetitive. A **pronoun** is almost always paired with an **antecedent**, the **noun** that a pronoun renames or replaces. As a result, pronouns must agree with their antecedent in both **gender** and **number**. This is known as **pronoun-antecedent agreement**.

> In this lesson, you will learn about pronoun reference and consistent pronoun-antecedent agreement.

Pronoun Reference

Pronouns must refer to a clear antecedent. Otherwise, your writing will become confusing and potentially misleading. Take a look at these examples:

Clear antecedent	Jennifer left the party and drove her car home.
Ambiguous antecedent	Jennifer left Susan's party and drove her car home.
Missing antecedent	She gave her the present, left her party, and then drove her car home.

The second example is ambiguous, or unclear, because there are two possible antecedents: *Jennifer* and *Susan*.

In the third example, pronouns rename other pronouns instead of antecedents, so we can't be sure whose car or party is being discussed.

On Your Own

Read the sentences in the table below. Then, replace *they* with a specific noun.

I went to the doctor's office, but they told me to see a dentist.		
I went to the doctor's office, but		told me to see a dentist.
After touring the ruins of the Roman Colosseum, they took a train to Florence.		
After touring the ruins of the Roman Colosseum,		took a train to Florence.

To learn more about pronoun reference and case, see Lesson 10.4.

Writing Environment: Professional

Pronoun-antecedent agreement is extremely important for professional communication with clients and coworkers. Memos, emails, and reports often address multiple departments in different locations. For instance, *marketing department* is a singular, gender-neutral noun (even though the department includes many people of both genders) so replacing it with the pronoun *it* is appropriate. *Members of the marketing team* is plural, so it could be renamed by the pronoun *they*.

Gender

The gender of a pronoun must match the gender of its antecedent. If a sentence includes a male antecedent, use male pronouns. If the sentence includes a female antecedent, use female pronouns. Otherwise, use neutral pronouns.

Male	Female	Neutral
he, him, his	she, her, hers	I, me, my, mine, we, us, our, ours, you, your, yours, it, its, they, them, their, theirs

Male   That man mows his yard every Saturday.

Female   Kayla left her purse on the subway.

Neutral   The maple tree is losing its leaves.

If the gender of an individual person is unknown, use the term *he or she.*

If a student is interested in volunteering, he or she can sign up in the school office.

An athlete should stretch before he or she exercises.

Because using the term *he or she* can sound wordy, this isn't always the best option. Instead, you can make the **subject** plural and use the neutral pronoun *they*.

> If students are interested in volunteering, they can sign up in the school office.

> Athletes should stretch before they exercise.

Writing Environment: Academic

In conversation, you probably use the neutral pronoun *they* for both singular and plural subjects.

> If anyone wants to ride with me to the game, they can.

While this is slowly becoming more acceptable, in formal writing it's best to use singular pronouns to replace singular subjects.

Number

In addition to gender, pronouns can also be singular or plural. *Singular* refers to one thing, and *plural* refers to multiple things. Singular antecedents are always paired with singular pronouns; plural antecedents are always paired with plural pronouns.

SINGULAR	PLURAL
I, me, my, mine	we, us, our, ours
you, your, yours	you, your, yours
he, him, his, she, her, hers, it, its	they, them, their, theirs

Here is an example:

> Devynne made some life-changing plans, but she has not shared them with anyone.

In this sentence, the word *plans* is renamed by the pronoun *them*. Both of these words are plural, so the sentence is correct.

Indefinite pronouns, pronouns that do not rename a specific noun, can be a little harder to use. These pronouns are also labeled singular or plural.

SINGULAR		PLURAL	BOTH
anybody	nobody	both	all
anyone	no one	few	any
anything	nothing	many	most
each	somebody	several	none
everybody	someone		some
everyone	something		
everything			

When a singular indefinite pronoun is used as an antecedent, make sure you rename it with a singular personal pronoun. Here is an example:

> Someone in the previous class left his or her backpack under the table.

In this sentence, the indefinite pronoun *someone* is singular. Since you don't know the gender of the person, it's best to use the singular term *his or her*.

Some indefinite pronouns can be both singular and plural depending on how they're used in a sentence. To decide how the words *all, any, most, none,* or *some* are being used, look at what the indefinite pronoun is renaming.

Singular

All of the cake has already been eaten.

Most of the floor is covered by carpeting.

Plural

All of the orders have been filled on time.

Most of the apartments are carpeted.

> **Helpful Hint**
>
> All the singular indefinite pronouns except *each* can be broken up into two word parts. For example, *some + one = someone.* Notice that the second part, *one,* is singular. If an indefinite pronoun fits this pattern, it is singular.

Finally, when a sentence contains a **compound subject**, you must use special guidelines to decide if the subject is singular or plural. A subject that is joined by the **conjunctions** *and* or *both/and* is plural.

Myra and John answer questions at the end of each training session.

Because *Myra* and *John* are joined by the conjunction *and*, they are a plural compound subject.

However, if the sentence uses any of the following conjunctions, use the subject closest to the **verb** to decide if the subject is singular or plural.

either/or	nor
neither/nor	or

Look at this example:

Either the bathroom or the kitchen is being remodeled this year.

This sentence uses the conjunction *either/or* to join a compound subject. The singular noun *kitchen* is closest to the verb, so the subject is considered singular. Notice that the highlighted verb is also singular.

Here's another example:

Amy or the twins are coming with us this afternoon.

In this sentence, the plural noun *twins* is closest to the verb, so the subject is considered plural. Notice that the highlighted verb is also plural.

On Your Own

Read the following paragraph and identify the sentence with a pronoun and antecedent that do not agree in gender and/or number.

Little is known about the subjective experience of breast cancer survivors after primary treatment. However, these experiences are important because it shapes their communication about their illness in everyday life. The study investigated this topic by combining qualitative and quantitative methods.

(Excerpt courtesy of "Breast Cancer Survivors' Recollection of Their Illness and Therapy" by Patricia Lindberg, et al.)

Lesson Wrap-up

Key Terms

Antecedent: the word that a pronoun renames

Compound Subject: a subject made up of two nouns or pronouns usually joined by a conjunction

Conjunction: a word that makes a connection between other words or a group of words

Gender: a way to divide words into three groups: male, female, and neutral

Indefinite Pronoun: a pronoun that does not rename a specific noun

Noun: a word that represents a person, place, thing, event, or idea

Number: a way to divide words into two groups: singular and plural

Pronoun: a word that takes the place of a noun in a sentence

Pronoun-Antecedent Agreement: when a pronoun and its antecedent in a sentence are the same in gender and number

Subject: who or what a sentence is about

Verb: a word that represents an action, relationship, or state of being

Writing Application: Using Consistent Pronouns and Antecedents

Read the following brief paragraph, paying special attention to the pronouns and antecedents. Does each pronoun agree in gender and number with the noun it replaces? Do any pronouns have ambiguous or missing antecedents?

Many people know that Serena Williams is a talented athlete. Her ability on the tennis court has made her legendary. However, Serena's versatility is even more amazing. She has developed her own line of clothing and promoted it on the Home Shopping Network. The tennis star also recently co-starred with Beyoncé Knowles in the music video for "Lemonade." Additionally, Serena has used her celebrity standing to help others. She recently made a generous donation to the construction of a school in Jamaica for underprivileged children. She volunteered to help build the school and cut the ribbon at the opening ceremony. Last, Serena and her sister Venus hold an annual dance competition together, and they have agreed to make a movie about the competition.

Lesson 10.4
Using Correct Pronoun Reference and Case

Pronouns are words that take the place of **nouns** in a sentence. Although they are often small in size, they can have a huge impact on your writing. Misusing them can be especially confusing for your reader. To ensure that your writing is as effective as possible, pay close attention to pronoun case.

Pronoun **case** refers to the form of the pronoun. Which form is correct depends on the function of the pronoun in the sentence: as a subject, an object, or to show possession. Consider these examples:

Subjective   He went to school in East Texas.

Objective   David's girlfriend gave him a new video game.

Possessive   Kyle lost his glasses again.

In this lesson, you will complete the following goals:

Identify Pronoun Case
Apply Correct Case with Difficult Wording
Use Correct Pronoun Reference

Identify Pronoun Case

Personal pronouns have three main functions in a sentence. They act as subjects, they act as objects, and they show possession. These functions match the three pronoun cases: subjective, objective, and possessive.

To avoid errors in your writing, make sure that the case of the pronoun matches the way the pronoun is being used in the sentence. Review the table below for examples of each case.

SUBJECTIVE	OBJECTIVE	POSSESSIVE
I	me	mine
you	you	yours
she	her	hers
he	him	his
they	them	their/theirs
we	us	our/ours
it	it	its

To learn more about pronoun use in sentences, see Lesson 10.3.

Subjective Case
Subjective pronouns are always used as the **subject** of a sentence.

I am heading to the gym right after I finish grocery shopping.

Last night, you told me you were going to finish cleaning these dishes!

Objective Case

Objective pronouns are used in two ways. First, they function as **objects of prepositions**: words that complete the meaning of a **prepositional phrase**.

> Unexpectedly, the mail carrier delivered a package addressed (to me).

> Did you mean to send this email (to him)?

The second function of objective case pronouns is as direct and indirect objects of **verbs**. **Direct objects** follow a verb and receive some kind of action. **Indirect objects**, on the other hand, receive the direct object.

Direct Object

> Don't forget to thank her for your new birthday gift!

> Jeanine found mold on the sandwich in the refrigerator, so she threw it in the trash.

Indirect Object

> Mia's soccer coach gave her a list of areas in which he wanted her to improve.

> The greasy pizza made us feel queasy.

Maybe you've been told never to use *my friend and me* and that *my friend and I* is correct. The truth is, it depends on how you're using *my friend and me*. How can you tell which is correct? Test the pronoun case by removing the noun.

The usage in each of these sentences is correct:

Subject

> (My best friend and) I can't wait to get a motorcycle one day!

Subject

> (My best friend and) I planned to study, but it turned into a binge-watching session of our favorite TV show.

Object of a Verb

> The teacher provided (my classmates and) me with some helpful writing strategies.

Object of a Preposition

> My grandma's surprise birthday party was pretty boring for (my brother and) me.

> ▶ If you remove *my classmates* and *my brother* from the last two examples, you'll see that using *me* is completely correct. You would never say, "The party was boring for I."

Possessive Case

The last personal pronoun form is the possessive case. **Possessive** pronouns show possession. They can function as **adjectives** or as regular pronouns.

Adjectives   Who put on her makeup?

My parents hid their holiday presents from one another.

Pronouns   His is on the table.

Mine was loud, but yours is quiet.

Possessive case pronouns are spelled the same way as both subjects and objects.

> I put our tickets in my pocket.

> Ours are in my pocket.

Helpful Hint

Notice that none of the possessive pronouns need **apostrophes**. In this way, possessive pronouns are the opposite of possessive nouns, which always need an apostrophe.

Apply Correct Case with Difficult Wording

Relative pronouns are used to introduce **dependent clauses**, groups of words with a subject and a verb that do not express a complete thought.

> My new cookie recipe that uses applesauce was a hit at the party.

> The teacher, who had lived in New York all her life, decided to move to China.

Here are the seven relative pronouns:

that	whoever
which	whom
whichever	whomever
who	

Although *who* and *whom* are relative pronouns and not personal pronouns, they do have case. *Who* is a subjective-case pronoun, and *whom* is an objective-case pronoun. To decide which one you should use in a sentence, try substituting *he* or *she* for *who* and *him* or *her* for *whom*. You may need to rearrange the words in the sentence slightly.

> Who vacuumed the house yesterday?

> He vacuumed the house yesterday.

> Whom are they looking for outside?

> They are looking for her outside.

Writing Environment: Academic

Academic writing tends to be more formal than professional writing. While a text for work must be concise and compelling, it's also more direct and brief. You're much more likely to encounter the use of *whom* in academic writing.

Demonstrative pronouns take the place of a noun phrase or serve as adjectives in a noun phrase.

Demonstrative pronoun

That is much heavier than this.

Demonstrative adjective

This piano is more properly tuned than that one.

Having so many pronouns available makes it hard to know when to use *which* and when to use *that*. However, these two pronouns are not interchangeable. Here's a good rule of thumb: *which* indicates unnecessary detail.

If the sentence doesn't need the clause, use *which*.

The dress, which had a rip in the side, was laying across the chair.

If the clause is essential for clarity, use *that*.

The dress that had a rip in the side was laying across the chair.

Writing Environment: Professional

Professional writing tends to be focused and concise. If you use a lot of clauses starting with *which*, you may be providing too much unnecessary detail. Consider these examples:

The funds, which were allocated for the project, were quickly spent.

The funds that were allocated for the project were quickly spent.

The first sentence requires two commas and interrupts the flow of information. The second sentence is more precise and requires no commas. Use this rule to edit cover letters, memos, proposals, and other professional documents.

Use Correct Pronoun Reference

Every time you use a pronoun, it must refer back to a clear **antecedent**, or a word that a pronoun renames. Otherwise, your writing will become confusing and potentially misleading. Read this example:

Last week, Monica accidentally hit Leslie's car when it was parked at the bank. She started worrying about how to handle the situation. Since they are friends, she wasn't sure how to get the money necessary to fix the car.

These sentences contain important information. However, their meaning has been completely mixed up by incorrect pronoun reference. Who was worrying? Who didn't know how to get the money? Monica or Leslie?

No Clear Antecedents

One common pronoun error is using a pronoun without any antecedent at all. Look at the following examples:

After the house was tragically burned down, they started to search the rubble for any treasured items.

Ross tried to get call his university, but they put him on hold.

> In both of these sentences, the pronoun *they* is unclear. Who exactly is *they*? To fix these examples, add a more specific noun in place of the pronoun.

> After the house was tragically burned down, the O'Brien family started to search the rubble for any treasured items.

> Ross tried to get call his university, but the secretary at the registrar's office put him on hold.

Another pronoun commonly used without an antecedent is *it*. Whenever possible, use a noun instead.

> There has been an ongoing debate about the use of chemical pesticides in the food we consume. In her article, "Chemical Dependency," Ariel Beck argues that "we ingest food in our system now that will one day become illegal." While many people support Beck's claim, there are only a small number of individuals who have actively rallied against this issue. It could change if more people speak up.

> The last sentence in the paragraph above is unclear because it starts with the word *it*. Replacing this word with a noun, like *policies*, would make the meaning much clearer.

Multiple Antecedents

A pronoun can also become confusing when it has more than one possible antecedent.

> Oscar revealed to Jonah that he had a new job offer.

> Who had a new job offer? From the information provided in this sentence, there's no clear way to know. The best way to correct this sentence is to replace the pronoun with a noun and/or re-word the sentence as necessary.

> As soon as Oscar got a new job offer, he told Jonah immediately.

> Jonah was glad when Oscar got a new job offer.

Antecedent Rules

Finally, the antecedent of a pronoun will always be a noun, not an adjective. This is because adjectives function differently than nouns or pronouns. Here's an example:

> I called Rob's all morning, but he never picked up.

> In this sentence, the word *Rob's* is an adjective and cannot act as the antecedent for *he*. This sentence can be fixed by replacing the pronoun with the correct noun.

> I called Rob's all morning, but Rob never picked up.

Using a noun instead of a pronoun may feel a bit repetitive in some cases. Keep in mind, however, that using correct pronoun reference will help your readers understand exactly what your sentence means.

On Your Own

Read the following paragraph and identify the sentence that contains an incorrect pronoun reference.

> Before the pair went out on stage, Elliot asked Jerry for some help. He listened closely during the conversation. After feeling much more confident, Elliot and Jerry performed a set that the audience loved.

To learn more about pronouns and antecedents, see Lesson 10.3.

Lesson Wrap-up

Key Terms

Adjective: a word that describes a noun or pronoun

Antecedent: a word that a pronoun renames

Apostrophe: a punctuation mark used for possessive nouns, contractions, and shortened numbers and words

Demonstrative Pronoun: a pronoun that takes the place of a noun phrase or serves as adjectives for that noun

Dependent Clause: a group of words with a subject and a verb that does not express a complete thought

Direct Object: a word that receives the action of a verb

Indirect Object: a word that receives the direct object

Noun: a word that represents a person, place, thing, event, or idea

Object of the Preposition: a word that completes the meaning of a prepositional phrase

Objective Case: a pronoun used as the object of a preposition, a direct object, or an indirect object

Personal Pronoun: a pronoun that renames a specific person, animal, object, or place

Possessive Case: a pronoun that shows possession or functions as an adjective

Prepositional Phrase: a group of related words that starts with a preposition and ends with a noun or pronoun

Pronoun: a word that takes the place of a noun in a sentence

Pronoun Case: the form of a pronoun, depending on how it functions in a sentence

Relative Pronoun: a pronoun used to introduce a dependent clause

Subject: who or what a sentence is about

Subjective Case: a pronoun used as the subject of a sentence

Verb: a word that represents an action, relationship, or state of being

Writing Application: Using Correct Pronoun Reference and Case

Read the following brief paragraph and pay attention to pronoun reference and case. Which pronouns are subjective, objective, or possessive? Does each one clearly refer back to an antecedent?

Although most people recognize Thomas Jefferson as the author of the Declaration of Independence, this was only one of his many achievements. Jefferson also designed his own home, Monticello. Studying architecture was a passion and hobby for him. He often remarked that he enjoyed "putting things up and tearing them down." Jefferson was especially impressed with the Neoclassical style, and many of the Romanesque Greek Revival-style government buildings were built under his influence. Their classical details communicate a sense of powerful and enduring strength. In his lifetime, Jefferson was often consulted about plans for building state capitols because the people who knew his passion for architecture respected his opinions.

Lesson 10.5
Correcting Misplaced and Dangling Modifiers

Modifiers are words or groups of words that add extra information to a sentence. The most common types of modifiers are **adjectives** and **adverbs**. However, some **phrases** and even some clauses can also be considered modifiers.

Here is an example of each type:

Adjective	My new, white sneakers are covered in mud.
Adverb	New York sports fans are occasionally known to get rowdy.
Phrase	Hiding under her umbrella, Sarah made a mad dash to her car.

All of the modifiers in the sentences above give additional meaning and clarity. Look at the sentences without modifiers:

> My sneakers are covered in mud.

> New York sports fan are known to get rowdy.

> Sarah made a mad dash to her car.

> ▸ Each sentence still makes sense; however, none of them have the same effect as the original version.

Each type of modifier describes a particular part of speech. See the chart below for the breakdown:

Part of Speech	Modifies
Adjective	Nouns
Adverb	Verbs
Adjective Phrase	Nouns/noun phrases
Adverbial Phrase	Verbs/verb phrases

It's also perfectly acceptable for a sentence to contain more than one type of modifier as in the examples below:

Adverb Phrase + Adjective:

> While driving home from class, I developed a splitting headache.

Two Adverbial Phrases:

> As I came into the kitchen, I saw my cat jumping quickly off the counter.

To be effective, modifiers must be placed close to what they modify.

Helpful Hint

As you proofread your own writing, you sometimes skip over mistakes without even realizing it. Consider asking a friend to proofread your work and help you find misplaced and dangling modifiers.

This lesson will help you correct two types of incorrect modifiers:

Misplaced Modifiers
Dangling Modifiers

Misplaced Modifiers

A **misplaced modifier** is placed too far away from what it modifies. This makes the sentence potentially confusing to your audience. Here's an example:

> Daniel saw a raccoon playing soccer.
>
> This modifier is misplaced because it suggests that Daniel saw a raccoon kicking around a soccer ball. To fix this sentence, move the modifier as close as possible to the word being modified.
>
> Playing soccer, Daniel saw a raccoon.

> **Helpful Hint**
>
> Don't forget to add the proper punctuation when changing the location of a modifier. If a modifying phrase is at the beginning of a sentence, it should usually be followed by a comma.

One-word modifiers should also be placed near the words they modify. Consider this sentence:

> Rebecca gave a presentation to her entire company, bravely.
>
> The meaning of this sentence would be much clearer to the audience if the modifier *bravely* were placed closer to the word it modifies.
>
> Rebecca bravely gave a presentation to her entire company.

Writing Environment: Professional

In your job or career, it's important to write as clearly and concisely as possible. While modifiers are sometimes important to make a specific point, they can become wordy. Cutting excessive adverbs is a "best practice" for professional writing. It's imperative, however, to be sure any modifiers you keep are properly placed. In the following sentence, the misplaced modifier makes an ambiguous point.

> The CEO said on Friday the company would publish their stock policy.

How would you reposition *on Friday* to indicate when this was said? How would you reposition *on Friday* to indicate when the stock policy will be published?

Sometimes, misplaced modifiers are harder to catch because both meanings seem realistic. Consider these two versions of the same sentence:

> The food in the cafeteria cannot be eaten.

> The food cannot be eaten in the cafeteria.

> ▶ In the first sentence, none of the food in the cafeteria can be consumed. In the second sentence, the food can only be consumed outside of the cafeteria. The intended meaning of your sentence will determine which version is the correct choice.

Here's a slightly trickier example:

> The hiring manager nearly had to review one hundred applications.

> The hiring manager had to review nearly one hundred applications.

> ▷ The first sentence implies that the hiring manager didn't have to look through any of the applications. The second sentence, on the other hand, states that the hiring manager did look through the applications, all ninety-nine of them.

Writing Environment: Everyday

Emails and conversations are often confusing when modifiers are misplaced. Although this can sometimes be good for a laugh, it's easy to see how misplaced modifiers cause breakdowns in communication as well. The following text raises a number of questions:

> I was drinking the coffee I had bought slowly while walking my dog without success. Drinking my coffee, the dog made me trip and fall.

* Why did the speaker buy coffee slowly?
* How is a dog unsuccessful?
* Why does the dog drink coffee?

Dangling Modifiers

The second type of incorrect modifier is a **dangling modifier**. In these cases, what's being modified is completely missing from the sentence. Look at this example:

> Before going to the doctor, the virus got worse.
>
> The modifier in this sentence is dangling because the sentence never identifies who is going to the doctor. To correct this sentence, simply add the missing information as close to the modifier as possible.
>
> Before going to the doctor, Henry thought the virus got worse.
>
> The sentence is now correct because the audience knows that Henry is the one going to the doctor.

On Your Own

Read the following sentences and identify the one with correct modifiers.

☐ Making the bed, my sheets were untucked at the bottom.

☐ Since announcing his presidential campaign, the phones have been ringing all day.

☐ After finishing the exam, students began collecting their materials.

Writing Environment: Academic

Although both types of modifier errors are equally problematic, it's wise to learn the difference between misplaced and dangling modifiers. This distinction helps you edit your papers more efficiently and give clear, specific feedback during peer reviews.

Lesson Wrap-up

Key Terms

Adjective: a word that describes a noun or pronoun

Adverb: a word that describes a verb, adjective, or another adverb

Dangling Modifier: a modifier that has no word to modify

Misplaced Modifier: a modifier that is too far away from the word it modifies

Modifier: a word or group of words that adds extra information to a sentence

Phrase: a word group that does not form a complete thought

Writing Application: Correcting Misplaced and Dangling Modifiers

Read the following paragraph, which has multiple modifier errors. Then, read the second paragraph, which is the corrected version.

Original:

I had suspected that the moving company was untrustworthy all along. Picking up the poorly packed boxes, they fell apart and my glassware shattered, which hadn't been taped shut. Without hesitating, my letter of complaint was sent the next morning. No one responded after waiting for 48 hours. I called and asked to speak with the customer service manager early Tuesday morning. She didn't seem surprised at the problems I had encountered with the movers when we talked on the phone. Her lack of professionalism and support proved my point about the company, which was obvious from her tone.

Corrected:

I had suspected all along that the moving company was untrustworthy. As I picked up the poorly packed boxes, which hadn't been taped shut, my glassware shattered. Without hesitating, I sent my letter of complaint the next morning. I waited for 48 hours, but no one responded. Early Tuesday morning, I called and asked to speak with the customer service manager. When we talked on the phone, she didn't seem surprised at the problems I had encountered with the movers. Her lack of professionalism and support was obvious from her tone and proved my point about the company.

Lesson 10.6
Using Active and Passive Voice

When you think of the words *active* and *passive*, what comes to mind?

The word *active* probably reminds you of outdoor activities or exercise. An active person is energetic and involved. The word *passive*, on the other hand, probably reminds you of someone who is quiet or timid. This person often avoids conflict and is less likely to be the center of attention.

In writing, active voice keeps your sentences energetic and exciting while passive voice slows them down. Too many passive sentences make a text slow and boring. Look at this example:

> In contrast, Antigone's actions are interpreted by Mary Dietz as an affirmation of the importance of politics over family. Antigone is established by Dietz's argument as a model for "citizenship with a feminist face" and as an advocate for religious and civil customs (1112). In Dietz's opinion, political reform rather than maternal awareness must be devoted to by modern feminists.

> This paragraph is written almost entirely in passive voice. As you read, you probably noticed that the sentences were tedious. Using active voice in the paragraph would make it more interesting and engaging.

> Read the revised version below:

> In contrast, Mary Dietz interprets Antigone's actions as an affirmation of the importance of politics over family. Dietz's argument establishes Antigone as a model for "citizenship with a feminist face" and an advocate for religious and civil customs (1112). In Dietz's opinion, modern feminists must devote themselves to political reform rather than maternal awareness.

While active voice can improve your writing, using *only* active voice would sound repetitive and aggressive. Learning to find a good balance of active and passive voice will help you refine your writing skills and communicate your ideas more effectively.

This lesson will teach you how to use both active and passive voice.

Active Voice

When a sentence uses **active voice**, the **subject** is performing an action.

> My basketball team won last year's championship game against our rivals.

> In this sentence, the subject, *team*, did the winning. Therefore, this sentence is considered active.

Active voice makes your writing more energetic. Look at the following examples. Which sentence seems more exciting?

> Despite the risks, cliff-jumping in Greece was completed by Autumn and me.

> Despite the risks, Autumn and I cliff-jumped in Greece.

> ▶ The second sentence uses active voice to show the subjects performing an action. This sentence has more energy than the first sentence, which is written in passive voice.

On Your Own

Read the following sentences and identify the one using active voice.

- ☐ The whole chapter was reviewed by my study group.
- ☐ The options were carefully considered by Erica.
- ☐ I ran home as fast as possible to catch the game on TV.

When you use active voice, your writing is often more direct and clear than when you use passive voice. Think about these sentences:

> I was reminded by my doctor's receptionist that I had an appointment.

> My doctor's receptionist reminded me that I had an appointment.

▷ Both of these examples express the same basic idea. However, the sentence in active voice communicates its meaning in a much more direct way.

To turn a passive sentence into an active sentence, make sure that the doer of the action is the subject. Sometimes, this information is already included in the sentence. Other times, however, you need to supply the new subject. Here are a few examples:

Passive   The research was conducted by a group of Yale students.

Active   A group of Yale students conducted the research.

Passive   At the convention, environmental issues were argued.

Active   At the convention, the politicians argued about environmental issues.

Writing Environment: Academic

In research writing and other academic writing assignments, active voice is preferred over passive voice. Particularly in **persuasive writing**, active voice will make you sound more authoritative and compelling. In contrast, passive voice can sound hesitant and unconvincing. Passive voice also usually requires more words, which may interfere with clarity and concision.

Passive Voice

When a sentence is in **passive voice**, the subject is receiving an action.

> The movie was made by a first-time director.

> In this example, the subject, *movie*, is not doing anything. Something else, the *first-time director*, is doing the action to the subject.

Sentences in passive voice contain a **helping verb** in addition to a main **verb**.

To learn more about types of verbs, see Lesson 9.1.

In your writing, passive voice can sound both wordy and vague. Look at this example:

> Henry's house will be renovated by the contractors after agreeing on plans with an architect.
>
> This sentence is confusing. A much better version would sound like this:
>
> The contractors will renovate Henry's house after agreeing on plans with an architect.

Passive voice can also confuse your audience when the person or object doing the action is not named in the sentence. Here are two examples:

> A cake was baked for the faculty meeting this afternoon.

> It has been argued that students should not have to wear school uniforms.

▸ These sentences never tell the audience who is doing the actions.

On Your Own

The following sentences are written in passive voice. In the table below, rewrite them so that they are in active voice.

Passive	Active
The trip was planned entirely by Frankie.	
The project goals were set out by the leader of the group.	
Laws for electricity usage are being changed by many corporations.	
The computer was restored by a brilliant technician.	

Writing Environment: Professional

In the United States, our style of interaction tends to be bold, assertive, and direct. We usually emphasize authoritative, confident writing. However, some cultures value passivity because it can show humility, unselfishness, and respect for authority. For example, saying, "The research was conducted by me," places more focus on the research than the person completing it. If people aren't aware of these cultural or personal differences, they might become frustrated or misjudge a coworker's competence and credibility. Therefore, awareness of this cultural difference may enhance your chances for success in various professional environments.

Why Use Passive Voice?

While active voice is usually a better choice for your writing, there are occasions when passive voice is better. First, you may want to keep the emphasis of the sentence on a word other than your subject. Look at these examples:

> Maddox was adopted from Haiti by Kyle and Lauryn last week.

> Kyle and Lauryn adopted Maddox from Haiti last week.

> ▸ The first sentence would be a better choice for an announcement sent to family and friends because they're probably more interested in Maddox than the fact that Kyle and Lauryn were the ones who adopted him.

Another reason to use passive voice would be to keep the meaning of the sentence deliberately vague. Look at this example:

> Due to employee oversight, your recent insurance claim was unable to be processed.
> This example purposefully uses vague language to make the insurance company sound less responsible for the oversight. Think about what the active version of this sentence might sound like:

> An employee overlooked your recent insurance claim.

Further Resources

Politicians often use passive voice to avoid taking blame for mistakes or scandals. One famous phrase, "Mistakes were made," has been used so many times, it has its own Wikipedia page (http://en.wikipedia.org/wiki/Mistakes_were_made).

Another reason to use passive voice would be to add variety to a text. Too many active sentences in a row can sound choppy. Adding a few passive sentences will help you keep your writing smooth.

> Jim will plan the rest of his school year next week. He will create lessons, tests, and projects for his students.

> Jim will plan the rest of his school year next week. Lessons, tests, and projects for students will be created.

> ▸ In the second example, one sentence is active and one is passive. Not only does the passive sentence add variety to the text, but it also helps the reader make a connection between the two sentences.

One final reason to use passive voice is to emphasize facts. You might see this in medical or scientific writing because it emphasizes certain information. Take a look at the example below:

> The patient's symptoms were exacerbated by low blood sugar and dizziness. The dosage of antibiotics was increased, and intravenous glucose was raised by 10 ccs.

Writing Environment: Everyday

You might sometimes see acknowledgements presented in passive voice. For example, an event or party may feature a menu with captions like *catering provided by*, *flowers arranged by*, or *instrumental solo by*. This draws attention to the service provided. Guests are more likely to recognize the service they received than the name of the company or individual who provided it.

Group Activity

As a group, decide which of the following sentences are active and which are passive. Then, rewrite each sentence in the opposite voice.

Carpentry school was much harder than Karissa had expected.

While finding a cure for cancer has been difficult, significant progress has been made.

Yesterday, Jane and I took turns reading aloud to our daughter.

Lesson Wrap-up

Key Terms

Active Voice: when a sentence is written so that the subject is performing an action

Helping Verb: a word that changes the form of the main verb so that it grammatically fits the sentence

Passive Voice: when a sentence is written so that the subject is receiving an action

Persuasive Writing: writing that uses argument to influence someone's beliefs and/or actions

Subject: who or what a sentence is about

Verb: a word that represents an action, relationship, or state of being

Writing Sample: Using Active and Passive Voice

In the following excerpt from a press release, active and passive voice work together.

Earlier this week, film industry representatives announced the rollout of a new video-hosting platform. Developed by World Vision Films in conjunction with the Firebrand Collection, this new subscription-based service features thousands of movies from Hollywood studios and independent filmmakers. Subscriptions are being offered via a monthly membership program, and members will have unlimited access to the library of films. Special categories contributed by World Vision include a "Bollywood" section with a large selection of subtitled movies from India; a "Retro Release" section featuring rare silent films from the 1920s; a "Film Noir" collection; and an impressive collection of sports footage from Super Bowls of the past thirty years. Comedies, musicals, documentaries, dramas, and Hollywood classics are also being added by Firebrand.

Lesson 10.7
Maintaining Consistency in Tense and Person

Words can indicate the past, present, or future, as well as perspective; that's why it's important for them to be consistent.
Photos courtesy of Wikimedia Commons (https://commons.wikimedia.org/wiki/Main_Page).

Filmmaker Quentin Tarantino is famous for non-linear storytelling. His movies often ignore chronological order, raising the level of suspense by slightly disorienting his audience with incomplete information. For example, *Pulp Fiction*, *Django Unchained*, and *The Hateful Eight* all use this technique.

Books sometimes do the same thing. Maybe the first chapter is set in the future while the second chapter is set in the past. Authors use flashbacks and flash-forwards to make a dramatic story more interesting. As the reader, you must piece the story together as you observe the events from different points in time.

Similarly, some stories unfold through the different perspectives of the main characters. In the first half of the book, you might observe the events from one character's point of view; then, in the second half, you see the events from another character's point of view.

While these shifts in time and perspective can make a fictional story more interesting, the same strategies in a text for work or school could confuse your audience. This is because in **academic writing** and **professional writing**, time and perspective are usually the same throughout the text. Maintaining consistency in your writing will help your main idea be as clear as possible.

This lesson will help you avoid two types of inconsistency in your writing:

Tense
Person

Tense

Take a look at the following sentence and decide whether the action takes place in the past, present, or future:

> The human resources director was shocked to discover the scandalous theft within the company.

You could probably tell that the action took place in the past, but how did you know?

Group Activity

As a group, try rewriting each of the following sentences in a different tense:

He is planning to complete graduate school and then pursue a doctorate degree.

Did you jump in the lake with all your clothes on?

It isn't fair to keep us from entering the concert!

Based on the group activity, what did you notice about changing the tense? What word determines the tense of each sentence?

Verbs use different **tenses** to tell the audience when an action took place: past, present, or future.

Past	Present	Future
swam	swim	will swim
jumped	jump	will jump
baked	bake	will bake

Switching tenses in the middle of the same thought is awkward. Look at this example:

> A normal shift at work consisted of standing behind the counter and taking customer's orders. Once in a while, it included making simple salads and sandwiches. I even ran a few deliveries. Usually, I clean up before I leave.

> Did you notice the shift? In the first three sentences, all the action is happening in the past. Then, an awkward shift to the present interrupts the flow of the writing. To correct this mistake, the writer should change the verb tenses in the last sentence so that they match the rest of the passage.

Past, Present, and Future Tense

Sometimes, writing in the **present tense** is the best way to communicate your message. In a narrative or a story, you may use present tense because you want the readers to feel as though the events are unraveling right before their eyes.

In a literary analysis or reflection essay, it may be necessary to use both present tense to discuss the literature and past tense to discuss any historical events or author information.

> Homer was a storyteller in ancient Greece who became famous for the story of Odysseus, a warrior who experiences many adventures as he travels home after the Trojan War.

Writing Environment: Academic

No matter how long ago a novel was written, references to literature should always be in present tense as if the story is currently happening. For example, an essay analyzing *The Kite Runner* might include a sentence like this:

> Khaled Hosseini explores the rich and complex history of Afghanistan through the eyes of the story's protagonist, Amir, and his path to personal redemption.

This example uses present tense because the author is currently sharing his or her opinions about the book.

The **past tense** is used to report an event or reflect on a past experience. Many fictional books are also written in past tense.

Here's an example of past tense from an article about an experiment:

> The majority of the research participants claimed that they were not treated fairly. This resulted in the experiment being prematurely shut down.

> The participants are not currently involved in the experiment; this event took place in the past.

> **Helpful Hint**
>
> The present and past tenses are usually the most logical options for most writing.

> **Further Resources**
>
> To talk about past events using the present tense is sometimes called using the "historical present" tense, and it's used more frequently than you might think. Check out this podcast from Slate's "Lexicon Valley" to learn about the historical present in every type of media from Charlotte Brontë to *Seinfeld*: (http://www.slate.com/articles/podcasts/lexicon_valley/2012/07/lexicon_valley_the_historical_present_in_seinfeld_and_the_novels_of_charlotte_bronte.html).

The **future tense** is often used to describe plans or instructions.

> After the holiday party, the social committee will discuss plans for celebrating the manager's birthday.

Regardless of the tense you use, be as consistent as possible. You don't want to confuse your readers by switching back and forth between two different points in time.

Writing Environment: Professional

In some professions, it may be necessary to provide background information for a new proposal, project, law, or policy change. This often involves making an introduction in the past tense and explaining previous conditions or policies before delving into the current situation or recommendations for future changes. If such a scenario is part of your job or assigned writing task, cue the reader by signaling the time change in your paragraphs.

> **Helpful Hint**
>
> Although certain tenses are more appropriate for specific types of writing, your instructor might have guidelines for the tense that you should use in a writing assignment. Always remember to double-check the instructions.

Appropriate Tense Shifts

Occasionally, shifts in tense are unavoidable. You might need to describe events that happened at two different points in time.

> Harry lifted one-hundred-pound weights at the gym last week, and this week he is going to try to lift two hundred pounds.
>
> The first part of this example happened in the past, and the second part is happening in the future. In this case, it makes sense to use two different tenses in the same sentence.

Similarly, you might need to show that a current or future action is the direct result of a past action.

> Carmen spent all night studying for his math final, so today he is feeling exhausted.
>
> In this example, Carmen studied in the past, so he is feeling tired in the present.

Finally, tenses can also shift within a paragraph. Consider this example:

> Iggy gave a poor public speech to her school with very little preparation. Next time, she will be sure to practice her speech aloud before she presents it.
>
> In the past, Iggy realized that she needed more preparation. In the future, she will prepare better.

On Your Own

Read the following passage and identify the paragraph that contains a shift in tense.

> Ralph tries to fill the role of authority figure by maintaining the signal fire and building shelters. He also assigns tasks to different groups of boys to ensure that they live in a civilized fashion. Unfortunately, since Ralph is only a young boy, his authority is not respected as much as an adult's authority would be respected.
>
> Piggy plays the role of the father figure, which is reflected in his appearance. He wears thick glasses, and his hair does not seem to grow. He also provides the voice of reason on the island. When the "littluns" got scared and started talking about the beast, Piggy tried to calm their fears. He maintains order by explaining that life is based on science. When Jack gets the rest of the boys frenzied about hunting, Piggy exhibits common sense by refusing to participate.

Person

In addition to consistent verb tenses, good writing also includes consistency in **person**, or point of view. There are three different points of view that you can use:

First Person   The narrator or writer is a member of the story or event.

Second Person   The reader is a member of the story or event. Questions can be directed to the reader.

Third Person   The narrator or writer is outside of the story or event. This writing strives to be unbiased.

On Your Own

Read the sentences below and identify the sentence that has a third-person point of view.

- ☐ If you've never gone skydiving before, this will be an experience like nothing else.
- ☐ My colleagues and I were concerned when we found the front door to the office wide open.
- ☐ Even after the crime was solved, the neighbors wondered if their neighborhood was actually safe.

Personal pronouns can be first-person, second-person, or third-person. (All **nouns** are considered third-person.) To determine point of view, look for these pronouns:

PERSON	SINGULAR	PLURAL
First person	I, me, my, mine	we, us, our, ours
Second person	you, your, yours	you, your, yours
Third person	he, him, his, she, her, hers, it, its	they, them, their, theirs

To learn more about pronouns and antecedents, see Lesson 10.3.

On Your Own

Read the following passage and identify all the first-person pronouns.

> "Who is that?" I thought. There was a man lurking around outside, his back facing me. Without hesitation, I jumped off the couch and snuck toward the door. After getting closer, I was relieved to see that it was just my Uncle Henry. He was trying to pull a prank on my dad. It's a good thing I didn't call the cops!

Different perspectives are appropriate for different types of writing. When writing or revising, double-check any assignment guidelines to make sure that you are using the correct one. Here are some examples of commonly used points of view in different genres:

- **First person**: Informal writing and personal reflections
- **Second person**: Instructions and advice
- **Third person**: Formal academic writing and professional writing

On Your Own

In the table below, rewrite each of the following sentences so that they use a different point of view.

Original	Re-written
Can you imagine if smart phones became illegal?	
We almost fell out of the cab when the driver sped away while we were still getting out.	
I always share accurate pricing when dealing with customers.	

If a piece of writing includes frequent shifts from one point of view to another, it can be difficult for your audience to follow. Consider the following example:

> The baseball team was disappointed in their loss, so we decided to cheer ourselves up with a night out.
>
> The word *team* is third-person because it's a noun, but the pronouns *we* and *ourselves* are first-person. To fix this shift in person, the word *we* should be changed to *they* and the word *ourselves* should be changed to *themselves*.
>
> The baseball team was disappointed in their loss, so they decided to cheer themselves up with a night out.

On Your Own

Read the sentences below and decide which person (first, second, or third) is being used. Check the box next to your answer.

> If you run several days a week, you will eventually get in shape.
> ☐ First Person
> ☐ Second Person
> ☐ Third Person

> If a person wants to get in shape, he or she will have to run several days a week.
> ☐ First Person
> ☐ Second Person
> ☐ Third Person

> If I want to get in shape, I need to run several days a week.
> ☐ First Person
> ☐ Second Person
> ☐ Third Person

Point of view should also be consistent within paragraphs. Read the following example:

> I will never forget my first trip to Disney World when I was ten years old. I was so excited to try out all of the rides. You got a pass for access to different rides in different parks. I also wanted to meet all the characters and get pictures with them.
>
> In this passage, the writer shifts the perspective from first-person to second-person. To correct the error, the third sentence should be revised so that it uses a first-person pronoun.
>
> I will never forget my first trip to Disney World when I was ten years old. I was so excited to try out all of the rides. I got a pass to access different rides in different parks. I also wanted to meet all the characters and get pictures with them.

> **Helpful Hint**
>
> Hearing your own writing is often a useful way to detect shifts in time and perspective. To check for consistent tense and person, try reading your paper aloud. You might hear issues that you missed while you were proofreading silently.

On Your Own

Read the following paragraph and identify the sentence that is inconsistent in person.

> It is not easy to make changes to the law. However, if people feel that something needs to be corrected, they should speak up. One way to do this is to appeal to local representatives. People can make phone calls to their senators or even go door-to-door to get neighbors' signatures and support. When I feel frustrated with something, I need to do a better job at taking a stand. Nothing will change if people don't speak up.

Lesson Wrap-up

Key Terms

Academic Writing: a text intended for instructors or students and often directed by specific prompts and requirements

Future Tense: when something has not happened yet

Noun: a word that represents a person, place, thing, event, or idea

Past Tense: when something has already happened

Person: a way to divide words into three groups: first-, second-, and third-person

Personal Pronoun: a pronoun that renames a specific person, animal, object, or place

Present Tense: when something is currently happening

Professional Writing: a text intended for managers, coworkers, or customers

Pronoun: a word that takes the place of a noun in a sentence

Tense: how a verb indicates when it took place: past, present, or future

Verb: a word that represents an action, relationship, or state of being

Writing Application: Maintaining Consistency in Tense and Person

Read the following passage, paying close attention to verb tenses and perspective. When did the actions take place? From whose point of view is the story being told?

Foliage in the Tennessee hills had begun to fade by November, but Chris still managed to spot a tree or two with a goldenrod crown. He pointed these out with enthusiasm, and I'd nod and smile, somewhat preoccupied. The weekend at the cabin hadn't been his idea, but his interest appeared to be growing steadily once we were out of town and on the road. My own enthusiasm was somewhat dampened by the prospect of bad weather. I also had work to focus on, so it wasn't going to be a complete pleasure trip. We had dinner plans with some friends that night, and Chris wanted to kayak on the lake in the morning.

It was dusk when Chris pulled into the driveway, and I clicked the remote to turn on the front porch light. As light flooded the stairwell, I noticed a large brown cardboard box at the top of the landing. It didn't look familiar, and we weren't expecting any deliveries.

Lesson 10.8
Using Parallelism, Coordination, and Subordination

When you write, one of your main goals should be to clearly show connections between ideas. Some ideas are equally important to your meaning while others are less important. The way that you structure a sentence can help establish those relationships and make your writing flow more smoothly.

Read the following examples. Which paragraph is easier to read and understand?

> We the people of the United States, in order to form a more perfect union, because we want to establish justice, insuring domestic tranquility, provide for the common defense, to promote the general welfare, and we secure the blessings of liberty to ourselves and our posterity, do ordain and establish this Constitution for the United States of America.

> We the people of the United States, in order to form a more perfect union, establish justice, insure domestic tranquility, provide for the common defense, promote the general welfare, and secure the blessings of liberty to ourselves and our posterity, do ordain and establish this Constitution for the United States of America.

> ▷ As you can see, the structure of these paragraphs greatly affects their meaning and flow. The first example is difficult to read, and the relationship between the ideas is unclear. In the second example, it's much easier to identify the ideas and see that they are all of equal importance.

In this lesson, you will learn three ways to add structure to your writing:

Coordination
Subordination
Parallelism

Coordination

Coordination is used to link two related ideas. Look at the following sentences:

> Billy, my little cousin, swam in the pool for the first time.

> He was scared.

Because these sentences are so closely related, they can be combined to form one sentence:

> Billy, my little cousin, swam in the pool for the first time, but he was scared.

> In this example, two sentences have been combined using a **comma** and a **coordinating conjunction**, which is a specific type of **conjunction** used to link ideas of equal importance.

Helpful Hint

To remember the seven coordinating conjunctions, memorize the acronym FANBOYS:

For
And
Nor
But
Or
Yet
So

To learn more about conjunctions, see Lesson 9.1.

Sometimes, the relationship between two ideas is so clear, you don't need to use a conjunction. Think about the following examples:

> Don't worry about what other people think of you, but worry about what *you* think of you.

> Don't worry about what other people think of you; worry about what *you* think of you.

▶ If you read these sentences aloud, you may notice that the second sentence sounds better. Because the relationship between both sentences is so obvious, you can simply join them with a **semicolon**. Using a comma and a coordinating conjunction in this case is both unnecessary and awkward.

Helpful Hint

Whenever you combine two independent clauses, you must join them with either a semicolon or a comma with a coordinating conjunction. If you use just a comma or just a conjunction, your sentence is grammatically incorrect.

To learn more about properly combining sentences, see Lesson 10.1.

Subordination

While coordination is used to connect related ideas of *equal* importance, **subordination** is used to connect related ideas of *unequal* importance. Here's an example:

> Dr. Peppercorn cannot work with any patients until he has his first cup of coffee.

> In this sentence, the **subordinating conjunction** *until* is being used to combine two independent clauses.

> Dr. Peppercorn cannot work with any patients.

> He has his first cup of coffee.

▶ Using coordination to combine these sentences doesn't work because the ideas are unequal. In this case, you need to subordinate one of the sentences by adding a subordinating conjunction.

> Dr. Peppercorn cannot work with any patients until he has his first cup of coffee.

> Until he has his first cup of coffee, Dr. Peppercorn cannot work with any patients.

Here is a list of the most common subordinating conjunctions:

after	even though	until
although	if	when
as	once	while
because	since	

Parallelism

You might already be familiar with the term *parallel* from geometry class, where you learned that parallel lines share certain mathematical characteristics. As a result, they run side-by-side without ever intersecting.

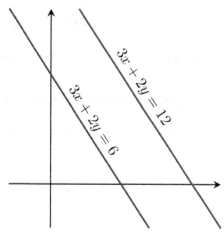

*Two ideas that are parallel are expressed
with similar words, phrases, or clauses.*

In writing, **parallelism** is used to create balance between two or more related ideas by using similarly-structured words, **phrases**, or clauses. Consider this sentence:

> My favorite season is the summer; the fall is what my husband prefers.

> The two halves of this example are **independent clauses** that express related information. In each, the speaker describes a favorite season. However, the clauses are structured differently, making it difficult to see the connection between the two ideas.

> Changing the second half of the sentence will make it easier to read.

> My favorite season is the summer; my husband's favorite season is the fall.

> Both halves of this sentence are now parallel because they follow the same basic pattern:

Person	Topic	Season
Me	favorite season	summer
My husband	favorite season	fall

Writing Environment: Everyday

Because parallelism adds rhythm and flow to your writing, it is often used in poems or song lyrics. Can you think of any specific examples?

Parallelism also includes using consistent coordinating conjunctions (*either/or, neither/nor*). *Neither* must be followed by *nor*, and *either* must be followed by *or*. *Not only* must be used with *but also*.

Not only did the company change its hiring policy, but also it adjusted its pay scale accordingly.

Either we will meet next week, or we will have to reschedule.

Neither our marketing department nor our advertising agency has approved the changes.

On Your Own

Use the items below to write a complete sentence with a parallel list. You may need to change the wording.

Getting a haircut
Going shopping
Picking up dog food

You should also use parallelism for lists.

Not Parallel   Before she could go to the beach, Beth had to eat breakfast, pass a math test, and running errands.

Parallel   Before she could go to the beach, Beth had to eat breakfast, pass a math test, and run errands.

Not Parallel   My neighbor's parakeet, the cat belonging to my grandmother, and my best friend's hamster came to my dog's birthday party.

Parallel   My neighbor's parakeet, my grandmother's cat, and my best friend's hamster came to my dog's birthday party.

These sentences are easier to read when each item in the list follows the same structure.

Each of the following sentences is *missing* parallel structure. This is jarring for the reader because it upsets the rhythm.

According to my mentor, my greatest strengths are negotiating, delegation, and I also solve problems well.

For relaxation, I like golf, fishing, and to watch TV with my friends.

Each candidate had to demonstrate his or her talent, poise was important, and have a competitive strategy.

Now consider the parallel versions of the same sentences.

According to my mentor, my greatest strengths are negotiating, delegation, and problem-solving.

For relaxation, I like golfing, fishing, and watching TV with my friends.

Each candidate had to demonstrate his or her talent, maintain poise, and have a competitive strategy.

Learning Style Tip
If you're a visual learner, try highlighting or underlining each item in a list. This will help you determine if you have used parallel language.

Writing Environment: Academic

For class assignments and research papers, your professors will expect strong organization in your ideas and arguments. It's essential for them to quickly find your thesis and follow it throughout your paper. Parallelism can be a great tool for organizing transitions, style, and length at the paragraph level. Keeping paragraphs similar in structure helps the reader focus on your convincing argument and compelling information.

On Your Own

Take a look at the following examples and identify the list item in each sentence that doesn't seem to fit with the others.

My favorite hobbies include playing the guitar, watching action movies, and anything with basketball.

The committee resolved to cut funding for after-school programs, decided to hold nominations for a new chairperson, and interviewing the recently hired police chief.

Lesson Wrap-up

Key Terms

Comma: a punctuation mark used to separate items in a list; join compound sentences; mark introductory words, phrases, and clauses; add extra or unnecessary details to a sentence; and separate similar adjectives

Coordinating Conjunction: a conjunction that joins similar words or groups of words together

Coordination: a method for combining similar ideas

Conjunction: a word that makes a connection between other words or a group of words

Independent Clause: a group of words with a subject and a verb that expresses a complete thought

Parallelism: a method for showing a relationship between ideas by using similarly structured words, phrases, or clauses

Phrase: a word group that does not form a complete thought because it is missing a subject and/or verb

Semicolon: a punctuation mark used to combine two independent clauses and separate long list items

Subordinating Conjunction: a conjunction that introduces a dependent clause

Subordination: a method for combining unequal ideas

Writing Application: Using Parallelism, Coordination, and Subordination

Read the following brief paragraph and look for coordination, subordination, and parallelism. How does each structure reinforce the connections between ideas?

Stress is a state of tension or worry often related to ongoing problems at home, work, or school. Stressors can cause not only physical and emotional responses, but also mental and psychological ones. These may include crankiness, insomnia, nervous disorders, and even depression. Prolonged stress can be unhealthy and even contribute to serious conditions such as heart disease, cardiac arrest, and stomach ulcers.

Stress is actually a natural and involuntary impulse; it's the body's instinct to avoid danger. When humans sense trouble, the sympathetic nervous system warns the body to react. This is the reaction known as "fight or flight." This reaction is triggered by cortisol and adrenaline entering the bloodstream, which increases the heart rate, quickens the pulse, and causes muscle tension. People respond differently; some sweat profusely, some clench their jaws or breathe harder, and some notice that their pupils dilate.

High stress is uncomfortable and negative, but a little burst of stress now and then can actually motivate us to get things done and take positive action.

Lesson 10.9
Proofreading Sentences for Grammar

Once you are comfortable with the rules of grammar and spelling, you can start applying this knowledge to your writing. Being able to correct your own writing errors will help you present yourself and your ideas in a more professional and academic way.

> Reflection Questions
> Have you ever noticed grammar or spelling errors in a book, article, or document? How did this affect your opinion of the text?

Keep in mind that proofreading skills don't happen overnight. As you continue to practice, you will find yourself becoming more comfortable with identifying and fixing grammar and spelling mistakes. Additionally, the more you write, the more you will learn from these mistakes, which will shape you into a stronger and more effective writer.

In this lesson, you will learn strategies for proofreading a text for grammar and spelling errors.

Further Resources

Missing even small grammar and spelling errors can lead to big problems. In one case, a man was sentenced to forty-two extra months in jail because of a typo in his paperwork. You can read more about the case here: (http://www.vox.com/2014/4/15/5617676/weird-federal-math-typo-3-and-a-half-extra-years-in-prison).

Proofreading Strategies

Proofreading a text for grammar and spelling can be a time-consuming task. There are a lot of rules and guidelines to keep straight. If you don't have a strategy for proofreading, you may find yourself feeling bored or overwhelmed. To become a more effective proofreader, use the following steps.

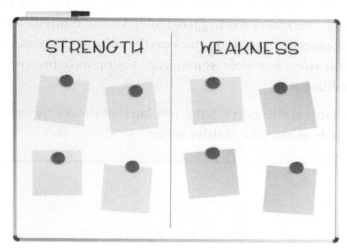

Making a list of common mistakes along with your strengths can be helpful when proofreading.

Make a List of Your Common Mistakes

Everyone struggles with certain grammar and spelling mistakes. Think back to the papers you've written; what errors did your teachers mark over and over again? Once you've identified where you struggle, you can use this information to make your proofreading time more effective.

If you're not sure what grammar and spelling mistakes you commonly make, ask a friend or tutor to review your work and share three to five areas of weakness.

Helpful Hint

Keep a copy of your common grammar mistakes saved on your computer or in a folder. Review this list anytime you proofread your writing and update it every time you receive grammar feedback from an instructor.

Proofread in Stages

Trying to catch all your grammar and spelling errors in just one reading is impossible. Instead, you should proofread your text in stages. During each stage, focus on correcting one type of grammar error.

To make the best use of your time, start with your most common grammar and spelling mistakes. For example, you might first proofread for **comma splices**, then **subject-verb agreement**. Once you've worked through your list of common errors, proofread these four general areas:

Sentence Structure	Comma splices, **fragments**, and **fused sentences**
Agreement	Subject-verb and **pronoun-antecedent agreement**
Punctuation	**Commas, semicolons, colons**, and **quotation marks**
Spelling	Spelling, capitalization, and numbers

Proofreading Checklist

☐ Are all the sentences complete?

☐ Have you avoided fragments, fused sentences, and comma splices?

☐ Are names spelled correctly and consistently?

☐ Is capitalization used properly?

☐ Do subjects and verbs agree?

☐ Are tense and person consistent?

☐ Do pronouns have clear antecedents?

☐ Have you avoided passive voice?

☐ Have you avoided vague pronouns?

☐ Have you used parallelism?

☐ Is the punctuation appropriate?

Writing Environment: Academic

Proofreading usually improves your grade. You may not like that some professors take off points for things like spelling, grammar, and sentence errors. After all, isn't it more important to know the material and possibly discover something that could change the world? Probably, but it's also important to express those life-changing ideas clearly and meaningfully. Taking the time to proofread shows respect for your audience and the important content you're covering. Additionally, a missing or misspelled word here or there could change the meaning of a sentence and compromise your message.

On Your Own

Read the paragraph below and identify any mistakes you find. As you're working, consider how you would fix these mistake(s).

> In November of 1963, President Kennedy was shot in Dallas, Texas, by a assassin. He was riding in a car with the governor of Texas, John Connally, that was also hit by a bullet. The motorcade was supposed to travel downtown through Dealey Plaza, where the shots were fired. The Warren Commission concluded that this was the work of a lone gunman and announced it to the public. Many details were unexplained, and they thought there were other shooters involved. Top secret investigations continued for many years and produced conflicting evidence. In 1979, the House of Representatives Select Committee on Assassinations concluded that the assassination was the result of a conspiracy.

Try Multiple Reading Techniques

When you proofread a text, starting at the beginning and reading all the way to the end isn't always the best strategy. It's easy to rush through your sentences without even realizing you made grammar or spelling mistakes.

To help yourself slow down and focus, try reading your text aloud to yourself. Your brain often supplies missing words or fixes mistakes automatically when you read silently. Actually saying the words can reveal errors you would have missed otherwise.

Another way to keep yourself focused on spelling and grammar is to read your text backwards. Read the last sentence first. Then, read the second-to-last sentence. Keep moving through your sentences in this order, looking for errors in each once. This strategy helps you focus on the contents of the sentence without getting distracted by the overall ideas in the paragraph or essay.

Finally, try printing out a paper copy of your text to proofread. Sometimes, seeing the words in a different location can help you find mistakes you previously missed. Mark any errors so that you can go back and fix them later.

Group Activity

Read the excerpt below. Practice using some of the previous strategies. Did you catch any mistakes? When you're done, compare your findings with a partner.

So, why don't we, as a society, continue to volunteer past adolescence and into adulthood. Many argue that lack of time is the bigest factor preventing college students and young workers from giving to others. However, when a person gives of his time. He learns to see the world through the eyes of those who benefit from his volunteering. For example, a woman who helps distribute food at a food pantry sees the need in her community. She sees the value of sacrificcing a couple of hours a month; to give to others who may need some temporary help in order to survive. Because she can put a face to that need, they are willing to give up some of her down time. the activities that used to take up her off-work hours, such as television, become less engaging than the satisfaction of improving another's life.

Take Advantage of Technology Tools

Most writing programs, like Microsoft Word, offer useful proofreading features. Spell-check scans your writing and identifies problems with spelling, capitalization, and punctuation. Keep in mind that a computer may not notice if you use a correctly spelled word in the wrong place. You should never rely on spell-check to do your proofreading for you.

On Your Own

Read the sentence below and identify the misspelled or misused words.

Some doctors will tell you two avoid fruit in the morning since it contans a high amount of sugar.

Most programs also offer a handy feature that allows you to find specific words or punctuation marks in a text. If you know that you always mix up *their* and *there*, use this feature to search for these words. You can then proofread each sentence to decide if you used the words correctly. This feature is also useful for proofreading less common punctuation marks like **brackets** or quotation marks.

Take frequent breaks

As you proofread your paper, don't be afraid to take frequent breaks. Five to ten minutes should be plenty of time for you to stretch your legs or get a drink. Don't allow yourself to take too much time, however, as you might become distracted.

You should also consider breaking your proofreading across multiple days. Getting a good night's sleep will give you fresh eyes and a clear head.

Now, let's take a look at a sample excerpt from an essay on the brain's role in processing depression. This is a good model for proofreading mistakes for spelling and grammar. Although the paragraph is focused and developed, the author has quite a few grammar issues to work through.

> Many self help gurus turn to notions of self-empowerment and willfulness to encourage depressed individuals to engage the world. However, this sort of instruction ignore what many current scientists and philosophers know: a person's ability to control his or her own thoughts is extremely limited. In his essay, Jack Burton explains that "lower-level brain modules can profoundly affect not only our ordinary sensory perceptions but also how we experience abstract symbols (65). He goes on to explain that these lower-level processes actually precede feelings of certainty when people make decisions, so unconscious thinking actually underwrites human actions Thus, it is not at all clear that positive thinking is within a person's control. While many people don't believe this to be true.

Considering the number of mistakes made in the paragraph above, let's now look at another excerpt from an essay on the prison system. Practice using multiple strategies to find and adjust any spelling and grammar mistakes.

On Your Own

Identify all the sentences in this passage that contain spelling and/or grammar mistakes.

> Most citizen do not think about the men and women behind the walls of prison systems, and they think much less about what is hapening in the prisons. Because of the lack of interest in prison policies. The system in effect in many penitentiaries today is not as effective as it could be. There are many ideas for how prisons should function, but a process needs to be enforced that is productive not only for prisoners but also society. The high rate of relapses, that results in overpopulated prisons has the potential to be lower. Rehabilitating prisoners is the key to a more productive change in the prison systems because it takes into account the prisoner's background and individuality and benefits both society and prisoners. When compared with other alternatives for prisons, the rehabilitation process actually changes the lives of prisoners, thus making it the best choice.
>
> When a prisoner is released back into society, they must learn how to thrive without reverting back to old behaviors. Violators can either change in the prison systm or remain in a career of crime. Because they are unlikely to change without intervention, inmates will most likely be put back into an overcrowded prison system in which they learn even more about breaking the law. Offenders need to be put into a situation where the ability to change is present. The best way to help prisoners change; is to make change a possibility.

Writing Environment: Professional

Sometimes, it's puzzling to see grammatical or spelling errors published in blogs, websites, or books. "Doesn't the writer have a spellchecker?" you might ask. "Why didn't he or she check for errors?" The truth is, they probably did. However, last-minute changes may have been added after the initial proofreading, or a tight deadline could have restricted the proofreading process. Regardless, errors diminish credibility. Carelessness with words suggests carelessness on the job. Sometimes, professional publications even offer apologies or retractions for misprinted or misquoted material.

Lesson Wrap-up

Key Terms

Antecedent: the word that a pronoun renames

Brackets: a pair of punctuation marks commonly used inside parentheses or quotation marks to add minor details to a sentence or insert missing text inside a quotation

Colon: a punctuation mark used to introduce a list or quotation, end a salutation, and join related numbers

Comma: a punctuation mark used to separate items in a list; join compound sentences; mark introductory words, phrases, and clauses; add extra or unnecessary details to a sentence; and separate similar adjectives

Comma Splice: a sentence error made when two independent clauses are combined with a comma but no conjunction

Credibility: what makes something or someone believable

Fragment: a sentence that does not express a complete thought

Fused Sentence: a sentence error made when two independent clauses are combined without punctuation

Parallelism: a method for showing a relationship between ideas by using similarly structured words, phrases, or clauses

Passive Voice: when a sentence is written so that the subject is receiving an action

Person: a way to divide words into three groups: first-, second-, and third-person

Pronoun: a word that takes the place of a noun in a sentence

Pronoun-Antecedent Agreement: when a pronoun and its antecedent in a sentence are the same in gender and number

Quotation Marks: a pair of punctuation marks used to repeat someone else's words

Semicolon: a punctuation mark used to combine two independent clauses and separate long list items

Subject: who or what a sentence is about

Subject-Verb Agreement: when a subject and verb used in a sentence are both singular or both plural

Tense: how a verb indicates when it took place: past, present, or future

Verb: a word that represents an action, relationship, or state of being

Writing Application: Proofreading Sentences for Grammar

Read the following brief passage and practice using the proofreading strategies discussed in this lesson. Write down any errors you find and discuss them with a classmate.

Those who say they don't like Indian food probably haven't sampled many dishes. Indian food's reputation for intense flavors may be intimidating. Why must it be so hot? The truth is, cooking varies by region and includes a wide range of styles, flavors, and textures, it's not always hot or spicy. Some of the most popular dishes include braised meats in creamy sauces made with yogurt and fruits, while others are strictly vegtarian. Indian cooks know the power of "layering" flavors and the potent impact of combining spices. *Garam masala* is a blend of dark spices used to flavor many dishes. Cayenne pepper and chili pepper are also used in many dishes, but surprisingly it is usually not the source of the high-level heat. The single most potent factor in Indian cuisine is actually mustard, which brings out the heat in the other ingredients. Combining mustard with other spices like cayenne and ginger makes a fiery combination. One uniquely spicy dish is called *Koftas*, which are meatballs served with rice or *naan*, which may help to tame the heat.

Notes

Notes

Notes

Notes

Notes

Notes